JOURNEY TO THE

HIGH SOUTHWEST

WITHDRAWN

MAR 0 6 2023

DAVID O. McKAY LIBRARY
BYU-IDAHO

DATE DUE

AUG 16 1994	

DEMCO, INC. 38-2931

RICKS COLLEGE
DAVID O. McKAY LIBR
REXBURG, IDAHO 8344

Journey to the

High Southwest

A Traveler's Guide
by
Robert L. Casey

Third Edition,
Revised & Enlarged

Illustrated by
Julie Roberts

A Voyager Book

The
Globe
Pequot
Press
Chester, Connecticut

Updated Summer 1990

The following publishers and authors have been kind enough to grant their permission for use of selected quotes from previously published material.

 p. 130: *National Geographic,* "Our People, Our Past" by Albert Laughter, and "The Navajos" by Ralph Looney.

 p. 306: Alfred A. Knopf, Inc., *Death Comes for the Archbishop* by Willa Cather. Copyright 1927 by Willa Cather. Copyright renewed 1955 by the executors of the estate of Willa Cather.

Copyright © 1983, 1985, 1988 by Robert L. Casey

All rights reserved. No part of this book may be reproduced or transmitted in any form by any means, electronic or mechanical, including photocopying and recording, or by any information storage and retrieval system, except as may be expressly permitted by the 1976 Copyright Act or in writing from the publisher. Requests for permission should be made in writing to The Globe Pequot Press, 138 West Main Street, Chester, Connecticut 06412. Previously published by Pacific Search Press.

Library of Congress Cataloging-in-Publication Data

Casey, Robert L.
 Journey to the High Southwest.

 "A Voyager book"
 Bibliography: p.
 Includes index.
 1. Southwest, New—Description and travel—
1981-   —Guide-books. 2. Mountains—Southwest,
New—Guide-books. I. Title.
F787.C37   1988   917.9′ 0433   87-30217
ISBN 0-87106-659-9 (pbk.)

Book design by Judy Petry
Cover illustration, seriograph entitled "Heaven and Earth" by Doug West
Maps and illustrations by Julie Roberts

Manufactured in the United States of America
Third Edition/Fourth Printing

In Memoriam

George Miksch Sutton
1898–1982

*His living legacy will always be
books like this written by students and
friends he inspired.*

CONTENTS

Preface to the Third Edition

This third edition is more than just a complete update and revision. There is new material as well. In Section I (Southeastern Utah, Canyon Country), the final completion of paved Utah Highway 12 from Capitol Reef National Park to Bryce Canyon National Park makes it possible to include tour data on what I believe to be one of America's uniquely scenic drives. Don't miss traveling this incredible one hundred miles through one of our nation's most remote locations. Section II (Northeastern Arizona, Indian Country) has been expanded more than any of the other segments of this book. High-altitude Flagstaff is steadfastly, but calmly, evolving into a genuine mecca for the traveler to the High Southwest. The recent quiet, but very discernible "explosion" there of restaurants, more intimate, charming places to stay, and a few, small quality shops and galleries make Flagstaff more than just a place to spend the night on the way to another destination. It is a fine destination in its own right and serves as a base from which to explore much of northeastern Arizona. This edition includes for the first time tour data on many interesting sights around Flagstaff, including Walnut Canyon National Monument, Sunset Crater and Wupatki National monuments, the Meteor Crater near Winslow, Arizona, and Oak Creek Canyon. It also details some of the activities in Flagstaff, including those of the prestigious Museum of Northern Arizona, the Coconino Center for the Arts, and Northern Arizona University.

Section II also includes a revised and much-expanded shopping and consumer's guide for those interested in purchasing southwestern Indian arts and crafts. This guide is useful not only in northeastern Arizona but throughout the High Southwest.

In Section III (Southwest Colorado and Northwest New Mexico) I have written about the new Anasazi Heritage Center near Dolores, Colorado, and expanded the listings of lodging, food, and shops in the historic up-and-coming summer resort and ski town of Telluride, Colorado. And for the adventurous who have more time, I have pointed out sights around Cortez, Colorado, such as Hovenweep National Monument and Crow Canyon Archaeological Center. Around Farmington, New Mexico, the reader is introduced to the Bisti Badlands.

In Section IV (North Central New Mexico, the Spanish Rio Grande Country) I have reviewed, updated, and expanded the listings of lodgings, restaurants, shops, and galleries in the Santa Fe–Taos corridor and have guided the traveler to new attractions there. In Santa Fe veteran and new visitors alike will enjoy the New Mexico Museum's new facility, the Museum of Indian Arts and Culture. And for the enjoyment of natural history aficionados I have included a detailed tour to the serene and peaceful Randall Davey Audubon Center in the hills, a few miles east of Santa Fe's plaza. But not neglecting hard-core shoppers, I have also extended one of the Santa Fe walking tours to include the new retail and restaurant activity centered around that city's newest shopping area, South Guadalupe Street. In addition to describing some of the new changes at Taos's prestigious Millicent Rogers Museum, I have included tour information on the incredibly beautiful historic home of Russian-born artist and longtime Taos resident, Nicolai Fechin.

But the major changes in Section IV are in Albuquerque, New Mexico. This pleasant city is truly becoming a worthwhile traveler's destination with its explosion of fine hostelries, restaurants, and shops over the past six years. Using Albuquerque as a base, I have added a variety of tours to some of its more unique sights. The breathtaking exhibits at the New Mexico Museum of Natural History (no kid, young or old, should miss it), the informative and peaceful Rio Grande Nature Center State Park, and the stunning examples of ancient Southwest Indian rock art at Indian Petroglyph State Park are all within your reach from Albuquerque. In addition I have included a day tour from Albuquerque to Ácoma Indian Pueblo, one of our nation's oldest and most dramatically situated villages.

Throughout all sections, listings of hotels, motels, restaurants, and shops have been updated and expanded to better reflect what you will find upon your arrival. Wherever possible I have included bed-and-breakfast homes and inns, since in my estimation, these smaller, more intimate hostelries sometimes impart a better sense of the ambience and culture of an area than the "standard" accommodations found there.

Acknowledgments

First I wish to thank my family, Mary, Dana, and Rob, for their unstinting support. This effort would have been impossible without their patience, understanding, and help.

I am deeply grateful to Julie Roberts for the fine illustrations she produced for the book. She went above and beyond the call of duty in striving for the very best evocative characterization of each scene. As a former university English teacher, successful potter, and now illustrator, it is mind-boggling to think of all her special talents. I hope this will be the first of many books to reveal her artistic abilities.

Kudos, and a lot of them, also go to Robbie Mantooth, a talented, energetic lifelong friend who took time from her busy work and family schedule to pore over early copies of the manuscript, offering suggestions and advising changes which almost always were on the mark. I eagerly await the production of her first book, because just about everything she has done in her writing career so far has seemed masterful to me.

I also want to thank Hugh Murray, who planted the seed which got me to thinking about writing this book, and Mary and Jim Finney of Santa Fe for being the most supportive and friendly hosts west of the Pecos.

There are some thank yous not related to the tangible manuscript. I am extremely grateful to my parents, who introduced me to the High Southwest. I am still in awe of my father's wonderful curiosity and special talent of befriending strangers that served him so well as he went knocking on unfamiliar pueblo or farmhouse doors. Pat Casey would have liked a book like this. And my mother will enjoy the book, for when we took her back to New Mexico last spring to visit some familiar haunts, I saw on her face an expression of delight stemming from her fond memories of the region. And, of course, I am also indebted to my lifelong friends Jim Warram, Jim Warram, Sr., and Ruth Warram, who opened up for me windows to the country west of the Rio Grande. That was a memorable summer!

In the 1950s, when "Doc" (Dr. George Miksch Sutton) took some of us out to Oklahoma's Black Mesa country on the New Mexico border, we didn't know what was in store for us. He convinced us that the very western tip of the Oklahoma Panhandle was part of the High Southwest. There he taught us about mesas, buttes, and alcoves and he introduced us to piñon jays, scrub jays, red-tailed hawks, and blue quail. I have had my eyes open ever since. In his sixties then, he shinnied up trees like a schoolboy to inspect bird nests, and he left us breathless and heaving behind him as he effortlessly negotiated steep inclines, probably with a twinkle in his eyes. Doc's timely suggestions about this manuscript before his death were most helpful.

I also wish to thank Andrew Gelfand, Will Johnson, Jim Mantooth, and Herb Wimberger for the use of their slides and photographs in preparing the illustrations for the book. And I wish to thank Jean Okimoto for her expert advice as a veteran author and Doug West, Santa Fe artist, whose evocative work graces the cover of this book.

I am greatly indebted to the many park rangers and park naturalists who patiently answered my many queries about the state and national parks listed in this book. I am equally indebted to the staffs of the Museum of Northern Arizona and Northern Arizona University in Flagstaff, the Heard Museum in Phoenix, and the Museum of New Mexico in Santa Fe for their cooperation and the information they supplied me. In addition, I would like to thank all of the authors mentioned in the bibliography whose works serve as part of the data base for the book. Special thanks go to Ekkehart Malotki of Northern Arizona University, Flagstaff, for information on the Hopi language, and to Dorothy A. House, librarian at the Museum of Northern Arizona for her help with the third edition.

And thanks to the many readers of the first and second editions of this book who not only expressed their appreciation of this kind of detailed travel guide, but who made many valuable suggestions about its revision. Some of these suggestions are included in this third edition.

Introduction

During several summers in the late 1940s, near the end of July when the Oklahoma sun had heated the asphalt to the point you could almost fry an egg on it and when even the largest of fans would not cool the bedrooms at night, we would pack the car and head for the high country in New Mexico. Sometimes on our way to Santa Fe or Taos we went by way of U.S. Highway 66 through Clinton, Oklahoma, Amarillo, Texas, and Tucumcari, New Mexico, while at other times we headed west through the Oklahoma and Texas panhandles to Raton, New Mexico.

It was always the same. Early in the morning with the car windows rolled down as far as they would go, we began the long, hot daytime drive through the flat prairie, the superheated wind parching us to the bone. Occasionally the monotony was broken by a mirage ahead of us on the highway, where it actually looked like water was standing on the road. Or sometimes we would drive under an isolated cloud in the sky, a giant umbrella casting a protective shadow which screened us for a few miles from the sun's scorching rays. Although we headed west along what seemed to be a flat, straight road, we were actually gaining altitude slowly, mile by mile, so that by late afternoon we had gained over five thousand feet elevation. There it was hot, but not unbearably hot, for the dry country had finally wrung the last miserable bit of discomfort-producing moisture from the air.

Just as the sun was beginning to set, the road began to climb noticeably and we found ourselves in country altogether different from that we had come from that morning. We were now in a high desert surrounded by lofty mountain peaks looming in the distance. Immediately we flatlanders would try to spot patches of snow on those distant peaks, sometimes mistaking, in our eagerness, billowy white clouds for the real McCoy. The next thing we noticed was the sky. In the high, dry, clear air it seemed bluer and brighter than we had ever known it and it spread across the country with such immensity that it did not even look like the same sky we had at home. On the horizon, that very blue sky dipped down to the earth, where it seemed to mingle with an infinite variety of varicolored landforms poking their tips right into its blue borders. As the road topped one high ridge after another, it seemed that we could see forever from those lofty viewpoints. There was a sense of boundless space and openness that was different from anything we had experienced before. Then, at some magic moment along that road as the sun made its magnificent exit behind the distant high mountains, the air suddenly chilled. For a few moments, exhilarated by the drop in temperature, we just gulped great deep breaths of that cool, high, dry air, pungent with the aroma of pine and sage. There in the deepening twilight and incredible silence of that big country, we knew we had reached the High Southwest.

I am not sure whether my love affair with the High Southwest began then at age ten with that first dramatic entry into the high country or whether it began earlier. For one day, sometime before that first trip to New Mexico, I had discovered, carefully wrapped and boxed in the attic of our home, a black pot which my parents had purchased in the late 1920s at one of the Indian pueblos along the Rio Grande north of Santa Fe. I recall being fascinated by the utter smoothness of that vessel's black, shiny surface. Over and over again, my fingers traced the beautifully executed serpent design that encircled it, somehow trying to discover its meaning. I could not imagine how an object of such rare beauty could have been fashioned by hand from raw clay.

On my first trip to the High Southwest, I could hardly wait to visit that Indian pueblo to see how it was done. Sure enough, on arriving there I saw Pueblo Indian women hand building and decorating fine pots and firing them in open bonfires, just as their ancestors had done for nearly a thousand years before them. Those and other sights and experiences there left indelible impressions on my memory that have lasted a lifetime. One in particular stands out. In Spanish New Mexico that summer I learned that the oldest public building in the United States was not along the East Coast of the United States, but right there on Palace Avenue in Santa Fe, New Mexico. That jolting discovery fully awakened what must have been a dormant sense of prairie pessimism, for from that day on I never again fully trusted history books to tell it the

way it really was. Later my pessimism seemed fully justified when I learned that the two oldest continually occupied villages or towns in the United States were not along the Atlantic seaboard as I had been led to believe, but instead were atop two high mesas, one in northeastern Arizona and the other in northwestern New Mexico.

After that first summer I was hooked. Over the next thirty-five years, I returned to New Mexico many times. Eventually I began journeying to the high desert and mountain country surrounding an area called the Four Corners region, where the borders of Utah, Arizona, Colorado, and New Mexico come together. In many ways, this country was a continuation of the high country around Santa Fe and Taos. Dramatic thunderstorms pounded the ground on hot July and August afternoons, cooling and refreshing the air there just as they did in New Mexico. Pygmy forests of juniper and piñon were just as prevalent at certain altitudes there as they were in the Rio Grande Valley and the zoogeological features were quite similar. And in both regions there were certain isolated canyons, mesas, and mountaintops that offered a solitude I had never experienced before.

But there were cultural similarities as well. Over time I learned that the early prehistoric Indian culture in the Four Corners area had given rise to the Pueblo civilization that is still intact on

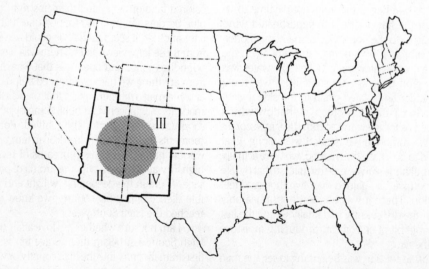

The Four Corners Area and North Central New Mexico

the Hopi mesas. And it also spawned the great Pueblo communities, which continue to flourish along the Rio Grande. Even the Navajo provided a link between the two areas. Their beginnings in the Southwest were centered not far from the Rio Grande. From there, they eventually migrated west and settled in the Four Corners area where they live today. Historically, the Spanish thought of the Four Corners high country as just another continuation of their New Mexico empire, as they traversed its boundaries from one end to the other, dropping names wherever they went just as if they owned it.

Within a few years, I discovered that I had the same boundless enthusiasm for the Four Corners region that I had earlier for the Rio Grande Valley. I found myself visiting my favorite spots in both areas with relative frequency. Eventually I came to know all of the high country bounded on the east by New Mexico's Rio Grande Valley and on the west by Utah's canyon and plateau country as the High Southwest. To me it seemed to be an area that transcended state borders and local interests and begged to be explored as a whole. As time went on and I traveled more on this continent and beyond, the High Southwest became all the more precious, for I discovered that most of its exotic landforms and cultural features were not duplicated any other place in the world. Many of its indigenous people continue to live out a lifeway that has been in existence for almost a millennium, while some of its adopted residents have brought their sophisticated culture to its highest peak in the nationally recognized art galleries, concert halls, and the well-known opera house of the region. In many ways the High Southwest is a land of contrasts and paradoxes unparalleled anyplace else in the United States, perhaps in the world.

As interest in southwestern travel began to pick up, I was approached by several friends about travel advice to the High Southwest since they were unable to find a comprehensive traveler's guide to the region. About the same time, while having breakfast in Monument Valley one morning, I met several European travelers who told me of their frustration in trying to find a helpful, detailed, European-style guidebook to the Southwest's high country. And not long after that, on a busy August weekend in Santa Fe, I took note of the large crowds there. It occurred to me that many of the people who returned there year after year possibly did not venture to other areas of the High Southwest because the last page of their guidebooks ended just south of the plaza.

So I decided to write this book. It offers to the reader the broader perspective of someone who loves that high desert and mountain country, yet who is an outsider. That perspective helps to transcend local interests and state boundaries and allows for a unified approach to the High Southwest as a single geographic and cultural entity. So finally there is a traveler's guide that places most of the scenic and historical sights of the High Southwest between the covers of one book. The material included generally represents a balanced presentation of my favorite places to visit, which are easily accessible by the standard family automobile or by short walking or hiking trails.

The selected sights range from Santa Fe and Taos on the east to Bryce Canyon National Park on the west, and from Arches National Park on the north to the Hopi mesas and Flagstaff on the south. It covers some of the highest of the high country from Red Mountain Pass, elevation 11,018 feet, and Telluride, Colorado, elevation 8,744 feet, to one of the lowest elevations of the high country at Moab, Utah, elevation 4,000 feet. The book touches on up-and-coming Flagstaff, Arizona, bustling Durango, Colorado, Santa Fe and Taos, New Mexico, and Mesa Verde National Park, Colorado. Yet it also details some of the more remote areas, including part of the Escalante Canyon system and isolated sections of Capitol Reef National Park, Canyonlands National Park, and Dead Horse Point State Park in Utah, as well as the remote Spanish villages of New Mexico. There the descendants of some of our nation's earliest European inhabitants still talk in halting English to visitors, while among themselves they speak remnants of a Spanish dialect that dates back to Cervantes's time.

But not everything is included. I take full responsibility for omitting certain sights from this book, such as the Grand Canyon. The Grand Canyon is so well known, has had so much written about it, and is so heavily visited that it needs no further boosting from this nor any other book. Goblin Valley State Park and Natural Bridges National Monument in Utah were omitted to conserve space in this already long book since many of the unusual landforms concentrated there can be seen in other areas. Although Chaco Culture National Historic Park is briefly mentioned in this guide, a detailed account of its ruins and how to see them will be added to future editions when a better all-weather road to the area is constructed. The wonderful high mountain country around Red River and Eagle Nest, New Mexico, has been bypassed in favor of similar, but higher mountain country in southwestern Colorado. But that does not mean you cannot go there!

In addition to the touring, accommodations, restaurant, and shopping sections of this book, I have tried to broaden the reader's perspective by detailing the geological and natural history of some areas, while flushing out the historical and cultural roots of others.

Although it is possible to make a whirlwind trip and see all of the sights listed here in less than three weeks, most people will want to focus on the areas that interest them. Consequently I have divided the High Southwest into four touring sections that reflect what I feel are the major interest features of each region. The first section details the exotic landforms which the High Southwest is perhaps best known for. The most intense concentration of these occurs in southeastern Utah. That section also contains a geological primer that will aid you in understanding what you see there, as well as in some of the other sections of the High Southwest. The second section, in addition to a detailed touring and ceremonial dance and festival guide, gives in-depth coverage of the history of the region's prehistoric indigenous people and their Indian ancestors who live in the area. Nowhere in America can you experience both Indian past and present so acutely as you can on the Hopi mesas and the Navajo reservation centering around northeastern Arizona. But for many, the High Southwest is intimately tied to the image of the American western frontier, including its prospectors, miners, and cowboys and its lofty mountains. Southwestern Colorado, the focus of Section III, is the geographical location which evokes the history and ambience of the frontier West better than any other place I know, and it is there that the grandeur of the Rocky Mountains reaches its climax. The

fourth section of the book concentrates on the interest feature of the Spanish, the first European explorers and settlers to penetrate the American heartland. You will see poignant evidence of their dynamic past wherever you go in north central New Mexico's Rio Grande Valley and you will witness the unique life-style of their Hispanic descendants, who are the majority population in most of the towns and cities there.

The tours in this book are, of course, suggested routes and you can either use them or, with the information provided, devise your own touring routes. The narrative accounts detail either some of the more adventurous or less well-known sights. They are written to provide you with the details of an in-depth experience so that from the comfort of your armchair you can gain a good sense of what to expect in the High Southwest. Although the narratives are based on actual experiences and give you some idea about what can be accomplished in a half or full day of touring or hiking, you may prefer to see more or less in a given period of time.

So choose the section or sections of the High Southwest you are interested in and proceed to use the enclosed maps and the "Travel Access" chart to help you make your plans. That chart and most of the information you will need to have a safe and successful journey are located in the "Practical Hints" section at the back of the book.

You will find that the High Southwest, except for one or two locations, is one of few areas in the country where families can still travel relatively inexpensively. Although the emphasis in this book is on moderately priced lodging which evokes the atmosphere of the Southwest, many other accommodations are listed which are inexpensive compared to other resort and vacation areas in the United States. And for families on a stricter budget, it is reasonably easy to camp one night and stay in comfortable lodgings the next night in the informal, casual atmosphere of the Southwest.

No attempt has been made to rate the quality of the lodging except to point out that the author and his family have either stayed in or inspected nearly all of the listings and found them to be more than satisfactory for the price category they represent. Lodging is rated according to the price of a room for two during high season, May through September. Generally, rates are lower at other times of the year. Some facilities have a wide range of rooms and span more than one category. Others, which are either at the very top or bottom of a category, are listed with the additional annotation of "high" or "low." To rate bed-and-breakfast establishments on a par with traditional hotel and motel accommodations, up to $8.00 has been deducted from the bed-and-breakfast daily rate for two. That rate may or may not include a room with a private bath. Where possible, the description of each bed-and-breakfast establishment indicates the status of private and shared baths. Usually a room with a private bath is costlier than one with a shared bath. And it should be pointed out that the American brand of bed and breakfast is generally more upscale and thus costlier than its European counterpart. The categories for all types of lodgings are: Inexpensive, $25.00 to $45.00; Moderate, $45.00 to $65.00; Expensive, $65.00 to $110.00 and up.

In peak summer months, if you are particular about where you stay, advance reservations should be made in the more crowded areas mentioned earlier. In addition, if you want to stay in Monument Valley, Canyon de Chelly, or the Hopi mesas, advance reservations should be made because of the limited number of rooms available. But do not feel you have to plan months ahead for every stop. If you are willing to be more flexible and take some risks, you might want to consider making reservations, as you go, from day to day. A call today for a room tomorrow, even in the summer, may net positive results. Remember that there are a certain number of cancellations each night, perhaps 5 percent, and if you have called ahead or are standing at the desk waiting at the right time, a room often can be yours. Rooms are generally available in the spring and fall without advance reservations, just as long as there are not any special events attracting people to the area.

Since the publication of this book in 1983, many travel-oriented establishments have acquired toll free (1-800) telephone numbers. Although the numbers may change quite frequently (sometimes once a year), I have included them anyway, because they are a real convenience in planning a trip. If the 1-800 number has been disconnected or changed, dial toll free information 1-800-555-1212 to find out if another number has been assigned. If not, dial the "regular" phone number listed.

I have tried or visited nearly all of the cafés and restaurants listed here. Some have been favorites for over twenty-five years. In many, you will be able to enjoy the food of the region, including some interesting and well-prepared Indian and Spanish New Mexican dishes. Although the price of a meal will vary according to what and how much you eat at a particular restaurant, a rough guideline to prices is presented throughout the book based on the price of a three-course dinner for two, not including cocktails, wine, or tips. The categories here are: Inexpensive, up to $20.00; Moderate, $20.00 to $38.00; Expensive, over $38.00.

It is my fondest hope that this will be a useful, hands-on guide for new travelers to the area, whether they be Americans who are just now discovering this region or Europeans who discovered it long ago, but who are just now getting there. And, of course, I hope that veteran Southwest travelers will also find the book useful for planning trips to areas they had thought were too far away or too remote to visit, short-circuiting the four decades it has taken me finally to make the complete circuit of the High Southwest. If you see most of the sights that are listed in any one section of the book, you will have had a genuine in-depth High Southwest experience, which will include many places not covered by other guidebooks.

So after reading this book, should you travel across the Continental Divide to the Rio Grande Valley or the Four Corners areas, keep an eye out for the ubiquitous High Southwest Spirit. For whether you ride a horse at sunset through the sagebrush near Taos Mountain or take the chill out of an August evening with a piñon fire laid in the adobe fireplace of your casita in Santa Fe, or eat a lunch of posole, fried bread, and mutton stew in the company of our nation's first citizens on the Hopi mesas, or take a walk up Capitol Gorge at Capitol Reef National Park to soak up the solitude there, you will be experiencing that omnipresent spirit of the American High Southwest, a spirit that well may hook you for a lifetime!

SOUTHEASTERN UTAH

Canyon Country

Southeastern Utah

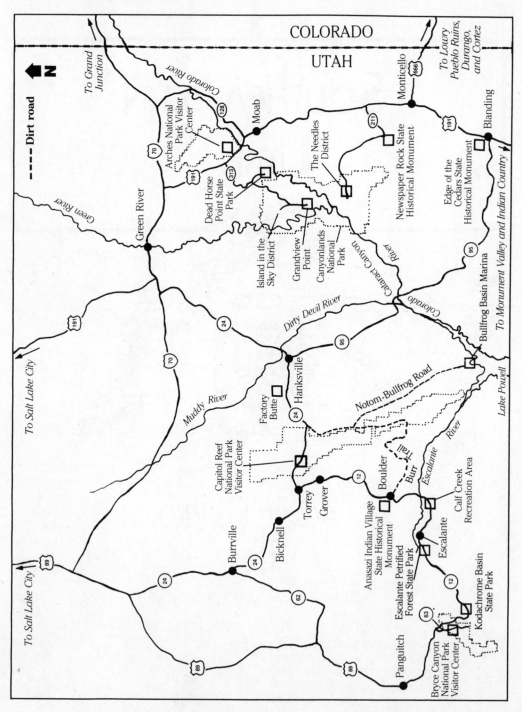

Introduction

If you like scenic landscapes and are a naturalist at heart, the Utah Canyon Country awaits you with a store of wonders unparalleled anywhere else in the United States. Southeastern Utah is one of the few places in the world where the casual traveler can become acquainted with the history of the earth's crust in an effortless way, on paved roads that penetrate its heart. But if you like adventure, there are well laid out walking trails through this slickrock wilderness that will fill you with excitement at every turn.

You will explore zigzag canyons leading so deep into the earth that the walls reveal in their well-defined rock layers 300 million years of the history of the earth's crust. You will walk to the rims of sandstone canyons where, thousands of feet below, ancient rivers meet and flow on to the Pacific Ocean over a thousand miles away. In the bottom of some of those canyons you will see weirdly eroded landscapes that you never imagined possible. Stone archways over a hundred feet high span desert expanses up to the size of a football field. Windows, larger than any manmade windows you have ever seen, open onto panoramas that defy the imagination. And you will see natural stone bridges spanning more than a hundred feet that have already outlasted all the bridges man has ever made in Utah or any other place in the world.

The dry climate holds back the growth of vegetation, exposing the clear skeletal shapes of the rock. When vegetation does survive this aridity, it does so with a rare dignity and beauty. The barrenness around it sets it off like a piece of well-displayed art in a fine gallery. Birds, lizards, and insects are easily seen and identified, as there is so little cover to camouflage them. But more than anything else, you will see rock. For the earth's crust is sculpted to an infinite variety of shapes in this natural showcase. If you have ever wondered about the geologic forces that have shaped the earth, southeastern Utah offers a classroom rich in example. Although good paved roads lead to many fine sights, this is country where you will want to walk the trails to touch, feel, and examine each chapter of the story that nature has spread out for you.

Technically speaking, the land you will be traveling in southeastern Utah and in most of the other sections of this book is part of a giant elevated rock table called a plateau. This giant plateau, almost as large as California and containing 130,000 square miles of high desert, is called the Colorado Plateau. It extends across the borders of four states—Arizona, New Mexico, Colorado, and Utah. The Colorado River for which it was named runs through it and drains it of its water. This high tableland is at an average 5,000 feet above sea level. It is encircled on the north and east by the Rocky Mountains, while to the south and west the table edge drops hundreds of feet in stair-step fashion to the lower deserts and basins. But nature did not stop after building the main plateau. In southern Utah, others soon formed atop the mother plateau, piggyback style, producing some of American's highest—the Paunsaugunt over

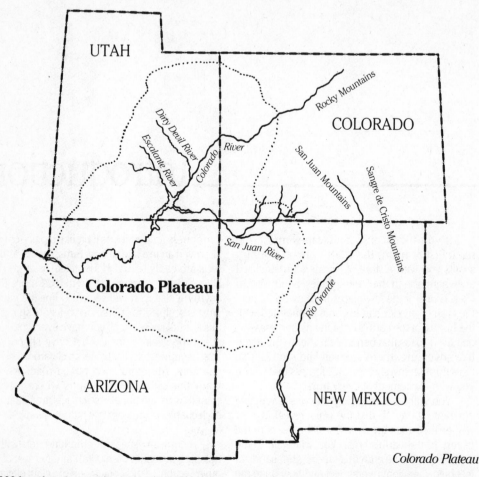

Colorado Plateau

9,000 feet elevation and the Aquarius at 11,600 feet elevation. The Paunsaugunt contains delicately carved Bryce Canyon, while the Aquarius is home to Boulder Mountain offering spectacular panoramas over the surrounding high deserts.

But the heart of the Colorado Plateau's scenic lands rests at lower elevations in southeastern Utah's Canyon Country. There in 28,000 square miles of canyon and rock wilderness, nature has wrested unbelievable beauty from sheer rock. The scenery is so varied that a stunning array of names has been coined for the area. These include Red Rock Country, Sliprock Country, Standing Up Country, Rim Rock Country, and Panoramaland. Attesting to the uniqueness of the region, four national parks have been created to acknowledge the superb scenery and preserve it. A map of south-

eastern Utah reads like a Who's Who of the national park system as it delineates Capitol Reef National Park, Canyonlands National Park, and Arches National Park, while Bryce Canyon National Park flanks its western border.

In addition, the Bureau of Land Management has become the steward of the Escalante Canyon system. Not allowing all of the scenic lands in its southeastern quadrant to be gobbled up by the federal government, the state of Utah has stepped in and preserved for your benefit even more scenic landscapes. Near Moab is a little-known slumbering giant, Dead Horse Point State Park, whose vistas over Utah's Colorado River Canyon easily rival those of the Grand Canyon to the south. Meanwhile Anasazi Indian Village State Historical Monument at Boulder, Utah, and the Edge of the

Cedars State Historical Monument at Blanding, Utah, preserve the heritage of the first people who roamed these canyons.

All of these parks are interconnected by good paved roads that pass through lands often as scenic as those set aside for preservation. This intense concentration of scenic parks in a relatively small area means that you can easily travel from one park to another in just a few hours. As you travel Utah's scenic roads, you will conclude that mile for mile southeastern Utah contains the most intense concentration of incredible, multicolored landforms in the world. You will see cliffs and buttes protrude skyward to heights that surpass the Sears Building in Chicago and that dwarf the Eiffel Tower. Conversely, you will see canyons that pull your eyes as far down as some mountains will pull them up, noting as some have said that much of the scenery in this corner of Utah's Canyon Country is "upside down."

Besides all this, southeastern Utah is a photographer's paradise. There even the most amateur of photographers come away with dramatic photographs of nature's handiwork. Professional photographers find ever-increasing challenges each time they visit. Tourists of all ages from many different places enjoy this country. Of the nearly one million people who visited Bryce Canyon National Park during a recent year, almost 20 percent were from Europe or Japan, while an estimated twenty-five to fifty thousand European visitors flocked to Capitol Reef National Park and the surrounding national and state monuments and parks. As you travel there, you will hear visitors gathered in cafés, motel parking lots, and campgrounds talk about rocks, sunsets, sunrises, and viewpoints with such excitement you would think they were talking about the final game of the World Series. You, too, may become a southeastern Utah fan after you follow the guideposts laid down in this section.

History

Although wonderfully scenic, the land in this area often has been too harsh for people to endure. Southeastern Utah is sparsely populated. The towns are small and have a "frontier" air about them. The ancient Indians, the early Mormon settlers, and the uranium "boomers," in that order, have left their mark on the land. Remnants of those past cultures are visible today. To aid in understanding those relics from the past and to gain a better understanding of the impact of man on this region, some historical guideposts are helpful.

The first known inhabitants were Indians of the so-called Fremont culture, named by modern historians for the river that first attracted the Indians to the area. That ancient river, the Fremont River, was named for the American explorer John C. Fremont. The Fremont culture generally is regarded as a subdivision of the Anasazi culture, most of whose people occupied Mesa Verde and other sites to the southeast. But the Fremont people lived further to the north and west, occupying this region from approximately A.D. 950 to sometime before 1200. They grew corn and made dwellings and storage houses like the Anasazi. But unlike the southern Anasazi, they wore moccasins rather than sandals and were more dependent on hunting. Their dwellings, like the pit houses at Mesa Verde, were constructed by digging a hole in the ground. Then they placed basalt boulders in a ring around the pit. These served as a foundation for rock walls and corner posts, which supported the roof. They built storage houses for corn and other food, high in the cliffsides.

You may see examples of these granaries along Calf Creek near Escalante, Utah, on the Hickman Bridge Trail at Capitol Reef, and at the Moki Ruin turnoff from Utah Highway 24, east of the Capitol Reef visitor center. Early archaeologists thought the small storage houses were the dwellings where the Indians lived and concluded that the people who lived in them must have been very small. They called these early people "Moqui" or "Moki." The term is thought by some to have been derived from a Paiute Indian word meaning "little people," while others believe it is a term that drifted north from the Hopi mesas (see Section II, "The Hopi: A Long and Continuous Past"). The term is still used today to label some of the remains of the Fremont culture. Probably because of drought or fear of hostile marauding tribes, these people left southeastern Utah around A.D. 1200. It is thought that they migrated to the south, where they probably mingled with the main-line Anasazi who are believed to be the forerunners of today's Pueblo Indians. The Fremont Indians left behind many fine examples of their culture through the medium of petroglyphs. You may see these on canyon walls in the Capitol Reef area, in the Escalante Canyon system near Calf Creek, and along the Colorado River near Moab, Utah.

From the time the Fremont Indians left this area in the late 1200s or early 1300s until the first white contact in the late 1700s, there are many blank pages. It is thought that sometime after A.D. 1000 nomadic Indian tribes, hunters and gatherers from the Great Basin—that huge desert area to the north and west—migrated to the higher plateau land. It is possible they were responsible for forcing the Fremont people to abandon the area. These nomads are thought to be the forebearers of the Utes and the Paiute Indians. The Utes claimed most of eastern Utah, but the Paiutes, who ranged over much of southwestern Utah, also pushed east as far as the Capitol Reef area, which they used for seasonal camps from 1600 on.

When the Ute Indians attacked Taos, New Mexico, in 1716, the Spanish defeated them and took some of the captured Indians into slavery, to be sold in Mexico. Thus began a practice that was to continue well into the 1850s. After this battle, the Utes maintained contact with the Spanish traders, later acquiring horses which allowed them to dominate the Paiutes. With horses, they became aggressive raiders, not only stealing more horses and livestock but also stealing or buying Paiute Indian women and children for the flourishing Mexican slave trade. The Paiute women and children sold as slaves were used as domestics in New Mexico and New Spain. In return the adaptable Utes received wool blankets, horses, and guns or "thundersticks" with which they later exacted tribute from the Mexican traders along the Old Spanish Trail. With their aggressive actions, they were able to so successfully fend off white settlement in southeastern Utah that the first permanent white community was not established until 1877, over one hundred years after the first white men had entered the area.

The first documented white contact in Canyon Country came in 1765, when Juan María Antonio Rivera, under orders from the governor of New Spain in Santa Fe, New Mexico, led a prospecting and trading expedition north into Ute country. The route he established from Santa Fe into what is now southwestern Colorado became the eastern leg of the route later known as the Old Spanish Trail. It is believed that Rivera reached the Colorado River near the vicinity of today's Moab, Utah.

Eleven years later, the priest at Zuni Pueblo, Fray Francisco Silvestre Vélez de Escalante, and his superior, Fray Atanasio Domínguez, set out from Santa Fe with a small expeditionary force. This group of ten, including the two priests, sought to find a land route for the establishment of a road from Santa Fe to Monterey, California, the two far-flung Spanish Provincial capitals. They followed Juan Rivera's route into Colorado near the current towns of Durango and Dolores. They continued in a northerly direction until reaching what is now northern Colorado. From there, they went westward to Utah Lake. At Utah Lake, they hoped to traverse southward to the latitude of Monterey and head west to California. But with winter fast approaching, they gave up and headed back to Santa Fe five months later. Except where they crossed the Colorado River near what is now Glenn Canyon Dam at Lake Powell, they made a complete circle around Canyon Country. The maps from this great circle tour into Uteland, which were made by Bernardo de Miera y Pacheco, were published in 1811 by a German scientist, Alexander von Humboldt, who had come to New Spain from Germany around 1804. Although he never visited New Mexico, he did have access to the data supplied by the Spanish explorers, such as Pacheco, as they returned to Mexico City. His maps were instrumental in stimulating new interest in the region, as New Mexican traders spread into the newly discovered and mapped country and stepped up trading with the Utes.

By this time, there was great interest in establishing a land route between Villa Real de Santa Fe de San Francisco (Royal Town of the Holy Faith of Saint Francis), known today as Santa Fe, and El Pueblo de Nuestra Señora de la Reina (Town of Our Lady the Queen of Angels), better known as Los Angeles. A number of variations on the Domínguez–Escalante route into Utah were tried in attempts to shorten the distance. Meanwhile, routes from Utah west to California were being explored. It is not known precisely when or by whom the important shortcut through southeastern Utah was discovered. But finding the practicable crossing of the Colorado River near today's town of Moab, Utah, allowed the traders to bypass the difficult terrain of central and northern Colorado. The new route may have been discovered by Manuel Mesta, who at age seventy-five led an expedition deep into Ute Country in 1805. Some believe the honors should go to the Arze–García party of 1813, while others credit the American mountain men for discovering this important shortcut. The result was a 1,200-mile route which came to be known as the Old Spanish Trail.

Although it was described as the longest, crookedest, most arduous pack mule route in the history of America and took more than two months to negotiate, the trail served as a major trade route for over twenty years. Mules loaded with New Mexican woolens went west to San Gabriel and Los Angeles, while horses and mules from California were driven to Santa Fe. Paiute Indian slaves went both directions. By the end of the Mexican epoch in 1846 and the beginning of the California gold rush in 1848, this rugged trail, which had been forged segment by segment over several decades by brave and hardy men representing a triad of cultures, fell into disuse as other, better routes to the West were established. But segments of the trail continued to play a role in Canyon Country history. Trappers, Mormon settlers, explorers, and scientists used it as a gateway to some of the remotest land in America.

With Spanish colonial restrictions removed after the independence of Mexico in 1821, American beaver trappers and mountain men began entering the Colorado Plateau and Canyonlands area in increasing numbers. In 1847 Brigham Young led his Mormon (Latter Day Saints of Jesus Christ) followers west to settle in northern Utah. This area had only been mapped three years earlier as a result of a United States Government expedition led by John C. Fremont of the United States Corps of Topographical Engineers. Fremont returned to the Colorado Plateau to explore the region of Canyon Country from 1853 to 1854, in his search for a shorter transcontinental railway route. During that expedition, he mapped and surveyed parts of southeastern Utah, one of the last land masses in the United States to be explored.

In 1855, the first white settlement in Southeastern Utah was attempted when Brigham Young sent 42 men down the Old Spanish Trail to the current site of Moab, Utah. Upon arriving in mid-June, they immediately built a stone fort, dug irrigation ditches, planted crops and began fulfilling their mission of preaching to the Ute Indians. This settlement, with all it implied, was too much for the Utes. Six months after they arrived, these hardy

Mormon pioneers abruptly left and abandoned their settlement when three of their members were shot and killed outside the fort by a band of Elk Mountain Utes. It was 22 years later before another settlement was attempted in the area. That attempt stuck, giving birth in 1877, to the town of Moab, Utah, which would later became county seat of Grand County, Utah.

In the late 1850s and 1870s, a number of trailblazers, cartographers, and geologists came into this area, recording what they saw. For the first time, they recorded in their journals the scenic beauty of the area's unique rock jungles. They wrote in awe-inspiring terms of the beauty that abounded everywhere. One of these visitors was John Wesley Powell, who navigated and mapped over one thousand miles of the Colorado River in its serpentine and treacherous course from its source in Wyoming southwestward through the Grand Canyon. He left names on the land wherever he went. At one point, near today's Capitol Reef National Park, Powell's men saw the mouth of a river. One of the men wondered if this was a trout stream. His comrade is reported to have replied that it was not fit for trout because it was such a "dirty devil." The name stuck. The river became known as the Dirty Devil River. But unknowingly, Powell had given different names to two different sections of the same river. In an earlier expedition along the Old Spanish Trail, some of his men had found an abandoned cache along a riverbank, the remnants of the earlier Fremont expedition. In honor of that group they named the river the "Fremont." Today the confusion continues. The upper section of the river is called the Fremont while the lower segment just below where the Muddy River (also known as Muddy Creek) dumps its silty load is called the Dirty Devil.

Prospectors looking for gold entered southeastern Utah as early as the 1870s. The main route through the impenetrable rock barrier known as Capitol Reef was by way of a narrow passageway known today as Capitol Gorge. In the gorge the cliff walls rise hundreds of feet as the channel narrows to less than twenty feet. As the prospectors passed through, many carved their names on the cliff walls. For decades after that, many of the early pioneers inscribed their names on the same rock walls. Pretty soon the walls of Capitol Gorge began to look like a government register. Today those walls full of signatures, which have withstood the test of time and the adversity of the elements deep in the protected gorge, are known as the Pioneer Register. Nearby and hundreds of years older are some Indian Petroglyphs, tell-tale drawings remind us who the first "pioneers" really were.

After the prospectors came the stalwart Mormon pioneers who began to settle in the Capitol Reef area along the Fremont River in the 1880s. Several structures remaining there today, Behunin Cabin and Fruita School, are testimony to the presence of the early white farmers who settled there. Later some of Capitol Reef's serpentine blind canyons served as hideouts for Morman polygamists, or cohabitationists as they came to be known, who fled from the law. Today you may walk up remote Cohab Canyon, named for the fugitives who sought seclusion in its hidden recesses.

Another Mormon pioneer, Ebenezer Bryce, built a cabin in the 1870s on a tributary that drained a large amphitheater or canyon of eroded rock. He has gone down in history for his remark that the rock jungle near his homestead was a "helluva place to lose a cow." Not only that, it was a marginal place to raise a cow, taking two hundred acres of land to feed one cow or a few sheep. Bryce's rock jungle is known today as Bryce Canyon. He and other early settlers left this land of abundant rock and meager grazing long ago, for the spare land soon became overgrazed and increasingly subject to devastating floods known as "gully washers." The life on this land was too difficult for homesteaders. Time would prove that it was fit only for tourists.

But in other parts of southeastern Utah, the cattle industry thrived until the 1900s. It was given a boost by the arrival of the Denver and Rio Grande Western Railway in 1883. That line was a spur from the first transcontinental railway to link the East and West, which was completed with the driving of a golden spike near Ogden, Utah, in 1869. The train opened up Canyon Country to exciting times. Cattle rustling became even more profitable and, as one historian pointed out, if there were no cattle to rustle, there was always the train or a bank to rob. Like the Mormon cohabitationists, Butch Cassidy, Utah's own frontier Robin Hood, and other assorted outlaws hid out in the canyons of the Capitol Reef area. The Grand Wash Canyon was one favorite spot as well as a place east of there which was used so frequently as a hideout it became known as "Robbers' Roost." Zane Grey, the famous western writer, has immortalized these rough-and-tumble days in several of his books.

Behunin Cabin, Capitol Reef National Park

By 1898, gold prospectors had discovered carnotite ore in the La Sal Mountains south and east of Moab, Utah. This greenish yellow ore, containing radon gas, vanadium, and uranium, began a small radium boom that ended in 1924. In the early 1900s a sample of radioactive ore from these deposits was sent to Madame Curie, who used it in her research on radium and radioactivity in France. After World War II, with the pressure of the cold war, there was a push to find more uranium and southeastern Utah became a target. Prospectors combed Canyon Country in the 1940s and 1950s, but Charlie Steen, a down-on-his-luck Texas geologist, started it all in 1952. After several frustrating, hard-luck years of prospecting in southeastern Utah, he borrowed a drill one day in Moab to explore a hunch. He returned with an ore sample that must have shocked the Moab ore appraisers out of their boots. For Steen had discovered a rich vein of uranium in his mine, soon to be called "Mi Vida." This sixty-million-dollar bonanza turned the peaceful Moab farm community of a few hundred souls into pandemonium. The boom had begun! The population of Canyon Country's largest town skyrocketed to over five thousand. People lived wherever they could, in tents, barns, and even caves. After the uranium bonanza, Moab settled back into a comfortable niche, until one of the world's largest supplies of potash was tapped in 1964. Once again Moab rode the crest of a miniboom. And when the potash industry leveled off, some of the economic slack was taken up in the late 1970s by oil and gas exploration in several nearby areas. But that economic bright spot was soon to be dampened by the oil patch depression of the 1980s.

So far industry has not significantly marred the clean air of southeastern Utah. Yet old-timers say that the coal fired over one hundred miles to the south in power plants in northern Arizona has encroached on southeastern Utah's clear atmosphere. And further encroachment may be coming. A decision to strip mine near Bryce Canyon probably means that the coal obtained there will be used to power coal-burning, soot-spreading, particulate-disbursing, power-generating plants and coal gassification plants nearby. And even if the coal is slurried to distant points like Las Vegas, Nevada, for processing, prevailing summer winds could blow the dirty air from those plants right back to Bryce Canyon. For now some of the worst proposals have been checked, but you can be sure that within time they will be back on the drawing boards, threatening the pristine air and solitude that is this area's special province. On some days you can no longer see forever from some of southeastern Utah's former crystal-clear viewpoints. So do not wait too long to see Canyon Country. Its wonder may not be there forever.

A Geological
Primer to
Southeastern Utah

In addition to your appreciation of the beauty of the landforms in southeastern Utah, you may want to know more about the geology of the area. Rocks exposed to view in river gorges, steep canyons, high cliff faces, and soaring rock outcroppings have a fascinating story to tell. I traveled for many years in this country without studying the region's geology. That was a mistake. Since boning up on the geology of the area, my appreciation has grown immeasurably and made the land a friendlier, more interesting place to roam. Before, I saw cold, hard rock. Except for its shape, I had little interest in it. Now when I see a sheer cliff wall in certain areas and recognize the Wingate formation, I immediately feel that I have found a trusted old friend. As a lay geologist I am not knowledgeable enough to identify all of the rock layers, especially when nature plays tricks and produces unconformities or irregularities in the rock structure. But I am able to read some of the simpler stories the rocks have to tell. With a little practice you can do the same by having the following orienting text, figures, and charts at your fingertips. First comes a geological history of the area. That is followed by a section which focuses on three important rock features that are helpful in identifying specific rock and formation layers. By carefully observing these rock features and cross-referencing them with the chart on p.36, you should be able to identify many of the rock layers you see. Once you know the name of the rock layer, you can look it up in the appendix at the end of this section. There the prehistoric scenes of Canyon Country geology will emerge as you read how that particular rock layer was formed millions of years ago.

Geological Overview

After walking a few miles in any direction in southeastern Utah's Canyon Country, you are apt to find yourself looking over the rim of an arroyo, a canyon, or a mesa, your forward progress stopped by the absence of land in front of you. You are confronted with a gaping chasm revealing many layers of rock in the side walls, descending to the depths below. One particularly dramatic and telling rim location is that of Dead Horse Point near Moab, Utah. There the role of time in the geologic process is illustrated graphically. From the rim of that six-thousand foot island in the sky, towering above the Colorado River two thousand feet below, you are looking at nearly a dozen layers of rock which took about 100 million years to form. Focus your eyes on the Colorado River and its immediate banks and you are looking at a rock layer formed over 275 million years ago.

As your gaze comes to rest on the rock directly under your feet, you might reflect that if you were standing there 170 million years ago, water from an ancient freshwater river would be flowing by your feet. It would deposit sand and silt that would eventually become the Kayenta sandstone you are standing on. But the stack of rocks under your feet and the rocks visible to you are only part of the original heap. At one time, beginning about 175 million years ago and ending less than 60 million years ago, there were another dozen layers that would have extended thousands of feet above where you are standing. At Dead Horse Point they have all eroded away over the last 10 million years, although near Bryce Canyon they are still intact. There you will walk on some of the very youngest rocks in Canyon Country, a mere 17 to 60 million years old.

So it has taken millions of years for most of the rocks you see in southeastern Utah to develop. Like a colorful multilayered cake, one rock has been forming on top of the other for the last 275 million years. From the exposed banks of the Colorado River below Dead Horse Point State Park to the rim of Bryce Canyon, nature has created a rock pile thousands of feet high, containing about two dozen different rocks. The amount of time represented by the scenery boggles the mind and is almost incomprehensible to those of us living in a fast-paced world in which our patience is often tried by a delay of a few minutes or hours. But rock historians who understand the cadence of nature's pace use the word "period" to signify a unit of time lasting many millions of years, such as the Permian or Cretaceous Period. And they have coined the term "era" for a longer span of time encompassing several periods, like the Paleozoic or Cenozoic, to help us comprehend the enormity of it all.

Most of the rocks in the plateau stack are sedimentary rocks formed in an astounding variety of environments. These rocks began taking shape in ancient deserts, salty oceans, fresh lakes, boggy swamps, fertile deltas, vast floodplains, and the tidelands and stream beds that once covered this land. Sedimentary rocks are formed from grains or fragments of older rocks scrubbed off by erosion and washed by rivers downstream. Then, with accumulated masses of organic materials and sometimes volcanic ash, they were deposited at the edges of floodplains or shallow seas. Water seepage from above carried chemicals such as calcium and clay, which acted as cements binding sediments together. But even with the proper ingredients, it took eons of pressure, heat, and chemical action to create the rocks we see today.

Sediments containing particles of sand produce sandstone, while fragments of shells and other limy remains of marine creatures form limestone. Ancient mud and silt deposits, when well compacted, form shales. When less well compacted, they form mudstones and siltstones. So paradoxically water, both fresh and salt, in copious quantities, has created the arid, skeletal landscapes you see today.

If the sediments that were laid down over several million years form a layer of rock that is of uniform composition, that sedimentary rock is named both according to the sediments that gave it its origin and by the location where the rock was first studied. For instance, Navajo sandstone was named for the region where the rock was first studied, the Navajo reservation, and for the sediments forming the rock, ancient sands. But if the sediments making up a layer of rock are not of uniform composition so that the layer contains several different kinds of rocks such as sandstone, siltstone, limestone, shale, or a conglomerate, the rock layer is called a "formation." Formations are named just like uniform rock layers. For instance, the Kayenta formation is named after the location where it was first studied near Kayenta, Arizona.

But the climax of this geologic story does not begin until after the formation of the sedimentary rocks. It is a saga about the forces within the earth that began to shape the earth's crust. Twenty-two to forty million years ago, molten rock pushed up the sedimentary rock of the plateau surface, doming it up thousands of feet, dotting the plateau with structures called laccolithic mountains. These scattered outcroppings, southeastern Utah's answer to the Rockies, include the Henry Mountains near Capitol Reef National Park, The Manti–La Sal Mountains east of Dead Horse Point State Park, and the Abajo or Blue Mountains south of Canyonlands National Park.

These mountains are the only mountains of igneous rock in the area. Igneous rock is formed from molten magma which has surfaced from within the earth. It is thought these rocks contained the radioactive element uranium, which water leached from them and spread into the surrounding area where over millions of years it became a part of the sedimentary rock formations. And as if that was not enough, beginning about ten million years ago, after the mountains were formed, dozens of consolidated layers of sedimentary rocks began to be slowly uplifted by forces in the earth's crust that are still not well understood. Over five million years at the rate of one-hundredth of an inch per year, the powerful pressures from within the earth raised thousands of square miles of flat lowlands from sea level to four thousand feet and higher above the surrounding land.

These elevated flatlands are called tablelands and are the locations of many of the Southwest's high deserts or plateaus. During this time of upheaval, the land was not only raised to great heights, but in some places it was warped and bent, while in other locations it was tilted and contorted. In some instances, huge blocks of the earth's crust fractured along fault lines and separated, opening the way for the further rising and development of higher but smaller plateaus like the Paunsaugunt. There, on the Paunsaugunt, standing on the rim of Bryce Canyon, you may sense the full impact of this incredible story about the powerful forces within the earth. The infinite tonnage of Wasatch rocks around the rim and below it were formed at sea level. Now they are with you, over eight thousand feet above today's oceans.

The rest of the story, probably the last eight to ten million years, is of the final shaping of the structures you will see today. After the great uplifting of the plateau, the Colorado River and its tributaries, the Fremont–Dirty Devil, Green, Escalante, and San Juan rivers, began to shape the land. Once a sluggish river, the Colorado became a forceful current. It began traveling mostly downhill from the newly formed Rocky Mountains at the eastern edge of the plateau and then picked up momentum as it descended, pell-mell, in its long journey down to the sea. With the land already fractured and ready for erosion, the increased flow of the river began the process of cutting down through the slowly uplifting sedimentary layers. It cut downward at approximately the same rate the land was rising so that today's riverbed that often is many thousand feet below the surrounding surface is, ironically, at about the same elevation it was when the whole process began.

In cutting down, the river exposed multiple layers of rock, creating the region's gorges and beginning the development of the canyons. If you stand on the canyon rim at Dead Horse Point and look down, you will see the Colorado River as it flows through the canyonlands two thousand feet below you. Draw an imaginary line out to the horizon from the rim where you are standing. That line for nearly fifty miles extends two thousand feet above and parallel to the Colorado River bed below you. Once that empty space defined by your line would have been filled with solid rock, extending miles and miles to the horizon. Some have said that the real testament to the forces of erosion is not what you see but what you do not see.

Throughout southeastern Utah erosion has created the vast, haunting spaces between canyon walls and the miles of open space between mesas and buttes that were once filled with solid rock. Literally hundreds of millions of tons of rock have been washed away by erosive forces. And it is still happening. It is estimated that the Colorado River, with its abrasive particles of sand and rock, erodes and washes away more than one million tons of sand and silt past any particular point every day. Even at that mind-boggling rate, the river is only washing away three cubic miles of rock each century. These silts are now being deposited or laid down as sediments in today's freshwater lakes, filling Lake Powell and Lake Mead at alarming rates. After millions of years, this sand and silt will be cemented into new sedimentary rock layers, to be studied and named by scientists of a future era.

But the river only accounts for part of the story of erosion by water. Although canyons are the children of rivers, the rivers do not play the only role. They may cut a gorge not too much wider than the river itself, but after that the forces of gravity and erosion take over. The river may undercut a cliff wall, but the root of a plant or tree or a wedge of ice may force a crack in the overhanging rock which, with gravity's help, finally topples. In this way gorges widen into canyons. So the river begins the process by opening the sedimentary rock layers to weathering. Seasonal moisture finishes the job.

Even the final precision sculpting of arches, monuments, spires, pinnacles, mesas, and buttes, and in some instances plateaus, is mostly the result of falling seasonal water. So as many have pointed

Lava boulders, Capitol Reef National Park

out, it is water that falls as snow over ten million icy winters which seeps into fissures, freezing and expanding to further split the rock. It is water in torrential downpours, driven by the gales of ten million windy springs, and water falling in huge, heavy drops (as you may well experience in your summer travels) during the course of ten million afternoon thunderstorms that pounds and abrades the rocks, which have no soil or vegetation to soften the blows. Rainwater courses down a path set by the cracks and fissures in the sedimentary rock. It scours the rock, dissolving the binding cements. It loosens grains of sand and washes them away, ever widening the cracks and fissures in the process, turning rivulets into gullies, gullies into washes, and washes into arroyos, lowering Canyon Country about one inch every four hundred fifty years. These are the major shaping forces for most of the scenery you will encounter.

But there are a number of phenomena you will see that are unexplained by this general summary. These include the lava boulders at Capitol Reef National Park, the unusual forces that created Bryce Canyon, and the great salt valley of the Moab region. Throughout Capitol Reef National Park, you will see round, black boulders strewn randomly about as though someone had turned loose thousands of bowling balls. The boulders are the result of volcanic activity about twenty million years ago south and west of the park near Boulder, Utah. Although the lava flows did not reach Capitol Reef, black basaltic boulders did. They are erosional remnants of the lava that caps Boulder Mountain, a segment of the Aquarius Plateau. They were pushed into the reef area by glacial meltwaters about ten thousand years ago after one of the last glacial ages. These forceful waters carried them many miles from their source, rounding and smoothing them as they tumbled along, depositing them in the Capitol Reef area. But nature did not stop its fanciful handiwork there. Many of the boulders, originally solid black in color, are now variegated, black and white. The white color that coats the boulder in interesting patterns is an alkali or lime coating that was deposited on those parts of the boulder's surface that have had contact with the soil over the last few thousand years.

Bryce Canyon is an exception to the rule that rivers are the mothers of canyons. At Bryce, the Wasatch sandstone formed between seventeen and sixty million years ago. That rock layer, hundreds of feet thick, consists of sand, silt, and lime sediments. It received the same powerful uplift phenomenon from within the earth as did the rest of the Colorado Plateau. As the earth rose, a series of north to south faults or zones of weakness in the earth's crust caused huge blocks of the crust to separate from one another. The Paunsaugunt fault was responsible for raising the land two thousand feet above the surrounding level, creating the Paunsaugunt Plateau. This faulting and fracturing, rather than a river, opened the plateau cliffs to erosion, creating the unusual shapes you see today. Thus Bryce is not a true canyon, but rather an escarpment at the very edge of a plateau. Erosion is eating away at the rim at a rate of about one foot every fifty years.

Most valleys are carved by the rivers that flow through them. But Moab Valley is different. Salt is responsible for creating its valley. Millions of years ago, a salt deposit as big as Maryland and about two and one-half miles thick was laid down, a legacy of ancient landlocked seas. Lighter than rock and like putty when put under pressure, the salt ascended via numerous faults and other weak places in the sedimentary rocks, doming and warping their surfaces upward. The salt supported the rock much as a hand supports the glove that it fills. But as surface moisture seeped through the sedimentary rocks, it invaded the supportive salt structures, dissolving them. This removed the support from the surface, which then cracked and dropped, leaving vast, sheer-walled valleys or trenches. In areas like Arches National Park, the surfaces were cracked along the edges of the domes, in evenly spaced lines called joints. The forces of erosion have worked on these joints, gradually widening them to leave fins, vertical slabs of harder rock, standing in rows between open, eroded spaces. From natural recesses in these fins, erosion has caused the formation of arches.

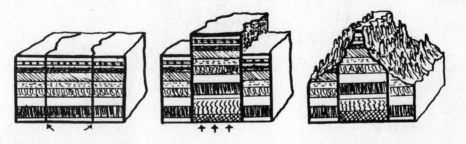

Bryce Canyon uplift and formation

Reading the Rocks

Now that you are acquainted with some of the ways sedimentary rocks are formed and shaped, the next step is to look at specific rocks and learn how to read their various clues. The accompanying chart (p.36) was devised to help in the identification of individual rocks or rock formations you may encounter. The chart details the age, thickness, color, characteristic shapes, surface features, fossil/mineral content, and some of the locations where the rocks can be seen. Having determined the identity of a rock layer that interests you, you may then turn to the appendix at the end of this section and read about environmental conditions prevailing when it was formed. You will discover that the arid landscapes you see before you, paradoxically, often had their origins in ancient fresh lakes, saltwater seas, or in verdant marshlands teeming with marine and other life-forms.

In order to identify a layer of rock, you must focus your powers of observation on four of its main features: shape, color, surface characteristics, and contents. By noting these features and cross-referencing them with the chart, you should be able to make a reasonably accurate identification. On the first try, you may not be able to narrow the identification to a single rock or formation since a number of the rocks have very similar features.

But suppose you narrow your identification to two or three rocks on the chart. Most likely these rocks will appear at different levels in the geologic time column. If so, return to nature for more clues.

Note the adjacent rocks above and below the rock you wish to identify. Cross-reference these features on the chart. A positive identification of one or both of the neighboring rock layers may resolve the ambiguity about the rock in question, for the latter will appear on the geologic time column just as it appears in nature. It can be identified as the rock just above, below, or sandwiched between the positively identified neighboring rock layers. It is not always possible to make a positive identification with the materials assembled in this book. There are complex geologic variables and exceptions to the usual patterns that this greatly simplified geologic primer does not accommodate. But this is a beginning to introduce you to some understandings that will, I hope, enhance your visit. If your interest goes beyond the scope of this primer, consult the geology resource section in the bibliography at the end of the book.

In order to read the rocks for clues to their identity, you must first look beyond their scenic beauty and focus on their physical characteristics. One of the most important features is rock shape. As you will recall, water erosion is instrumental in shaping the sedimentary rocks. But the precise shape sculpted by the water is determined by

Butte

Mesa

several factors within the rock layer itself. These include its thickness, as well as how hard or soft the rock is. Harder rock layers contain more of the natural cements such as iron oxide, silica, or calcium carbonate, while softer rocks contain fewer of these binding agents. In some rock layers, the quantity of these natural cements varies throughout the rock so that some portions which are softer than others erode at a different rate, producing a variety of interesting shapes and in some instances where the rock is very soft, creating pockets or tanks in the rock.

In addition to its hardness or softness, the shape of a particular rock layer is also affected by the hardness or softness of the rock layers immediately above and below it in the sedimentary rock

stack. You will see these exposed alternating layers of hard and soft rock along the walls of canyons and on the steep sides and slopes of plateaus and mesas, either formed by faulting and uplifting of the land or by the action of a river cutting down on all sides of a land mass, leaving it elevated above the surrounding land. If the top of one of these elevated land masses is composed of soft rock, it will erode away until a layer of erosion-resistant harder rock under it emerges to the surface, usually forming a flat protective cap over the rock layers below it. But since this cap may be many feet thick, it also serves as part of the vertical cliff wall.

It is this flat-topped cap which gives this landform its name since the Spanish thought these flat-topped hills that were wider than they were high looked like tables or mesas. The slopes or sides of a mesa below the cap are often made of shales or softer sandstones. Within time, even the durable cap of a mesa reduces in size, for as its softer base recedes with erosion, the edge of the cap rock is undermined. With nothing to support it and with the help of ice and root wedging, it eventually cracks, splits, and falls. As a mesa is shrunk in size by seasonal erosion, it may also be cut into smaller landforms by rivers and their tributaries. If these smaller mesa remnants are at least as high as they are wide, they are called buttes.

Further erosion may narrow a butte to a monument, tower, pinnacle, or spire. The shaft

Monuments and spires

Rock and Formation Profiles

Time	Rocks or Formation	Thickness	Sediments	Shape(s)
Cenozoic Era — Tertiary Period 63,000,000 years ago	Wasatch group	600 feet	Limestones, siltstones	Spires, pinnacles, balanced rocks, intricate shapes
Cretaceous Period 135,000,000 years ago	Mancos shale	3,500 feet	Shale with some sandstone and limestone	Fluted mesa cliffs, rounded mounds, badlands, smooth slopes
	Dakota Formation	350 feet	Conglomerate, sandstone, shale	Low cliffs, bluffs, slopes
Mesozoic Era	Morrison Formation	400 feet	Mudstone, shale, sandstone, volcanic ash	Hills, slopes, ridges
	Summerville Formation	300 feet	Interlayered sandstone, siltstone, mudstone, shale, gypsum	Ledgy cliffs, slopes, open desert
Jurassic Period 180,000,000 years ago	Entrada/ Moab tongue	150 feet	Sandstone	Low cliffs, sheer walled domes, petrified dunes
	Entrada/ Slickrock member	350 feet	Sandstone, siltstone	Arches, rounded fins, domes, spires, bluffs, cliffs

Color(s)	Surface Features and Mineral/Fossil Content	Location(s)
Pink, red, white	Mammal bones	Bryce Canyon National Park
Blue-gray, gray, black	Petrified wood, sea fossils (shark's teeth), quartz pebbles	Capitol Reef National Park. Between 8 and 30 miles east of visitor center along Utah Highway 24 to about 10 miles east of Caineville.
Light brown to white, gray, green	Fossilized oyster shells and ferns, petrified wood and bone, agate	Capitol Reef National Park. 12.5 miles along Utah Highway 24 from visitor center, then turn right on Notom Road 2 miles to see Dakota Formation.
Variegated green, red, gray	Dinosaur bones, petrified wood and bone, agate, chert	U.S. Interstate Highway 70 and Utah Highway 24 junction and south of junction on 24 about 3 miles; east of U.S. Highway 163/191 just north of 163/191 and Utah Highway 313 junction; about 9 miles east of Capitol Reef National Park visitor center on Utah Highway 24 as road cuts through high ridge; and Wolfe Cabin area, Arches National Park
Red-brown (definite brownish cast)	Ripple rock, mud crack casts, agate beds, thin horizontal bedding `	12 miles south of Moab, U.S. Highway 163/191 cuts through this rock and at 14 miles appears to right of highway. Also, trail to Delicate Arch, Arches National Park.
White	Cross-stratified	Found in Arches National Park in Salt Valley and Klondike Bluffs areas and the top 4 feet of the crest of Delicate Arch.
Salmon, buff		Most of the arches in Arches National Park, including Delicate Arch; rock structures in Cathedral Valley, Capitol Reef National Park.

(continued on next page)

Time	Rocks or Formation	Thickness	Sediments	Shape(s)
Mesozoic Era — Jurassic Period 180,000,000 years ago	Entrada/ Dewey Bridge member (related to Carmel Formation)	100 feet	Siltstone, mudstone	Severely contorted shapes
	Carmel Formation	650 feet	Siltstone, mudstone, shale, limestone	Red deserts, pedestals, or bases
	Navajo sandstone	850 feet	Sandstone (quartz sand)	Rounded humps, domes, knobs, sheer high cliffs, butte forms, petrified dunes
Triassic Period 230,000,000 years ago	Kayenta Formation	350 feet	Sandstone, shale, siltstone	Stone wall cap rock atop Wingate sandstone; ledgy slopes, small cliffs, natural bridges
	Wingate sandstone	375 feet	Sandstone	Sheer vertical walled cliffs with vertically cracked or fluted surface; towering spires; boulders litter slopes below

Color(s)	Surface Features and Mineral/Fossil Content	Location(s)
Dark red	Thin wavy bands of sediment layers, i.e., distorted horizontal layering or "wrinkling"	Arches National Park. In pedestal of Balanced Rock and in entrance of park, as well as in the Windows and Devil's Garden areas. Also, at base of Monitor and Merrimac buttes on Dead Horse Point State Park Road.
Gray-green to reddish brown	Occasionally cross-bedded	Not seen too frequently in this area. Forms the pedestal for Balanced Rock in Arches National Park. Also, in outcrops 7.5 miles east of visitor center at Capitol Reef National Park.
Mostly white, but may be lightly tinted with yellow, red, brown	Large-scale high-angle cross-bedding; pterosaur and other tracks	Entire Escalante Canyon system. At Capitol Reef National Park, Capitol Dome, and base of Golden Throne. Buttes and domes rising above mesa at Dead Horse Point State Park and Canyonlands National Park. In Arches National Park, petrified dunes 4.5 miles from visitor center.
From whitish/ grayish to dark reds and browns	Small-scale cross-bedding; dinosaur tracks	Throughout area caps Wingate sandstone cliffs; at Capitol Reef National Park forms Hickman Natural Bridge. Forms walkways at Dead Horse Point State Park and Grandview Point, Canyonlands National Park. Dinosaur tracks north and west of Moab on Utah Highway 279 (Potash Road).
Light orange to red-brown, pinkish	Often cross-bedded	Forms the high, sheer cliffs of Dead Horse Point State Park, Island in the Sky, Canyonlands National Park, and Capitol Reef National Park. High cliffs across highway from Arches National Park visitor center. Petroglyphs at Newspaper Rock, Canyonlands National Park region, are pecked on Wingate.

(continued on next page)

Time			Rocks or Formation	Thickness	Sediments	Shape(s)
Mesozoic Era	Triassic Period 230,000,000 years ago		Chinle Formation (includes Shinarump member)	650 feet	Shale, siltstone, mudstone, conglomerate, volcanic ash	Steep ledgy slopes at base of Wingate cliffs; low, rounded hills
			Moenkopi Formation	1,400 feet	Mudstone, siltstone, sandstone	Steep slopes with many protruding, hard ledges; buttressed cliffs; low ridges; columns
Paleozoic Era	Permian Period 280,000,000 years ago		Kaibab limestone	300 feet	Limestone	Deep in canyon walls
			White Rim sandstone	250 feet	Sandstone	Vertical or undercut cliffs; balanced rocks, towers
			Cedar Mesa sandstone	1,200 feet	Sandstone	Vertical cliffs, natural bridges
			Cutler Formation	1,400 feet	Sandstone, mudstone, shale	Strangely rounded walls columns
	Pennsylvania Period 310,000,000 years ago		Honaker Trail Formation	3,000 feet	Interlayered shale, limestone, sandstone	Near-vertical cliffs; narrow shelves, terraces

Color(s)	Surface Features and Mineral/Fossil Content	Location(s)
Variegated dark reds, browns, blue-green and gray-green	Marine fossils and fossilized plants; uranium	At Capitol Reef National Park and Dead Horse Point State Park and Canyonlands National Park, appears as grayish sloping base below Wingate sandstone cliffs. At Capitol Reef National Park, Shinarump caps Chimney Rock and makes up Twin Rocks. At Capitol Reef National Park, Slickrock Divide caps red Moenkopi. At location of Olyer Uranium Mine, Capitol Reef National Park.
Brick red (reddish brown)	Ripple marks, mud crack casts; occasional tracks	The base rock along highway between Fruita and Torrey, Capitol Reef National Park. Forms the base of Chimney Rock spire at Capitol Reef National Park. The ledgy slopes just above the white rim at Dead Horse Point State Park and Canyonlands National Park.
Grayish white		Only visible deep in canyon walls west of Fruita, Capitol Reef National Park, as viewed from Goosenecks Trail.
White	Cross-bedded layers	The White Rim as seen from Dead Horse Point State Park and Grandview Point, Canyonlands National Park.
White		White bands of the Needles, Canyonlands National Park. Base of north Sixshooter Peak and surrounding flatland, Canyonlands National Park.
Dark red		Along U.S. Highway 163/191, ½ mile north of Arches National Park entrance and north to Utah Highway 313 junction. Fisher Towers east of Moab. Red bands of the Needles, Canyonlands National Park.
Red, white, gray or a combination of the above	Marine fossils	Below Dead Horse Point State Park in Colorado River Gorge. Just beyond end of pavement of Utah Highway 279 (Potash Road), out of Moab.

of a monument or spire is usually harder than the base on which it stands and, like a mesa or butte, is capped with a narrow rim of even harder rock. Erosion of the softer rock under the cap may reduce a spire to a variety of interesting and weird forms called hoodoo rocks. Hour-glass-shaped balanced rocks, delicate mush-room-shaped demoiselles, and strangely eroded pillars and pedestals are all hoodoo variants. Over time erosion finally topples hoodoo rocks to the ground. There they remain as boulders until further seasonal erosion demolishes them altogether and they disintegrate into pebbles and finally into the sand you will walk on as you explore the surface of the Colorado Plateau.

Another example of the importance of hard–soft layering is in the formation of canyon walls. When canyon walls contain many alternating hard–soft layers stacked on top of one another, erosion proceeds at a different pace for each level, creating a stair-step effect as it shapes the sloping sides of the canyon. In Canyon Country sheer steep cliff faces of canyons are often of Wingate sandstone. Although it is topped by a rim of harder Kayenta sandstone, it rests on a base of softer Chinle formation rock which erodes so easily it undercuts the Wingate, leaving it extended un-supported in space. Eventually it splits off in giant pieces, leaving sheer, vertical cliffs.

Window

Each layer of rock, then, erodes to character-istic shapes that aid in its identification. Other com-mon shapes that aid in identifying a particular rock layer are as follows: badlands, rounded mounds, bluffs, ledgy cliffs, slopes, domes, fins, rounded walls, terraces, fluted cliffs, columns, ridges, towers, arches, windows, bridges, and pinnacles. Some of these shapes are self-explanatory, but a few need some elaboration.

A badland is a waterless area usually without vegetation, filled with monotonous repetitive slopes and hills, formed from soft, half-hardened rocks such as shales or limy siltstones. Badland topography has narrow gullies and sharp ridges and is often formed on the side of a plateau, hill, or mesa. You will see some incredibly beautiful badlands just east of Capitol Reef National Park near Caineville, Utah. You will also see giant rock walls with holes right through the middle of them. These holes are created by seasonal erosion and are either called arches or windows, depending on the perspective of the people who first discovered them. One person's "arch" might be another's "window." Generally if the hole in the rock opens to the ground below or if the hole is close enough to any of the rock's edges to influence its shape, it is called an arch. Windows are holes in the rock that are higher up from the rock's base. Their apertures are far enough away from the top of the rock that they do not affect the shape of the rock's edge. In Canyon Country, arches form in Wingate, Navajo, Cedar Mesa, and Entrada sandstones.

The Entrada gives birth to most of the arches in Arches National Park. There, the Entrada sand-

Demoiselle

Sandstone fins, Arches National Park

stone has been extremely fractured and jointed in the vertical plane by a variety of forces. Some believe that the vertical cracking in the Entrada began after the many layers of rocks that had previously formed on top of it eroded away. Experts think that the release of weight from above the Entrada caused it to slowly "rebound" or expand, thus creating many vertical cracks or faults in the rock. In other instances, the joints or cleavage lines were thought to have been caused by the collapsing of rock surfaces when their underlying salt support dissolved. But whatever the cause of the vertical fracturing, all are agreed that the next step involves seasonal erosion or weathering. Erosion eventually widens the cracks into narrow canyons, which separate the rock into vertical partitions called fins. Fins are relatively narrow sandstone walls which may be one hundred feet tall and two or three times as long. Small recesses in the vertical surface of the fins are enlarged by erosion to form alcoves or shallow caves. This process may occur on one or both sides of the fin. Eventually, quarrying by water and ice persists until the fins are perforated. The perforations eventually enlarge to become graceful arches or high clerestory windows.

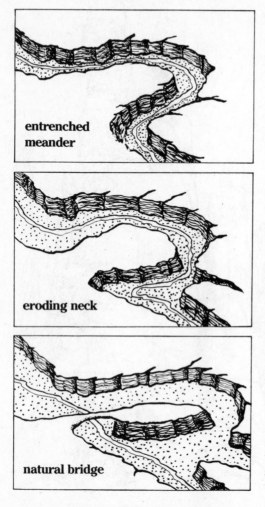

entrenched
meander

eroding neck

natural bridge

Evolution of a natural bridge

Natural bridges also are perforations of rock, but are formed by running water instead of rain. These natural bridges occur on streams where rivers have gouged deep winding curves known as meanders. The stream carves a great curve in its streambed, which comes back almost as if to meet itself before coursing on. At the point where it almost meets itself, it works away at the rock barrier to create a thin wall of rock between the curves. Eventually water on both sides of the thinning rock wall cuts and gouges away at it, until one day there is a breakthrough and the stream leaves its old curving course for a shorter straighter one

through the rock wall, flowing under a bridge of its own creation. Often you will see the old abandoned channel to the side of most natural bridges, as the river follows its new course under the bridge.

After noticing the shape of the rock layers you wish to identify, note their color. This second identifying feature is a characteristic that makes Canyon Country rocks unique in the world. For nowhere else will you see the intense coloration of varicolored rock you see there. Rocks acquire color from the minerals they contain. Consequently a rock may have several different colors, depending on where it is found. Iron in its many forms is responsible for most of the coloration you will see. In its oxide form, it colors many of the red and red-hued rocks. In its other chemical states, iron creates some of the blacks, browns, yellows, grays, and greens you will see. Carbon gives a black or gray color. Manganese gives black, brown, red, and purple, while copper gives green. Grayish layers mixed with more colorful sandstone strata usually contain volcanic ash. This material fell on Canyon Country from the Arizona area, hundreds of miles south, where volcanoes were extremely active millions of years ago. White or whitish colors represent rock layers formed from relatively pure sand of either beach, beach dune, or offshore sandbar origin. Red-hued layers within such sandstone represent land sediments rich in iron oxide which have been washed over the white sand by freshwater streams.

The white coloration you will see on some rocks is a superficial coating of alkali deposited on the rocks from the soil they have been in contact with. Sometimes alkali will coat level areas of the ground, giving the appearance of snow. Another colorful feature you often will see in Canyon Country is a huge streak of light brown to purplish-black pigment on the side of a cliff. This phenomenon is called desert varnish. It looks like someone took a pail of varnish and poured it down the cliffside, leaving the face of the cliff dramatically streaked. Desert varnish at its darkest is thought to take thousands of years to form and for years was thought to be the result of either manganese or iron oxides slowly leached by water from the rock and deposited on its surface. More recent research has provided an alternative theory. Some think

Desert varnish

that much of the streaking on cliff walls is due to fine windblown particles of clay which have settled on the rough porous faces of the cliff walls. Then water from runoff or seeps, containing manganese and iron oxides, penetrates the clay. The water evaporates, leaving the oxides to stain the clay particles and cement them to the cliff wall, producing a lustrous coating that resembles a burnished Pueblo Indian pot.

Rocks also may be colored by lichen or algae which grow on their surface, often imparting a green cast. And of course the colorful sandstones are greatly affected by the sunlight, giving off different hues at different times of the day. Some have said that at certain times of the day the sandstones do not just reflect light, they seem to glow as if they had their own light source.

Rock shape and color are the easiest identifying marks to use since they can often be seen from a distance as you travel along. But the third rock characteristic requires a closer examination of the rock surface, for you will be looking for some identifying marks imprinted on the rock surface or captured within the rock millions of years ago. In your close-up examination of the rock layer, you will be looking for clues to the rock's history such as cross-bedding lines, ripple marks, mud crack casts, dinosaur tracks, and the fossils or minerals imbedded in the rock. When you find a rock surface feature, look it up in the rock identification chart under the column of "surface features." Then follow the column horizontally to the left to find the names of the rocks that are known to contain that feature. These rock features truly open windows on the prehistoric settings in which the rocks were formed.

When you walk up to a sandstone wall or a slab of sandstone on the ground, look carefully at

Cross-bedded sandstone

On the surface of some sandstone slabs, you may be fortunate enough to find "ripple marks." This is a handsome feature with delicate, wavy ridges coursing across the rock surface. Mud and silt at the edge of a shallow sea, millions of years ago, were rippled by the water's action as it continuously advanced and retreated. The ripple pattern was preserved when it was buried under the forming sediments. After turning into rock, it later was exposed to erosion where the overlying sediments were washed off revealing intact, after millions of years, the indelible evidence of an inland sea lapping at its own shoreline. From time to time you may see a surface feature resembling crinkled glass or mud cracks in a dry riverbed. These are fossilized mud cracks representative of shallow water conditions during prehistoric times. They formed in mud and silt sediments that were wet and then dried out, cracking in typical patterns. The cracks and depressions were filled by overlying sediments of a different type. When the sediments turned to rock and were exposed to erosion, the softer, original mud sediments washed away, leaving a cast of the cracks with raised edges in the more resistant covering layer. Other surface features to look for are dinosaur tracks, fossilized oyster shells and ferns, as well as petrified wood.

its surface. The surface of some sandstone appears as if it was laid down evenly. But the surface of other sandstone is composed of many layers or strata sloping at different angles to one another, sometimes overlapping or interfingering. This cross-bedded or cross-stratified sandstone is thought to have been laid down during howling sandstorms millions of years ago when Sahara-like desert conditions prevailed in southeastern Utah. There, as winds changed direction, sand blew over already-existing dunes, each new layer being deposited at a variety of cross angles to the previous layers. The cross-angle configuration in the sediments was then covered and preserved by the later formation of a shallow sea. Over time the protected sediments hardened to create the surface features you see today in these petrified sand dunes.

Ripple rock

Seeing Canyon Country

Moab, Utah, is an excellent place to stay while seeing many of the sights in the eastern portion of this section. From there, by taking half-day or full-day trips, you can explore Arches National Park, Dead Horse Point State Park, Edge of the Cedars National Monument, and two accessible areas of Canyonlands National Park. Moab is also headquarters for many raft trips down the Colorado River.

But to see Capitol Reef National Park, the Anasazi Indian State Historical Monument at Boulder, Utah, the Escalante–Calf Creek country, Bryce Canyon National Park, and other sights, it is best to spend several nights in the western portion of southeastern Utah. All of these sights are now connected by one of America's most scenic paved highways, Utah Highway 12. This one-hundred-mile long stretch of highway leaves Grover and Torrey, Utah, near exotic Capitol Reef National Park, crosses through high forest and meadowland over Boulder Mountain on the flank of the Aquarius Plateau (offering incredible views of the desert below), dips deep into the Escalante Canyon system, and winds through picturesque and remote southern Utah towns until it reaches Bryce Canyon National Park. And if you plan to visit Bryce Canyon, it is best to spend at least part of a day and a night there since the changes in the sunlight best reveal its beauty. For more details about overnight stays at both Capitol Reef National Park and Bryce Canyon National Park, see "Staying There" at the end of this section.

Moab—The Hub of Canyon Country

Close to the Colorado River in a green valley surrounded by pink and red sandstone cliffs, Moab is on the way to or from most of the scenic sights of southeastern Utah. One of the lowest spots on the Colorado Plateau, at four thousand feet elevation, it is the largest town in Canyon Country, with a population pushing five thousand. It offers a wide variety of good accommodations and decent cafés and restaurants. From early times, Moab has exuded a western ambience because of its location on the frontier of the slickrock jungles that surround it. It has been host to prospectors of all sorts and booms of many kinds since the rocks around it began yielding a wide variety of valuable minerals.

Farmers, cowboys, and rustlers have walked its tree-lined streets along with outlaws like Kid Curry and Butch Cassidy. Cassidy once boarded the old Moab Ferry by force and took it across the Colorado River as he fled from the scene of his first bank robbery just over the border in Telluride, Colorado. With such an eclectic history it is no wonder that Moab is the tolerant, open, and friendly place it is. The business people there will cater to your needs in the same friendly manner they used in the past to host thirsty and tired, dust-covered prospectors, miners, and cowboys.

So do not hesitate to "bed down" a few nights

in the western town of Moab. As you tour the national and state parks and monuments by day, you will return each evening to a typical southwestern farming and ranching town that offers a number of attractive amenities. Away from the busy, urbanized sprawl of U.S. Highway 191 that bisects the town, you will find streets lined with giant old cottonwoods and fragrant Catalpa trees. There you will see many of the early Mormon pioneer homes made from either hand-hewn red or brown sandstone blocks or from bricks molded from the local clays. These sturdy buildings must have offered a sense of security to the early settlers who named their town after the Old Testament kingdom of Moab, a "far country" beyond the Jordan and Dead seas, situated on the edge of Zion and surrounded by flat-topped mountains. The early Mormons must have felt that they, too, were occupying a remote country far from civilization as they established southeastern Utah's first white community smack-dab in the middle of the mysterious and foreboding Canyon Country in a valley ringed with flat-topped mesas.

Moab has two easily accessible and well-maintained parks. The "City Park" or Moab Park is located several blocks west of U.S. Highway 191 at 400 North Street and 100 West Street. The Moab public swim center is at that corner of the park where, for a modest sum, you can take a dip on a hot summer day. Along Park Drive, on the south side of the park, is a large expanse of green grass rimmed by stately old trees shading a number of picnic tables under them. This oasis is a pleasant place to spend part of a warm summer evening slicing up and devouring watermelon purchased and chilled upon request by one of the nearby grocery stores. More picnic sites are available in another tree-shaded park maintained by the Moab Lion's Club along the south bank of the Colorado River just east of U.S. Highway 191.

Take a brief tour of downtown Moab where there are some interesting shops and craft stores, as well as the always instructive Moab Museum at 118 East Center Street. Along Main Street are several excellent "rock" shops specializing in many of the unusual rocks and fossils found in the area. One of them provides a free slide show each evening depicting some of the geological wonders of the region. Moab is an excellent place to buy rock and mineral specimens, including petrified wood and certain fossilized plants and insects. And increasingly, Moab is becoming a place to purchase American Indian handicrafts. However, if you are a collector or are looking for the very finest in Indian arts and crafts, you may want to spend part of a day driving to Blanding, Utah, eighty miles south. There, one or two shops carry some of the finest Indian jewelry, pottery, and weavings available. From Blanding south, into the area covered by Sections II and III of this book, the opportunity increases for finding high-quality, authentic Indian crafts. For more information about Moab, write Moab Visitor Center, Grand County Travel Council, 805 North Main Street, Moab, Utah 84532. Telephone: 1-801-259-8825. Or the Moab Chamber of Commerce and Convention Bureau, 59 North Main, Second Floor, Moab, Utah 84532. Telephone: 1-801-259-7531.

Arches National Park

Arches National Park lies approximately four miles northwest of Moab just east of U.S. Highway 191. It contains in its one hundred fourteen square miles of rock wilderness an amazing array of natural stone arches, windows, bridges, spires, and pinnacles. But the most remarkable features are its approximately ninety natural arches whose varied and graceful spans are a photographer's delight.

Many of the more picturesque arches may be seen from the eighteen-mile paved road that starts at the visitor center and ends at Devil's Garden, elevation 5,355 feet. Paved laterals from the main road into other parts of the park extend the all-weather road system for another five miles. At Devil's Garden and several other major stops in the park, relatively short, well-laid-out trails are available for your use. At several of the trailheads, self-guiding maps and pamphlets are available that will lead you to some of the park's more interesting sights and most famous arches. One of these, Landscape Arch, is the largest known natural stone span in the world, stretching almost a football field from end to end. It is also the highest span in the park, arching 106 feet above the ground. Yet another well-known arch in the park that has graced the covers of many magazines is unbelievably beautiful Delicate Arch. The foot trail leading to it is chock-full of excitement and scenic beauty at every turn and is the subject of the narrative that follows.

Many of the arches were known by the end of the nineteenth century. But it was not until the 1920s that a European-born prospector became so enthused about these scenic wonders that he alerted officials to their rare beauty, setting off a chain reaction that has led to their preservation. With the help of many local residents, the area achieved National Monument status in 1929 and National Park status in 1971. Since then the number of visitors to the park has been constantly on the increase. Last year around 500,000 travelers enjoyed the park. In some years approximately 15 to 20 percent of the visitors were from other countries, the largest number coming from Europe, reminding us that the park's first enthusiast, the man who put Arches on the map, was European born. For more information, write Arches National Park, Box 846, Moab, Utah 84532. Telephone: 1-801-259-8161.

Seeing the Park

After paying the entry fee (which also allows you access to Canyonlands National Park), stop off at the visitor center. It offers a good natural history display and further augments this text on the formation of the arches and other geological phenomena you will see. The center has many books on display which are for sale. Numerous free mimeographed sheets about various aspects of the park are available for the asking. Above all, before you leave the center area, do not miss the excellent nature trail nearby. Ask for a guide to the trail before leaving the visitor center, and with guide in hand, go out the front door and turn right. Walk a short distance toward the rising cliffs to this extremely educational trail.

The common vegetation of the area is well marked. You will see and learn about rabbitbrush, squawbush, sage, yucca, blackbrush, cliffrose, and Mormon tea. In addition you will learn about cryptogamic soil or brown sugar soil, a common phenomenon in the high desert. Cryptogams are plants which reproduce other than by making seeds. Some cryptogams are algae, fungi, and lichens. These minute plants often form gardens which will completely cover the soil or streak the face of a rock, giving the surface a crusty look. Soil rich in these crusts absorbs more moisture, making it easier for plants to grow in this arid land. In addition the cryptogams hold the soil in place, as well as providing it with nutrients.

Before leaving the visitor center, you may want to purchase for a small fee a booklet entitled "The Guide to an Auto Tour of Arches National Park." This booklet is keyed to all the numbered pullouts and major sites of the park. You can do a

Landscape Arch, Arches National Park

Cliffrose

quick auto tour of some of the major sites from the road and walk one or two of the trails in a long half day. But to see and walk to most of the major sites in the park requires a full day or two half-day visits. Some stay for a week or more. If you travel from Moab to the park, tour the principal paved roads, and return to Moab, you will have traveled approximately fifty miles. Because of its relatively low elevation, some parts of the park are like a hothouse in the summer. So prepare for your visit accordingly (see "Practical Hints" at the back of the book).

The Adventuresome Trail to Delicate Arch: A Narrative Account

It is 7 A.M. here in Moab. We seem to wake up early in this land of bright, morning light. But this morning we are awake a little earlier than usual as we eagerly anticipate our trip to Delicate Arch. Although we went there many years ago and have periodically reviewed the colored slides we took then, there has been a strong urge to go back again to experience some of the magic of that magnificent landform which can only be felt in its presence. So today is the much-awaited day.

Although Moab is quiet this morning as we drive north out of town, my thoughts are racing. I have just finished reading Edward Abbey's stimulating book *Desert Solitaire*. The book was

written a number of years ago and recounts Abbey's experience as a ranger at Arches National Park. It is a well-written book, rich in descriptive language and filled with information about the plants, animals, birds, and rocks of the area. It is the best nature guide anyone could have for the Moab area and I am anxious to put it to use.

We cross the bridge over the Colorado River and the bridge over Court House Wash, which drains one of our favorite areas in the park. At the entrance to Arches, we pay our fee and then follow the excellent road as it zigzags up the cliff face. In about one mile we stop at the first pullout, labeled the Moab Fault. From this vantage point, a valuable geological lesson is laid out before our eyes. At one time the heap of rocks we are standing on and the rocky cliffs over there on the other side of this narrow part of Moab Valley, across U.S. Highway 191, were part of the same contiguous rock mass. At that time there was no valley. There would have been no space for the railroad tracks, the highway, or Arches visitor center.

About six million years ago, forces in the earth's crust caused a fracture or a fault in the solid rock bed where the highway is now. The side we are standing on sank thousands of feet, while the side across the highway probably rose. This side ended up twenty-six hundred feet or almost one-half mile lower than the other side. The space between the fractured and cracked walls was probably very small at first. The huge gap we see between the cliff walls this morning was created by seasonal erosion or weathering over millions of years. The fault extended south of here, too, opening that area to weathering and the eventual creation of Moab's wide valley.

Moab Valley is a geographical oddball because the Colorado River runs perpendicular to it. Usually rivers run parallel to valleys since most valleys are formed by the rivers that cut through them. But it was different for the Moab Valley. Although the Colorado River was there first, it did not create Moab Valley. The valley was formed as a result of the faulting and the weathering mentioned above. At that point, the Colorado River, crossing the north part of the newly formed valley, might have left its channel to flow south down the valley. But that was impossible, for when the valley was formed the land collapsed in such a way that the south end of the valley was considerably higher than the north end. The Colorado River was thus forced to cross the top of the valley, never really penetrating its long axis. Valleys and rivers that have this kind of relationship are called paradoxical valleys. From the bridge where we crossed the Colorado River this morning, the river flows through a gap in the valley's southwestern cliff walls a little over a mile from the bridge. That gap, similar to a mountain pass, is called the "portal" and it is there that the Colorado River enters its canyon system that stretches 270 miles before terminating just below the Grand Canyon in Arizona.

Now we turn our attention to the rock layers. I point out that the top layers in the cliffs across the highway look like Wingate formation rocks topped by Kayenta sandstone. But on this side of the road, those formations are nowhere in sight. They are still deep in the ground. What we see over here on the surface are Entrada formation rocks and some Navajo sandstone, younger rocks that were formed on top of the Wingate and the Kayenta as the sedimentary rock pile was assembled. On the opposite side of the highway where we should see the Entrada and Navajo rocks and other younger rocks in the pile, we see nothing but blue sky. Those rocks which protruded for hundreds of feet were unprotected and were so vulnerable to weathering over millions of years that they have all eroded away. But on this side of the highway, the Entrada and the Navajo remain, for they were on the bottom of the heap protected by still younger rocks like the Summerville, Morrison, Dakota, and Mancos which topped them. Many of those younger, unprotected top layers that have eroded away here along the fault line can be seen in other areas of the park.

Content that we have learned something new, we pass in another mile the maze of rock fins known as South Park Avenue. These fins resemble many American cityscapes as they reach skyward, blocking the sun in many places below them. In yet another mile we catch glimpses of the Manti–La Sal Mountains, the youngest rock mass in view, formed from the action of molten magma only twenty-two million years ago. Mount Peale at 12,721 feet is the highest peak in the La Sals. Now at 3.3 miles from the visitor center, we see Court House Towers. On a previous visit here we made a

long stop, for it is a fine example of how erosional forces carve a variety of evolving forms from what was once a huge solid wall of rock called a mesa (see "Reading the Rocks"). Shortly we pass "petrified dunes" or cross-bedded Navajo sandstone and then pull over to look at Balanced Rock at 8.5 miles from the visitor center. We all heave a sigh of relief that it is still here for it looks like it could topple any moment. And that will certainly be its fate when the attached, softer base weathers to a thinness that will not support it. When that 58-foot-tall oblong ham-shaped piece of Entrada sandstone takes a dive from its 73-foot-high rock perch, it is going to make a resounding noise as its 3,600 tons hit the ground below.

Just beyond Balanced Rock, about 9 miles from the visitor center, we bypass the spur road into the Window Section of the park. Last year we took that road, traveling its 3-mile length to the two parking areas where it dead-ends. From the first parking lot, we followed a trail to see The Spectacles (North Window and South Window) and Turret Arch. From the second parking lot on the north side of the dead-end loop, we walked an easy 400 yards to view Double Arch or Double "O" Arch, one of the most geometrically interesting arches in the region. Our kids remind me that on that route they saw the "Parade of Elephants," a series of whimsically shaped stones resembling animals in a circus parade. From the Windows intersection we drive down into Salt Valley, where some of the younger formations like the Summer-

Balanced Rock, Arches National Park

ville and Morrison, which were eroded away along the fault line, can be seen. We bypass several of the overlooks and reach the turnoff to Wolfe Ranch and Delicate Arch trailhead at 12 miles from the visitor center. We recall that last year, when we had less time on our hands, we passed by this turnoff and continued on the Scenic Drive road past the Fiery Furnace area, with its maze of sandstone walls, to the Devil's Garden area at the end of the road. There, in a shaded picnic spot, we refreshed ourselves with food and drink from our small styrofoam icebox before taking the somewhat level 2-mile, one-hour round-trip walk along an "avenue" of smaller arches to the world's largest natural rock span, Landscape Arch. But perhaps more than anything else we remember returning, sweating hot, to our Moab motel for a refreshing swim.

Now we swing off the main road onto the Delicate Arch spur road. We travel 1.8 miles to the Wolfe Ranch–Delicate Arch parking area. There are only a few cars in the parking area this morn-

ing so we should have plenty of solitude along the Delicate Arch trail.

Before starting up the trail, we notice the green shale behind the parking area, which belongs to the Morrison, one of the youngest formations in the park. Ordinarily the Morrison is drab in color, but here it is tinted a beautiful shade of blue-green by the copper it contains. The Morrison was laid down over 135 million years ago and often contains dinosaur bones. It is already very hot in this little valley this morning. We walk down to examine the ruins of Wolfe Ranch. The cabin, a small root cellar, the corral, and an old wagon are the only reminders that an early settler occupied this site from 1888 until about 1910. We marvel that anyone could have sustained himself here for over 20 years.

We cross the 100-foot-long swinging bridge that spans Salt Wash on the way to the 1.5-mile-

Double Arch, Arches National Park

long trail to Delicate Arch. We stop on the bridge, which is swinging and swaying a little and look into the wash. We see the feathery leaves of the tamarisk shrub and a large clump of reeds growing out of the moist, alkaline soil. We understand that there is quicksand under the wetter areas. On the other side of the bridge, we step off the trail to follow footprints through the rabbit brush to the low cliff faces about 50 yards to our left. The petroglyphs pecked in the desert varnish are of more modern origin that those we saw at Capitol Reef. The horse with a rider is the clue to the date. These carefully carved pictures were probably produced by the Utes after they had obtained horses from the Spanish. Except in pre-, prehistory, there were no horses on our continent until the Spanish arrived (see Section II, "A Prehistory of Indian Country").

We return to the trail, which crosses a sandy flat area for about 100 yards before it begins to climb. We will gain 500 feet in elevation by the time we reach Delicate Arch. We huff and puff up the excellent asphalted trail, taking time to notice opuntia (prickly pear) and fishhook cacti as well as small clumps of luminescent green snake-grass and wispy Indian ricegrass that are on the left side of the trail. Soon the trail levels out. We stop to catch our breaths. It is already a little cooler just this far out of the valley as a gentle breeze hits our moist skins. My wife spots a small bottle plant to the right. We all admire its weird shape and see the bottlelike nodules along the stem just below each major

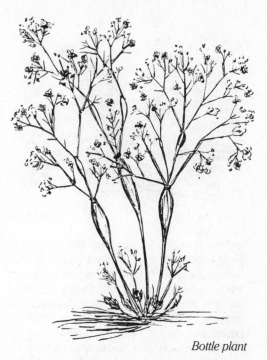

Bottle plant

branching joint for which it is named. As we traverse this higher ground, there are good views of the surrounding Entrada sandstone eroded into many strange forms, and we see alcoves in the cliff walls streaked with desert varnish. We continue along the good trail on flat ground, passing several low areas in which the dirt is covered with white alkali, looking for all the world like newly fallen snow on this eighty-five-degree day.

Now the trail climbs again. This time it means business. But it soon levels out, offering good views back over the valley where we started. Pausing to catch our breaths, we notice several eight- to twelve-inch-long lizards. One is a collared lizard with two black bands encircling its neck. My son thinks one of the other ones was a whip-tailed lizard with its characteristic orange-colored back. These lizards are having fun today, scurrying from rock to rock, occasionally crossing the trail. They are perfectly harmless and are a delight to watch. To the left we see giant alcoves or shallow caves in the sandstone. The backs of the caves are covered with dark desert varnish, but the seeps there have streaked the varnish with alkali giving an interesting three-dimensional effect. We see the green "garden" under the seeps where tender,

Fishhook or devil's claw cactus

Collared lizard

delicate moisture-loving plants like maidenhair ferns, columbine, and monkey flower grow. Now the trail goes across a slowly rising plateau until we reach the next ascent. The trail for this next elevation gain is across the face of a huge sandstone outcropping called slickrock. It is not slick when dry, but can become tricky when wet. We all have tennis shoes on today with good treads, but trail boots would offer more security for the less surefooted.

We feel the heat, now, reflecting back up from the rock. We see a few black-blue ravens soaring above us as we stop for a cool drink from our canteens on this waterless trail. Continuing on through the slickrock wilderness, the kids both yell at once, "There it is." They have seen one of their favorite

arches, Twisted Donut Arch. This small arch, 11 by 14 feet, magnificently frames Delicate Arch below and beyond it. We climb a few sandstone steps up to the arch and are silenced by what we see. There is Delicate Arch on the far side of a smoothly rounded sandstone amphitheater, perched on the very edge of a canyon wall that plummets 500 feet to the mighty Colorado River below. In the background, the snowcapped La Sal Mountains soar nearly 13,000 feet into one of the clearest blue skies imaginable. We sit down a few minutes in this comfortable place, which offers some shade and is exposed enough to catch a breeze if there is one. We drink more of our cool water and munch on candy bars, enjoying the relief from the intense sun.

Twisted Donut Arch, Arches National Park

We round the corner of Twisted Donut Arch and walk down the eroded sandstone bowl that dips gracefully to Delicate Arch. Slowly, almost reverently, we approach it. I feel the same tingling sensation in the back of my neck that I had when I first saw this beautifully carved piece of stone sculpture a few years ago. We stand directly under it and stretch our necks to see the roof of the arch, 45 feet above us. It is well named. Ironically, this arch containing tons of stone has the appearance of floating on the edge of the canyon. There is a light, airy, delicate quality to it. How fragile it is we do not know, but it is an old arch carrying the patina of age gracefully.

How many more summer thunderstorms

Monkey flower

Delicate Arch, Arches National Park

and winter frosts will it take before it topples? After all, nature creates beautiful spans like this and then works to level them. As we stand dwarfed by this monument to time, we slowly back away from it, trying to once again record on film what our senses will never let us forget. We walk back up the sloping surface of the amphitheater and take one last admiring look at it through Twisted Donut Arch. We comment that the thirty minutes we have spent up here this morning at the arch have more than compensated for the two days of driving it took us to get here. We walk back down the trail, arriving back at Wolfe Ranch a little more than two hours after we started. It is now 11:30 A.M. We drive the 1.8 miles back to the paved road with the air-conditioner on full blast. We feel tired from the heat, but exhilarated. The trail was as exciting as we remembered it and the sight of Delicate Arch was the kind of natural "high" we have come to expect here in the Southwest.

Dead Horse Point State Park

One of the major reasons people travel to Moab is to visit this state park perched on one long arm of a giant mesa sometimes called Island in the Sky. From Dead Horse Point, you will witness spectacular views out over the Colorado River and much of Canyonlands National Park, 2,000 feet below. This overview of what many call Utah's Grand Canyon rivals the vistas of another stretch of the Colorado River Canyon system seen from the rim of Arizona's Grand Canyon over 250 miles to the southwest. The park, located 33 miles from Moab at an elevation of 6,000 feet above sea level, contains 4,630 acres of land. This land was set aside for the public in 1959 and is managed by Utah State's Department of Parks and Recreation. A small entry fee is required. The park contains an excellent picnic area. Its well-situated campground requires a fee. Water is available but since it is hauled in from a source 70 miles away, you are requested to help conserve it.

The visitor center is to the left of the entrance station. It is helpful to stop by there for orientation purposes. In addition to offering up a wealth of helpful information about the geology and natural history of the area, they have plotted a well-designed nature and orientation trail nearby. The self-guiding booklet for the trail is excellent. From the visitor center it is only a short drive on to Dead Horse Point. There, several markers and displays help explain the sea of rocks that unfolds thousands of feet below you. For more information, contact Park Superintendent, Dead Horse State Park, P.O. Box 609, Moab, Utah 84532. Telephone: Dead Horse Point State Park Visitor Center, 1-801-259-6511.

Visiting the Colorado River and Dead Horse Point State Park: A Narrative Account

The daily thunderstorm was particularly vigorous this afternoon, leaving the August air fresh and dropping the temperature from the nineties down to the seventies. There are still some beautiful, but ominous white cloud formations to the north. One of the darker ones appears to have a silver rim around it. And to the west an enormous rainbow crosses the sky, a post-storm phenomenon we have come to expect here in the High Southwest.

Deciding that the storm had passed, we prepare for our visit to Dead Horse State Park to view Utah's "Grand Canyon." We attempted this trip a few years ago, but miscalculated the time and the distance, traveling halfway there only to discover that the sun was sinking rapidly and that our gas gauge was on empty. Faced with the prospect of running out of gas on that remote mesa after dark, we did an about-face and dejectedly drove back to Moab, vowing to return someday. Today is the day. I check the gas gauge. It is nearly full. It is a little before 5:00 P.M. We have plenty of time to drive the thirty-plus miles to the point and return before dinner.

As we head northwest out of town along U.S. Highway 191, the sun is low and to our left. We pass by many old cottonwood trees whose bright, almost acid green leaves give color to the whole valley, making it look like a shining desert oasis from a distance. We notice the contrast this evening between these green trees and the surrounding cliffs and bluffs of red, pink, off-white, and tan sandstone. A few seconds ago we passed the headquarters of Tag-A-Long Tours, run by the son and grandson of Doc Williams, a pioneer Moab physician who was instrumental in the development and preservation of the arches northwest of town as a national monument. A large rubber raft like the one we took down the Colorado River last year is out in front this evening. At the very edge of town, on top of a hill to the right, we notice Mi Vida, formerly the home of Charlie Steen, the Texas geologist who put Moab on the map with the discovery of his Mi Vida uranium mine in the 1950s. Then, we pass a lovely old home, the residence of an early Mormon settler, nestled in the coolness of some tall cottonwoods. It is now converted to a restaurant and is our destination following this evening's excursion.

Just beyond the northwest edge of town, the Colorado River comes into sight. Right on the banks of the Colorado is a park with a picnic and recreation area. We remember a fine Fourth of July evening spent there a few years ago, under an unbelievable canopy of stars. We stop to read the

Grand Old Ranch House Restaurant, Moab

sign erected on the south side of the bridge. It tells about the early Mormon settlers and the establishment of Grand County in 1890, with Moab as the county seat. It tells of the importance of cattle and sheep grazing before Moab became the capital of the western uranium boom. It points out that Moab was the hub of Colorado River traffic years ago. But the sign does not tell us about the Ute Indians who roamed and lived in this land for several hundred years before and after white contact.

No doubt the river's accessible banks served to water the horses the Utes acquired from the Spanish traders in the eighteenth century. But the Utes have been remembered in another way. This state did not forget its important Indian heritage. For when Utah became a state in 1896, it kept the name that had been on the land so long—the land of the Yutas, the Spanish name for the people of the area. Horses ridden by Spaniards probably found this river a welcome oasis in 1765. That year the first known white contact with this region was made by the Spanish soldier, Juan María Antonio Rivera, and his men. The road we are traveling tonight approximately parallels a segment of the Old Spanish Trail. Not far downstream from today's modern steel bridge is the site where a "practicable crossing" of the Colorado was discovered in the early 1800s. Which Spaniard, Mexican trader, or American trapper or mountain man made this discovery is unknown. But it is known that this crossing of the Colorado was a vital link in the Old Spanish Trail, joining the two far-flung cities of the northern Spanish Mexican empire, Santa Fe and Los Angeles.

It is now 5:30 P.M. The sun is still warm this evening. It is quiet. In this early evening stillness, we can imagine shouting men and hundreds of heaving animals swimming across this river. Perhaps the men are hanging on desperately to the newly constructed rafts to which the trade goods have been lashed. The swift undercurrent would have made an arduous day's work of this river crossing. Now we walk to the river's edge. This evening the river is flowing salmon red to brown, looking for all the world like a vast stream of tomato soup. Some have characterized the river's muddy waters as being "too thick to drink and too thin to plough." Stained by the minerals

from the red rock surrounding it, it was first seen in the High Southwest in the region of Arizona's Grand Canyon by members of Coronado's expedition in 1540. How it got its name is still uncertain. But one story has it that it was named by a Spanish priest, Friar Francisco Garcés, in 1776. While our Declaration of Independence was being framed, he debated about what to call this reddish gruel. He did not name it the Rio Rojo or "red river." He was more precise. He named it the Rio Colorado or "reddish river." The name stuck.

The surface of the river appears smooth, but it has strong undercurrents along this narrow passage above Moab as it cuts across rather than parallel to Moab Valley. At Arches this morning we learned how the Moab fault created this paradox. From where we are standing, just a mile or so downriver, the Colorado flows through a break or portal in the eight-hundred-foot-high cliffs and leaves the valley to enter the Colorado River Canyon system. That almost three-hundred-mile-long series of canyons finally peters out just south and west of one of its most dramatic stretches, Arizona's Grand Canyon.

The segment of the Colorado River flowing in front of us originates about three hundred miles northeast of Moab, near Grand Lake, Colorado, not far from Denver. A little more than thirty-two miles downstream from us, it makes a great wild loop in the canyon called an entrenched meander as it goosenecks its way around the rocks just below Dead Horse Point, our destination this evening. From there the river drops one foot every mile for thirty miles until it reaches the confluence with its main tributary, the Green River. The Green River, flowing through most of eastern Utah, originates seven hundred miles northeast of the confluence in the Wind River region of southwestern Wyoming. Three miles below the confluence, rapids take shape as a prelude to the river's entry into Cataract Canyon. There the Colorado contains some of the wildest white water in the West, popular with rafting enthusiasts from all over the world. Calming itself at Lake Powell, the river then builds up steam as it churns through Arizona's Grand Canyon country.

As we return to the car, we discuss the fact that the river here at Moab, from the confluence up to its Colorado source, was once named the Grand

River. In fact, we are now in Grand County, Utah, named in the 1890s after this river. How the name got changed to the Colorado is a story with as many uncertain twists as the river itself. But it goes something like this. The Spaniards named the river they saw from the Grand Canyon, the Colorado. The name stuck for that stretch of the river south to the Gulf of California. Later, the Domínguez–Escalante party were the first white men to come across a large river to the north. They named it El Rio San Buenaventura, the "river of good fortune." Known for a while by the American trappers as the Spanish River, the Spanish relabeled this river of good fortune, calling it the Rio Verde or Green River. To the northwest another large river was discovered, perhaps by French trappers. It was named the Grand River. At that time it was not known that the Green and the Grand joined to form the Colorado. In the 1860s Colorado Territory was formed. It was named after the great western river of the same name which many thought ran through the territory.

Statehood came to Colorado in 1876, the same year that Captain J. N. Macomb's report of his 1859 Utah expedition was published. He had discovered the confluence deep in Utah's canyonlands where the Green and the Grand joined to become the Colorado. It was now clear the Colorado River did not flow through Colorado. Embarrassed and increasingly sensitive to this discrepancy, Colorado pushed for renaming the Grand after the Colorado River which it joined. But to do so would have defied tradition. For in the 1890's the Federal Board on Geographic Names had established a policy of naming rivers after their longest tributary. According to this rule the lower segment of the Colorado, that named by the Spanish, would have to be changed to the Green since the Green River was the largest tributary. But they decided that historical precedence should rule and kept the older name of Colorado for the river below the confluence. Uncertain, they made no decision about changing the name of the river above the confluence.

By 1920, the Colorado legislature, chafing at the bit, declared that the river between Grand Lake and the Utah border would be named the Colorado. About the same time, the Utah legislature voted down a proposal to rename the Green River

the Colorado. Jumping into the breach, the Colorado legislature convinced its Utah neighbor to name the forty-mile stretch of Grand River between the Utah border and its confluence, the Colorado. Armed with this support, Coloradoans took the fight to Washington, D.C. There on July 25, 1921, Congress voted to change the name of the Grand River to the Colorado River. The people of Colorado now had possession of their namesake, while the people of Grand County, Utah, simultaneously lost theirs. The United States now had one river, its fifth largest, called the Colorado, that stretched deep from its mountainous interior to the Pacific Ocean.

As we drive across the bridge, we wonder if Grand County residents ever resented the change. Doubtful. It is more prestigious to be located on the banks of the Colorado River and to raft the Colorado River than some obscure tributary named the Grand River. But in spite of being well known, the Colorado River, unlike the Nile River to which it is so often compared, has not attracted settlement along its banks because of the rugged terrain around it. Except for Hite Marina on Lake Powell and the recently constructed "company" towns at Glenn Canyon Dam, Arizona, and Boulder Dam, Nevada, there is not a single, major commercial town between Moab, Utah, and Needles, California, a distance of over one thousand miles.

Looming in front of us to the left, just beyond the junction of U.S. Highway 191 and Utah Highway 128, is a giant uranium processing mill and tailings pond, producing concentrated uranium yellow cake. Now everyone is wondering if we will ever get to Dead Horse Point. Approximately ten miles northwest of Moab we reach Utah Highway 313, the road to Dead Horse Point State Park and Grandview Point in the Island in the Sky District of Canyonlands National Park. Immediately, 313, a good paved road, heads west twenty-one miles to the park. No traffic here. We drive up Sevenmile Canyon. It is scenic in its own right, bordered by tall, Wingate cliffs and numerous interesting rock formations. The road climbs out of the canyon in a series of steep switchbacks.

On the way up we catch glimpses of two large salmon-colored, flat-topped buttes to the northwest. They are named after the Civil War ironclad vessels, the Monitor and the Merrimac. The large butte to the west is called the Merrimac, while the smaller one to the east is the Monitor. The sheer cliff faces of both are of Entrada sandstone. They are each thinly capped with Summerville and Morrison formation rocks. Now we switchback through Kayenta sandstone ledges until, true to our geologic chart, we reach massive outcroppings of whitish cross-bedded Navajo sandstone, taking the form of smoothly rounded beehive mounds. As the road reaches the top of the switchbacks it levels out on the mesa top, truly an Island in the Sky. Soon we enter a semibarren stretch of sand and grassland. To the right, red slopes are studded with bright green Utah junipers. Beyond them about seven miles from the U.S. Highway 191 junction, at the base of the steep Entrada bluffs to the right, are several large alcoves. White alkaline stains on the dark desert-varnished back walls of the alcoves create a toothlike design which gives the illusion of white stalactites protruding from the alcove ceiling.

The road continues on south with a very gradual incline. Piñon pines begin to appear along with Utah junipers. In this "pygmy forest" the trees are dwarfed due to a lack of moisture, poor soil, and widely fluctuating temperatures. These lovely trees, with interesting and contorted features, are small but very old. Trees with a diameter of six to ten inches are often 150 years old and some with only slightly larger diameters may be 250 to 350 years old.

We think of the wonderful aroma of piñon when its smoke fills the air in some southwestern communities on chilly fall and winter evenings, and we remember the first time we experienced the delightful, pungent smell of freshly cut juniper when we visited a Navajo Indian who was using that resilient wood for the construction of his hogan (see Section II, "Monument Valley: A Narrative Account"). As the miles pass by, we look for cliff rose, yucca, and Mormon tea among the vegetation. We see many doves and a few desert cottontail rabbits. The road forks at a well-marked junction 14.5 miles from the U.S. Highway 191 junction. The right fork goes to Canyonlands National Park's Island in the Sky District and Grandview Point. The road to the left continues about 6.5 miles to Dead Horse Point State Park.

Reaching the park, we pass the entry station

after paying the small fee. We pass the excellent visitor center which is closed this evening and drive the short distance to the point. The view to the east is magnificent with the Manti–La Sals rising to almost thirteen thousand feet. We take time to look at our map and realize that in traveling this evening we have come full circle and a little more. Although we started our trip by driving northwest out of Moab, we are now several miles south of Moab but on a different plane, over one thousand feet above Moab Valley.

Near the neck of the point, we pass a sign right next to a beautiful old piñon pine tree. The sign says, "Stop, look, and listen. Listen to the sounds of the not too distant past. Listen for the thunder of horses' hooves running across the mesa top and the screaming cowboys behind them running in the blinding and choking dust. Look at the flaring nostrils and rippling muscles on the powerful mustangs' legs and sides as they run past you heading for the point. So it was during the late 1800s when the cowboys used to herd the wild horses that roamed throughout the area across the narrow neck of land that separates the point from the mainland. The point served as a natural corral. Once the mustangs were on the point, the cowboys fenced it off and captured the horses they wanted for their own use. The legend of Dead Horse Point states that a group of horses left stranded on the waterless point died there within sight of the Colorado River, 2,000 feet below." So now we know how this jutting peninsula of land, really a flat mesa top, obtained its name.

With the sun descending lower in the west, we pass through the narrow neck of the peninsula, only thirty yards wide, and begin to see for ourselves how this thin bottleneck could easily be blocked to create a natural corral. We park the car and walk—almost run—on the Kayenta sandstone to the rim. We are stunned by the view. Alone now, the sun dropping quickly, a slight breeze, utter silence, we gaze out over the point. As I stand there, I know what it means to "see forever," five thousand square miles of Canyon Country laid out before us. In the distance, the Manti–La Sal Mountains to the east. They were named by the early Spaniards who likened their snow-covered peaks to piles of salt. To the south, the Abajo Mountains, fifty miles away. Between

Dead Horse Point

those far distant mountains of molten magma origin, time and erosion have carved an immense sea of canyons, labyrinths, and mazes. There are protruding towers, mesas, monuments, and monoliths in ever-changing colors of reds, purples, whites, pinks, and grays as the sunlight casts lengthening shadows. The sheer cliffs expose almost every rock formation created in the Colorado Plateau over the last 250 million years.

Then my eye catches the river, serpentine-like, two thousand feet below and thirty-two river miles downstream from Moab. Sometimes pink, sometimes brownish red, as it changes with the progression of twilight. It bullies and forces its way, cutting deeper and deeper through the sedimentary rock layers over eleven hundred miles from here to the shoulder of Mexico's Baja California, where, after being drained to the point of depletion by California's thirsty Imperial Valley, it trickles into the Pacific Ocean's Sea of Cortez, better known in this country as the Gulf of California. A mighty river, this "Grand," "Colorado," or what-

ever you want to call it. The fifth longest river in the United States demands respect as it makes a wild 180-degree turn, goosenecking around an enormous rock outcropping right before our eyes.

From up here on the point, the whole world is made up of sheer, steep cliffs, stratified walls, and stone staircases in multicolored layers. The Grand Canyon of the North, the Upper Grand Canyon, Utah's Grand Canyon—call it what you will, it is magnificent. We have been alone this evening until now when one other visitor, a man from Germany, joins us at the rim. He is as awed as we are. Our mutual respect for what we are experiencing transcends the language barrier. Trading glances, each of us knows and understands what the other is feeling at this moment as we gaze out over the horizons of the High Southwest. Now the red sandstone is acid pink in color, while the sky behind it is a dark vibrant blue. An almost full moon is rising in the east. Here at the top of the peninsula we feel we are at the fulcrum of the universe. As the sun goes down gradually in the west, the moon ascends slowly to the east, both lending their light to this panorama before us.

Far, far below we see a small whitish line curving and bending, a jeep trail left over from the uranium fever days that now carries adventurers into Canyonlands National Park. Down to the east, we see some green pools. Too regular and too structured to fit into this natural landscape, they momentarily jar our mood. They are potash solar evaporation ponds at the end of Utah Highway 279. Much of what we are seeing from up here is Canyonlands National Park. Some say it is one of the best overviews of that park. Certainly it is one of the most accessible panoramic overlooks.

We notice a nice picnic area on the way back to the car. The rabbitbrush and snake-grass are taking on phosphorescent colors in the early twilight. Then we see a juniper loaded with bluish purple luminescent berries. It has been said that some of the rare beauty in this big country is to be found by searching out its smallness. Tonight, in the cool of the evening, we see an occasional whitetailed antelope, ground squirrel, and a few lizards scurrying about, although we see no kangaroo rats. As we drive out, the only car on the road, we see more doves and a few bluebirds. We notice on the road in front of us some small creatures. We stop to look. They are spadefoot toads who are enjoying the rainwater that pooled this afternoon in some of the small holes beside the road.

The descent back down to U.S. Highway 191 is a treat—deep pinks and purples on the left with the full moon rising to the right. In front of us, directly north, intermittent streaks of lightning dance across the sky in both vertical and horizontal directions. We drive carefully, alert for any deer that might cross the highway. There is

silence in the car as we drive back down to Moab. Each of us is reflecting in some way on the beauty and solitude we have experienced, thankful that this "grand canyon" is still pristine and reasonably untouristed. We arrive back in Moab at 8:30, sixty-six round-trip miles and 3.5 hours later. Having feasted visually, we are now ready to feast gastronomically!

Canyonlands National Park

Canyonlands National Park is the largest national park in Canyon Country. It contains in its 525 square miles some of the world's most isolated, yet scenically beautiful rugged land. Once occupied by the ancient Indians, it was never thought suitable for settlement by white pioneers. The first known white man brave enough to walk through the heart of it and who lived to record his visit was Captain J. N. Macomb of the U.S. Topographical Corps, who lead an expedition there in 1859. Scorched by the heat and jarred to the bone by the unevenness of the terrain, Macomb wrote tersely, "I cannot conceive of a more worthless and impracticable region than the one we now find ourselves in."

The expedition went up and down an endless series of "deep and great cañons," compelling Macomb to write, "I doubt not that there are repetitions and varieties of this for hundreds of miles." His expedition discovered the confluence of the Green River and the Colorado River, flowing through deep canyons in a riverbed rimmed with rocks of the Hermosa group, the oldest layers of the earth's crust to surface in southeastern Utah. But Macomb was right. He had only seen the beginning of this up-and-down land. He never made it to the desolate heart of Canyonlands, a thirty-square-mile area of hell on earth called the Maze. There a labyrinthian world of dry, desolate, skeletal rock creates an unbelievable concentration of canyons which twist and turn, divide and redivide like some baroque sandstone puzzle. But somehow those indomitable prehistoric Indians of the

Spadefoot toads

region eked out a living there, leaving pictographs of rare beauty on the canyon walls for modern-day adventurers to see and wonder about.

Understandably the area remained unexplored a decade after Macomb's visit. Then John Wesley Powell, a one-armed Civil War veteran, led an expedition in search of a more direct rail route across the Southwest. He went down the Green River to the confluence and then on down the Colorado River where he got the surprise of his life. Three miles below the confluence the quiet river becomes increasingly rough. It moves faster and faster as the riverbed drops eight feet each mile. Then in one last giant step down, it races even faster as it drops thirty feet in one mile, deep in Cataract Canyon. Powell lived to tell about it but several accompanying him on the expedition were killed by Indians on the way out.

Seeing Canyonlands

This huge park of unusual beauty receives only about 250,000 visitors each year, fewer than at the other parks in the region. But there are not many visitors for a good reason. Most of the sights within the park, like the Maze section, Monument Basin, the Totem Pole, Druid Arch, and Angel Arch, are beyond the reach of the average traveler. Numerous paved roads lead to this park and circle it, but only one penetrates it. There are several good paved roads that take you to various parts of the elevated rim around the park to panoramic overlooks. But the roads to most of the major sights are four-wheel-drive-vehicle roads. Some visitors,

Totem Pole, Monument Basin,
Canyonlands National Park

like Major Powell, prefer to explore the park by river, others choose to fly over it. Some discover it on guided horseback tours, while other hardy souls elect to hike through it. Moab serves as a base for many commercial tour companies designed to fit just about every adventurer's needs (see "Moab—Tours"). But for the average traveler with limited time and funds, the following two routes can be explored with great satisfaction. For more information, write Canyonlands National Park Headquarters, 125 West 200 South Street, Moab, Utah 84532. Telephone: 1-801-259-7164.

Grandview Point—Island in the Sky District, Canyonlands National Park

Approximately 10 miles northwest of Moab, U.S. Highway 191 turns left on to paved Utah Highway 313 at a junction marked Dead Horse Point State Park and Canyonlands National Park, Island in the Sky District. Travel approximately 14.5 miles to the well-marked Dead Horse Point junction, with the paved Canyonlands road taking off to the right. To see all of the sights listed here, you will travel on good, paved roads 52 round-trip miles from this junction. From the junction travel 7.5 miles to the ranger station through level high desert grasslands. Stay on the road, as the sandy shoulders are soft and could entrap you. Along the route you will be rewarded with the views of three mountain ranges formed from molten magma upthrusts. The Henry Mountains rise in front and to the right, the Manti–La Sals loom behind you, and the Abajo Mountains appear to the left.

Stop at the ranger station-visitor center to pay a fee (which also allows access to Arches National Park), see more detailed maps of the region, and pick up some of the helpful brochures relating to this section of the park. Some books about the area are for sale there. From the ranger station continue along the Island in the Sky road past several scenic pullouts and the interesting Mesa Arch Trail at 6.4 miles from the ranger station. At the Mesa Arch trailhead you can pick up an excellent self-guiding booklet which will lead you down the 0.5-mile round-trip trail. It identifies and explains most of the plant life along the way. At trail's end perched on the very rim of Canyonlands Park, twenty-one hundred feet above the Colorado River, Mesa

Arch, beautifully carved in the Navajo sandstone, frames the canyonlands below as well as the Manti–La Sal Mountains over 35 miles away. This trail is somewhat confusing, so follow the self-guiding instructions carefully and take note of your bearings. Do not let small children out of your sight because of the steep drop-off at the rim.

From Mesa Arch trail parking lot to the junction road is only about 0.3 mile. Take the left fork and continue in a southwesterly direction for 6.4 miles past a nice picnic area to Grandview Point. This overlook should not be missed. Although similar to the view from Dead Horse Point State Park, the vantage point there penetrates the park deeper, offering quite a different perspective. From the rim you see the cliffs drop to the White Rim, the top of a sandstone escarpment capped by White Rim, Cutler formation rocks twelve hundred fifty feet below. That rim drops another one thousand feet to the Colorado River, which is buried deep in the canyons and is not visible from this viewpoint. The 35-mile-wide basin you see was carved from the rock by the Green and Colorado rivers with the aid of other erosive forces. The truly incredible view opens out to the Abajo peaks, Cathedral Butte, North and South Sixshooter peaks, and the Needles section of the park. Immediately below is a view of the Totem Pole. This three-hundred-five-foot-high spire of sandstone, one of the Standing Up Rocks in Monument Basin, looks like a miniature from Grandview Point.

Return by way of the same road to the junction with the Upheaval Dome and Green River Overlook roads to see one of the most peculiar geologic entities in Canyonlands Park. Drive northwest 5.3 miles to the Upheaval Dome Overlook parking lot. Just before reaching the parking lot you will see Whale Rock, a very good likeness to that sea mammal sculpted by nature from Navajo sandstone. There is a primitive trail from Whale Rock to the Upheaval Dome crater. From the parking lot and pleasant piñon-shaded picnic area, pick up the Upheaval Dome information brochure and walk five hundred yards, mostly uphill, to a junction in the trail. One path leads to a viewpoint 0.5 mile to the left, while the other one leads to an overlook only sixty yards to the right. What you see before you from either trail is the closest thing to a moonscape on earth. There in the center of a great crater several miles wide, sharply angulated whitish green-gray rocks protrude upward. What happened there is still not entirely clear. Some believe this strange phenomenon was created by a meteor. But the prevailing theory holds that the creative force was salt. Under pressure from the thousands of feet of rock that had formed above it, salt, the consistency of toothpaste, oozed up through a weakened area of the earth's crust, pushing up the ten layers of rock above it to form a dome 3 miles wide. Six of the rock layers were so distorted by the movement they were turned almost on edge. Eventually the surrounding area from which the dome rose slowly sank to form a trench or syncline around it.

Over the next forty million years erosion stripped away the overlying crust to expose the upturned and fractured faces of the domed rocks to further erosion. Near the center of the dome the stack of upturned and broken rock eroded more easily, washing away into the canyon that extends from the fractured west wall of the crater. This created an inner void, an erosional basin fifteen hundred feet deep and a mile wide, circled by cliffs of the harder, more erosion-resistant Wingate

sandstone. Today, ringed by a floor of colorful Moenkopi formation rocks, you will see the weird central core of Upheaval Dome with its multicolored, five-hundred-foot-high, eroded, otherworldly spires extending from the White Rim, one thousand feet below. Many of these gray-green rock forms are Organ rock shale.

The round-trip, nonstop walking time to the closer overlook and return to the parking lot is thirty minutes. Keep your eye open for black swifts in this area as they dart through the air. From the parking lot return to the main road. You have now seen all the main sights except the Green River Overlook. It is a 3.6-mile round-trip drive from the junction. Besides the campground near the overlook, there are rim views west out over the Green River. From the junction you are 14.2 miles from the paved Dead Horse Road and 35 miles from Moab. From Moab allow well over two hours round-trip driving time and two and one-half hours of sight-seeing time. If you want to combine this trip with a visit to Dead Horse Point State Park, add another thirty minutes driving time plus an additional hour for seeing the sights. (Telephone: Canyonlands National Park Island in the Sky Visitor Center, 1-801-259-6577.) Be sure to bring

Upheaval Dome, Canyonlands National Park

your own water since none is available on the Island in the Sky. And fill your gas tank before leaving Moab.

The Needles District, Canyonlands National Park

The Needles District road is the only paved all-weather road that actually penetrates Canyonlands National Park. Although it will take you closer to many of the best sights in the park, like the Needles, it will not take you to them. The end of the Needles District road is the beginning of numerous four-wheel-drive-vehicle roads and hiking trails to some incredible landforms. But the hiking trails to those sights are generally long and strenuous and probably are not appropriate for the average traveler. What does this road offer the average visitor then? It offers some spectacular views of the park at near-canyon level rather than rim level. It provides eye-level views of the Needles in the distance and several short, but interesting nature trails through the slickrock.

From Moab drive south through beautiful red rock country that someone forgot to put in a national park. In approximately 39 miles you will reach a well-signed junction road to the right, Utah

Highway 211. The sign indicates that Newspaper Rock State Park is 12 miles from the junction and Canyonlands National Park is 34 miles away. The first up-and-down 12 miles take you to Newspaper Rock. Pull in the parking area to the right. Shaded picnic grounds are on the left side of the road. Walk a very short distance to the desert-varnished Wingate cliffs in front of you. You will see more petroglyphs than you ever thought imaginable, from the earliest prehistoric times through modern times, scratched in the sandstone. The variety is amazing. Even more amazing is that these writings are still intact. This large collection of petroglyphs is well worth seeing. Just to the left of the petroglyphs is a box with self-guiding booklets for a nature trail 0.25 mile long. The booklet is well researched and the trees and plants are clearly marked. You will see rabbitbrush, mountain mahogany, squawbush, gambel oak, box elder, river birch, and sandbar willow.

From Newspaper Rock the good paved road soon gets even better and continues 22 miles to the park. The road, which follows Indian Creek as it flows from the Abajo Mountains to the Colorado River, eventually enters a wide valley with many large cottonwoods. The road passes over several cattleguards. These narrowly spaced parallel

Newspaper Rock, Newspaper Rock State Park

pieces of pipe spook cattle belonging to the few ranchers in this remote valley and keep them from straying too far. The valley gives way to more open, picture-perfect western movie country as twin Sixshooter Peaks come into sight. These are really buttes, their unusual peaks carved from Wingate sandstone resting on Chinle and Moenkopi bases. Scenically this area resembles Monument Valley, Utah. Just before entering the park, you will pass a junction road to the north leading about one-half mile to the Needles Outpost, the only seasonal watering hole, general store, and auto services facility for miles around. At approximately 34 miles you will enter the park, where you will soon come to the ranger station located in a trailer to the right of the road. Stop to see the small natural history exhibit and bookstore and pick up free maps and information folders about the area.

After leaving the ranger station, travel a short distance to the first parking area on the left, the Roadside Ruin Nature Trail. Pick up a self-guiding booklet from the box and walk the 0.25-mile round-trip trail to the Anasazi Indian granary, constructed of stone sometime between A.D. 950 and 1200. Along the trail you will see yucca, Fremont barberry, and big sagebrush.

Return to your car and drive about 0.5 mile to the junction of paved Salt Creek Road. Turn left and in a short distance turn left again onto a dirt road marked Cave Springs Environmental Trail. In about 1 mile, enter the parking lot at the road's end. This is an interesting trail, taking you through some of the typical slickrock country at this elevation. The self-guiding booklet is informative, but it leaves out several important points. First carry insect repellent. The wet nature of the springs attracts mosquitoes. Next watch for cairns, small stacks of rocks which help guide the way. Part of the trail is over slightly steep sandstone slickrock. Wear shoes that offer good traction. The trail is up and down requiring two ladder descents. One ladder has eight steps while the other has twelve.

This 0.5-mile-long round-trip trail does bear out the notion that some of the beauty in this big country is found by searching out its smallness. Look for piñon pines whose bark has been stripped by porcupines. Look for pack rat nests in the cliff alcoves. It is hard to believe, but studies of some of these nests have established that they date back ten thousand years, giving the pack rats at least squatter's rights to this area. And no doubt you will see numerous scrub jays, white-tailed antelope, and ground squirrels. Keep an eye out for rare golden eagles that may soar above. At the end of the trail is a large cave or alcove in the Cedar Mesa sandstone, its ceiling blackened from many kitchen fires. This cave served as a cowboy line camp, a temporary base for cattle operations in the late nineteenth and early twentieth centuries.

Return to your car and drive back to the main park road. From there drive 1.5 miles to the

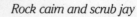

Rock cairn and scrub jay

White-tailed antelope ground squirrels

junction with the paved Pothole Point and Big Springs Overlook road. Drive approximately 2 miles to the Pothole Point parking area. There a short walk out onto the sandstone flats gives good views of the spectacular Needles area, where you will see a forest of tall, red (Cutler formation) and white (Cedar Mesa sandstone) banded rock pinnacles. The self-guiding booklet obtained from the box in the parking area explains the formation of the potholes that surround you at every step. When a pothole dries up, the dirt in its bottom contains many microscopic eggs waiting for sufficient moisture to hatch. If you arrive just after a shower when there is water in these rock basins, they may be filled with living creatures such as fairy shrimp, snails, and beetles.

Return to the road and follow it to its end, where there are good views out over the canyons. Not far from this point, to the southwest, hidden in the canyon, is the confluence of the Green and Colorado rivers. From Big Springs Canyon Overlook to the Confluence Overlook is a 9-mile round-trip hike over a "primitive" foot trail. Inquire at the ranger station before taking this hike. Drive 3.7 miles back to the main road and enter Squaw Flat Campground and picnic area. Fine, shaded campsites backed up to nicely rounded Cedar Mesa sandstone bluffs are available there. From the southwestern section of the campground, numerous foot trails, many along dry creek beds, extend into the park's most scenic sights, such as Chesler Park and Druid Arch. These are long hikes over rough country and should not be attempted in wet weather. The Druid Arch Trail is 14 miles round trip. For further information about the hiking trails and four-wheel-drive-vehicle roads,

consult with the ranger.

Having seen the major sights, return to Utah Highway 191 over the same road you came. From Moab this trip is a 170-mile round-trip drive that takes three-quarters of a day. If you are traveling from Moab south to Mesa Verde or Monument Valley, this is a trip you might want to take on the way, early in the day, before proceeding south. Telephone: Canyonlands National Park Needles District Visitor Center, 1-801-259-6568.

The Potash Road: An Introduction to Dinosaur Tracks, Petroglyphs, and More

If you have an hour someday between major half-day trips or at the end of the day, be sure to sandwich in this scenic and educational trip close to Moab. Drive out of Moab across the Colorado River Bridge and then cross the Court House Wash Bridge to the junction of U.S. Highway 191 and Utah Highway 279. Turn left onto paved Utah Highway 279, called the Potash Road. This well-engineered highway won an award some years ago as one of the most scenic drives in the country. The railroad tracks you see serve the potash mines fifteen miles west at the end of the road. The tailing pits of Atlas Uranium Ore Reduction Plant are to the right. Leaving all of that behind, in about a

Druid Arch, Canyonlands National Park

mile, the Colorado River closely parallels the road as it prepares to exit Moab Valley. Both the river and you will enter the Portal, an opening in the cliffs on this side of the valley through which the river and the road enter the Colorado River Canyon system. The sheer walls are Wingate sandstone. The base of the walls rests on a variety of Chinle formation shales. At approximately three miles is a pullout to the left. A viewscope is zeroed in on petroglyphs and a prehistoric Indian granary on the steep canyon walls across the river. Binoculars are helpful.

At the next stop the sign says "Indian Petroglyphs." Pull off to the left side of the road. The petroglyphs are on the wall to the right. This is a very large, well-preserved gallery of many petroglyphs, possibly pecked in the desert-varnished Navajo sandstone wall by the Fremont Indians who flourished in this area and by the Utes who roamed this country later. This panel of petro-

glyphs is well worth seeing. The next well-marked pullout is to the right, marked by a sign that reads "Dinosaur Tracks." Viewscopes are fixed to reveal dinosaur tracks on a large slab of Kayenta sandstone on the cliffside above the parking area. You will not see dinosaur tracks anywhere else in the area. The next parking areas are for trails leading to Corona and Bowtie arches. At thirteen miles from U.S. Highway 191 is the Jug Handle Arch parking area. The configuration of Jug Handle Arch is interesting since it occurs on a vertical plane and is one of the few known arches in this area to have formed in the usually resistant Wingate sandstone. At the end of the paved road to the right is the potash plant and its nearby evaporation ponds, which can be seen from Dead Horse Point State Park. This forty-mile round-trip drive from Moab with stops takes about 1.5 hours.

If you have seen all you want to see and have more time, you may want to take a raft, sportyak, or boat trip down the Colorado River or a four-wheel-drive-vehicle trip into one of the more remote scenic areas around Moab. Half-day, day-long, and longer tours are available. Some of the tour operators are listed at the back of this section.

Rafting the Colorado: A Narrative Account

It is a few minutes before 9:00 A.M. We just arrived here at the raft tour office and are waiting for the bus that will take us 22 miles upstream from Moab to the launching site. We are well prepared for a day on the water in the July sun. In addition to camera and film, our day pack contains plenty of sunscreen, and sun lotion. We all have hats with brims, sunglasses, and are wearing shorts under our long pants. The rest, the water, lunch, and the waterproof containers for our valuables, are provided by the tour operator. We feel a little anxious this morning. No wonder. We have avoided doing this for years. Each year as we crossed and re-crossed the narrow band of the Colorado River at Moab, passing the numerous signs advertising Colorado River trips, we discussed but quickly dismissed the possibility of such a trip. Somehow "rafting the Colorado" had always seemed connected with high adventure not suitable for a family with young children. But over time, we came to know numerous ecstatic survivors of raft trips who extolled the safety as well as the fun, the pleasure, and the scenic beauty of such trips. So yesterday I took the plunge and made reservations for all four of us for today's oar-powered raft trip.

The bus arrives on time and we climb aboard with about a dozen other hardy souls and several well-tanned raft guides who inspire confidence just by their weathered appearance, looking for all the world like veteran Huck Finns. The bus leaves U.S. Highway 191 at the bridge and turns up Utah Highway 128 as it takes us up the Colorado River Gorge, passing below the high rim of Arches National Park. Soon the gorge opens into wider valleys, offering striking views of such stone monuments as the Priest and the Nuns, Castle Tower, and the Fisher Towers. We are told that many of these sights have served as backdrops for a variety of western movies. At the launching site we exit the bus and explore, while our erstwhile river pilots prepare for the launching of the two large nylon and neoprene rafts, with their many individually inflated chambers. The river rocks are fascinating. We ask about several of them and discover that our guides are well-educated natural historians. One particularly beautiful whitish rock

Colorado River raft trip

with many parallel cross striations is identified as a piece of oil shale, rounded and smoothed by the river's powerful grinding and cutting action. Our son finds several beached channel catfish that have given up the ghost in the silty water. The water is so thick with silt and debris today that it looks like gruel. It is almost surprising that it is wet! We are told that yesterday's big thunderstorm, the first in many weeks, has washed all kinds of matter into the river.

The boats are ready. We are given life jackets and safety instructions before we board. Now that we are comfortably seated in the raft, our guide rows us skillfully into the main channel. He points out a variety of rock formations, including the Fisher Towers in the distance. He tells us that one of those towers, the Titan, is a nine-hundred-foot spire of ancient Cutler formation rock with a Moenkopi cap that stands up three hundred feet taller than the Washington Monument. In a few miles, we meet the first rapids, which slowly build up to the liveliest run on the trip, White Rapids. We hold on as the raft picks up speed, bouncing us up and down. The front of the raft is elevated some as we plunge through the rapids, Colorado River soup thoroughly spraying us. In the churning waters are small tree branches, medium-sized burls of wood, detached juniper roots, pine cones, grass, and numerous small plants washed down from their native environments many miles away. Yesterday's storm must have cleared out every gully, wash, arroyo, and canyon for miles around. Now in calmer waters, I reach over the side of the raft for a gnarled, twisted piece of wood. Success! It is a beautiful tree root smoothed to an exquisite fineness by the abrasive action of river and rocks. I place it on the floor of the raft preparing for the next series of rapids. They are less intense and are followed by a wide, calm section of river where we pull ashore for lunch.

After exploring the shorelines and devouring a tasty lunch, we once again head for the main channel. The water is very still now and the guide is forced to row. The sun is directly overhead and we are grateful for our protective clothing. Soon we pull over to a wide, sandy beach where we see the bus waiting for us. This is the end of the trip. We have been on the raft for about five hours. While the boats are put back on the bus, we wade and swim a short distance from the beach. We are told to be cautious because of the swift undercurrents beneath the water's placid surface. We climb aboard our vintage bus and arrive back here at Moab around 4:30 P.M. Confident that we can survive the moderate rapids above Moab, we are tempted to try a more difficult stretch of the river. Perhaps next time we will attempt Cataract Canyon!

Edge of the Cedars State Historical Monument, Blanding, Utah

If your travels will not take you further south into Indian Country (see Section II) and you would like to sample some of the region's Indian prehistory, take a short day trip to Edge of the Cedars State Historical Monument, Blanding, Utah. Even if you are going south to Indian Country, this monument, placed on the National Register of Historic Places in 1971, is well worth a stop.

Drive U.S. Highway 191 south seventy-eight miles through Monticello, Utah, and the beautiful Abajo or Blue Mountains. Follow the signs in Blanding to the monument, which is located just northwest of town. The Monument is open daily except Thanksgiving, Christmas, and New Year's Day. It is located on the site of an ancient Anasazi Indian ruin that was occupied from A.D. 750 to A.D. 1220. An ongoing excavation and stabilization program is still in progress.

You can walk among several clusters of buildings and ceremonial ruins. The handsome monument building houses an excellent museum. The museum contains dioramas and other well-designed exhibits showing how these early people lived. In addition, many artifacts from the ruin are on display. Be certain to visit the second floor, for there you will see the Shumway collection, one of the finest exhibits of prehistoric Anasazi Indian

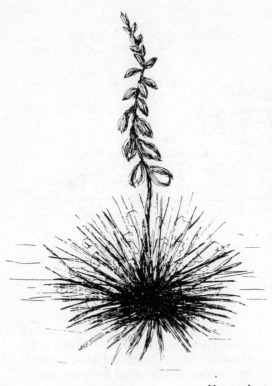

Yucca plant

pottery in the Southwest. This is a stunning collection and should not be missed. Besides the museum shop, there are several Indian Arts and Crafts stores in Blanding (see "Moab—Shopping"). From Moab the round-trip driving time is approximately four hours.

The Road between Moab and Capitol Reef National Park

Capitol Reef is almost directly west of Moab, but to get there you must make an arc to the north on paved U.S. Highway 191 to I-70 near Crescent Junction. Then travel west on I-70 past Green River, Utah, to the intersection of Utah Highway 24. Follow Utah Highway 24 south through Hanksville and Caineville to Capitol Reef. Along the way, you may want to stop at Green River, the

melon-growing capital of eastern Utah, approximately one hour out of Moab. It rests alongside the Colorado River's longest tributary and takes its name from that great river. It is an interesting, very small, old Utah town which slumbers in the midday heat as the traffic whizzes by on nearby Interstate Highway 70. (That interstate connects Denver, Colorado, with Interstate Highway 15 to Los Angeles, California.)

From Green River, travel Interstate Highway 70 to Utah Highway 24 and turn south. The sights along Utah Highway 24 could very well be in a national park (see "Utah Highway 24 East of the Capitol Reef Visitor Center"). Near Hanksville, about an hour's drive from Green River, you will pass close to the junction of the Fremont and Muddy rivers where they join to become the Dirty Devil River (see "History"). From Hanksville to Capitol Reef the driving time is less than an hour through some very scenic territory that includes good views of the moonscape badlands and Factory Butte that stands taller than any of America's skyscrapers. Allow three hours, total, for driving time between Moab and the Capitol Reef visitor center.

Capitol Reef National Park

One hundred and fifty miles west of Moab, Utah, and 225 miles southeast of Salt Lake City is Utah's second largest national park. It is one of the nation's most exotic, but least known scenic areas. Containing an unbelievable variety of landforms in its 378 square miles, the park stretches like an elongated teardrop for over 80 miles from its northern border to the south, where its constricted tip comes within just a few miles of Lake Powell.

Within its borders the land ranges from 3,800 to 8,600 feet in elevation. It contains the 100-mile-long water pocket fold, part of an elevated, elongated, and grossly distorted mass of rock that gives the park its name. Early prospectors trying to cross from east to west came face to face with this monstrous outcropping of rock rising from the

Factory Butte

desert floor, Utah's version of the Great Barrier Reef. Because it obstructed their forward progress and frustrated their journey westward, some of these fortune seekers who had previously known adventure on the high seas, likened it to a reef rising from the ocean's floor. The reef was such an effective deterrent to travel that the lands west of it were some of the last to be explored and settled in the continental United States.

When the early explorers did penetrate the area in the 1870s they were dumbfounded by what they saw. Especially Captain Clarence Dutton who reached the Aquarius Plateau's Boulder Mountain area just southwest of Capitol Reef with the last exploration group formed to map unknown regions of the contiguous United States. Climbing to the lava rim on top and looking out over the weirdly eroded cliffs, the reef's water pocket fold, and miles and miles of canyon and plateau country, he wrote, "It is a sublime panorama...It is a maze of cliffs and terraces lined off with stratification, of crumbling buttes, red and white domes, rock platforms gashed with profound canons, burning plains barren even of sage—all glowing with bright colors and flooded with sunlight." The beautiful essence of what he saw made him feel like a poet rather than a geologist. Putting his feeling into words he later wrote, "The Aquarius should be described in blank verse and illustrated upon canvas."

Some have likened the Capitol Reef area to a symphony in sandstone. An unfinished symphony at that, with many variations on the theme.

In Capitol Reef National Park erosion continues to carve some of the most unusual features in Canyon Country, making liars out of the geology books. Canyons and cliffs take on sizes and shapes not found elsewhere. Even buttes, ordinarily easy to recognize, defy the norm and take on otherworldly shapes. One of Capitol Reef's most common butte shapes occurs when the Navajo sandstone erodes to the shape of a dome. The frequent occurrence of these symmetrical, sometimes 1,000-foot-high shapes, which resemble the domes on top of the principal government buildings in Washington, D.C., gives this national park the first part of its name, "Capitol." And there are even variations on the dome theme. Many exotic rounded buttes have protuberant points, while others are squared off and look like cylinders standing on end. The Indians picked up on another unique aspect of the Reef. They called it the "land of the sleeping rainbow." To them this long reef of geological whimsey resembled a colorful, sprawling rainbow, resting near the earth's surface, tinted by the multicolored Chinle shale, one of the most colorful rock layers on earth.

The scenic and geological wonders of this area were first set aside for preservation in 1937 as a national monument. The monument received national park status in 1971. For a number of years, this remote, isolated park languished in solitude and peace attracting loyal followers from Utah, California, and the Federal Republic of Germany (in that order during one year of heavy European travel to this country). But when the last segment of Utah Highway 12 was paved, opening an easy, all-weather route from Bryce Canyon National Park, the number of visitors to Capitol Reef increased so that in a recent year the figure soared close to 500,000. But this large park absorbs crowds easily, and even during the busiest summer months, there is a sense of peacefulness and remoteness not found at many of the other parks. You can still walk some of the park's less frequented short trails to unique scenic landscapes and have plenty of moments to yourself. Gas stations, restaurants, and motels have been removed from the park, which further enhances its sense of remoteness. The closest gas station is at Torrey, Utah, eleven miles west of the park. In the summer it is open daily, but it is sometimes known to close on Sunday. Inquire at the visitor center. For further information, write Superintendent, Capitol Reef National Park, Torrey, Utah 84775. Telephone: 1-801-425-3791.

Seeing the Park

The park is open all year. Two all-weather roads penetrate its north half. The paved road, Utah Highway 24, crosses it for fourteen miles from east to west, while the unpaved gravel and dirt Scenic Drive road probes its long axis for twelve miles. Both routes provide magnificent scenery from the road. But the park's uniqueness can best be appreciated by driving the short spur roads off the main roads and by taking short, safe walks into washes, slots, gorges, and canyons, and over slickrock outcroppings to high canyon rims, natural bridges, and Indian ruins.

It is the special province of Capitol Reef that there are many interesting things to see concentrated in a reasonably compact area. This means that really long drives within the park are not required and that many locations of special interest can be revisited with ease. In addition, the scenic roads and trails there provide an intimacy with the land you will not encounter elsewhere in the Southwest. If southeastern Utah is nature's classroom, then surely Capitol Reef is its "hands-on" laboratory.

In addition to the two all-weather roads for family autos, a good seventy-mile-long unpaved road will take you down the east side of the reef. It then climbs steeply over the Waterpocket Fold through beautiful country to Boulder, Utah. The last section of the road is marked on the maps as the Burr Trail Road. There are many four-wheel-drive roads that crisscross the park leading, unbelievably, to even more sights of rare scenic beauty (see "Remote Capitol Reef").

The junction of Utah Highway 24 and the Scenic Drive road is the location of the Capitol Reef visitor center, elevation 5,400 feet. The center is dramatically situated across the highway and south of the "Castle," an unusual Wingate butte with fluted and crenellated towers, sitting on top of colorful, ledgy Chinle formation slopes and fronted by a sculpted red Moenkopi base. These are three of the four most common rock formations you will see in the park. In addition to its setting, the visitor center provides an interesting ten-minute narrated slide show about the history and geology of the park. The display area in the center has some good natural history and cultural exhibits. Be certain to see the buffalo hide shields that were found within the park's borders. It has not yet been established who owned them. Probably they were made either by the Fremont Indians or the Utes who roamed this area in later times.

The bookracks in the center and off to one side offer a very good selection of information about the park and the High Southwest. A handsome self-guiding booklet (with color and black and white photos) entitled "This Ancient Rock—Guide to the Scenic Drive" can be purchased for a small fee. It is printed in German, French, and English. Much of the same information is available in a small, plain, pamphlet, which is sometimes given out upon paying the entry fee to the park. Many mimeographed, free materials not on display are also available for the asking—provided you know what to ask for. Some of the subjects covered are plant life, birds, trail guides, and lists of accommodations and services outside the park.

Utah Highway 24 West of the Visitor Center

To gain an overall impression of Capitol Reef Park, you can do a fairly quick reconnaissance by traveling approximately 2.5 miles west of the visitor center to the Panorama Point and Gooseneck Point junction. At the junction, turn left and

The Castle, near Capitol Reef National Park visitor center

drive the short distance to the Panorama Point parking area. Walk to the viewing area, where you will find laid out before you the heart of the park, including the huge curving spine of Capitol Reef as it extends southward. Many of the whitish, swirling, rising domes, knobs, and cylinders are sculpted from the Navajo sandstone for which the park is best known. From this vantage point, you can see why the reef presented such an impenetrable barrier to early settlers.

Beyond the reef to the southeast are the Henry Mountains, to the southwest is the Aquarius Plateau and Boulder Mountain. Return to the parking lot. Drive out the way you came for a very short distance to the dirt and gravel junction road taking off to the right to the Gooseneck's overlook. It is only three-quarters-of-a-mile long and easily passable. At the parking lot there are two trails. One short trail leads about 0.1 mile to a protected, fenced overlook of the Sulphur Creek Gorge. The second trail, labeled the Sunset Point Trail, extends about 0.5 mile alongside the gorge and is a double wide trail (with benches along the way) that has been made as level as possible for those who are

not steady on their feet. The trail leads through a veritable garden of Moenkopi rock as it follows the gorge rim at 6,400 feet elevation. The rim drops over 500 feet to Sulphur Creek below, the dark reddish brown of the raindrop-pocked Moenkopi rim giving way to the contrasting whitish gray to tan layers of the Kaibab limestone. This is probably the only place where you will have a chance to see a broad expanse of the Kaibab limestone in southeastern Utah. This trail offers fine views and at sunset you can watch the sun's ever-changing glow on the faces of the distant rock cliffs.

The sinuous, meandering curves made by Sulphur Creek deep in the gorge are called "goosenecks." As the creek sliced through this section of Miner's Mountain uplift, cutting its gorge, it kept the widely looping and curving course it had followed for millions of years across the surface of an ancient flat plain. As the land rose, the river cut down, much like an S-shaped cookie cutter. As it cut deeper, the river could not overflow its banks to reduce the curves. It became trapped in the deep recesses of its own curves. In other words, the meandering curves became entrenched. When entrenched curves are so close to one another that they almost meet, they are called goosenecks. These goosenecks are clearly visible from the rim.

As you walk along the longer rim trail, keep an eye out for some interesting rock formations. Several giant slabs of Moenkopi have fallen in such a way as to produce forms that look like dolmens or ancient tombs. Other giant slabs show the separation of their formative layers, looking for all the world like cross sections of flaky, multilayered pastries. Along this trail also look for such regional plants as Mormon tea, Utah juniper, piñon pine, and roundleaf buffaloberry. Return to Utah Highway 24 and turn left. Travel approximately 0.3 mile to the Chimney Rock turnoff. Pull into the parking lot to view the spire that rises 200 feet from its base.

At one time this spire was attached to the nearby cliffside. The large gap you see between the two is a testament to the power of seasonal erosion or weathering (see "Geological Overview"). The whitish cap on top of the chimney is a Chinle formation rock, Shinarump member. Just a little further west on Highway 24, you can see Twin Rocks from the road. The Shinarump is prominent there, too. The shaft of the Chimney Rock spire and the eroded red beds in front of you belong to the Moenkopi formation. The 3.5-mile round-trip Chimney Rock Trail that takes off from this area is rated as "fairly strenuous," gaining 540 feet elevation in 0.75 mile. From the ridge at trail's end are fine views of the reef face and Chimney Rock below. Return to Highway 24. Turn left and drive back to the visitor center junction. To drive and see all of the sights, excluding Chimney Rock Trail, along this segment of the highway, takes about 1.5 hours.

Now you can choose to continue on Highway 24, east of the visitor center, or take the 25-mile round-trip Scenic Drive southeast alongside the face of the reef. Each of the next two segments as presented here will take half a day, but can be seen piecemeal in a shorter span of time. For instance, just driving up the Scenic Drive road and back offers some good sights and only takes about an hour.

Scenic Drive Road

Turn right or southeast at the Capitol Reef visitor center and follow the signs along the Scenic Drive road to the picnic area 0.75 mile and the campground at 1 mile. On a hot day, this area of the park is a veritable oasis. The translucent green of the giant old cottonwood trees (one with a girth greater than twenty feet) and the lovely old orchards watered by the ever-flowing Fremont River which passes nearby, make this area a good resting spot for a picnic or camping. Both early In-

"Pastry" Moenkopi, rim of Sulphur Creek Gorge

Utah juniper

dians and white settlers recognized the amenities of this location. The settlers established the community of Fruita there. With the development of the park, almost all traces of that early settlement have been removed. But from this area you can take a footpath leading to a bridge across the river, then through the fruit orchards to the old Fruita School Building across Utah Highway 24. The orchards still produce some of the largest, juiciest, sweet cherries, peaches, apricots, and pears you will ever taste, and if you are there during the fruiting season, you can pick these morsels for a small fee. Inquire at the visitor center. If you arrive in April or May when the orchards are blooming, the visual feast is free of charge.

Some afternoon if you want to "sit out" an afternoon thunderstorm, pull into the parking-picnic area. If it has been a "gulley washer," as those storms often are, water will begin to cascade over the surrounding high cliff rims. Those instant waterfalls crash hundreds of feet down to the valley floor. After witnessing an event like that, you will never again question the role of seasonal water as the powerful shaping force of all that you see around you. Keep an eye out for colorful yellow-headed blackbirds, and redwing blackbirds, as well as western bluebirds and black-billed magpies.

Driving on through the Fruita area, you will come to the Cohab Canyon Trailhead (see "History") in approximately 1.2 miles. The trail is 3.5 miles round-trip and is rated as "strenuous" for the first 0.25 mile. It leads to a hidden canyon above the campground and a maze of narrow side canyons. At 1.4 miles you will pass the pleasant Capitol Reef campground on the right, well situated in the midst of orchards and lawns. At the end of the campground, the pavement ends and an unpaved but well maintained all weather dirt and gravel road continues. Average speed along this road is from 15 to 25 miles per hour. Approximately 2.5 miles from the visitor center, the road reaches the top of Danish Hill. Pull into the designated pullout. This is a good place to stretch your legs and orient yourself to the surrounding country.

From the direction you have just come, look back to the northwest to nice views over the Fruita area. Across the road to the northeast are massive, steep, pinkish sandstone cliffs of the Wingate formation resting on greenish gray and purplish-appearing layers of Chinle formation rocks. They in turn rest on the dark reddish brown Moenkopi rocks that erosion has sculpted to a variety of interesting shapes. In the distance, to the south, all along the ridge of the reef are several strangely eroded outcroppings of whitish Navajo sandstone. Early settlers pulled no punches when they called one of the more prominent protuberances, Fern's Nipple.

Continue south along the road. At approximately 3.4 miles is the spur road leading up Grand Wash. A wash is a dry water course larger than a gully and smaller than a canyon. When it rains, it is subject to flash flooding and can become a raging river capable of washing away everything in its path, including automobiles. Heed the sign and do not enter if rain is threatening. Just as you enter the wash, look carefully at the cliffside to the left, near the base. There you will see several old uranium mine tunnels, closed off with gates. Those mines are in the uranium-containing Shinarump member of the Chinle formation. Exploration for uranium was carried out in this area from 1904 up through the 1950s.

As you travel the 1.2 miles to the parking lot through the gap between the high, desert-varnished Wingate cliffs, you will notice an increasing amount of vegetation, particularly some fine stands of stunted Utah juniper. Also watch for Apache plum, Fremont barberry, rabbit brush, and dwarf yucca. As you travel up the wash, you will catch glimpses of smoothly sculpted Navajo sandstone buttes in a variety of shapes along the skyline in front of you. Look for the pullout or the Cassidy Arch viewpoint. You'll have to look hard to see the arch. Just before reaching the parking lot is a sign marking a shallow depression in the rock wall to the right. This is "Echo Cliff." Try it. It works.

From the parking lot, a short and pleasant walk continues on up the wash leading 0.25 mile to the Cassidy Arch trailhead and 2.25 miles on through the wash to Utah Highway 24. The trail takes you through widely spaced junipers which offer good shade for a picnic on a hot day. In May, the spaces between the junipers showcase a wide variety of wild flowers. As you continue along the trail, the sandstone appears "moth-eaten" in some areas. This honeycomb effect is caused by erosion as water "melts" parts of the sandstone rocks that are not tightly cemented together. Further on you will see where erosion has gone wild, creating potholes and gigantic vertical tanks in the sandstone the size of phone booths. Many of these are

Erosional potholes and tanks

large enough to sit or stand in. The Cassidy Arch trailhead sign is a good place to turn around, unless you want to continue on through the "narrows" for about 2 miles where the trail slips between five-hundred-foot-tall cliff walls that are only twenty to thirty feet apart. Eventually the wash will deposit you onto Utah Highway 24, approximately 4.5 miles east of the visitor center. Another alternative is to take the 3-mile round-trip "strenuous" hike to Cassidy Arch, in the Navajo sandstone about one thousand feet above the elevation of the trailhead. Whether Butch Cassidy, the outlaw, ever saw the arch named for him is a matter of conjecture, but he did apparently frequent Grand Wash where he allegedly built a hideout shelter.

Return to the Scenic Drive road and turn left, following the road as it ascends gradually up to Slickrock Divide, paralleling a gully to the right. The gully is filled with large slabs of Moenkopi rock, many having prominent "ripple marks" (See "Reading the Rocks"). Now at approximately 2.5 miles from Grand Wash junction, pull into the parking area to the right. This location is the divide between the Grand Wash and the Capitol Gorge drainage areas and is named "Slickrock" because of the prominent smooth sandstone outcroppings.

The divide offers fine views of the reef, with many formations in the Navajo sandstone visible above the Wingate cliffs. The land rising to the west, called Miner's Mountain, is dotted with vegetation and is part of a large uplift that extends from Sulphur Creek Gorge all the way up to this point. It was given its name Miner's Mountain because of its uranium and copper deposits.

From the Divide it is only a little over 2 miles to the Capitol Gorge junction. Along the way you will pass the Egyptian Temple, a structure, like Chimney Rock, carved from the Moenkopi and capped with the Shinarump member of the Chinle formation. In addition you will see some light-colored Shinarump boulders carved by nature into a variety of shapes, one resembling a dinosaur. Approximately 4.6 miles from Grand Wash is the Y junction to Capitol Gorge and Pleasant Creek. Take the left branch. Stop at the Capitol Gorge display pavilion to the right of the road. It houses a detailed and excellent summary of the history, geology, plant, mammal, bird, and reptile life of the area. Spend some time at this informative interpretive center. You will read about rock squirrels, spiny lizards, prince's plume, and roundleaf buffaloberry.

Do not enter Capitol Gorge if rain is threatening. For eighty years this gorge, cut through the reef by water, was the only feasible route for

Rock wren

wagons and autos to pass from one side of the reef to the other. Even at that it was always fraught with difficulties. Flash floods and falling boulders made travel through the gorge very difficult. As you travel down the gorge along the 2-mile unpaved road to the parking area, look for rock wrens, canyon wrens, mountain bluebirds, and the seldom seen golden eagles. Although some eagles nest in the high cliffs in the park, they seem to stay out of sight much of the time, relinquishing their air space to the ravens which are commonly seen.

Soon the road passes between high Wingate cliffs rising abruptly on both sides. To the right is "Tapestry Wall," where desert varnish (see "Reading the Rocks") has streaked the cliff walls with beautiful vertical designs. Also, as you drive along, look for evidence of cross-bedding in the sandstone next to the road. Much of the scenery along the skyline, including the Golden Throne off to your left, is sculpted from the smooth, cream-colored Navajo sandstone. Look for a parking pullout from which you can walk to the short trail which leads to views of the Golden Throne, one of the reef's best-known sculpted Navajo buttes and one of the most visible points along the reef at sixty-five hundred feet. In this area, the cliff walls are in the Kayenta sandstone, topped by the Navajo. Drive on to the end of the road and the parking area.

From the parking area, a foot trail leads beyond the small information booth through the gorge's narrow walls for about 0.75 miles to the tanks where most visitors turn around. You will walk through areas where the cliff walls rise more than eight hundred feet above you. From the tanks you can walk another 3 miles to Notom, the Gorge's portal on the east side of the reef. From the parking area, signs also lead to the Golden Throne

Roundleaf buffaloberry

Trail, a "strenuous" 4-mile round-trip hike that gains eleven hundred feet in 2 miles. Some say that this trail really penetrates the heart of the Capitol Reef country, offering incredible views of the awesome and beautifully eroded Navajo sandstone in all of its shapes and colors.

The trail up the gorge is a flat one, the Kayenta rocks giving way to the Navajo sandstone. Further down the gorge, the Navajo will be at eye level. There, again, look for cross-bedded surface marks (see "Reading the Rocks"). These are sweeping lines on the rock's surface that intercept one another at varying angles, revealing the origin of this rock millions of years ago (See "A Geological Primer to Southeastern Utah"). Notice how the Navajo cliffs erode to smooth, rounded shapes rather than the steep abrupt configurations of the Wingate sandstone. It is believed that if the Navajo rested on the same soft Moenkopi rock that underlies the Wingate, it too would fracture into giant pieces, forming steep cliffs. But the Navajo's base, the Kayenta, is harder and erodes more slowly, allowing subtle, rounded shapes to develop (see "Reading the Rocks," hard-soft layering).

As you walk down the gorge, you will pass Fremont Indian petroglyphs on the north cliff wall, and a little further on at 0.5 mile you will reach the Pioneer Register (see History). Beyond the Register at 0.75 mile are the "tanks," erosional basins that collect water similar to those in Grand Wash. Water pockets like these are common throughout the "folded" and uplifted areas of Capitol Reef.

Return to the parking lot and drive back to the Scenic Drive road at the Y junction. Turn left on to the branch leading to Pleasant Creek. In about a mile from the Capitol Gorge junction you will catch good views of the Golden Throne from a pullout to the left. Continue on approximately 2.3 miles to another Y junction. Bear right there and continue to keep to the right as you drive through the corrals of the Sleeping Rainbow Ranch and on to Pleasant Creek. The road for conventional vehicles ends at the creek. There is plenty of space to park.

Hiking Down Pleasant Creek: A Narrative Account

It is 9:00 A.M. and the sun is already beaming down on us with a vengeance. We left our motel at 8:15, arriving at the visitor center just before 8:30. In the last thirty minutes we traveled the thirteen-mile Scenic Drive road nonstop from beginning to end. Today is going to be a scorcher. But for now it is very pleasant alongside this perenially flowing stream, aptly named Pleasant Creek. The stream has its origin up along the high escarpments of Boulder Mountain. There at elevations several thousand feet higher than here, rainfall is more plentiful, keeping this stream flowing year-round. Down here the precipitation is only a meager five to seven inches a year. The stream has helped carve this beautiful wide valley, and like Capitol Gorge, has cut right through the reef. Cattlemen used to drive their herds to market along this well-watered route all the way to the old settlement of Notom on the east side of the reef, over six miles away. The water is plenty cold. We were told that it is not drinkable so we have our own water in quart containers in our day pack. Park officials recommend a gallon of water per person per day along backcountry trails like this one. Since we are only going to hike four hours, we have planned accordingly and are grateful each of us does not have to carry an entire gallon!

We douse ourselves with insect repellent and suntan lotion and head down the creek. There is not a maintained trail here, but the cattle hooves and intrepid travelers' boots have worn a path through the brush. Just north of us we notice the ranch house perched on the mesa top which extends like a peninsula into, but above the valley. The site was once occupied by the early Indians of the region and later settled by Mormon pioneers. Since the late 1930s it has been developed and occupied by Lurt and Alice Knee. For many years, until it closed, they operated the Sleeping Rainbow Guest Ranch from that site. We recall with fondness our stay with them years ago when we first began coming to Capitol Reef. Natural historians of the best kind, they educated their guests about the reef and environs. In many ways, they have been instrumental in putting Capitol Reef on the maps. It was there one unforgettable night that we met a family of kit foxes who had come in the shadow of evening hoping to pick up a morsel or two. They stayed long enough for us to observe them in some detail and then disappeared quickly back into the canyon.

Kit fox

Now we leave the stream and walk across the valley floor to the high cliffs on the northeast side, just below the ranch. We reach the talus slopes below the cliffs and spread out as we search the cliff walls for some of the most unusual petroglyphs in southeastern Utah. Our daughter yells out first. Sure enough she is standing in front of one of the petroglyph panels. We climb the jumbled heap of rocks to get a closer look. In one area we see several figures that look like "smiley faces." Now we see a number of concentric circles resembling a target with a bull's-eye. Unfortunately it is marred by someone's bullet. We have been told that many of these pictures may have been made by an ancient Indian stargazing and tracking cult. This may have been one of many "stations" in the Southwest to record the data of the heavens.

Even today the events in the heavens determine the time for planting and certain ceremonial

Fremont Indian petroglyphs

functions for many Pueblo Indians. Perhaps the mouth in the "smiley figure" is a crescent moon and the two pecked holes above it are two stars or planets as they appeared in relation to the moon some starry night nearly a thousand years ago. The concentric circles baffle us, but we do remember reading that they may represent the sun. My son spots some interesting animal and human forms, many of which we have seen in other locations. We marvel at the ability of these people to incise the rock so precisely with little more than a piece of chert or flint that has been "worked" into the shape of a chisel.

Looking at our watches, we pull ourselves away from other possible petroglyph discoveries and return to the creek to explore the valley further downstream. We walk through sage, tamarisk, and willow. Monarch butterflies, as large as we have ever seen, flit nonchalantly in the purple tamarisk blossoms. One monarch, completely absorbed with the blossoms, catches my daughter's eye. She sneaks up behind it and is able to photograph it from less than two feet away. Now the valley's southern wall and the creek come close together as we enter Pleasant Creek's canyon. There are numerous shallow caves here large enough for us to enter and rest in the shade. We speculate that the Indians may have used these caves in a similar manner.

In the back of most of these caves are pack rat nests. Those pesky little rodents have probably occupied this valley longer than anyone. Now farther downstream the canyon walls narrow and block the sun. The shade is refreshing, for even at the lower elevations here in the park it is considerably cooler in the shade than in the sun. Now we reach an area where the creek narrows and flows down slippery sandstone steps. It drops a few feet at a time until it finally cascades into several large, deep pools before it continues its meandering course as Pleasant Creek.

It is 11:00 A.M., warm and getting warmer. We are sweating profusely. The pools look inviting. The cold water feels good as we immerse ourselves. The smooth sandstone creek bed is slippery, the water instantly refreshing. As the kids wade upstream, we dry off by stretching out on a huge slab of sandstone. The warm rock feels good on our cold, wet bodies as the hot sun beams down

Pack rat or desert wood rat

from a bright blue sky. Colorful butterflies flit from one side of the creek to the other. We relax completely. Scanning the horizon we notice several massive, white dome-shaped rock formations looming in the distance against a backdrop of one of the bluest skies we have ever seen. With no other people around, we have the valley to ourselves this June day. We savor these moments of total solitude, unique on this earth, deep in the remote canyon recesses of Pleasant Creek, Capitol Reef National Park.

Utah Highway 24 East of the Capitol Reef Visitor Center

In many ways the drive east of the visitor center on paved Utah Highway 24 is one of the most satisfying in terms of gaining an overall impression of sights the park has to offer. It is one of the busiest sections of the park and can even be downright crowded midsummer. From the visitor center to the park boundary is about eight miles. From there you may want to continue a few more miles on paved Utah Highway 24 to see an excellent "Moki" Indian ruin and the moonscape-otherworldly badlands around Caineville and Hanksville. That drive will reward you with a view of massive and famous Factory Butte, rising over fifteen hundred feet above the desert floor. Several

picnic sites both inside and outside the park dot the road from the visitor center to Caineville. Along the way there are many sights close at hand to the left and right of the road, but also keep your eyes focused on the skyline for magnificent views of the eroded white Navajo sandstone forms that have made this area so famous. The road follows the Fremont River most of the way. That river provides the essential moisture for the relatively lush vegetation and cottonwood groves you will see on the way.

From the visitor center drive east a little less than a mile through many pleasant tree-shaded areas to the first pullout to the left. There you will find an old, log, one-room schoolhouse built in 1896 by Fruita's Mormon settlers and last used in 1941. The next pullout a little further on puts you within a few steps of being face to face with a fine panel of Fremont Indian petroglyphs pecked into the Wingate sandstone cliff wall. A little further on and in front of you, the space between the walls of the Fremont Canyon at skyline level is filled with a symmetrically rounded whitish dome that is startling in its immensity. This is Capitol Dome, probably the best example of the dome-like Navajo sandstone structures found throughout this park.

Approximately two miles from the visitor center is a large parking area to the left. This is the trailhead to Hickman Bridge. If you have time to take only one longer hike in the park, take this "moderate" two-mile round-trip walk to see Hickman Bridge and an amazing array of other sights. The elevation gain is four hundred feet in a mile. The following narrative details this hike.

Hiking the Trail to Hickman Bridge: A Narrative Account

We just arrived here at the Hickman Bridge trailhead. It is now 4:00 P.M. The air is fresh and it is a little cooler now as a gentle breeze pushes the last few clouds from the sky, remnants of this afternoon's thunderstorm. We notice that the Fremont River that has been to the right side of the road so far is now on this side of the highway. We look at the map on display here at the trailhead and drop a coin in the wooden box for a copy of the self-guiding booklet that will help us identify

Fremont Indian petroglyph panel

numerous plants and natural phenomena.

Booklet in hand we start out on the flat, well-maintained trail and follow it as it parallels the river. We sidestep small pools of water created by this afternoon's brief but heavy rain. We are impressed with the vegetation here along the river. Cottonwoods, willows, and tamarisk grow profusely. Especially tamarisk. Tamarisk or tamarix or salt cedar is a southern European, Mediterranean import which has its origins in the deserts of the Middle East. It was introduced into the Southwest early in the century as an ornamental and for erosion control.

Between 1910 and 1930, this pesky plant whose abundant seeds have "wings" in the form of small tufts of hair became established throughout the High Southwest as seasonal breezes spread the seeds everywhere. It is a beautiful plant when it blooms and even out of bloom its sparsely filled juniperlike branches are attractive, lending a nice

Tamarisk

green color to many a dry and drab creek bed. But its growth has become so prolific that it is squeezing out native willow trees and its moisture consumption is so high that it is now thought to be an undesirable plant in the arid Southwest.

Looking up we see very little vegetation above the river. The river provides a narrow band of sustenance for life in this dry country. Now we pass by rabbitbrush, a fall-blooming plant that is found everywhere in this arid land. Rabbits use it for food and shelter. We also identify four-wing saltbush, with its distinctive winglike bracts and narrow leaves, and squawbush or skunkbrush, so named for its use by Indian women for basket materials. Its malodorous plant stems give rise to its other less attractive name. Now the trail begins to climb abruptly. Winding our way up the cliffside, we catch good views of Capitol Dome.

As we near the top, we catch sight of numerous rounded, black as well as black and white lava boulders looking for all the world like randomly strewn bowling balls. They seem to be everywhere (see "Geological Overview"). They are stuck here and there on the benches and ledges above the Fremont River which brought them here. My daughter spots a small, narrow-leaf dwarf yucca off the trail to the right near the Whiskey Spring Trail junction. The yucca may well have been the single most useful natural plant to both the early Indian and settler. Amazingly, the early Indian got beyond the yucca's warlike, bayonet appearance and found that the pods, flowers, and young stalks were edible. Strips of the inedible leaves were twisted into cords and used in sandals, mats, and baskets. Not wasting any part of the highly prized yucca leaf, the sharp tips of the leaves were used as needles. The early settlers discovered that yucca roots also supply a soapy lather when placed in water—instant desert shampoo!

Staying to the left at the trail junction, we soon come to an area with vistas to the north. Looming up in front of us are several impressive Navajo sandstone monoliths. We take numerous pictures of these awesome rocks before going on. Now we spot a prickly pear cactus as well as a small barrel-shaped fish hook cactus as we walk into a sparse pygmy forest of Utah junipers and piñon pines. We see a large clump of roundleaf buffaloberry with its jadelike leaves. In addition we notice numerous tufts of Indian ricegrass. The early Indians harvested the seed heads by thrashing them. Then they cooked the grain or ground it into meal. We also spot several nice specimens of Mormon tea, which is closely related to the piñon and juniper trees around it. Mormon settlers brewed a tea from the tough, rounded stems of this plant.

The trail takes us onto the face of a large outcropping of sandstone. We travel over this slickrock easily with our tennis shoes. Now the trail parallels a wash to our right. Our son spots a Fremont Indian granary, a construction of sticks and mud built in a small alcove in the cliff wall. These storage cysts, mistaken for the homes of early Indians, led to the misnomer Moki or Moqui, thought by some to mean small person. Beans, corn, and squash, the staples of the early Indian diet, were probably stored here, safe from marauding animals. As we continue up the wash, many potholes and water tanks at the bottom of the wash come into view. Some of these natural storage tanks can hold thousands of gallons of water. They are formed when sand and gravel abrasives, powered by the force of running water, scour the surfaces of rocks. Continued abrasion over thousands, even millions, of years dissolves the sandstone where it is less well cemented together and hollows it out into these huge pots and tanks.

Walking mostly over rock along a narrow twisty segment of the trail, we spot Hickman Bridge in the distance. We are surrounded by a sea of rock. The trail guide waxes poetic: "Rock, it

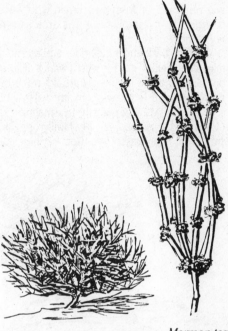

Mormon tea

dominates your view of Capitol Reef. Naked, ungiving, overwhelming rock. Perhaps the feeling that the place arouses depends on that, the scarcity of life, the immensity of bare and broken rock." As we approach the bridge we are awed by its presence. It is a huge, but graceful stone semicircle spanning 133 feet between its bases. It is set amidst a backdrop of rock slabs, boulders, and cliff faces— a true rock jungle. Now we are at the base and can appreciate its other dimension. This sturdy Kayenta sandstone bridge and its strong support averages 15 feet in thickness. We notice the stream bed under it. As it passes under the bridge, it continues its precipitous downward course.

At a high point, immediately under the bridge, the inside of the arch is 72 feet above us. As we move east of the center of the bridge, it is nearly 125 feet above us. We feel completely dwarfed by its size. Now we discuss the difference between an arch and a bridge (see "Reading the Rocks") and decide that this is a bridge since the river runs under it. We assume the abandoned river channel followed a course west of the bridge before it created a hole and established its path through this sandstone wall. Originally known as Broad Arch, it was renamed for Joseph Hickman who was instrumental in establishing this area as a national monument.

I climb back under the bridge and ascend the talus slope behind it to the west. I want a picture of our family framed by this giant hole in the rock wall. As I turn to look back, I am amazed by what I see. From this vantage point the true magnificence of this bridge is apparent. My family appear so small that I can barely see them as they stand under it. Rising in the background, perfectly framed by the graceful curving lines of the red stone bridge, is the massive presence of Capitol Dome. The light is perfect now, the scene beautiful if not poetic. I snap this perfect picture, compliments of Mother Nature.

Everyone is up here now. We stand in silence soaking it all in. As the sun begins to go down, the colors become richer with each passing minute. The bridge frames the white cap of the dome as it

*View of Capitol Dome
through Hickman Bridge*

turns golden in the evening light, while the color of the sky behind it deepens to an incredible shade of blue. The silence is as powerful as the shapes and the colors. But we break the silence as we clamber noisily down the rock slopes back to the bridge and retrace our steps down to the trailhead. We should be down by 6:30 P.M., giving us ample time to drive back to Panorama Point to see the last rays of sunlight on Capitol Reef's west face.

From the Hickman Bridge parking area continue east on Utah Highway 24. In the next few miles are several parking areas offering views of many of the park's landmarks such as swirling, pointed Navajo Dome with its pleated skirt base. Almost 4 miles from the visitor center is a shaded picnic area on both sides of the highway. There are picnic tables and toilets but no water. In less than a mile farther you will come to a parking pullout to the right which is at the end of Grand Wash. For those hiking through from the Grand Wash Trail off the Scenic Drive road, this is the exit. This 2.25-mile one-way trail can be walked in either direction. A little over 6 miles east of the visitor center, on the right, is the Elijah Behunin Cabin and parking area. Built of sturdy sandstone blocks in 1892, this home is another testimonial to the hardy Mormon pioneers who attempted to settle near the Fremont River. After much backbreaking labor to divert the river and then plant fields and orchards, violent floods washed away just about all their efforts in the third year of their residence. But that was not unusual, as this harsh land resisted most efforts to tame it.

A half mile farther up the road, approximately 6.4 miles from the visitor center, is a parking turnoff to the left. There you will discover one of the true hot-weather delights of the park, a swimming hole on the Fremont River. Notice the warning sign. Its admonition is applicable to the rocky areas to the left of the sign. Go to the right of the sign, instead, where you will notice a well-used, short footpath to a small waterfall and wide wading area. There the cascading Fremont River forms a large shallow pool at the base of a sloping sandstone wall. Enjoy! Do not attempt to climb the rocks above the pool. This is slickrock which is slippery and dangerous when wet.

About 8.5 miles east of the visitor center is the eastern border of the park. But do not stop there. The sights and the scenery continue even if the park does not. In another 0.5 mile is a shaded picnic area on the right. Then about 9 miles from the visitor center is the junction road to Notom, only a geographical place-name now and the location of a ranch. This unpaved road, the Notom–Bullfrog Road, heads south toward Lake Powell. Approximately 34 miles from its junction with Utah Highway 24, the Burr Trail leads west from it to Boulder, Utah. Family autos can travel this scenic route from the Capitol Reef visitor center to Boulder, but be prepared for 70 miles of sometimes difficult driving over dirt roads. Although these are usually well-maintained roads, you will want to check at the visitor center before starting out, especially if it has just rained or is threatening to rain, since the roads are not passable to all vehicles when wet.

Continue east on Utah Highway 24. In less than 2 miles you will see a parking turnoff to the right labeled Moki Ruin. This is a picnic area as well. Close to the road, only requiring a short walk, is one of the best Fremont Indian granary structures to be seen in the area. About 11 miles from the visitor center on the left are another parking area and picnic table in a shaded area. Just east of the picnic area is a junction with Utah Highway 12 leading to Cathedral Valley in the park's northern district. Continue straight ahead until you cross the Fremont River where you will begin to see over the next 4 miles some of the most distinctive landscapes in the Southwest.

Entirely different from those in the park, these Mancos shale badlands look like moonscapes with their wrinkled, fluted, blue, gray, pyramidal-shaped structures lined up in rows for miles and miles. This scenery reaches a climax 5 miles east of Caineville where Factory Butte, with its crenellated towers, rises with great power and strangeness over 1,500 feet above the surrounding desert. If you do not enter or leave Capitol Reef on this route, be certain you drive this far east. Near Factory Butte you are approximately 25 miles from the visitor center and 20 miles from Hanksville. Hanksville, 40 miles from the Capitol Reef visitor center and situated near the junction of the Fremont and Dirty Devil rivers has lodging and food (see "Staying There"). As you return to the

Fremont River swimming hole

visitor center from this eastern segment of Highway 24, you will be rewarded with some superb views from the highway that were not visible to you as you traveled in the other direction.

Remote Capitol Reef

The all-weather paved and dirt and gravel roads open up only a small part of the park's immense area to most visitors. Additional spectacular country can be seen on the network of four-wheel-drive roads that more thoroughly cover the park. These remote roads will lead you to areas of fossilized dinosaur bones and oyster shell beds as well as to agate beds and agate caves. Some of them will take you face to face with several stunning monoliths in Cathedral Valley, like the Temple of the Sun, Temple of the Moon, and Solomon's Butte, that have helped make the park famous. Some of the Cathedral Valley roads can be driven by family automobiles if the road surface is

dry and the driver is experienced in handling rough, rocky, and sandy spots. You should inquire at the visitor center before you start out on such a venture. The average motorist will probably feel more comfortable taking a half- or full-day jeep tour from the tour operator listed at the end of this section.

Granary, Fremont or Moki Indian ruin

Scenic Utah Highway 12 From Capitol Reef to Bryce Canyon

If you have the time, travel Utah Highway 12 approximately one hundred miles from Capitol Reef National Park to Bryce Canyon National Park. This exceptionally scenic route offers dramatic views at almost every turn and takes you through remote southeastern Utah towns, where time seems to have stood still. This is perhaps the most interesting and scenic one hundred miles you can drive in Utah's Canyon Country. The paved two-lane road takes you over the 9,200 feet elevation crest of Boulder Mountain, which flanks the Aquarius Plateau to Boulder, Utah (see Boulder Mountain and Boulder, Utah below), and then plunges you deep into the Escalante Canyon system (see Calf Creek Recreation area: the Escalante Canyon System below). The road then emerges from the canyon depths near the town of Escalante, Utah (population 650) with its restaurants, motels, and shops (see "Staying There" this section) before it winds by the Escalante Petrified Forest State Park one mile west of town. There you will find a small visitor center, self-guided (trail guide pamphlets provided) trails through an area laden with petrified wood and a nice shaded picnic and camping area around a lake, Wide Hollow Reservoir. (For more information, contact Utah Parks and Recreation, P.O. Box 350, Escalante, Utah 84726. Telephone: 1-801-826-4466.)

From there the route passes through a number of small southeastern Utah towns until it reaches the road junction to Kodachrome Basin State Park between Henrieville and Cannonville. You can follow that improved dirt-and-gravel road (check road conditions if storms are threatening) seven miles to the park where there are pleasant picnic and camping sites in the midst of unique freaks of nature called petrified geyser holes— eroded, white, misshapen plugs of stone and sediment standing upright everywhere you look. Fee. For more information about the park, telephone: 1-801-679-8562. After Cannonville comes the interesting and historic old town of Tropic (popula-

tion 420) with its shaded picnic areas and historic log-and-stone homes. Then Utah Highway 12 enters more scenic country and winds through a five-mile segment of Bryce Canyon National Park before reaching the créme de la créme, Bryce Canyon.

Utah Highway 12 is a scenic road, not a speedway. Although it is a good, paved two-lane road, there are some segments with narrow to no shoulders. And some parts of the roadbed wind and twist and are without guardrails. Allow two and one-half hours one-way driving time and more, if you plan many stops. For more details about this route, including hiking trails to more remote areas, write Scenic 12 Chamber of Commerce, P.O. Box 146, Escalante, Utah 84726. Telephone: 1-801-826-4210.

Boulder Mountain and Boulder, Utah

Boulder Mountain at 9,220 feet elevation rises from the northwestern edge of the Aquarius Plateau, which tops out at 11,600 feet above sea level, making it one of America's highest plateaus. Its high mountainous terrain with rushing mountain streams, wide green meadows, and great stands of quaking aspens and stately evergreens offers a stark contrast to the park below it. Even on the warmest of summer days, the temperature up there is pleasant. The views of the surrounding countryside as described by Captain Dutton and quoted in the introduction to the Capitol Reef section of this book are truly magnificent. You can reach this genuine mountain country in less than an hour from the Capitol Reef visitor center on Utah Highway 12 from Torrey to Boulder. There are numerous pleasant places that you will find for picnicking along the way.

If you go as far as the summit, you might just as well continue on Utah Highway 12 to Boulder, Utah, approximately fifty miles from the visitor center. Almost all the popular tour books have missed this town. You should not. This small farming and ranching mountain community, population 125, high up on the side of the Aquarius Plateau at 6,000 feet elevation, has the distinction of being the last town in the United States to have a road built to it. That was in 1938–1939. Until then it was the only town in the continental United States to still receive its mail delivery by pack mule and packhorse. The town is scenically situated among evergreen trees and numerous mounds and ridges of white Navajo sandstone.

But more importantly, Boulder is the home of the Anasazi Indian Village State Historical Monument (known to some as the Coombs Site). This was a distant Kayenta Anasazi outpost on the northwestern frontier of that great prehistoric culture (see Section II, "A Prehistory of Indian Country"). The monument is located on the site of an ancient village dating back to somewhere between A.D. 1050 and A.D. 1200. The excellent visitor center on the site has some good displays of early Indian life (including replicas of a prehistoric granary and a petroglyph panel) as well as displays of artifacts found on the site. Outside a six-room life-size replica of an Anasazi dwelling has been constructed on the path that leads to the excavated prehistoric village. There eighty-seven rooms have been unearthed by University of Utah archaeologists, who are still intermittently involved with the site for research and training purposes. A small entry fee is charged to walk the interesting self-guided trails (trail brochure provided) of this ancient village. There are several shaded picnic tables convenient to the visitor center. For more

*Anasazi dwelling, Anasazi Indian
Village State Historical Monument*

information, contact Park Superintendent, Anasazi Indian Village State Historical Monument, P.O. Box 393, Boulder, Utah 84716. Telephone: 1-801-335-7308.

Utah Highway 12
Calf Creek Recreation
Area: The Escalante
Canyon System

From Boulder, Utah, it is an easy twenty-mile drive over paved Utah Highway 12 to the Calf Creek trailhead in the Escalante Canyon system. When you come this far, you know you are truly in some of the most remote country in the United States. Calf Creek feeds the Escalante River, the last river in the lower forty-eight to be discovered and mapped. The Escalante canyon system is conveniently situated between Capitol Reef and Bryce Canyon National parks. It is spectacular country which beautifully captures the spirit of the High Southwest, yet it is overlooked by most tour guidebooks.

Entering the canyon system from either direction is a dramatic event as the road winds deeper and deeper through beautifully sculptured Navajo sandstone, each turn of the road revealing some new configuration and each approaching turn offering tantalizing views of some spectacle ahead. Down, down, down through layers of rock until finally you see a lush green paradise with the Escalante River flowing through it. The early Fremont Indians found this little bit of paradise as evidenced by the numerous storage huts and petroglyphs that abound in this deep canyon system. Look for the sign to Calf Creek Falls Trail and Calf Creek Campground. Follow the road to the tree-shaded campground alongside Calf Creek. This is a good place for a picnic or just to take a stroll.

If you have time, take the 5.5-mile round-trip walk along the flat canyon floor to lower Calf Creek Falls. A self-guiding booklet is available in a small box at the trailhead. The trail follows the creek as closely as possible as it winds up the canyon between sandstone walls which contain numerous alcoves, caves, and petroglyphs. Look for horsetail in the wetter areas. It is a plant that dates back to the dinosaur age and which thrives in the seeps

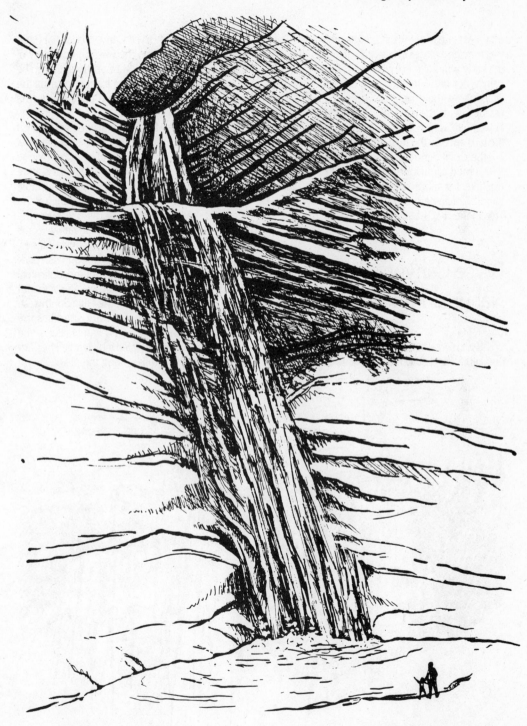

Lower Calf Creek Falls

and moist areas of the canyon floor. Occasionally you may find pieces of barbed wire, a reminder of the early white settlers who used this natural box canyon for pasturing their calves. Calf Creek they called it. At the end of the hike you will be rewarded with the rare beauty of 126-foot-high Lower Calf Creek Falls. You can feel the cool mist of the falls and see the lush hanging gardens around it—the oasis penultimate of southeastern Utah. You should allow four to six hours for this round-trip hike. For more information, contact Bureau of Land Management Office, Escalante, Utah 84726. Telephone: 1-801-826-4291.

Bryce Canyon National Park

If you travel to Capitol Reef National Park or to the Calf Creek–Escalante area, you will be within a few hours' drive of Bryce Canyon National Park, which rests just beyond the western boundary of Utah's southeastern quadrant. Although it can be jammed with tour buses and travelers during the summer months, this unique park should be visited if you have time.

It is Utah's smallest national park, yet yearly it receives the second largest number of national park visitors in Utah. In a recent year, nearly one million visitors roamed the park's fifty-six square miles. In the summer it is probably the most densely populated national park in Utah. Yet the elongated shape of the park seems to disburse the crowds in such a way that the traffic rarely seems overburdensome. And even at the busiest times, pockets of peace and quiet can be found. It is a park well worth seeing for its truly stunning, delicately carved sandstone landforms that offer a visual feast not found elsewhere in the High Southwest.

Bryce Canyon National Park straddles the eastern edge of the lofty Paunsaugunt Plateau, one of America's highest elevated tablelands. The park extends for twenty miles along the plateau's rim

Bryce Canyon National Park

and high escarpments, providing you with superb views over the surrounding Colorado Plateau country over 2,000 feet below. On a clear day the country unfolds in front of you as you look out from Yovimpa Point, elevation 9,105 feet. Eighty miles in the distance you can make out the Henry Mountains to the northeast, while ninety miles away near the Arizona border, Navajo Mountain rises into view.

But the park is better known for its "badlands" or its erosional forms than it is for its views. Not a "canyon" in the true sense of the word (see "Geological Overview"), the delicately carved sculptured forms that have made the park so famous occur along the eroding cliff faces of the uplifted Paunsaugunt Plateau. Paunsaugunt is a Paiute Indian word meaning "home of the beaver." Most of the unusual and extremely delicate rock forms have been carved from the Wasatch formation sandstone, one of the youngest in the sedimentary stack (see "Geological Overview"). Its varied composition includes soft layers of silt and clay with very little calcium carbonate-binding cement, as well as hard layers of limestone and dolomite that are well cemented together. The differential weathering of those alternating hard-soft layers accounts for many of the unusual shapes you will see. Perhaps "exquisite" describes the eroded forms better. Some have called this crenellated escarpment a fairyland, as beautiful demoiselles, delicate spires, minarets, pinnacles, and weird hoodoos reach for the sky. Some of the formations are so unusual that you will probably be caught up in the game of "name it yourself." Why not? Others have.

Early on, Paiute Indians letting their imaginations run wild read so much into these rock forms that they developed an enchanting legend about them. They believed this area was the home of exotic lizards, birds, and manlike creatures who fell into evil ways and were all turned into stone. Accordingly, they named this area Unka-timpe-Wa-Wince-Pock-ich which means "red rocks standing like men in a bowl-shaped canyon." Settlers and early park visitors also unleashed their creative minds on these rock forms coming up with The Turtle, The Gossips, Alley Oop and Dinny, The Happy Family, The Organ Grinder's Monkey, and in one single leap of fantasy someone called a

large, stony presence Queen Victoria. This fascination with the park's landforms made it highly popular very early in the century. The area was set aside as a national monument in 1923. By 1928, the monument was doubled in size and was declared a national park.

One of the early surveyors of the park put aside his tripod long enough to write, "There are thousands of red, white, purple and vermillion colored rocks, of all sizes, resembling sentinels on the walls of castles, monks and priests in their robes, cathedrals and congregations. . . presenting the wildest and most wonderful scene that the eye of man ever beheld." The unusual and dramatic coloration of the landforms is due to the different stages of oxidation of iron and manganese that have stained and colored these once drab rocks. Bryce's highly colored rocks are extremely sensitive to the nuances of changing light. In the early morning you will see them change from a reddish brown to light gold with traces of purple, blue, and lavender. Around noon, those hues are replaced by flaming yellows and oranges as well as brick reds and tans. In the evening those colors change to the many shades of pinks and reds for which the park is most famous. Even clouds crossing the sun's path in the daytime change the coloration from yellows and oranges to reddish browns and rusts. Some formations are topped with white, giving the impression of a winter scene.

All of the colors stand in contrast to the fresh green provided by the stands of juniper, ponderosa and piñon pine, Douglas fir, spruce and aspen which dot the canyon rims and floors. Add to all of this the intensely clear blue sky found at this extremely high elevation, and you have a picture whose subtleties challenge even the best photographer's skill.

Bryce's high altitude, averaging more than 8,000 feet above sea level, means cooler day and nighttime temperatures, a real bonus in the summer. Summer comes late with an explosion of wild flowers in late June and July. During those months you can see blue columbine, sego or mariposa lilies (Utah's state flower), yellow evening primrose, wild iris, and Indian paintbrush. In the winter the main park roads are kept free of the high altitude snows as Bryce Canyon is covered with a mantle of snow providing it with yet another

Sego or mariposa lily (Utah State flower)

8,000 feet. Park in the designated area and walk the short distance to the rim. There you will catch your first glimpse of what Bryce Canyon is all about. As you look out on the enormous amphitheater of delicately carved miniature canyons giving rise to thousands of fanciful shapes, you will begin to understand the powerful sculpting force of seasonal erosion.

The very rim you stand on is eroding away at the rate of one foot every fifty to sixty years. Continue to walk south along the almost level rim trail. The one-half-mile section of trail between Sunrise Point and Sunset Point is not only fairly level but it is also paved, allowing handicap access to this particularly dramatic section of rim trail. Or you can choose to take the Navajo Loop Trail from the

contrasting color. For more information, write Superintendent, Bryce Canyon National Park, Bryce Canyon, Utah 84717. Telephone: 1-801-834-5322.

Seeing the Park

Although Bryce Canyon can be seen as part of a day trip from some other base location, its rare beauty is best appreciated by spending part of an afternoon, an evening, and part of a morning there. In that length of time, you can not only see most of the sights that have made Bryce Canyon so popular with travelers (particularly along the 5.5-mile rim trail, which follows the canyon edge from Fairyland to Bryce Point), but you can hike several interesting short trails into the heart of Bryce's beautiful badlands as well. The only entry point into the main section of the park is near its north border from Utah Highway 12.

After paying an entry fee, drive to the visitor center. There you will find geology and natural history exhibits and can view a narrated slide show about the natural history of the park. A list of interpretative programs offered in the summer is also posted there. From the visitor center, drive to the Sunset Point portion of the rim trail, elevation

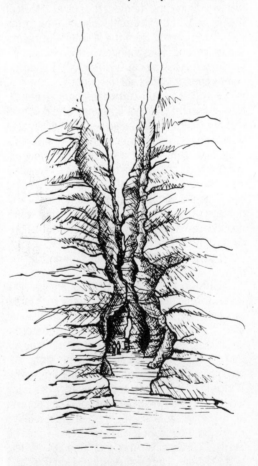

"Wall Street," Bryce Canyon National Park

Douglas firs growing out of gorge, Bryce Canyon National Park

Sunset Point area, one of the favorite walks in the park. This trail, rated as "fairly strenuous," is easy to negotiate. Just below the rim, take the trail to the right. It descends several hundred feet below the rim by way of many well-designed switchbacks to a narrow gorge, called Wall Street, from which the trunks of several large Douglas fir trees rise over 100 feet above the canyon floor between the narrow 200-foot-tall canyon walls to the light above.

After Wall Street there are two trail junctions. Always stay to the left to complete the Navajo Loop. Along this route you will see The Turtle, Camel and Wisemen, the Organ Grinder's Monkey, Thor's Hammer, and the Temple of Osiris. Keep an eye out for round-leaved manzanita, mountain mahogany, and ocean spray, a few of the plants which thrive in this environment. Of course, at the end of this 2.2-mile round-trip loop you must regain the 521 feet in elevation that you lost on the way down. The tread is good and there are places to rest along the way as the trail switchbacks up to the rim. This round-trip hike takes about one and one-half hours.

Back on the level rim trail, you can walk a short distance south to Inspiration Point, which offers some different views of the amphitheater, or walk north to Sunrise Point where the morning sun places much of the canyon in favorable light. From there you can take the Queen's Garden Trail, which leads 320 feet down into the canyon past views of Queen Victoria, Queen's Castle, and Gulliver's Castle, where, in addition to the rock formations, you will see several of the rare, almost extinct bristlecone pine trees, one of the oldest living things on our continent. This is the easiest hike below the canyon rim, taking less than one and one-half hours for the 1.5-mile round-trip excursion. It also connects with the Navajo Loop Trail. The rim trail goes on another 5 miles to Fairyland View near the park's entrance station. If you spend an evening at the park when the moon is bright, be sure to take a walk along the rim. You will see yet another variation on the theme of the canyon's ever-changing appearance.

Before leaving the park, you may wish to drive south a few miles to Bryce Point and Paria viewpoint where additional panoramas of the eroded pink escarpment can be seen. Two longer trails, both rated "strenuous," begin at Bryce Point. One, the hike to the Hat Shop along the Under-the-Rim Trail is 4 miles round trip (about four hours hiking time) and takes you through a region rich in demoiselle erosional forms. The other, Peek-a-boo Loop, is a 5-mile round-trip trail (three and one-half hours hiking time), which leads to views of Alley Oop and Dinny, Three Wise Men, Bryce Temple, Cathedral, and Hindu Temple. This trail also connects with the Navajo Loop Trail. Horseback rides are often scheduled along this trail.

The park's main paved road extends south through aspen groves and spruce and fir forests to Rainbow Point and Yovimpa Point, elevation 9,105 feet, where excellent views open up in all directions out over the Colorado Plateau. While there, you can take the easy to moderate Bristlecone Loop walk trail along the plateau top through a fir-spruce, bristlecone pine community. This almost level trail is one-mile long and takes about one hour to complete. Allow about an hour for this round-trip drive (more if you plan to stop often or walk a trail or two), obeying the park's 35-mile-per-hour speed limit. From Yovimpa Point you can truly see forever.

And should you decide to stay longer at Bryce Canyon National Park, there are over 60 miles of trails to remote caves, hollows, canyons, prairie dog villages, and of course, to more of those weirdly eroded hoodoos!

Staying There

In some areas of southeastern Utah lodging and food are listed under one heading. But in Moab, where there are many choices, they are each listed separately. Generally, you will take meals in a cafélike atmosphere or in a restaurant or dining room serving very basic fare. Try to remember that your visit to southeastern Utah is to savor the visual landscapes. Let that visual feast compensate for some of your gastronomic needs. You will not be entirely starved for quality food and superb cooking, for the scene is changing rapidly especially in and around Moab, where several high-caliber restaurants, cafés, and dining rooms, which would get along famously in any large American city, have sprung up in the last few years.

Wine, beer, and cocktails are available in all areas covered by this book, except on the Indian reservations, where alcohol is illegal. The legal drinking age in all the states is twenty-one. The most restrictive liquor laws are in Utah, where there is a system of state-owned liquor stores that accept only cash. Restaurants in Utah cannot serve liquor per se, but many have their own liquor stores on the premises where you can buy wine or liquor to be served and consumed with the meal. Setups are provided by the restaurant, but liquor can be consumed in restaurants only in conjunction with a meal.

Moab, Utah

Lodging

Green Well Motel (Best Western). Open all year. One of the nicest and most comfortable motels in Moab, this very pleasant oasis is surrounded by enough trees and shrubs to help soothe the summer's blistering heat. It is staffed by pleasant, courteous, and knowledgeable Moabites. The swimming pool (heated when required) is circled by a brick wall and nice plantings. From there you have a good view of Moab Valley's colorful cliff walls in the distance. Its seventy-one air-conditioned rooms with TV's and phones and full bath facilities fill up fast in the summer. Queen and king beds are available in many rooms. Although located on U.S. Highway 191, most of the rooms are a considerable distance away from the busy highway and are quiet. The adjacent coffee shop and restaurant serve three adequate meals a day. Mailing address: Green Well Motel, 105 South Main Street, Moab, Utah 84532. Telephone: Toll free in the United States 1-800-528-1234 (Best Western Reservations Center) or call 1-801-259-6151. Moderate.

Cedar Breaks Condos and Canyon View Cottage (Bed and Breakfast). The six modern Cedar Break Condos are spiffy if not luxurious air-cooled units located in an attractive two-story building in a quiet location away from the highway, but close to restaurants and shops. They are spacious, splen-

Moab, Utah

didly furnished, and very comfortable. Most have two bedrooms (either king or twin beds), living-dining room, and kitchen. Some have view balconies. Canyon View Cottage is located south of town on an escarpment above the golf course and offers fine views. The interior is handsomely designed and configured much like the condo units. The efficient and friendly owners who are very knowledgeable about the area stock the refrigerator with all the fixings you will need to prepare either a full or continental breakfast. No detail is overlooked, so preparing breakfast in these modern kitchens is as easy as pie. All units have telephones and color TV's and are as comfortable as home. You should reserve well ahead of time. Reservation deposit required. Mailing address: Cedar Breaks Condos/Canyon View Cottage, Center and Fourth East, Moab, Utah 84532. Telephone: 1-801-259-7830. Inexpensive.

The Rustic Inn. Open all year. Located just off U.S. Highway 191 one block behind the Green Well Motel. Twenty-four air-conditioned rooms with TV's and telephones. All rooms with queen beds. Some waterbeds available. This motel is in a very quiet location. The large, well-furnished rooms are a bargain for the price. Swimming pool on the grounds. Mailing address: The Rustic Inn, 120 East First South Street, Moab, Utah 84532. Telephone: 1-801-259-6177. Inexpensive.

Ramada Inn. Located along U.S. Highway 191 south of downtown. Eighty-three air-conditioned rooms with heated pool, TV's. Pets allowed. Restaurant adjacent. Attractive. Mailing address: Ramada Inn, 182 South Main, Moab, Utah 84532. Telephone: 1-801-259-7141. Moderate.

The Virginian. Open all year. Located one-half block off U.S. Highway 191. Twenty air-conditioned rooms with TV's. All have kitchenettes. Mailing address: The Virginian, 70 East Second Street, Moab, Utah 84532. Telephone: 1-801-259-5951. Inexpensive.

Apache Motel (Friendship Inn). Located in a pleasant area several blocks off the main highway. This is a thirty-three-unit air-conditioned motel with swimming pool. The rooms are small and the exterior of the building looks a bit tired, but the Apache provides an adequately comfortable night's lodging. Mailing address: Apache Motel, 166 South 400 East, Moab, Utah 84532. Telephone: 1-801-259-5727. Inexpensive.

Bowen Motel-Best Value Inns. Open all year. Located on U.S. Highway 191 near the north side of town. This locally managed motel is right on the highway, yet is able to buffer most of the problems that come with the location. Its forty-one attractive, air-conditioned rooms with TV's, phones, and full baths offer a variety of queen and double beds. In addition, some rooms have kitchenettes. The motel has a heated swimming pool. Mailing address: Bowen Motel, 169 North Main Street, Moab, Utah 84532. Telephone: 1-801-259-7132. Inexpensive and moderate.

Pack Creek Ranch-A Country Inn. Located sixteen miles south of town. When you turn into the gate at Pack Creek Ranch and look around at the tall mountains and pink cliffs in the midst of a green valley cut by a clear mountain stream you may think you have died and gone to heaven. Then you realize you are in the foothills of the La Sal Mountains at a considerably higher and cooler elevation (six thousand feet) than Moab, which is less than thirty minutes away. On this spacious property (three hundred acres), there are five differently configured western-style cabins housing twenty-six beds all together. One large cabin has four bedrooms, living room, dining room, kitchen, and fireplace. While another smaller cabin has a sitting room-bedroom and kitchen. All cabins have private baths and are nicely furnished. Four have fireplaces. The attractive and comfortable ranch lodge-dining room is handsomely furnished, southwestern style, and also has a book and gift shop. The dining room, open for breakfast and dinner, offers some of the best victuals in Southeastern Utah (see "Food"). And there's more. Swimming pool, horseback riding (trail rides, dinner rides, moonlight rides), pack-supported hikes, stream fishing, hikes into the La Sals, river-raft trips, and the helpful advice of the two hospitable owners who know the country and the horses like the back of their hand. Reservation deposit required. Mailing address: Pack Creek Ranch-A Country Inn, P.O. Box 1270, Moab, Utah, 84532. Telephone: 1-801-259-5505.

Campgrounds

In addition to the campgrounds at Arches National Park (Devil's Garden, 53 sites. Telephone: 1-801-259-8161), Dead Horse Point State Park (21 sites. Telephone: 1-801-259-6511), and Canyonlands National Park, Island in the Sky District (Willow Flat, 12 sites. Telephone: 1-801-259-7164), there are several commercial campgrounds including two south of downtown, Canyonlands Campark (113 sites. Telephone: 1-801-259-6848), and the K.O.A. campground south of town along U.S. Highway 191 (60 sites. Telephone: 1-801-259-6682). Located one mile north of downtown is Slickrock Campground (120 sites. Telephone: 1-801-259-7660).

Food

Sunflower Hill Pantry. This superb lunch and snack restaurant is conveniently located right downtown in the Grand Emporium shopping mall on the corner of North Main Street and Center Street, diagonally across from the Western Plaza. Telephone: 1-801-259-5066. The care and use of quality fresh ingredients that go into the preparation of the food here changes the face of eating in downtown Moab. Their fresh fruit salad supreme

with a cool cream dressing is the most soothing concoction this side of the La Sals on a hot day. Homemade breads enclose delicious, fresh sandwich fillings (ham, turkey, and others) and can be accompanied by delicious, made-from-scratch soups and salads. Outstanding homemade desserts. Fresh fruit slushes. Ice cream. Will pack lunches to go. Closed Sunday. Inexpensive.

Poplar Place Pub and Eatery. Located on the corner at 10 East 100 North Street and Main Street. Telephone: 1-801-259-9971. For years this award-winning pub has produced outstanding pizzas and sandwiches for lunch and dinner. And they still do. Now, however, the whole family can partake in the Top of the Pop family dining room above the pub and eatery. The scene is always casual and fun here, where you'll brush shoulders with the Pop's regulars: park rangers, river guides, wranglers, and assorted others. Inexpensive.

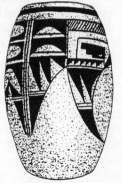

Hopi pot

The Grand Ice Cream Parlor and Restaurant. On South Main or U.S. Highway 191 south of the Green Well Motel. Telephone: 1-801-259-5853. Good for breakfast or lunch. Homemade sweet rolls and pies. Many flavors of ice cream. Hamburgers. Carryout. Inexpensive.

Canyonlands Café. A lively place on Highway 191 midtown at 16 South Main. Telephone: 1-801-259-5167. Best for breakfast. Inexpensive.

JR's Restaurant. Located south of town on the east side of U.S. Highway 191 is this likely spot for breakfast. Telephone: 1-801-259-8352. From ranch-style breakfasts and omelets to lighter fare, you'll find something on the menu to get you going in the mornings. Also open for lunch and dinner. Closed Sunday. Inexpensive.

The Grand Old Ranch House. North of town at 1266 North U.S. Highway 191. Telephone: 1-801-259-5753. Moab has many cafés and restaurants that serve basic, wholesome food. This place tries to do a little more and does it with reasonable success. It is located in a lovely old home listed in the National Register of Historic Places. Built between 1896 and 1898, this tree-shaded home, which backs up to colorful cliffs, has seen a lot of history from its location alongside the wagon road that led to the Colorado River Ferry. It is said that members of Butch Cassidy's Wild Bunch once hastily visited the ranch to change horses before fleeing from the law. In addition to beef, chicken, and seafood, the menu lists several German specialties including wiener schnitzel, spare ribs, and homemade sauerkraut. And do not miss the Ranch House's "mud pie" for dessert. Beer, wine, and liquor may be bought on the premises. Lunch and dinner only. Reservations advised in the summer and on weekends. Moderate.

The Sundowner Restaurant. Located a little farther north on U.S. Highway 191 is another popular restaurant. Telephone: 1-801-259-5201. Chicken, steaks, and some fancy desserts make up the fare in this large, convivial, family-oriented restaurant. Open for lunch and dinner. Inexpensive and moderate.

Pack Creek Ranch-A Country Inn Dining Room. Located sixteen miles south of Moab in a picturesque, tranquil mountain setting in the foothills of the La Sal Mountains. It is worth every mile of the way to this dining room which is open to the public by reservation. This restaurant at Pack Creek Ranch has put Moab on the map as a gourmet's paradise. The large, genuinely western ranch-style dining room with its giant stone-faced fireplace is a treat in itself as are the friendly staff who make you feel right at home. From outstanding veal, beef (tournedos, prime rib), and fish entrées to the barbecued chicken and baby back pork ribs (cooked like the ranch potatoes on the

massive outdoor cowboy grill), this is a menu that James Beard not only would have recommended, but would have savored. The owner's love of fine food and the ability to prepare it well from the freshest ingredients are evident throughout, especially at dessert time when you will choose between a heavenly Swedish crème and fresh raspberries, fresh strawberries with zabaglioni, ice cream with homemade chocolate sauce, and other tantalizing sweets. You may want to arrange a horseback ride before dinner. Reservations required. Dinner only. Setups available or bring your own favorite wine. Call for directions. Moderate and high moderate. Telephone: 1-801-259-5505.

Tours

Tag-A-Long Tours. River and four-wheel-drive-vehicle tours. Rubber rafts and other conveyances with experienced and knowledgeable guides packaged for just about any tour you can imagine along the Colorado and its tributaries. They specialize in one-day raft trips on the Colorado around Moab. Just as comprehensive are the jeep tours to many Moab area and canyonland sights. Located at 452 Main Street on U.S. Highway 191. Mailing address: Tag-A-Long Tours, Box 1206, Moab, Utah 84532. Telephone: Toll free in the continental United States 1-800-453-3292 or call 1-801-259-8946.

Lin Ottinger Scenic Tours. Four-wheel-drive-vehicle tours only. Tours into Canyonlands National Park, Dead Horse Point State Park, special geological, fossil, and rock-hunting tours, as well as many others. Ottinger's longtime experience in the area, and his knowledge about geology and dinosaurs make the cross-country jeep rides come alive. Tours leave from his Moab Rock Shop, 137 North Main Street, Moab, Utah 84532. Telephone: 1-801-259-7312.

Ken Sleight Expeditions. From horseback rides in Arches National Park and Pack Creek Ranch to trail rides in and around Moab featuring Indian rock art and ruins to hiking with pack stock, this tour guide touches most of the bases. River raft trips on the Green, San Juan, and Colorado rivers. Motorized boat tours of Glen Canyon and Escalante Canyon. Mailing address: Ken Sleight Expeditions, P.O. Box 1270-A, Moab, Utah 84532. Telephone: 1-801-259-5505.

Tex's River Expeditions and Riverways. River tours only. Two miles north of Moab on U.S. Highway 191, north of the Colorado River Bridge. Jet boats, canoes, rafts, and Tex's large "wonder" tour boat. Mailing address: Tex's River Expeditions, Box 67-T, Moab, Utah 84532. Telephone: 1-801-259-5101.

North American River Expeditions-Canyonlands Tours. This expedition group offers numerous multiple-day rafting and white-water adventures on the Colorado River as well as one-day river adventures nearby. Mailing address: North American River Expeditions and Canyonlands Tours, P.O. Box 1107-B, Moab, Utah 84532. Telephone: 1-801-259-5865.

Sherri Griffith Expeditions. This tour outfitter specializes in overnight river raft trips on the Colorado, Green, and Dolores rivers but also offers some day trips on the Colorado near Moab. Mailing address: Sherri Griffith Expeditions, P.O. Box 1324, Moab, Utah 84532. Telephone: 1-801-259-8229 or 1-800-433-6316.

Western River Expeditions. Featuring one-day river trips on the Colorado River near Moab. Do-it-yourselfers can rent canoes, rafts, sportyaks, and other equipment. Located one mile north of Moab next to the Slickrock Campground. Mailing address: Western River Expeditions, 7528 Racquet Club Drive, Salt Lake City, Utah 84121. Telephone: 1-801-259-7019.

Canyonlands Field Institute-Ed-Ventures. This nonprofit educational organization, which focuses on the natural and cultural heritage of the Colorado Plateau region, offers a series of seminars and trips in and around Moab. Some seminars/trips are: Canyon Country Photography, In The Footsteps of John Wesley Powell (smooth-water canoe trip), Desert Wild Flowers, Naturalist Guided Mountain Bike Trip, and others. Trips may include rafting, jeeping, or hiking with pack stock. Also

classes in river rescue skills and rock climbing. Mailing address: Canyonlands Field Institute, P.O. Box 68-F, Moab, Utah 84532. Telephone: 1-801-259-7750.

The Canyon's Edge. In the air-conditioned theater-in-the-barn at the downtown Western Plaza shopping center (59 South Main Street) you can view a multi-media slide production featuring computer-synchronized projections and stereo sound. See canyon country come alive as you view some superb photography of the area. Produced by the Canyonlands Field Institute (see address above). Fee. Telephone: 1-801-259-7750.

Canyonlands by Night Tours. Scenic sound and light tours of the Colorado River by boat, starting around 8:00 P.M. or 8:30 P.M. Fee. Mailing address: Canyonlands by Night Tours, P.O. Box 328, Moab, Utah 84532. Telephone: 1-801-259-5261.

Rim Tours. Guided mountain bike tours ranging from one-half day tours in Arches National Park to overnight tours to destinations in Canyonlands National Park. Or take combined bicycle-riverboat trips. Mailing address: Rim Tours, 94 West First North, Moab, Utah 84532. Telephone: 1-801-259-5223.

Redtail Aviation Scenic Air Tours. Eighteen miles north of Moab just off U.S. Highway 191 at Canyonlands Airfield. Mailing address: Redtail Aviation Scenic Air Tours, P.O. Box 681, Moab, Utah 84532. Telephone: 1-801-259-7421.

Red Rock Balloons. See the Canyon Country from the high-rise perspective of a hot-air balloon. Mailing address: Red Rock Balloons, 452 North Main, Moab, Utah 84532. Telephone: 1-801-259-8946.

The Moab Museum. 118 East Center. Small but rich in historical detail, the museum is staffed by some very knowledgeable volunteers. Exhibits focus on prehistory, history, geology, uranium mining and milling, minerals, and gemstones. Telephone: 1-801-259-7378.

Moab Golf Club. Tour yourself around eighteen

holes at this scenic golf course. Telephone: 1-801-259-6488.

Rental Cars

North Main Conoco. Four-wheel-drive-vehicles, sedans, and camper rentals. Mailing address: North Main Conoco, 284 North Main, Moab, Utah 84532. Telephone: 1-801-259-5242.

Fairs, Festivals, and Events

Annual events during the tourist season include the Moab Stage Race (bicycle) and the Canyonlands Quarter Horse show in April. Then comes the Friendship Cruise in May. Private boaters enter the Green River near Green River, Utah, for a 196-mile jaunt down that river and eventually up the Colorado River to Moab. The Canyonlands Rodeo is held sometime after the middle of June. In July there is, in some years, the Little Buckaroo Rodeo (ages four to fourteen), and centering around the Fourth of July is a grand fireworks display. Toward the end of July comes Pioneer Days (parade and carnival), which is staged to celebrate Moab's early western frontier history. In the middle of August, there is the lively Grand County Fair with a rodeo and horse show followed in September by a two-day four-wheel-drive camp-out into the red rock country and the La Sal Mountains. In October the Moab Rock, Gem, and Mineral Show is held.

The precise dates and locations for these annual events and other information may be obtained by writing or calling the Moab Visitor Center operated by the Grand County Travel Council. Mailing address: 805 North Main Street (U.S. Highway 191), P.O. Box 550, Moab, Utah 84532. Telephone: 1-801-259-8825 or in Utah 1-800-635-Moab. Or you can contact the Moab-Central Services Unit, Western Plaza, Moab, Utah 84532. Telephone: 1-801-259-7531, ext. 29.

Shopping

Moab Rock Shop. North Main Street. Much like a museum, except you can buy what you see. Specializing in rocks, minerals, and fossils of the area. Lin Ottinger and his staff are regional geology experts. Each night at 8:00 P.M. they give a free slide show focusing on the canyons of the Colorado River. Their four-wheel-drive-vehicle trips are legendary. Telephone: 1-801-259-7312.

Marc's Gallery. Located at 59 South Main in the downtown Western Plaza shopping area. Telephone: 1-801-259-8614. This gallery has an excellent selection of southwestern prints and posters and regularly features regional and local art. There is also an extensive collection of miniature southwestern Indian baskets and pots, and one room is devoted to the display and sale of Zapotec weavings from Mexico.

Ken Sleight Books. Located at Pack Creek Ranch, sixteen miles south of Moab is this full-service bookstore. Telephone: 1-801-259-5505. Although it has many general book selections, it focuses in depth on the Southwest and the Colorado Plateau. There is an unusually comprehensive selection of books on natural history, regional archaeology, western Americana, and the Southwest Indians. Mail orders accepted. Mailing address: Ken Sleight Books, P.O. Box 1270, Moab, Utah 84532.

Lema Indian Trading Co. Located at 60 North Main in downtown Moab. Telephone: 1-801-259-5217. Here you will find a wide selection of Indian crafts from all over the Southwest including jewelry, Pueblo pottery, sand paintings, and baskets.

Blue Mountain Trading Post. Located in Blanding, Utah, eighty miles south on U.S. Highway 191 South. Telephone: 1-801-678-2570. This museum-caliber shop with its outstanding selection of Indian jewelry, Navajo rugs, Pueblo pottery, sand paintings and other southwestern Indian arts and crafts, shows that the experienced owners of this family-run gallery know quality when they see it. Mailing address: Blue Mountain Trading Post, Box 263, Blanding, Utah 84511.

While in Blanding pursuing fine Indian arts and crafts, you may also want to visit Edge of the Cedars State Historical Monument (see "Seeing Canyon Country"), and Huck's Museum and Trading Post (on U.S. Highway 191 South. Telephone: 1-801-678-2329), as well as several other shops specializing in Indian crafts. While there you may want to chow down at the popular Elk Ridge Restaurant (breakfast, lunch, and dinner. Closed Sunday).

Capitol Reef National Park

There are no services in Capitol Reef National Park. To find accommodations, food, gas, and supplies you must travel outside the park. There you will find the basics but do not count on modern, upscale, "citified" accommodations and restaurants. Instead you will find inexpensive, clean, usually well-run, friendly establishments, which reflect the level of services required by the farming and ranching communities they serve. Café food, not gourmet food is the order of the day, just as adequate rather than luxurious seems to be the standard in lodging. In many ways it is a relief not to see a gentrified resort looming up on the border of the park. Capitol Reef is a special, remote, uncommercial place so enjoy it as long as it lasts!

Aside from one motel and restaurant eight miles out, most of the facilities are in the small towns near the park. Torrey and Bicknell, Utah, eleven and nineteen miles, respectively, from the Capitol Reef visitor center offer services to the west along Utah Highway 24, while Hanksville is the commercial center thirty-seven miles to the east along the same highway. Probably the most consistent facilities for food and lodging at this writing

are in Bicknell, Utah. If you tire of the two restaurants there, or if the motels are full, it is only eleven miles on to Loa where you will find several more food and lodging choices. And should you travel on scenic Utah Highway 12 to Bryce Canyon, this section lists a good recuperative spot in Escalante, Utah.

Groceries, gas and diesel fuel, ice, and laundromats can be found in Torrey. Propane fuel is available in Bicknell and Hanksville. There is a medical clinic in Bicknell while the nearest hospital is in Richfield, seventy-five miles west of the park.

For further information contact: Superintendent, Capitol Reef National Park/Visitor Center, Torrey, Utah 84775. Telephone: 1-801-425-3791.

Lodging and Food

Rim Rock Motel. The Rim Rock, open all year, is conveniently located just eight miles west of the Capitol Reef visitor center. Although just off the highway it is situated in a scenic location which affords almost all of the twenty-four rooms a view. None of the rooms are air conditioned, and some are small and poorly ventilated (especially on warm summer nights), while others are looking tired and worn. TV's. The ranch has a lake for fishing, horses for hire, jeep tours of the park, and a coin-operated laundromat. The restaurant there serves three meals a day. Advance reservations are recommended. Reservation deposit is required. Mailing address: Rim Rock Motel, Tor-

Badlands around Cainville, Utah

rey, Utah 84775. Telephone: 1-801-425-3843. Inexpensive.

Sunglow Motel and Café. Open all year. Located just off Utah Highway 24 in the pleasant little town of Bicknell, Utah. This spic-n-span motel with eighteen nice rooms with TV's (nine are air conditioned) provides a restful spot not far from the park. The adjacent café/restaurant offers good home-cooked food with friendly service and is well known for its scones and pies. Breakfast, lunch, and dinner. Mailing address: Sunglow Motel and Café, 55 East Main, Bicknell, Utah 84715. Telephone: 1-801-425-3821. Inexpensive.

Aquarius Inn and Café. Open all year. Also located in Bicknell just off the highway. Ten rooms with air conditioning and TV's. Some kitchenettes. Coin laundry and RV spaces at Aquarius Mobile Park. The café/restaurant adjacent serves three meals a day and is a pleasant place to dine. Mailing address: Aquarius Inn and Café, 230 West Main, Bicknell, Utah 84715. Telephone: 1-801-425-3835. Inexpensive.

La Buena Vida. Located on the west side of Torrey to the left of the road is the Mexican-style restaurant which offers a change of pace from the regional café food. A lively little spot filled with locals, off duty rangers, and travelers. Telephone: 1-801-425-3759. Inexpensive.

Capitol Reef Inn. Torrey. Second closest to the Park. A good bet. Seven clean, spacious motel rooms. Fresh, well prepared food in the cafe. Homemade baked goods. Mailing address: Capitol Reef Inn, Box 100, 360 W. Main, Torrey, Utah, 84755. Telephone: 1-800-425-3271.

Redrock Restaurant and Camp. Located in Hanksville, along Utah Highway 24 is this nicely designed restaurant, which serves three meals a day. The service is friendly and efficient and the food is up to par. Telephone: 1-801-542-3235. Inexpensive.

Circle 'D' Motel and Restaurant. In Escalante, Utah, seventy-seven miles south of the visitor center. Should you decide to take that exceptionally scenic route (Utah Highway 12) to Bryce Canyon, you'll enjoy knowing of a good place to eat on the way. This very nice restaurant with good food and caring owners is quite a surprise in the small town of Escalante. For breakfast, lunch, dinner, or just a snack or a cold drink, you can't go wrong here. Telephone: 1-801-826-4297. Inexpensive.

Campgrounds

In addition to the excellent campground just south of the visitor center in the park, there are several other campgrounds located in the surrounding National Forest Service and Bureau of Land Management lands.

Fruita Campground. One of the most pleasant campgrounds anywhere in the Southwest, the seventy-one units here are right in the park, less than a mile from the visitor center. The campground is beautifully situated in a lush valley under towering pink cliffs with large cottonwood trees and fruit orchards just steps away. And the Fremont River courses through nearby. The nice amphitheater sets the scene for evening programs prepared by the park rangers. Telephone: 1-801-425-3871.

Sunglow Campground. This campground is located twenty-two miles from the visitor center just out of Bicknell, Utah, two miles off Utah Highway 24. It rests at a cooler elevation of 7,500 feet. Six units. Open all year.

Singletree Campground. This is the next closest campground to the park. It is located twenty-two miles from the visitor center just off Utah Highway 12, the highway to Boulder, Utah. It is in the pines at 8,200 feet elevation and has twenty units. Farther south on the same road are Pleasant Creek and Oak Creek campgrounds with eighteen and eight units, respectively.

The Rim Rock Campground. The Rim Rock Motel has a fee trailer park just east of the motel. Fifty spaces with hookups are available. Men's and women's restrooms and showers are provided. For a small fee any traveler can use the showers. Tent spaces may also be rented in this area. See motel listing for description of property.

Tours

Pine Creek Tours. Air-conditioned, four-wheel-drive-vehicle tours of Capitol Reef National Park and environs. Both half-day and full-day tours include many of the remote gems of the Capitol Reef mother lode, including Cathedral Valley, the Blue Dugway, and the sights along the Burr Trail. Customized tours also arranged. Minimum of three fares required. Water and soft drinks provided. Box lunches for a reasonable fee. Pick up at Capitol Reef visitor center parking lot or Rim Rock Ranch. Reservations must be made and confirmed ahead of time. Mailing address: Pine Creek Tours, 58 North 100 East, Loa, Utah 84747. Telephone: 1-801-836-2629 or 1-801-425-3843.

Bryce Canyon National Park

Lodging and Food

Bryce Canyon Lodge. Conveniently located in the national park close to the scenic Bryce Canyon rim. Open mid-May to the first of October. There are 110 units nestled in the pines only yards away from the portion of the canyon rim detailed in the "Seeing Canyon Country" section. There are two types of units. You may stay in one of the forty large historic stone and timber duplex "Western" cabins complete with gas log fireplaces, two double beds, private bath, and nice, wide front porches, or you can bed down in one of the attractive and spacious "motel" rooms with two queen beds, private bath, and small, private porch. Several rooms are designed for the handicapped. There are seventy of these very nicely decorated and comfortable rooms located in two handsome two-story stone and timber buildings. No air conditioning as it is not required at 8,000 feet elevation. From any of the 110 units, you can view the birds in the pines or stroll over to the canyon rim.

The handsome lodge building, restored to the historic 1930s period, has a large dining room with two mammoth fireplaces, a lobby area with a post office, a small auditorium, and a large gift shop that carries curios and some southwestern Indian crafts, particularly jewelry. The informal dining room serves three meals a day and will fix box lunches on request. Dinner reservations are necessary. Call ahead the evening or morning before you arrive (1-801-834-5361) to reserve space. Snacks can be obtained at the Camper Store several blocks away. There is also a coin-operated laundromat there. Horseback rides available (fee) as well as scenic tours in comfortable vans (fee). Park ranger programs most evenings. If you arrive by 4:00 P.M., you can avoid some congestion by checking in before the tour buses arrive. Reservation deposit required. Mailing address: TW Services, 451 North Main, P.O. Box 400, Cedar City, Utah 84720. Reservations telephone: 1-801-586-7686. Lodge desk telephone: 1-801-834-5361. Moderate and high moderate.

Ruby's Inn (Best Western). Located one mile from the park entrance near the junction of Utah Highways 12 and 63. Open all year except Christmas Day and New Year's Day. In a fine location ad-

Western cabin, Bryce Canyon National Park

jacent to a freshwater lake near the pines. Of the motels outside the park, this is the closest one to it, within short driving distance to the canyon rim. It is almost as historic as the park itself, since its pioneer owners began greeting park visitors as early as 1924. There are 120 air-conditioned, modern units with queen and king beds located in several one- and two-story motel buildings around the spacious property. Two units have kitchens but do not provide utensils. Guests may enjoy the heated indoor swimming pool. The large, handsome main building of the inn contains a spacious lobby, large gift (an excellent selection of Indian arts and crafts including Pueblo Indian pottery, Indian jewelry, and Navajo rugs) and bookstore (good selection of regional titles). In the same large space there is a store with groceries and sundries. There is an art gallery in the loft upstairs. Also offered for a fee are go-cart rentals, helicopter scenic flights, horseback rides, mountain bike rentals, paddle boat rentals, wagon rides, cookouts, and rodeos. The large, very attractive western-style restaurant serves three meals a day. Reservation deposit required. Mailing address: Best Western Ruby's Inn, Bryce Canyon, Utah 84764. Telephone: Toll free in the continental United States 1-800-528-1234 or call 1-801-834-5341. High moderate.

Bryce Canyon Pines. Open all year. Located on Utah Highway 12, six miles from the park entrance. Nicely located with good vistas out over the plateau countryside, the forty-seven units are nicely furnished and well maintained. Most units are air conditioned and have TV's and full baths or showers. One kitchen unit (without utensils). Coin-operated laundry. Heated swimming pool. Very nice dining room and coffee shop as well as a comfortable and relaxing space to lounge. Horseback rides and western wagon rides (sometimes with cookout) can be arranged. Advance reservation deposit required. Mailing address: Bryce Canyon Pines, Scenic Route 12, Panguitch, Utah 84759. Telephone: 1-801-834-5336. Inexpensive.

Campgrounds

The park has two campgrounds. One, North Campground (107 sites), is located just east of the visitor center, while the other, Sunset Campground (107 units), is one mile south of the visitor center. Both have tables, fire pits, and nearby water and restroom facilities. There is no water available between October 1 and May 1. Campers are required to bring their own firewood or purchase it in the park. There is a fourteen-day camping limit. A small camping fee is levied. Groceries and a coin-operated laundromat are available at the Camper Store located in the Sunrise Point parking area. Showers are also available there. No reservations are taken. You are advised to arrive early in the day to obtain a space. The North Campground can accommodate small trailers, but hookups are not available. Outside the park you will find hookups at Ruby's Inn Campground Trailer Park (80 sites, see "Ruby's Inn").

Appendix:
Prehistoric Scenes of Canyon
Country Geology

During one of the very earliest periods in this region, the Permian Period, a series of shallow seas covered the region we now call the Colorado Plateau, laying down marine deposits of beach, offshore, and sandbar sand (Cutler formation, Cedar Mesa sandstone, and White Rim sandstone). Meanwhile freshwater sediments accumulating in the tidal flats, following the retreat of the seas and sand dunes, one thousand feet thick, began to be cemented into rock (Cutler, de Chelly sandstone). Then, during the early Triassic Period, the sea retreated and the area became a broad floodplain, a tidal flat, and then, later, returned to a shallow sea.

During this time, shallow marine, mudflat, and tideland sediments were laid down (Moenkopi). Then meandering streams and shallow lakes laid down sediments carried from the ancestral Rockies to the north and east on the vast, level floodplains. These were layered with volcanic ash from Arizona which dusted the land (Chinle).

During this prehistoric time when the vegetation was lush and today's treeless land was covered with swamps and forests, the scene was set for the deposition of a yellowish hard sandstone, the Shinarump, a Chinle formation member. As time wore on and the timber died, fell, and decayed, it was the decaying wood that collected the radioactive mineral uranium that was leached by water from the igneous rock which had been thrust upward from the earth's interior to form the laccolithic mountains.

During the later Triassic Period, the land experienced an uplift, draining the seas and becoming a vast, Sahara-like desert. Forceful winds blew sands into deep drifts or dunes which over time became cemented into sandstone (Wingate sandstone). Later, freshwater sediments were deposited by a system of sluggish streams that covered most of the country following the desert interval (Kayenta). But returning desert dunes, containing dry lakes, built up again. Time and mysterious geologic forces froze the dunes into immobile rock or petrified dunes (Navajo).

In the early Jurassic Period, the land tilted again and a shallow sea advanced and retreated many times. Rivers from the sea, flowing into lower areas, deposited a variety of marine sediments (Carmel formation). Then came a time of more tranquil activity in which the land was covered with a series of landlocked basins in which marine mudflat deposits were made (Entrada/Dewey Bridge member). Forming out of marine tidal flats and the remaining reddish-colored desert dunes, soft siltstone and sandstones were laid down (Entrada/Slickrock member). From white dune sand of sea-coastal origin, another variety of sandstone was formed (Entrada/Moab tongue). Then another shallow sea deposited marine origin sediments (Curtis formation). This was followed by another layer of coastal marine origin sediments (Summerville formation) which was deposited in the tidal basins and mudflats of the retreating Curtis Sea. This was the final and youngest of the great red bed sediments deposited in this region aptly called Red Rock Country.

The land was again lifted in the later Jurassic Period to create a wide freshwater floodplain which eventually became a swampy lake. Reptiles were numerous in this environment called the Age of the Dinosaur. At the same time, volcanic ash once again layered the region and the freshwater lake and stream systems deposited several sediments (Morrison formation).

Then eighty million years ago, one of the newest layers began forming. This occurred with the slow encroachment of the sea in the Cretaceous Period. A multilayered sediment was laid down from erosion products from higher ground and by shale deposited from tidal lagoons and marshes and by beach sand (Dakota formation). Then as the last Cretaceous sea alternately and sluggishly advanced and retreated, sometimes stagnating it, it made deposits of marine origin (Mancos shale). During its fitful retreat from the area, it laid down marine, lagoon, and beach sand sediments (Mesa Verde formation). Now a whole new system of freshwater lakes began to build up in the late Cretaceous and early Tertiary periods. Deposits of freshwater or brackish lake water were laid down (Wasatch group) from which most of the formations at incredible Bryce Canyon have been carved.

Northeastern Arizona

Indian Country

Northeastern Arizona

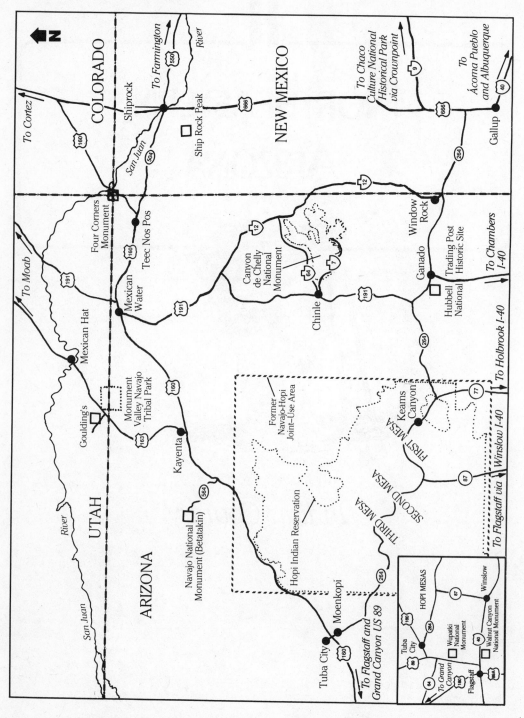

Introduction

Stretching south from the scenic sights mentioned in Section I, the Colorado Plateau extends into northeastern Arizona. The terms "remote" and "scenic," which so aptly describe southeastern Utah, also are applicable to some extent in Indian Country. But it is not as scenic and remote as it is foreign and different. It is the scenery that boggles your mind in southeastern Utah. But it is the culture that surprises and astounds in this part of the Four Corners area. Some consider this area an undeveloped nation within a nation. Others have called it the land of room enough and time enough. But more than anything else it is a region in which the people make the real difference. The land is not much more forgiving than the land which ran off the hardiest of the white settlers in Utah. It is not easy living in this arid, windblown, eroded country. But a sturdy group of people have learned to live with the harshness of the environment there, adapting their culture and lives to it . . . living in harmony with it. So with a sense of patience and understanding that has endured for generations, 170,000 Navajo and 8,000 Hopi continue to live out their lives there.

The amazing Hopi live in the same villages and settlements and farm the same land their ancestors did in the twelfth and thirteenth centuries. The continuity of the present with the past is more evident with the Hopi than with any other cultural group in America. These very first Americans found white man's ways strange to them and from the time of white contact until now have maintained such a positive sense of identity that only a trickle of western traditions, philosophy, and religion have penetrated the high Hopi mesas.

The adroit, adaptable, and tenacious Navajo have held on to and survived in this land, which they adopted much later in time. Forming a strong bond with the land they fought vigorously against white intrusion but it was a losing battle. When they were finally defeated, they were rounded up and marched to eastern New Mexico for "deprogramming." After that protracted social experiment failed, they were returned to their homeland. Although they had adopted a few white customs, they still retained the essence of their culture.

It is no wonder, then, that we speak of the Hopi Nation and the Navajo Nation. These independent and powerful cultures are very different from the rest of mainstream America. The melting-pot theory did not hold up there as it did with other distinct cultural groups. The Irish and Poles longed to become "Americanized," as did the Germans and Swedes. But the native Americans, these first Americans, have had great faith in their roots and have clung to a lifeway that has enriched them spiritually for centuries.

So, visiting Indian Country is like entering a different country. Each time I visit and return home, I have trouble dealing with the cultural shock. I have crossed no oceans nor international borders, yet when I travel to Indian Country, I experience a very foreign way of life. When I first traveled to this area, I would return home and begin to think about what I had seen. Women in bright, long skirts and colorful blouses herding

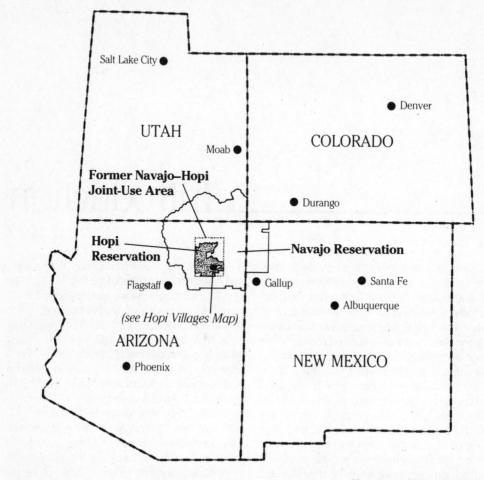

Salt Lake City ●

UTAH

Moab ●

Former Navajo–Hopi Joint-Use Area

Hopi Reservation

Flagstaff ●

(see Hopi Villages Map)

ARIZONA

● Phoenix

● Denver

COLORADO

● Durango

Navajo Reservation

● Gallup

● Santa Fe

● Albuquerque

NEW MEXICO

Navajo and Hopi Reservations

sheep across the highway. Indian men with braided hair gathering around a filling station, talking in a language unfamiliar to me. Road signs that point the way to Kin-Li-Chee, Beclahbeto, Teec Nos Pos, and Shungopovi and maps telling about the location of Dzilidushzhinih, Ziltahjini, and Dzilintsah peaks. Back home, a thousand miles from Indian Country, it all seemed like a dream. I began to doubt that I would ever see these things again. Yet year after year, they continue to be there.

Although they have lived side by side for generations, the Navajo and Hopi are just as distinct from each other as they are from the rest of America. They come from different stock, have a different history, speak different languages, and have different religious and cultural ways. The

Hopi, soon to celebrate almost nine hundred years of continuous living in the area, speak a language belonging to the Uto-Aztecan language group. Many native people from Mexico speak a language derived from this same linguistic stock. The Hopi always have farmed and lived in villages. The Navajo, on the other hand, are relative newcomers, having arrived in the Southwest sometime around 1500. They speak a language that derives from Athapascan linguistic stock. Today, some of the native people in northern Canada, up to the Arctic Circle, and in the northwestern part of the United States speak languages derived from this same stock. The Navajo ancestors were hunters and nomads tending to live in widely separated family clusters rather than in villages.

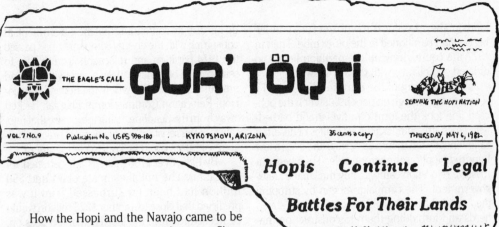

THE EAGLE'S CALL **Qua' Tööqti** SERVING THE HOPI NATION

VOL. 7 No. 9 · Publication No. USPS 998-180 · KYKOTSMOVI, ARIZONA · 35 cents a copy · THURSDAY, MAY 6, 1982

Hopis Continue Legal Battles For Their Lands

Hopi newspaper, Qua' Toqti

How the Hopi and the Navajo came to be neighbors in conflict is an interesting story. Since around A.D. 1100-1300, the Hopi have continuously occupied a small parcel of rugged mesas and desert country in northeastern Arizona, which is surrounded by a vast no-man's-land. Today, they occupy the same territory, but now it is completely surrounded by Navajoland. This has produced great conflict. Although conflict and enmity between the two groups goes back to the nineteenth century when the Navajo raided Hopi villages and encroached on their lands, it is neighbors disputing over land occupancy and ownership that keeps the conflict going today. You may occasionally read about it in one of the sporadically published Navajo or Hopi newspapers. Or you may hear about it at the community center in Tuba City or in the coffee shop at the Hopi Cultural Center. In many instances the fire of conflict has been fanned by the United States government's well-meaning, but misplaced efforts to help settle the land disputes that are behind most of the ill will.

The germ of today's conflict began in 1882 when President Chester A. Arthur gave to the Hopi 2.4 million acres of land, which were west of the lands that had been granted the Navajo in 1868. This included lands they had occupied for generations. But the language of the Hopi grant stated that the lands were not only for Hopi Indians but for "such other Indians" that the government might "see fit to settle thereon." The farming- and village-oriented Hopi did not expand into the area surrounding the mesas. The restless, nomadic Navajo did. Not only did they fill the vacuum around the mesas, but they also made raids and encroached on the Hopi villages.

The Hopi complained to the government, for fear of being gobbled up by their neighbors. So in 1943, the government allocated 640,000 acres outright to the Hopi. Instead of being pleased, the Hopi were offended since they felt this would forever rob them of using or possessing the remaining 1.8 million acres from their earlier grant. Predictably, the Navajo said they should be considered the "other Indians" mentioned in the 1882 grant and proceeded to occupy lands around the Hopi reservation. The conflict remained unresolved for years. Finally the courts designated the disputed area as a "joint-use" area. That is the way it appeared on most maps for years. But the failure of that solution was obvious from the beginning. How could two such disparate peoples, who had never agreed on anything, all of a sudden bury the hatchet and work harmoniously to manage jointly held property?

As might be predicted, the joint-use area became a focal point of even more bickering between the two groups. When the management and maintenance of the area became paralyzed by the dispute, the area began to look once again like a no-man's-land as roads deteriorated and wells dried up. So the government came to the "rescue" again in 1974. That year, Congress, in passing the Navajo-Hopi Land Settlement Act, authorized the partitioning of the disputed 1.8 million acres according to population density and allocated funds for the relocation of members of one tribe living on land partitioned to the other tribe. Then in 1977 the courts drew up the partition lines and ordered compliance with the 1974 law.

The drawing of the partition line in 1977 seemed easy enough on paper. But when the penciled line took the form of a five-strand barbed-wire fence stretching across 300 miles of desert, it caught nearly ten thousand Navajo and even a few hundred Hopi on the wrong side. Thus began a massive relocation campaign by the United States government. The campaign began by stripping the "offside" Navajo of 90 percent of their sheep herds and forbidding them to construct permanent homes on the disputed land. Then the government sweetened the pot with promises of free housing and cash incentives. For the most part, the government plan worked. By the mid-1980s, all but about one thousand Navajos had relocated or had promised to do so. But those who relocated to the government-provided tract homes in subdivisions outside of towns, on or near the reservation, had not fared so well. Uprooting them from their native homesteads was unsettling enough. But stripped of their herds and their land, they had no skills to generate income. Many who were uprooted did not speak or read English. Utility bills and property tax statements often went unheeded since they were not written in Navajo. (For a parallel experience involving the Spanish in New Mexico, see Section IV, North Central New Mexico, "History.") Unscrupulous real estate entrepreneurs had a field day. Soon, many relocated Navajo, who had given up their herds and had no urban job skills, were not only out of work but also homeless. By 1986, there remained over one thousand Navajo who refused to relocate. They became even more adamant in their refusal when they saw what was happening to their newly relocated friends and relatives. Their staunch and well-publicized refusal to move from areas such as Big Mountain gained support from activist groups around the United States. As the legal deadline for completion of the relocation process loomed closer in 1986, it was apparent that a nasty confrontation was at hand. There were rumors that the government might use army helicopters and that the National Guard might be sent in to force the Big Mountain Navajo off the land. The Navajo heated up the dispute contending that the government, in conspiring with the energy companies, had passed the 1974 partition and relocation act as a ruse to seize control of the land that was rich with coal and uranium deposits. But wisely the Federal Navajo-Hopi Relocation Commission in Flagstaff backed away from the deadline, using the excuse that relocation of the resistant Navajo was not practical until new houses could be constructed for them.

By 1986, over $100 million had been spent for relocation. The initial estimate of around $50 million had been far surpassed, and it was predicted that close to another $275 million would be needed to finish the job. The conflict goes on, and you will see evidence of this painful relocation as you travel through Indian country.

History of the People

First a word about the historical materials which follow. Much of our knowledge about this part of the Southwest has come from two sources. One is the anthropological and archaeological information stemming from the studies of the ruins found in the Four Corners region. This information is not always consistent because in many cases there is wide disagreement between the "experts" about what a certain piece of historical evidence means. There are many gaps in the historical chain of evidence, leading to much speculation about what may or may not have happened. Consequently, I have presented in the brief summaries offered here what seems to be the dominant or prevailing view.

The second source of information comes from the people native to this area, the Hopi and the Navajo. Since they had no written language, there is a rich history available only in the oral tradition. Certain rites, prophecies, legends, and sayings are still handed down from the elders to the young people. Many white anthropologists, writers, educators, and others with a genuine interest in the Indians have interviewed numerous native people to learn about their history and culture. Much of the information has been published. The problem is that, beyond a very general framework, the Indians have not told a consistent history to their white interviewers. There are many inconsistencies in the "truths" about Indians that have been recorded by white authors.

It may be that the oral tradition has been inconsistent and that indeed there are several versions of the same myth or ritual going around among the Indians. Or, and I can believe this to be very likely, the Indians have told any tale that came to mind to their white interviewers, keeping the genuine and authentic details of the myths and legends to themselves. In other words, this information is hidden from the white man's view. But even if the published body of information does reflect the genuine views of the Indians about their own mythology and history, that data is quite often in conflict with current archaeologic "evidence." Of course the academicians generally imply that their "science" gives a more accurate picture than the Indians' oral history as told to white interviewers. Yet it should be remembered that the scientists are often at odds with one another in the interpretation of their "data." So read these pages of history as though they represent the best that we outsiders know at this time. These are the facsimiles of facts, not facts themselves.

A Prehistory of Indian Country

The history of the indigenous people of the Southwest brings us at once to the question of the emergence of early man on the North American continent. The current, best theory is that sometime between twelve and thirty thousand years ago, some advanced Stone-Age people came down from today's Asia in the region of Siberia. They had fully developed brains and a spoken language. In addition to their coppery skins, dark eyes, black hair, and wide cheekbones, they possessed distinctive, shovel-shaped incisor teeth. They probably crossed what is now the Bering Sea on either a land bridge, a stretch of glacial ice, or possibly at a later time they may have crossed that fifty-five-mile-wide channel by boat. Slowly migrating southward, their travels may have taken them along an ice-free corridor, either paralleling the eastern side of the Rocky Mountains or stretching down the coast of Alaska through present-day British Columbia.

After several thousand years, perhaps at a pace no faster than ten miles every year, these hardy people spread over this new land from Alaska to the tip of South America, a migration trail over ten thousand miles long. As they were heading south, some of the animals native to North America were moving north. These animals, including the camel and the horse, were dwindling in numbers as the environmental conditions changed. They finally became extinct on this continent as the new immigrants grew in numbers, slaughtering more of the animals as their need for food increased.

In South America, where the ice from the great Ice Age receded first, the wandering migrants took strong root, possibly fourteen to twenty-five thousand years ago in the fertile soil and warming climate of Patagonia. These earliest civilizations, nurtured under less hostile conditions after the Ice Age, grew and developed until they were the most advanced of the Asian immigrant civilizations of their time. As the ice receded further north, civilization in what is now Central America and Mexico began to take shape and flourish.

In today's Southwest, the ice melted somewhat later. Before the Ice Age was completely over, a group of people who have come to be called the Clovis culture was living there some eleven to twelve thousand years ago. They had developed fluted spearpoints and a special spear-thrower called the atlatl. They hunted camels, horses, and mammoths just east of the land you will be traveling through. The finding of their relics in New Mexico, especially their fluted spearpoints, is the earliest irrefutable evidence for the existence of man in the New World. Similar sites have been found at Naco, Arizona, and the Lehner sites in Arizona.

Next, the prehistorians tell us a people called the Cochise emerged about nine thousand years ago in the Southwest. The name was derived from Cochise, Arizona, a town in southeastern Arizona near which many of the artifacts of these people were found. This culture existed in that region for about seven thousand years until 500 to 300 B.C. These people were initially hunters, using the same types of weapons used by the earlier Clovis people. But as it became drier and as other environmental conditions changed over time, the animals became extinct and the Cochise were forced to convert their life-style or perish.

They chose to change. In addition to hunting deer, mountain sheep, rabbits, and birds they became food-gatherers, seeking berries, seeds, and nuts. They used these natural vegetables until about 2000 B.C., when it is thought they began to plant a primitive form of corn called "pod" corn which was probably introduced from meso-America where it had evolved from natural grasses over a period of many years. The Cochise also learned about squash and beans from those great civilizations to the south.

Probably the adaptable and innovative Cochise desert culture spawned the next developing group, the Mogollon culture. And about the same time, the first Anasazi, who may have had their roots in the Cochise culture but who probably developed from the Desha and Oshara prehistoric traditions of southeastern Utah and northwestern New Mexico, were settling in on the high desert. These first Anasazi residents of the Colorado Plateau were called the Basketmakers. They were given this name in 1893, when Richard Wetherill, a local cowboy who previously had made some outstanding discoveries at Mesa Verde, decided to explore a blind canyon stemming off Grand Gulch in southeastern Utah. There, this unschooled archaeologist discovered a cave with ninety mummified bodies. Wrapped in fur blankets, they had large, exquisitely woven vegetable fiber baskets over their heads.

These Basketmakers lived between A.D. 200 to 700 in the Four Corners region, their culture peaking between A.D. 500 to 700. Before A.D. 500, they used the atlatl spear-thrower and made snares and nets to trap field mice, gophers, rabbits, and prairie dogs. In addition to using yucca, cactus, and bulb plants, they grew corn and, later, beans and squash. Their houses, so-called "pit" houses, were built partially underground. They made superb, even somewhat ornate, square-toed sandals and the men wore their long hair divided into three sections, one on each side and one in the back, each section wound into thick bobs and tied in place.

In their drive toward domestication, they advanced the art of basket weaving to an all-time high. Crafting finely woven jars, trays, bowls, and baskets of all sizes and shapes, they also developed the intricate technique of coil weaving with binding splints. Weaving so finely that many of the vessels held water, they sometimes waterproofed their vessels further with pine pitch. It is thought that the development of the bean, which would have been difficult to eat when shelled and dried, led to the innovation of filling the woven vessels with water and then dropping hot rocks into them to raise the temperature suficiently to cook and soften the beans.

The later Basketmakers developed fixed communities with permanent pit house structures three to five feet deep. These houses had a smoke hole in the roof and a covered entry hole on the side. Eventually the side hole was reduced to a ventilation-sized opening and the top hole was used for entry and exit. Between the fire pit, located in the middle of the house, and the ventilation hole was an upright piece of flat stone, a deflector stone. These pit houses also had a hole in the floor filled with clean sand. Archaeologists speculate that these holes represented the "sipapu," through which the Pueblo people believe they made their first entry into this world. Sipapus are also found in underground ceremonial rooms called "kivas," which evolved from these early pit house structures. At the acme of the Basketmaker period, the bow and arrow replaced the atlatl and fire-resistant pottery began to replace the basket. Decorating their pottery with the same designs they used on their fine baskets, the Basketmakers used geometric lines, circles and dots, and animal figures. A favorite subject was the turkey. But unlike the first white settlers to the New World, the Anasazi probably did not eat the turkey for, like the dog, it was kept as a pet and its feathers were used for ceremonial purposes.

The Pueblo culture, emerging from the Anasazi Basketmaker tradition in A.D. 700, peaked in the so-called classic period between 1100 and 1300. When people think of the term Anasazi, they often associate it with this period of time. For during those years all the people living in the High Southwest probably were Basketmaker descen-

Atlatl

Kiva

dants of the Anasazi. Ironically, Anasazi is a Navajo word meaning "ancestors of the alien people." These were the people whose deserted villages were found by the Navajo when they migrated onto the Colorado Plateau sometime after 1500. Although the Anasazi are sometimes referred to as the "Cliff Dwellers," archaeological evidence indicates that only certain groups spent the last fifty years or so of their one thousand years of existence as a cultural entity in that type of dwelling. For the most part, they lived in communities in mesa-top homes. Even when some of the people lived in the

Wild turkey

cliff dwellings, many others continued to live on top of the mesas (see Section III, "Mesa Verde National Park") close to their corn and cotton fields.

As the Pueblo culture flourished, so did their neighboring group, those Cochise descendants, the Mogollon, who lived in the mountains south of the Colorado Plateau. Probably because of their proximity to the highly developed civilizations to the south, in the land that would eventually become Mexico, they were the first group in the region to make pottery. It is likely they passed their advanced knowledge on to the early Basketmakers and their later Pueblo culture descendants who took pottery making to heights never known before in the Southwest. It is possible they borrowed other ideas from the Mogollon people, as well as from the Hohokam culture, another group who lived to the west and south. Hohokam is a Pima Indian word meaning "those who have vanished." They, too, were greatly influenced by the advanced cultures further south, developing an elaborate irrigation and canal system. In addition to growing cotton and weaving garments from it, they learned to etch delicate designs on the surface of seashells with cactus juice, thus preceding the discovery of that art in Europe by four hundred years.

So the Anasazi culture developed not in isolation, but most likely in conjunction with these other cultures as they traded back and forth over long distances. There is also evidence that from time to time some of these different groups actually commingled and lived near one another as they migrated throughout the Southwest.

The Sunset Crater-Wupatki ruin area near today's Flagstaff was one such cultural frontier. Cinders and ash from the Sunset Crater eruption of A.D. 1065 blanketed the arid soil, creating a moisture-preserving mulch that greatly enhanced the productivity of the land. When news of this farming bonanza spread, splinter groups from the Kayenta Anasazi, the Hohokam, and possibly the Mogollon cultures moved into the area and lived side by side with each other and the area's native inhabitants, the Sinagua people. After several generations, this region became a melting pot for early southwestern culture. There is evidence that both goods and ideas were assimilated among the different groups. So with a touch of Mogollon here and a tinge of Hohokam there, the Anasazi were able to develop a complex and productive society from a rich blend of cultural traits.

The Anasazi have been grouped into subtypes by modern scientists. These subgroups are based on differences of geographic location, pottery, and architecture. Four of the major groups are Mesa Verde, Chaco, Kayenta, and Rio Grande. (Section III of this book will detail the Mesa Verde Anasazi, while Section IV will cover the Rio Grande Anasazi.) The ruins of the Chaco area, located within a half day's drive of Sections II, III, and IV, are not so dramatically situated, but they are nevertheless some of the most extensive of the Anasazi ruins. Their buildings contained as many as eight hundred rooms and towered four and five stories high, exhibiting the finest craftsmanship in all of Anasaziland. Although in prehistoric times the highly developed Chaco community had an elaborate road system, today the ruins are somewhat difficult to reach by conventional vehicle, especially in wet weather.

But a few of the most compelling Anasazi ruins were left by the Kayenta group in the area covered by this section. Some of the most accessible remains of the Kayenta Anasazi culture are found at Navajo National Monument just south of Kayenta, Arizona, and in Canyon de Chelly, the heart of Navajoland. Although the Kayenta Anasazi group seem to represent a simple, less-sophisticated culture, the dramatic sites for their villages are unparalleled in the Southwest. And some of their handiwork, especially their pottery, is exceptionally fine.

In the mouths of great caves in steep canyon walls, the Kayenta Anasazi built multistory dwellings above the ground in addition to pit houses. Often they built several rows of buildings, each containing twelve to fourteen rooms, with some rows reaching several stories high. When the Spanish saw apartment house villages like these in caves, on mesa tops, and in river valleys, they called them "pueblos." Although early Anasazi construction was of the primitive "wattle-and-daub" type, where rows of upright sticks were bound together with string and plastered with mud, by later Kayenta times stone construction had gained a strong foothold. Even at that, the wattle-and-daub method continued to be used occasionally.

Most of the ruins you will see represent construction with stones and mortar. Verdant green valleys and great groves of trees were scarce, but stones were plentiful. Work crews apparently gathered these rocks, mostly sandstone, and then shaped them using a sharp-edged piece of chert, a flintlike rock. After a deep groove was scratched in the sandstone rock, it was placed over a smaller rock or pebble, the fulcrum located at the incised groove. The groove was then tapped with a hammer rock directly above the pebble, usually breaking the building stone neatly to the desired size and shape. But the procedure was done somewhat carelessly among the Kayenta Anasazi, so the stones are not shaped as carefully or as uniformly as they are in Mesa Verde and Chaco structures. And the walls are not as straight nor the corners as uniformly square as those found at Mesa Verde and Chaco Canyon. The chinking between the rock was accomplished with mud mortar containing potsherds and pebbles for additional strength.

These sedentary village farmers planted seeds with digging sticks and diverted water to their crops through intricate trench systems. They harvested their crops and stored them in stone granaries. Using the metate, a flat rock with a con-

Wattle-and-daub construction

cave surface, and a mano, an oblong piece of stone held in the hand, they ground cornmeal. Although they wove clothes from cotton and continued to make baskets of high quality, more and more the Kayenta people turned their efforts to pottery. Using the coil-and-scrape method in which unsmoothed coils were systematically pinched, they developed beautiful and functional corrugated pottery as well as pottery decorated with a variety of colors. Although black on white was commonly used, the Kayenta Anasazi are renowned for their polychrome pottery where three or four colors were used. In several of the area's museums you will see examples of pottery with black, red, and white pigments applied in a variety of designs on top of orange, yellow, or buff bases.

As you stand on the canyon floor at Betatakin and view the dramatic and complex structures built into the remote canyon alcoves and as you admire the graceful and even exquisitely beautiful pottery of the Anasazi, you are aware that civilization was marching along there at a rapid pace, although it never reached the zenith of the prehistoric cultures in meso-America. A forceful, determined people had learned to master one of

the harshest environments in the world by developing a life-style in harmony with nature rather than in conflict with it.

But then something happened. Sometime between the late 1100s and A.D. 1300, many of the great Anasazi sites you can visit were suddenly and abruptly abandoned. All aspects of everyday life were left just as they were the day their inhabitants abandoned them. It was as if one morning, someone you know left his house with only his clothes on his back, never to return again. The reason for this abandonment is not known, but it is speculated that a great and prolonged drought hit this already moisture-poor region whose soil had been depleted from overuse due to the expanding population.

Faced with starvation, there was no choice but to leave and search for more fertile living sites. So over a period of several hundred years, the Anasazi people of the Four Corners area migrated to other locations. Some migrated to the Rio Grande Valley, joining the few Anasazi people who had lived there for several centuries, establishing the furthest eastern outpost of the Pueblo people, while others migrated south, joining

Kayenta   **Mesa Verde**   **Chaco**

Anasazi masonry styles

migrants from other areas to establish the most southwesterly community, a pueblo known today as Zuñi. It is thought that the Anasazi in the Kayenta area who had spread as far north as today's Boulder, Utah (see Section I, "Boulder Mountain and Boulder, Utah," Anasazi Indian Village State Historical Monument), also migrated south along with small groups from the Mesa Verde, Chaco, and other areas. When they reached the southernmost ridges and mesas of the Black Mesa, they stopped. Perhaps from this high outpost, seeing even more desolate regions below them to the south, they felt they must make their last stand. Besides, small groups of people had been in and around these mesa extensions for several hundred years and had no doubt discovered the life-giving springs and the moisture deep under the sands. The coalescence of many disparate Anasazi groups into one unified Hopi culture is the next part of the story.

The Hopi: A Long and Continuous Past

There seem to be no breaks, no lost chapters between the Hopi's prehistoric past and their present lifeway. This is supported both by Hopi mythology and modern archaeology. Hopi mythology has it that the Hisatsinom (the Hopi term equivalent to Anasazi), the ancestral, early Hopi, entered this, the Fourth World, at a sacred spot in the Grand Canyon region, near the confluence of the Little Colorado River and the Colorado River. They entered the world, as the story goes, through a sipaapuni or sipapu or a hollow reed in the ground.

From this emergence, they began their diverse and scattered migrations to the four directions, forming a "Sacred Circle" of settlements. They called themselves Hopitue or Hopi, which in their Shoshonean, Uto-Aztecan language means well-behaved or well-mannered.

According to the myth, eventually they all would reunite at the center of the sacred circle or the "center of the universe," where they would live out their lives until Purification Day and entry into the Fifth World. So after years of wandering, they finally did reunite near three mesa extensions of the Black Mesa. From the north came the Bear, Bluebird, and Spruce clans from Mesa Verde, the Snake Clan from Hovenweep in Utah, and the Flute society of the Horn Clan from Canyon de Chelly. From the west came the Fire, Water, and Coyote clans from Betatakin and Keet Seel. From the south came the Sidecorn, Cloud, Sand, Tobacco, Rabbit, and other clans from Homol'ovi near today's Winslow, from Wupatki near modern Flagstaff, and possibly from Casa Grande south of

Kayenta Anasazi black-on-white storage vessel

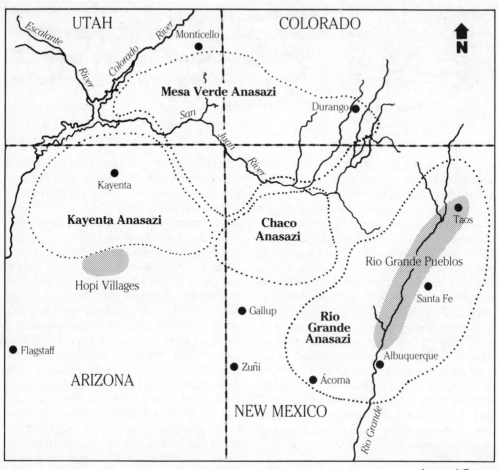

Anasazi Groups

Phoenix. From the east came a few clans from Chaco Canyon and the Salmon Ruins area.

Both archaeological findings and Hopi mythology are in general agreement that many groups of people migrated to a single location at the south end of the Black Mesa where they formed villages and the unified culture represented by today's Hopi. The archaeologists also tell us that even before this time, a number of people from surrounding areas already had migrated there, inhabiting Antelope Mesa, fifteen miles to the east as early as A.D. 700.

After the clans began migrating to the mesa area between 1100 and 1300, villages were formed. One of the first villages established below

the mesas after the migration was ancient Masseba, which later became Schomopovi or Shungopovi when it was moved to the mesa top where it is today. By 1150, the first village to be established on the mesa top, Oraibi, was formed. Although sparsely inhabited today, this ancient community is probably the oldest most continually inhabited village or town in the United States. Later, other villages were established along the terraces of the mesa edges and below the mesas.

At the acme of the early pre-Hopi or Hopi civilization, there were over forty villages populated by several thousand people. With intermarriage and time, the people began the process of coalescing into a single culture. When this began

Awat'ovi mural fragment

to happen, smaller villages were abandoned in favor of larger, more centralized villages. In fact, by 1300, thirty-six villages had been abandoned, the population concentrating in the eleven remaining villages plus three new ones to be formed after 1300. Some of these larger villages had multistory buildings, plazas, and kivas, all mirroring the "cave dwelling" structure from which these people so recently had migrated.

Today's Hopi villages reflect many of these same organizational and architectural ideas. In the excavations carried out at Awat'ovi, a Hopi village founded in 1332, the link between the late prehistoric villages and the religious and ceremonial symbolism of today's Hopi was well established through the two hundred painted murals found in about twenty different kivas. Most of these murals were removed from the excavation site and a number were placed in the Museum of Northern Arizona located in Flagstaff, Arizona, where they may be viewed.

During this period, when many disparate peoples unified and settled in larger, more densely populated villages, some kind of social organization was required. It is thought by scholars that this is the time ceremonial ritual was laid down, eventually leading to the establishment of the katsina or kachina cult. Where the cult had its beginnings before coming to the mesas is not known, but Hopi mythology and archaeological evidence point to an origin further south. The Hopi depiction of gods with masks and costumes is very reminiscent of one of the other Uto-Aztecan groups, the Nahuatal-speaking Aztecs. Their culture, in what is now Mexico, flourished and peaked about the time scholars believe the Hopi were organizing themselves.

It was the development of the kachina cult that began to distinguish the Hopi Pueblo people from other Anasazi Pueblo descendants, especially the ones who settled along the Rio Grande Valley. The Hopi believe the kachinas are ancestor deities who live in the San Francisco peaks and they fervently believe that the kachinas will return yearly to the mesas with clouds of rain if the Hopi people have given them their due with sincere thoughts and prayers throughout the year. The kachinas also are associated with reproduction and the redistribution of food among the Hopi people. About the same time the kachina cult was established, the clan system developed, cutting across village boundaries and providing all the Hopi villages with a sense of harmony or unity not seen by the casual observer. The clan groups are matrilineal, meaning that a Hopi is born into his mother's clan and knows his mother's sisters also as "mother" and their children as "brothers and sisters." The clan system, which may once have had as many as fifty clans within it, continues today with thirty active clans.

Secure in their villages and with constant ongoing development of their ceremonial and ritual system, the Hopi lived several centuries in relative peace. During this period of amalgamation and cultural growth, agriculture was expanded and coal was dug to heat homes and fire pottery. Then one day, Pedro de Tovar and Juan de Padillo, two Spaniards, and their entourage arrived without notice on horseback, possibly at the easternmost now-extinct village of Kawayka. They had been dispatched by Coronado from the Zuñi village of Hawikuh in that year of 1540 to explore further north (see Section IV, "History"). This first "white contact" must have confused the Hopi. For in Hopi mythology, the story is told of two brothers who had the same mother: one brother had a light complexion and the other was the color of mother earth. Each brother was given a stone tablet and each tablet was marked with symbols portending the future. The older white brother took his stone and left the Sacred Circle for another land. The younger brown brother stayed in Hopiland and left his stone tablet at the Hopi mesas, where it is today.

There is an ancient Hopi prophecy related to

this myth which states that until the other stone tablet is returned or until the True White Brother or "Pahaana" returns, the Hopi will lose interest in their language, ceremonies, and rituals. When the white brother returns, he will judge the people on how well they have kept their traditions. If they have not been faithful to their beliefs, he may punish them, but if the white brother stays, he will eventually dispel the evil among the people becoming, in effect, their savior. He will lead the Hopi to Purification Day so they can enter the Fifth World and on that special day, all will rise from their graves and meet the Giver of the Breath of Life. If they have been true to the Hopi way, they will live forever on a purified earth, free of famine and illness. Love will prevail then and there will be water everywhere. If this comes to pass, the Hopi people will, at last, not have to labor so much.

No doubt the Hopi, who had never seen a white man but whose legend had deified the idea of a white brother returning some day, wondered what to make of these unexpected visitors astride strange animals they had never seen before. But on this day the village chief sensed something more than a myth come true and drew a line that the white men were not to cross. The air was tense. A Spanish horse whinnied and moved suddenly. A fight ensued and the Hopi were subdued. But the Spanish saw no riches, so they left and did not return for almost a century. By that time the Spanish had named these people living along the remote mesas the Tusayan, derived from the name "Tucano" which they had given to one of the Hopi villages. In time the name Moqui was also given to the Hopi by the Spanish. This name was probably derived from a term used by other Pueblo people for their Hopi neighbors. But since the Spanish corruption of the term sounded like the Hopi word Mokee, which means to die, it came to be spelled Moki as well as Moqui and took on a derogatory slant, especially when used by the Hopi's Spanish enemies. For another use of the term Moqui or Moki, see Section I, "History."

But the Hopi were not forgotten altogether, for in 1630, an edict came from the Spanish Franciscan order in Santa Fe. It declared that the Pueblo people, including the Hopi, needed to have their souls saved. In a short time, the Spanish established a mission at the largest village, Awat'ovi. At that time there were only five or six Hopi villages and a population of around three thousand. A church was built there and an intense effort to convert the Hopi was made for over fifty years. But in 1680, the Pueblo people had had enough of increasing Spanish domination and they revolted. The Hopi, who had never before or since been aggressive to other Indian tribes or whites, joined in. In a rare act of violence against others, they allegedly slashed the throats of the priests and hurled them over the mesa cliffs and then set about to destroy all evidence of the Spanish occupation. But ten years later, the Spanish, who had been chased out of the Southwest altogether (see Section IV, "History"), returned and by 1692 had retaken most of the Pueblo villages of the Rio Grande.

With the return of the Spanish, most of the Hopi villages that had been established below the mesas moved to the mesa tops, for they feared Spanish reprisals for harboring some of the Rio Grande Pueblo people who fled for their safety to the Hopi mesas. There were enough of these immigrants to the Hopi mesas to form a new village, Hano, still in existence today. In 1699, the Spanish reestablished a tenuous foothold at Awat'ovi.

But the collaboration of Awat'ovi with the Spanish was not to be tolerated by the other villages. Consequently in 1700 civil strife occurred. The villagers of Oraibi and Walpi descended on Awat'ovi in the night, systematically killing most of the village men in the kiva and irreparably wrecking and burning the village to remove all traces of the Spanish. The women and children were captured and divided between the villages. In doing this, the Hopi blotted out forever any dominant or meaningful Spanish influence on the mesas. Although the Spanish never gained a foothold there again, they did make peace with the Hopi late in the eighteenth century.

Since those early contacts, the Hopi have had an ambiguous relationship with the white man. On the one hand there has been the desire to find the True "Pahaana." On the other hand, the Hopi experience with all whites has been somewhat similar to their first experience with the Spanish. Other Spaniards, then Mexican traders, then American government officials, and finally some of the tourists on the mesas, have duplicated the negative aspects of that first white contact. So the Hopi have learned to be a bit leery of whites, wondering who each white man is and what he wants. But perhaps there can be no rejection of all white people, for some day as the legend says, the True White Brother will return and lead the Hopi to their paradise in the Fifth World.

Even though the Hopi rejected the Spanish, they nonetheless retained some of their culture. They learned from their enemies how to raise watermelon and peach trees. Within time, wool replaced cotton in weaving, and sheep and goats introduced by the Spanish replaced antelope meat. For about another one hundred years, the Hopi lived in security until a drought of major proportions hit the area between 1777 and 1780. Then in 1781, the legacy of white contact, smallpox, hit the villages. This deadly disease resulted in a massive depopulation of the villages. The survivors left the mesas temporarily to live with their friends, the Zuñis and the Ácomas to the south. From about 1750 to 1863, raids by alien Indians exerted a disruptive influence on the Hopi. By 1853, another smallpox epidemic hit First Mesa, reducing the population by 50 percent. Between 1864 and 1868, another severe drought struck the area, forcing the Hopi once again temporarily to abandon their villages. This time the villages were abandoned almost completely.

Indian agents of the United States government began visiting Hopiland by 1870 and government-operated boarding schools were opened in that year. Desirous of "integrating" the Hopi to white society as soon as possible, Hopi children and their parents were bribed to increase school attendance with the stated goal of "re-educating" Hopi children to white ways. The idea was to break up the traditional lifeway. This interference from the United States government and certain religious groups split the Hopi into two warring factions reminiscent of the earlier strife at Awat'ovi. The Hopi began disputing among themselves as to who was following the Hopi way most diligently.

Because the disputes often centered around issues introduced by the United States government that were foreign to the Hopi way, the Hopi divided into two camps. One group came to be known as the "Hostiles," or those who were against government interference. The other group was known as the "Friendlies," or those who supported some of the changes wanted by the government. This split among the Hopi did not lead to loss of life but rather to the splintering of one group away from the other to form new villages. Old Oraibi felt much of the tension between old and new values. By 1896, the progovernment members and the antigovernment members of the village were holding separate ceremonies. In 1906, the tension had become so great that the two groups engaged in a "pushing" match, the loser having to leave the village. The Hostiles, or antigovernment faction, lost and split from Oraibi to form a new village, Hotevilla.

The white traders who came to the villages in the late 1800s began to affect the Hopi way drastically. Machine-made cloth began to replace much of the handwoven cloth. Even Hopi architecture was altered in that the roof entrance was replaced by side wall doors. Around 1910, several new villages were formed below First and Third mesas, and in 1943 land disputes with the Navajo began in earnest.

By 1943, the Hopi were wearing the clothing of the dominant white culture and were speaking and reading English. World War II found the Hopi fighting the war as well as helping out in worthwhile wartime industries off the reservation. Paved roads constructed in the 1950s and 1960s opened up the reservation to the outside world via the automobile. The mid-1980s saw the construction of the first high school on the Hopi Reservation. With its completion, many of the students who formerly traveled 160 miles round trip each day to Holbrook or Winslow, Arizona, or who attended boarding school in Flagstaff, Phoenix, or California could, for the first time in this century, complete their secondary education close to home. And today, plans are being made for a new hospital on the reservation, which will cater to the needs of the Hopi people.

In spite of adapting to some modern ways, the Hopi have maintained the land and the villages their ancestors inhabited nine hundred years ago. They continue to resist being swept under a wave of white modernism. So in the face of great obstacles, elaborate rituals, ceremonies, and dances are still carried on by these people so diligently faithful to the hard, but rewarding Hopi way.

The Navajo: Nomads and Survivalists

The Navajo are relative newcomers to the Southwest, probably arriving there sometime after 1500. They are Athapascan-speaking people who came from the north, where they occupied land near the Arctic Circle in the north and west of what is now Canada. No one knows why they headed south, but it is speculated that today's Navajo represent a group of these northern nomads and hunters who split off from the others and followed the buffalo south until they reached the plains of New Mexico, east of the Continental Divide. There, these plains-dwelling people traded with Rio Grande Pueblo people in the 1500s and later moved and settled west of the Rio Grande on the Colorado Plateau. From there, one group moved to the mountains south and east of the Colorado Plateau, becoming the predecessors of some of today's Apache Indians. Still another group moved across the Colorado Plateau to the San Juan River watershed to an area that had been abandoned previously by the Anasazi, settling in the region that is now northwestern New Mexico probably sometime in the 1600s.

This group supplemented its hunting with farming. They learned about farming from their Pueblo neighbors, with whom they traded and whose villages they sometimes raided. It was there around Gobernador Canyon that much of Navajo religion and symbolism had its beginnings. For on top of Gobernador Knob, an ancient rock outcropping of molten magma origin, is the sacred spot where Changing Woman, the principal Navajo deity whose aging represents the progression of the changing seasons, was first found as a baby. Not far away at Huerfano Mesa, which the Navajos call mountain-around-which-traveling-is-done, is the symbolic home where she was raised.

When the Spanish arrived in 1539–1540, they made little mention of these people. But since they lived in small, clustered groups of extended families widely spread over this vast country, they were not as visible as the Pueblo people who lived in more densely populated villages made of stone on top of high mesas. The Navajo called themselves "Dineh" or The People. The Spanish had earlier named some of these more nomadic Indians "Apache," a Spanish word possibly derived from the Zuñi "Apachu," which literally means "enemy." When they found these Indians in

Navajo sheep and goats

northwestern New Mexico who were nomadic but who also farmed, they named them Apache de Navajo or literally Apaches of cultivated fields. The Spanish borrowed the word Navajo from the Tewa-speaking Pueblo people whose word Navajo means "great cultivated fields."

During the time of great conflict with the Spanish in the late 1600s, which was detailed earlier in the Hopi section, many Rio Grande Pueblo people such as those from Jemez Pueblo, fled westward seeking refuge with the Navajo in the San Juan River Basin. This period of Pueblo unrest greatly aided the Navajo. From the Pueblo emigrés, they learned and incorporated many skills and ideas that enhanced their own lifeway. From the Pueblo people who brought their Spanish goats and their scrawny, spindly-legged, Spanish churro sheep with them, they learned about sheepherding. And Navajo women learned from Pueblo men how to shear sheep, make yarn, and weave it into blankets, skills the Pueblo people had learned from the Spanish.

Probably through close contact and intermarriage, they assimilated some of the ritual and religious ceremonies from the Pueblo people as well as learning about pottery from them. The Navajo took to sheepherding like thirsty men to water. Later Spanish contact also offered "The People" another opportunity, the horse. Reintroduced to this country by the Spanish after becoming extinct in North America following the last glacial age, the horse became like one with the Navajo. Their nomadic instincts sensed bright possibilities in this new combination of horse and man.

With the ever-increasing need for new pasture for their sheep and under constant pressure from the hostile Utes to the north who attacked them often, the newly mobile Navajo were prodded to move steadily westward until they reached the Canyon de Chelly area by the early 1700s. There in the bottom of the canyon they found seclusion, built their hogans, and cultivated fields that had been abandoned long ago by the Anasazi. The swift Spanish horse allowed the Navajo to step up their raids on other Indian villages for the purpose of increasing their animal stock. Their raids on the Hopi pueblos began an enmity that has lasted to this day. Later, unhappy with white encroachment on their lands, they raided white settlements, first Spanish, then Mexican, and later American. Their profligate raiding of Spanish settlements became such a problem that in 1805 the Spanish government sent an expedition led by Lt. Antonio de Narbona to quell them (see "The North Rim of Canyon de Chelly").

But the Spanish and later the Mexicans were unable to stem the tide of Navajo raiding. The harrassed white settlers dubbed the Navajo the "Lords of the Earth." After this area became a part of the United States, the raiding intensified in the 1840s. In 1860, over one thousand Navajo attacked Fort Defiance. Alarmed white settlers demanded that the government do something. In 1863, Col. Kit Carson, previously a friend of the Navajo, was enlisted to systematically destroy Navajo orchards, fields, and hogans wherever he found them. In this way he broke the back of Navajo resistance so that in the winter of 1864, over eighty-five hundred starving, half-frozen, beleaguered Navajo (out of an estimated total of twelve thousand) surrendered and were forced to relocate to Fort Sumner in eastern New Mexico. Men, women, and children (all except babies and debilitated elderly) were forced to walk nearly three hundred fifty miles to a concentration camplike settlement in an area called Bosque Redondo on the Pecos River near the fort. This trail of tears has come to be known as the "Long Walk."

For four years, the vanquished, uprooted Navajo eked out an existence on the ungiving land. They fell prey to white man's diseases and suffered from a shortage of fuel and good water. Many starved. Yet the unhappy but adaptable Navajo learned something from this experience. In addition to acquiring more knowledge about agriculture, they discovered the usefulness of wagons pulled by horses and they learned to construct more long-lasting hogans, which would later replace the ancient forked-stick hogans. Introducing a style of dress you will still see in Navajoland today, the Navajo women, imitating the white officer's wives, began wearing long, wide, full-length skirts, which were either tiered or pleated. These skirts, often called squaw dresses or skirts today, were given to the Indian women at Bosque Redondo by missionaries who had collected cast-off, fashionable hoopskirts from the East and by military officers' wives who discarded this style of

Forked-stick hogan

dress in anticipation of a new style. The Navajo women wore the skirts without the hoops, much as they do today. During this period, the men began wearing pants from unbleached muslin they had received at the fort. They topped these with colored velvet shirts and tied bright satin scarves around their foreheads.

The experiment to deprogram the Navajo and to change them into an agricultural people was by and large an expensive failure. When the government finally recognized this, a treaty was signed between the government and the Navajo as an autonomous people. Because the preamble states that the treaty is between two sovereign powers, the Navajo have claimed to be a nation within a nation. Thus today, they refer to themselves as the Navajo Nation. So in June of 1868, after the Navajo were given 3.5 million acres of the lands they had formerly occupied around Canyon de Chelly, these proud people walked back home to resume their lives amid their cherished red rock canyons. Except for a few sheep and goats given to each family, the Navajo had to start over from scratch.

In the 1870s, trading posts began to spring up on the new reservation. White traders attempting to befriend the alienated Navajo learned the Navajo language and often served as interpreters of white culture for them. The Navajo traded wool, rugs, silver, jewelry, and livestock for flour, coffee,

utensils, and bright machine-made cloth. In some instances, traders would advance credit as long as there was collateral. For collateral the Navajo pawned saddles, rifles, and jewelry. If the debt was not paid, the pawn was sold. But the debt often was paid in raw wool, woven blankets, and piñon nuts. The trading post of Lorenzo Hubbell, one of the most revered early traders, is still in operation today, thanks to the National Park Service (see "Back to Navajoland: Keams Canyon to Ganado via Hubbell Trading Post. . ."). Because of his great respect for the Navajo people, his counsel and guidance were well accepted by them.

By the late 1800s, the Navajo once again were tending their flocks, their peach orchards, and their farms. White missionaries and schools came on the scene about this time. At the suggestion of the traders, the skilled women weavers, whose finely woven blankets were legendary by that time, began making heavier blankets called "rugs" which the traders could sell easily. These rugs represented an incredible array of startling geometric patterns, which the Navajo weavers picked up from the more than one thousand blankets designed and made by the Spanish weavers along the Rio Grande that the United States government sent to Fort Sumner. Their weaving became so popular that there was little left for their own personal use, so they began buying brightly colored, Oregon-made, Pendleton blankets which the trading posts carried.

Meanwhile Navajo men further developed silversmithing skills learned earlier from Mexican silversmiths in the 1860s. The making and selling of beautiful silver and turquoise jewelry, along with the rugs, gave the tribe a new economic base. In addition to making artistic jewelry for sale, the Navajo have a great affection for their own jewelry. Adorning themselves with their hand-crafted finery at ceremonies and social events, the jewelry has come to symbolize Navajo wealth.

Prior to the 1920s, the United States government zealously wanted to "educate" the young Navajo so they could enter white society. Many Navajo children were sent away to boarding schools at an early age. Sometimes they were dragged kicking from their homes. Their long hair was cut short. The Navajo language was forbidden and they were forced to learn English. In many cases the results were disastrous, producing people who could not live in either society. The emphasis has changed somewhat since the 1930s, with schools being provided on the reservation and with more emphasis on teaching children to live in both cultures. An increasing number of Navajo children attend day schools sponsored by the state-operated public school systems, religious missions, and the tribal government. Bilingual education has become an integral part of the curriculum in some schools, especially those administered by the tribe. Still, because of bad roads and long distances many Navajo children leave their homes at an early age to attend boarding schools sponsored by the United States Bureau of Indian Affairs.

The Navajo reservation, unlike other Indian lands, has continued to grow in size. Through executive order of the United States government and various congressional actions, numerous additions have been made to Navajoland. Since 1868, the reservation has increased fourfold from 3.5 million to over 14 million acres. For a number of years, the Navajo population increased at a rate five times as fast as the national birth rate. Although full citizenship was conferred on all Indians including the Navajo in 1924, rewarding

Hubbell Trading Post

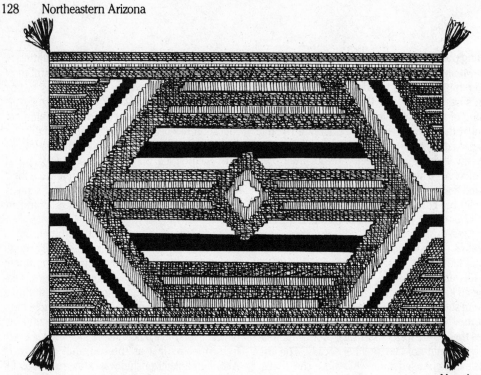

Navajo rug

them for their participation in World War I, they and all the other Indians in Arizona and New Mexico were not allowed to vote in state and national elections until 1948 when restrictive state laws were struck down.

As the Navajo population grew, the population of their sheep and horse herds grew with them. The sparse land was heavily overgrazed by the early 1930s and severe erosion was beginning to take its toll. The government started a stock reduction program which made little sense to the Navajo, whose prestige and very life were intertwined with their sheep herds. For the "good" of the Navajo people, government agents shot and killed thousands of animals, leaving their carcasses to rot. The Navajo were embittered, and once again a barrier of distrust with the United States government was raised. Over time, programs to breed higher-quality, more wool-productive and meat-efficient sheep have been successful. But the Navajo began to realize that they could not live by sheep alone. Still an integral part of Navajo life, sheep have become less important economically, as more cattle have been introduced.

In 1934, under the Indian Reorganization Act,

the Navajo were offered a constitution drafted by the United States government to help structure their tribal government. This constitution was voted down by the skeptical Navajo. Asserting their autonomy on the basis of the language of the preamble of the 1868 treaty, they formed their own council. They declared that they were a part of the United States yet separate with full rights of self-determination.

The reservation took a quantum leap in terms of Anglo contact during World War II, when thirty-six hundred Navajo served in the Armed Forces and fifteen thousand more were tapped for work in war-related industries. With these people returning after several years away, the reservation saw drastic changes. In addition, after World War II, uranium and oil were discovered on the reservation, further increasing white contact and helping to fill tribal coffers. Then the tribe began to develop business enterprises including timber, power plants, oil and gas production, as well as a park and recreational department, staffed by Navajo rangers. Today, the Navajo receive approximately four million dollars annually from strip coal mining in the Black Mesa and Four Corner operations, which generate power for the Southwest and southern Arizona. Ironically, in giving the Navajo their original land grant, the United States government thought that it was giving away a piece of worthless land which nobody else would want.

In 1972, the government offered to let the Navajo begin to run their own reservation. The tribal government is represented on the local level by "chapter" houses throughout the reservation. Each district or chapter house elects a representative to the tribal council in Window Rock. The tribal government is headed by an elected chairman. The tribe has a police force, tribal court system, and a tribal welfare department. Nonetheless, the Bureau of Indian Affairs still has considerable authority over the tribe. Reservation lands, held in trust for the Navajo people, are managed by the United States Bureau of Indian Affairs. As individuals, the Navajo do not own the land they occupy. Instead, the tribe assigns traditional use areas to Navajo families, which are usually the lands the families have occupied for generations.

_____Seeing Indian Country

Flagstaff

For most travelers coming up from the south or approaching Indian Country from the east or west via Interstate 40, Flagstaff is an ideal stopping place before heading north to the Four Corners area. This relaxed friendly city of 41,000 citizens is perched amid the pines at a cool 7,000 feet. But more than its cool climate and its western ambience, Flagstaff offers the visitor an outstanding introduction and overview to the Four Corners Indian Country just to the north of it. Its Museum of Northern Arizona is a gem of a place, widely known for its focus on the prehistoric peoples of the Southwest and its ongoing involvement with the Hopi and Navajo people. This forward-looking museum has often moved out of the staid, traditional museum role to become a dynamic force in the preservation of Northern Arizona's traditional communities. Forever keeping a concerned eye toward helping the Hopi and Navajo people preserve their past, the museum has reached out numerous times to offer its support and specialized services to its Indian neighbors to the north. In the 1930s, when it appeared that some of the Hopi crafts were languishing and losing their indigenous character, the museum initiated the, by now almost legendary, Hopi Craftsman Exhibition, which has been an annual summer event in Flagstaff for almost sixty years. That event was soon followed by the equally prestigious Navajo Craftsman Exhibition. For several weeks in July

and August, these events plus the recent addition of the Zuñi Craftsman Exhibition in late May, turn the city into one of the largest Native American marketplaces in the country. Then in the 1960s, the museum lent its assistance in obtaining National Historic Site status for the Hubbell Trading Post on the Navajo Reservation. And in the 1980s, the museum staff assisted the Hopi villagers of Walpi on First Mesa in identifying and preserving culturally significant artifacts as they stabilized and restored their village.

But the museum is not the only Flagstaff institution involved with the Four Corners Indian tribes. Resting on a large, handsome campus west of town is Northern Arizona University. This university, with its 13,000 students and a complement of over 600 full- and part-time faculty, also plays a major role in collaborating and supporting these southwestern Indian cultures. Of course the university has its special regional research-oriented programs like the Center for Colorado Plateau Studies and the unique "Quaternary Studies" master's degree program, which takes an interdisciplinary approach to the last two million years on the Colorado Plateau. But more importantly, it provides an educational environment at the college level for over 800 Native American students, most of whom are from the Southwest. So it is no wonder that the university offers courses in the Navajo language and has been hard at work trying to improve bilingual instruction techniques for both Hopi and Navajo primary and secondary school students. And it is not too surprising that the outcome of a decade-long linguistic research project involving both Hopi and Anglo staff resulted in the publication of the one-volume Hopi-English dictionary with its more than 30,000 entries. In the absence of a universally accepted Hopi language dictionary, it is hoped that this alphabetical dictionary, which for the first time writes and spells words the way they sound and defines them in terms of the traditional culture, will find acceptance among the Hopi people. This may be just the ticket needed to preserve the ancient Hopi language, which many say is in danger of extinction. No doubt much of the university's linguistic and educational research will stay right at home to facilitate instruction of Navajo and Hopi students attending day and boarding schools in Flagstaff and to aid in assimilating some of Flagstaff's non-English speaking Navajo families who have been newly uprooted from their homes on the reservation because of the Navajo-Hopi land dispute.

But not all of the university's research has been cultural. The university's College of Engineering and Technology has been encouraging its Native American students to take on projects that will help make life on the reservations a little easier. One such project recently completed included the installation of electrical generating solar panels in a remote part of the Navajo reservation, where the only light available had been kerosene lamps. For the first time in history, Navajo weavers there can turn on an electric light to work in the evening while their children have light to read and do their homework.

While the Museum of Northern Arizona and Northern Arizona University have played such vital roles in the preservation and development of the Four Corners cultures, they are not the only Flagstaff institutions that focus on Indian Country. The Coconino Center for the Arts promotes both traditional and contemporary Indian arts from the Four Corners and beyond through its excellent rotating exhibits. And in the summer it joins with the Flagstaff chapter of Native Americans for Community Action to sponsor the well-known Festival of Native American Arts.

When visiting Flagstaff, you may have your first encounter with some of the Navajo and Hopi families who, in spite of a growing number of commercial stores and shops on the reservations, still come to Flagstaff, one of their favorite market towns, to shop and sell their crafts. Although Flagstaff's resident Native American population is less than 5 percent, on some summer weekends and over certain holidays and special university days such as graduation, you will see so many Navajo and Hopi families that you will begin to think you are in the middle of reservation country rather than fifty miles to the south of it. And while visiting "Flag," as everyone likes to call it, take a trip to the casual downtown area where you will see an egalitarian mix of Anglo businessmen, ranchers, lumberjacks, and students along with Native Americans of several tribal persuasions and some of the town's hispanic citizens who comprise about 8 percent of the population.

Although influenced by the sophisticated, Anglo sunbelt cities to the south, the remote "room enough and time enough" Indian cultures to the north, and the mix of mainstream America as it flows east and west on the interstate, Flagstaff has maintained an identity of its own. It has carved out a prominent position as the leading commercial and cultural city in Northern Arizona. Even if it does not always seem certain of its vision, it appears to be getting there anyway. If not a beautiful city, Flagstaff is a genuinely warm and friendly western town in a scenic high-altitude environment rich in history and tradition. So there is more to Flag than meets the eye of the one-night-stand traveler who drives bleary-eyed down Santa Fe Avenue seeing only the city's sprawl of motels and fast-food joints. Flagstaff's true spirit lies off the interstate and its feeder arterials in the pleasant tree-lined residential districts, the historic downtown area, and the surrounding ponderosa pine-clad hills and mesas, which shelter pleasant parks and homes with stunning views of snow-clad mountains.

Despite its beautiful location, Flagstaff is quite different from its charming high-altitude sister city to the east. Unlike Santa Fe, Flagstaff did not develop slowly over several hundred years in a multi-cultural environment. Just about the time Santa Fe was being rediscovered and gentrified, the new town of Flagstaff was just beginning to find itself. So it is a young city. Like many frontier towns, its settlement, although resolute and purposeful, was somewhat hasty. Its early growth and

Using camels to help survey the High Southwest (1857)

development yielded to the practical economical and geographic demands of the western frontier that spawned it.

In 1857, the United States government sent Lieutenant Edward F. Beale west to plot a practicable wagon road across New Mexico and Arizona (along the thirty-fifth parallel) that settlers could follow to California. In what was possibly one of the most unusual expeditions ever mounted in the west, Beale led twenty-five camels imported from Asia Minor through the High Southwest desert country. It was the first time a camel's hoof had touched American southwest soil since prehistoric times. (See "History of the People" and Section IV, "Seeing the Spanish Rio Grande Country.") One of the places they stopped to rest was near a spring not far from today's Flagstaff. Over the next few years the newly blazed trail, called Beale's Wagon Road, was followed by many different wagon trains heading west. Some stopped near the location of today's Flagstaff but then moved on. In the 1870s a group of fifty prospective settlers called the Boston Party rested near another spring in the same area. They found only one other settler

there, Thomas F. McMillan, a rancher from Prescott who had come into the area to graze sheep. Together they celebrated the one hundredth birthday of the United States on July 4, 1876, by felling a pine tree, stripping it of its limbs, and attaching the stars and stripes to it. Other parties coming to the area continued the tradition so that when it came time to name a town, "flag staff" was chosen.

But the evolution from settling parties to town was to take longer. It was not until 1881 that a town was finally settled at Antelope Springs just a little west of today's downtown Flagstaff. That year a giant sawmill was pulled into the area by oxen to begin cutting ties for the new transcontinental railroad that was being constructed along Beale's earlier route. The railroad arrived in 1882, and because of the steep grade at Antelope Springs, the rail depot was located about one-half mile east, adjacent to the new tracks. A new town developed there. Both "Old Town" at Antelope Springs and "New Town" grew up together until July of 1884, when a fire burned down much of Old Town. From that time on, New Town was the primary focus of growth, and it prospered until a disastrous fire in 1886 leveled most of its commercial core. Out of the ashes grew an even larger town until the next downtown Flagstaff fire in 1888. The town rebuilt again, and with the advent of running water, was not to be plagued by more fires.

Although earlier ranchers like Thomas F. McMillan had raised sheep in the area, pressure to raise beef did not come about until railroad and timber crews in the West began to demand more beef. Meanwhile the ranching and commercial opportunities of the area leaked to the East Coast and by 1886, two members of the Babbitt family from Cincinnati stepped off the train and began to make history. They, along with other family members who came later, developed an empire of retailing and ranching seldom to be equalled in the West. Defying tradition by successfully grazing both cattle and sheep, the Babbitt family, today, still lays claim to 850,000 acres of deeded and permit land in their CO Bar Ranch and owns mercantile stores spread throughout Arizona as well as a string of trading posts on the Navajo Reservation.

In the 1890s, Flagstaff became the county seat of Coconino County; geographically the second largest county in the United States. Shortly thereafter, Flagstaff was chosen as the site for a reform school. The lovely stone building constructed for that purpose was never utilized in that way. A teacher's school was established there instead, and eventually, it evolved into thriving Northern Arizona University, one of the chief mainstays in Flagstaff's economy. In the mid 1890s, the first tourists began coming to the area to enjoy its cool summer climate and take the stage line to the Grand Canyon. The Weatherford Hotel was built to accommodate some of the tourists after the local newspaper had cried loud and hard for more hotels and guest houses. It was also in the 1890s that Percival Lowell (brother of American poet Amy Lowell), noted astronomer and internationally known expert on the planet Mars, decided the Flagstaff air was so clear he would locate an observatory there atop a mesa west of town. His research, which led to the discovery of the planet Pluto, helped Flagstaff's observatory gain an international reputation among astronomers.

By the 1920s, most of the downtown buildings had been constructed, and a stable community was developing when an economic slump hit the area. To bolster the community economically and take advantage of its unique location near the Grand Canyon and Indian Country, Flagstaff built a new rail depot and the Monte Vista Hotel. Indeed the ploy to attract travelers worked and a number of them stayed in the area. One such early traveler-turned-resident was Dr. Harold S. Colton, a zoology professor from the University of Pennsylvania. By 1928, this energetic natural historian had founded the Museum of Northern Arizona to preserve the natural and cultural history of the Colorado Plateau. The museum has evolved into one of the finest in the region with its focus on Southwest archaeology and ethnology and its dedication to educating the public. Through her interest in art and ethnology, Mary-Russell F. Colton (Dr. Colton's wife) was instrumental in helping to revive the crafts on the Hopi mesas, which had drastically declined in the early 1900s. Under her guiding hand, Flagstaff became renowned as a nurturing center for southwestern Indian crafts.

By the late 1920s, Flagstaff's main arterial, Santa Fe Avenue, became part of a national road system called the Old Trails National Highway. When the route was finally paved from Chicago to Los Angeles in 1932, it was designated as U.S. Highway 66, one of America's legendary thoroughfares. Over time it was dubbed the "Main Street of America" and "The World's Longest Traffic Jam" as it carried mid-America's impoverished depression-era migrants west in the 1930s and their affluent vacation-bound children east in the 1950s and 1960s. With the explosion of automobiles after World War II and the development of

The Monte Vista Hotel, Flagstaff, Arizona

Depot, Flagstaff, Arizona

Route 66 as the major east–west highway, Flagstaff's downtown business district dried up as the town's growth sprawled east and west along Highway 66. That sprawl is still evident today as over eighty motels along with numerous convenience stores and shopping centers line Santa Fe Avenue and other major arterials near the exit ramps of the interstate highways. But in recent years with a shift in the city's economic base away from timber and toward the University of Northern Arizona (whose expanded summer programs offer a cool haven for hundreds of students) and tourism, there has been a renewed interest in the historic downtown area as well as the area south of the railroad tracks. The downtown development of the handsome new library in a beautiful parklike setting, the renovation of several downtown historic buildings to accommodate new lodging facilities, restaurants, and several upscale shops and galleries, and the development of a prestigious luxury resort on the city's eastside suggest that Flagstaff is on the move. There is now good reason to spend more than just a quick "overnight" in Flagstaff as travelers discover the real charm and beauty of this high-altitude city and use it as a base to see the many worthwhile sights in and around the city and the region.

Touring Flagstaff—A Few Short Tours

If you are interested in the Indian cultures and the natural history of the Colorado Plateau to the north, you must visit Flagstaff's Museum of North-ern Arizona. It, alone, is the most compelling reason to make a stop in Flagstaff. Described by the knowledgeable as one of the jewels of the museum world, this sixty-year-old museum, beautifully situated in the ponderosa pines three miles north of town on U.S. Highway 180 (North Fort Valley Road), offers the best introduction and overview of the region available anywhere. The vast number of artifacts you will see in the museum are but a handful compared to the total collection stored in over twenty nearby warehouses. Over the years the museum's large crew of over sixty dedicated staff persons has been composed of some of the region's outstanding archaeologists, geologists, botanists, paleontologists, and anthropologists. Their special mission has been to present objects within the context of an articulated story line so that the viewer comes to understand not only the significance of a certain artifact but also how it relates to other artifacts from different time periods in the same culture. This special emphasis on education makes this museum a delight for both adults and children.

Upon entering the distinctive, native, gray-brown basalt stone building with its red-tiled roof, you will notice high ceilings supported by massive beams. The overpowering feeling of the Southwest provided by the architecture of the building is further enhanced by the view of the ponderosa pines and the San Francisco Peaks through the large picture window in the lobby. This is just the beginning of a museum adventure that will prepare you well for the Indian Country sights you are going to see, or help you fill in the information gaps you may have accumulated after touring the region. The first thing you may notice is that the lobby is filled with books—one of the most complete selections of southwest titles in the Four Corners region. If you have children, ascend the stairs from the lobby-bookstore to the balcony where you will find the children's loft. There the younger set can play Native American games, learn about a Navajo loom, create their own "rock art," and learn how to date artifacts by counting tree rings.

The heart of the museum's permanent collection, which begins in the room to the right of the lobby is the award-winning exhibit, "Native Peoples of the Colorado Plateau." There you will encounter in the archaeology and the archaeology and ethnology sections one of the clearest and most comprehensive exhibits relating to the history of the native peoples of the region. One of the many interesting displays in this exhibit is a fascinating time line focusing on the evolution of native foods. After viewing many well-displayed prehistoric and historic artifacts of the region you will next see an exhibit displaying the history and evolution of Navajo textiles. There you will view beautiful Navajo rugs from the early classic period (1700 to 1840) to the present. And if you are in the market for a Navajo rug, information from this revealing exhibit will help you make a more knowledgeable purchase. The next highlight of the exhibit is a replica of the Hopi Kiva or ceremonial chamber at the ancient village of Awat'ovi. Be certain to see this exhibit, for it contains the original wall mural fragments from the kiva at the abandoned village of Awat'ovi. Elements of these remarkably complex and artistically sophisticated murals are found in many of the Hopi design motifs used today. And, more than any other artifacts you will see in your travels through the Southwest, these few fragments with their well-preserved, exquisite artwork open a revealing window on the dynamic and incredibly rich prehistoric Native American cultures in the Four Corners region. Just a few feet from the kiva is an interesting exhibit of Hopi textiles and a Hopi weaver whom you can observe working at his craft.

From the textile room you can enter the outstanding museum shop and sales gallery, which is stocked annually from the Hopi, Navajo, and Zuñi craftsman shows, or exit to the museum's central patio, which features a live outdoor botany exhibit displaying specimens from the six major life zones of the Colorado Plateau. Passing through the lobby-bookstore enter the geology wing, where another permanent exhibit documents through dioramas and fossils and mineral specimens the geological and paleontological history of the Colorado Plateau. This exhibit is centered around an unusual prehistoric specimen—the skeletal remains of a Pleistocene giant ground sloth. The next two galleries provide space for rotating exhibits covering special subjects and fine arts. Many of these special exhibits come from the 2,000 paintings and sculptures, 40,000 biological specimens, and 20,000 fossil, rock, and mineral specimens stored in the museum's warehouses. In the past, the rotating exhibits have ranged from presentations about "Trading Posts" to displays of contemporary Native American and Anglo artwork depicting images from the Colorado Plateau.

For further information on the museum gift shop and bookstore, see "Shopping," this section. The museum is open daily from 9:00 A.M. to 5:00 P.M. except Thanksgiving, Christmas, and New Year's Day. To get there from Santa Fe Avenue downtown, turn north onto Humphreys Street (U.S. Highway 180 North to the Grand Canyon), which then becomes Fort Valley Road. In approximately three miles you will see the sign to the museum, which is just left of the road. Mailing address: Route 4, Box 720, Flagstaff, Arizona 86001. Telephone: 1-602-774-5211.

And while you are in the neighborhood you should definitely stop by the Coconino Center for the Arts located in the Fort Valley Cultural Park, 2300 North Fort Valley Road (see "Shopping" and "Fairs, Festivals and Events"). Their superb rotating exhibits featuring western Americana as well as the Indian cultures of the Southwest offer yet another perspective on the culture and art of the region. And if you should be in the region during the Festival of Native American Arts (co-sponsored by the center), you may want to attend one of the special Native American pottery, weaving, or basket-making workshops, watch outstanding Indian dancers accompanied by Indian drummers, or attend a concert given by contemporary Indian artists such as flute player, Carlos Nakai.

During that summer festival you will also want to see the large juried show in the center's spacious gallery where the very finest in contemporary Indian jewelry, weaving, and pottery are displayed. For up-to-date information about exhibits, write P.O. Box 296, Flagstaff, Arizona 86002. Telephone: 1-602-779-6921. Sharing the same driveway with the Art Center is the Northern Arizona Pioneers' Historical Museum, where, in addition to Flagstaff memorabilia, you can see a replica of a frontier blacksmith's shop as well as an early settler's cabin.

In addition to the Museum of Northern Arizona and the Coconino Center for the Arts, you may want to visit the well-known Lowell Observatory located just one mile west of downtown on Santa Fe Avenue and up to the top of Mars Hill. The visitor center is open five days a week (closed Sunday and Monday) and offers two lecture-tours per day in the summer and one thereafter. Lecture and slide programs are offered on Friday evenings in the summer, and visitors may look through the telescopes the first evening of each month if the weather permits. It is best to call to check on times. Telephone: 1-602-774-3358.

Another site, less than a fifteen-minute drive from the observatory, is the U.S. Geological Survey's Center of Astrogeology, better known as the "moon lab." No tours are available, but exhibits in the reception area describe some of the moon's geographical and geological features as well as aspects of the center's training program for lunar astronauts. From downtown drive north on Beaver Street to Cedar Avenue. Take a right onto Cedar Avenue and follow it up the hill by Buffalo Park to Gemini Drive. The center is located at 2225 North Gemini Drive. Telephone: 1-602-527-7000.

Half-Day Trip to Meteor Crater

If the Lowell Observatory and the lunar aspects of the universe tickle your fancy, and you are driving east to Albuquerque, or if you are using Flagstaff as a base and wish to take a half-day trip, consider visiting the Meteor Crater. Drive thirty-five miles east on Interstate 40 to the Meteor Crater exit and then five miles south on a good paved road to one of the world's largest and best-preserved meteor craters. The Meteor Crater

visitor center, which is perched on the rim of the giant crater, houses the excellent Museum of Astrogeology. It offers films and exhibits of how the meteor impacted and displays some of the meteorite fragments responsible for gouging this huge hole in the earth's surface. The Astronaut Hall of Fame (also in the visitor center) depicts man's exploration of space and describes the training received at this moonscape site by the Apollo astronauts. The exhibit includes a NASA space capsule and other space gear. For a number of years astronauts used the meteor crater as a hands-on classroom to learn crater mechanics. The site is impressive. The 22,000-year-old circular crater, which drops from the rim to a depth of 570 feet, could easily contain a sixty-story building. The crater spans more than 4,100 feet across and has a circumference of three miles. If converted into a stadium, it could seat two million spectators. Although it is not possible to hike to the bottom of the crater, you can hike around the rim and view its center from the high-powered telescope located there. Telephone: 1-602-774-8350.

**Half-Day Trip to
Walnut Canyon National Monument**

To whet your appetite for Indian Country, you may wish to take three hours out of your Flagstaff schedule to see a treasure trove of prehistoric Indian cliff ruins magnificently situated near the rim and down the steep walls of Walnut Canyon. Drive 7.5 miles east of Flagstaff on Interstate 40 until you see exit 204, the exit to Walnut Canyon National Monument. From the exit travel 3 miles over an all-weather road to the monument's visitor center. Plan to spend some time in this informative center to view the natural history displays, particularly the botany exhibit, which is one of the best in the region. There are also displays of relics from the Sinagua, Hopi, and Navajo cultures. Petroglyphs, which are found in the canyon but are not visible from the hiking trail, are reproduced in the visitor center. They include the image of the humpback flute player who is associated with fertility and the abundance of crops.

From the visitor center you can take a three-quarter-mile round-trip hike around a peninsulalike protuberance in the canyon wall. This

Petroglyph,
Walnut Canyon National Monument

island-in-the-sky provides magnificent vistas of this intimate canyon and its verdant vegetation, which includes groves of Arizona black walnut trees growing up alongside Walnut Creek 360 feet below the rim. The creek flows at a trickle nowadays because the water is held back in Lake Mary, which holds an important part of Flagstaff's scant water supply.

More importantly, the island trail takes you directly to twenty-five of the cliff-dwelling rooms and provides visual access to approximately one hundred others. The Sinagua Indians, possibly related to the Hopi farther north (see this section, "History of the People"), emigrated to this well-watered canyon from the Sunset Crater area sometime after A.D. 1120. They inhabited these dwellings for almost 150 years. It is thought that the band of nearly five hundred Sinagua Indians who lived in the canyon left their former home when it became overcrowded with opportunistic farmers from other areas who sought the arable lands created by the volcanic eruption in A.D. 1065. Throughout the canyon, the Sinagua built nearly four hundred rooms. Using masonry techniques borrowed from their Anasazi neighbors, they constructed double thickness stone walls at the openings of the many recesses and alcoves in the Kaibab limestone formation cliffsides. With the front walls closing in the recessed spaces, they then built perpendicular sidewalls, thereby closing up the sides and partitioning the long spaces into rooms.

The trail descends via a series of good paths and stairs about 180 feet before it starts up again. Although only moderately difficult, you may find yourself huffing and puffing on the way back up. But rest assured, your tax dollars have purchased several nice benches along the way. As you walk you will see fossils, remnants from an ancient sea

that covered this area over 250 million years ago, as well as a wide variety of high-desert plants such as yucca, cacti, barberry, Mormon tea, and in the spring, Indian paintbrush. Parents should watch children carefully along the trail as it meanders close to the edge. An excellent trail guide is available at the trail head. For more information, write Walnut Canyon National Monument, Walnut Canyon Road, Flagstaff, Arizona 86001. Telephone: 1-602-526-3367.

Half-Day Trip to Wupatki National Monument via Sunset Crater National Monument

Another prehistoric Indian ruin you should not miss if you are in Flagstaff is the Sinagua Pueblo of Wupatki located thirty-eight miles to the northeast off U.S. Highway 89 North. This site is an easy half-day round trip from Flagstaff or can be seen as you drive north toward Tuba City and Indian Country. On the way you will pass by the Sunset Crater cinder cone volcano and its associated lava fields. Leave Flagstaff by traveling east on Santa Fe Avenue past the Flagstaff Mall to U.S. Highway 89 North towards Page, Arizona. In approximately fifteen miles from downtown Flagstaff, you will see the sign to Sunset Crater on the right. Travel approximately two miles to the Sunset Crater visitor center. The rim of the crater, about one thousand feet above the surrounding surface, rises three hundred feet above the crater floor. It is covered with reddish cinders colored by the oxidation of iron particles found in the area's basaltic rocks. This is in contrast to the remainder of the cone which is black due to the deposition of cinders from the more abundant nonoxidized basaltic rock. In both instances, the cinders feel and look the same—typically lightweight and frothy in appearance. On the east side of the crater, deposits of gypsum, sulphur, and limonite, which evaporated out from the hot gasses and steam, tint the multi-colored rim yellow, purple, and green. Upon seeing this crater from a distance, the nineteenth-century American explorer, John Wesley Powell, could not help noting that at certain times of the day the rim seemed "to be on fire" and to "glow with a light of its own" much like a sunset.

But Sunset Crater, formed in A.D. 1065, is only

Sunset Crater,
Sunset Crater National Monument

the youngest of over four hundred cinder cones in the San Francisco Peaks Volcanic Field, which includes 2,200 square miles of cinder cones, lava flows, hills, and even the magnificent San Francisco Peaks themselves. Formerly a single, gargantuan volcano rising to over 15,000 feet, the San Francisco Peaks were formed when the volcano collapsed a half million years ago. These peaks, which dominate the Flagstaff skyline, can be seen from as far away as the Hopi mesas to the north and from much of the Navajo Reservation. They are sacred to both groups. The highest peak, Humphreys Peak, which tops out at 12,633 feet above sea level, is Arizona's highest mountain. Before gracing these beautiful peaks with the name of their favorite saint, Saint Francis of Assisi, the Spanish had dubbed these volcanic outcroppings the Sierra Sinagua. The term means "mountains without water" and was coined because, in spite of their size, no major streams flow from them.

The Sunset Crater visitor center has an excellent geological and seismological exhibit as well as a working seismograph. There are also exhibits focusing on the plants and insects of the area. There is a one-mile-long loop trail that bends through one of the lava flows taking visitors to a 225-foot-long cave called a lava tube, which is sometimes encrusted with ice. In recent years these ice caves have been closed to the public due to unstable conditions. Check with the ranger on duty. You will also be introduced to squeeze-ups, spatter cones, and lava blisters as you hike this informative self-guided trail. Although it was formerly possible to hike up to the rim, it is not allowed now because the heavy traffic was beginning to cause erosion of the cinders. Stay on the paved roads because driving on the cinders can be dangerous. Open daily throughout the year. For information, write Sunset Crater National Monument, HC 33, Box 444A, Flagstaff, Arizona 86001. Telephone: 1-602-527-7042.

From the Sunset Crater National Monument you will drive northeast about 18 miles to Wupatki National Monument. The road winds through numerous lava formations, pygmy forests of piñon pine and juniper carpeted with black cinders and finally, wide-open country offering scenic vistas of the Painted Desert to the east. At 7.5 miles from the Sunset Crater visitor center is the Painted Desert Vista turnoff with its handy picnic area.

The ruins of Wupatki Pueblo, built of Moenkopi sandstone, rise from an open, exposed, and often windy section of the high desert. The multistory pueblo, once three to four stories high, contained over one hundred rooms. It was erected by the Sinagua Indians following the volcanic eruption of A.D. 1065. The building techniques reveal traces of both Anasazi and Hohokam cultures. (See this section, "History of the People.") The pueblo was occupied from A.D. 1120 to A.D. 1210. Housing over three hundred inhabitants, Wupatki or Tall House, as the Hopi called it, was anchored on the east by an amphitheater and on the north by a ball court. It is the oval ball court unearthed in 1965 that gives this ruin its fame, as this feature is a rarity among the ruins found on the Colorado Plateau. It is a typical feature in the ruins found to the south in the Sonoran Desert area. There, however, the walls of the courts are made of adobe rather than masonry. In the Sonoran Desert area, the Hohokam, hearty desert dwellers and persistent irrigators, developed ball courts in many of their communities as did their neighbors to the south in today's Mexico and Central America. The large, oval ball courts were used for a strenuous ball game that probably had religious significance. The presence of the ball court and evidence that parrots and macaws were kept at Wupatki are further testimony that this area was a melting pot for many different groups of Indian farmers following the Sunset Crater eruption. The fallout from the eruption covered the parched soil with a moisture-preserving layer of cinders and ash making it ideal for farming.

Wupatki National Monument contains over eight hundred ruins in its fifty-six square miles of territory and in its heyday it was populated by over four thousand residents. Several of the other ruins such as Citadel (still unexcavated) and Lomaki were built and occupied by Anasazi people and are easily visited just off the road northeast of Wupatki as the road stretches toward its northern junction with U.S. Highway 89. These Anasazi ruins probably represent the southernmost settlements of the Kayenta Anasazi. The visitor center at Wupatki is well worth seeing. It contains a replica of an early pueblo ruin, displays of prehistoric pottery found in the area, and an interesting natural history exhibit. Open daily. For further information, write Wupatki National Monument, HC 33, Box 444A, Flagstaff, Arizona 86001. Telephone: 1-602-527-7040.

Half-Day Trip to Oak Creek Canyon

The beginning of this popular sixteen-mile-long canyon, noted for its red rock formations and scenic beauty rather than prehistoric ruins, is located about thirteen miles from Flagstaff. Like a long twisting slide, U.S. Highway 89A takes you from an elevation of 6,000 feet on the Colorado Plateau's southern rim through several life zones to an elevation of 4,500 feet on the bottomlands of Oak Creek in the Verde Valley. But more than that, it takes you into another world represented by Sedona, an Anglo outlier of the sunbelt cities to the south. There, elegant restaurants, resorts, galleries, and shops signal that you have left the quietude and remoteness of Indian Country far behind. In the canyon, twenty-one miles from Flagstaff, is popular Slide Rock. There, as the creek makes its rapid descent through the canyon, children of all ages wearing durable cutoffs slide with joy down the algae-covered slickrock chutes into quiet pools below. Watch for signs to the parking lot and recreation area on the west side of the highway about eight miles north of Sedona. Sedona is less than thirty miles from Flagstaff but the driving is slow because of the twists and turns in the road.

Full-Day Trips to the Navajo and Hopi Reservations and the Grand Canyon

For years Flagstaff has served as one of the major gateways to the Grand Canyon. In fact, it is estimated that several million or more tourists a year pass through the Flagstaff corridor on the way to the Grand Canyon. Should you want to travel to that scenic wonder of the world, you may want to consider a day trip there using Flagstaff as a base. If so, take the scenic route from Flagstaff to the canyon via Fort Valley Road (U.S. Highway 180). On the way out of town you will pass by the Museum of Northern Arizona. The highway then takes you directly to the commercial hubbub and scenic center of the Grand Canyon's South Rim, a little over eighty miles away. You can then return by way of the Little Colorado River Gorge and the Cameron Trading post via Arizona Highway 64 and U.S. Highway 89. The round-trip distance for this route is less than two hundred miles. Alternatively, you can spend the night at the canyon in one of the dozen or so inns, lodges, or motels there, or incorporate a trip to the canyon with plans to explore Indian Country to the northwest. For information about the Grand Canyon, contact: Superintendent, Grand Canyon National Park, P.O. Box 129, Grand Canyon, Arizona 86023. Telephone: 1-602-638-7888. Or for lodging, contact: Grand Canyon National Park Lodges, P.O. Box 399, Grand Canyon, Arizona 86023. Telephone: 1-602-638-2631, ext. 6577.

It is possible to use Flagstaff as a base for taking day trips into Indian Country. One recommended trip is to travel U.S. Highways 89 and 160 via Cameron, Arizona, to Tuba City, Arizona, the Western Capitol of the Navajo Nation. From Tuba City you can travel on Arizona Highway 264 to the heart of the Hopi Mesas, returning to Flagstaff through the Painted Desert by way of Arizona Highway 87 (to Winslow, Arizona) and Interstate 40. The round-trip mileage for this tour (all over paved roads) is approximately 270 miles.

Alternatively you can travel to Tuba City and continue north on Arizona Highway 160 to the intersection with Arizona 564, which takes you to Navajo National Monument and the magnificent Anasazi cliff dwelling, Betatakin. Round-trip mileage for this excursion is approximately 270 miles. Other sights, such as Monument Valley and Canyon de Chelly, which are farther from Flagstaff and which require a considerable amount of sightseeing time, are best seen by planning to spend more time there, possibly even overnight.

All of the Indian Country destinations mentioned above, their lodging and restaurant facilities, as well as a detailed discussion of their connecting routes are described in detail in the sections that follow.

Traditional hogan

The Navajo Nation

Within the United States' borders is a growing vibrant nation, the Navajo Nation. It is home to an estimated one hundred seventy thousand people, making it the largest Indian reservation in the United States. Navajo reservation lands are as large as the states of Vermont, Massachusetts, and New Hampshire combined, twice the size of Israel, and as large as the state of West Virginia. They extend across the borders of three states, resting mostly in Arizona, where they comprise 20 percent of that state's lands. These fourteen million acres lie at a base altitude of thirty-five hundred to four thousand feet and ascend to over ten thousand feet at Navajo Mountain. The reservation is surrounded by four directional mountain peaks sacred to the Navajo. To the north is Debe'ntsa or the La Plata Mountains in Colorado. To the south is Tso'dzil or Mount Taylor in New Mexico. To the east is Sis na jin or Blanca Peak in the Sangre de Cristo range in Colorado. To the west is Dook Oslid or the San Francisco Peaks in Arizona. The eastern portion of the reservation is the most developed in a modern sense. But in the western reaches of the reservation, firewood must still be hauled and water carried twenty or thirty miles from paved roads to remote, traditional hogans which have neither electricity nor plumbing.

The scenery almost rivals that found in portions of southeastern Utah, but the main reason to visit has to do with a culture who call themselves Dineh or "The People" and their very different lifestyle which permeates the land. I do not mean to say that the Navajo are living today as they did in the 1500s. That is not the case. Modern civilization has made its mark. But where that has happened there has been a Navajo imprint, softening the blow and retaining a distinctive Navajo flavor. One of the first indicators that you are in a different country comes when you see the traditional Navajo home. It is called a "hogan," which means home in Navajo. The traditional hogan you will see today is a rounded six- or eight-sided structure of logs, chinked with mud or clay, while the roof is formed with cribbed logs and then covered with mud.

By building a many-sided structure, short logs, which are the only kind available in this land of "pygmy" forests, can be used to produce the maximum amount of interior space. As in a geodesic dome, there are no center supports and all of the interior space is open and usable. Always facing east to the rising sun, the door is the only source of light in some of the older, windowless hogans. The smoke from the open cooking and warming fire in the middle of the hogan is vented through a hole or pipe, in the center of the rounded roof. In the more remote hogans, kerosene lanterns are still used when electricity is not available and at night, sheepskins are piled on the hard packed dirt floor for sleeping.

The shape and style of the hogan is thought to reflect certain religious sites occurring in nature. A very early style of hogan, called the four-forked beam hogan, resembled an inverted cone or a mountaintop. It was thought that it was modeled after the holy mountain, Gobernador Knob, in northwestern New Mexico. Later, probably during the internment at Bosque Redondo in the late 1800s, the hogan changed to the perpendicular-sided hexagonal or octagonal structure described above. Some speculate that this shape was modeled after another of nature's creations, the holy place called Huerfano Mesa, also located in New Mexico.

Today, even more changes are taking place in hogan construction. Although the basic, rounded shape is being maintained, the walls are often framed in traditional modern style and the cribbed, mud-plastered roof is giving way to modern structural and composition materials. Consequently, you will see many interesting and innovative variations on the theme, showing the creative, independent, and adaptive forces at work among the Navajo.

Through the addition of extruding bay windows, modern skylights, and large sliding glass doors, the traditionally shaped hogan has taken on a new look in many areas. And, of course, television antennae adorn many hogans. You will also see alongside many hogans, modern rectangular homes in the western tradition. But no matter what the shape of the hogan or house, the chim-

ney remains resolutely in the center, because that is where the cooking fire has always been. Also you often see windowsills, doors, or roofs in various shades of blue. This characteristic is possibly derived from either the traditional Pueblo Indian or Spanish belief that the color blue helps keep evil or the devil away.

To the Navajo, the hogan is more than a wall-less one-room entity warmed by a fire or stove in the middle. It is also a social place, a religious symbol, and a sanctuary where many Navajo ceremonies and rites are performed. According to Navajo legend, the hogan was created first, then came the order and planning of all creatures. In the summer, the dark hogan with its stale air gives way often to a brush shelter called a shade house or summer house. This breezy structure, often constructed of willows, provides shade from the hot sun yet allows air and light to penetrate.

So today, as you drive along, you will see the modern version of a Navajo camp, a scene passed down from this ancient nomadic culture's long past. There may be a single, traditional, many-sided, geodesiclike dome hogan along with several other buildings. These may include a traditional modern or western home or a modern trailer home, as well as a summer house. The clustering of these various homes usually represents an extended family living arrangement, which may include an elderly couple and their married daughters along with their husbands and children.

In the traditional family structure, a clan system is at work. Probably from their early contact with the Pueblo people, the Navajo adopted a clan system similar to that of the Pueblo. The Navajo, then, have a matrilineal society with children being born into their mother's clan and property passing through the wife's clan. This usually includes the hogan and the land. It is said that the husband owns only his clothing, jewelry, and saddle. In this system, fellow clan members are called "brother and sister" even though blood relationships may be distant.

The children and women of the traditional family often take care of the sheep from herding and shearing to dyeing, carding, spinning, and finally weaving the blankets. The child-care and household duties belong to the female, while the husband is the manager or trustee of the property and generally works in the fields growing corn, squash, and peaches, as well as tending to the horses and cattle. In the more remote sections of the reservation lacking modern conveniences, the men carry water and haul wood to the hogan.

So the Navajo hogan is at once the place where all aspects of living, including religious ceremonies, take place. But it is not for the dead. The Navajo fear the dead and the hogan may be abandoned if someone dies in it. Often the dying person is removed from the hogan at the last minute so as not to contaminate the home. The Navajo believe that the dead person's ghost may be a threat to the living, for ghosts who appear at night can either chase people or make them ill. So it is best to die outside the hogan and it is best to have someone else bury the dead. It is not even wise to speak the name of the dead person after he is gone. This Navajo aversion to the dead and superstition about death possibly played an important role in the preservation of the abandoned, dead cities of the Anasazi, which the Navajo discovered but never touched in the many years they lived in the San Juan River Basin. The ghosts of those ancient village people protected those great ruins, which were left unmolested for centuries until the arrival of the early white settlers who often plundered and destroyed valuable evidence from those pages out of the past. Moonlight

Navajo camp

requisitioning of Indian sites in the Southwest is still a considerable problem, even with many strict laws on the books to protect against such activity.

Off the highway, in trading stores and towns, the Navajo give other signals of their differentness. Today you still will see beautiful Navajo horses ridden side-saddle by Navajo women in long colorful skirts or by a Navajo rancher in his cowboy garb. More commonly you will see young Navajo boys riding bareback. But most frequently you will see what the Navajo jokingly call the Navajo "convertible," the ubiquitous Navajo pickup that replaced the horse and wagon in the 1950s, but which probably never will replace the horse in the more remote areas.

Modern clothing is replacing traditional dress for the younger children, but middle-aged and older women wear traditional Navajo garb daily. Navajo men wear the adaptable clothes of the rancher, including cowboy boots and hats. This produces interesting comments from white children visiting the area for the first time. Once my son asked, "Dad, why are all the Indians here dressed like cowboys?" But at ceremonies, the same men might wear dark velvet shirts and white trousers with bright satin or rayon scarves tied across their foreheads. As you overhear conversations in the trading posts, gasoline stations, or any of the places you have contact with The People, you will most likely do a double take. For the King's English is not for the Navajo. Over 90 percent of the people speak the Navajo language fluently. For many, English is a second language or often spoken haltingly and with considerable accent.

More subtle differences from the white world also prevail. The Navajo religion and philosophy does not place much emphasis on material goods nor on competition. There is a Navajo saying that a man can't get rich if he looks after his family right. This pretty well sums up the sense of sharing in the Navajo community. Of course, the Navajo like to wear and display fine silver and turquoise jewelry on their persons and it is certainly true that they take pride in the number of sheep or cows they have. But having isn't everything there. Wealth often is counted in terms of sharing or knowing ritual songs or in taking care of one's family. The Navajo feels especially blessed in his land. Land

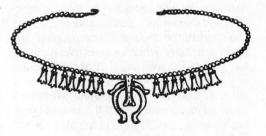

Navajo silver squash blossom necklace

that any travelers might consider as barren and desolate, the Navajo sees as the most beautiful and magnificent land on earth. Much of it is and a lot of that beauty is reflected in the Navajo people.

Yet it is a poor land. The land will only support one out of four Navajo. Overgrazing by sheep has so denuded this marginal land that many Navajo have switched from that traditional source of income to raising cattle. The average annual income of the individual Navajo is considerably below that of the rest of the country. It is said that about 50 percent of the Navajo live below the poverty level. At times, the unemployment rate reaches above 40 percent. Fifty percent of the people have neither electricity nor water in their homes. There are millions of acres of beautiful landscapes, but there is not enough productive land to support the needs of this, the fastest-growing Indian group in America, where the average age of all tribal members is estimated to be between eighteen and twenty.

Although the people are poor, the reservation itself is the richest Indian reservation in America. This land often described by government agents many years ago as "worthless" has turned out to be richer than anyone ever imagined. For years the tribe received millions of dollars from the mining of oil, gas, uranium, and more recently, coal. With the cuts in federal aid programs and the drastic slump in oil and gas prices during the mid-1980s, the financially hard-hit Navajo government began talking about making the reservation a haven for opportunity and private investment by wooing light industry to the reservation or by building a world-class luxury resort to attract more tourist dollars. Income received by the tribe does not go directly to individuals but to the tribal government for the development of roads, dams, schools, and hospitals. The tribe engages in logging and operates profitable sawmills, a utility authority, and the one-hundred-thousand-acre Navajo Agricultural Products Industry, which includes massive irrigation projects. The spending of tribal monies in this way has provided jobs for some of the people. When a Navajo family is employed, one or both family members may work in the sawmill operation at Navajo, New Mexico, or the plants at Fort Defiance or Page, Arizona.

In addition, the reservation hosts several hospitals, health centers, and over one hundred medical clinics. There are many schools on the reservation including two Navajo community colleges at Tsaile and Many Farms, the latter being the first Indian-owned and -operated college for Indians in the United States. Other jobs are provided through the large bureaucracy of the Navajo Nation's governmental center at Window Rock, Arizona. Yet these opportunities do not provide enough jobs for the Navajo. Many drive daily to Flagstaff, Arizona, or Gallup, New Mexico, in search of work. Some live in the city during the week and return to the family hogan on the weekends. Some never return, for the lure of modern amenities and opportunities elsewhere is so great that it tends to threaten the life-style you see today.

But some say that the independent Navajo will never be subsumed by the dominant culture. History bears out this notion. Spanish horses and other alien traditions were adopted by The People, yet they remained resolutely Navajo. There is little of the Spanish in their culture today. At Bosque Redondo, they were programmed to live in settlements and become primarily an agricultural people like the Pueblo Indians. Today they do farm, but they also continue to raise sheep and graze cattle and live as their nomadic ancestors did, in widely separated family groups. Hospitals and clinics are being built, yet many Navajo prefer traditional healing ceremonies. Supermarkets have come to the reservation in the more populated areas, but the trading posts still outnumber them and continue to provide a social center and gathering place for the people who live in remote areas and who are isolated from one another.

The pickup you will see so often on the reservation has not anglicized the Navajo any more than the horse did in the seventeenth century.

Look past the exterior of today's pickup truck on the reservation. On the inside you will notice the braided hair of the father or grandfather and the long calico or sateen, tiered skirts topped by brightly colored velveteen blouses worn by the mother or grandmother. Observe the pickup bed where the kids usually ride. See the sharp bright eyes and quick smiles as they converse in their native tongue. They reflect that the beautiful Navajo tradition lives on. Be aware that the pickup may be headed to a particular spot of land where on a warm summer's evening, a traditional Sing, such as the Enemy Way Dance, may be performed. Although this is a social dance where some of the traditional Navajo courtship rites will unfold, these so-called Squaw Dances may serve a curing function as well. The pickups will come in slowly, pull off the highway, and park. The Dineh gather and build a bonfire as darkness approaches. Not even the pickup has speeded up that wonderful slow, even tempo of Navajo life, which by comparison makes the average tourist look frenetic, if not crazed.

In many ways, the Navajo of today lives in two different worlds. In the same extended-family hogan complex, two cultures often live out their lives under one roof. One Navajo park ranger commented on how he had adapted to the dominant culture. He wrote, "I pushed myself to accept it. I live in two worlds. One is yours and one is my grandmother's. In our hogan, these two cultures live together under one roof."

"There, although I often eat and drink like the white man, I am called by my Navajo name. We still call ourselves the Dineh—the People. Our skin is brown like our mother earth. Our eyes are black like the universe at night. Our smiles are like the stars. And we speak like the voice of the wind."

This testimonial to the difficulty of living in two worlds is amplified over and again in the half-dozen or so very engaging Navajo mystery novels by New Mexican author and journalist, Tony Hillerman (see bibliography). Although each of these absorbing books details different facets of the Navajo lifestyle, they almost all focus on the conflict and pain associated with bridging two disparate cultures in today's complex world. This conflict seems to permeate many aspects of Navajo life and almost all Navajo families are affected.

One elderly Navajo woman whose children had left the reservation was heard to say that when her children and grandchildren returned home, they were afraid of the sheep and thought her hogan was a "dirty place." But the grandmother, who has herded sheep for decades and who still lives inside of and prays to the four sacred mountains, sees beauty wherever she goes. She does not see herself as being disadvantaged, but rather feels rewarded that she can live out her life there. Perhaps when she is alone herding her sheep, under the giant, red monolithic sandstone memorials to time, she may chant a favorite old Navajo song. "I will be happy forever, nothing will hinder me.

"I walk with beauty before me, I walk with beauty behind me, I walk with beauty below me, I walk with beauty above me, I walk with beauty around me, my words will be beautiful. . ."

Monument Valley (Navajo)

Some call it the eighth scenic wonder of the world. Others refer to it as the land of "room enough and time enough." Still others know it as the penultimate in cowboy-Indian western landscape through such movies filmed there as *How the West Was Won, Stagecoach, Billy the Kid, She Wore a Yellow Ribbon, The Searchers, My Darling Clementine, The Trial of Billy Jack,* and many others. But no matter what this area is called, it is impressive.

Resting on the Colorado Plateau at an elevation of more than five thousand feet, Monument Valley is located along the northern border of the 14-million-acre Navajo Nation. It lies in one of the most remote sections of the Navajo reservation, halfway between Mexican Hat, Utah, and Kayenta, Arizona, and fifty miles from the Four Corners Monument.

There, arising from the flat tableland, are over forty named and dozens more unnamed red and orange monolithic sandstone skyscrapers jutting skyward hundreds of feet. Indeed this valley of skyscraping monuments testifies as much as anything to the mighty forces of erosion and time in the Southwest. For there great expanses of Cutler formation rock, especially de Chelly sandstone, capped with Chinle formation rocks like the Shinarump or occasionally with Moenkopi rocks have been carved into giant monuments found nowhere else in the world. And in the southern part of the valley there are strangely shaped outcroppings of igneous rock of molten magma origin, like the magnificent El Capitan or Agathlan peak, an ancient volcanic neck or feeder pipe to a much larger volcanic structure that once rested here. As erosion continues its work, most of the monuments you see here today will be leveled to the ground over time. Until then, this will remain a valley of rare beauty (see Section I, "A Geological Primer to Southeastern Utah").

In 1958, recognizing the unusual scenery there and desiring to protect it from any encroachment that could spoil it, the Navajo Tribal Council established Monument Valley as its first Tribal Park, setting aside approximately 30,000 acres of their more than 14-million-acre reservation for the park. Straddling the Utah and Arizona border, most of the park is on the Arizona side. But which state it is in is a moot point, since all of the Park is on Navajo reservation lands and the visitor center there is staffed by Navajo park rangers and Navajo assistants.

Monument Valley is home to many Navajo whose families have occupied this territory continuously since the 1800s. Not even the diligent raids of Kit Carson rounded up all the Navajo in this far northern section of Navajoland. Consequently, pastoral life and sheepherding went on even during the troubled times of the 1860s. In Monument Valley and on Hoskinnini Mesa to the west, the "Lords of the Earth" have reigned for more than a century.

In addition to the scenic delights Monument Valley offers, a whole brimful of historical and cultural gems await your exploration. After all, over one hundred ruins of the ancient prehistoric Indians, the Anasazi, have been found in the valley area. So there is a rich prehistory there as well. Beauty and desolation seem to go hand in hand on the Colorado Plateau. But the Anasazi knew that although the surface was desolate and dry, there was subsurface moisture that could be used to grow crops. They must have realized the importance of the sand dunes as "insulators" and protectors of that moisture. By the time the Navajo came to this area, the Anasazi had been gone centuries before. They left what you will see today, remnants of buildings containing relics of their inhabitants such as flaked pieces of stone, potsherds, and a host of magnificent petroglyphs. The ruins of these once-thriving communities were left to slumber in the dry desert air.

But the drama of the landscape is somewhat overpowered by the people living there today. Far from the busy Navajo capital of Window Rock, Arizona, the Monument Valley inhabitants retain in their remoteness a staunch traditionalism that would be difficult to match anywhere else on the Navajo reservation. If you can stay in this area for a day or two, you will begin to see some of the people and their way of life unfold before your eyes. You will see Navajo women and their children tending flocks of sheep and goats close to or across the road. You will see numerous hogans and some of their modern counterparts being built alongside them. Some of these Navajo sheep have been inbred for so many generations that they sport strange genetic mutants such as curled, double horns. You will see young Navajo children riding bareback with the agility of West Coast Motocross racers. About dusk you will see Navajo pickups parked along the side of the road where a "Sing" or ceremonial dance is to be performed. You will see brush shelters—called summer or shade houses—erected next to the hogans for the purpose of more comfortable summer living. And you will see Navajo women weaving their excellent rugs in intricate geometric designs. In many ways, Monument Valley epitomizes what you will see in the rest of Section II. Scenery? Yes. But more than that, a people, a culture whose coexistence with the harsh land there is more dramatic than the land itself, making the valley a wonder even without its scenic virtues.

The Navajo Tribal Park visitor center levies a fee for each car, but sometimes there is not anyone to collect it. The center contains a geological exhibit, and occasionally some crafts made in the area are on sale. A good picnic area and a nice campground are adjacent to the center. But primarily the center serves as a panoramic viewing spot of the valley's monuments and as an access point to the seventeen-mile valley loop road that allows as good a view as you can get from your private car.

This road is rutted badly near the visitor center but improves as you go along. If the weather is clear and the road dry, you should have no problem negotiating it as long as you drive slowly. On the loop drive be certain to take the fifteen-minute round-trip walk from the North Window around the tip of Cly Butte, which opens up some magnificent views. This sight and others are detailed in the Monument Valley booklet available for sale at the visitor center. You will also be able to see and, in some instances, for a small fee enter a hogan and observe a weaving demonstration. Allow at least three hours for the loop trip.

This leads me to point out that one way to see the valley is via a four-wheel-drive vehicle. You can use your own or one hired out with a guide for a half-day or day tour. A busy and reliable tour operator can be found at Goulding's Ranch, five miles away, which also offers the only accommodations and food in the immediate area. Tours can also be arranged at the visitor center or from Kayenta, twenty-five miles to the south, and from Mexican Hat to the north (see "Tours" at the end of this section). The tours are well worth the cost for they allow you, in some comfort, to see the landscapes and many monuments that cannot be viewed from the loop roads and to observe more closely how the Navajo live in their rural camps in the high desert miles from any cities or roads. In this area you may also visit the interesting old Oljato Trading Post by following the paved road nine miles further past Goulding's Ranch. For inquiries about Monument Valley, write to the Tribal Park Headquarters, Box 93, Monument Valley, Utah 84536. Telephone: 1-801-727-3287.

Monument Valley: A Narrative Account

This morning as I pull back the drapes in front of the picture window of our motel room here at Goulding's Ranch, I see the faint shadow of the monuments to the east. I dress hurriedly to get outside so I will be ready to take some pictures when the light is just right. The air is cool against my face as I climb the talus slope below the high red rock cliffs just behind our room. I find a huge, flat-topped sandstone boulder, plop myself down on it, and wait for the prime moment. The silence out here this morning is deafening.

As I sit waiting, I think about the twentieth-century frontiersmen who first settled here. Like Lurt Knee at Capitol Reef, Harry Goulding, who died in 1981, is somewhat of a legend in these parts. He came here in the early 1920s. Shortly after that, the Paiutes were moved out of this region. The Navajo were expanding their reservation then and wanted this area. The state of Utah put 640 acres or one section of land up for sale. Harry Goulding bought it for two dollars an acre. Below a towering six-hundred-foot red rock escarpment, Harry Goulding pitched a tent and settled in. In a few years he built the stone house that is now the lodge's lobby and craft store, and it was here that he started a lodge and a trading business. For awhile he even traded goods out of the back of a horse-drawn wagon. He was known as an honest trader among the Navajo, who called him "Long Sheep."

Now there is enough light to see the long, black asphalt road, looking for all the world like a piece of decorative ribbon or a snake twisting its way to the east. With increasing light I can make out Sentinel Mesa and further north, Big Indian,

Castle Butte, Bear and Rabbit, Stagecoach, King on his Throne, and Brigham's Tomb, and most northerly, Eagle Rock. I snap several pictures. A slight breeze comes up and as the sun begins to ascend behind the monuments, the light changes dramatically, shifting colors over this broad panorama of the high desert and its rock projections.

The sun is up. The light is bright and when I feel the sun's rays, already warm, I realize we must prepare for another typical July day with temperatures in the nineties. By now my family is up. The breakfast gong breaks the silence at the old ranch house built many years ago for the movie set of *She Wore A Yellow Ribbon*, which serves as the dining room here at Goulding's. We eat a hearty western breakfast. Sitting near our table are two Belgian women and a family from France. Around the adjacent table this morning is part of a tour group from Germany. The atmosphere is warm and convivial. There is eager anticipation of the day's activities. We are going on a half-day jeep tour deep into the valley. Others are going to a little gem of a place called Mystery Valley, an area particularly rich in prehistoric ruins.

We meet our guide for the day and the couple who will accompany our family of four in the air-conditioned four-wheel-drive vehicle. We drive five miles over to the visitor center, where we spend some time looking at a geological exhibit

Monument Valley

before heading into the valley. As we begin the trip, we are immediately glad that we did not attempt to negotiate the park roads in our private vehicle. The road is badly rutted in places and, following yesterday's heavy rains, like a quagmire in some spots, so occasionally we divert from the road into the surrounding desert in order to make our way.

Shortly we reach a splendid area of high buttes and numerous monuments where many of John Huston's movies were made. There can be no doubt that this is the ultimate in "western scenery." Now we see a young Navajo boy riding bareback at a fast clip alongside the road. His pony is chasing along behind. Our driver hails him. He speaks Navajo and broken English. We ask him if we can take a picture. He agrees. We tip him, for our driver tells us that he will not allow his picture to be taken without a fee.

Now we seem to be in a forest of monuments not visible from the lodge. Rising four hundred feet from the desert floor is a spire hardly wider than

our vehicle that is called the Totem Pole. It is flanked by the Yei-Bi-Chei formation which resembles a group of Navajo dancers. Soon, we round a bend and come to a Navajo encampment. An extended family lives here. We stop and ask if we can enter one of the hogans. The response is friendly. A young Navajo girl about twelve or thirteen takes us into the hogan, where an upright loom is set up and an intricate tightly woven Navajo rug is in progress. It's cool inside the hogan. With the door open, there is barely enough light to work by in this windowless structure. A sheepskin covers the hard-packed dirt floor where the weaver sits. As our eyes adjust to the darkness and we look around, the efficiency of the hogan architecture is evident immediately. Built somewhat like a geodesic dome, there are no center supports or joists, so all of the inside surface is usable. The hogan is noticeably cooler this morning than it will be this afternoon when the sun heats up the desert outside.

From here, we head out cross country. We are

Navajo boy, horse, and pony

Navajo weaver

dicates that he, too, likes to savor the pleasant aroma of juniper.

More cross country. The way is very rough and bumpy now. We hold on to anything solid in the vehicle to keep from smashing each other. Then we arrive at the base of an enormous rock outcropping. A fantastic natural window high in its wall opens to the blue sky above. A short distance from here we see an incredible number of petroglyphs carved through the desert varnish into the cliff wall. We stop and explore this area carefully. The sand under our feet yields potsherds from Anasazi times and pieces of chert that obviously have been "worked" and shaped by the former residents of this area. But the petroglyphs capture the day. With the sun to our back, good photographs are possible. I click away, using almost a roll of film as I move along the cliff wall to a variety of figures resembling goats, sheep, and turkeys and to stick figures of people as well as a host of other designs.

bounced and jostled around as we traverse this rough terrain. Shortly we come to another site where a large hogan is being constructed. A young man and his friend are doing the work. Meanwhile his family is living in a recently built brush shelter for the summer, awaiting completion of the hogan. The aroma of the newly cut and peeled juniper wood is heavenly and we ask if we may take a small chip. The gracious owner indicates "yes" with a broad smile and gives us a handful. He is pleased that we truly like what he is doing and in-

It is nearing noon, our time is running out, and it is very hot. The air-conditioned vehicle feels good as we head across country along a rough trail down a dry creek bed. We seem to feel every boulder the truck laboriously negotiates. Along the way we stop at some incredible pink sand dunes, while our children climb partway up them and

Hogan under construction

Anasazi petroglyphs

slide down. Sweaty and dusty, we arrive back at the ranch in time for lunch. We feel we have seen some magnificent scenery, but we are most pleased that we have been able to see close up how the Navajo live. With this introduction to Navajo life, we feel we will more thoroughly enjoy the rest of our visit to Navajoland.

Navajo National Monument: Betatakin

From Goulding's Lodge in Monument Valley, drive south along paved U.S. Highway 163, twenty-five miles to Kayenta, Arizona. Along the road you will see several interesting rock formations. One of them, on your left nearer Kayenta, is a towering formation of darker volcanic rock, Agathlan Peak or El Capitan, which rises to 7,100 feet elevation. The Navajo call this structure "Much Wool," derived from the times when The People scraped deer and sheep hides on the rough rocks at the peak's base, leaving an accumulation of hair or wool there. According to Navajo legend, this is where the Two Came for Water Clan met up with the Western Water Clans, before journeying eastward. Hoskinnini Mesa looms to the west. Watch for sheep, goats, and cows along this somewhat narrow up-and-down road. If it is raining, do not negotiate this road until the rain subsides, for parts of the road, about halfway between Kayenta and Goulding's Junction, are subject to flooding. The signs which indicate this are to be heeded.

Kayenta, which in Navajo means "Spraying Water," is a sprawling town of over a thousand inhabitants. In a wide-open location, where the wind seems to blow much of the time, this Navajo frontier town seems about as remote as any place in the United States. Yet with its Navajo Boarding School and medical clinic, it is a useful and necessary shopping and trade center for this northwestern corner of the reservation. In addition it serves as a rest stop and transportation hub for the many trucks along U.S. Highway 160, as they travel in and out of Arizona. Kayenta's pattern of sprawling growth makes it look larger than it actually is. Most of the growth has been on the north side, consisting of residences and modern buildings that blend reasonably well into the high desert landscape. For many years there have been several motels that also offer food service. But with the recent development of the modern H'indee shopping center along the highway, with its pizza parlor, small shops, and large supermarket, trav-

Agathlan Peak

elers are more apt to stop in Kayenta to shop and soak up some aspects of contemporary Navajo living. While there, you can browse in one of the Indian arts and crafts outlets including Black Mesa Indian Arts and Crafts store, which is located just across the road from the big shopping center and next to the convenience store on the east side of U.S. Highway 163.

From Kayenta, head southwest on U.S. Highway 160, a good paved, all-weather road. Look for Navajo sheepherders along this road. This is pretty country as the road climbs through a pygmy forest of piñon pine and juniper to Marsh Pass (elevation 6,750 feet). Approximately eleven miles south of Kayenta you will notice Tsegi Trading Post, the first of several Navajo trading posts you will see along this stretch of road to Tuba City.

The canyons to your right are part of the Tsegi Canyon system. Tsegi Canyon consists of a large group of finger or dead-end canyons formed in the rock of Skeleton Mesa, which lies just east of Navajo Mountain. The small canyon that holds Betatakin Ruin to the south feeds into this canyon system. On your left, you are traveling alongside the northern portion of the Black Mesa. Coal is being mined there now. About sixty miles south, the Hopi villages hug this mesa's high cliff walls as it abruptly ends at the desert's edge. This road is a bit windy and twisty and large trucks often ply their way between Kayenta and Tuba City on the way to Flagstaff, so the going can be slow.

About nineteen miles south of Kayenta, you will come to a sign and junction road on the right leading to Navajo National Monument. Across U.S. Highway 160 from the junction is Black Mesa Trading Post, gas station, and fast-food center. Now head west on Arizona Highway 564, nine paved miles through another pygmy forest of juniper and piñon pine. At the end of the paved road, elevation 7,268 feet, are a parking lot and monument visitor center. You are now several thousand feet above the elevation of Monument Valley. Your body will make you aware of the difference.

I have seen many prehistoric dwellings in the Southwest, but the two that have inspired me the most are this one at Betatakin and Lowry Pueblo Ruins at Pleasant View, Colorado. There may be better ruins, larger ruins, or more intact ruins, but the dramatic site of Betatakin, coupled with its relative inaccessibility and solitude and its direct relationship to the Hopi villages to the south, make it one of the major attractions in the Southwest. Try to plan your schedule to include the four hours necessary for a Betatakin tour down into the canyon. The monument is on Mountain Daylight Savings Time in the summer. Navajo National Monument is also the departure point for Keet Seel, Arizona's largest and best-preserved ruin with 160 rooms. Only twenty-five hikers and fifteen horses and riders are allowed entry permits each day for this sixteen-mile round-trip hike or horseback trip. Hikers are advised to make this a two-day trip. Advance reservations are required for both hikers and horseback riders. During peak season, reservations should be made up to two months before the planned trip. All canyon trails are closed after the first snowfall and remain closed until all snow melts in the spring. However, the visitor center and canyon overlook trail are open all year. For updated information, write Superintendent, Navajo National Monument, National Park Service, HC63, Box 3, Tonalea, Arizona 86044. Telephone: 1-602-672-2366.

Betatakin: A Narrative Account

After a filling, ranch-style breakfast at Goulding's this morning, we left the ranch about 8:45 A.M. and arrived here at the Navajo National Monument visitor center by 10:00. Yesterday we called from Goulding's to learn the exact time of the Betatakin tours since tour times and frequency may vary from year to year. We decided to aim for the midday tour, rather than early morning or afternoon tour. We were told that only twenty-four people would be allowed on the tour, so we decided to show up about an hour or two early. The air is bracing this morning at this altitude. The small, but well-run visitor center is a delight. It serves as a tour headquarters and museum for the three ruin sites, Betatakin, Keet Seel, and Inscription House. The latter is closed for stabilization purposes. Most people come here to take the Betatakin tour. But I notice a few people with advance reservations have come to hike the Keet Seel trail.

We register for the next Betatakin tour (no ad-

Betatakin Ruins

vance reservations accepted) and, while waiting, view the excellent displays in the center. The exhibit of Kayenta pottery is one of the best I have ever seen with some incredibly large pieces as well as some exquisite, smaller, polychrome pieces. The display reveals Anasazi life, the Anasazi migration, and summarizes the evidence that links the Betatakin people to the Hopi. It is well done and instructive. While waiting we also make some purchases at the excellent Navajo craft shop.

I learn from the museum exhibit material that the six hundred acres comprising this monument are on the Navajo reservation. The monument is named "Navajo" National Monument, but it is a United States government enterprise rather than a Navajo tribal enterprise. It was established as a national monument in 1909. The ruin we are to see today has nothing to do with the Navajo. It belonged to a people whose descendants are often at odds with the Navajo, the Hopi. The exhibits here in the visitor center are about the ancestors of the Hopi, but it is the Navajo who have the craft concession here. The name for this ancient Hopi-related ruin is "Betatakin" which is a Navajo word meaning "Ledge House." The Hopi refer to the ancient dwellings in this area as "Kawestima" or North Village.

Many of the rangers here are white, but those who are not are Navajo. Fifty miles south of here are today's Hopi villages surrounded by and in constant conflict over land disputes with their age-old adversaries, the Navajo. Here Navajo rangers help protect Hopi history. All very confusing, I think, for first-time visitors. I vow that if I ever write a book about this area, I'll try to set the record straight. Although this part of the United States is referred to as "Indian Country," there are two very distinct Indian groups here. Understanding that makes many things clearer (see Introduction).

With a little time left before the tour, we scurry along a well-graded viewpoint trail, the Sandal Trail, one mile round-trip, to view Betatakin Ruin from the rim. From this vantage point, it looks very small in the distance and we are thankful we have our binoculars with us.

Aspen leaves

Douglas fir

At the appointed hour, our ranger guide gathers us together and informs us that we are about to embark on a 2.5-mile round-trip, four-hour tour. Sounds easy. But she goes on to say that we will be descending seven hundred feet into the canyon in less than a mile. That means an elevation gain of similar proportions on the way back out. A bus will take us to the trailhead (only a few minutes away), where we will begin the steep descent into the canyon. People with heart disease and physical problems that might be aggravated by this much exercise at this elevation (over seven thousand feet) are urged to stay on the rim.

We begin the descent. We are walking down into one of the finger canyons of the Tsegi Canyon system, part of the same canyon we saw at Marsh Pass this morning. In the distance looms Navajo Mountain, a sacred mountain and the highest point on the Navajo reservation. From this vantage point the canyon looks long and narrow as it disappears on the horizon. Looking into the canyon bottom, we observe the color of green I have come to associate with deciduous trees that receive ample water—a vibrant chartreuse green. Indeed, as we near the bottom, I can make out aspen, oak, and elder. Somehow, it seems strange to see aspen in the canyon when none exist anywhere on the rim. Indeed we are going from a high, dry, pygmy forest desert environment down into a moist valley environment, which contains Douglas firs (the tree that grows prolifically on the moist Northwest Coast of the United States), and horsetail, that ancient fernlike plant found anywhere in the West where there is a great deal of moisture.

Horsetails

We saw magpies and bluebirds near the road this morning, and already we have observed them and several ravens from the trail. Near the top of the canyon walls, we note the cross-bedded Navajo sandstone and beneath it we see the purple-red of the Kayenta strata of rock. Deep in the canyons, we are told that Wingate sandstone can be seen (see Section I, "A Geological Primer to Southeastern Utah"). We are also told that the Navajo sandstone is permeable, so that rain water goes down through it until it hits the denser Kayenta stone. There the water stops its vertical descent and begins to seep horizontally on top of the Kayenta, until it reaches cliff faces or cliff bottoms where it either emerges on the surface as seeps or springs or continues underground.

Finally, when we reach the bottom of the steep trail, we sit and rest in the cool shade of the canyon forest. The ranger tells us about the ruin. This was a typical village of the Kayenta Pueblo Anasazi, who lived here about A.D. 1260. They built and abandoned the village before 1300. Now, as we walk along, we top a small rise and from here can see the alcove for the first time. This naturally formed, erosion-carved alcove faces southeast. It is of magnificent proportions. It was probably right about this spot where John Wetherill, a Kayenta rancher and trader and younger brother of Mesa Verde's "discoverer," and Bryan Cummings, an anthropologist, acting on a tip from a Navajo friend, rode on horseback up this long finger canyon in 1909 and saw what we are seeing right now. The sight is overwhelming. The roof of the alcove is five hundred feet above the floor of the cave. Walking a little further, we now catch a glimpse of many boxlike apartments, some several stories high and at different levels in this gaping aperture in the sandstone. There is silence as our group of twenty stands, transfixed. None of us expected to see anything quite this dramatic. The canyon is still. Only a gentle breeze sets the aspens quaking.

I wonder how they produced a small city deep down in this remote canyon. Not until this moment had it really struck me how innovative and hardworking the Anasazi must have been to produce this edifice. I remember something I read about the Hopi being hardworking and patient. We round the bend and, on an ascending path, enter the village. Most of the village is very much intact after these seven hundred years. There are six tiers of rooms and a balcony of rooms high and to the back of the cave. We are told that some of the original 135 rooms were destroyed by a rock fall. At one time, 125 inhabitants occupied this alcove. They farmed the narrow strip of land just below the village. We see a rectangular kiva similar to the ones in the Hopi villages. The tall mortar-and-stone tower was probably a granary for storing corn and other staples. We marvel at the tight construction, even though these people were not known to produce the finest of the Anasazi buildings.

In the village, I look up and see the high protective cliff roof. Now when the midday summer sun is the hottest, we are in a pocket of shade under this huge alcove umbrella. But in this region of cold winters, when the low winter sun shines, this alcove would catch most of those warming rays and no doubt the stone would retain some of the heat. We shout and hear our reverberating echoes. One hundred twenty-five noisy Anasazi would have filled this empty alcove with a great vibrancy of sound and life. We explore for another thirty minutes or so. We touch large hand-hewn timbers whose concentric rings reveal that they were probably living trees here in this canyon sometime around A.D. 1100. We see soot from cooking fires that stained the apartment walls over seven hundred years ago. We are gratified that there are only twenty of us down here rather than the masses who go tramping through some of the better-known ruins.

Now we begin the hard ascent back up the steep trail equivalent to climbing the stairs of a seventy-story building. We take our time and enjoy the pleasant surroundings, chatting about our newly found discoveries. At the top, we spread a picnic lunch in the shade near the visitor center. We refresh ourselves and push on to the Hopi mesas. We want to see and feel the relationship between the Hopi ancestors here at Betatakin and today's Hopi people. We are spanning the gulf of hundreds of years today in just a few short hours.

Navajo Trading Post Row and Tuba City

From Navajo National Monument, return nine miles to U.S. Highway 160, turn south. Just across the highway are a gas station and several

places to find cold refreshment. The road now follows Klethla Valley, once known as "trading post row" of western Navajoland. Along the road you will see ample evidence of the coal mining going on at Black Mesa. Some of the Hopi are concerned that the amount of water it takes to produce and transport the coal will lower the water table of Black Mesa and cause a reduction in their farm production. This coal is being shipped by rail on the tracks which parallel the highway to fire generators at the Navajo Power Plant, Page, Arizona, which produces electrical power for distant sites in Arizona and California.

Because this is one of the most remote sections of the reservation, you may see Navajo women in their colorful blouses and long, flowing skirts herding sheep on either side of the road. From now on you may begin to experience the feeling of being in a country with people whose customs are very different. A sense of timelessness begins to set in, too, when you realize that you will be in one time zone in Monument Valley, Mountain Daylight Savings Time, and that you will be in still another zone by the time you reach the Hopi mesas, where they are on Mountain Standard Time.

In about twelve miles you will pass the junction to Page, Arizona. In approximately twenty

The Old Red Lake Trading Post, Tonalea

Tuba Trading Post

miles look for the Cow Springs Trading Post on the left-hand side of the road. Eight miles farther down the highway from Cow Springs are two large outcroppings of cross-bedded Entrada sandstone resembling elephant's feet.

Just one mile beyond Elephant's Feet on the left-hand side of the road is the old Red Lake Trading Post. The old trading post building has been abandoned, and the Red Lake Trading Post operates out of the modern building about one-quarter mile southwest of the old site along U.S. Highway 160. It is now called Tonalea General Store. Trading posts are an integral part of Navajo life so stop either here or at the historic Tuba Trading Post in Tuba City. Many trading posts operate nowadays out of buildings such as this one that resemble those found in large urban shopping centers. Yet, if you spend a little time in these modern grocery store posts, you will find they contain not only a wide range of goods similar to those found in your own local stores, but unique items that have been part of the trading post scene for over a hundred years. There may be saddle blankets, galvanized buckets, large bolts of velveteen cloth, brown sugar candies, an extensive Indian arts and crafts sales area, and a host of other items unique to the area. The name of the post office at Red Lake is "Tonalea," which means in Navajo, "where water comes together." The old trading post was named for the small silted lake to the north of it. Established in 1881, this trading post had several trader-owners before being permanently established at this exact site in 1891 by the Babbitt Bros. Trading Co. of Flagstaff, Arizona. They still own the Red Lake post's successor, the Tonalea General Store, as well as the Tuba Trading

Post. Zane Grey often visited the old Red Lake Post, and it is the setting for the first chapter of his book, *Rainbow Trail,* published in 1915.

Back on the highway notice the San Francisco peaks beginning to loom up to your left as you drive the thirteen miles to Tuba City, population five thousand, elevation 4,936 feet, where it's always very hot in the summer afternoon sun. But this vibrant and bustling center of western Navajoland, with its crowds of Navajo and their pickups, is a good place to people watch without being intrusive or feeling too self-conscious. So stop awhile. You will see women in long ankle-length skirts with bright blouses and Navajo men in western garb with hair braided down their backs, all going about their daily business.

Tuba City, once occupied by Hopi people, was named for the Hopi leader, Chief Tuvi, whose name was somehow changed into Tuba by early-day Washington bureaucrats. In fact the Hopi village, Moenkopi, lies just a few hundred feet east of the highway that bounds Tuba City on the east. The Navajo name for the town is "zigzagging water" because of the springs found in the area. Tuba City is the capital of western Navajoland and has a number of Navajo tribal services, including the always busy Navajo Community Center and a tribal law and order agency. It is also home to the United States Public Health Service Indian Hospital. There are several large grocery stores and trading posts there, as well as a good motel and several cafés. If you arrive there around lunchtime, be sure to stop at the small Tuba City Truck Stop Café ("Let's Eat," the sign says) on the east side of U.S. Highway 160 near the junction of Arizona Highway 264, also known as Navajo Highway 3.

From the café's parking lot, you look east over to the Hopi village of Moenkopi, just a few yards away. The café's specialty is the Navajo taco. Partake of one of these special tacos built atop Navajo fry bread and you will know why this is one of the best eating establishments west of Window Rock.

Now with a taco or cold drink in hand, drive out of the glaring sun west into Tuba City proper to the shaded main street that runs alongside the historic Tuba Trading Post, about one mile west of Arizona Highway 160. This large, octagonal-shaped trading post building houses one of the most interesting posts on the reservation. It is an historic trading establishment, which has been on this site for over one hundred years. Inside, be sure to focus on the center of the room, where you will find a large number of high-quality, handwoven Navajo rugs, including saddle and double saddle blankets. And often, excellent, well-crafted pieces of Navajo pottery and jewelry are available. Behind the trading post is the modern, recently constructed Tuba City Motel and Pancho's Family Restaurant, which put Tuba City on the map as a place to stay for a few days while touring the area. Be certain to observe the strictly enforced 15-mile-per-hour speed limit in sections of the town.

As you drive back to the highway, you will pass Monongya's Jewelry on the southwest corner of the intersection of U.S. Highway 160 and Arizona Highway 264. Turn right onto U.S. Highway 160 and drive south for approximately five miles, where you will see the unpaved road to Moenave taking off to the right or north of the highway. In just over one-eighth mile this road will take you alongside a set of dinosaur tracks, compliments of the Pleistocene Age. Seventy-five miles to the south and west of Tuba City is the Grand Canyon Village. Flagstaff is approximately eighty miles to the south of Tuba City. If you are headed to either destination, you might want to make a stop at the busy, restored Cameron Trading Post, twenty-six miles south of Tuba City. Besides having a nice selection of regional Indian arts and crafts and a gallery section devoted to both historic and contemporary Indian art, there are forty-five updated motel rooms, a lovely garden area, and a welcome restaurant for travelers and hungry locals.

The Hopi World

High atop the Colorado Plateau in northern Arizona, another gigantic tableland is superimposed. It is called the Black Mesa. From its origin in northern Arizona, it extends over sixty miles to the south through much of Navajoland. At its southern end, the mesa divides, like fingers on a hand, into several phalanges that extend high above the desert. At their tips where they abruptly end, the mesa cliffs drop 600 feet to the valley below. There, the Hopi villages lie, many clinging to the edges of this rocky escarpment over 6,200 feet above sea level. The mesa tops, the terraces along the steep mesa walls, and the interconnecting desert between the three mesas comprise the small, but significant Hopi reservation. Many of the villages are as isolated from one another as they are from the rest of the modern world in this remote region of Arizona.

From these mesa-top villages, you can look out over thousands of square miles of brown and multicolored painted desert, punctuated with mountains, mesas, and buttes rising on the horizon. From these high promontories, at night, the stars are the biggest and the brightest you will ever see, as though the mesas are stepping-stones to the heavens. For the first time visitor who is willing to spend enough time to absorb some of the aura, this is heady stuff. There is a sense of mystery and eternity among these rocky, dry mesa tops that are completely exposed to the full force of the elements.

What you feel may only be reflecting what the Hopi have known for almost nine hundred years. In Hopi mythology, this is the Center of the Universe, Tuuwanasavi. This is the center of the vibrations of the world. This is the Sacred Circle, a holy place in tune with the Hopi universe. From here all the landmarks of the Hopi religious world are in full view. From the twin shafts of sacred Corn Rock close at hand to the mighty San Francisco Peaks looming in the distance over eighty miles away, where the kachinas live out their lives, you will view much that is sacred to the Hopi. To the southeast, an extended ridge arises containing

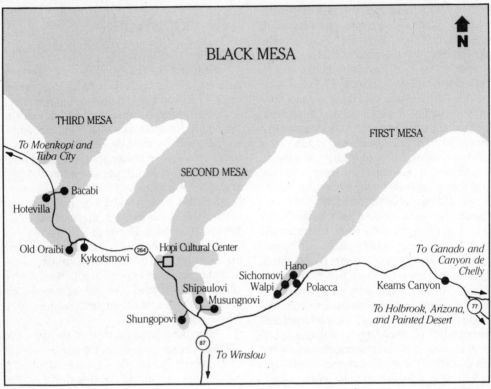

Hopi Villages

numerous small buttes and mesas (see White Cone on your map), giving the appearance of a notched calendar stick.

This is the Hopi calendar that only the village chiefs or appointed "sun watchers" are trusted to read. They watch this ridge carefully as the sun moves along it, as their ancestors have for generations before them. Especially, they watch it in December as the sun moves from notch to notch, north to south, looking for the day when the sun reaches a particular spot along the ridge, reverses its direction, and begins heading north again, the harbinger of longer and warmer days. When the sun reaches a certain notch, a prayer is sung and the planting season begins. When it reaches still other notches, it signals the beginning of certain age-old ritual ceremonies and dances. Also in the distance are two curved buttes, The Giant's Chair and Montezuma's Chair. Sometimes they appear as one in the distance, like a giant pair of horns or wings. Horns like these are thought to transmit

power from the heavens to the earth. At sites like these and others to the north, young Hopi men capture symbols of some of that power when they catch golden eagles for ceremonial purposes and bring them back to their rooftops and kivas.

If you drive through without stopping in this area on a hot summer's day, you will think you have not missed anything. All you will see is a certain drabness of brown rocks giving way to arid brown desert. Even Maasaw, the Hopi deity of life, death, and fire who led the Hopi into this world and who is their guardian, recognized that. In a Hopi legend, he is quoted as saying: "My land is a wasteland. Look at it. There is nothing attractive. It is harsh land. However, if you are willing to live my way of life, you may stay here. Even though it is harsh land, beneath it are riches. For that reason do not ever allow it to pass into anyone else's hand." Maasaw also prophesied that there the Hopi would "live in poverty but in peace." After wandering in the four directions, it was prophesied

Hopi kachina dolls

that the Hopi clans would meet up eventually and settle on the mesas. So it is there that the Hopi took a stand to live out their lives in this, the Fourth World, to await Purification Day and entry into the Fifth World.

Maasaw was right. Beneath the land, riches have been discovered. Coal and uranium are now mined from the Black Mesa. But the real resources there are the Hopi people, who have in the fastness of their subterranean kivas learned how to use the land and the water wisely. Ironically, this seemingly dry land has sustained thousands of people for hundreds of years. For the early Hopi, the Hisatsinom, discovered that water at this southern end of the Black Mesa comes out in the form of hidden seeps and springs along the mesa edges and below the mesas.

The Black Mesa serves as a giant subterranean water reservoir, collecting rainwater from its extensive surface. The water filters through the permeable sandstone and then courses between the rock strata to the Hopi mesas, where it waters the small plots of farmland. Below the mesa, sand dunes have piled up against the mesa walls. These dunes act as an insulating blanket to help retain the water that seeps from the bottom of the mesa. In these sandy areas, the early Hisatsinom discovered that eight or ten inches below the very dry-appearing surface was a layer of moisture ready to be tapped for agricultural pur-

poses. When they found that corn, beans, and squash grew well there, they discovered a sustaining richness that far exceeds the value of any minerals being mined today.

But the dramatic setting of the Hopi villages is only one of the rewards awaiting the traveler. The other rewards are wrapped up in the most valuable resource there, the Hopi People, their history, culture, and religion.

By the time you get to the Hopi mesas, the colorful landscapes of Navajoland have faded to a dull, drab beige and brown. Jumbled heaps of rock make the land seem even more desolate. The people also seem less colorful. Simple, plain cotton dresses replace the long, colorful dramatic dress of the Navajo women. Khaki and polyester slacks replace the Navajo cowboy dress. A cotton scarf may be tied around the forehead, but there is no dramatic display of clothing, silver jewelry, or other adornments. But just as these dry mesas paradoxically give water from deep springs, the Hopi people project a richness that cannot easily be verbalized. The drama is so underplayed there, that when it hits you, it is all the more powerful.

Deep in the kivas and deep in the hearts and spirits of the Hopi are some of the most colorful and dramatically overpowering scenes I have ever witnessed. How can it be, I ask myself, that a man in simple, everyday modern dress, who by western and even Hopi standards holds a menial job, can undergo such a complete transformation that after only a few hours in the kiva, he becomes a figure of regal beauty and awesome power? As he ascends from the kiva to perform an intricate, ancient, complex dance, he commands the respect of all. For in Hopiland, respect is often tied to the Hopi way rather than to success in the modern world.

The Hopi way probably will never be completely known or understood by an outsider. But from time to time, the outsider catches a glimpse of what it is. The Hopi way is really a life pathway with several divergent branches. Each branch or byway demands some kind of special obligation or responsibility from the people. The various branches of the Hopi way are reflected in the organization of the Hopi culture and villages. Through the matrilineal clan system, the Hopi have certain kinship duties, responsibilities, and loyalties. Through the ceremonial societies and the religious leaders, the Hopi have certain responsibilities toward the religious and ceremonial life of the village, the Hopi community as a whole, and to mankind in general. To his village he has certain secular responsibilities symbolized through the kikmongwi, the hereditary village father or chief, who in his autonomy only gives way to certain revered religious leaders regarding ceremonial functions. The Hopi also has certain social responsibilities to those in and beyond his own village. In addition, he has certain agricultural or farming responsibilities to the family farm plots that have been handed down for generations on his mother's side of the family.

In the absence of a written language, these highly structured and complex nine-hundred-year-old responsibilities and traditions have been passed down through personal example, oral traditions, and in many ceremonies and rituals. These responsibilities are for a lifetime and with them go daily tasks to be fulfilled. Discharging one's responsibilities and performing one's immediate tasks are most important to living the Hopi way. A Hopi woman told me several years ago that she and her family could not go on vacation that summer because her husband and sons had major roles in the ceremonial dances. This means the family had to provide money for refurbishing costumes and to purchase the many gifts to be given out by the clowns to the village people

and its visitors. In addition, many man-hours are required in the kiva to learn and practice to perfection the very precise and intricate nine-centuries-old choreography that you may see performed in the village. Many dances reflect weeks spent in the kiva making ceremonial preparations. Many other hours are spent there patiently refurbishing the ceremonial masks and costumes. It has been said that a traditional Hopi may spend most of his life in preparation for his ceremonial and other duties.

The rigors of the Hopi way begin early when a child is born into his or her mother's clan. Whether it is the Corn, Bean, Badger, Water or any one of thirty or forty other clans, the Hopi child inherits the ceremonial and community responsibilities that were given to each clan years ago in exchange for the farmland each clan received. It is the duty of the mother's relations, especially her brother, to teach these duties to the child. As he grows up in the village, the child learns another set of obligations relating to village life and he gains respect for the powerful village father or chief, the hereditary kikmongwi.

It is said that a Hopi knows about music and dance from birth. Well he might, for almost from the very beginning of life, he is exposed to a dazzling array of dances and ceremonies in the village plaza each year. During these times, especially during the kachina ceremonies, more responsibilities are taught. Kachina dancers give kachina dolls to infants of both sexes and later to the female children. The dolls, carved from cottonwood roots, and then painted and clothed are not only beautiful to look at and fun to play with but they also serve an educational purpose. They introduce the young Hopi child to the power and sacredness of the kachina spirits by teaching her about the costumes, masks, and other details of these deities. At other times, the dolls are occasionally given to older females as fertility symbols.

Between the ages of six and ten, both boys and girls are initiated into the kachina cult. At this time they learn the obligations of the kiva. They acquire a ceremonial father or mother who have been picked by the child's parents and who is from a different clan. The ceremonial parent has the responsibility of preparing the child for the rites of passage from childhood to adulthood. As the child reaches adulthood, he or she will be initiated into a priesthood or ceremonial society such as Wuwtsim for men or Maraw for women, all a part of the Hopi spiritual world.

In addition to these social, religious, and ceremonial responsibilities, the Hopi child, especially the male, has been learning right along from his father the responsibilities of planting, nurturing, and harvesting good crops. If the term "Hopi" means anything to me, it means above all a people who excel in dry land farming. So it is no accident that a Hopi father will teach his son about corn, soil, water, and prayers for rain and good crops. Farming not only provides staples for the table, but it also provides products that are essential to the religious and ceremonial life of the Hopi.

The Hopi farmers raise a variety of products, but the one you will see most frequently in the fields is corn. Corn is not just a dietary staple there, it is an integral part of Hopi ritual and ceremonial life. Traditionally, cornmeal, laboriously handground from ears raised on nearby small farm plots, is a symbol of fertility and friendship and plays an important role in the marriage ceremony. Symbolically the Hopi speak of corn as "Corn Mother." At birth, an ear of corn is given to the newborn baby and corn pollen is used in christenings. Later the same child receives another ear at the time of initiation. In ritual dances, cornmeal may be used as body make-up while corn stalks and husks may be used in making the "paaho" or plumed prayer stick which is used in a variety of ceremonies.

Hopi cornfields are not like the ones in Iowa. And the corn is not the same either. A Hopi cornfield may be planted in very sandy soil and may only be from one-half to ten acres in size. Even today, tractors are used only sparingly to prepare the ground. Most of the planting is done by hand as the ancient Hopi did it centuries ago. The traditional planting stick is made from a sturdy stick cut from one of the high desert shrubs and whittled to a wedge-shaped point on one end. Sometimes a short piece of pipe or metal is flattened at one end for the same purpose. The two yearly plantings are done by the boys and men on land belonging to the mother's clan, passed down through the female lineage for generations. The corn is planted eight inches or more deep in areas where the soil is subirrigated and has good capacity to retain water

and where it will receive good surface run-off. Prayers are said after the planting and ceremonies are performed to insure a good harvest. The patient Hopi farmer tends his corn diligently, with great care. More prayers are said to ward off too early or too late frosts, summer floods, drought, wind- and sandstorms.

Hopi corn is short and stout and comes in a variety of colors including yellow, red, white, and blue. These colors coincide with the Hopi symbols for the four cardinal directions. The colors, which represent north and south respectively, are yellow and red, while white and blue are the colors for east and west. It is blue corn that you will see used here and along the Rio Grande for a variety of southwestern Indian foods. On the cob, the kernels look bluish black, but when they are processed they have a definite bluish cast. Hopi corn is descended from the "pod corn" which dates back to 2500 B.C. in the Southwest, where each kernel is individually sheathed, not looking too dissimilar from the seeds found in the heads of the wild grasses from which it was patiently developed.

Many dedicated people in the villages continue to live out the hard, but rewarding Hopi way that has gained for the Hopi a reputation among their fellow Indians for spiritual purity and superiority. Even the neighboring Navajo and distant Pueblo tribes recognize the Hopi's spiritual pureness and often ask them to weave special ceremonial garments for them. But the drive towards purity of ceremonial life creates problems that may, ironically, lead to its demise in our modern world. For instance, other American Indian tribes feel no inhibition performing their dances away from the reservation, wherever their people may be. But the Hopi do not do this. A Hopi must return to the sacred ground of the mesas for his religious ceremonies. It is only in this setting that these ceremonies are held. It is only in village kivas that they are practiced. So understandably, modern jobs are cutting into ceremonial life. It is hard, if not impossible, for a Hopi to take several weeks off from an hourly job so he can return to the mesa to prepare for the ceremonies. Consequently some of the villages have given up some of the more intricate ceremonies. Others though, like Shungopovi and Hotevilla remain steadfast.

This decline of the Hopi way and ceremonial

life is firing once again the age-old controversy of being "true" to the Hopi way. The "Hostiles" of yesterday are known today as "Traditionalists" and the "Friendlies" of the early 1900s are known as the "Progressives." The Traditionalists are opposed to mining coal on Black Mesa and are against the introduction of industries on the reservation. They are against the quest for new homes, cars, and economic development in general. A graphic example of this occurred some years ago when money was made available to bring electricity to one of the villages. The village protested, but the trucks came anyway and began the necessary preparatory work. Shortly after the holes were dug for the utility poles, the women of the village got down in the holes, thereby stopping the work.

Many of the Hopi feel that all this modernization will detract from spiritual responsibilities. The Progressives, however, believe that modernization can occur with certain modifications so as to preserve most of the cultural and spiritual life of the tribe. Many of these differences are played out in the activities of the Tribal Council. The Council was mandated by the United States government to represent the whole reservation. It was hoped that it could help unite the politically independent villages. Although each village is supposed to elect representatives to the Council, not all villages are represented there. These elected representatives are frequently in conflict with the hereditary village chiefs who often go their own way. But the Council has been useful in presenting a united front for the reservation in its legal battles centering around land disputes with the Navajo.

Change is evident today as you drive from one mesa-top village to another, but it is not overpowering. Many of the older mud plaster-and-stone homes are being replaced with homes made of manufactured concrete blocks. Electricity has been installed in most of the villages. There is an increasing amount of indoor plumbing. Cars and pickups seem abundant. Hopi men and women dress, for the most part, like westernized whites. But as the new comes in, the old remains. Early in the morning, a few of the Hopi women who are nurses depart for work in their white uniforms, while some of the older women are carrying buckets of water to their homes from a communal faucet and still other Hopi women prepare to fire

their pottery in the age-old method, using sheep dung for fuel. Some of the men in hard hats depart the village in pickups, headed for work a hundred miles or more away, while other men can be seen weaving ceremonial garb or carving kachinas in their homes. Today, you still will hear the friendly chatter of a community starting the day. And you will see in the center of things, integrated into village life, the ancient religious kiva, its ladder reaching skyward from the heart of the village.

Without a doubt, the Hopi have an unshakable sense of identity. On the mesas today, a Hopi can point to a certain cornfield, a special rock, or even a particular house, and say with assuredness that his ancestors farmed this field, frequented that spot, or lived in that house for over nine centuries. These rocky escarpments are home to the Hopi. Their agelessness renders a sense that this is a sacred spot. I am sure I am not the only visitor who experiences a tingle up and down his spine as I approach this high tableland from the desert below, or who is drawn back time and again to these mesas. The mesas, the villages, and the people are likewise magnets for the Hopi themselves, holding a sense of mystery and sanctity. Those Hopi who have left their mesa homes for jobs outside frequently come back home for good. Those who have left and live elsewhere in the Southwest often journey hundreds of miles to return to the mesas, seeking the personal fulfillment found in watching or participating in the various age-old dances and ceremonies.

The Hopi Villages

Starting just east of Arizona Highway 160 at Tuba City is Moenkopi, the first of the twelve recognized Hopi villages you will encounter as you travel from west to east over a span of about seventy miles. Each of the villages will be described in its order of appearance. All are situated on or just off Arizona Highway 264, also known as Navajo Route 3.

Moenkopi (Hopi: "running water all the time"). One of the largest of the Hopi communities,

Moenkopi was not founded until the late 1800s when villagers from Old Oraibi left that increasingly crowded village to form a new village. But this was not new territory for the Oraibi Hopi. They had planted corn in the fertile fields around Moenkopi Wash for generations. It is said that villagers in those early days ran the forty-five miles between Oraibi on Third Mesa to their fields of corn, beans, squash, and melons at Moenkopi.

Moenkopi is the only village not situated directly on or beneath Black Mesa and is widely separated from the other villages. It is actually divided into two village units, Upper Moenkopi and Lower Moenkopi. Upper Moenkopi is one of the least traditional villages, as it snuggles up to the busy main north–south highway in this region and the Navajo tribal center of Tuba City. Lower Moenkopi is more traditional, as the kachina cult still is followed there and the village women continue to make fine wicker baskets.

As you are leaving Moenkopi, you will see for the first time on your journey, on the east side of the village just above the wash, homes made mostly of stone and plaster which represent the kinds of homes found in most of the Hopi villages further east. You also will see fields of Hopi Indian corn for the first time on the sides of the wash. Notice the short but sturdy stalks and remember that these fields and others like them have grown corn and sustained the Hopi people for almost nine hundred years.

Third Mesa (forty-five miles east of Moenkopi)

Bacabi (Hopi: "place where the reeds grow"). This village was founded during the troubled times of the early 1900s, when the internal conflict between the "friendlies" and the "hostiles" at Old Oraibi became so intense that several dissident groups split from that village to form several new villages. In 1909, some of the dissident villagers who had left Old Oraibi in 1907 to settle Hotevilla decided they wanted to return to Old Oraibi. Old Oraibi refused to let them come back, so they formed this new village. It sits well into the mesa top and has good springs, providing moisture for its arable fields. This is a very traditional village. It has the reputation of having some of the best

ceremonial dancers in Hopiland. The women here weave wicker baskets of high quality.

Hotevilla (Hopi: "a slope of junipers" or alternatively "a scraped back," referring to the topography of the land here at the mesa's edge). This village was formed in 1906 by a "hostile" or anti-United States government group who, after great conflict with the progovernment faction, lost a "pushing match" and left Old Oraibi to form this new village. With naturally irrigated farmlands spilling below the village on the mesa's terraces, this village on the mesa's edge, the Hopi's largest, is well worth a visit. The terraced fields are most impressive and strongly resemble oriental terraced fields as they descend the slopes behind the village. This community has the reputation of being the most conservative and traditional of all the villages. It is the village that most staunchly defends the ancient Hopi way. Many Hotevilla men still put up their hair in the old style with a bob in the back and square cut bangs in the front. The women make excellent wicker baskets. The older section of the village is still without electricity.

Old Oraibi (Hopi: "place of ourai," a type of rock). For almost a decade now the following sign has been in place on the spur road leading to the village:

> WARNING   WARNING
> No outside white visitors allowed
> Because of your failure to Obey the
> Laws of our Tribe
> As well as the Laws of Your Own
> This village is hereby closed.

At times, the village has been sporadically open to the public. You may want to check the status of the village when you visit. If you are fortunate enough to find the village open, you will be asked to pay a small fee before entering. This was the first mesa-top village, settled about A.D. 1125–A.D. 1150. It has remained occupied since that time, claiming the title of the oldest, most continuously occupied village or town in the United States. For many years there were only a few people living there, but now many old houses are being rebuilt and it is once again beginning to

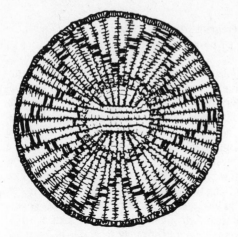

Hopi wicker plaque

come to life. Although it is definitely the oldest mesa-top village and the oldest continuously inhabited village in the same location, there is some dispute as to whether it is the first Hopi village (see "Second Mesa, Shungopovi"). At one time Oraibi, with its narrow streets and multistoried buildings, definitely had an urban scale.

New Oraibi or Kykotsmovi (Hopi: "place of the hill ruins"). This somewhat sprawling, modern settlement at the base of Third Mesa accommodates the Hopi tribal office and a tribally owned trading post. Several gas stations and a quick-food store are also located there. Formed around 1910, this and other valley villages became modernized much more quickly than the mesa-top villages. From here, at New Oraibi, or from the highway just west of New Oraibi, as you enter town, you can look back to the west and catch glimpses of Old Oraibi and the ruins of the old church in the distance on the mesa top, as well as its terraces stepping down to the desert below.

Second or Middle Mesa (five miles east of Third Mesa)

Shungopovi (Hopi: "water place where reeds grow"). Although some Hopi identify Old Oraibi as the first Hopi village, others would point their finger at Maseeba and its modern-day counterpart, Shungopovi. It is believed by many Hopi that Maseeba was the first village to be formed by the people known today as the Hopi. It was established in the 1100s, below Second or Middle Mesa. The village moved several times and after the Pueblo Revolt in 1680, surfaced on the mesa top as today's village of Schomopovi or Shungopovi. Some call this venerable village the "vatican" of the Hopi World. In the middle of the Sacred Circle, the center of Hopiland, it is situated at the tip of Second Mesa with a commanding view over the desert and the sacred Hopi monuments to the south.

Second Mesa juts its fingerlike projection further into the desert than any of the other mesas. Being on Second Mesa is more like being on an island in the sky, rather than on a peninsular extension of a larger mesa. There is a certain sense of timelessness there and from its vantage point, all of the visual cues to the Hopi universe can be seen. This is a commanding position with the site of old Maseeba just below Shungopovi's ridge. Although many of the ancient stone and stucco houses are being stabilized or replaced with new cinder block homes, traditional village life is very much intact. Second Mesa women still make beautiful, coiled baskets, while some of the men continue to weave beautiful ceremonial garments and sashes and carve kachinas. This village is the site of many dances. Ceremonial traditions are carried out here with diligence and rare beauty.

Shipaulovi (Hopi: "place of mosquitoes"). This village was formed by a dissident group of Shungopovi villagers when that village moved to

Hopi coiled basket

the mesa top. It also has a commanding view from its mesa-top position. Unfortunately, in the last few years, modern housing built by the United States Department of Housing and Urban Development below the mesa has attracted most of the villagers away from the mesa top. The village is now almost abandoned, except when it is used for ceremonial purposes and dances. The women make coiled baskets there.

Mishongnovi (Hopi: "place of the dark man"). Settled around A.D. 1200, it was moved to the mesa top after the last Pueblo Revolt. It is one of the best-situated villages. The twin shafts of the sacred Corn Rock, visible for miles around, are just above the Mishongnovi graveyard on the terraces below the village. Many of the traditional rough-hewn rock houses can be seen there. As at the other Second Mesa villages, the women there make well-crafted and artistic coiled baskets and plaques.

First Mesa or East Mesa (eight miles east of Second Mesa)

Polacca (Hopi: "butterfly"). This is a modern suburban village founded by Thomas Polacca, a Hano village resident who moved down from the mesa in the early 1900s. Today this suburban off-shoot of the three mesa-top villages is home to many fine Hopi potters. It is an active, busy community and seems to grow every year as residents move from the mesa top to this more accessible location below the mesa.

Hano or Tewa (Hopi: "place of the eastern [Tewa] people"). This village was formed after the Pueblo Revolt by Tewa-speaking Rio Grande Pueblo people who emigrated to escape Spanish reprisals after the Pueblo Revolt. Over the years they have assimilated completely with the Hopi. They learned the Hopi language, but the Hopi at Walpi never learned Tewa. Since the original Hano villagers brought their highly developed pottery skills from the Rio Grande Pueblos, some of the best Hopi potters, including the renowned Hopi potter Nampeyo, have come from this village.

Sichomovi (Hopi: "hill place where flowers grow"). This village is the newest on First Mesa, being

Hopi pot

formed as a suburb of Walpi sometime after 1700. It lies between Walpi and Hano up on the mesa and is the last village to which you can drive. You must walk the few yards from there to the mesa tip where Walpi village is located. Since Sichomovi is a satellite village or colony to the older village, Walpi, its residents join with the Walpi villagers for many of the ceremonial society functions. Sichomovi is also a pottery village and there, as in the other two First Mesa villages, pottery "for sale" signs are often seen in the windows of the houses.

Walpi (Hopi: "place of the gap"). Perched at the very tip of First Mesa, Walpi is the most dramatically situated of all the Hopi villages, appearing to be an extension of the mesa itself. Its stone-and-mud plastered buildings hug the narrow ledge above precipitous cliffs on all sides. The village was founded in 1417, but did not move to the tip of the mesa top until sometime between 1680 and 1690. Except for Sikyatki, an earlier now-extant village founded a little to the north below the mesa, Walpi is the oldest First Mesa village. A few stepped-back multistory buildings in the village shape to a somewhat pyramidal form that for some echoes the pyramids of the Aztecs. Unquestionably, this is the most photogenic of the Hopi villages, if only it were allowed. Recently Walpi has undergone stabilization and some reconstruction. Because many of the centuries-old buildings were deteriorating, the Economic Development Administra-

Walpi

tion spent about a half million dollars to restore many of the weakened walls. Rock was cut by hand from the mesa itself, just as in ancient times, in order to be true to Hopi tradition. At Walpi, you can see the "kiska," a covered passage between the buildings used frequently in ancient times to interconnect parts of the village to the plaza. Walpi, where excellent pottery and beautiful kachinas are made, is truly a five-star village of the world.

Visiting Hopiland: A Narrative Account

Somewhat refreshed after a cold drink in Tuba City, and with a full tank of gas, we head back into the glaring sun and drive east on Arizona Highway 264 to the Hopi mesas. We quickly drive through Moenkopi, the first and most removed of the Hopi villages, separated from the other villages by forty-five miles of Navajo grazing lands and some of the controversial partitioned lands. We note the new homes being built at Upper Moenkopi, and toward the west end of Lower Moenkopi, further down the wash, we see the old stone-and-mortar houses handsomely situated above a fertile valley of green cornfields. There is more green here than we have seen all day. The villages are quiet this terribly hot afternoon. We reflect that Moenkopi Wash, which provides the moisture for the corn we see, is a tributary of the Little Colorado River. Not far from here, about twenty-five miles south, the Little Colorado empties into the Colorado River not far from the Grand Canyon. At the confluence of the two rivers is the ancient "sipaapuni" or the place in Hopi mythology where the Hopi people entered this, the Fourth World, from the Third World, through a hollow reed. From that sacred point according to Hopi legend, they began migrations which would eventually take them to the mesas forty-five miles east of here.

At approximately fourteen miles, we pass the short spur road on the left (unsigned and unmarked except for a nearby windmill) to beautifully eroded, colorful Coal Canyon. Also known as Coal Mine Canyon, this eroded sandstone escarpment is often referred to as the "Little Bryce Canyon." Here and in other spots like it on or near the Black Mesa, nature has opened up canyon walls to reveal vast seams of coal. For centuries the Hopi have used coal obtained from canyons like this one. Although the canyon and an adjacent picnic area are only about one-half mile north of the highway by a good dirt road, we decide to bypass it for now since the best viewing times are in the early morning and late afternoon, not midday. Now the road climbs gradually until we reach a sign, forty miles from Tuba City, that tells us we are entering Hopiland. In just a few more miles we reach Third Mesa. A little further on we pass two spur roads. The road to Bacabi to the left and the road to Hotevilla to the right. We remember that a few years ago, we visited Hotevilla in search of a wicker basket. We were greeted diffidently by several people in the plaza of this very traditional village. We did not feel unwelcome, but we did feel we must put our best foot forward and do nothing disrespectful. The lady we were looking for that day wasn't home. Although we did not linger too long, we found Hotevilla to be one of the more interesting villages and were quite impressed with the terraced gardens behind the village.

A little further on, we arrive at the spur road leading to Old Oraibi. The sign that prohibits pahaanas or whites from entering is in place today so we honor it and turn back to the highway. As we continue east, we pass the excellent Monongya's Gallery before descending into the valley between Third and Second mesas. We catch glimpses of Old Oraibi to our right as we drive down the hill into Kykotsmovi or New Oraibi, a thriving modern community complete with a gas station and grocery store. This is the home of the Hopi Nation's headquarters. Continuing on towards Second Mesa, we come to the Hopicrafts Workshop and crafts store where much of the Hopi "overlay" silver jewelry is made. A stop here a year ago resulted in an interesting impromptu tour of the workrooms.

Now we start up again, fairly steeply, to the top of Second Mesa. To the left is the Hopi Arts and Crafts Silvercrafts Cooperative Guild Shop, with the Second Mesa campground separating it from the well-designed Hopi Cultural Center and Motel. I pull into a parking space. As usual, several Hopi seeking refuge from the afternoon sun are standing in the shade provided by the buildings. After registering in the motel, I return to the car to drive it around to the other side of the complex where our room is located. I put it in reverse and start to back

out. Bang—crash! I receive a tremendous jolt and my seat is knocked back a notch or two. At first I just feel stunned. Then I turn to see what happened. I have backed into a steel light pole.

As I sit trying to gather my wits, an older Hopi man comes out of the shade and ambles slowly to the car window. For a few minutes, he just stands there quietly and looks at me. I think to myself, "Maybe he thinks I'm the True Pahaana." Then in a friendly but definitely serious way, he admonishes me for drinking too much that time of the day "in all of the heat." Defensively, I try to explain that I'm just fatigued from the long drive and hot weather and that I have had nothing to drink. He smiles as though to say, "Sure you haven't," and goes back to stand in the shade.

I get out of the car to see what damage I've done. To my relief, the dent and blue paint left on the pole by my car is matched by an artful array of many other varicolored dents up and down the pole, looking for all the world like a Hopi version of the totem pole. I am relieved that I have only done what others who have parked in the same space before me have done. After checking in, I walk to the air-conditioned room, drink a large glass of ice water, and take a siesta. In this country, there is indeed a time just to stand quietly in the shade or take a siesta!

Rested, I inquire at the desk from a handsome young Hopi man if there are any dances this weekend. He replies that a dance is about to begin at Shungopovi and that if we hurry we can get there in time. Shungopovi is an easy five-minute drive away. We arrive at Shungopovi, where the streets of the village are the stage and the roofs are the grandstands. While waiting for the dancers to emerge from the kiva, we remember that last year we observed an outstanding ceremony that would make a born-again Hopi out of anyone. We saw some of the most dramatically costumed dancers we have ever witnessed, as they surfaced from the top of the kiva, their feet moving, with staccatolike cadence as they danced their way into the plaza. We heard some of the strongest, most otherworldly sounds known to man and then witnessed the dancing and chanting of some extremely complex rhythms, by a group of more than fifty of the Hopi faithful.

With two golden eagles in full view, tethered

on the adjacent rooftop, with costuming that matched and excelled anything we had ever seen at the Santa Fe Opera, and with the buzz of the chorus gaining in momentum and speed, filling the air with that ancient music, we felt ourselves transformed, mesmerized, goose bumps forming, spines tingling. The Hopi around us were equally serious, showing great reverence and respect for this primordial enactment. Then a break in pace and the clowns emerged in the plaza throwing gifts of food, cigarettes, candy, even toys up to the crowds on the rooftop and in the plaza. There was laughter then as everybody reached out to catch the generous gifts from the clowns. We were treated warmly and hospitably by our Hopi hosts that day, who even helped, at one point, to clear a viewing path for our youngest so he could see what all the fun was about.

With that as background, we are looking forward to today's Snake Dance. The same village, the same plaza. The same intense afternoon heat. The sky is clear and the air is quiet, the audience hushed, as members of the Antelope society emerge from the kiva in full, glorious costume. The sense we have is of strange creatures emerging from the bowels of the earth. With intricate rhythms, the Antelope society chants and dances in place, while the Snake society members dance

Snake Dance

with snakes. Sidewinder rattlesnakes and other poisonous and nonpoisonous snakes from the Colorado Plateau are all here in their natural state.

We are told that these snakes were caught on and around Second Mesa many days ago and have been kept in the kiva until today. The handling of the snakes and the rhythmic chant builds to a crescendo as the snakes are placed in the handlers' mouths. Now with human teeth pressing their midsections just below their heads, their bodies suspended in space, the snakes writhe with fangs bared as they turn their heads back and forth perilously close to their handlers' faces. But with great patience, each handler's accomplice, the guide, bends down intently following every move of the snake's mouth, using the power of his eagle's feather to divert the snake and his poisonous fangs from the handler's face.

The audience is quiet, reverent. We and the other pahaanas present are seeing a harmony between man and nature we have never witnessed nor ever thought possible. We gaze with great concentration now as the drama unfolds before us and we forget the heat, forget that we had failed to buy sunglasses. The events in the plaza transfix us. There is a silent reverence among us, the spectators, white and Hopi alike. No carnival atmosphere here. This is the holiest of the holy.

The dance continues, lovingly, intensely. It is now almost 6:00 P.M. A shadow passes over the plaza. I look up and see large clouds forming in the

Hopi clowns—Koshare, watermelon kachina, and mudhead kachina

distance as a huge, black cloud moves toward Second Mesa. Now the wind begins to come up as the dance is about to conclude. Large raindrops start falling. After being sanctified with cornmeal, the younger members of the Snake Clan grab up the snakes and race pell-mell out of the plaza toward the mesa's edge, where they release the dozens of snakes to the four directions, back to nature, grateful to them for helping to bring the rain. Now it is raining in torrents. We rush to our car and head back to the motel. Dry, inside, we comment on how welcome this rain is on this August Saturday evening in Hopiland. We, too, are thankful to the Antelope and Snake society members, as well as nature's snakes, for this wonderful moisture they have brought through their hard work and diligent efforts.

After an excellent Hopi dinner of posole, lamb, and fry bread, we take a walk. The rain has stopped, the air is clean and is at its purest. The early evening sky is absolutely clear and the bluest of blues. We admire the architecture of Ben Gonzales who designed the Hopi Motel and Cultural Center. He has truly captured, in a modern way, some of the essences of Hopi Pueblo living. The sun is sinking in the West and, at sixty-two hundred feet altitude, it is becoming much cooler. We walk across the road through a sandy field to the mesa's edge. Far below us is the desert floor stretching out to the Painted Desert to the south. We look straight down. There are ledges and cliffs and piles of rock all the way down to the valley floor. We climb down from the mesa's edge to a small sandstone ledge and sit down.

It is very quiet now. A hawk is circling above us. Strewn on the ground around us are some of the most unusual pieces of sandstone we have ever seen. These contorted rocks look as if they had been cooked in a pressure cooker, their insides bubbling up and then popping, leaving jagged edges and craters in all assortments of shapes. Sitting on this high escarpment, we sense the respect the Hopi have for their beautiful mesas. It doesn't take too much imagination to turn some of the square-topped mesa buttes in the distance into villages and, with a little more imagination, step back almost a thousand years to when the Hopi first occupied these mesas. It is so quiet now that maybe, if we listen carefully, we can hear the distant sounds of a village full of life. Our reverie is abruptly ended with the realization that twilight is fading fast into darkness. As we silently make our way back to the motel, we have a sense that we are reentering civilization from some prehistoric time where we have stood on the edge of the universe and felt the vibrations of the Hopi world.

Visit to a Hopi Village: A Narrative Account

This morning after breakfast, we visit the Hopi museum here at the cultural center. For a small fee, we view a display of both new and old crafts and absorb some interesting historical points. But our interest in Indian crafts will be pampered today, for there are several craft shops here in the complex, as well as the Hopi Arts and Crafts Silvercraft Cooperative Guild about one hundred yards away just beyond the campground. In one of the shops, we spot a pot we particularly like, but it is being held for another buyer. We inquire about the pot's maker and discover that she lives at Walpi village on First Mesa. We ask if it is all right to visit her there. We are told that she sells from her home and sometimes takes special orders from there. We receive instructions about finding her home.

Following Arizona Highway 264 across the top of Second Mesa, we pass Shungopovi and then drop to the valley below, where to our left another high spur of Second Mesa protrudes. Atop this promontory are the old villages of Shipaulovi and Mishongnovi. Near the junction of Arizona Highway 87 to Winslow and Flagstaff, we pass the Secakuku Trading Post complex with its supermarket, restaurant, gift and craft shop, and gas station. In a few miles, First Mesa looms up on our left. It is narrow, steep and dramatic, rising abruptly from the desert floor.

At first, we do not see Walpi on the western tip, but as we get closer we understand why. Its rock-and-mortar buildings blend perfectly with the mesa, looking almost like an extension of the mesa top. Now we notice wisps of smoke coming from the very top of the mesa and wonder if a Hopi potter is "firing" her wares this morning. Soon we come to a sign welcoming us to the First Mesa villages which reads, "Respect our privacy. Absolutely not permitted: Photography, recording, hiking foot trails, removal of objects, sketching, drawing—Clan Leaders." After that sign is another directing us to turn left off the highway to the villages and informing us that recreational vehicles, commercial buses, trailer campers, and motor homes are not allowed on the Mesa.

We now make an immediate right turn up the narrow paved road to the mesa top. At this point the way is steep, narrow, and without guardrails. There is a sheer drop-off on the downside. We hug the rock-strewn cliffside, just hoping we won't meet another vehicle. We pass a few Hopi girls walking down the road who smile and wave. We have heard that these eastern villages are the most receptive and friendly to strangers. Finally, at the top, we drive through the narrow streets of Hano or Tewa village. Here we see numerous women firing pots in their bonfires near the mesa edge. Just a few yards further, we pass through the narrow streets of Sichomovi village where children are already playing outside their stone-and-mortar houses, as the morning comes peacefully to the mesa. In another minute or two we pass through the village and come to the gap in the mesa.

Here the road ends. We stop, park the car, and walk a few paces across the narrow stretch of land bridging the "gap" or walpi into Walpi village. There are houses here several stories high, all built of stone from the mesa. We see one pyramidal-shaped complex of stone-and-mortar houses, which we learn has been occupied since around 1690, and we see the kiska or passageway under it dramatically cutting through this stony edifice.

On this bright, sunny morning, the children are playing in the narrow streets and in the small plaza. Several are selling pottery. We ask to see more pottery and are taken up some steps to an open screen door. The child calls his mother. She greets us warmly and invites us inside. We see her wares and talk with her briefly about life on the mesa. Our children purchase a small pot from her daughter. She knocks on the neighbor's door to see if she knows the whereabouts of the potter we're looking for this morning. Inside this home, an older Hopi man is carving a kachina doll from a cottonwood root. He tells us that the root is becoming very expensive and hard to get. Formerly he traveled over one hundred miles to get his own,

but now has to rely on others for his supply. Some of the completed kachinas in the room are exquisite. Most of the kachina dolls are for sale, but a few of the special ones will be given at the right time to some very lucky Hopi child.

We find the woman we are looking for. She is dressed in a cool gingham dress and flat shoes, firing pots out at the very tip of the mesa. The open fire which she tends carefully is burning with intensity, the flames licking the air. Occasionally she backs away from the fire when the wind blows the smoke into her eyes. We notice on both sides of us that the rock ledge we are standing on drops off precipitously to the desert below. The smoke spirals upward and curls off the mesa as it floats high above Pollaca below us. She is firing three large pots this morning, she says, and using sheep dung for fuel. She points to the valley below and tells us that is where she used to gather the dry dung fuel; but now that she's too old to do that, she buys it from the Navajo, who charge a hefty price for a gunnysack of dung.

She invites us to her house, which also serves as her "studio." There are pots drying in the sun on the steps outside. After she tells us about digging her clay and making the slip she uses to coat the pots, she shows us several yucca brushes she uses to apply the decoration. These well-designed pots made by the coil method are thin walled and as smooth as glass. There is no need for pottery wheels here in Hopiland! Although she does not have the shape we are looking for, she says she can make it for us.

We talk about prices. She sells for a little less than the craft stores on Second Mesa, but not much less, and she tells us she is amazed how much she is receiving for her pots, compared to what she used to sell them for. We all agree that in the past she received too little for the amount of work and time she puts into a pot. She is just now getting adequately compensated. So now, for the first time, she is making enough money to "put back" for her grandchildren's education. She sees us to the door and points out sacred Snake Rock in the plaza, where we see carefully wrapped fetish bundles resting in its hollows. We thank her for her generosity and return to the car.

We wind our way back through the villages and then start the descent to Pollaca. We are thankful for good brakes and go as slowly as we can on the way back down to the highway. We reflect that these three villages perched up on the mesa, safe from revengeful Spanish and marauding Navajo, are reasonably safe from today's tourist hordes. With considerable regret, we turn east, leaving the Hopi villages behind as we head for Keams Canyon, 11.5 miles east of Polacca. We stop at Keams Canyon, primarily a government town, for lunch and a cool drink in the pleasant Keams Canyon Trading Post, Café, and Arts and Crafts Store. We are always amazed by the excellent Indian handicrafts found here. Today we skirt the town where a bank, a motel, the Indian Health Service Hospital, and the Hopi Indian Agency are located, as we leave this otherworldly setting of the Hopi Nation and head 43 miles east to Hubbell Trading Post near Ganado, Arizona.

Snake Rock, Walpi

Back to Navajoland: Keams Canyon to Ganado and on to Window Rock and Canyon de Chelly

Heading east from Keams Canyon on Arizona Highway 264, you will come to the junction with U.S. Highway 191, which leads thirty-two miles north to Chinle, the gateway to Canyon de Chelly. Continue four miles east past the junction to a sign indicating Hubbell Trading Post. Turn right and follow the dirt road across the bridge of the Pueblo Colorado Wash, a short distance to the trading post. Park in front of the old stonewall building. This National Historic Site is definitely worth a stop.

Although the Navajo mistrusted many whites, they never seemed to stop revering "double glasses" or "Old Mexican" as they affectionately called him. Don Lorenzo Hubbell began trading at Ganado in 1876. When he died in 1930, he was buried on top of a small hill overlooking the trad-

ing post next to his wife, two sons, a daughter, and his very close Navajo friend, Many Horses.

His respect for the Navajo and their way of life led to their respect for him. When the Navajo returned from their Long Walk in the late 1880s, Hubbell, more than any other white person, helped them get through that difficult transition time. He served many roles for the Navajo. He translated and wrote letters for some and helped settle family quarrels for others. He helped in time of sickness and acted as interpreter of the government and its policies. Moreover, he helped set the standards in color and design that would bring the best market price and continuous business to the Navajo weavers. To this day, the Hubbell Post is still operating. Owned by the United States National Park Service since 1967, it is operated on a nonprofit basis by the Southwest Parks and Monuments Association. It is still a functioning trading post and, in my estimation, still carries one of the best supplies of Navajo rugs in the area.

Upon entering the post, you find yourself in a somewhat dark, rectangular space closed on three sides by counters. This space is called a "bullpen." It contains all kinds of necessities of living, including large bolts of the rayon and velveteen cloth Navajo women use for making their skirts and blouses. To the right and through a doorway is a room leading to the "rug room." There you will see one of the largest and best supplies of Navajo rugs anywhere on the reservation.

Guided tours of Hubbell's home are available

and are instructional as to the way of life of the early white traders. You will see some beautiful old Navajo rugs there, as well as many mementos of the early West. Return to the parking area, for on the west side of the complex is a small museum run by the park service. There you will find an excellent selection of books relating to the area. But the central focus is several weaving looms which are used daily during the summer by neighboring Navajo women. Their work is beautiful to watch, and they are often helpful in describing what they are doing and how they do it. All in all, the park service has done an excellent job in preserving the old traditions of the post, yet adding some unique educational features that are in harmony with the setting.

From the trading post, return to Arizona Highway 264. A few miles east is the settlement of Ganado, elevation 6,400 feet, population one thousand. The town is named after one of the old Navajo chiefs, Ganado Mucho, who signed the 1868 treaty between the Navajo and the United States government. A Presbyterian mission and hospital are located there. To the north of town are the buildings of the area's parochial schools. Continue east from Ganado twenty eight miles to Window Rock, capital of the Navajo Nation. There is considerable traffic along this road since it leads to the eastern, more populated region of the reservation. Near the junction of Navajo Route 12 and Arizona Highway 264 is the sprawling commercial center of Window Rock (Navajo: nee Alneeg: Earth's Center), population twenty-five hundred.

Coming up to this junction, you can see Window Rock in the red sandstone formations to the northeast, and you will pass the Navajo fairgrounds and rodeo site on your right. On the northeast corner of the intersection are the main shop of the Navajo Arts and Crafts Guild and the excellent Navajo Tribal Museum, depicting many aspects of the Navajo way of life. Books and journal reprints pertaining to the Navajo culture can be obtained there. In addition, you will find gas stations, fast-food cafés, and the tribally owned motel. You may wish to visit the tribal government seat just north off of Navajo Route 12, located beneath the beautiful natural window in the red sandstone formation there.

This window in the rock is the source of the town's name. This gaping hole in the rock and the spring below it are important in Navajo ceremonial rites. There are some thirteenth-century Anasazi ruins just below the window. But more important than the geological and archaeological treasures is the large administration headquarters for the entire Navajo Nation. Of special interest is the well-designed Navajo Tribal Council Building, shaped like a hogan and containing murals depicting the history of the Navajo tribe.

From Window Rock, you are 92 miles from the historically rich mesa-top Ácoma Indian Pueblo (which rivals Old Oraibi for "oldest city" honors) and 164 miles from Albuquerque, mostly by way of U.S. Interstate 40. And Chaco Canyon's Chaco Culture National Historic Park is 110 miles to the northeast, the last twenty miles being over a very rough unpaved road that is not negotiable with a standard car during wet weather.

Leaving Window Rock, head north on the Fort Defiance Road, Navajo Highway 12. This excellent paved, all-weather road will take you to Canyòn de Chelly. Along this road, you will see a more modern version of Navajo life than you saw in the west. Small clusters of modern homes and trailers have sprung up. At certain hours, the traffic

Navajo rug

can be fierce. In five miles, a spur road to the left leads to Fort Defiance. Today, Fort Defiance is a bustling, picturesque modern community with no remains of the old fort (once called Fort Canby) which Kit Carson used for headquarters and which served as an early day "concentration camp" for the Navajo he rounded up for the Long Walk. There are a number of tribal agency offices in Fort Defiance. Return to Navajo Route 12 and drive north through beautiful forested ponderosa pine country, dotted with lakes. Approximately 50 miles from Window Rock, turn left at the junction of Navajo Route 12 and Navajo Route 64. Now drive 25 miles to the visitor center, paralleling the north rim of Canyon de Chelly most of the way. If you have time, you might want to tour the north rim (see "The North Rim of Canyon de Chelly").

Canyon de Chelly

The Rio de Chelly and its tributaries descend from their origin in northeastern Arizona high in the Chuska Mountains, which are known locally as the "Navajo Alps." They have carved one of the most spectacularly beautiful canyon systems in the world. Canyon de Chelly is not the largest, nor the deepest, nor the widest of canyons, but it is one of the best proportioned and aesthetically beautiful canyons you will see anywhere. In addition to being a canyon whose size humans can relate to, it is a canyon with a human element. Wherever you look into Canyon de Chelly and its tributary canyons, there is evidence of human existence. Whether it is the ancient apartmentlike cliff dwellings that dot the floor and walls of the canyon, or the hogans, cornfields, and peach orchards in the canyon bottom being actively farmed today, you know that the canyon has given warmth and shelter to people for generations. Somehow Canyon de Chelly National Monument epitomizes the geography in Section II, beautiful landscapes that have been enhanced by people who have known how to blend and live with their environment.

The canyon and its three branches measure over one hundred miles long. The three tributary canyons of Canyon de Chelly are Canyon del Muerto and Black Rock Canyon to the north and Monument Canyon to the south. You can follow this canyon from its shallowest westernmost part about 30 feet deep to its deepest, southeasterly part where it plunges 1,100 feet into the earth, revealing eleven million years of geological history and over a thousand years of human history.

Navajo Tribal Council building and Window Rock

From its barren and dry sandstone rim, you will observe a lush oasis of green cornfields, large trees, and flowing water far below. It is this sense of contrast that adds another unique dimension to Canyon de Chelly.

Canyon de Chelly National Monument, over 130 square miles in size, was established in 1931. Historically the Navajo have called it "Tsegi" meaning "rock canyon." "De Chelly" is a Spanish corruption of the Navajo word "Tsegi." The canyon contains over one hundred prehistoric sites dating from A.D. 350 to 1300. Some are in shambles, others are still standing, while several appear untouched by time. The steep and extensively varnished canyon walls are filled with some of the richest and best Anasazi Navajo rock art in Arizona. Because Canyon de Chelly is more remotely located than many other canyon sites, you can view all of this in relative peace and quiet.

For a geological view of how canyons on the Colorado Plateau form, see "A Geological Primer to Southeastern Utah," Section I. Specifically, most of the rock you see at Canyon de Chelly is sandstone by the same name. It was formed from ancient sand dunes and is dramatically cross-bedded in places. A harder rock, the more durable Shinarump conglomerate of the Chinle formation, makes up the rim of the canyon and overlies the de Chelly sandstone. In a few areas such as the visitor center and the first overlook, you will see the Chinle sandstone on top of the Shinarump. Although it has eroded away almost everyplace else, leaving a predominantly Shinarump rim, the softer Chinle sandstone still rests on top of the Shinarump there.

The canyon and its environs are owned by the Navajo people, so all tourists are guests of the Navajo. During the summer months, several hundred Navajo and their families farm in the canyon bottom, living there daily or on weekends. Although its cool, watered recesses make it a fine place to spend much of the day during the hot, dry summer, there are virtually no inhabitants during the winter when snow makes access difficult. Cold winter air often is trapped in the canyon bottom, which is so deep in places that the low winter sun never penetrates it. Up on the rim as well as in the canyons, you will see plenty of Navajo life. Hogans in camps or clustered settlements can be found in and around the town of Chinle, which is just a few miles from the canyon. The large Chinle Trading Post offers a good look at a more modern version of the Navajo reservation trading post business.

Seeing Canyon de Chelly

Chinle, elevation 5,500 feet, population 2,800, is the place to mark on your map if you want to tour Canyon de Chelly. Chinle in Navajo means "running out," for it is there that the Rio de Chelly emerges from its deep canyon recesses. Chinle is a sprawling Navajo settlement with schools, medical clinics, gas stations, and a few cafés. Southeast of town, about two miles on Navajo Route 7, is the educational Canyon de Chelly visitor center. In the summer, Navajo women are at work weaving rugs there that may take over four hundred hours from start to finish. Just outside the center is a Navajo hogan which you may enter and examine, while inside the center is an excellent visual display of the geology, natural history, and history of the canyon. Since you are not allowed to travel in the canyon without a park ranger or authorized guide, stop at the visitor center if you plan any extensive

Shrub live oak

travel on the canyon floor. There is one exception to this rule. The White House Ruin Trail winding down to the canyon floor is a foot trail which you may travel unescorted (see "The South Rim of Canyon de Chelly: A Narrative Account"). The park ranger often will take visitors on morning hikes up the canyon's outer reaches, approximately 3.5 miles round trip.

From the visitor center, go down the hill and follow the signs to Cottonwood Campground and the Thunderbird Lodge. The campground is one of the most tempting on the Colorado Plateau, as it is nestled at the outlet of the canyon in a grove of large, old cottonwood trees. During the summer, park rangers present lectures and slide shows about the canyon in the evenings. Just beyond the campground, the Thunderbird Lodge is another oasis. Formerly the site of the old Chinle Trading Post (1896), it is now a haven for those wishing to explore the canyon. There you will find motel accommodations, a crafts shop, and a Navajo rug room, as well as a good and economical cafeteria, open to the public. The motel office is also headquarters for four-wheel-drive-vehicle tours into the canyon. Half- or full-day tours may be arranged

there. Full-day tours also enter Canyon del Muerto. From a nearby concessionaire, it is possible to take all-day guided horseback trips to White House Ruin.

The canyons to be viewed are roughly Y-shaped, with the visitor center and motel located at the bottom of the Y where the river exits the canyon. From this main stem, you can choose to follow the left branch or the right branch of the canyon. The left branch is known as the North Rim and the right branch as the South Rim. It is possible

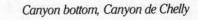

Canyon bottom, Canyon de Chelly

White House Ruins

to tour both branches and be on your way to another destination after about five hours of viewing and walking time. Or you could easily spend more than a day there. If you are particularly ambitious and short of time, it is possible to view the South Rim, then the North Rim, visit Window Rock, the Hopi villages (fleetingly), Tuba City, and be in Monument Valley by 10:00 P.M.—if you dare! For inquiries about campgrounds and tours write: Canyon de Chelly, National Park Service, United States Department of the Interior, Attention: Superintendent, Box 588, Chinle, Arizona 86503. Telephone: 1-602-674-5436 or -5213.

The South Rim of Canyon de Chelly: A Narrative Account

Last night, we arrived at Thunderbird Lodge about 7:30 P.M., checked in, and immediately drove two and a half miles up the south rim to see

the canyon at sunset from Tsegi Overlook. On the way over, we saw several Navajo homesites, complete with hogans. The view from Tsegi was startlingly beautiful. Standing on that high rim, we saw a broad expanse of canyon, the buff reds of the Navajo sandstone giving way to the pink, mostly sandy canyon bottom 275 feet below us, where we could make out a Navajo hogan and cornfields. As the sun dropped and a slight breeze came up, the colors became even more dramatic. A few minutes later, we were back at the lodge, where we ate a filling and plentiful meal at the excellent cafeteria. Navajo tacos topped the list. After dinner, we browsed in the well-stocked craft shop, located in the building adjacent to the cafeteria, made inquiries about local artisans, and then went outside to sit under the stars beneath the giant cottonwood trees. Another star-studded, comfortably cool night here on the Colorado Plateau.

It is now 8:00 A.M. We have finished breakfast

and are ready to return to the South Rim. As we drive to the South Rim road, we realize that the canyon at its westernmost end is only twenty or thirty feet deep. We make a quick pass at Tsegi Overlook where we were last night and continue on to Junction Overlook at 3.5 miles. We stop for another view. It is still cool this morning, but the sun is warming things up quickly. We walk over to the rim. We notice that the canyon is tens of feet deeper here than at Tsegi. Here we see the junction of Canyon del Muerto, which stretches 26 miles to the northeast, and Canyon de Chelly directly below us.

Canyon del Muerto, or Canyon of the Dead, was named by a Smithsonian expedition member in 1882, when numerous remains of prehistoric Indian burials were found there. About the same time, the well known archaeologist, Cosmos Mindeleff, visited Canyon de Chelly. He discovered and wrote about "first ruin," which we see this morning to the left and on the far side of the canyon. His writing helped spread the word to both Americans and Europeans about this unique part of the Southwest. About the same time, Karl May in Germany was writing fantasy stories about the American Indians and the southwestern "desert." These writings, plus the many western movies filmed in the Southwest that have been so popular in Europe, have greatly influenced the visitor population here. Last night at dinner and this morning at breakfast, there were more visitors from Germany and France than from the United States. We mused to ourselves that many Americans go traveling in Europe without even seeing what the Europeans consider a prime attraction in this country.

At 6.4 miles, we reach White House Overlook. We scurry down to the rim and see what is in store for us. This is a stunning overlook, down and across the canyon. For up from the sandy canyon bottom, beyond the Rio de Chelly, emerging from the brilliant green of the cottonwoods on the opposite wall of the canyon, is White House Ruin. Above it, in another canyon recess, is a well-preserved ruin with one of the best towers you will see in this area. After some debate, we decide we have time to take the 2.5-mile round-trip hike 500 feet down into the canyon to see the ruin. We bring our day pack with water bottles and a small first-aid kit.

We follow the well-marked trail called the "women's trail," which is a section of the canyon's rim that offers such easy access into the canyon that even sheep can be driven up and down it. The trail starts down fairly rapidly. But we are all doing fine even though some of us have on tennis shoes rather than boots. As we begin our descent, we notice it is 8:30 A.M. and the day promises to be hot.

This morning we comment on how bare of vegetation the rim is. But as we start our descent along the south face of the 600-foot cliffs, we are aware of considerable and varied plant life, as well as signs of animal and bird life. The trail is wide, the tread is good and not at all "scary" as we had anticipated. The trail cuts first northwest and then southeast as it switches back and forth on the gentle descent. There are piñon pines and junipers on both sides of the trail, and we see many large sandstone rocks displaying the cross-bedding of the de Chelly sandstone, representing those vast "frozen" sand dunes of ancient times, which were sculpted and hardened by nature into these surreal rounded masses. To our right, adjacent to the trail, is an ancient gnarled tree, its trunk shaped like a contorted piñon; but its moisture-preserving leaves, tough, green, and serrated like a holly tree, help us identify it as a shrub live oak. Above, two ravens we had spotted earlier are now soaring in the currents rising from the canyon. Walking along, we spot some well-defined animal tracks in the sand and, after some controversy, identify them as belonging to the gray fox. Now, near the end of the trail, we enter a small, dark, and pleasantly cool tunnel in the sandstone, which

Canyon wren

ends in a few yards at the bottom of the canyon, putting us face to face with a Navajo farm and hogan.

As we look back up, extending our necks to see the route we have traveled, we see no evidence of a trail, just a jumbled heap of boulders and rocks on a slant, topped by the steep edges of the ridge. Quickly, but quietly we walk past the hogan so as not to disturb the occupants. For about the length of a football field, we walk in packed sand across the river bottom, dodging a few trickles of water but continuing to move forward as we watch for quicksand, a hazard here in the canyon bottom. On the other side of the canyon floor, we step up the small bank into a thicket of tamarisks, their pink blossoms nodding in the gentle breeze. As we emerge from the thicket into the cottonwoods, we find the trail to the ruin where we see some willows and Russian olive trees. Much of this vegetation was planted to aid in erosion control. Even with the summer sun at its zenith, there is considerable shade down here this morning in the deep recesses of the canyon. Although the shade makes it cooler, it is still humid here by the riverbed. We are told that in the winter cold air is trapped down here and, as icy winds blow through the canyon, it becomes a veritable freezer, for even the elevation of the canyon floor is a lofty 5,500 feet.

We find a welcome set of bathroom facilities just below the ruin, near the historical markers. Over several hundred people apparently lived in this multistoried apartment house constructed around A.D. 1100 by the Anasazi. It was built in two sections along the lower part of the 600-foot south-facing canyon wall. In the well-preserved upper section is a central room with a long wall that was mud plastered many years ago. This distinctive wall gives the ruin its name, for it stands out as a prominent, white, crenellated tower high above the canyon floor and is easily visible from afar. The signs below the ruin tell us that the first white man to record seeing the ruin was United States Army Lt. James Simpson, in 1849, while the first authoritative archaeological exploration and map of the ruin was made by the well-known archaeologist, Cosmos Mindeleff.

We explore the accessible small ruin below in some detail. We realize that years ago it was a story

or two taller than it is now. A small ladder connected the roofs of the lower complex to the upper section of apartments. On the wall between the upper and lower ruins are several large, well-executed petroglyphs. The cliff face above the upper ruin has been nicely varnished (see Section 1, "Reading the Rocks"). On the ground, buried in the sand, are numerous pieces of flaked chert, obviously worked by hand in making arrowpoints. We also see many pottery shards in the sand. They belong to the ruin and to the Navajo owners, so we leave them in place.

We are the first ones down here this morning, so we sit in the sun by the ruin, surrounded by solitude, and try to reconstruct what life down here would have been like. If we raise our voices, they echo and reverberate off the canyon walls. No doubt one hundred or more people, including children, turkeys, and dogs, would have raised quite a din in the echoing depths of Canyon de Chelly. We realize why the Anasazi may have felt safe here and why the Navajo used the canyon to hide from the Spanish, Mexicans, and later Americans who attempted to retaliate and punish them for their injurious raids to white settlements. A few inches under the hot, dry sand, we feel moisture, the lifeline of the earlier peoples in the canyon and the reason the Navajo still, to this day, farm the canyon bottoms. We have read that somewhere in this vast labyrinthian canyon, on some obscure wall, is the locust sign of the Hopi Flute Clan, placed there before they migrated south to the mesas. We look again carefully at the building techniques and observe elements of Hopi architecture that we have seen at Walpi and in parts of Shungopovi. The tree-ring data from the roof logs here go back as far as A.D. 1060, while the latest date found here is 1275.

We turn, now, to cross the canyon bottom so as to make our ascent. Several canyon wrens dart in front of us. The way up is a little more challenging, an elevation gain of 500 feet in less than 1.25 miles. The sun is warm and, as our thirst increases, we are glad we have our water bottles. As we hike up, many people are just coming down. It is a little like a mini-United Nations. First, a couple from Japan. Then three young men from France. Now we pass a couple from Germany. Occasionally we stop and drink a little water from our canteens and then push forward and upward. We pass several other people before we reach the top, but only one of them is an American! Now on top, we rest on a large sandstone rock, literally gulping water.

We are glad we have been able to enjoy the solitude of the ruins by ourselves and there are even a few apologies from some family members for the disgruntlement they had expressed in having to get such an early start this morning. We notice that our round-trip hike plus our stops and wandering, have taken us about three hours. It is just after 11:00 A.M. as we sit here enjoying the little breeze that has come up. We return to the car to find that all is well. We had been warned that we should place everything of value out of sight and lock the car if we were planning to be gone for any length of time. Too bad, but a reality that has to be dealt with here and in the trailhead parking lots in the Cascades and Sierras as well.

Back to the South Rim drive, we reach Sliding Rock Overlook in another 6.5 miles. On the short walk to the rim, we look for some of the aquatic life we have been told we would see in the numerous water-filled potholes or sandstone basins along the trails. Even though these are fresh pools and perhaps for that reason we are unable to spot any fairy shrimp, spadefoot toads, or other interesting aquatic specimens. Now at the rim, we see a small ruin on a narrow ledge across the canyon. This ruin has yet to be excavated. We return to the rim road and drive 9 miles further to the turnoff to the parking lot at Spider Rock Overlook.

After walking 200 yards to the rim, we are overawed by what we see, for protruding 800 feet straight up out of the canyon bottom is Spider Rock with its cap reaching within just 200 feet of the rim. It towers magnificently, like a sentinel post, above the junction of Canyon de Chelly and Monument Canyon. It is a geological remnant of the downcutting of the two canyons. For often in areas where two canyons merge, a lone, isolated spire remains, somehow missed by the onslaught and ravages of the rapier-like streams of water which cut through the stone around it. The Navajo call this 230-million-year-old monument to rock history "Tse Na'ashje'ii" or Spider Rock. It is the home of a Navajo deity, Na'ashje'ii Asdzau or Spider Woman, who is thought to live at the top of the taller of the two needles, while

"Talking God" lives on top of the shorter spire.

To the left and on the far side of the canyon is another spire called Speaking Rock. From here, with our binoculars, we see a few Anasazi ruins across the canyon to the left of the overlook. A volcanic plug, Black Rock, is visible on the horizon a little to the left of Spider Rock. Now as we turn to walk back to the car, our son spots a large bird soaring in the air currents above the canyon. With the binoculars we identify it as a golden eagle, a rare find here and a nice end to our tour of the canyon. We retrace our route twenty-two miles back to the lodge for a refreshing lunch, before heading on to the North Rim.

The North Rim of Canyon de Chelly

From the visitor center, travel northeast on Navajo Highway 64, five miles to the turnoff to Ledge Ruin Overlook. Park your car and take the short walk to the rim. Across the canyon, about one hundred feet above the canyon floor, is a complex of twenty-nine rooms. Archaeological evidence from ceramic fragments suggests the ruin was probably occupied from 1150 to 1275. The other viewing point here is of Dekaa Kiva. You will see it high above the canyon bottom in an alcove. Although the kiva looks isolated today, it should be noted that the alcove directly to the west contains Anasazi remnants and that the two alcoves were probably connected by a toe- and hand-hold trail. It is thought that this was probably a male ceremonial chamber since it contains remnants of weaving looms which it is thought were used solely by the Anasazi men.

Now return to the highway and drive one mile to Antelope House Overlook Turnoff. Park and walk to the rim. Below and to the right is the site of the ninety-one-room, four-story Antelope House. It acquired its name from the well-executed pictographs of antelopes on the canyon wall to the left of the ruin. Binoculars help here. These antelope drawings are not of Anasazi origin, but were done by a well-known Navajo artist, Di be Yazhi, in the 1830s. The other wall pictures were done by the Anasazi. Occupied from A.D. 693, the site includes circular kivas and a main plaza. It was abandoned before the great drought sometime before 1260, probably because of flood damage it incurred because of its location near the river bottom. Its fleeing residents have probably become members of today's Hopi and Zuñi Indians. There is some evidence to suggest that the area was used sporadically by the Hopi after 1300, probably for the purpose of growing crops in the summer.

Just across the wash from Navajo House is the Tomb of the Weaver. It is also in an alcove about fifty feet above the canyon floor. This single burial site contained the mummy of an old man who was probably a weaver. He was buried with a blanket made mainly of eagle feathers. In addition, a bow and arrow and numerous foodstuffs were found, such as cornmeal, corn on the cob, salt, piñon nuts, and beans. Under the feather blanket was a finely woven cotton robe, along with a skein of cotton yarn more than two miles in length. The tools of his trade, including a spindle whorl, were also found buried with him.

Now walk a little further around the rim to the display sign for "Navajo Fortress." The "Fortress" refers to the single, high red stone butte on the other side of the canyon. The Navajo often had good reason to hide from whites seeking retribution after devastating Navajo raids. This was a fine place to retreat. Although not visible from the rim, there is a trail that ascends to the top of the fortress. The trail is segmented, so as the Navajo climbed from one level to another, they could pull the ladder up behind them. While some pulled ladders, other Navajo hurled rocks at the enemy from behind stone fortresses built at each level. This was truly an effective defense system.

After returning to the highway, drive 5.5 miles to Mummy Cave Overlook turnoff. From the rim, you will see Mummy Cave across the canyon. This cave was so named because a United States archaeological expedition in the late 1800s discovered two mummies in the talus slopes below the ruins. The Navajo call this ruin Twy Kini or House under the Rock. Some believe that the

Spider Rock

people who occupied this site were migrants from Mesa Verde, and certainly the three-story tower is reminiscent of that kind of architecture. There are fifty rooms and three kivas in the largest, eastern alcove. It is thought that access was via a hand-and-toe trail up the face of the cliff from the top of the talus slope. Excavations there have revealed evidence of Basketmaker habitation since A.D. 100.

At the same turnoff is the viewpoint to Massacre Cave and Yucca Cave. Massacre Cave tells even more dramatically the history of conflict between the Navajo and whites. For there, in 1805, the Spanish military leader, Lt. Antonio de Narbona, led a Spanish expedition from Santa Fe into Canyon de Chelly, hoping to halt the Navajo raiding on Spanish settlements as they spread east. Receiving word that the Spanish along with some Zuni Indian allies were on the march, the Navajo took refuge in a remote cave, 500 feet high up on the canyon wall, yet several hundred feet short of the rim. This cave, which you can easily see, is 300 feet long and 8 feet wide at its widest point. Protected from the rim by the angle of the cave's roof and from below by large rocks at the rim of the cave, about 150 Navajo, including many women and children, climbed the arduous route and took refuge there that day.

Exactly what happened is not known, but it is said that by the end of the day, Narbona's force had spotted the hideout and his sharpshooters had massacred 115 Navajo. Narbona supposedly delivered the ears of 84 Indians to the government in Santa Fe. Navajo legend asserts that only 25 of their people were killed there. The rest were captured. It is thought that Narbona's men fired from the spot where the overlook is, after one of the elderly Navajo women had given their position away by shouting taunts at the soldiers in the canyon below. Indeed, the cave was safe from the canyon rim directly above it, but not from its flanking rim.

Yucca Cave, a small Anasazi ruin, is the last of the historic sites you can see from the North Rim road. From there you can either return 11.5 miles to the visitor center or continue northeast on Navajo Highway 64 to the junction with Navajo Highway 12 leading to Window Rock to the south or Lukachukai and Mexican Water to the north.

From Chinle to Mexican Water, Teec Nos Pos, and the Four Corners Monument

The drive north of Chinle on U.S. Highway 191 leading 63 miles to the junction with U.S. Highway 160 is one of the best routes to view the scenic and everyday life of today's Navajo. Although less crowded and more traditional than the Window Rock area, this stretch is not quite as remote as the Monument Valley region. This north-central portion of the Navajo reservation is still in transition and retains a rich cultural flavor alongside some of the best scenery in Navajoland. Just 12.6 miles north of Canyon de Chelly is the community of Many Farms. The Navajo call this location "Water Stringing Out." It is indeed such a well-watered place that there are many carefully tended and productive farms there, making it the breadbasket of the reservation in terms of its arable land. Many of the acres are irrigated, providing a belt of green when the rest of the country is brown and dry. The Navajo Community College there was the first college for American Indians to be owned and operated by the Indians themselves.

The road soon gives way to beautiful red rock country, dotted with Navajo hogans and farms. There are enough hogans of all shapes, sizes, and descriptions strung out along this route on both sides of the highway to make you a hogan expert by the time you complete this route. You often will see flocks of sheep or goats alongside the road being tended by Navajo women and children and, with luck, you will see young Navajo children riding bareback in the long stretches of open land along the road. Where U.S. Highway 191 meets U.S. Highway 160, you have a choice. You can either go west through fairly uninteresting country to Kayenta, or you can head east 31.2 miles to Teec Nos Pos, gateway to the Four Corners Monument and home of a well-known trading post where intricately designed Teec Nos Pos rugs can be purchased.

At Teec Nos Pos junction, turn north on U.S. Highway 160 for a geography lesson you will not soon forget. At approximately 6 miles, you will see a sign marking the spur road to the Four Corners Monument. Turn left and follow the short distance to the road's end and a large parking lot. Almost every day many Navajo are there, having set up tables around their pickups for the purpose of selling jewelry and other items to the tourist trade. This is the only place in the United States where the borders of four states are so aligned that you can be in all four states on one time. Walk up to the monument, place both feet in two of the four quadrants. Now comes the hard part—bend over and place each hand in the remaining two quadrants. You are now, literally, standing, squatting, or perhaps "panting" in four states at one time.

From there you can either continue north into the geographic area covered by Section III of this book, or you can retrace your steps to Highway 160/504 and head southeast to Shiprock, New Mexico. On the way, you will see a most impressive geological monument, 1,700-foot-high Ship Rock. This volcanic plug or throat has fins of igneous rock running north and south which resemble wings. There are numerous Navajo legends concerning this rock which the Navajo call "Winged Rock." Although its soft volcanic rock represents a dangerous challenge, it was first climbed in 1939 by the California Sierra Club. Topping out at 7,178 feet, this imposing rock structure was named by early white settlers who thought it resembled an old windjammer under full sail. Indeed in the evening just before sunset, after a hot summer's day, an optical illusion is created which makes it appear as though this gigantic monolith is rising off the desert floor and floating.

All along New Mexico Highway 504, you may see oil well pumps as they bring barrels of "black gold" to the surface. In several areas, particularly around Red Mesa, you will see traditional hogans within a few yards of these pumps. The royalties from many of these wells have helped to enrich the Navajo tribal government. At 26 miles from the Four Corners Junction is the sprawling modern community of Shiprock, New Mexico. There, amidst the traffic and the suburbanlike sprawl you will note that the northeast corner of the reservation has not been able to resist some of the less desirable aspects of white, modern culture. Nonetheless, the Shiprock Trading Post is still an excellent repository for Navajo handcrafts.

From Shiprock you can travel 25 miles to Farmington, New Mexico, and enter the geographic area covered by Section III. Or alternatively you can head north on U.S. Highway 160/666, 41 miles to Cortez, Colorado, another gateway to Section III.

Or to reach the sights in north central New Mexico you can drive south 92 miles to Gallup, New Mexico and then 138 miles east on U.S. Interstate 40 to Albuquerque. Or you can drive 40 miles east to Bloomfield, New Mexico, and then 167 miles southeast on New Mexico Highway 44 to Bernalillo, New Mexico, where you are just a short distance from either Albuquerque or Santa Fe. This route also takes you by the unpaved road leading to Chaco Culture National Historical Park.

Staying There

Lodging

The total tour covered by Section II is over five hundred miles in length. Accommodations outside of Flagstaff are few and far between. But among these few accommodations are some real gems that place you in the midst of settings that evoke the scenic and cultural essence of this area. If you are going to travel in this area in the busy summer season, and where you stay and what kind of room you get makes a difference, it is wise to reserve ahead of time. On the other hand, if you have not tied down reservations before arriving, you might be lucky enough to get some sort of accommodation on the spur of the moment, even in the peak of the summer season. I have done that several times by calling ahead the morning I plan to be there and guaranteeing my reservation with a credit card. But, if you really want to be certain about it, phone or correspond with the establishment before you begin your trip, and prepay either by personal check or credit card. This way your room will be held for you no matter when you arrive. In lieu of any of the above, arrive before 4:00 P.M. on the day you want to stay and inquire about space and the possibility of any cancellations. There are always cancellations, but there are almost always people wanting those cancellations during the peak travel season. Many tourist-oriented facilities on the high desert do not operate full services or are closed from early November through February. If for any reason you are travel-ing to this area in the winter months you should check ahead of time to determine what facilities are open. And, of course, be prepared for snow and winter conditions.

Food

Restaurants outside of the Flagstaff area are sparse. Most of them are listed with the lodging they are associated with. A few independent cafés are listed separately. In Indian Country there are some special foods you may want to watch for. Staples of the Navajo diet are mutton stew, fry bread, fried potatoes, coffee, and soda pop. A recent innovation is the Navajo taco. This is a piece of fry bread covered with a variety of condiments including lettuce, tomatoes, beans, and either a chili or tomato sauce. On the Navajo reservation, you may not find fish, fowl, or eggs readily available, as the more traditional Navajo often do not eat these "taboo" items.

On the Hopi reservation keep an eye out for "posole." Posole is corn that resembles hominy. The Hopi also relish stews and have their own version of fry bread. Look for the excellent pik'ami pudding made of cornmeal. And if you have the chance, try the piki bread, a small bluish cylinder of paper-thin bread resembling parchment paper rolled up into a scroll. This is a real delicacy. It is made of blue cornmeal, which is spread thinly on a stone griddle. After cooking just a few seconds, it is deftly lifted and rolled while soft.

Hopi Ceremonial Dances

Although the ceremonial dances of the Hopi begin for the new year in December, most travelers will only be on the mesas for the spring and summer dances. Nonetheless, it is helpful to view these summer dances in the context of the Hopi ceremonial cycle.

The Hopi New Year, beginning at the time of the winter solstice, December 21, is celebrated with the Soyal Ceremony. During this time of longer days, as the sun starts back north again, the symbol of renewed life is further reinforced as a single kachina returns from his underworld home in the San Francisco Peaks, a harbinger of more deities to come in future months. And this is the beginning of the six to seven months in which the kachinas take the responsibility for village ceremonies from the Bear Clan.

Some of the kachinas are said to represent the dead and some are cloud kachinas who can bring rain, while others are thought to be intermediaries between the Hopi and their gods. The kachina dancers are symbolic representations in human form of the kachina deities and consequently resemble otherworldly beings with their masks and elaborate costumes. It is said that the kachina dancers are so well prepared through meditation and purification in the kiva that they feel themselves to be not just impersonators but actually personifications of the 250 to 300 different kachinas. During Soyal, prayer sticks or paahos are exchanged among the villagers to honor the return of the kachinas and to wish for each other's well-being.

By February, so many kachinas have returned that the largest kachina ceremony, Powamu or the Bean Dance, is staged. As many as two hundred kachina dancers may appear at this time, thereby dramatically announcing the return of most of the kachinas to the village. During this ceremony, beans are sprouted in the warm nurturing environment of the heated kivas, while the cold winds howl and snow blankets the plaza outside. This symbolic act presages the richness of the coming growing season. If the beans sprout well and grow tall in the kiva, then it follows that the corn will be strong and grow tall in the summer. But the

View from Goulding's Ranch

concern is not just for crops. There is also a deep concern for renewed spiritual life as young children are initiated into the kachina cult. During this time, the carved kachina figures or dolls are given to the young girls in the village, while other gifts are given to the boys.

Following Powamu is a constant series of kiva and plaza dances, as well as races in late winter and early spring. During some of these more social dances, marvelously costumed Hopi represent their neighbors or enemies. From May through July there are kachina dances almost every weekend in one or more of the villages. From April through July there are a variety of dances for good weather and good crops. These are usually daytime kachina dances. They are often held on Saturdays so that the Hopi who live off the reservation can return to see them. The public is often welcome.

The kachina dances culminate with the Niman or Home Dances held the last three weekends in July in several of the villages. This, the second most important ceremonial during the year and the last of the masked dances, is held to thank the kachinas for their help in producing crops that are ripening by then, and to bid them good-bye as they leave their villages for their spiritual home in the San Francisco Peaks for the remainder of the year. When the kachinas leave, responsibility for the ceremonial cycle returns to the Bear Clan. Usually on the third weekend of August the Snake-An-te-lope Dance occurs alternating with the Flute Dance every other year. The public is usually invited to attend the last day or two of the sixteen-day Snake Dance ceremony made famous by the likes of D. H. Lawrence and others.

In September the Women's Society performs several dances, including the Knee High Dance in late September and the Basket Dance around the middle of October. Morningtime Butterfly Dances are also performed during this time. The Hopi year ends in late November when the Men's Societies seek the solitude of the kiva to initiate young Hopi men into the important ceremonial societies and to pray for the renewal of life in a ceremony called Wuwtsim. With new initiates to keep these centuries-old ceremonies going, the new year is greeted once again with the Soyal Ceremony.

Many of the dances in the Hopi ceremonial calendar are open to the public, even though they are not advertised. Most summer visitors are able to see some of the Niman or Home dances in July, as well as the Snake Dance in August and some of the family and women's dances in the fall, such as the Butterfly and Basket dances. Dances usually fall on Saturday, with an occasional extra day on Friday or Sunday. So if you want to see Hopi ceremonial dances, plan to go to the mesas on the weekends. Do not rely on any of the dates listed above until you have checked them out a short time before the event is to occur. The Hopi Cultural Center Motel is often a good source of information, as is the Museum of Northern Arizona in Flagstaff. Should you not find the information you are seeking from these sources, try the agencies of the Hopi Reservation. (See "Telephone Numbers," this section.)

But not every traveler visiting Hopiland will want to or be able to spend the time to attend one of the Hopi ceremonial dances. You must be prepared to sit or stand at least two or three hours in the afternoon sun on a rooftop that you reach by climbing a ladder. If you are not there very early, all the good viewing positions will be taken, and you will have to rubberneck it for the afternoon. For in addition to visitors, the dances are extremely well attended by the Hopi themselves. In fact, the story is told that one weekend the Hopi people were supposed to attend an important meeting of the tribal council to decide how five million dollars' worth of land grants were to be distributed. The Hopi newspaper reported that only a few people showed up for this important tribal meeting, while over five hundred people attended a basket dance that same weekend. So the dances are well attended and the crowds, which can be fierce, somehow materialize out of what appear to be deserted mesas and underpopulated villages.

However, if the above are not obstacles and you are willing to attend with peace in your heart, as the Hopi say, and in a sense to become a Hopi for an afternoon, you will witness one of the most moving experiences of your lifetime.

Any reservation at the Hopi Cultural Center Motel for a dance weekend in the summer should be made well in advance. If you cannot get a reservation there, you may want to try the small motel in Keams Canyon or the very nice modern Tuba Motel in Tuba City.

Shopping (Consumer Tips for Buying Indian Arts and Crafts)

In the late 1920s and early 1930s, my parents made several forays over rough, dusty unimproved roads to the Pueblo villages along the Rio Grande Valley in New Mexico. The Pueblo Indians there, like those in western New Mexico and Arizona, had not too many years before discovered their "roots" in nearby archaeological diggings. Greatly influenced by their Anasazi ancestral art, beautiful pottery once more became a hallmark of the native southwestern people. In those days, some amount of trading still went on. My father took candy (especially jelly beans) with him, for in the more remote areas, candy was quite a luxury for the Indians. With some cash and candy, he acquired numerous pottery pieces, which have been treasured by my family since then. Later he took me back to the same Pueblo villages, where I can vividly remember buying small pots from children my own age in the dusty plazas of the pueblos. Still later and with greater appreciation of Indian crafts, I have taken my family to the doorways of Indian homes along the Rio Grande and on the Hopi mesas in the search for fine handcrafted items. Today, with good, paved village-to-town roads in Arizona and New Mexico, a number of excellent craft shops are available along major highways, as well as in the center of some Indian villages. And, of course, just as earlier in the century, it is still possible to buy from the doors of the homes of the craftspersons.

But most travelers will probably make their purchases in one of the many convenient shops or galleries that specialize in Indian crafts. These shops, found in the major towns and cities, serve as marketplaces for today's Indian craftspeople. There the traveler will be aware, possibly for the first time, not only of the wide assortment and variety of crafts to choose from but of the large selection available of each of the different types of crafts. And it is probably there too that the traveler will first be aware of the price structure of authentic Indian-made crafts in today's marketplace. The confusion that comes from trying to make a single purchase from so many items, and the "sticker shock," which so many travelers experience after looking at a few price tags, are two of the complexities in today's market that were not present twenty or thirty years ago. In today's market Indian craftspeople are beginning to receive, for the first time, fair prices for their skillful and time-intensive work. These prices, which allow for adequate but not excessive compensation, along with the personal satisfaction that comes from the increasing popularity and recognition of their work have led to today's thriving southwestern Native American art movement (it is estimated that there are over twelve thousand Navajo weavers at work today). This country's indigenous traditional craft movement is no longer dying on the vine as it was when rugs and pots sold for a pittance. In fact, southwestern Indian arts and crafts have become so popular that the marketplace has attracted not only manufacturers of legitimate curios and souvenirs but opportunistic and unethical individuals as well, who by their dishonest but well-publicized abuses, have hurt the reputation of the southwestern Indian arts and crafts movement and instilled an unfortunate element of doubt and skepticism in the mind of the unknowledgeable buyer. That is too bad. With a little planning most travelers alert to the problem of either manufactured or handmade imitations from this country or abroad should fare quite well in purchasing an authentic craft item to fit their budget. So arm yourself with some basic knowledge about the crafts you are interested in (for starters read the paragraphs that follow), obtain a list of reliable shops (some thought to be reliable are recommended in this book), and proceed to search for the item that captures your heart and soul and yet fits your pocketbook. There is a wide range of prices available in today's expanded market. Do not hesitate to shop and cross-compare among the numerous reliable dealers on your list. You deserve to pay the lowest price possible that still provides the dealer and craftsperson a fair but not excessive profit. A good dealer recognizes this. For ultimately the viability of the southwestern Indian arts and crafts movement rests on satisfied buyers like yourself who enthusiastically spread the good word about the beauty and pleasure derived from our country's most popular indigenous artwork.

You will see two broad classes of "Indian made" items. In some shops you will be presented with an overwhelming array of commercially made items, which can be classed as souvenirs and curios. Although these items are evocative of Indian Country and the American Southwest, and some are produced by hand in other countries, most are manufactured in assembly line fashion in this country or abroad for the southwest tourist market. Some of them may actually be made by small manufacturing companies on or near the reservation where local Indians apply stereotyped Indian designs to production line pieces. Most of these items are not expensive to make and do not command the price of Native American handcrafted work. The other broad class of items is authentic one-of-a-kind pieces meticulously handcrafted by individual southwestern Indians using techniques and designs handed down through several generations in their families or villages. The difference in both quality and price of these two broad classes of "Indian made" items is in most instances marked. But sometimes the imitation pieces are not clearly or accurately labeled and are pawned off, at higher prices, as genuine Native American handmade crafts. While there is nothing wrong with buying a piece that is manufactured or handmade in another country you need to make certain that the price you pay reflects the origin of the item and does not carry the price tag of the more expensive time and labor-intensive Native American craft item. Usually the differences are relatively easy to spot if you can spend just a little time to educate yourself. If you have time before your trip use the bibliography in this book, or with the help of your local librarian, find books that illustrate with good color photographs examples of authentic Indian handcrafts. There are also a number of consumer guides that can help you sort out the differences. One such book is *A Consumer's Guide to Southwestern Indian Arts and Crafts* by Mark Bahti. Alternatively when you reach Indian Country visit one of the museums listed in the text and spend some time there acquainting yourself with the real McCoy. You will find that for the most part there are a spirit and dynamism that live in the better southwestern Indian handcrafted pots, rugs,

and baskets that cannot be duplicated by commercially made look-alike items.

If you are in the market for an authentic Indian craft item, a basic knowledge of how the craft is created will help you choose the piece that best suits your needs and your pocketbook. You will see authentic handcrafted items ranging from less expensive pieces created by younger artisans just learning their trade to very expensive, museum-quality show pieces handcrafted by master artist-craftspeople whose work is so extraordinary that it would be classified as fine art by almost anyone's standards. There seem to be no hard and fast rules for determining the price of a handcrafted piece. But in general, the more craft hours applied to producing the piece, the higher the price. Other factors that determine the prices may be the artist's skill, experience, and reputation (in that order) as well as the cost of the materials (silver and turquoise for jewelers, bags of dried sheep dung for some potters). To have some idea of the time involved in making a Navajo rug or a pottery vessel, I have listed below the time-consuming, labor-intensive steps used to create these two forms of Native American art.

Weaving. The weaver usually raises her own flock of sheep and goats. After shearing, the raw wool is cleaned, carded, spun, washed, and then dyed with either natural or manufactured dyes. If natural dyes are used there is additional time in gathering the plant material and processing the dyes. The rug is then woven on a hand loom. Generally the intricate pattern is woven from memory. The preparation and weaving time for a three-by-five-foot rug may be nearly four hundred hours. Usually a tighter weave represents both more advanced skill and more time. Today a growing number of weavers are purchasing ready-made yarns in order to achieve more refinement in the final product. Of course this saves a great deal of time. You should be on the alert for Navajo rug look alikes or imitations from Mexico that use Navajo designs. It is certainly all right to purchase these rugs as long as they are properly labeled and priced according to their method of manufacture and country of origin.

Pottery. The traditional potter in this century has

dug her own clay from a special place on the reservation, processed it by hand, and then hand built the vessel, giving it shape by using the coil and scrape method. After the clay slowly dries, the potter makes a slip from clay and water and applies it to the vessel's walls. The slip may then be meticulously burnished or polished with a smooth round stone or a piece of plastic. Pigments are prepared from both mineral and vegetable materials (depending on the color desired), and the pot is then decorated using yucca brushes to apply the design. Once the design has been painted on the vessel, it is then taken outdoors where it is fired in a bonfire fueled by manure, usually dried cow or sheep dung. This traditional painstaking method of firing pots is very tricky because of the difficulty in controlling the intensity of the fire. Many pots

can be lost in the process. The walls of traditionally fired pots are porous and should never be filled with water. Many of the older potters are still producing their work using all the steps mentioned above. But some younger potters are taking shortcuts either by firing their work in electric kilns, using commercial clays, or wielding manufactured paint brushes rather than yucca brushes. All of these changes reflect the desire to produce finer work and to save time. It is sad to see the diminished use of bonfire firing, for there are wonderful (albeit unpredictable) surface changes that occur with that kind of firing that can never be duplicated in an electric kiln. Some southwest potters have abandoned the coil and scrape method of handbuilding the vessel and are now slipcasting pieces (making them in molds, production line

Museum of Northern Arizona, Flagstaff

style), hand decorating them and firing them in an electric kiln. These pieces are best classed as souvenir items and should not bring the price of a handcrafted piece fashioned in the traditional way.

And just a word about Indian jewelry. It is here that the buyer beware dictum should be applied in full force. Some aspects of the Indian jewelry market have become so confusing that at times, not even reputable, knowledgeable dealers can always be certain of a piece's authenticity. In order to sleep well at night, some dealers purchase bulk silver, turquoise, and coral, which they then parcel out to Indian jewelers who ply their trade either individually or in small workshops under the dealer's supervision. Through this arrangement the dealer can best protect his reputation, and the consumer is certain of getting what he is paying for. Most Indian jewelers make their jewelry by hand, but they use modern machines and tools to help them in their tasks just as their anglo counterparts do. The consumer should buy jewelry only from a reliable dealer or a recommended source. And if you are going to buy very expensive jewelry, it might be best to have it evaluated by another dealer or a knowledgeable gemologist.

Whether you are seeking a gem quality piece or just a nice piece of relatively inexpensive cast or hammered silver jewelry, it may be useful to know about some of the materials used in making Indian jewelry. Sterling silver is 92.5 percent pure silver. Generally it is marked in some way indicating that it is sterling silver. Yet I have seen pieces that are sterling that have not been marked. Coil silver is 90 percent pure and should be slightly less expensive than sterling. The next cheapest form of silver is silver plate, a mixture of nickel and silver, which is much cheaper than the other two kinds but is often the silver of choice for certain items that receive a lot of wear, such as money clips. Turquoise is one of the most difficult minerals to evaluate. On today's market there are three types of turquoise. Natural turquoise or gem turquoise is by far the most expensive and is becoming increasingly difficult to find. Probably the most common variety of turquoise you will see on the market today is stabilized turquoise. This non-gem quality but genuine turquoise is chemically treated to make it harder and more durable, because it is too soft in its natural state to be used in jewelry. It is,

of course, less expensive than gem-quality turquoise and because of its availability is one of the more popular and common types you will see. It can be easily confused with gem-quality turquoise. The next type, reconstituted turquoise, is not turquoise at all but rather an aggregate of other mineral or plastic particles dyed to look like turquoise. It is very cheap. Do not think you can judge the difference between these three types of turquoise. Do rely on the judgment of a knowledgeable jeweler, dealer, or gemologist if you are contemplating the purchase of an expensive piece of jewelry. Equally difficult to determine are the authenticity of coral in jewelry pieces and the hand-carved stone fetishes in necklaces. Some fetish pieces are being mass produced cheaply in the Philippines and should not demand the high price of carefully crafted Zuñi fetish pieces.

Increasingly, Indian artists are bringing innovative new designs and techniques to their work. These innovations are often in the form of contemporary treatments of older designs that reflect the unique viewpoint of the artist. These pieces, although different from those produced in the last eighty years are all a part of the evolving culture of the Native American people in the southwest. The life of the Indian crafts movement depends both on artists who preserve the old teachings and styles as well as those who incorporate new ideas with the old methods. The high quality contemporary work of today may well become the standard for the "traditional" work of tomorrow.

Navajo Arts and Crafts

The Navajo make beautiful and finely crafted jewelry. In addition to turquoise and coral necklaces, look for the popular silver and turquoise and coral combinations found in bracelets, concha belts, and in the squash blossom necklaces. Less well known are Navajo sand paintings and the fragile Navajo pottery, brown in color because of its glazing with piñon pitch. In addition, the Navajo weave beautiful sashes and make purses constructed out of woven materials. They also make a few baskets covered with piñon pitch to make them waterproof. These baskets often have small handles made of horsehair.

Navajo silver concha belt

But the tightly woven, durable, well-designed Navajo rug is probably the most sought-after item. Not too many years ago, trading posts in each corner of the reservation carried rugs woven only in that area. Today almost all trading posts carry a variety of rugs. Because of paved roads and better communication, Navajo weavers may travel all over the reservation trying to get the best price for their fine work. Also, with increased communication, the weavers in one region may often weave a rug that has been the specialty of another region. And, today, throughout the reservation, a few weavers are incorporating into their work mohair

from the Angora goats in their herds. Although mohair gives a rug a softer look and feel, many weavers dislike it because the longer fibers of the silky mohair often blur or obscure the sharp edges of a complex design. The following are some of the rug types you will see in most of the shops listed below.

Ganado Type Rug. This famous rug often known as "Ganado Red" is what most people think a Navajo rug should look like. Traditionally, it is a tightly woven, mostly aniline-dyed rug with a bright red background enclosed by geometric crosses, diamonds, and stripes, all in colors of gray, white, and black. Today, gray often replaces the red background, but the bright reds are still present.

Crystal Rug. These rugs are thought to be some of the finest on the reservation. These distinctive rugs are borderless and are woven from wool dyed with the soft browns, golds, and oranges of the vegetal dyes. The vegetal dyes are the ones the weavers extract from native plants.

Two Gray Hills Rug. These popular, high-quality expensive rugs, woven east of the Chuska Mountains in New Mexico not far from the Chaco area, combine beautiful natural tones of brown, black, and white wools (the sheep are often bred to produce the color needed) to create most of the design, which is then bordered by aniline black dyed wool, providing a fine contrast for the more subtle colors. The design focuses on the intricate central panel, which often is triangular or diamond shaped.

Yei Rug. These rugs have traditionally been woven in the Lukachukai area and in the Shiprock area. They depict the "Yei" gods of the Navajo religion. Mostly aniline dyes are used, and they may be bordered or unbordered. The Yeis woven in the Lukachukai area are heavier and better suited for

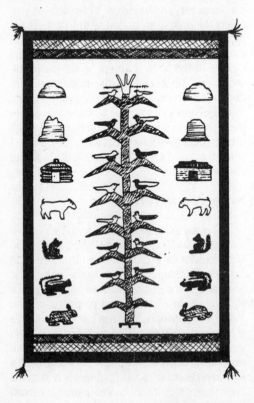

Navajo pictorial rug

the floor while the Yeis woven in the Shiprock area make excellent wall hangings.

Teec Nos Pos Rug. These rugs are usually very busy and intricate in their design and are woven mostly from brightly colored aniline dyes.

Wide Ruins Rug. This is another rug that is woven with wool that has been colored with vegetal dyes. Mostly borderless, these rugs contain endless combinations of subtle, natural colors using a variety of forms of arrows, chevrons, and squash blossoms in the design motif.

Storm Pattern Rug. Originally a pattern found in the Red Lake area, it is now found throughout the reservation. This bordered, highly symmetrical rug contains mostly aniline dyes in bright colors. The designs include zigzags, diamonds, swastikas (an ancient Indian symbol referring to the four directions), arrows, and stepped terraces. Red and black as well as yellow and black combinations are in evidence. Some of these bold designs are now being made with more subtle vegetal dye colors.

Hopi Arts and Crafts

The quality of crafts in the Hopi villages is extremely high. In the various shops on the reservation you can purchase some of the finest handwoven sashes being made in the Southwest today. These tightly woven pieces are made by the Hopi men, as are the beautifully carved and decorated Hopi kachinas that are carved in all of the villages. If you want a Hopi kachina, you will find the prices and selections very good on the mesas. Several young Hopi wood-carvers also are making some outstanding contemporary pieces. In addition to these crafts, Hopi men make the handsome Hopi overlay silver jewelry in a stunning series of shapes and designs. Other Hopi artists such as Charles Loloma design and craft beautiful contemporary jewelry. But possibly the acme of all Hopi handwork is reached by the Hopi potters working in the tradition of the renowned Hopi potter, Nampeyo, who revived pottery making on the mesas. The delicately beautiful hand-coiled Hopi pot is often intricately designed and is usually of the highest quality. The walls of some of the pots are so thin

Hopi sashes

they almost ring when tapped gently. Some Hopi potters also use a surface decoration called corrugation, an old Anasazi pottery technique where the fingernail is used to make a series of small pinch marks in the unsmoothed coils of the wall of the vessel. And then there are Hopi baskets. There are probably no finer baskets being handwoven today in the Southwest than those on the Hopi mesas. The varieties of baskets, including the unique coiled baskets, and where to find them are listed in the subsection on Hopi villages.

Flagstaff, Arizona

Until recently the only lodging available to travelers in Flagstaff was in somewhat nondescript motels (at last count more than eighty) strung out along the route of old U.S. Highway 66 (Santa Fe Avenue) or situated close to the freeway interchanges. Fortunately the scene is changing as reflected in the listings below. The rehabilitation of some of the historic downtown buildings has led to the creation of one comfortable hotel and several restaurants that offer the warm ambience of this historic southwestern town. In addition, the bed-and-breakfast movement, which has caught on with a fury in the rest of the country, has just recently reached Flagstaff. Far from the commercialism of motel row and decidedly different from the downtown historic area, these accommodations reveal yet another slice of Flagstaff. One imparts the charm of Flagstaff's intown residential districts, while the other demonstrates the breathtaking beauty and solitude of the outlying areas. In addition to the two excellent bed-and-breakfast establishments listed here, write or call the Flagstaff Chamber of Commerce for an update of additional listings that may have just appeared on the scene. Write: Flagstaff Chamber of Commerce, 101 West Santa Fe Avenue, Flagstaff, Arizona 86001. Telephone: 1-602-774-4505. In spite of its three thousand rooms for visitors, Flagstaff's accommodations can fill rapidly during any of the times listed under "Fairs, Festivals, and Events." So if your travel plans coincide with those dates, plan to make reservations well ahead of time.

No longer do travelers have to complain that there is no place to eat except in fast-food joints or motel dining rooms. Over the past few years, a number of quality restaurants have opened up offering a wide variety of food in pleasant surroundings, which elicit the spirit of the area. And you will note that Flagstaff is also a transportation hub served by Amtrak's Southwest Limited, commuter airlines from Phoenix, and several major bus lines. Should you arrive without a car, Flagstaff now has convenient lodging and good food service within walking distance of the bus and rail stations. Taxi service is available from the airport, and there is a convenient bus system within the city. Of course rental car services are also available. And there are several tour bus operators who have daily scheduled runs to just about all the major attractions in the immediate area plus the Grand Canyon and most of the sights listed in this section for Indian Country. As the southern gateway to the Colorado Plateau and Indian Country, Flagstaff is home to many tour and expedition services offering excursions and adventure trips to the Grand Canyon

and the Four Corners area. The city itself hosts many premiere fairs, festivals, and events, which are detailed below.

Because Flagstaff is at the crossroads of several different highways and interstate freeways and is divided down the middle by the transcontinental Atchison, Topeka, and Santa Fe railroad tracks, and further subdivided by hills and mesas, some orientation to this sprawling city is useful. It is helpful to know that Interstate 40 passes to the south of the town and south of Northern Arizona University. It intersects with Interstate 17 on the west side of town near the university while Flagstaff Mall anchors the east side of town. U.S. Highways 89, 150, and 66 merge into one and become Santa Fe Avenue (also known as Business Interstate 40), Flagstaff's major east–west arterial, which divides the town north and south. Downtown, Leroux Street runs north and south dividing Flagstaff east and west. U.S. Highway 89A coming up from Oak Creek Canyon merges with traffic from the Interstate 17 and Interstate 40 interchange exits to become Milton Road, which then intersects and merges with Santa Fe Avenue. The San Francisco Peaks, the high mountains that can be seen from many places in town, are to the north.

Lodging

Monte Vista Hotel. Situated in the heart of unpretentious and friendly downtown Flagstaff is this historic hotel (circa 1926), which recently has been thoroughly remodeled and refurbished to evoke the ambience of bygone years. Once a haven for decades of Highway 66 travelers, the rejuvenated Monte Vista brings back the spirit and excitement of the early 1900s to the downtown area. The restoration has been tastefully carried out with both antique western and contemporary touches. Elegant ceiling fans reminiscent of yesteryear help cool most of the newly air-conditioned rooms. Brass light fixtures and oak furniture abound. The final result is a small, friendly European-style hotel smack-dab in the middle of this easy-to-take, bustling western city. The Monte Vista's central location gives you a room with a view not available on Motel Row. From the Monte Vista, you can experience firsthand both the casual aspects of high-altitude western living as you stroll the downtown streets. Located two blocks north of busy Santa Fe Avenue on North San Francisco Street, the hotel has forty-one guest rooms with TV's. Some rooms are quite small, others much larger. Suites are available. All rooms are handsomely decorated. A few rooms without private baths are available and are less expensive. The popular Monte Vista Lounge and the new One Hundred North Restaurant are located on the premises. No pets. Mailing address: Monte Vista Hotel, One Hundred North San Francisco Street, Flagstaff, Arizona 86001. Telephone: 1-602-774-9086. Inexpensive and moderate.

Dierker House Bed and Breakfast. Just a few blocks west of downtown, this centrally located bed-and-breakfast home offers the convenience of downtown and the privacy of a residential district. The modest, older, Victorian-style house with its antique-filled rooms, garden room, and warm fireplace offers three bedrooms, all sharing a bath. From Dierker House you are within walking distance to the transportation depots, downtown, Lowell Observatory, and for the hearty, Northern Arizona University. Write or call ahead for reservations. Continental breakfast included. Mailing address: Dierker House Bed and Breakfast, 423 West Cherry, Flagstaff, Arizona 86002. Telephone: 1-602-774-3249. Inexpensive.

Quality Inn. Out near the university on U.S. Highway 89A (the Sedona Highway) and one-half mile north of the Interstate 17 and Interstate 40 junc-

The high-altitude Abert squirrel

tion near Green Tree Village shopping center, is this handsome two-story motel set back from the highway amid the pines. South and west of downtown, it can be reached from Interstate 40, Exit 195B. There are ninety-six nicely appointed air-conditioned rooms (some with excellent mountain views) with TV's and oversized beds. Swimming pool. There are several restaurants adjacent, including one that is open twenty-four hours a day. Mailing address: Quality Inn, 2000 Milton Road, Flagstaff, Arizona 86001. Telephone: Toll free in the United States (Quality Inns reservations) 1-800-228-5151 or call 1-602-774-8771. High moderate and low expensive.

Walking L Ranch (Bed and Breakfast). The Walking L offers still a different view of living in the Flagstaff area. Located several miles north of downtown just a short distance off the scenic Grand Canyon Road (U.S. Highway 180 or North Fort Valley Road) and near the Museum of Northern Arizona is this peaceful bed-and-breakfast haven. Nestled in the shade of tall ponderosa pines and adjacent to the Coconino National Forest, this spacious, contemporary western-style home (hand built by its owners) is on a large tract of ponderosa-studded land, where you are just as apt to see a handsome Colorado Plateau squirrel scurry from tree to tree as a beautiful scarlet western tanager flit from pine bough to pine bough. Your hosts are two knowledgeable, gracious, and long-transplanted Arizonans, whose hospitality is as warm as the spa provided for their guests. He is a professor at Northern Arizona University, and she is a skillful and artistic knitter. Three bedrooms each with private bath. One bedroom equipped for handicapped. Full American western breakfast included. Write or call ahead for reservations. Mailing address: Walking L Ranch. RR4, Box 721-B, Flagstaff, Arizona 86001. Telephone: 1-602-779-2219. Low moderate.

Fairfield Flagstaff Resort. This one hundred-unit condominium resort is located at the edge of town in East Flagstaff, south of the Flagstaff Mall and Interstate 40 (take Exit 201 to 2580 North Oakmont via Country Club Drive). It is beautifully situated in a quiet, spacious, 2,200-acre pine tree-studded location that offers fine views of the mountains and surrounding countryside. It is Flagstaff at its best. All of the nicely designed, tastefully appointed units contain either a kitchenette or a full kitchen. Touting itself as one of Arizona's destination Four Season Resorts, this attractive if not luxurious resort complex offers almost everything. Two outdoor heated swimming pools, golf course, tennis, and horseback riding are all available along with skiing in the winter. In addition, breakfast, lunch, and dinner are served in the resort's clubhouse dining room, which offers beautiful views of the mountains and the pines. Reservation deposit required. Mailing address: Fairfield Flagstaff Resort, P.O. Box 1208, Flagstaff, Arizona 86002. Telephone: 1-602-526-3232, toll free 1-800-526-1004, or from Arizona 1-800-352-5777. Expensive.

Best Western Little America. Situated on four hundred pine-covered acres near Interstate 40 (Exit 198) in an area rapidly filling up with other motels is one of Flagstaff's best. Follow Santa Fe Avenue east and turn north on Enterprise Road to 2515 East Butler Road. The neat but sprawling two-story complex looks for all the world like a transplant out of the Midwest with its brick facade and white painted gables. This luxury motel has 241 air-conditioned spacious rooms (some with good views of the mountains, some suites with fireplaces and saunas) with TV's. It also boasts many reception, party, and convention rooms that get repeated use by Flag's citizens for weddings, anniversaries, and other special occasions. The giant heated outdoor swimming pool must be one of the largest in Coconino County. The equally gargantuan gift shop carries everything from fine Indian crafts to chewing gum. And it is open twenty-four hours a day as is the coffee shop. For finer fare there is the Western Gold Dining Room with its luncheon buffet and upscale dinners. No pets. Do not let the size fool you. This motor hotel fills up fast during the summer and early fall. So do reserve ahead of time. Mailing address: Best Western Little America, P.O. Box 850, Flagstaff, Arizona 86001. Telephone: Toll free in the United States 1-800-528-1234 (Best Western Reservations Center) or call 1-602-779-2741. Expensive.

La Quinta Motor Inn. Near Little America and close to Exit 198 on Interstate 40 is this moderately priced, older two-story motel with 101 air-conditioned units with TV's. Heated swimming pool. Reservation deposit required. Mailing address: La Quinta Motor Inn, 2350 East Lucky Lane, Flagstaff, Arizona 86001. Telephone: Toll free in the United States (La Quinta Motor Inns reservations) 1-800-531-5900 or call 1-602-779-3614. High moderate and low expensive.

Allstar Inn. Near Little America and close to Exit 198 on Interstate 40 is this economically priced two-story motel with its 121 air-cooled rooms with TV's and oversized beds. Heated swimming pool. Mailing address: Allstar Inn, 2500 East Lucky Lane, Flagstaff, Arizona 86001. Telephone: 1-602-779-6184. Very inexpensive.

Best Western Pony Soldier Inn. This ninety-unit, two-story air-conditioned motel is located along Santa Fe Avenue's motel row and is three miles east of downtown. The rooms are nicely furnished and maintained. All rooms have TV's. Heated swimming pool. A Chinese American restaurant, Afton House, is on the grounds. No pets. Reservation deposit required. Mailing address: Best Western Pony Soldier Inn, 3030 East Santa Fe Avenue, Flagstaff, Arizona 86001. Telephone: Toll free in the United States (Best Western Reservations Center) 1-800-528-1234 or call 1-602-526-2388. Low moderate.

Best Western Kings House Motel. Closer to downtown and offering an informal continental breakfast with your night's stay is this fifty-nine-room air-conditioned motel with TV's. Heated swimming pool. Reservation deposit required. Mailing address: Best Western Kings House Motel, 1560 East Santa Fe Avenue, Flagstaff, Arizona 86001. Telephone: Toll free in the United States (Best Western Reservations Center) 1-800-528-1234 or call 1-602-774-7186. Moderate.

Campgrounds

Flagstaff K.O.A. This K.O.A. is located five and one-half miles out on the northeastern fringes of town just beyond Flagstaff Mall on U.S. Highway 89 (the Sunset Crater Highway). Use Exit 201 from Interstate 40 to find this large modern multi-facility campsite in the pines. It includes some camping cabins for rent. There are two hundred tent and recreational vehicle sites spread out over ten acres. Reservations recommended. Telephone: 1-602-526-9926.

Fort Tuthill County Park. Located three miles south of town just off Interstate 17 (Exit 337) and just off U.S. Highway 89A, the Oak Creek Canyon–Sedona Highway. This 355-acre park has nature trails, racquetball courts, sixty-five tent sites, and ten recreational vehicle sites with hookups. Telephone: 1-602-774-5139.

Bonito Campground. Located near Sunset Crater twelve miles north of Flagstaff on U.S. Highway 89 and then two miles east on FR 545 is this National Forest Service campground with forty-four sites in the pines for tents and recreational vehicles. Telephone: 1-602-527-7470.

Pineflat Campground. Sixteen miles south of Flagstaff and just off the scenic Oak Creek Canyon–Sedona Highway (89A) is this National Forest Service campground with fifty-eight sites for tents and recreational vehicles. Swimming in the creek, nature trails, and fishing are some of the extras. Reserve ahead of time. If this campground is full ask about Cave Springs and Bootlegger campgrounds immediately to the south. Telephone: 1-602-282-4119.

Food

Cottage Place. This excellent dinner restaurant resides in an early twentieth-century home located across the railroad tracks from Santa Fe Avenue, immediately west of the Amtrak station and just off Beaver Street on Cottage Place. 126 West Cottage Place. Telephone: 1-602-774-8431. If you want to sample some of the best continental-style food in Flagstaff in a charming setting that evokes the elegance of bygone years in a warm, friendly way, make a reservation for dinner at Ron Freeman's Cottage Place. With a full and well-selected wine and beer list, the Cottage Place offers up everything from rack of lamb to Hungarian-style pork loin. And in addition to the excellent seafood menu and the superb soups that accompany din-

ner, there are vegetarian specialties such as eggplant parmesan and fettucini alfredo. The delicious desserts, made daily on the premises, are outstanding and include such chocoholic delights as chocolate soufflé cake and German chocolate pie. Reservations recommended. Dinner only. Closed Monday. Moderate.

Buster's. Located at 1800 South Milton in Green Tree Village shopping center southeast of downtown on U.S. Highway 89A leading to Sedona. Telephone: 1-602-774-5155. This family restaurant, with flair and a lot of hubbub, serves delicious, high-quality food. Buster Keaton, the restaurant's namesake, probably never ate this well nor this creatively. For instance, the luncheon menu features delicious and unique items such as the guacamolecheeseburger or the ham and Swiss cheese croissant sandwich. The dinner menu, in addition to hamburgers and sandwiches, offers champagne chicken, veal Marsala, and cajun shrimp Diane. The restaurant does wonderful things with fresh fruit and omelettes. There is "kids stuff" for those under twelve. And for any age there is an outstanding Sunday brunch. The modest wine list is well selected, and the dessert menu ranges from Buster's bigtime hot fudge sundae to chocolate mousse. Closed Monday. Inexpensive and moderate.

One Hundred North Restaurant. Located at One hundred North San Francisco Street in the venerable Monte Vista Hotel. Telephone: 1-602-774-8840. This attractively restored restaurant serves three meals a day. Breakfast may include huevos rancheros or homemade ranch biscuits with sausage gravy, as well as traditional offerings. Sandwiches dominate the menu at noon while the dinner menu offers a balance between steak and seafood as well as specialty dishes featuring veal and chicken. Inexpensive and moderate.

Charly's. Located downtown at 23 North Leroux in the historic Weatherford Hotel. Telephone: 1-602-779-1919. Although the nicely renovated space that houses the restaurant is reminiscent of the late 1890s, it is the modern western spirit of the place that hooks you. Perhaps it is the lively piano music that sometimes accompanies the meals, or possibly it is the crowd of regular locals who seem to love this place that gives it so much life. At any rate, this popular lunch spot serves up an excellent assortment of sandwiches, delicious homemade soups, and salads for the midday meal. Breakfast includes many old favorites as well as a long list of pancake and waffle specialties. And for dinner there are steaks, prime rib, scampi, and swordfish. Open daily. If Charly's is crowded try their satellite restaurant next door, The Weatherford Café, which offers more indigenous southwestern dishes including the popular Navajo taco. Inexpensive and moderate.

Alpine Pizza-Spaghetti Station. Located at 7 North Leroux in the historic district area. Telephone: 1-602-779-4109. This casual café turns out a variety of delicious pizzas as well as a number of Italian pasta specialties. Outdoor streetside dining, weather permitting. Inexpensive.

Café Espress. Located at 16 North San Francisco Street. Telephone: 1-602-774-0541. This 1960s café is funky but a lot of fun and a good place to catch up on the local scene at breakfast or lunch. With a bakery right on the premises, breakfast naturally features freshly baked breakfast rolls as well as omelets. Lunch includes salads and sandwiches on homebaked breads. Limited outdoor dining, weather permitting. Inexpensive.

Bun Huggers. Located at 901 South Milton Road (west end), telephone: 1-602-779-3743, and 3012 East Santa Fe (east end in Kachina Square), telephone: 1-602-526-0542. Flee the national fast-food chains for this regional version of the charcoal-broiled hamburger house. Sit on log benches (what else in this land of lumberjacks) and design your own hamburger. Or try the soups, chili, salad bar, or deep-fried vegetables. Open daily until 10:00 P.M. Inexpensive.

Kachina Restaurant. Located right along busy Santa Fe Avenue at 2220 East Santa Fe Avenue. Telephone: 1-602-779-5790. This unpretentious (in Albuquerque they would say "hole in the wall") Mexican restaurant is immensely popular with the locals. But besides the local scene, which may include Navajo and Hopi families visiting town for a day, the down-home food of this family-run café is some of the best in the area. Inexpensive.

Fairfield Flagstaff Restaurant. See driving instructions to Fairfield Flagstaff Resort listed in the "Lodging" section above. Telephone: 1-602-526-9324. This restaurant and dining room serves breakfast, lunch, and dinner and is open to the public. The comfortable dining room in this contemporary Arizona-style building has outstanding views out over the green oasis of the golf course, the pines, and the mountains. The views from this other slice of Flagstaff will tantalize you and so will the food. There is a wide choice of breakfast and luncheon favorites and a dinner menu featuring prime rib and other favorites as well as some special continental entrées. Reservations recommended. Moderate and expensive.

Garland's Oak Creek Lodge (Dining Room). Located about twenty miles from Flagstaff on Oak Creek Canyon Highway 89A. Turn right or west from the highway when you see the sign. Telephone: 1-602-282-3343. Not for everybody; the dining room at Garland's is for adventurous gourmands who not only demand fresh ingredients but who also delight in creative gourmet food. The dining room, which serves lodge guests on the American Plan, is open to the public. Although breakfast here is a treat, it is dinner that deserves your attention. Each evening there is only one sitting for dinner. The meal is a fixed-price, single, multi-course dinner with only a few possible choices. But do not worry, the variety and assortment of unique and delicious courses will make you think you had a choice even if you did not. The first appetizer is free if you take into account the visual feast placed in front of you as you drive the approximately twenty miles from Flagstaff to Garland's. Oak Creek Canyon serves up a palette of colors and ruggedly beautiful sights, which make this thirty-five to forty-five-minute drive seem like it only lasted a few. Arrive a little early to walk around the spacious tree-shaded, log cabin-studded grounds of this unique lodge. The older log-and-Arizona-stone building, which serves as the office, reception area, and dining room is almost worth a visit by itself with its wonderful fireplace and American Southwest Indian furnishings. With a visit to Garland's you feel as though you have met the northern Arizona of your dreams. You may stay there, too, but reservations must be made months in advance. Reservations required for breakfast and dinner. Reserve well ahead of time, especially for weekends. Garland's Oak Creek Lodge, P.O. Box 152, Sedona, Arizona 86336. High moderate and expensive.

Tours

Nava-Hopi Tours. This major bus tour line offers tours to many of the sights around Flagstaff, including Walnut Canyon, Sunset Crater, and Wupatki National monuments. It also offers tours to the Grand Canyon as well as Monument Valley farther to the north and Oak Creek Canyon to the south. For further information and schedules, write Nava-Hopi Tours, Box 339, Flagstaff, Arizona 86002. Telephone: Toll free within the United States 1-800-892-8687 or 1-602-774-5003.

The Seven Wonders Scenic Tours. This tour director with a seven-passenger van is willing to customize tours to your liking. Tours may include every place from the Grand Canyon to more distant sites on the Indian reservations and beyond. Telephone: 1-602-526-2501.

Museum of Northern Arizona. The museum offers a series of half-day and full-day summer adventures for children. Some of the programs include basketmaking, natural history lessons, and solar energy projects or full-day activities such as archaeological camp, geology hikes, and learning to live outdoors. In addition there are nature hikes for families, which include exploring several ruin sites and hiking the wildflower meadows in August. For further information, write Museum of Northern Arizona, Education, Route 4, Box 720, Flagstaff, Arizona 86001. Telephone: 1-602-774-5211.

Expeditions. Choose from Grand Canyon Youth Expeditions, kayaking, backpacking, or support trips on the Colorado Plateau. These tour outfitters operate the Kayak and Raft Equipment Sales at 624 North Beaver Street. As an authorized National Park Concessionaire at the Grand Canyon, they offer a variety of five- to eighteen-day hiking and white-water trips in that area. For further information, write Expeditions, Route 4, Box 755, Flagstaff, Arizona 86001. Telephone: 1-602-779-3769.

Wild and Scenic Expeditions. This broad-ranged expedition company offers white-water trips on the Colorado River in the Grand Canyon, at Cataract Canyon, and on the San Juan and Green rivers. Depending on the trip, you will travel in a manually powered or motorized raft or a sportyak. This company also offers some overland tours by jeep into Indian Country and Utah's canyon lands. For further information, write Wild and Scenic Expeditions, P.O. Box 460, Flagstaff, Arizona 86002. Telephone: 1-800-231-1963 or 1-602-774-7343.

Arizona Raft Adventures. This company's specialty is white-water raft trips on the Colorado River near the Grand Canyon. Both motorized and oar-paddled trips are available. For more information, write Arizona Raft Adventures, P.O. Box 697, Flagstaff, Arizona 86002. Telephone: 1-602-526-8200.

Horseback Riding

Hitchin' Post Stables. Located four and one-half miles east of Flagstaff on Lake Mary Road. These outfitters provide rides of various lengths including rides through Walnut Canyon, the site of prehistoric cliff dwellers. In addition, horseback rides or horse-drawn wagon rides are available for a special Sunset Steak Ride. Or if you want to start the day with a western flair, try a cowboy breakfast ride. Reduced prices for children ten and under. For further information, write Hitchin' Post Stables, 448 Lake Mary Road, Flagstaff, Arizona 86001. Telephone: 1-602-774-1719 or 1-602-774-7131.

Fairs, Festivals, and Events

Pine Country Pro Rodeo. This professional rodeo takes place about the middle of June each year. It provides a lot of real western thrills. Located at the fairgrounds, Fort Tuthill Park. Telephone: 1-602-774-4505.

Festival of Native American Arts. For seven weeks,

from the middle of June to the first week of August, Flagstaff hosts Native Americans from the Four Corners area and other parts of Arizona and New Mexico in a series of events sponsored by the Coconino Center for the Arts and by NACA (Native Americans for Community Action). There are many premiere events taking place during this festival that secure Flagstaff's place as one of America's most important centers for the advancement of American Southwest Indian culture. Events at the Coconino Center for the Arts include a series of Native American craft demonstrations, special exhibits, workshops, films, lectures, dances, and musical and dramatic performances. The Coconino Center for the Arts is open all year and hosts a variety of art and photography exhibits, music concerts, and lectures. The center is located at 2300 North Fort Valley Road, just south of the Museum of Northern Arizona on the east side of U.S. Highway 180, north of town. For precise date and details each year, write Festival of Native American Arts, P.O. Box 296, Flagstaff, Arizona 86002. Telephone: 1-602-779-6921.

Annual Hopi Craftsman Exhibition. This excellent juried show is sponsored by and held at the Museum of Northern Arizona, three miles north of downtown just off U.S. Highway 180 (North Fort Valley Road). The best of Hopi traditional and contemporary pottery, basketry, weaving, and carving (kachinas) are brought in for display and sale from the Hopi Reservation. It is held over the weekend closest to the Fourth of July. The Fourth is the biggest day of this event, which has been held annually for almost sixty years. Mailing address: Museum of Northern Arizona, Route 4, Box 720, Flagstaff, Arizona 86001. Telephone: 1-602-774-5211.

Annual Navajo Craftsman Exhibition. This premiere event, sponsored by the Museum of Northern Arizona, occurs three weeks after the Hopi event during the last week of July and the first few days of August. It hosts the best in Navajo rugs, jewelry, and pottery for display and sale. This event has been held annually for almost forty years. Mailing address: Museum of Northern Arizona, Route 4, Box 720, Flagstaff, Arizona 86001. Telephone: 1-602-774-5211.

Annual Zuñi Craftsman Exhibition. This recently established exhibition features the outstanding jewelers, potters, and carvers from the Zuñi Reservation southeast of Flagstaff. It is staged annually for five days in late May over Memorial Day weekend. Mailing address: Museum of Northern Arizona, Route 4, Box 720, Flagstaff, Arizona 86001. Telephone: 1-602-774-5211.

Flagstaff Festival of the Arts. For over twenty years Flagstaff has attracted visitors to its cool summer climate with a five-week (July to August) series of music, drama, film, dance, and arts events held throughout the city and on the campus of Northern Arizona University. There is, of course, an emphasis on regional art and music (including the excellent Flagstaff Symphony Orchestra). In addition, world-famous artists and musicians take part in this midsummer art and music storm. For an updated calendar, write Flagstaff Festival of the Arts, P.O. Box 1607, Flagstaff, Arizona 86002. Telephone: 1-602-523-5055.

Annual Coconino County Fair. This annual event, held at the nearby Fort Tuthill County Fairgrounds, draws folks from all over this huge county for contests, competitions, and just plain fun. Usually held around Labor Day weekend in early September. For further information, write Flagstaff Chamber of Commerce, 101 West Santa Fe Avenue, Flagstaff, Arizona 86001. Telephone: 1-602-774-4505.

Shopping

The Museum of Northern Arizona Gift Shop. Route 4 (Box 720), North Fort Valley Road. Telephone: 1-602-774-5211. This shop is known for purchasing the best southwestern Indian handcrafted work available. You will find many unique items here not found elsewhere. Although beautiful craftwork from other tribes is available, their extensive selection of Navajo and Hopi jewelry, Hopi pottery and kachinas, Navajo rugs and Hopi weavings is exceptional. The gift shop's reputation is impeccable, so you can be certain that what you buy is the real thing. The museum also has a bookstore in its lobby with a large selection of regional books and periodicals for sale, including current and back issues of the museum's own outstanding magazine, *Plateau.* The museum is on Arizona Highway 89 just three miles north of Flagstaff city center. It is set among ponderosa pines, and the shade they provide makes this an excellent place for a picnic.

Gift Shop. Coconino Center for the Arts. 2300 North Fort Valley Road. Telephone: 1-602-779-6921. Located north of town in the Fort Valley Cultural Park. In this very nice gift shop adjacent to the exhibits gallery, you will find a broad range of southwestern Indian crafts as well as regional crafts from the area. There are many gift possibilities in this wide-ranging shop, from T-shirts and posters to Indian jewelry and other Four Corners crafts. There is also a nice selection of regional cards.

The Art Barn. Located on the grounds of the Fort Valley Cultural Park in a building adjacent to the Coconino Center for the Arts. This interesting shop seems to carry a little bit of everything. From Four Corners Indian crafts and jewelry to utilitarian pottery and crafts from the Flagstaff area, this large emporium offers the buyer many choices.

Old Town Traders/Old Town Gallery. 2 West Santa Fe Avenue. Telephone: 1-602-774-7770. This outstanding shop and gallery, located in a renovated historic, downtown corner building, has a wide and distinctive selection of Four Corners southwestern Indian fine arts and crafts. The owner wears two hats, one as an anthropologist and the other as a contemporary jeweler. In his spacious gallery he has brought together a collection of well-selected Navajo rugs, Pueblo pottery, kachinas, Indian jewelry, and paintings, many of which are of museum quality. He is extremely knowledgeable about Indian art and, like a good teacher, is willing to share that knowledge with his customers. The gallery represents some of today's finest Native American artists from the region and hosts numerous Indian art shows and musical concerts. The selection of contemporary Indian jewelry is stunning.

Spirit Gallery. 9 North Leroux Street. Telephone: 1-602-774-7114. The distinctive look and "feel" of this gallery, located in the historic downtown district, probably reflects the way the district will eventually develop. This gallery of contemporary southwest crafts features the works of both local and regional artists. The owners have brought together a splendid selection of pottery, glass, jewelry, weavings, and handcrafted wood pieces, which adds immeasurably to the new level of excellence cropping up in the downtown shops.

Landmark House. 7 Riordan Road. Telephone: 1-602-779-4474. Kill two birds at one time while soaking up a little Flagstaff history by shopping in this historic Flagstaff residence-turned-shop southeast of downtown. Besides prints, paintings, fine collectibles, and antiques, there are many gift items reflecting the region and beyond.

Anasazi Gallery of Art. 2710 North Steves Boulevard. Telephone: 1-602-562-0718. Located in the Kachina Square shopping center out east on Santa Fe Avenue. This large gallery carries a wide range of American Indian crafts including Pueblo pottery, Navajo rugs, kachinas, and Indian jewelry. There is also a nice selection of gift cards and gift items from the region.

McGaugh's Newsstand and Tobacco Shop. 24 North San Francisco Street. Telephone: 1-602-774-2131. Located in the downtown area across the street from the Monte Vista Hotel. This old-time newsstand specializes in a truly outstanding selection of regional books and maps covering the local area, the Four Corners region, and the Southwest in general. In addition, this down-home establishment, with its popcorn machine, children's books, comic books, and candy selection, also stocks out-of-town newspapers to keep you in touch with the rest of the world.

Telephone Numbers

Flagstaff Chamber of Commerce. 101 West Santa Fe Avenue. Telephone: 1-602-774-4505.
Coconino National Forest. 2323 East Greenlaw Lane. Telephone: 1-602-779-3311.
Pine Country Transit (Flagstaff bus company). 113 West Clay Avenue. Telephone: 1-602-779-6624.
Budget Rent-A-Car. Telephone: 1-800-527-0700 or 1-602-779-0306.
Bargain Rent-A-Car. Pre-owned rentals. 23 North

Leroux, second floor. Telephone: 1-602-526-2323.
Northern Arizona University. Box 4084, Flagstaff, Arizona 86001. Telephone: 1-602- 523-9011.
Taxi Service. 1-602-774-1374 or 1-602-774-7329.
Motel information. 1-602-779-5125 or toll free from the Phoenix area. Telephone: 233-FLAG.
Fairfield Flagstaff Golf Course. 1-602-526-3232.
Municipal swimming pool. 1-602-635-9958.

Monument Valley

Lodging and Food

Goulding's Lodge and Tours. Goulding's is the only accommodation in the valley and just a few minutes away from the monument's entrance. Located in an enviable spot on the high desert, close to the Arizona-Utah border, it is situated directly beneath soaring eight-hundred-foot red sandstone cliffs and offers panoramic views out over the valley and its many monoliths. The lodge is surrounded by high open desert, which is dotted here and there with hogans and modern Navajo houses that are spaced wide apart. There is no hustle and bustle, just peace and solitude. The older ranch buildings house the office, craft store, and part of the dining room, while the sixty air-conditioned lodging units (all with two double beds) are in typical motel style. The original nineteen, single-story motel units (called lodge rooms) are nicely refurbished and are close to the dining room, which is on the same level. The forty-one newer units (called motel rooms) are in a handsome two-story building in a more open location a short distance down the hill from the older units. All rooms have spectacular views and picture taking is made easy by the rooms having sliding glass doors that open to small balconies overlooking the valley.

All three meals can be taken at the lodge in the recently renovated and enlarged dining room. No reservations required. The menu is broad, offering everything from Navajo tacos and fried chicken to green pepper steak. The dining room is often closed from November through February.

Goulding's Lodge, Monument Valley

Liquor and wine cannot be sold on the Navajo Reservation. You may, however, bring your own. The curio and craft store specializes in items made by the Navajo (see "Shopping"). In addition to serving as a Monument Valley tour center (see "Tours"), the lodge also operates a convenience store with gas pumps, a laundromat, and a car wash just down the hill from the motel units. You should note that in the summer the ranch, which is in Utah, is on Mountain Daylight Time (as is all of the Navajo Reservation) while Arizona, immediately to the south of the Navajo Reservation, is on Mountain Standard Time. Pets allowed. Advance reservation deposit required. Deposit refunded upon twenty-four-hour notice of cancellation. Mailing address: Goulding's Lodge and Tours, Box 1, Monument Valley, Utah 84536. Telephone: 1-801-727-3231. Moderate.

If Goulding's is full, the following are the only alternatives, definitely second-best in my view.

The San Juan Inn and Canyon Country Scenic Tours. Located twenty-five miles northeast of the Monument Valley Visitor Center on U.S. Highway

163. This is a basic, modest, but adequate motel situated along the banks of the San Juan River. It has twenty-two air-conditioned rooms with TV's and an adjacent restaurant. The inn offers daily tours of Monument Valley and the entire canyon lands region (see "Tours") as well as river trips. Advance reservation deposit required. Mailing address: San Juan Inn, Box 535, Mexican Hat, Utah 84531. Telephone: 1-801-683-2220. Inexpensive.

Wetherill Inn Motel. Located twenty-five miles southwest of the Monument Valley Visitor Center on U.S. Highway 163. This two-story motel with fifty air-conditioned units with TV's is just north of the main Kayenta junction. Café adjacent. Pets allowed. Advance reservation deposit required in summer. Mailing address: Wetherill Inn Motel, Box 175, Kayenta, Arizona 86033. Telephone: 1-602-697-3231 or 1-602-697-3232. Moderate.

Campgrounds

Mitten View Campground. Located one-quarter mile southwest of the Monument Valley Tribal Park visitor center. Inquire at visitor center. Reservations necessary in the summer for the one hundred tent and recreational vehicle units. Telephone: 1-801-727-3287.

Goulding's Monument Valley K.O.A. Located a short distance west of Goulding's Lodge in scenic Rock Door Canyon with fine panoramas of Monument Valley. Fifty sites with full hookups available. Convenience store and gas pumps nearby. Telephone: 1-801-727-3280.

Tours

Goulding's Lodge and Tours. Goulding's offers two half-day tours to Monument Valley and a full-day tour to Monument Valley and Mystery Valley (both starting at 9:00 A.M.) in a variety of four-wheel-drive vehicles. In the summer, a sunset tour of Monument Valley is also offered between 4:00 P.M. and 7:00 P.M. (See narrative section of Monument Valley for detailed information about sights on the Monument Valley tour.) Special tours to certain other sites in the region can also be arranged. Tours operate only if minimum numbers (six for

daytime tours, eight for sunset tour) of adult passengers are reached. Tours for children are one-half the adult price. Advance reservations are recommended but are not essential if room is available. Mailing address: Goulding's Lodge and Tours, Box 1, Monument Valley, Utah 84536. Telephone: 1-801-727-3231.

Canyon Country Scenic Tours. This group offers half- or full-day tours to Monument Valley and Indian ruins in the San Juan Basin. River tours. Mailing address: Canyon Country Scenic Tours, P.O. Box 426, Mexican Hat, Utah 84531. Telephone: 1-801-683-2226.

Crawley's Navajo Nation Tours. Offers tours of Monument Valley and surrounding sites. Mailing address: Crawley's Navajo Nation Tours, Box 187, Kayenta, Arizona 86033. Telephone: 1-602-697-3463.

Adventure Trails of the West. This far-reaching outfitter from Wickenberg, Arizona, offers deluxe guided tours that last several days through both Monument Valley and Canyon de Chelly. Geared for adults and older teenagers. Mailing address: Adventure Trails of the West, Box 1494, Wickenburg, Arizona 85358. Telephone: 1-602-684-3106.

Shopping

Goulding's Lodge. The curio shop/craft store, in conjunction with the office of Goulding's Lodge, usually has a small stock of good handcrafted items. The small rug room in the back contains a wide selection of rugs from throughout the reservation. A large selection of Navajo jewelry is available as well as a good supply of regional books and cards. Mailing address: Goulding's Lodge and Tours, Box 1, Monument Valley, Utah 84536. Telephone: 1-801-727-3231.

Black Mesa Indian Arts and Crafts Shop. This craft shop located next to the Thriftway Convenience Center at the Kayenta highway junction is new, but the owners are seasoned traders who know the real thing when they see it. They carry a wide assortment of Indian crafts. Telephone: 1-602-697-3435.

Betatakin (Navajo National Monument)

Campgrounds

Navajo National Monument Campground. Located amid piñons and junipers near the Betatakin visitor center at a cool elevation of 7,286 feet are thirty tent and recreational vehicle sites. No fee. Telephone: 1-602-672-2366.

Tours

Keet Seel. All-day horseback trips are available if reservations are made considerably in advance. Mailing address: Superintendent, Navajo National Monument, HC 63, Box 3, Tonalea, Arizona 86044. Telephone: 1-602-672-2366.

Shopping

Navajo National Monument Craft Store. Located adjacent to the visitor center is this small, Navajo craft store, which specializes in Navajo jewelry. Mailing address: Navajo National Monument Craft Store, Tonalea, Arizona 86044. Telephone: 1-602-672-2366.

Tuba City, Arizona

Lodging and Food

Tuba Motel. Located in an enviable part of Tuba City just behind the trading post is this new, modern, and well-designed multistoried motel that offers more comfort than you could ever imagine in the western capital of the Navajo Nation. There are forty air-conditioned rooms, all with queen beds and TV's. Restaurant adjacent. Mailing address: Tuba Motel, Box 247, Tuba City, Arizona 86405. Telephone: 1-602-283-4545. Moderate.

Pancho's Family Restaurant. Conveniently located between the Tuba Trading Post and the Tuba Motel, this restaurant is housed in a new air-conditioned building somewhat reminiscent of a large hogan. The food is basic American, some Mexican and some southwestern regional with a Navajo twist. Telephone: 1-602-283-5260. Inexpensive.

Let's Eat/Tuba City Truck Stop Cafe. This modest little place down on the highway near the junction of U.S. Highway 160 and Arizona Highway 264 with a view east toward the Hopi village, Moenkopi, serves up the best Navajo taco around. Telephone: 1-602-283-4975. Inexpensive.

Fairs, Festivals, and Events

Western Navajo Nation Fair. Tuba City, Arizona. The western Navajo community hosts this large fair, similar to the other tribal fairs, on the second or third weekends in October.

Shopping

Tuba Trading Post. Located one mile west off U.S. Highway 160. Well worth a visit, this active trading post is as much a relic of the past as it is a bustling commercial hub. Navajo rugs, Navajo jewelry and pottery, southwestern Indian baskets, Pueblo Indian pottery, and kachinas are all available, as well as cold soda pop. Mailing address: Tuba Trading Post, P.O. Box 237, Tuba City, Arizona 86045. Telephone: 1-602-283-5441.

Monongya's Jewelry. Located on the southwest corner of the junction of U.S. Highway 160 and Arizona Highway 264 is this very fine Indian arts and crafts shop. It is operated by an outstanding Hopi artist who knows his business. There is a very nice selection of traditional and more contemporary Navajo and Hopi jewelry. Also, this spacious shop has Navajo rugs, an excellent selection of Hopi pottery, and, of course, kachinas, in both traditional and contemporary styles which have brought fame to the owner. Mailing address: Monongya's Indian Jewelry, Tuba City, Arizona 86045. Telephone: 1-602-283-4637.

The Hopi Reservation

Lodging and Food

Hopi Cultural Center Restaurant and Motel. If you have any desire to explore the Hopi mesas and villages, you may want to stay at this centrally located motel, the only accommodation on the Hopi mesas. High atop Second Mesa near the ancient village of Shungopovi, the Hopi, with the help of Arizona architect Ben Gonzales, erected this interesting complex of buildings. Built over two decades ago, they evoke the ancient Hopi architectural style in a modern way. From the exposed second-story porches you can see forever out over the high desert, while in the enclosed courtyard, you feel a sense of the protection and comfort offered by the village plazas. Over the years, the motel has suffered from a lack of maintenance. But no longer. At this writing, close to $1,000,000 has been allocated by the tribe to restore the motel and grounds to their former levels of comfort and beauty. The work is scheduled to be completed in the spring of 1988. Since the motel and adjacent restaurant, craft shops, and museum are tribally run, this is a fine place to meet the Hopi. The thirty-three units are all air-conditioned. Most of the rooms have TV's.

The newly enlarged and air-conditioned restaurant offers friendly, efficient service in a very pleasant well-maintained dining room. The waitresses wear uniforms that have a real Hopi flair.

The food is Hopi-American, and the tunosvongya or menu is interesting. Be sure to try the posole, fry bread, and special lamb stew, as well as the blue cornflakes and the sa qua vi ka vike or blue cornmeal pancakes. Liquor and wine are not available there or anywhere else on the reservation. At the counter there is often lively talk among the Hopi who frequent the café, as well as the Navajo, who find this Hopi watering spot attractive.

The adjacent museum is informative. It tells the history of the Hopi people and displays some of the traditional crafts. Adjacent to the museum are several Hopi craft shops that are well worth a visit. Just west of the cultural center is the Hopi Arts and Crafts Silvercraft Cooperative Guild. The desk in the motel office is happy to supply information about Hopi dances and ceremonies that are open to the public. They also can help you locate a particular craftsperson whom you may wish to visit. In the summer, the cultural center and the Hopi reservation are on Mountain Standard Time rather than Mountain Daylight Time. Although it is possible at times in the summer just to walk in and get a room, it is best not to risk it, especially if you are going to be there on Friday or Saturday night. Advance reservation deposit required sometimes. Mailing address: Hopi Cultural Center Motel, P.O. Box 67, Second Mesa, Arizona 86043. Telephone: 1-602-734-2401. Inexpensive and low moderate.

Keams Canyon Motel. If the motel at the cultural center is full and you badly need a place to stay nearby, drive twenty miles east on Arizona High-

Hopi Cultural Center Restaurant and Motel, Second Mesa

way 264 to Keams Canyon. There you will find a twenty-two-unit air-cooled motel. The rooms are quite modest and several steps below the rest of the lodging listed in this section. Two units have kitchenettes. Mailing address: Keams Canyon Motel, Box 188, Keams Canyon, Arizona 86034. Telephone: 1-602-738-2297. Inexpensive.

Campgrounds

There is a modest campground adjacent to and operated by the Hopi Cultural Center and Motel as well as another campground, tribally operated, at Kykotsmovi. Inquire at the Keams Canyon Shopping Center about directions to several picnic areas located in the canyon.

Fairs, Festivals, and Events

For information about the Hopi ceremonial dances, please refer to the text at the beginning of "Staying There."

Tours

Hopi Village Tours. Tours to several of the Hopi villages are by reservation only. This Hopi-operated guide service can help the traveler become more knowledgeable about the history of the mesas and the people. But services like this come and go so check it out before counting on it. Mailing address: Hopi Village Tours, Box 668, Second Mesa, Arizona 86043. Telephone: 1-602-737-2633.

Shopping

Monongya's Gallery. Situated in view of Arizona Highway 264 on Third Mesa just east of the turnoff to Old Oraibi. This excellent shop has carefully selected Hopi pottery, kachinas, and jewelry. The owner, Von Monongya, a prizewinning contemporary Hopi wood-carver, also has many outstanding pieces on display and for sale. Mailing address: Monongya's Gallery, P.O. Box 287, Kykotsmovi, Arizona 86039. Telephone: 1-602-734-2344.

Shalako's. Located in the cultural center complex on Second Mesa. This shop has a small, but outstanding selection of Hopi crafts that range from pottery and jewelry to kachinas. Well worth a stop if you are at the cultural center. Mailing address: Monongya's, P.O. Box 82, Second Mesa, Arizona 86043. Telephone: 1-602-734-2384.

The Hopi Arts and Crafts Silvercraft Cooperative Guild. Located just west of the Hopi Cultural Center and Motel. This shop is dedicated to handling nothing but Hopi handwork of all kinds. It carries an extensive selection of Hopi pottery, baskets, weavings, kachinas, and jewelry, all made by some of the best-known Hopi craftspeople. Mailing address: Hopi Arts and Crafts Silvercraft Cooperative Guild, P.O. Box 37, Second Mesa, Arizona 86043. Telephone: 1-602-734-2463.

Keams Canyon Arts and Crafts. Located just west of town on Arizona Highway 264 in the Keam's Canyon Shopping Center complex. This shop carries a wide selection of Hopi, Navajo, Ácoma, Zuñi, and other handcrafts from the Southwest. Under the ownership of the McGee family, longtime traders in the area, it is one of the most complete general craft stores in Indian Country. Be sure to ask permission to enter their museum-quality crafts salesroom. It is a good place to see some of the best of what is available in Indian jewelry, pottery, and kachinas. Good regional book and card selection. Mailing address: Keams Canyon Arts and Crafts, Box 607, Keams Canyon, Arizona 86034. Telephone: 1-602-738-2295.

Telephone Numbers

Hopi Indian Agency, Keams Canyon, Arizona. Telephone: 1-602-738-2228.
Hopi Tribal Headquarters. Kykotsmovi, Arizona. Telephone: 1-602-734-2441.

Canyon de Chelly/Ganado

Lodging and Food

Thunderbird Lodge. What Goulding's is to Monument Valley, the Thunderbird is to Canyon de Chelly. If you want to explore the canyons and ruins, this is the ideal base. Located in a lovely, remote spot at the mouth of the canyon, less than one-half mile down the road from the visitor center and near the campground. The lodge, with its seventy-one air-conditioned rooms with TV's is an oasis in a grove of cottonwood trees. The cafeteria occupies part of the old trading post built in the late 1800s. The older motel units were built from native stone in the 1920s and circle a tree-filled, grassy courtyard. The newer units are in adobe-style construction and are very well placed on the periphery of the property. In addition they are handsomely furnished. The atmosphere is peaceful, and the staff is friendly and helpful. The novel idea of a cafeteria instead of a restaurant adjacent to the lodge is worthy of praise. After facing numerous menus, which all begin to look the same after a while, it is a real pleasure to be able to select exactly what you want to eat. Children will be delighted with the choices, which include some Navajo favorites, as well as excellent French toast for breakfast. The cafeteria is also open to the public and many Navajo from the surrounding area come to eat here. The lodge owners and their staff are well informed about the area (see "Tours"). Four evenings per week in the summer, park rangers give a series of talks about the Navajo culture. No pets. Advance reservation deposit required. Mailing address: Thunderbird Lodge, Box 548, Chinle, Arizona 86503. Telephone: 1-602-674-5841 or 1-602-674-5842. Low moderate and moderate.

Canyon de Chelly Motel. If the Thunderbird is full, as it often is, you can try this clean fifty-room air-conditioned motel with TV's. It is located just out of Chinle one-quarter mile east of Arizona Highway 63 and three miles from the visitor center and the canyon. You can take your meals at Thunderbird Lodge. Pets. Advance reservation deposit required. Mailing address: Canyon de Chelly Motel, Box 295, Chinle, Arizona 86503. Telephone: 1-602-674-5288. Moderate.

Campgrounds

Cottonwood Campground. This campground at Canyon de Chelly National Monument is a superb one. It is beautifully situated in the trees at the mouth of the canyon. There are picnic tables, nature trails, and nightly campfire programs presented by the park rangers. Horseback riding can be arranged through the visitor center. Reservations for the ninety-four tent and recreational vehicle sites are essential during the summer. Telephone: 1-602-674-5436.

Tours

Thunderbird Tours. Navajo guides lead tours from Thunderbird Lodge in large, twenty-four-passenger, open-air four-wheel-drive vehicles through the bottom of the canyon. There are opportunities to get closeup views of White House Ruin, Mummy Cave, Antelope House, and Navajo Fortress. Half-day (both morning and afternoon) and all-day tours are generally available. Mailing address:

Hogan, Canyon de Chelly

Thunderbird Lodge, Box 548, Chinle, Arizona 86503. Telephone: 1-602-674-5843 or 1-602-674-5841.

Other tours. You may drive your own four-wheel-drive vehicle through the canyon if you are accompanied by an authorized Navajo guide. Guide services can be arranged through the Canyon de Chelly visitor center. There are guide fees. You may also tour the canyon by horseback. Hourly, half-day, day-long, and more extensive overnight horseback trips are available. Make arrangements through the visitor center. Mailing address: Canyon de Chelly Visitor Center, National Park Service, Box 588, Chinle, Arizona 86503. Telephone: 1-602-674-5436 or 1-602-674-5213.

Hubbell Trading Post. This historic, but still active trading post is located thirty-five miles south of Chinle just outside of Ganado, Arizona. Daily tours of Hubbell's home, lasting about forty minutes, are free of charge and are offered several times throughout the day. There you will see paintings of some of Hubbell's rug designs, which Hubbell displayed visibly inside the post as models to guide the Navajo weavers. In addition, there is almost always something interesting happening at the visitor center, which is in the small building to the right as you drive up to the post. Often Navajo weavers or other craftspersons will be at work demonstrating their considerable expertise. Mailing address: Hubbell Trading Post, Box 150, Ganado, Arizona 86505. Telephone: 1-602-755-3475.

Shopping

Thunderbird Lodge Rug Room and Craft Shop. Located next door to the cafeteria. The craft shop features an excellent selection of Navajo and Indian jewelry. A separate rug room features a wide selection of rugs. The lodge owners have considerable experience with Indian jewelry as well as other crafts and it shows. Mailing address: Thunderbird Lodge, Box 548, Chinle, Arizona 86503. Telephone: 1-602-674-5841 or 1-602-674-5842.

Hubbell Trading Post. Hubbell offers one of the consistently best selections of handwoven Navajo

Thunderbird Lodge

rugs and Navajo jewelry in the Southwest. The quality control is excellent, which means that Bill Malone, the trader here, really knows what he is doing. The large rug room holds just about every type of Navajo rug known to man, ranging from less expensive saddle and half-saddle rugs to museum-quality rugs and tapestries. If you want to invest in a Navajo rug, but know little about the subject, this is definitely a safe place to buy. You can trust the dealer's judgment. The post also has one of the best selections of Navajo piñon pitch-glazed pottery available, as well as a nice selection of Navajo sashes. Mailing address: Hubbell Trading Post, Box 388, Ganado, Arizona 86505. Telephone: 1-602-755-3254.

Window Rock, Arizona

Lodging and Food

Navajo Nation Inn. If you get in a pinch and need a place to stay on the east side of the Navajo

Reservation, try the adequate, tribally owned Navajo Nation Motor Inn. Modern in appearance, it has forty-four air-conditioned units. Heated swimming pool. Café on premises and several fast-food cafés nearby. Mailing address: Navajo Nation Inn, Box 1687, Window Rock, Arizona, 86515. Telephone: 1-602-871-4108. Moderate.

Fairs, Festivals, and Events

Annual Navajo Nation Fair. This celebration is held over the second weekend in September. The Navajo Queen is selected and ceremonial dances are performed. Both weaving and silversmithing are demonstrated and those crafts are for sale. For more information about this fair, the Fourth of July fair, or any of the other Navajo fairs, write Navajo Nation Fair Office, P.O. Drawer U, Window Rock, Arizona 86515. Telephone: 1-602-871-4417.

Shopping

Navajo Arts and Crafts Enterprise. Located just beyond the northeast corner of Window Rock's main junction (intersection of Arizona State Highway 264 and Navajo Route 12) is this very large tribally owned Navajo crafts shop. You will find Navajo rugs and an extensive selection of Navajo jewelry. At times you may find pine pitch-covered Navajo baskets and piñon pitch-glazed Navajo pots. In addition, the shop handles a variety of posters, cards, and books. Mailing address: Navajo Arts and Crafts Enterprise, P.O. Drawer A, Window Rock, Arizona 86515. Telephone: 1-602-871-4090 or 1-602-871-4095.

Navajo Tribal Museum. Whether you go into the Navajo Arts and Crafts shop or not, do not miss seeing this gem of a museum, which is located just down the hall from the shop. Tracing the history of the Navajo people from their earliest existence in the Southwest to modern times, the exhibit gives you a flavor for the Navajo culture seldom found elsewhere. In addition, there are rotating exhibits showcasing the works of contemporary Navajo artists. Some monographs and other hard-to-find printed materials about the Navajo culture are available for sale. Telephone: 1-602-876-6673.

Gallup, New Mexico

Fairs, Festivals, and Events

Annual Intertribal Indian Ceremonial. Red Rock State Park, Gallup, New Mexico. This world's fair of the American Indian world is held for four days, including the second weekend in August. In addition to the sale of Indian arts and crafts, there are Indian dances, parades, and rodeos. Mailing address: Annual Intertribal Indian Ceremonial, Box 1, Church Rock, New Mexico 87311. Telephone: 1-505-863-3896.

Telephone Numbers

Navajo Tourism Development Office. P.O. Box 308, DOR Building, Window Rock, Arizona 86515. Telephone: 1-602-871-6659 or 1-602-871-4941 ext. 1659 or 1359.

Shiprock, New Mexico

Shopping

Foutz Trading Company. Telephone: 1-505-368-5790.

Shiprock Trading Company. Telephone: 1-505-368-4585.

Fairs, Festivals, and Events

Northern Navajo Nation Fair. Shiprock, New Mexico. Held the last week of September, this seven-day event includes a rodeo and dancing.

Southwestern Colorado and Northwestern New Mexico

Rocky Mountain Frontier Country

Southwestern Colorado and Northwestern New Mexico

Introduction

If it is a taste of the wild and woolly west you want, head straight to southwestern Colorado. There in that mountainous, historically rich quarter slice of the Four Corners treat, you will see ghosts of the area's colorful past at every turn and experience as pure a culture of western ambience as you will find anywhere in the United States. That ambience stems from a long history of western frontier traditions forged in the fiery hell-bent-to-leather years between the end of the Civil War in 1865 and the turn of the century. Those colorful, but tumultuous years had their beginning when news of the mineral-rich San Juan Mountains spread like wildfire across the country, igniting an unprecedented stampede of fortune seekers to southwestern Colorado.

Those early prospectors, dropping out from all walks of life, came from everywhere imaginable, their carefully concealed life savings staked on their hopes and dreams of striking it rich. These robust men were not the least bit shy about their motives. Along the way west to Colorado, they spread the word, talking so openly and excitedly about where they were going and why that you would have thought they had been hired by a chamber of commerce or some New York advertising agency. Those who traveled in covered wagons must have thought of their wagon covers as canvases, stretched and ready to paint. For with crude brushes they daubed on those semicircular mobile billboards, in large, bold letters for all to see the slogan "San Juan or Bust."

Even now the San Juan Mountains continue to excite and tantalize modern-day fortune seekers. Whenever gold and silver prices shoot up, parking spaces along the wide streets of southwestern Colorado's towns fill with a variety of four-wheel-drive vehicles, as merchants do a land office business selling gold pans and other prospecting paraphernalia. Local property owners pull their hair as scores of strangers and out-of-staters stomp across their land searching for gold, trying to hit pay dirt in "them thar hills and streams," for the region is still rich in minerals. Commercial miners continue to truck away tons of ore every year for substantial profit.

Just outside of Silverton, southwestern Colorado's oldest town, is the largest active gold mine in Colorado today. Silver, lead, copper, and zinc also continue to be produced commercially for profit and help to fill the local coffers. While around Farmington, New Mexico, a short distance to the south, diamond drilling bits have punched thousands of holes into the San Juan Basin's crusty surface in search of "black gold." Over the last few decades over 11,000 oil and gas wells have been spudded and completed there, fueling Farmington's economy when oil and gas prices are up and dramatically depressing it when they are down.

You will see part of southwestern Colorado's lively past in the scores of old mining shafts, fallen-down shaft houses, mining trams, and pyramidal heaps of mine "garbage" or tailings that dot the mountainsides. Many of these mining ghosts, perched on the cliffsides in some of the most remote and inaccessible locations imaginable, can be viewed from modern highways that follow the routes of the narrow old mining roads of yesteryear, blasted mile by arduous mile out of solid rock. Be thankful that a few inches of smooth as silk asphalt separate you from those narrow, dusty trails of the 1880s that were so rough and rutted they snapped axles like matchsticks and shredded prospectors' tough leather boots like they were paper. And when they were wet, stretches of those old roads were so boggy that men, pack animals, and stagecoaches sank ankle and axle deep in oozing mud.

But the highway is not the only place you will come face to face with southwestern Colorado's exciting history. You will also meet its past if you travel on the narrow-gauge steam train that has huffed and puffed its way from Durango to Silverton since the 1880s. It got its start in 1882 when, after months of back-breaking, death-defying labor, the rails finally were laid over some of the North American continent's roughest terrain. The past also lives on in many of the buildings you will see and hotels and saloons you may visit in the old boomtowns, which were built when this was the rough-and-ready Wild West. Those were the days when it is said one hundred men were killed almost every month by either stray or intended bullets. That was when lynching sprees followed on the heels of hastily organized vigilante groups and when desperadoes like Butch Cassidy and lawmen like Bat Masterson walked the very same streets you will be exploring.

Memories of the past are even closer at hand when you stay in some of the old hotels and inns. Relics of the boom days of the 1880s and 1890s, they still offer comfortable lodging for tourists who are prospecting for memories of the Old West. And as you drive along from town to town, you will catch glimpses of working "cowboys" in the lower valleys carrying out their cow-punching activities just as their fathers and grandfathers did before them. While in the small towns, you will see many of the local citizens wearing cowboy hats and boots purchased in stores that were selling those duds long before it was fashionable to dress like a cowboy. These citizens, from all walks of life, are modern western Americans whose broad smiles and spontaneous "howdy's" and "hi's" are part of a western tradition of openness

which reflects the wide valleys and broad vistas you will see at every turn.

In spite of the honest-to-goodness authentic past of this area, much has been refurbished and embellished in the past decade to attract the tourist. Since the tourist "lode" was discovered around 1968, it has been mined with great enthusiasm. The same creative western ingenuity that saw the settlement of this area is now directed at the visitor. Much of the restoration is in very good taste. But the hokey, the cheap, and the claptrap also have crept in. Fortunately, for every curio place, there are at least a dozen other genuine, rewarding experiences for the traveler.

The area is so beautiful and historically rich that it is easy to sort the wheat from the chaff. For this is no Disneyland! It is a land forged by the indomitable courage, patience, and hard work of the early settlers. For every road or trail blasted from the mountainsides, for every foot of railroad track laid and for every mine dug, there were hundreds of men who lost their lives. Blinding snowstorms, avalanches, rockslides and crumbling rocky ledges, desperadoes, gamblers, stray or intended bullets, and high altitude pneumonia all took their toll. Indeed, as many have noted, death was the sidekick of every man, woman, and child who sought their fortunes and a new life in this mountainous western stronghold.

Yet when you pull into Durango, the area's largest town and tour base, to find heavy traffic at certain times of the day, crowded eating establishments, and already-booked overnight accommodations, you may begin to wonder where the past is hiding. But you will not wonder too long, for soon you will begin to sense a certain frontier excitement in those "boom" summer months which, along with the genuine warmth and friendliness of the local people, offsets much of the commercial atmosphere. The hustle and bustle fades after the summer tourist season is over, and the resilient mining and ranch towns like Durango return to the more relaxed style of western life they have known for decades. These towns would exist whether you or I ventured there or not. Their economic base has always been and will continue to be from the land. The consistent strength of the region rests in its beef cattle, pinto beans, and alfalfa, as well as in its precious metals and the refreshing resourcefulness of its people.

Although the overwhelming cultural essence of this section is that of white western America, you may want to travel to this region to seek out another chapter in the history of America's first citizens. Before the explorer, before the prospector, miner, settler and cowboy, the Indians, known as the Anasazi, inhabited the lower mesas and river basins of southwestern Colorado and northwestern New Mexico. This dry land has helped preserve in a magnificent state of intactness the homes of those early inhabitants at Mesa Verde, Colorado; Pleasant View, Colorado (the Lowry Pueblo Ruins); Aztec, New Mexico (Aztec National Monument); and at the Salmon Ruins just outside of Bloomfield, New Mexico.

Although this area is rich in remnants of the Indians' past culture, you will see little of their traditional way of life in southwestern Colorado today. You may catch a glimpse of a few Navajo from Arizona and New Mexico in traditional dress, as they bring goods to sell at one of the trading posts in Cortez or Farmington, but that is about it. The Utes, who proudly roamed this land after the Anasazi but before the Spaniards, Mexicans, and Americans, are not very visible to the traveler today. This once-powerful group has been divided and placed on two small reservations removed from most of the major tourist traffic. For the most part, they live a modern agrarian life, donning traditional dress only for special ceremonies a few times a year.

The Setting

The rich cultural heritage of southwestern Colorado has unfolded in a spectacular setting. From the Four Corners Monument at an elevation of 4,500 feet, the desolate, sparsely populated high desert of the Colorado Plateau gives way to rolling hills and rich farmlands in southwestern Colorado. This transition zone has been dubbed the "Pinto Bean Capital of the World" for its prodigious production of that southwestern American staple. From there, the plateau continues to rise, even as numerous mesas and small plateaus arise from it. Then, through pine-clad foothills, the Colorado Plateau ascends to higher, lusher valleys—the Dolores, the Mancos, and the Animas, where cattle graze in pastures of rich, abundant grass. As it continues to ascend into the foothills, the Colorado Plateau comes to an abrupt halt. For there it meets the towering sheer walls of the Rocky Mountains, whose lofty peaks stand as great sentinels on the eastern edge of the plateau overlooking the high desert to the west for hundred of miles. These incomparably rugged mountains impart to southwestern Colorado its most unique physical characteristic. For to meet the Rockies there is to see them at their most majestic, rugged, bare bones best.

As you drive through the mountains on excellent, wide, paved highways, you will appreciate their ruggedness. Some have said that the mountains of southwestern Colorado, with their incredibly steep and weirdly eroded angular faces and with their wildly descending deep canyons, make the rest of Colorado's mountain country pale by comparison. The country is literally standing on

its end with such an intense concentration of twelve-, thirteen-, and fourteen-thousand-foot peaks that the concept of "flat" has been squeezed right off the face of the earth. In the six hundred to seven hundred square miles that comprise San Juan County, the flattest, widest spot is a small piece of land one mile wide and less than two miles long between the two old mining towns of Silverton and Eureka.

Technically speaking, the mountains you see around you are part of an unbelievably long and high rock outcropping resulting from three cataclysmic upheavals, the last one occurring just seventy-five million years ago. The Rockies extend from the Bering Sea in northwest Alaska to central New Mexico, dividing most of the North American continent into two watersheds. East of the line known as the Continental Divide, all rainfall and snowmelt courses its way to the Atlantic Ocean. West of that line, nature's water eventually reaches the Pacific Ocean. At Silverton, Colorado, you will only be five miles west of the Great Divide. There you will see the Animas River as it courses southward to the San Juan River, which empties into the Colorado River, which flows on down to the Pacific Ocean's Gulf of California. A few paces east of that mountainous dividing ridge, the rains and snowstorms feed rivers such as the Rio Grande. It snakes its way along the Rio Grande Valley, skirting Santa Fe and passing Albuquerque as it courses on to El Paso, Texas. There it forms the border between the United States and Mexico, before emptying into the Atlantic Ocean's Gulf of

Continental Divide

Mexico.

The Rockies reach a show-stopping climax in Colorado, which boasts over fifty peaks above 14,000 feet, culminating in the grandest of them all, Mount Elbert near Leadville, Colorado, which at 14,433 feet is the highest mountain in the whole Rocky Mountain chain. Not far from Mount Elbert, the Continental Divide makes a distinct turn to the southwest. There it enters southwestern Colorado, riding on the backs of the ridge tops and towering peaks of the San Juan range, which sweeps more than one hundred miles from east to west and seventy miles from north to south. Its soaring, rugged peaks, like Uncompaghre Peak, Colorado's sixth highest at 14,309 feet, form a barrier that has delayed settlement and kept this region remote and isolated from the mainstream of civilization. Even today the only gateways from the east to southwest Colorado's San Juan region are over mountain passes that top out above 10,000 feet.

The San Juan range generally is thought to extend as far west as a line drawn between Durango and Ouray. Although many people refer to the mountains west of there as the "San Juans," they are actually parts of three separate ranges of magnificent proportions, which nudge the eastern border of the Colorado Plateau and finger out westward onto the high desert where they can be seen for almost one hundred miles. Southwest of Ouray, Colorado, around Telluride, are the San

Miguel Mountains, boasting Mount Wilson at 14,246 feet and Diente Peak, which at 14,159 feet was the last of the 14,000-foot peaks in the Rockies to be climbed by man. To the south of there are the Ricos and the La Platas.

Hesperus Peak, which looms above the La Platas, is one of the four sacred directional peaks of the Navajo. Its snowfields spawn rivers which flow many miles southward to the ancestral home of the Navajo in today's northwestern New Mexico. According to Navajo legend, the La Plata range was fastened to the earth with a rainbow. Then The People," as the Navajo call themselves, spread a blanket of darkness over the mountain and decorated it with obsidian. On a very clear day, the La Platas are visible from as far distant as Boulder Mountain on the Aquarius Plateau near Capitol Reef National Park. This is a distance of over one hundred fifty miles as the crow flies.

· In addition to the relics of man's bygone days, you will see an incredible array of flora as you ascend from one "life zone" to another. If you take the mountainous Silver Circle trip from Durango through the old mining towns, you will ascend in this up-and-down land, in just a few miles, from 6500 feet to over 11,000 feet, passing through four life zones and possibly five if you do any day hiking from the road. Since temperature diminishes three degrees for each 1,000 feet of elevation gain and moisture increases proportionately at higher altitudes, the flowers and trees and other living things are different at various levels or zones of elevation.

In fact, going up 1,000 feet is like driving north approximately two hundred miles. So if you drive or hike high enough, you will see vegetation that resembles that found in the Arctic at sea level, over two thousand miles north. From the Four Corners Monument, one of the lower elevations in the High Southwest at 4,500 feet, to Red Mountain Pass between Silverton and Ouray at 11,018 feet, you will travel through four life zones and be in easy view of the fifth one. From 4,500 feet to 6,500 feet near Durango, you will travel through the zone called the Upper Sonoran or Plains Zone. In addition to the piñons and junipers in this belt, you will also see willows and cottonwoods, as well as some cacti and yuccas. From 6,500 feet elevation to 8,000 feet, you will travel through the Foothills or Transition Life Zone into the ponderosa pine, Gambel oak belt, while from 8,000 feet elevation to 10,000 feet you will sometimes see in this Douglas fir-aspen belt called the Canadian Life Zone a few Colorado blue spruce, the Colorado state tree. But that tree is more common as you drive over the higher mountain passes into the spruce, subalpine fir belt, which occurs between 9,500 feet elevation and 11,500 feet.

Large trees like the Engelmann spruce thrive in this, the highest, coldest, windiest, and wettest zone in which trees will grow, where the rainfall may exceed thirty inches a year compared to eight

Columbine

or ten inches at lower elevations. Living at this elevation is similar to living in Canada's Hudson Bay area, ergo the Hudsonian Life Zone. From the high mountain passes, you will look up to see timberline beginning between 11,500 feet elevation and 12,000 feet, ascending to a point where the air is so rarified and dry, the winters so windy, cold, and severe, and the soil so rocky that larger, upright trees cannot grow there. Only tundra and low-lying mat-forming plants such as sedge and dwarf willow, similar to the vegetation found in the Arctic at sea level, survive there. Consequently timberline is sometimes called the Arctic Life Zone.

Spring breaks early near the Four Corners Monument, sometime around late February or early March. But similar signs of the sap's rising do not occur in the high mountains until June or later. There, especially in July or August, a splendid profusion of wild flowers can be seen, including the delicately beautiful Colorado state flower, the blue columbine. You also may see red columbine, Indian paintbrush, alpine forget-me-nots, and literally dozens of other species in the wild flower meadows.

Aspen grove

History

The first known people to leave a mark on southwestern Colorado were America's first and foremost masons and apartment builders, the Anasazi. They occupied the deserts, river valleys, and mesas of this region for over a thousand years, building structures that have weathered the test of time. Their history is well detailed in Section II.

After the Anasazi abandoned the area in the late 1200s or early 1300s, history's pages are blank. Sometime after the Anasazi left but before the Spanish arrived, the Utes inhabited much of this country. Seminomadic, they no doubt hunted in the higher mountains, but made their camps at lower, warmer elevations. It is not known exactly when the Utes met up with the Spanish. But probably sometime in the 1700s they acquired Spanish horses and from that time on distinguished themselves as aggressive warriors and raiders of the first rank. Doggedly they held onto their territory, frequently menacing the Spanish settlements in northern New Mexico. Rugged, hostile mountains, plus aggressive, hostile Utes, had a lot to do with the slow encroachment of white settlers into this region.

The ever-restless, ambitious Spanish were the first whites to visit southwestern Colorado as they sought gold, pelts, and Indian slaves. In 1765, under orders from the Spanish governor in Santa Fe, Juan María Antonio Rivera led a prospecting and trading party up the Dolores and Uncompaghre rivers to the Gunnison River. Near the Dolores River in southwestern Colorado he found some insignificant silver-bearing rocks, and it is thought that it was he who named the mountains nearby the Sierra de la Plata or the Silver Mountains. This expedition and others to follow left names on the land which are the only reminders we have today that the Spanish once explored this region.

Rivera found little of commercial value that would interest his superiors in Santa Fe. But he did open up a route that would soon lead to the establishment of the Old Spanish Trail (see Section I, "History"). Some of the men in Rivera's party made additional trips into Colorado after 1765, leaving many other names on the land. In 1776, one of the men who had accompanied Rivera earlier, André Muñiz, acted as a guide for the Domínguez–Escalante expedition. That party entered southwestern Colorado in search of a route west to California, traveling near today's towns of Durango and Dolores. Along the way, they camped at the base of a large green mesa which today carries the name Mesa Verde. They observed and were the first whites to record the discovery of an Anasazi archaeological site in southwestern Colorado. That site, near Dolores, Colorado, is known today as the Domínguez–Escalante Ruin, and is also the location of the excellent Anasazi Heritage Center (see "The Lowry Pueblo Ruin: A Narrative Account"). Some of the names you will find on your map were dropped on the land during that expedition. When a member of Escalante's group injured his hand when he fell from his horse while fording a river, the Spanish dubbed the river "mancos," meaning one handed or crippled.

By the early 1800s, American mountain men and trappers were exploring the area in their quest for beaver pelts. Men like Peg-leg Smith were outfitted with supplies in the crossroads trapping town of Taos, New Mexico. From there they would head west to Colorado's San Juan, Dolores, and San Miguel rivers. These adventurous American trappers were a tough bunch. They, possibly more than any other whites, penetrated deeply into the mountain fastness of southwestern Colorado, bringing back invaluable information about the area and helping to find new routes through the mountains. One of the trappers, William Becknell, the father of the Santa Fe Trail, camped in the area of Mesa Verde, where he found pottery shards, stone houses, and other Anasazi remains.

By the late 1820s, the more direct route from southwestern Colorado to the crossing of the Colorado River at Moab had been discovered and traffic through the area increased with this opening of the Old Spanish Trail in 1830. The Ute Indians became very active in the expanding trade business, providing slaves to Mexican traders and often obstructing trade caravans, demanding payment for crossing their territory. It is also possible that a few prospectors found their way across this area in the 1840s headed for the California gold rush. The next recorded visitor was Captain J. N. Macomb who entered southwestern Colorado in 1859 with a United States government exploratory party.

Then, when gold was discovered in 1859 and 1860 in eastern Colorado, fortune seekers headed west in large numbers. Learning from the Indians that there might be gold in the San Juan Mountains, Charles Baker, a veteran of the gold rush in eastern Colorado, led a prospecting party over the Continental Divide. The relatively flat valley they explored with the Animas River flowing through it became known as Baker's Park, site of today's Silverton, Colorado. Baker's dogged determination kept the group prospecting in spite of their meager findings. Finally, in the spring of 1861, the discouraged group moved downstream to a site in the Animas Valley about seventeen miles north of today's Durango. Although they found little gold there, they did build the first log cabins in southwestern Colorado. Disappointed and with mounting concerns about trespassing in Ute territory, they abandoned the site after a few months. They

headed back to Fort Garland, Colorado, where they discovered that civil war had broken out. Baker left the area to enlist in the Confederate Army. But the San Juan was still firmly entrenched in his mind as a region that would some day cough up millions.

When the war was over, in 1865, Baker returned to the San Juan Mountains with several other men. They explored the Gunnison, Animas, and La Plata rivers, looking for gold. Once again they found little to encourage them. Most of his party deserted this doggedly determined man and headed for home. But Baker pushed on. Only when the group had dwindled to Baker and two others did he finally give up and head home. But on the way out of the San Juans, as he was trespassing on Ute territory, Baker was killed by the Utes. His two companions narrowly escaped.

Historically, most of today's state of Colorado was Ute country. But with the rush of American settlers into eastern Colorado, the United States government removed the Utes from the lands east of the Continental Divide. They were "given" the lands west of the Rockies in 1868. From that time on, the Utes became increasingly territorial. Prospectors who worked the streams west of the divide were taking great risks. Nonetheless, men like Baker continued to trespass in their search for gold.

The next attempt to find gold in southwestern Colorado was led by Calvin Jackson. With a large group of men, he left Prescott, Arizona, in 1869. Harassed by Indians every step of the way, some of the group were killed. Others abandoned the expedition. Only eight made it to southwestern Colorado. Arriving in the dead of winter, they holed up in the cabins which Baker's group had abandoned. Their efforts to locate a promising source of gold were equally unsuccessful. Nonetheless, from Baker's time on, word had spread that some gold had been found in the area. Baker's vision of gold in the San Juans, more than his insignificant discoveries there, served as the kernel for rumors which grew into tall tales that kept the prospectors coming to the area.

Fed by just such rumors, Miles T. Johnson entered the western San Juans in 1870 and prospected in the Baker's Park area. There, after months of searching, he found the first profitable mineral lode in the San Juans in remote Arrastra Gulch, three miles northeast of today's Silverton. Somehow he was able to keep his gold strike a secret. But two years later when he packed his ore out, news of his Little Giant Gold Mine spread. A slow boom was on. Besides Arrastra, other gulches were being explored and given colorful names such as Maggie Gulch and Minnie Gulch. By 1873, nearly four thousand claims had been staked in this remote mining region, hundreds of miles away from civilization.

Prospectors had to be hardy souls to conquer the ruggedness of these mountains with their steep, sheer rock walls and precipitous canyons. These men were subjected to rock slides, dangerous ledge trails, and early snows with deep drifts which lasted until summer. Snow slides frequently sent down tons of snow in killer avalanches. Horses on steep trails would bolt, throwing their riders into gulches hundreds of feet deep. Attacks by bears were not unheard of. Death from exposure in this land of unpredictably extreme weather was a constant hazard. It is no wonder that the rush to the San Juans was said to be one of the most difficult migrations ever chronicled in western history. The early prospectors, miners, and settlers were said to have needed courage, patience, and strength in this remote land. But they also needed "white lightning" or its facsimile to bolster their courage, judging from the scores of saloons that sprang up in the sparsely populated mining camps.

In addition to these hardships, this was still Indian land west of the Rockies. The prospectors were trespassing and therefore subject to harassment by the Utes. In 1872, the great Ute chief, Ouray, rejected an attempt by the government to get back some of the lands they had given the Indians in 1868. But in 1874, Ouray saw the handwriting on the wall and did agree, in the Brunot Treaty, to give up a piece of land sixty by seventy-five miles in size, which included the prime mineral areas. The Utes were paid twelve cents per acre for these three million acres of especially valuable land.

With the Indians no longer posing a threat, hundreds of fortune seekers thronged to southwestern Colorado. The stampede had begun with the beginning of serious mining in 1874. But by

1875, the boom was really on. Pioneer wagons from the east headed west carrying the slogan "San Juan or Bust." The only way into this remote region was over the Continental Divide at Stony Pass (see Section IV "The Setting"). At an elevation of 12,000 feet, it was one of the meanest and most difficult passes to negotiate in the Colorado Rockies.

The descent on the west side of Stony Pass was especially precipitous, the wagon road dropping 2,300 feet in the first two miles. This was the way many pioneer prospectors came in and it was the exit route for the ore-laden packtrains. Sometimes these packtrains contained as many as one hundred fifty plodding burros, each laden with two hundred pounds of ore on the way out or coal and supplies on the way in. But the burros were not the only beasts of burden subjected to such misery. Oxen pulled their heavy loads in crudely made wagons whose wooden wheels crushed and groaned over the rough terrain.

Though it was gold most prospectors searched for, it was silver they found. With the discovery of more and richer deposits of silver, the area became known as the "Silvery San Juan." In the dramatic mountain-rimmed valley called Baker's Park, a town was born. The first cabin was built in 1871. The mining camp of Silverton, elevation 9,032 feet, was platted in 1874 and is the oldest major settlement in the San Juans. A hotel was built in 1874 and by 1875 a newspaper was established in Silverton. Today the *Silverton Standard and Miner* stakes its own "claim" as the longest continuously published newspaper west of the Continental Divide.

It has been said that in the 1880s wherever there was a rumor and a hole in the ground, a mining settlement would pop up. The small settlements were called "camps." The ruins of these camps can be seen today, for they are the ghost towns of southwestern Colorado. Around Silverton, many camps sprang up overnight in the gulches of the Animas River. Camps such as Howardsville, Eureka, Animas Forks, and Mineral Point were at extremely high altitudes. A story is told about a man in Animas Forks, just north of Silverton, who was arrested for drunkenness and brought to court. The judge levied a fine of ten dollars plus costs. Refusing to pay, the man said he

Early-day prospector

would appeal to a higher court. The exasperated judge retorted that there was no such thing as a higher court, that at 11,300 feet, his was the highest court in the land. Today stories like this and nostalgic memories are the only remains of many of these camps. Most of them have disappeared completely through the ravages of time and weather.

But Silverton remains. It lives up to its reputation as "the mining town that never quit." There, as in other mining towns, one-story buildings were constructed with their fronts higher than the building itself. False fronts, so typical of the early western towns, lent a touch of elegance to these rugged frontier settlements, offering partial compensation for the miserable living conditions. Wooden sidewalks so familiar in western movies were a necessity to keep from sinking knee-deep in the mud during certain times of the year. Saloons and places to buy liquor mushroomed in overwhelming numbers. At one time, Silverton had thirty-four watering holes. Eventually, hotels,

restaurants, assay offices, churches, and schools completed the scene. Over and over again, necessity was the mother of invention. Drinking water was frequently carried by a dog team pulling a wagon in the summer and a sled in the winter. Mail in the winter was often brought in by men on skis. Because these early towns constructed of wood were extremely subject to fire, Silverton wasted no time in bringing in the first hook-and-ladder fire truck over Stony Pass in 1878.

Thus far the mining activity described is that of men from the East heading west to find their fortunes. Ironically, another thrust into southwestern Colorado was going on at the same time. On the West Coast, veterans of the 1849 gold rush to California began to look east with greedy eyes to the Rockies they had bypassed a decade earlier in their pell-mell rush to Sutter's Mill. In 1856, almost one hundred years after Rivera passed by the La Plata Mountains, a Captain Moss left California to explore the west slope of the Rockies. He found good traces of minerals at the mouth of the La Plata

River, possibly not far from where Rivera had passed. He returned in 1873, no doubt aware of the new mining activity in the Silverton area. He obtained good samples of quartz, which were predictive of lode mining. Since he was in Ute territory at the time, he negotiated a treaty with the Utes, who gave him permission to mine and farm a piece of land in the La Plata region, thirty-six miles square. For this permission, he paid the Indians one hundred ponies and many blankets. With treaty and mineral samples in hand, he returned to San Francisco and enlisted the patronage of a wealthy man, Tiburcio Parrott. Captain Moss and his party returned to the La Plata River well equipped. They were responsible for discovering the first gold and silver lode there in 1875 which they called the Comstock. Another boom was at hand and Parrott City, named after Moss's benefactor, was born.

The year 1875 was significant for southwestern Colorado. For in that year major discoveries were made near today's Ouray and Telluride. Restless prospectors from Silverton began spilling over the mountains looking for more riches. And they found them in another parklike valley, cut by the Uncompaghre River. By 1876, Uncompaghre City, later called Ouray, was rapidly expanding. In one spot called the Mineral Farm, gold ore was found lying on the ground. Like digging potatoes, only a hoe or shovel was needed to reap the golden harvest.

In Ouray, as in all the mining areas, both fortune and misfortune occurred. Fortune often meant hitting it big. There were numerous rags-to-riches stories there. One of the most famous ones concerns the immigrant son of a poor Irish farmer who discovered gold in the form of telluride ore in the discarded tailings and waste dumps of other miners. Walsh's Camp Bird mine became one of the richest in the region. From its proceeds he bought his daughter the famous Hope Diamond.

In the summer of 1875, new discoveries were made in the San Miguel region. Later two towns cropped up. San Miguel City was the first, followed by Columbia. Columbia, later renamed Telluride for the rare sulphurlike element, telluride, found in the gold ore there, became the center for the area that included mines with such exotic names as the Smuggler, the Liberty Bell, the Tomboy, and the Hidden Treasure. Later, in 1879, a boom came to

False fronts

Rico. This area had been explored earlier in 1866 by a party of Texans and in 1869 by another group. But not until 1879 was a rich deposit of silver found on Nigger Baby Hill. It was called "Nigger Baby" because the rocks on the hill contained large quantities of black oxide of manganese. That year, men in Silverton, Ouray, and the San Miguel areas dropped their picks and shovels and headed for Rico. Within a month, over six hundred people had gathered there. Twenty-nine buildings, seven saloons, and four assay offices were quickly constructed to serve the new citizens. One of the newspapers in a neighboring town commented on how fast the town developed and stated that the town had "gotten there before it was sent for."

With discoveries at Rico, the Silver Circle was complete. From this time on, more lodes were discovered around the already-established mining camps and thousands of tons of ore were shipped out by mule and oxen trains. In the 1870s a man by the name of Otto Mears, later called "the pathfinder of the San Juans," began building a series of toll roads connecting the major mining centers to one another and to the "outside." In less than ten years, Mears engineered and built four hundred fifty miles of toll roads over this rugged up-and-down country, which were used by thousands of mules and burros, horse-drawn stage wagons, and

Otto Mears's toll road

panting prospectors. The toll road fees varied, but over one short stretch from Silverton to Ouray, later to be dubbed the Million-Dollar Highway, the fee was five dollars for a four-horse stagecoach and two dollars for a single rider and horse. With increasing traffic on the new toll roads, stagecoach robberies became commonplace.

Southwestern Colorado was booming. More and more people were attracted to the San Juans. In spite of the new roads and frontier settlements, the harsh land continued to take its toll. Many who came west were really not prepared to face the harsh life there. It is said that the first preacher in Ouray walked into town one winter in a blizzard, clinging to the tail of his donkey. He feared he would freeze to death if he sat quietly and rode the animal. Others soon became frustrated with the difficulty of everyday living in this cold, unforgiving, high-altitude country. K. C. Gillette was one of those early prospectors who became frustrated and left. The story is told that as he was shaving himself one morning, his hands were shaking so much from the cold that he cut himself. In anger and frustration, he threw the razor to the ground, chipping the finely honed blade. The idea of a razor you could throw away after each use occurred to him. He abandoned the prospects of riches in southwestern Colorado for the industrial denizens of the East. There he found other riches in marketing his Gillette throw-away razor blades.

In 1869, the transcontinental railway was completed at Promontory, Utah. With the main east–west connection completed, north–south spur lines from towns like Denver could be considered. The Denver and Rio Grande Railway was organized in 1870. By 1871, it was constructing track from Denver south and planning to extend it through Sante Fe and Albuquerque to El Paso. But as the silver boom in southwestern Colorado grew by leaps and bounds, a railway was needed there. The Denver and Rio Grande stopped its southerly march and made an abrupt turn west to accommodate this new lucrative market in southwestern Colorado.

There were other railways competing for the San Juan bonanza. But the Denver and Rio Grande, with its narrow-gauge, three-foot-wide tracks, outpaced its standard competition whose four-foot-eight-inch-wide tracks took longer to lay and when finished were more difficult to negotiate around the steep mountain curves than the narrow-gauge tracks. The new tracks went from Alamosa in eastern Colorado, over Cumbres Pass, zigzagging along the New Mexico–Colorado border to Chama, New Mexico (see Section IV, "Taos–Tours"). There they turned northwest to the new smelter–railroad town of Durango. Two thousand seven hundred men laid one hundred fifty miles of track across some of North America's roughest territory in just a little over seventeen months.

The workers lived in railroad camps. These were rough-and-tumble affairs. Merchants, following the camps as they moved along, sold vast quantities of whiskey. Heads fuzzed with liquor led to loose tongues, which sparked quarrels and fights. It was said that in one camp alone, thirteen men died of bullet wounds in less than a month. Desperadoes followed the camps and robbed unsuspecting workers indiscriminately. Snow, mud, and rock slides were the terror of all. In spring, fall, and winter several feet of snow and ice had to be cleared before the ground could be exposed to lay the railroad ties.

Men worked under these conditions, as well as along narrow rock ledges inches away from precipitous one-thousand-foot-deep "sudden death" canyons. This was more than most workers had bargained for. The desertion rate was astronomical. Many went home, while others dropped

Narrow-gauge train beside water tower

off the line and homesteaded in Colorado's rich agricultural valleys. But replacements were always available from Chicago, St. Louis, and Kansas City. There was no lack of men wanting to go west to find their fortunes. By the time the century was over, 1,635 miles of narrow-gauge rail line had been laid in the Rockies.

The track reached the new town of Durango in July of 1881. Founded in 1880, this rugged town was ready for the railroad. It had passed through some of the growth pains of a new town and had begun to settle down a bit. In May, before the railroad came, an ordinance was passed which was intended to bring tranquility, if not law and order, to the new town. The ordinance stated that any person carrying or concealing a pistol, bowie knife, dagger, or other deadly weapon would be fined no less than five dollars and no more than thirty-five dollars. There also was evidence that Durango was hoping to boom some day and become a peaceful community. Newspapers advertised for young women to come to this manly town and, sure enough, young ladies began arriving from all over the country.

While the track was being laid to Durango, the route from Durango to Silverton was being surveyed. Steel, instead of iron, rails were used on this forty-five-mile stretch of track which had an elevation gain of two thousand feet. The train chugged into Silverton in July of 1882, after nine months of backbreaking track-laying work. Silverton, settled in 1873 and incorporated in 1876, had six hundred hardy souls on hand to greet the new train.

It is often pointed out that although many of these southwestern Colorado towns got their starts from mining activities, they did not really flourish and grow until after the railroad came in. By 1885, Silverton's population had grown from five hundred to two thousand and would eventually expand to five thousand. With the new railway, it became possible for Silverton's citizens to reach Denver, the acme of civilization, in just less than thirty hours. As time went on, Silverton, Colorado, became increasingly "civilized" and connected with the rest of the United States. With the railway, white prospectors and entrepreneurs realized for the first time the riches that had eluded the early Spanish conquistadores in the High Southwest.

As the mining communities boomed and rejoiced in the prospect of new riches, the earliest inhabitants of the region had fallen onto bad times. By 1879, with more and more white settlers pushing into Colorado, the Utes became a nuisance to the United States government. At the Ute agency near Grand Junction, Colorado, a man by the name of Meeker had become the Indian agent for the region. It was his view that the Indians should learn to farm. Not understanding that these were proud, seminomadic hunters who thought of farming as women's work, Meeker took their lack of interest as a sign of active resistance. He retaliated by plowing up the Ute horseracing track, thinking that if he could discourage the Utes from their favorite gaming activity, they would farm. That was the straw that broke the camel's back. The Utes retaliated with a vicious attack on Meeker's agency, killing Meeker and nine others.

This incident was all the United States government needed to purge all the Utes from the potentially rich mining and farming areas in western Colorado. The Ute removal agreement of 1880 spelled the end to traditional Ute life. Under the force of arms, the Utes were literally run out of northwestern Colorado into Utah, where they were placed on the small Unitah–Ouray Reservation. The Utes in southwestern Colorado were driven from their green valleys to the arid and less desirable lands on the very southern border of Colorado adjacent to New Mexico. There they were placed on two reservations, the Southern Ute Indian Reservation southeast of Durango and the Ute Mountain Reservation just south of Mesa Verde. The land the Utes were forced to evacuate was occupied almost immediately by miners, while sheep and cattle ranchers homesteaded the lush grazing country north of the Ute reservations.

Ranchers from Texas had known about Colorado for some time. In 1866, Col. Charles Goodnight, known as the "Father of the American cowboy," drove two thousand Texas longhorns to the rich grazing meadows in Colorado. Their profitable enterprise soon became known as Colorado's second gold rush. The first large cattle operation reached the San Juan area in 1875. Before this time, the only meat in the developing mining and railroad communities came from mountain sheep or trail-worn oxen. The Colorado prospectors, miners, railroad workers, and large segments of the United States Cavalry wanted beef.

Numerous cattlemen flocked to Colorado. Pretty soon, range wars and rustlers completed the cowboy scene. In addition to problems with rustlers changing cattle brands, there were also feuds over innocent mistakes involving brands. In one instance, two ranchers whose operations were miles apart in the Durango area came to discover they had the same brands. The cattlemen's "law of the range" prevailed. One of the ranchers was forced to change the brand on twenty-two thousand head of cattle! For months the air must have been redolent with the smell of burned cowhide. Later, the land was found to be suitable for sheep, which set the scene for numerous feuds between sheepmen and cattlemen. Just as many of the mines came to be owned by English syndicates, so many of the large cattle operations were eventually supported by English money.

Many who worked on the railroads and some

Colorado cowboys

who had come to find riches in minerals were impressed with the richness of the land. The Homesteader's Act and the shipment of barbed wire into the area by 1878 attracted more and more settlers to the region. Homesteading 160-acre tracts, they cleared the land, built log cabins, brought in chickens and pigs, and planted orchards and crops. Potatoes, cabbage, tomatoes, and other vegetables grew extremely well. Apricots, peaches, and plums also flourished there. Not since the 1200s when the Anasazi lived there had such a stable and productive farm people settled in this region.

But eventually, feuds broke out between the wide-ranging cattlemen and the barbed-wire-loving homesteaders, who erected fences everywhere to protect their crops from the stampeding hooves of cattle. By the early 1880s, the open range was quickly becoming a memory of the past. Nonetheless, in the Dolores area, the cattle business was still so good that the bank there once recorded the highest per capita deposits in the United States. But that boom faded in a few decades when the cattlemen realized they had badly overgrazed the land. In doing so they had killed much of the formerly abundant grass. Eventually, the bare land became eroded and many of

the cattlemen moved out.

But the scene was being set for another boom that over the years would send millions of people flocking to the area, far surpassing the earlier mining and cowboy stampedes. The findings of an ancient culture in southwestern Colorado by Fray Escalante and his men were probably buried in some dusty book stashed in Mexico, when, almost one hundred years later in 1874, William Henry Jackson, a member of a United States Geological Survey party, tromped through the Mancos Valley looking for cliff dwellings rumored to be in the area. Jackson, a photographer, recorded sighting one ruin that he labeled "Two Story Cliff House." The picture of this ancient stone building, later printed and distributed in the East, led to another kind of "rush."

Although curiosity seekers from the East descended on the area in 1875 and in some instances recorded their findings of ruins, it was not until 1888 that the bonanza really got its start. In that year Richard Wetherill and Charles Mason, ranchers from Mancos, stumbled onto Cliff Palace, a multistoried dwelling up on the Mesa Verde. The artifacts they found were astonishing. They immediately began a campaign to let the world know of their rich strike. In 1890, they took a collection of their Anasazi artifacts to Durango. The exhibition failed. The busy miners and smelter operators were not interested. Undaunted, they went on to Pueblo, where they were ridiculed. In Denver, they were met with indifference. Nonetheless, the word was out and people began coming . By 1906, partly through the persistent efforts of the ladies' societies in Durango, the importance of the Wetherill find was so firmly established that Mesa Verde National Park was created by that great perpetrator of national parks, Theodore Roosevelt.

The late 1880s and 1890s saw the further development and refinement of the railways in the region. Silverton soon became the only town in the United States with four separate narrow-gauge rail lines serving it. In the 1890s another narrow-gauge line, the Rio Grande Southern, was completed. Over 162 miles of track were laid, giving birth to another railroad town, Ridgway. The route from Durango through Rico to Ridgway was so rugged that 130 bridges were needed to complete the line. With these new rails in place, all the ores dug in southwestern Colorado now could be brought to Durango's smelter. Between 1890 and 1891, the mineral output of the area was so prolific that even the railroads could not move the ore fast enough.

But the Silvery San Juan and its booming growth were shocked perilously when the silver panic of 1893 hit. That year the United States Congress voted for a gold standard, and the government stopped buying silver. With silver demonetized, the silver crash was inevitable. Fortunately for the Colorado miners, a rich gold strike

was made that same year in eastern Colorado at Cripple Creek. Since some gold had been found in the San Juans from the 1860s on, efforts to find more were intensified. These were so successful that by 1897, half the mineral output of the area was in gold. But that did not keep William Jennings Bryan from making an impassioned plea for the silver standard in 1896 in front of the Sheridan Hotel in Telluride. But by this time, lead and copper were also being produced, along with the increasing quantities of gold. By the turn of the century, the area had a new moniker, the Golden San Juan.

Mining reached its peak between 1900 and 1912. At that time, San Juan County boasted five thousand people. The story is told that in 1904, when Andrew Carnegie stopped in Grand Junction, Colorado, on a rail trip, a messenger from Silverton was on hand to tell him how badly a library was needed in that rapidly growing town. Carnegie was apparently impressed, as he donated ten thousand dollars for the library. It was built in 1905 and still stands today. But by the 1920s many mines had either slowed down or closed down as the boom began to fade. Towns began to dwindle in size, many of them barely surviving the depression of the 1930s.

The Rio Grande Southern also had problems. It had to discontinue its passenger trains, replacing them with "galloping geese." These contraptions were made from parts of old buses and cars and fitted with flanged wheels. They carried small amounts of freight and a few passengers to

Galloping Goose

Ridgway and Telluride. One of the better-known vehicles was the Casey Jones, which had a Cadillac engine, a cowcatcher, and, of course, flanged wheels. Another popular "goose" had a Pierce Arrow engine. By 1952, the Rio Grande Southern Railway had shut down altogether, although some mining activity continued to sputter along. But there was renewed interest in the area when uranium ore was mined from the vanadium plant in Durango during World War II. From this material, U324 was refined to be used in the atomic bombs that were dropped on Hiroshima and Nagasaki in 1945. But by the 1950s many of the boomtowns already were aging ghost towns. Eventually, in 1952, the Durango to Silverton Railway was forced to suspend year-round operations. But summer operations continued, for by that time a trickle of tourists had begun to discover the region.

Dormant since 1938, the Sunnyside Mine at Eureka, near Silverton, was reopened in 1959 and the American Tunnel was dug from Gladstone to Eureka. This mining operation currently is rated as one of the largest gold producers in Colorado and helps sustain the year-round population of Silverton, numbering around eight hundred. In recent years, numerous movies have been made in and around the historic towns of southwestern Colorado, including such popular westerns as *True Grit, Tribute to a Badman, How The West Was Won, The Denver and the Rio Grande,* and *Night Passage.* Parts of *Ticket to Tomahawk, Naked Spur,* and *Around the World in Eighty Days* were also made there.

In 1961, residents of Durango and Silverton, the railway companies, and the Interstate Commerce Commission saved the last regularly scheduled narrow-gauge line in the United States from extinction. Of the original several hundreds of miles of track between Alamosa and Silverton, only the sixty-five miles linking Chama, New Mexico, and Antonito, Colorado, and the forty-five-mile link between Durango and Silverton remain today. In a recent year, over 200,000 passengers rode "the rails to Yesterday." Fortunately, Silverton and Telluride were designated as National Historic Landmarks, so much of their frontier atmosphere has been saved. The 1970s and early 1980s have seen the development of a winter tourist business based around skiing. The much dreaded snow that claimed so many lives in the early days now provides a new and important source of economic renewal for the region.

Seeing Southwestern Colorado

Durango

Durango, population 12,500, lies nestled in the Animas Valley, surrounded by the foothills of the San Juan Mountains. With the Animas River flowing through the center of town and evergreen-forested hills and high mountain peaks visible in all directions, Durango is attractive by the very nature of its location. At an elevation of 6,512 feet, it offers an ideal summer climate for residents and visitors. Moreover, its location is suited ideally for a base from which to view most of the sights listed in this section. In the summer, there are many tourists and accommodations are tight. In spite of these two shortcomings, Durango is an enjoyable place to stay and its historic genuineness shines through the modern and sometimes "hokey" tourist establishments.

This is a town with a fascinating Old West history. With a little imagination, you can see and feel the old, wide-open, rowdy kind of a place Durango used to be. Although Silverton was the center of the precious metal boom of the 1870s, its mountain fastness made it an impractical smelter and freight center. The officials of the Denver and Rio Grande Railroad looked for a site along the lower Animas River as being more congenial to

Durango

their interests. For there, coal deposits had been discovered, along with lime and iron deposits. With coal readily available for fuel, a large smelter plant could be built to serve the entire region. So in 1879, the smelter at Silverton was brought down the mountains by mule train. A new smelter was built at a site two miles north of Animas City. Animas City, the only community in the lower Animas Valley, was an offshoot of the settlement founded by Charles Baker and his group further up the river in the early 1860s. Eventually, the new smelter site location and the site of the first rail terminus in southwestern Colorado was given the Spanish name "Durango" by railroad officials.

Although it seems unusual that this Anglo rail town was given a Spanish name, it is even more ironic that the name was not derived from neighboring Spanish New Mexico, whose citizens had traversed this region for over a century. Instead, it is thought the name was imported from Mexico, where the widely traveled Colorado territorial governor, Alexander Hunt, had visited. While there, he had been impressed with a thriving, prosperous city named Durango, which was a mining and commercial city whose mountainous location next to a river was similar to that of the new town to be built in southwestern Colorado. For, you see, Durango is a word of Spanish-Basque origin meaning a "well-watered place." Perhaps the Denver and Rio Grande officials who named the town took Hunt's suggestion, hoping that somehow their new town would become as prosperous and successful as its namesake in Mexico.

In 1880, with the railroad under construction from Alamosa, Colorado, to Durango, the town was laid out. Many of its first inhabitants were veterans of the Leadville, Colorado, gold rush. By the spring of 1881, Durango's population had swelled to over one thousand somewhat thirsty citizens. With fifty-nine saloons and other establishments where liquor could be obtained, it was said that Durangoites drank the Winchester way, "fire and repeat." Above the sea of saloons, one lone church lifted its modest steeple to the sky that year, but it was not much of a moderating influence in that violence-prone town. For cowhands, gamblers, prospectors, and railway workers mingled together in an explosive sea of mud, tents, shanties, saloons, and dance halls.

One gang of outlaws was so violent that a vigilante committee was formed to curb their excesses. Naming themselves the committee of safety, these three hundred men decided to close in on the gang. But before they could do so, a gambler shot and killed a local citizen in one of the saloons. Taking the law in their own hands, the vigilantes apprehended the gambler. Then, meting out frontier justice, they hung him from a tall pine tree right in front of the post office that same night. The next day, the Durango newspaper reported the incident in the following poetic terms. "A ghastly sight it was! A scene never to be forgotten. The slight wind swayed the body to and fro. The pale moonlight glimmering through the sifted clouds dotted the ghastly face of a ghostlier pallor. The terrible retribution stopped not in its pursuit. The foully murdered man was revenged ere the day in which the deed was done had flown."

There are ghosts of Durango's historic past wherever you go in this mountain town. Many of the original buildings were destroyed in the disastrous fire of 1899. The pine tree where the lynching was performed was approximately in the spot where today's City Market on Ninth Street now stands. The large smelter on the Animas River was located just across from today's Durango and Silverton Narrow-Gauge Railway depot. And a United States Cavalry Army Field Hospital was erected on the site of today's Landmark Inn when there was a threat of Ute hostilities. Every western town had sporting houses or houses of prostitution. Some of Durango's most famous houses were located near the site of today's Town Plaza Shopping Center, at Narrow Gauge Avenue and Eleventh Street. These houses of ill repute carried such colorful names as the Hanging Gardens of Babylon and the Silver Belle. One obviously more reputable house was called Mother's. The top floor of the Strater Hotel served the same function more informally and was for many years known as the Monkey Hall.

The site of the first platted city in the Animas Valley, Animas City, is located just a few blocks off U.S. Highway 550 or Main Avenue, where the railroad tracks cross Thirty-second Street. That old town was annexed to Durango years ago so that today there is no evidence that it even existed. Six-

Joy Cabin, Durango

teen blocks north of the Strater Hotel adjacent to the building at 2301 North Main Avenue is the Joy Cabin, a one-room log structure, which is the only surviving building from Animas City.

Another of Durango's earliest landmarks is easier to find. The Strater Hotel has been situated on the same site, the corner of Seventh and Main, since the day it was constructed in 1887. It is testimony to Durango's rich past and thriving present. By 1885, Durango's population had nearly reached three thousand and was growing by leaps and bounds. An ambitious twenty-year-old by the name of Strater came to Durango and saw the need for a fine hotel. With few funds but lots of grit, he constructed the Strater House, a fifty-room hotel with wood-burning stoves and comfortable furniture. The hotel has been in continuous operation under local ownership since that time. Now beautifully restored to its past grandeur, and possibly beyond, it is an anchoring Durango landmark that accommodates visitors from all over the nation.

When the first railroad came to Durango in the summer of 1881, a silver spike was driven at Ninth Street near the location of today's depot. Today, the oldest railroad car on the narrow-gauge trip to Silverton is coach and baggage car 212. Built in 1878, it is the oldest railroad car in Colorado. The wooden interior of handsome ash and the original oil side lamps are today's reminders of a not-too-distant past. Numerous other old cars make the forty-five-mile run to Silverton. In case you wondered, the car just behind the locomotive is the tender. It carries eight tons of coal and five thousand gallons of water. The fireman shovels coal from the tender into the firebox. Water is pumped into the boiler from the tender, where the burning coal in the firebox makes steam by heating the water. The steam is diverted into the cylinders which push the pistons. Since the pistons are connected to the wheels by means of rods, the wheels begin to turn and the trip to yesteryear begins.

Durango has a number of nice parks for picnicking. My favorites are Schneider and West Side Park along the Animas River, just off Roosa Avenue between Ninth and Fifteenth streets, and Fassbinder Park located just off Main on Seventeenth Street and Park Avenue. A nature and jogging trail, the Opie–Remes Nature Trail, parallels the Animas River from Alamo Drive north to East Third Avenue at Twenty-ninth Street. The trail is reached from Main Avenue by turning east one block past Twenty-first Street at the Vagabond Inn onto Alamo or by turning east onto Thirty-second Street to reach East Third Avenue.

If you are intrigued by Durango's early history, visit the interesting Animas Museum operated by the La Plata County Historical Society. The museum is located at Thirty-first Street and West Second Avenue in the old Animas City School House. The museum is well worth a visit. It is open daily between Memorial Day and Labor Day with a reduced schedule the rest of the year. Call for hours (telephone: 1-303-259-2402). Useful brochures (even some with historical guides incorporated into them) can be obtained at the Durango Area Chamber/Resort Association visitor center.

Mailing address: P.O. Box 2587, Durango, Colorado 81302. Telephone:1-303-247-0312. It is located in a parklike setting along the Animas River south of town at 111 South Camino del Rio (U.S. Highway 550 South) in a modern building identified by an old steam locomotive parked nearby. Another interesting side trip is a visit to Fort Lewis College, located on top of a hill east of town, offering fine views over the Animas Valley. There are some southwestern Indian relics on display in the library there and there is a picnicking area. Access to the college is from Main Avenue, where you turn south on Eighth Street. Drive up Eighth to Eighth Avenue and follow the signs all the way to the college.

There are a variety of shops, stores, and galleries in Durango offering up everything from fine Indian crafts, cowboy clothes, and railroad memorabilia to cheap curios. Durango's many restaurants are generally of high caliber and serve up some of the best food you will find in the whole Four Corners area. As in the old days, the bars and saloons are plentiful, many of them capturing the atmosphere of a bygone century. Early morning and late evening are excellent times to walk the streets to absorb some of Durango's genuine, historic atmosphere. And if you happen to be in Durango on a warm summer night when the moon is full and the silhouettes of the surrounding mountains are visible, listen for the sounds of muffled voices and tinkling glasses coming up from the entrance of the Diamond Belle Saloon at the Strater Hotel. As you walk up to the entrance and push open the swinging doors, see if you do not

Diamond Belle Saloon

have the distinct sensation of entering a time warp, a sense of being transported to another Durango, an earlier Durango, over one hundred years ago.

Traveling the Silver Circle: A Narrative Account

Last night at dusk we arrived in Durango from Taos, New Mexico. The first two motels we tried were full, but fortunately there was one room left at the Durango Inn just east of town. After a late dinner, we walked the moonlit streets and viewed the Rockies, dramatically silhouetted above the low-rise profile of the town. No skyscrapers here. Just two- or three-story buildings, some with modified false fronts that are so typical of old western towns like this one. It was a quiet unhurried evening as we strolled through the nearly deserted streets.

But this morning things are different. Summer visitors crowd the streets and the traffic is heavy for a town of just over twelve thousand residents. On our way to breakfast at the Strater Hotel, we note that there is a chill in the air this bright August morning. Over the breakfast table we make our plans for the day and then adjourn to the beautiful old hotel lobby where I inquire at the registration desk about a room for tonight. Fortunately there is a cancellation. In a quick trip up to our room, we find a handsome Victorian-style room furnished with antique walnut furniture. The kids are impressed with the ornate handcarved headboard and the claw-foot bathtub.

With assurance of a bed tonight, we prepare to leave Durango to tour the "Silver Circle," a 225-mile round-trip drive which will take us on an all-paved loop through the heart of some of the highest and most ruggedly scenic parts of the Rockies to the silver boomtowns of the late 1800s. The highway is well engineered and easy to drive. This morning we saw the Durango–Silverton narrow-gauge train depart the depot. The shrill sound of the steam whistle and the accompanying puffs of smoke made us sad we were not aboard. We had tried to get reservations before coming to Durango, but even three months ago the train was fully booked for today. This morning we stood in the cancellation line, but earlier birds got the few cancelled seats. So our plan this morning is to drive to Silverton and attempt to get seats for our

Durango–Silverton Narrow-Gauge Railway

children on the return trip to Durango, since we understand that many of the morning passengers make a one-way trip on the train, returning by bus to Durango. We will complete the Silver Circle loop by car.

Now with picnic lunch in hand, we leave Durango by way of Main Avenue, heading towards U.S. Highway 550 north and Colorado Highway 789. About sixteen blocks from the Strater Hotel, we see the historic old, log "Joy" Cabin, an important remnant of Durango's past. After passing La Plata County's fairgrounds we head north out of Durango on U.S. Highway 550, the so-called Million Dollar Highway. It is a road into the mountain fastness of the San Juan range of the Rockies.

Just out of Durango, we enter a particularly wide, beautiful section of the Animas River valley. Somehow valleys like this one are so typical of the Colorado scene. With the narrow-gauge tracks to our right, we glimpse views of the Animas River as it meanders through the valley. Today in its peaceful setting, it does not seem to live up to the dramatic name the Spanish gave it, the Rio de las Animas or the River of Lost Souls. We see numerous ducks flying up from the river and several redwing and Brewer's blackbirds along the road, as one graceful red-tailed hawk soars above us.

As we gain altitude and the valley narrows, small ranches and summer homes dot the valley

floor. They are colorfully backed by red rocks with dark green pines and junipers dotting their tiered, ledgy slopes which rise to meet the sheer cliff walls behind them. Green grasslands, tall ponderosa pines, and small blue ponds and lakes help com-

Ponderosa pine

plete this idyllic scene. Horses and sheep graze idly in the lush meadows, as trout rise in the lakes, leaving their tell-tale ripples in the shape of small, concentric rings. In these rich green meadows, which the Ute Indians must have prized before the coming of the white settlers, we note the barbed-wire fencing nailed to spindly juniper posts. Barbed-wire fences like these, hastily erected by early homesteaders on their newly deeded lands, sometimes brought those early settlers into violent conflict with the region's first cattlemen who fought to maintain the "open range." Sadly we note the increased ski and tourist developments in this once quiet valley. But it's not yet too commercial for our favorite high desert bird, the magpie, who goes sailing in front of us and across the meadow to our right, dressed in formal black and white.

Now, as this excellent highway takes us further up the valley, we gain altitude, slowly but surely, until we catch fine views of Windom Peak, elevation 14,091 feet, one of the many "four-teeners" we will see today. Nearing Hermosa, Colorado, we see an old wooden water tank, used to replenish the water supply of the narrow-gauge steam locomotives. Just beyond Hermosa, we cross the narrow-gauge tracks for the first time. We reflect that just a little north of here the region's first prospector, Charles Baker, and his party made a bridge across the Animas River and established the first settlement in the western San Juan Mountains known as Animas City. Animas City was a placer mining camp, occupied only a few months before it was abandoned. Later a town by the same name was platted further down the Animas, approximately where Thirty-second Street intersects Main Avenue and the river in Durango. In another few miles, the narrow-gauge tracks cross under the highway and it is here that the train takes its own course to Silverton as it heads through the Animas Canyon Gorge rather than paralleling the highway.

Now the road ascends rapidly, taking us into increasingly beautiful high mountain country,

Magpies

Narrow-gauge train in Animas Canyon

where spruces cover the high slopes and where for the first time today we see isolated stands of aspen. Now about halfway to Silverton, we see a bonanza of high peaks cropping up in the distance all around us. We pass by several small mountain lakes as well as large Electra Lake. Almost twenty-four miles from Durango now, we pass the Purgatory ski area road and are reminded, as we see the many ski cabins in the area, that skiing has made Durango and this valley an active center for travelers, even in the winter.

Just beyond the Purgatory road, the peaks that seemed so distant are now staring us in the face, including 12,972-foot Engineer Mountain and 14,086-foot Mount Eolus. Now we drive over Coal Bank Hill Summit at 10,640 feet, over 4,000 feet higher than Durango. On the other side of the pass, we get better views of Engineer Mountain, but the sight that takes the scenic award for the day is magnificent Twilight Peak, topping out above 13,000 feet. As we travel now just below the 11,500- to 12,000-foot timberline, surrounded by this sea of craggy, bare, unforgiving "thirteeners" whose crevasses still hold some of last winter's snow, we have that exhilarating feeling of being on top of the world. Surrounded by barren rock in all directions, we know that this is the heart of a mountain chain that could not have been named anything else but "Rocky."

As we continue our ascent to Molas Pass, elevation 10,910 feet, we are surprised that the road has no guardrails. In several places there are sheer drop-offs beyond the shoulders. But the wide road is well engineered since, in all of our

Chipmunk

Blue spruce

driving today, we have had only to negotiate a few horseshoe curves. We see bluebirds flit over the tarns from one stunted alpine tree to another and a few brave chipmunks scurry across the road. As we descend past Molas Lake, we observe more stands of Colorado blue spruce, the Colorado state tree, and mountains clad with stately Engelmann spruce.

Now we descend rapidly in a zigzag course to Silverton. In a few miles, we spot that old mining town far below us to the right, nestled in a small valley surrounded by high peaks. The valley is named Baker's Park after Charles Baker, the first prospector to enter this area. As we stop to soak in this dramatic view, we notice Indian paintbrush just off the roadside. Descending further, we get a view of the valley, one mile wide and two miles long. We are told it is the flattest piece of land in San Juan County. Not only is the valley flat, but it is also

Indian paintbrush

treeless, dry, and almost desolate looking in contrast to the green mountainside. The aerial view from here allows us to see the road we are traversing a mile or two ahead as it snakes its way down to elevation 9,318 feet to the oldest continuously inhabited community in southwestern Colorado.

Silverton occupies the western side of this very flat valley, while five miles to the northeast over a passable road when it is not wet is one of Colorado's largest and best-preserved ghost towns, Animas Forks. From our high perch, we see Silverton's symmetrical gridiron street system laid out before us, looking more like a piece of graph paper than a town. The Animas River courses through the valley just south of town, its red-streaked banks testimony to the iron oxides being washed down from the surrounding red mountains. We can see a series of roads leaving Silverton, extending like spokes from a hub, eventually winding through the numerous gulches that have produced an unbelievable amount of wealth over the years.

But according to Navajo legend, these gulches produced more than mineral wealth. That legend states that somewhere in this convoluted mountain country around Silverton, perhaps up one of these gulches, the Dineh or The People first emerged into the world from a hole in the ground. Snowmelt and water in these gulches spawn the Animas River which flows seventy miles south into northwestern New Mexico to the San Juan Basin, near where the Navajo made their ancestral home in Gobernador Canyon (see Section II, "The Navajo: Nomads and Survivalists").

We drive across the flat valley floor and cross iron-laden, red Mineral Creek, as we enter Silverton. We crane our necks looking at the mountains which encircle us. High and to the northwest is Anvil Mountain, to the northeast are Boulder and King Solomon's mountains. To the southeast is Kendall Mountain and to the southwest are Sultan and Grand Turk mountains. Silverton's streets are wide and flat. After all the up-and-down driving we have done this morning, it seems strange to find such a level piece of ground perched up here in the heart of the mountains.

As we focus on the town, we are instantly taken with the frontier, western character of this place. There are not any horses, but there are not many modern vehicles either. The few cars and trucks, most of older vintage, are pretty well banged up from their use on the mountain backroads. Main Street or Greene Street is paved, but the few side streets and auxiliary streets are not. Even the pavement we see seems about to return to dirt as it is pretty well covered in spots with dust and gravel. A cool breeze is blowing and whipping up the dust in the streets. Although we see several buildings with typical western false fronts, we particularly notice some of the elaborate Victorian buildings and quaint churches which gave the mining camps an aura of elegance.

We decide to tour the public rooms of the Grand Imperial Hotel on Main Street, which was built in 1882. Restored to much of its former glamour, it is well worth seeing, particularly its massive mahogany bar, the oldest in the region. Crossing the street, we walk by the Teller House, built in the early 1900s as a guesthouse and still used in that capacity today. The courthouse, the library, and the newly refurbished city hall were also built in the early 1900s. Today it is difficult to imagine that this was once such a wealthy and well-known area that financial syndicates in England bankrolled many of the mines and even built some of the buildings here.

Exploring the town, we are drawn immediately to the boxy tower and spire of the United Church of Silverton. It is Silverton's oldest, the first church being erected on this site in 1880. The

United Church of Silverton

simple design of the church, with its two multi-level, peaked roofs and its tall, pointed bell tower, almost seems to echo the shape of Kendall Mountain looming up behind it. Whether intended or not, there is a wonderful symmetry here between the natural and the man-made lines. As we leave the church, we note the galvanized metal roofs on many of the houses and speculate that they must make quite a din in the middle of a Rocky Mountain hailstorm.

We walk to the town hall and make an inquiry at the Silverton Chamber of Commerce (P.O. Box 565, Silverton, Colorado 81433. Telephone: 1-303-387-5654). Then we head toward the rail depot. I recall the story that led to hiring Bat Masterson as sheriff of Silverton. In the 1880s, the sheriff from Durango came up here looking for two desperadoes. He ordered Silverton's night marshal to help him out. The Silverton marshal saw several suspicious-looking men standing in front of a dance hall. Upon approaching them, they both opened fire, killing the marshal. The enraged citizens formed a vigilante committee. That night they caught and lynched an apparently innocent man. The desperadoes escaped. Because of incidents like this, the town of Silverton decided to hire Bat Masterson, the famous lawman from Dodge City, Kansas. Masterson was able to chase most of the undesirables away from Silverton and the town became more peaceful after that. We look at our watches and realize that it is about time for the train to return to Durango. We inquire and find that space is available. Our children hop aboard. The train spews great clouds of cinders and smoke as it prepares to leave the station. With a final shrill whistle blast, it is off.

Walking back to the car, we are aware of numerous shops for the tourists. We see everything from rock and railroad memorabilia shops to craft and curio shops. Although the town is thriving on the trainloads of passengers who disgorge here daily, we learn that many of its eight hundred full-time residents are largely supported by the continuation of mining activities. The Sunnyside Mine, a few miles outside of Silverton, continues to employ over two hundred people. It is rated as one of the largest gold producers in Colorado.

We regret we cannot linger a little longer here, but we have seen much of what the town has to

Mining relics

offer and we are eagerly anticipating the next twenty-four-mile stretch of road to Ouray, which some claim to be one of the two most scenic drives in Colorado. Driving out of town, we follow the signs to U.S. Highway 550, which parallels South Mineral Creek a few miles. Along the creek, we come across some of the most extensive mining ruins we have seen today, backed by the orangy, red hillsides. Now the highway starts up as though it meant it. Before this road was paved, one of the local newspapers described segments of it as being dangerous even to pedestrians. It went on to say that the grade was four parts vertical and one part perpendicular. We allow as how its designer, Otto Mears, was quite an engineer, as we drive along today's wide, paved but curving, climbing road. Although the stretch from Durango to Ouray is often touted as the Million Dollar Highway, the term was first used for this stretch of road between Silverton and Ouray. No one quite knows why the "Million Dollar" name was coined. Some say it was because the construction of the modern road in 1923 over these few rugged miles was so astronomically expensive. Others say that it was because the gravel used for the roadbed was later discovered to be like a rich placer deposit, containing enough gold to be worth a million dollars or more.

Now, climbing more steeply, we reach 11,018-foot Red Mountain Pass. This area is loaded with large numbers of old mines on the left and right of the highway, as well as up and down the mountainsides and up just about every gulch. Many of these mines are in absolutely unbelievable locations, hugging the vertical faces of steep rocky cliffs. We see phantoms of the boom days everywhere we look. Old shaft houses and other ghost relics of the mining heyday remain to remind us of this area's mineral riches. With the limited technology available in the 1800s, it is a marvel that this heavy mining equipment could have been lugged hundreds of feet up to these cliff-hanging sites. We are impressed that those fortune seekers worked hard for what they got—if they got anything at all!

The afternoon sun gives the mountains an incredible redness, bringing out many different shades of red and orange in the rocks. No problem figuring out how these mountains got their name. Now in a series of switchbacks, we descend the other side of the pass. One of the first things we see is the sign leading to the Idarado Mining Company's mine, which is one of Colorado's leading copper producers today. In a few miles, we come to a relatively flat area called Ironton Park, where we spot a water ouzel or dipper bounding along the surface of the water. This valley was named in honor of the mineral that has so generously stained the dirt, rocks, mountains, and rivers in this area. Even the stream is orange as it runs through the marshy meadow here. We are reminded that there were towns all along this route, as well as stagecoach stops. The mines were named for the loves, fantasies, hopes, and fears of their discoverers. The names are as colorful as the soil and the men who named them: The Micky Breen, The Yankee Girl, The Orphan Boy, and The National Belle.

Now in a few more miles, after two exciting double-horseshoe curves, the highway takes to a ledge or a shelf that was blasted out of the vertical side of the mountain by the indomitable Otto Mears in 1883. He called this testament to the power of dynamite the Rainbow in the Sky Highway. There was literally a pot of gold at both ends of this rainbow—and in-between as well! The original ledge was very narrow, barely admitting a stagecoach, and it was steep with a grade of 21 percent. As I ride the brakes down the pass, I am grateful that the slope of this modern highway is only 6 percent. I look up and see huge sheer rock walls to my right. Sometimes out of sight and hundreds upon hundreds of feet down on the left is the river. Someone once described this view as looking into the jaws of death. They weren't far from wrong.

In a few more miles, we round a curve and come face to face with an overwhelming view of a lush green-clad valley hundreds of feet below us, encircled by high peaks. We know in an instant from this high perch we are looking at our destination. Ouray often is called the "Switzerland of America," and no wonder. Deep in this mountainous amphitheater sits Ouray town, surrounded by red rock ledges and cliffs arising from the valley in stair-step fashion to the lofty heights of the surrounding peaks. Just two miles from Ouray, we stop at Bear Creek Falls. This spectacular waterfall plunges 227 feet into the canyon below. It was right around here that Otto Mears placed his toll booth collecting five dollars for stagecoach and horses and two dollars for a horse and rider, as men and animals traveled the new road linking Silverton and Ouray.

With the dramatic pass we have just negotiated and with Ouray in front of us, we reflect that we are pleased to have come this far rather than just stopping at Silverton. It seems impossible, but the scenery is getting better and better. Now as we descend rapidly, each curve brings the town closer into view. In Ouray, we see a pleasant western town that exudes warmth and a sense of community. About the only sign of life we see this afternoon is the Uncompaghre River as it flows lustily through the town. But this perennial river is more than just a place to catch a fish or two or cool your tired and dusty feet; it is responsible for turning this valley a shade of green not seen for miles around. The seven to eight hundred full-time residents here (striking a nice balance between retirees and young families with children) have chosen not only a well-watered place to live, but a cool haven at 7,800 feet elevation.

In many ways Ouray is our favorite family-oriented Colorado mountain town. It is old, Western, and yet very civilized. After all, we recall, Ouray has depended on tourism quite a bit longer than the other nearby towns, so making travelers comfortable and happy seems to come natural in Ouray town. The few days we spent here several years ago in this mountain oasis, with its many historic Victorian-style buildings, was a relaxing, enjoyable experience we would like to repeat. But today we only have time to see a few favorites like the Box Canyon. Instead of driving in from the first switchback south of town along U.S. Highway 550, we turn left from Highway 550 or Main Street just as we enter town, onto Third Avenue. We decide to park our car near the river and walk the short distance up to Box Canyon Park. Paying a small entry fee, we take the lower shorter trail down into the canyon bed at the base of the 285-foot falls, rather than the trail to the top. This 21-foot-wide "canyon" is really more of a gorge or a slot than it is a canyon. The narrow trail, partly over a suspension type of bridge, leads us deeper and deeper into the earth, the deafening pounding of the water becoming louder with each step. Now so close to the falls that the spray is hitting our faces, we look up as far as we can see to where the water starts its long course downward. By the time it gets down here, it has a tremendous force. If you want to witness the power of water, this is the place to

Old Beaumont Hotel, Ouray

come. As we stand here looking at this marvel of nature, one of the locals tells us that the water for the large hot springs swimming pool north of town is piped from this location.

As we walk back out, we comment that this is one of the finest natural sights in southwestern Colorado. We stop and rest for a few minutes at the pleasant picnic tables before walking back to the car. Driving through town, we notice more renovations of older buildings than we had remembered. Several of our favorite buildings, the old Beaumont Hotel and the Saint Elmo Hotel built in the 1890s are still very much intact. We recall that this town, too, had money and that one of its more fortunate and flamboyant citizens, Thomas Walsh, pulled so much gold out of his Camp Bird Mine that when he went to buy the pricey Hope Dia-

mond, it was like buying glass at the dimestore.

Now we turn off Main to the right and drive up Sixth Street, where we pass the excellent Ouray County Museum which details much of the mining history of the region. We turn left on Fifth Street and see the Wiesbaden Hot Springs Spa and Lodge. A few years ago, we walked from the motel lobby down into a series of subterranean chambers below the motel where there are numerous natural grottoes filled with hot springwater. Less soothing but just as fun are the many hikes which radiate out into the mountains from Ouray. We remember particularly the short hike we took to 200-foot-high Cascade Falls, on the trail by the same name, which begins at the end of Eighth Avenue. We return downtown and stop for a short time at one of the several fine regional craft and art galleries.

Sorry that we do not have time to stay and eat dinner, we drive north out of town, passing the huge mineral hot springs swimming pool which is breathtakingly situated so that as you stand neck-

Fire station, Ridgway

deep in the warm, soothing water, you can look out on an array of peaks that would cure even the most homesick Swiss immigrant. We note that the helpful Chamber of Commerce (P.O. Box 145, Ouray, Colorado 81427. Telephone: 1-303-325-4746) is still located at the pool. As we drive on north, we discuss the pronunciation of the name which lies on the mountains and river here and which used to label the town until Ouray citizens discarded that long Ute name for a shorter one, Ouray, to honor the great Ute chief. In Ute, Uncompaghre means "unca" for hot, "pah" for water, and "gre" for spring. Breaking it down this way, we come up with a pronunciation which satisfies us.

On the ten-mile drive to Ridgway, the road first parallels the glistening Uncompaghre River. Then we pass lush meadows which provide feed for horses and cows. Rustic ranch houses become part of the scenery as we move away from the mountains into the open country around Ridgway, population three hundred, altitude 6,985 feet. Once a rail and transportation center in the nineteenth century, Ridgway is now a sleepy little town. Just as we enter town, seven or eight youngsters on horseback are racing furiously around the corner of the old fire station, leaving a huge cloud of dust behind them. As the dust settles, we notice that the red front and bell tower of the old rock-walled fire station are set off beautifully by the exceedingly lush, green park across the street. The scene looks so inviting that we stop to stretch, sit, and eat a snack in the park before moving on to Telluride.

The ascent is gentle as we head west on Colorado Highway 62 to Dallas Divide, Placerville, and Telluride. Just a few miles out of Ridgway, we come to a rise which gives us a view over a vast valley, rimmed with a stunning array of peaks. We have seen powerful mountain scenery all day, but this scene stops us in our tracks. I get out and click away, hoping to capture the essence of what we are seeing. These Uncompaghre Mountains are truly magnificent. The highest peak, rugged and foreboding at 14,100 feet, is Mount Sneffels, named for the volcano in Jules Verne's *Journey to the Center of the Earth.* We linger a little longer before continuing up to Dallas Divide, named for the United States vice president under President Hayes. The divide tops out at 8,735 feet. Now heading down the other side, we pass through the remains of Placerville, established in 1876 as a mining camp, but pretty well wiped out by fire in 1919.

We turn southeast on Colorado Highway 145, following the San Miguel River for most of the remaining twelve miles to Telluride. From a few miles outside of town, we catch our first view of Telluride across wide San Miguel Park in a six-mile-long glacier valley at the foot of numerous rock walls, rising precipitously to Ajax, Telluride, and Ingram peaks. Just about two miles out, we glimpse another view of town, framed in the foreground by a few weathered old buildings and corrals. This is the approximate location of old San Miguel City. Founded in 1876, it was the first mining camp in the area. In the same year, another

Corral outside Telluride, Colorado

little camp called Columbia cropped up. Being closer to the mining area, it grew up and outstripped San Miguel City. In time, the name Columbia was changed to Telluride. Today's city, at 8,744 feet elevation has around 1,300 permanent residents and is listed in the National Register of Historic Sites. As we drive futher toward town, we see ski condominiums that have been built just outside the Historic District. In 1972 Telluride was chosen as the site for a major ski development. The winter snow that was so oppressive to the early miners is now viewed as a form of "white gold," bringing new life and money to this otherwise snowbound town, which can receive up to two hundred inches of snow in one season.

We stop briefly at the Telluride Chamber Resort Association visitor center (P.O. Box 653, Telluride, Colorado 81435. Telephone: 1-303-728-3041) located on the west side of town in an attractive modern building containing a restaurant and grocery store. As we drive in on the main street, Colorado Avenue, we immediately are impressed that Telluride is a little larger than both Silverton and Ouray. Numerous homes and older buildings reflect the richness of past bonanza times, while row after row of condominium units tell us that this town is in the middle of a ski boom. The mines, which produced the early opulence were christened with names as colorful as their discoverers: The Pandora, The Smuggler, Hidden Treasure, The Tomboy, and The Liberty Bell are but a few. And at one, the Gold King, a Telluride citizen developed the world's first successful line to transmit alternating current. Driving through town, we reflect that had this been 1889, the very road we are on might have been the escape route for Butch Cassidy's first bank robbery after he and two cohorts looted the San Miguel County Bank, making off with $22,500. Emboldened by this success, he repeated his stellar performance over and over again, becoming one of the West's most notorious outlaws.

After parking, we get out of the car and stand for a few moments, just taking in the high peaks encircling three sides of the town like a giant stage set. Ingram Falls, 3,000 feet above us, plummets several hundred feet down the rocky face of Ingram Mountain. Although it is several miles away, that mountain seems to be just at the end of the street. To the right of this impressive falls is another cascade of water which is even more breathtaking. Bridal Veil Falls streaks 450 feet down another vertical rock wall and takes the record as the highest unbroken waterfall in Colorado. We are told that in the summer, hang gliders descend from lofty Ajax Peak, elevation 12,785 feet, to land here on Colorado Street in front of the Sheridan Hotel.

Next to the courthouse, we see the Galloping Goose with its Pierce Arrow parts. It has been on display here permanently since 1951 when it was mothballed following the removal of the narrow-gauge tracks. In the early days, passengers arriving at Telluride were greeted by a stationmaster who would yell out "To Hell you ride." But there is no hell in this pleasant mountain community today.

Time spent in this old town with its fascinating array of nineteenth-century buildings, already restored or in the process of restoration, is nothing but pleasure. We walk from the old courthouse to the Sheridan Hotel next door. This three-story hotel, built in 1895, is one of the nicest we have seen all day. It was in front of this shrine in the "City of Gold" as Telluride was sometimes called, that William Jennings Bryan made several of his famous speeches, including a version of his "Cross of Gold" speech, in support of the silver standard in the late 1800s.

Adding to the sense that some kind of boom is going on here now, Telluride is very busy today. There are many young people gathering in front of the cafés and on the street corners. Yet in spite of all the people, we seem to be the only ones in a hurry. The atmosphere is more laid back than bustling. Perhaps, as one resident pointed out on our trip here last year, Telluride still has one foot in the 1960s. So it does, as evidenced by the young, relaxed, friendly, and open Telluride locals we have met today. Yet the other foot seems to be well in the grasp of the real estate developers who have already come close to overdeveloping the periphery of the town. From the standpoint of summer travelers it would be too bad to see the historic section of town dwarfed by the new, modern section. From what we see today there is still a balance between the old and the new, which possibly can be kept since the more aggressive developers are setting their sights on developing Telluride Mountain Village. It is over five miles away, out of sight, in another small valley southwest of town. There, Telluride residents are quick to point out, "they" (the developers) can have their Vail (referring to the chic, elegant ski development at Vail, Colorado), leaving the historic Telluride community to develop in a way more commensurate with its past.

From the material we picked up at the visitor center, we note that Telluride is quickly becoming a very pleasant place to stay with over two dozen restaurants, cafés, and bars, several dozen shops and gift stores and over fifty hotels, inns, bed-and-breakfast establishments, motels, and resort condos capable of housing over three thousand people. We walk down a few blocks from Colorado Avenue to the banks of the San Miguel River, which at this point in its journey is a beautiful mountain stream. We sit down on the grassy banks and just soak it all in. In every direction we look there are elements of magnificence and beauty we have not seen in the other mountain towns along our route today. There are outstanding views in every direction. And just across the river the steep mountainside, cut with hiking and ski trails, is lush with a dense mixture of conifers and aspen. The trails beckon us to explore them but we will have to wait for another day. No wonder everyone wants a piece of the action here. When we first came in this afternoon we drove just east of town to City Park. There we walked in a huge area of open space dotted with tennis courts, walking paths, picnic benches, and an outdoor concert stage, which serves as a platform for the jazz, bluegrass, and rock musicians who perform here during Telluride's many summer festivals. After a few more minutes listening to the cold, rushing mountain water, we reluctantly get up, leave the riverbank, and walk back to Colorado Avenue.

We look at the clock in the courthouse tower and realize that it is 5:30 P.M. and time to go if we are to be back in Durango to meet our kids for dinner. Although we have to leave Telluride the way we came in, we alter our route a little by driving up a few streets to one of the dirt roads heading in the same direction. In this somewhat residential part of town, we see a beautiful brightly painted Victorian-style home absolutely covered with "gingerbread." Although the house seems out of

Victorian home, Telluride

Lizard Head Peak

place in this rugged country, it lends a touch of elegance to this rocky glacial valley and no doubt was a great morale booster for its creative owner.

Now at the junction, approximately three miles from town, we interrupt our westerly course and turn south or left to New Ophir and Rico. The road rises steadily and we see in the distance Sunshine Peak at 14,000 feet and Mount Wilson at 14,246 feet elevation. Soon we see New Ophir along the road with its mining and railway relics just off the road. There are a few homes, some old buildings, and a post office here. We remember reading a story about a postman who, on Christmas Eve in 1883, set out from Silverton with the Christmas mail for Ophir. He never made it. Two years later his body was found with the mail sack still strapped to his back. Some crushing Christmas Eve avalanche had done him in.

From New Ophir, we pass through some of the prettiest forest land we have seen yet. Lining the road are beautiful groves of aspens or "quakies," as the cowboys used to call them in their attempt to describe the way their leaves move with the wind. We pass by Trout Lake with its thick grove of aspens leading up the slope to timberline. Beyond there, we see some of the most contorted peaks we have come across today. A half-moon is

rising above these mountains this afternoon, visible even in the bright blue sky. The road takes us in a traverse around these peaks so that at one point we view them end on. We are struck by the peak on the very end, Sheep Mountain, elevation 13,182 feet. It is almost perfectly triangular in shape and for a moment, the way the shadows are falling on it, it looks like an ancient pyramid in this high alpine country.

We now cross Lizard Head Pass at 10,250 feet elevation. It's very wide open up here on top of the pass. In its quiet isolation this afternoon, with the tops of 13,000-foot peaks looking close enough to touch, we once again have that special feeling of being on top of the world. The map reveals that many of these mountains surrounding us are part of the San Miguel range. Looming up now on the right is the grotesque rock formation for which the pass was named. Lizard Head Peak at 13,113 feet elevation looks at first glance like some giant brooding bird, sitting on a rock pedestal. I stop the car and get out in an attempt to absorb more fully what I am seeing. Gazing at the strange rock formation in the fresh, rarified mountain air, I have that spine-tingling sensation that comes when the senses are overwhelmed. I remember that it also caught the eye of a member of the Hayden Expedition in 1874. Hayden remarked that the pass was "marked by a curious monument of trachyte 290 feet high." Curious indeed. It looks like a giant pagan bird or lizard god sitting there. With great dignity, his awesome commanding presence rules the surrounding valleys, mountains, and sky. With some imagination, the stately spruce and fir lined up in the foreground look like loyal subjects standing at attention before the awesome figure above them. I know now that, for me, this is the most exhilarating experience of the day. For the third or fourth time in my life I am experiencing at this moment a "Rocky Mountain High."

With insufficient time to hike the several-mile-long trail to Lizard Head, we descend Lizard Head Pass, following the Dolores River to Rico. At Rico, we see a town that has many of the old buildings of the mining days. A modest church, the plain fire station, and the many tin-roofed homes are quite intact. Some of the buildings are occupied. Some are abandoned. There has been little done to restore this town, but it is maintained sufficiently that it does not yet deserve the ghost epitaph. The great boom that occurred here in 1879 is definitely over. But if silence is golden, then this town is indeed "Rico" or rich as the name implies! This afternoon everything is still and quiet here. We sense the peace and solitude. Quite a change from the rough-and-tumble mining boom days.

In another thirty-six miles, we pass through Dolores, an active, thriving agricultural and cattle town of around eight hundred people where there is a monument marker detailing the Domínguez–Escalante expedition through here in 1776. It is now quite clear, in this broad valley of rolling hills and wide vistas, that we have left the mountainous mining country for cattle country.

Just south of Dolores, we notice the signs to the new Anasazi Cultural Center and McPhee Reservoir west along Colorado Highway 184 (see "Indian Past: The Anasazi Circle Tour, The Lowry Pueblo Ruins: A Narrative Account," this section). But before reaching that intersection we turn left to head east on Colorado Highway 184 to Mancos, where in a few miles we see towering Mount Hesperus. On the way, we pass through a beautiful region of valleys and lakes, seeing numerous resorts and guest ranches. Mancos is quiet this evening. From the beginning, it has been a farm-

ing and ranching community, somewhat removed from the great mining bonanza higher up and to the north, although some disgruntled miners were among the first to homestead the fertile grasslands here. We learn that fishing and horseback riding are bringing many tourists here, sparking a mini-boom in this area where most of the matchsticks in the United States are made. They are split from aspen wood, logged from those quaking groves high up on the slopes of the mountains. From the Mancos Valley, we have a good view of the La Plata Mountains and Mount Hesperus at 13,232 feet.

The last few miles take us back to Durango, where we arrive shortly before 8:00 P.M. The narrow-gauge train has arrived from Silverton at 6:30. We find our children sitting happily in that grand old lobby of the Strater Hotel, eager to tell us about their return rail trip from Silverton. At dinner, over eight hours and 225 miles after we left Durango this morning, we share our tales of the Silver Circle. As we end our day, the old train depot, visible through the restaurant's windows, reminds us again that southwestern Colorado's past is very close to the present.

Indian Past: The Anasazi Circle Tour

Unquestionably, the essence of southwestern Colorado rests in its rich frontier history and its modern western ambience. Yet the area is best known both here and abroad for its ancient Anasazi Indian cliff dwellings in Mesa Verde National Park. This was the first national park in the United States to be dedicated to the preservation of the works of man. So it is a historical park dedicated to a people called the Anasazi who, for unknown reasons, began to leave the mesas in small numbers, possibly as early as the eleventh century, building to a mass exodus in the thirteenth century, which left the mesa abandoned by A.D. 1300. And they never came back. So when you visit Mesa Verde and its immediate environs, you will not see any Indians whose ancestors lived on the mesa. It is thought the Mesa Verde people

Mesa Verde Anasazi pottery

eventually migrated to other areas, resurfacing on the Hopi mesas and in the Rio Grande Valley, where they became the ancestors of some of the southwest Indians you will see in those areas. The history of the Anasazi and the speculative reasons for their leaving this area have been reported in Section II of this book. And the discovery of Indian ruins in the Mesa Verde region has been discussed in the history portion of this section.

Over 700,000 people visit Mesa Verde each year. There are many reasons to add the Mesa Verde scalp to your touring belt. The ruins are easy to reach. In a small area there is a rich concentration of well-preserved and, in some cases, restored ancient multistoried living quarters in large caves or alcoves along the cliff walls. The talks by the rangers are interesting and educational. The scope of the ruins is magnificent. The crowds, the signs, the erected fences, the restrictions, and the prohibitions are the distractions. But by visiting in May, September, or October you will avoid much of the summer congestion and find the ruins almost as peaceful as they were over nine hundred years ago. But do not miss Mesa Verde, especially if you will be unable to see the Anasazi cliff dwellings at Betatakin or at Canyon de Chelly.

Mesa Verde National Park

Mesa Verde National Park was founded in 1906 with the primary purpose of preserving the remains of an ancient pre-Columbian culture. Following the rediscovery of the ruins in 1888 by the Wetherill brothers, Mesa Verde became the stomping ground for both genuine scientists and entrepreneurs. Early visitors to the ruins often carted off relics by the basketful to sell for profit. By 1899, even the Wetherills were selling rare artifacts they had found there. In 1891, a Swede, Baron Gustav Nordenskiold, performed the first systematic excavations at Mesa Verde, opening the way to future archaeological expeditions. But upon leaving to return to Sweden, Nordenskiold crated up box after box of invaluable relics to take home with him. The people of Durango protested this move and tried, through the courts, to block shipment of the antiquities. There was no law to support their protest. The looting continued until the Federal Antiquities Act was passed in 1906, prohibiting the removal of ancient artifacts, and the park was established. By that time many fine, intact relics had disappeared from the site. Nonetheless, other fine artifacts have been found since that time and they are on display at the Chapin Mesa Museum.

The park contains approximately 52,000 acres. There are over twenty major ruin sites open to the public that have been excavated and stabilized. There are scores more which are inaccessible and not open to the public. It is believed that there are more than one thousand individual ruin sites on Chapin Mesa alone, and perhaps over four thousand ruins within the park border. From 1908 to 1922, Spruce Tree House, Cliff Palace, and the Sun Temple were stabilized. The authenticity of some of these changes made in the name of "stabilization" has been questioned, since docu-

Corrugated pottery vessel

mentation found in the archaeological field notes often does not back up the reconstruction that was done. Nonetheless these reconstructed sites are well worth seeing. Yet it is satisfying to know that the research and excavation being done these days employs the best of modern know-how and technology so that mistakes made in the past will not recur.

Mesa Verde's outstanding Chapin Mesa Museum is open year-round. With the exception of food service at Spruce Tree Terrace, lodging, food, and gas are available only from mid-May to mid-October. Except for Spruce Tree House, the cliff ruins are closed in the winter. Wetherill Mesa can be visited only from early June through either Labor Day or late September. Check with the Park.

Durango makes an excellent base for a day trip to Mesa Verde National Park, Cortez, Colorado, and the Lowry Pueblo Ruins at Pleasant View, Colorado. You could also use Cortez, Colorado, as a base for a similar day trip. But if for reasons of time, convenience, or romantic inclinations you want to stay on Mesa Verde, lodging is available there, while a campground is provided near the entrance below the mesa.

From Durango drive west on U.S. Highway 160, the San Juan Skyway (a national scenic byway) thirty-five miles to the Mesa Verde turnoff. One mile from the turnoff is the entry booth, where you will pay a small fee and receive some information about the park. From there it is twenty miles to the major ruin sites over a narrow, but paved mountain road which often is so congested and has so many sharp curves and steep grades that it takes about forty-five minutes to travel it. The speed limit in the park is thirty-five miles per hour in most areas and slower in others. It is strictly enforced. If you drive this road after dark, be particularly cautious, for deer seem to think this road is also theirs. Telephone: Mesa Verde National Park Visitor Center, 1-303-529-4465 or 1-303-529-4463, evenings.

Seeing Mesa Verde National Park

When you arrive at the park's entry station, you are at the north end of Mesa Verde. As the mesa reaches southwest, it, like the Hopi's Black Mesa, is cut by many deep canyons so that the southern edge fingers out above the desert below, creating several islands in the sky. Each of these island fingers of Mesa Verde is also called a "mesa." The two which you may visit are Chapin Mesa, named after an early amateur archaeologist, and Wetherill Mesa, named for the ranchers who were the first white men to "rediscover" the ruins on the mesa. The ruins on Chapin Mesa were restored early in the century, while those at Wetherill Mesa were not restored until the 1950s and 1960s.

From the entry station, the winding and twisting road ascends up the north escarpment of the mesa, gaining almost 1,000 feet in elevation by the time it reaches Morfield Campground. From the campground, the road eventually passes through a stand of ponderosa pines and after entering a short tunnel it begins the climb to the mesa top. At 6.4 miles from the entry station is a pulloff to the Montezuma Valley Overlook, providing splendid aerial views north and west out over the Cortez, Colorado area, and the Colorado Plateau beyond. Both the valley and its major city, Cortez, were named by early settlers who thought that Aztecs from Mexico had built the many ruins that lay on the land.

Now, still climbing, the road reaches the mesa's top at elevation 8,512 feet where there are a turnout and parking area. This is Park Point. Take the time to stop here, for you will be rewarded with an unobstructed one-of-a-kind, 360-degree aerial view of some of the major sights on the Colorado Plateau. The viewpoint is located at the end of an excellent uphill trail, dotted with benches, which only takes about five minutes to walk. If it is a clear day, when you reach the top you will be rewarded by how far you can see. Sixty miles to the north and west are the Abajo or Blue Mountains in southeastern Utah and looming up on the horizon, 110 miles to the north, are the Manti–La Sal Mountains, near Moab, Utah. Only 45 miles away is one of southwestern Colorado's famous fourteeners, Mount Wilson, elevation 14,246 feet. To the south, rising from the desert floor on the Navajo reservation in northwestern New Mexico, is a rugged giant of a monument, Shiprock, whose fractured top rises 1,700 feet into the sky. And in the same direction, 90 miles away in Arizona are the Lukachukai Mountains. With views out over four states, Park Point adds an extra dimension to this geographic region known as the Four Corners.

From this high point, the road descends approximately 5 miles to the Far View Visitor Center, a modern circular building. From the visitor center you can choose to visit the ruins on either Chapin Mesa or Wetherill Mesa. If you plan to spend a full day at Mesa Verde, you will have time to see most of the sights on both mesas. But if you are going to be there for a half day, you will probably have to decide whether to see the ruins on one mesa or the other in depth or just scrape the surface of both. In general, the Wetherill Mesa ruins were stabilized later in the century and profited from the application of more advanced archaeological techniques. The ruins there probably represent more accurately the way things were. But the Chapin Mesa ruins, while thought by some to be overly restored, often are more dramatic, and because there are more of them, render a fuller, more varied picture of early Anasazi life. They are also easier to reach since the Chapin Mesa road is relatively easy to negotiate and takes you, in most instances, right up to the short walking trails that give access to the ruin sites.

The Wetherill Mesa parking lot is reached via a slow, twelve-mile drive over a typical mountain road with lots of twists, curves, and steep grades. The road is open only in the summer between the hours of 8:00 A.M. and 4:30 P.M. Vehicles weighing more than 8,000 pounds GVW and/or over twenty-five feet in length are prohibited. Sandwiches and cold drinks are available on Wetherill Mesa. From the parking area you can walk a short distance to take the one-half-mile self-guided tour of the cliff-side dwelling, Step House (containing ruins from two periods in the Anasazi time line) or board the tram or minibus for the short ride to the cliff dwelling, Long House (a dramatic ruin second only in size to Cliff Palace and containing a large central plaza), where you will join a one-half-mile, round-trip ranger-guided tour. From there you can board the bus again to reach the starting point for a three-quarters-of-a-mile self-guided tour of Badger House Community, four clusters of pit houses spread out on the mesa top.

To the right of the visitor center, spread out along a ridge offering good views, is the Far View Motor Lodge with its very good restaurant. There is a small, high-quality Indian arts and crafts shop

there as well as another at the Far View services center, adjacent to the cafeteria and the mesa-top's only gas station, which has Indian crafts of equal quality. For information about buying southwest Indian arts and crafts, see the "Shopping" sections in Sections II and IV.

As you drive south from the visitor center to see the major ruins on Chapin Mesa, look for an access road to the left of the highway at approximately 1.3 miles. There is a sign on this road marking the road to the Far View Ruins, but it is south of the spur road and faces south. Although these ruins are apparently intended to be seen upon exiting the park, seeing them on the way in places the ruins you will see later in better chronological perspective, providing an excellent introduction to them. So turn left and follow the road a very short distance to the Far View Ruins, area where there are remnants of mesa-top pueblos that preceded the cliff dwellings in time.

Although often bypassed by visitors as they rush pell-mell to the more famous sites, these ruins far from the "madding crowds" offer some solitude the others do not. There you can wander in relative peace, explore, and touch several ruins of the Pueblo III or Great Pueblo Period, which spanned the years A.D. 1100 to 1300. Some of the structures had additions of up to three and four stories, as the Anasazi slowly abandoned many smaller village sites to live together in larger communities. As the population increased, these new rooms were added probably without the modern-day fear of reassessment and higher taxes. The Anasazi seemed to dote on these mesa-top pueblos, living in comfortable villages like this until, inexplicably, they abandoned some of them in the thirteenth century and new homes were built in great alcoves in the cliffs which were only occupied for a short time.

For a moment, take time to examine the hand-hewn rocks in the walls of Far View House, carefully cut to rectangular building block size and then shaped with exactness to fit the corners and curved walls (see Section II, "A Prehistory of Indian Country"). Mud mortar, sometimes containing strengtheners such as small rocks and pottery shards, was then used sparingly to cement the building blocks together. Contemplate how people who did not have the benefit of the wheel carried the thousands of tons of sedimentary rock and the huge Douglas fir timbers for roof supports that were required to construct multistoried apartment buildings containing more than fifty rooms and several kivas or ceremonial chambers.

Erecting these huge buildings with the limited technology available at the time is a feat that boggles the mind. But what is just as amazing is the construction of nearby Mummy Lake, a man-made reservoir ninety feet in diameter and twelve feet deep, estimated to have held a half million gallons of water. And as if that were not enough, the Anasazi diverted the water to the lake by way of a man-made canal, part of an extensive irrigation system that channeled water five miles south as far as Spruce Tree Canyon. If you have more time, you may want to walk a few hundred feet to another ruin, Pipe Shrine House, circa A.D. 900 to 1300, or take the short footpath to Far View Tower, one of fifty-seven towers of unknown function that once were scattered across the mesa top.

Returning to the main road, turn left and continue a little over three miles, following the signs to the Chapin Mesa Museum and Spruce Tree House. Although hard to comprehend, you are now at the

Masonry walls and doorway, Far View House

same elevation as when you entered the park at the entry station. This section of the park has picnic tables, restrooms, a lunchroom and small grocery store, and an excellent Indian arts and crafts shop. Be certain to take time to see the Chapin Mesa Museum, a real gem, which contains many of the artifacts that have been excavated and removed from the ruins you will be seeing. You will note the six wall murals upon entering the museum. These were executed by eight historically significant Native American artists who were associated with the Santa Fe Indian School in the 1920s and 1930s. Julian Martinez, one of the artists, was the husband and co-worker of Maria Martinez, the renowned San Ildefonso potter. And another of the artists, Jack Hakeah, was Maria's adopted son. Now take time to see the ceramic collection. The size and design work of the ceramic pieces on display are truly stunning. And do not miss the exhibit in one showcase that contains objects found in a leather bag, which belonged to an Anasazi healer or medicine man. Also, be certain to see the lifelike dioramas, which reveal how the building structures were incorporated into the lives of the prehistoric Anasazi people.

Although there are many beautiful artifacts there, it is sad to think that many others have been removed from Mesa Verde. Some Mesa Verde relics can be found in the galleries of the Museum of New Mexico's Palace of the Governors in Santa Fe, while others are in the Colorado State Museum in Denver and at several other museums throughout the United States. Surprisingly, one large group of relics resides in the National Museum in Helsinki, Finland, the legacy of a scientific study of the Mesa Verde ruins in the 1890s by the Swedish scientist Nordenskiold. Never displayed in Sweden, these well-traveled artifacts were stored there until 1938 when they became the property of the Helsinki Museum. But the Swedes were not alone in their enterprise, since both before and after them the Wetherill brothers and other Americans dug relics from the mesa like they were potatoes and sold them for a pittance.

From the museum you can take a self-guided walk to Spruce Tree House, a cliff dwelling built in the giant alcove of a sandstone cliff. One of the best-preserved ruins in Mesa Verde, it also is the third largest of the ruins, with over 114 living rooms and an estimated population of 100 to 150 people at one time. Spruce Tree was one of the earliest ruins to be discovered by Richard Wetherill, who found it in December 1888, shortly after finding Cliff Palace. Naming it for a large spruce tree that had grown up in front of the ruin, he must have wondered why these early people chose to live in these remote, almost inaccessible locations. For reasons not well understood, some of the mesa-top dwellings were abandoned in the early 1200s for these alcoves.

Echoing their life-style on top of the mesa, they built the same type of pueblo buildings within the caves. Ironically, the craftsmanship was not nearly as good in these later efforts. But since the stone walls were plastered over with a thin wall of mud, perhaps it made little difference. Some say the reduced quality in workmanship may have been due to the fact that in the great caves, the buildings were less exposed to weather and did

not need to be so carefully constructed. Others point out that the buildings may have been built in great haste to avoid potential enemies. Detractors of this argument point out that Spruce Tree House defies the notion that the Anasazi abandoned the mesa tops in fear of their enemies to seek the protection offered by the cliffsides. They argue that its location is not defensible at all and if anything might have led to entrapment.

Note the kivas at Spruce Tree House. They offer a dramatic sight, with their ladders protruding skyward out of the ground. Note, also, that the roofs of the kivas serve as the floor of the plaza. What reverberations there must have been in the kiva below, with the dancers pounding their feet in rhythm above. Early on, the kivas were square or rectangular like the living areas. Then in the Classical Period, with better techniques at hand, the Anasazi began building round kivas. In some instances during that period, however, such as in

Kivas of Spruce Tree House

the Fire Temple Ruin in Fewkes Canyon, rectangular kivas continued to be built. The migration patterns from Mesa Verde to other regions are still somewhat in question. But it is interesting to note that rectangular kivas began to appear in the region to the southwest at Betatakin and later on at the Hopi mesas, while the circular motif was used at the prehistoric Bandelier site and in many of the pueblos along the Rio Grande.

You may note that the stonework of some of these former three-story structures is not as fine as at Far View House. Nonetheless, it is impressive. The small T-shaped doorways indicate that the Anasazi may have carried wide loads on their backs, the wider aperture at the top allowing the burden to pass through. Although these openings appear small, you must remember that the average Anasazi male is thought to only have been 5 feet 4 inches tall, while the average female was

Anasazi doorway, Spruce Tree House

around 5 feet tall.

After completing your tour of Spruce Tree House, return to the museum parking lot. If you want to visit more cliff ruins, return to the main junction and take a right to the Ruins Road. Continue south until you come to the first intersection. There you can either continue straight on to the mesa-top ruins to turnouts offering views of cliff dwellings, or you can turn left at that intersection to reach Cliff Palace and Balcony House. Cliff Palace is a ten-minute drive from the museum. There you can take a self-guiding walking tour about one-quarter of a mile in length, lasting approximately forty-five minutes, during which visitors must climb four 10-foot-high ladders. Picnic tables and restrooms are near the parking lot.

Many of the pictures you have seen depicting the cliff dwellings are of this dramatic site. Not only was it the first dwelling to be found by the Wetherill brothers in December 1888, but it is also the largest cliff dwelling in the Southwest. Because of its many rooms and dramatic honey-colored, golden-hued stone towers, it was dubbed Cliff Palace. It was not a palace to the Anasazi. It was just the site of another agrarian, Anasazi community built along fairly standard lines during the Classic Pueblo Period. Its cave is 325 feet long and 90 feet deep. The cave entrance is over 60 feet tall at its highest point, allowing for structures that were four stories high in places. It contained twenty-three kivas and over two hundred rooms, but typically the living spaces were very small and some rooms probably were used for storage. Note the high ledge up and to the back of the cave. An ingenious attic space squeezed out of the cave's dimensions, it contained fourteen storage rooms. It is estimated that a population of between 200 and 250 people lived there.

The towers at Cliff Palace are especially impressive. Both square and round towers were found on Mesa Verde, but their function is unknown. Under the alcove roof, the towers rise from the earth and extend to the earth reaching for the cave ceiling, not the sky. Some have speculated that this intense recontact with the earth had religious or ritual significance. Look for the window in the base of the tallest square tower. Peek in that window and you will get some idea of the room size. While peering in, note high up on one

Cliff Palace

of the original plastered walls the fine Anasazi painting. After almost eight hundred years, this superbly designed painting is still mostly intact. Upon finishing your tour of Cliff Palace, retrieve your car and return to the Ruins Road. Continue in a southerly direction towards Balcony House. There are several places to park along this road to view ruins from the mesa rim across the canyon. As you round the very southern tip of Chapin Mesa, you can look down on the Mancos River Valley below before heading north along the east face of the mesa finger above Soda Canyon. You will arrive at the Balcony House parking lot after about a ten-minute drive from Cliff Palace.

Balcony House, sometimes known as the "Fortress," is perhaps the most interesting ruin on the mesa. The remarkably intact second-story walkway, which looks like a balcony, gives the ruin its name. There often are fewer crowds at Balcony House since touring it requires a thirty-two-foot climb up a sturdy, wide Anasazi-style ladder and a hands-and-knees scramble through a ten-foot-long tunnel. Skirts and high-heeled shoes are not compatible with either of these activities. Neither are people who have fears of heights, tun-

nels, or climbing ladders. But if none of the above apply, stand in line to take your turn as a modern-day Anasazi. Children delight in the exciting aspects of this ruin and adults are usually intrigued with the entry and exit routes. The entry ladder is provided compliments of the park service, since experts believe that today's exit was the only access path to and from the ruin, making it almost impregnable. The exit is through a narrow cleft in the rocks with improved toeholds for the modern visitor.

In spite of its inaccessibility, Balcony House, unlike many of the other cliff dwellings, seems to have been built with care and without haste. You will notice that the Anasazi stonemasons demonstrated a very high quality of workmanship there. Also notice the ancient timbers projecting from the stone walls. Small core samples drilled from those Douglas fir timbers were used to date the ruin by means of comparative tree ring growth patterns. While the men cut and hauled in the timbers, the women in this village processed the corn, using a mano or grinding stone and a metate or grinding basin, both of which are on display at Balcony House.

Entry to Balcony House is by ranger-conducted tours accommodating only fifty people on a first-come, first-served basis. The total walking distance is one-half mile and the round-trip tour takes approximately one hour.

From the parking area, continue north to the junction with the Ruins Road. At this junction, you can turn left and take the six-mile loop trip, which includes numerous modified Basketmaker pit house ruins on the mesa top, dating from A.D. 575 to 750, that precede the cliff dwellings by many centuries. If you take this road, you may want to turn off at the Square Tower House parking area. After a short walk, you will see Square Tower House, the tallest cliff structure in the park. Back to your car, wind your way through numerous other ruins, eventually reaching the Sun Point View area. From that location, which is thought to be the spot from which the Wetherill brothers first glimpsed Cliff Palace, you will catch your first view of the Sun Temple, the next stop along the Ruins Road. This haunting mesa-top structure probably

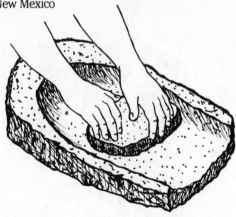

Metate and mano

served a religious function for many of the Anasazi communities. From the Sun Temple, return down the Ruins Road, past the Cliff Palace junction and past the museum junction, approximately twenty-four miles, to exit the park.

Provided you have time and are not too saturated with Anasazi ruins, you may want to spend a few hours seeing another Anasazi gem,

Balcony House

Lowry Pueblo Ruins

well off the tourist track. Lowry Pueblo Ruin at Pleasant View, Colorado, approximately thirty-five miles northwest of Mesa Verde, should not be missed. It can be seen as part of a Mesa Verde circle tour or as you enter or exit southwestern Colorado going to or from southeastern Utah.

The Lowry Pueblo Ruins: A Narrative Account

From the Mesa Verde spur road, we turn left and head west on National Scenic Byway, U.S. Highway 160, through the Montezuma Valley toward Cortez, Colorado. We are tired and hot. It has been an exhausting day so far. We arrived at the Chapin Mesa Museum and Spruce Tree House at 9:30 A.M. Except for a quick picnic lunch, we have been viewing ruins and hassling with crowds for five hours. But now we long for some seclusion. In spite of the reconstructions and museumlike displays at Mesa Verde National Park, we conclude that the experience was an exceptionally worthwhile one and certainly an educational one. The information on the signs and from the ranger talks was most helpful in further understanding the people who once inhabited this land. But we all agree that the experience was educational rather than inspirational. Now we yearn for some solitude and peace and quiet to reflect about what we

have learned. Isolated Lowry Pueblo Ruins will help us do just that.

We relax as the car's air-conditioner takes over. There's a storm building to the west and every few minutes we drive under the welcome umbrella of a cloud and then back out again into the hot, bright afternoon sun. Passing through the outskirts of Cortez, we see several of the trading posts and shops where we have purchased Indian crafts. These posts cater mostly to the Navajo further south, but occasionally Jicarilla Apaches from New Mexico or Utes from the area immediately south will trade here. As we pass pleasant Cortez Park with its shade trees and picnic tables and the modern Cortez visitor center (Cortez Area Chamber of Commerce, Mildred and Main streets, Cortez, Colorado 81321. Telephone: 1-303-565-3414), we notice the slower pace in Cortez and the lack of traffic this afternoon. Although it is an active farming and ranching community and a center for oil and gas production, it is a sleepier town than Durango and about half the size with a population of 6,800.

There is a good mix of Anglos, Mexican Americans, Navajo, and Utes here today. Tourism is also beginning to boom, since Cortez is well situated to serve as a base for many of the attractions in southwestern Colorado. At an altitude of 6,198 feet, it is lower and consequently hotter and not as picturesquely situated as Durango. The chamber of commerce, fond of promoting Cortez as a place where the mountains meet the desert, emphasize the latter when they point out that you need sunglasses in the winter as well as the summer. Those claims are not exaggerated. It is dry here with an annual rainfall of only twelve inches.

We drive through town, following the signs to U.S. Highway 666N, Pleasant View, and Dove Creek, Colorado. In less than two miles from Cortez we pass the junction road (County Road K) to the left, heading west a short distance to the outstanding Crow Canyon Archaeological Center. We recall that just a few days ago we met and visited with one of the Southwest's leading archaeologists who helped develop the center. He told us of the pleasant lodging and dining facilities there (see "Staying There," "Cortez, Lodging," this section) for travelers who want to dig a little deeper into the Southwest's prehistory. Visitors who are willing to spend a week there can actually participate working side by side with skilled professionals in the ongoing excavation and analysis of artifacts found at Duckfoot, a ninth-century Indian village and Sand Canyon, a vast thirteenth-century pueblo. No previous archaeological experience or knowledge is required. We decide that it would be fun to follow up next summer.

Now heading northwest, we drive across the high plains approximately twenty-one miles to Pleasant View. On the way, we have more good views to our left of the Sleeping Ute Mountains. These rounded outcroppings are well named, for

Western red-tailed hawk

their pleasing shapes combine to form an image of a giant man lying on his back, with emphasis on his arms folded and resting on his chest.

At Pleasant View, we see the sign to the Lowry Pueblo Ruins, turn left, and drive west nine miles to the site. The flat, relatively straight road (paved halfway and a recently graded dirt and gravel road the rest of the way) is in good shape as it cuts through the farm and scrub desert country to the site. Dust swirls around us as we pull into the parking area. Although it is hot this afternoon, the wind which has been kicking up the dust also makes the temperature tolerable. The breeze feels good on our backs as we get out of the car.

We are relieved that we are the only people here. In fact, the only other living creature in sight as we walk to the ancient pueblo is a western red-tailed hawk circling lazily above us. Our tour will be self-guided, with several small reader boards telling us about the main ruin. Operated by the Bureau of Land Management rather than the National Park Service, there are no rangers regularly on duty here. The ruin appears like a diminutive pile of rubble compared to some of the grand reconstructions at Mesa Verde. But we are drawn to it. Its scale is more human in size than the larger ruins we saw this morning. It speaks to us as no signs, brochures, or rangers can in this spectacularly understated setting here on the lonely high plain.

It is eerily quiet this afternoon. Out of crowds and alone for the first time today, we are able to get a keen sense of what it must have been like to live in one of these remote Anasazi villages. Silently, we walk through some of the forty rooms which have been excavated, their thick, almost nine-hundred-year-old walls casting cool, refreshing shadows under the hot afternoon sun. Although the Anasazi farmers who lived here probably appreciated the shade these walls provided in the summer, they were probably even more grateful for the protection they provided in the winter as blinding snowstorms howled outside.

Climbing to one of the highest parts of the ruin we are allowed to visit, fine vistas of the wide agricultural plain open up before us with the mountains looming up in the distance. For over fifty years the Anasazi farmers who occupied this village must have been able to scan the horizon as

Painted wall, kiva, Lowry Pueblo Ruins

we are doing now, perhaps spotting their neighbors and friends in the distance as they traveled on pilgrimages to the beautiful kiva here.

Stepping down, we decide to search for the underground painted kiva we have read so much about. Finding its location, we descend the few steps to take a look. We are pleased to see that although chipped and fading, some of the painted plaster walls are still sufficiently intact that the geometric designs can still be made out. The basic design of one painting is reminiscent of the steps of an Aztec pyramid. Or could it be a zigzag pattern representing lightning? My son wonders if it is a picture of a snake. Certainly it could be that, too.

We read that this pueblo was probably a religious center for people who gravitated here from neighboring places. In fact, over a period of time, it is thought that two of the major Anasazi groups inhabited this village. Some of the relics found here reflect Mesa Verde Anasazi influence, while others reflect Chacoan influence. The beautifully wrought masonry of the kiva is thought to be Chacoan. For unknown reasons, these ruins were abandoned by the middle of the twelfth century, long before the great drought of the thirteenth century which is thought to have contributed to the mass abandonment of Mesa Verde.

Now we walk in a wide circle on the somewhat sloping ground around the ruin. The only noise is the wind. A cottontail rabbit scurries into the brush. The dusty ground below our feet is honey-colored like the sandstone building blocks. We find an old tree, long dead, its stiff branches still reaching to the blue sky. Behind it are the stone remains of an ancient pueblo, its ladders pointing upward, its kivas firmly anchored in the ground.

And for a few minutes, alone and miles from civilization, we sit in the warm, loose sand at the base of the old walls.

We can imagine these people of the earth and the sky, climbing ladders to their second- and third-story dwellings. Perhaps they stood on the high walls, assessing the meaning of the clouds over the mountains. Or perhaps, just as we are doing this afternoon, they sat here in the open to catch a cool breeze, soaking in the pleasant view and gazing out over the horizon where the brown plain meets the intensely blue sky. Our son digs his feet into the warm sand. When he kicks the sand away, a small pottery shard surfaces. There is just a trace of a design on it. Indeed someone did use this barren ground we are sitting on. Maybe eight hundred years ago another small boy broke his mother's best bowl here. We wonder about that as we rebury the shard, laying it to rest where it has been for over eight centuries.

Returning to the car, we drive back toward the highway. After a few miles we see the junction road heading off to the south, which would take us over twenty-one miles of graded dirt road to Hovenweep National Monument, which straddles the Colorado-Utah border. That Anasazi area is known for its many varied-shaped tower ruins. But with rain threatening and the possibility of the road becoming difficult to negotiate when wet, we drive back to the highway. Retracing our route for about ten miles toward Cortez, we then turn left and head southeast on Colorado Highway 184 toward Dolores and Mancos. On our left about five miles from the junction with U.S. Highway 666, we see the Anasazi Heritage Center set into the hillside near the Domínguez and Escalante ruins. We have taken the short walk through these ruins many times before, giving them a special priority since they were the first prehistoric ruins in southwestern Colorado to be discovered by non-Indians when the Domínguez-Escalante expedition came upon them in 1776. And we all remember the wonderful vistas from the ruins out over the Dolores River Valley, now the McPhee Reservoir. We have just enough time this afternoon to make a quick reconnaissance of the Anasazi Heritage Center (27501 Highway 184, Dolores, Colorado 81323. Telephone: 1-303-882-4811). We enter the large, handsome, modern, Pueblo-style building and quickly discover that it is not a part of the National Park Service. Rather it was built by the Bureau of Reclamation (but managed by the Bureau of Land Management) as part of the McPhee Dam Reservoir Project mitigation. We learn that McPhee Reservoir, located just outside of Dolores, Colorado (created by damming the Dolores River), is the second largest freshwater lake in Colorado, and it is claimed to be fully stocked for fishing. The Anasazi Heritage Center is divided into public exhibit areas and collection, storage, laboratory, and administrative areas. Many of the materials in the permanent exhibit were recovered from the McPhee Dam and Reservoir site and some of the materials on exhibit here are from the Domínguez–Escalante site. Other materials are from other public lands in southwestern Colorado and the Four Corners area, representing the San Juan Anasazi tradition. We quickly view the permanent exhibits, learn of the slide programs scheduled for the small auditorium, browse in the bookstore, and then exit sooner than we would wish. But we will return. We are pleased that there is now a showplace and center for archaeological artifacts from the varied public sites in this part of the Four Corners region, including those from one of our favorite sites, the Lowry Ruins. We drive on toward Mancos, on a course that roughly approximates the trail blazed by those brave Spaniards from Santa Fe, New Mexico, who trudged across this land searching for a route to California. Glad that we are tourists headed for grub at Durango and not Spanish explorers riding into the unknown, we rush through Mancos, connect with U.S. Highway 160, and arrive back in Durango at dusk.

South of Durango: A Brief Visit to the "Fourth" Corner, Northwestern New Mexico

To view some other interesting Indian ruins and visit a town that serves as a market center for part of the Navajo reservation, you may want to visit northwestern New Mexico.

Leave Durango to the south via the busy U.S. Highway 550, which leads to the largest town in the Four Corners area, Farmington, New Mexico. It is approximately thirty-seven miles to Aztec Ruins National Monument from Durango. You will travel through the Southern Ute Reservation since the highway bisects it as you travel south. East of the highway is Ignacio, Colorado, the home of the Southern Ute Tribal Headquarters, where a visitor center and tribally owned motel and restaurant are open to the public. For most of the way, the road runs parallel to the Animas River. Pass through the small town of Aztec and follow the signs to the monument west of town where the large tree-shaded parking lot is always a welcome sight on a hot day. There is a small entry fee to be paid at the desk in the visitor center.

Declared a national monument in 1923, this site has coughed up some exceptionally fine ceramic artifacts which you should take time to see in the small museum just off the lobby. The ruins resemble those at Lowry Ruins and the three- and four-story surface ruins at Mesa Verde. The Chacoan influence is strong here, from the careful preplanning of the architecture to the open plaza and the fine-banded stonework. But there also is evidence that people from Mesa Verde lived here later in time, rebuilding some of the walls in their style and leaving much of their distinctive pottery behind.

But it is the Great Kiva here at Aztec that catches your attention and holds it. Entering its chambers is a sacred experience not dissimilar from walking through the doors at Chartres or Notre Dame. With a diameter of nearly fifty feet, the main floor is eight feet below the surface of the ground. Do take time to visit this wonderfully reconstructed kiva and experience some of the grandeur that was a part of this ancient high desert civilization. Early settlers to the area thought these and other ruins were built by the ancient Indian civilizations from Mexico, so they named them after the Aztecs. Average touring time at Aztec Monument is less than one hour.

Now continue down U.S. Highway 550 to Farmington, New Mexico, at 5,390 feet elevation, population 31,000 (Farmington Convention and

Great Kiva, Aztec National Monument

Business Bureau, 205 West Arrington, Farmington, New Mexico 87401. Telephone: 1-505-326-7602). This oil, gas, coal, and power-generating corner of New Mexico centers around this farming and ranching community. Although Farmington is situated in a well-watered spot near where the La Plata, Animas, and San Juan rivers come together, it is often dusty and dry, receiving less than eight inches of rain annually. In the 1950s, when I first passed through Farmington, New Mexico, the oil and gas boom was just beginning. Much of the town was a trailer city, ugly and sprawling in the hot sun, resting at the lower and hotter altitude of 5,500 feet. I swore at the time that I would never go back there. But in the early 1970s, after visiting Aztec National Monument, we drove to Farmington for lunch. What we found then and since that time is a modern, progressive town, showing its best side. It is also one of the leading trade centers for the eastern half of the Navajo reservation. Consequently, this is a good place to see some genuine trading posts and to purchase Navajo as well as Hopi crafts.

In spite of the scarred, rough-looking edges coming into town, Farmington is a friendly western town and you will feel welcome there. Perhaps you will want to have lunch at one of the air-conditioned restaurants or one of the many fast-food outlets. By all means, visit one of the Indian arts and crafts shops or trading posts. Browse the streets. Most likely you will see many Navajo in traditional dress doing their shopping and trading in this up-and-coming boom 'n' bust town bordering the northwest corner of the Navajo Reservation. And you'll see a lot of travelers passing through town on the way to some of the nearby sights such as the Bisti Badlands, thirty-two miles south along New Mexico Highway 371. There, in a paleontological paradise of 30,000 acres of geological whimsy mirroring some of the beautiful badlands formations found in southeastern Utah, your explorations may turn up unusual varieties of rocks, fossils, and petrified logs. There are no facilities so you will want to carry plenty of water.

Leave the traffic of modern Farmington and head east toward Bloomfield on U.S. Highway 64 to the well-marked Salmon Ruins. This site is still being excavated. Therein lies its uniqueness. Enter the air-conditioned visitor center with its welcome cold-water fountain and restrooms. The museum in the center is one you should not miss. In it you can see the best of the artifacts removed from this ancient pueblo. To date, none of the artifacts found there have been removed permanently to other locations. If you have been disappointed with the quantity or kind of artifacts displayed in the museums at Mesa Verde or Aztec, you will dote on the relics at Salmon. Sensing the cultural value of the ruins he found on this land which he homesteaded in the late 1880s, George Salmon and later his family protected them from pilferers and fortune hunters. The ruins were kept intact until they could be purchased by the San Juan County Museum Association in 1967. But it was not until 1971 that the voters of San Juan County passed a bond issue to investigate, excavate, and improve the site. Full-scale excavation began in 1972 and continues intermittently to this day.

The flat, arid ruins site, about one hundred yards from the visitor center, is just a few hundred yards from the fabled San Juan River that spawned many of the ancient Anasazi pueblos. You can spend several hours watching the excavation and stabilization work proceed. There you will see good examples of Chacoan masonry, with its wide layers of large rectangular blocks alternating with

narrow bands of smaller and thinner, finely spalled pieces of sandstone. Note how this differs from Mesa Verde masonry, which uses little mortar and consists of large sandstone blocks almost exclusively.

You may marvel that the stone for this 600- to 750-room mud-and-stone pueblo was brought by the Anasazi from thirty to forty miles away. The timbers may even have been carried from as far as today's southwestern Colorado. The Anasazi had not developed the wheel so, for a moment, contemplate what their options must have been. One theory supports the idea that all these materials were probably hand-carried over a network of specially constructed roads.

Although they do not have to build roads, many of the archaeology students at Salmon Ruins labor just as hard in their efforts to excavate and restore the site. Only about 40 percent of the original pueblo has been excavated. Even though these ruins may not be as dramatic or impressive as those you may have seen elsewhere, the fact

Interior of Great Kiva, Aztec National Monument

Salmon Ruins

that the site is sometimes being excavated makes it interesting to see. For even while you are there, discoveries of one sort or another may be made as stonemasons continue to stabilize and reconstruct toppled walls using age-old techniques.

Leaving Salmon Ruins, proceed 2.5 miles to Bloomfield. From there, partly by way of New Mexico Highway 44, you are 56 miles from Chaco Culture National Historical Park. The Chaco Anasazi probably reached a higher peak of development than the other Anasazi and left many large ruins that are architecturally impressive. However, part of the route there is unpaved, requiring a drive of over 29 miles from Blanco Trading Post (36 miles from Bloomfield on

New Mexico Highway 44) or 22 miles from Nageezi Trading Post, 8 miles further south (many prefer this shorter route in a conventional vehicle but for either route call the park visitor center for the latest road update). These sandy, dirt roads are sometimes very rough but are generally safe for a conventional vehicle when dry. They are not safe to drive in a standard vehicle during or just after rainstorms. Telephone: Visitor Center, Chaco Culture National Historical Park, 1-505-988-6716.

From Bloomfield take New Mexico Highway 44 to Aztec where you can reconnect with U.S. Highway 550 to Durango. This round-trip circle tour from Durango with stops and lunch takes approximately six hours. The total round-trip distance is 112 miles.

But if you are not returning to Durango, you may wish to continue on to Santa Fe or Albuquerque, New Mexico. From Bloomfield you can travel east on U.S. Highway 64 through the picturesque Jicarilla Apache Reservation to Dulce, Chama, Abiquiu, and Española, New Mexico, on the way to Santa Fe. Or alternatively, you can drive southeast from Bloomfield on well-traveled New Mexico State Highway 44 through the Jemez and Zia Indian reservations and by Coronado State Monument. From there you can drive to Corrales and Albuquerque or to Bernalillo and Interstate Highway 25, which runs south to Albuquerque and north to Santa Fe.

Staying There

Durango

The logical touring base for Section III is Durango, Colorado. There are numerous modern and well-run motels, inns, and hotels there. But during the height of the summer tourist season, it may be difficult to find the exact accommodation you are looking for. Consequently, reservations made ahead of time are advisable. Often a telephone call made the day before or the morning of your arrival will put a hold on the accommodation you prefer.

Listings for lodging (some of which date back to the turn of the century), food, and a few of the more interesting events in Silverton, Ouray, Telluride, Mesa Verde, and Cortez are entered below. They are also interesting places to stay, especially if you are wanting to stay in an even smaller and more remote location than Durango. In addition, several of the area's more interesting dude ranches are mentioned. Rates for these ranches are different from the usual accommodations in this book. Usually the rates are based on a week's stay, which includes three meals a day and may include a variety of activities. Because the rates are so highly individualized, no attempt has been made to provide price ratings. For detailed color bro-

View of the Rockies

Strater Hotel, Durango

chures and up-to-date rate sheets, write to the individual ranches at the addresses given. A more complete listing of these dude ranches as well as additional bed-and-breakfast establishments and current information about events in the area can be obtained from the Durango/Area Chamber Resort Association. Mailing address: P.O. Box 2587 (111 Camino del Rio), Durango, Colorado 81302. Telephone: 1-303-247-0312. Reservations for some but not all of the accommodations listed below (and some that are not listed) may be made by calling Purgatory-Durango Central Reservations 1-303-247-8900 or toll free in the United States 1-800-525-0892 or toll free in Colorado 1-800-358-3400. Or you may telephone ResWest, toll free in the United States 1-800-228-4524 or toll free in Colorado 1-800-247-7846.

Lodging

The Strater Hotel. Anchoring the oldest restored section of downtown Durango at the corner of Seventh and Main avenues, just two blocks from the rail depot, is the impressive four-story Strater Hotel. It was built in 1887 as a showplace hotel during Durango's boom years. It has been a hotel continuously since that time. But you no longer have to go outside to reach the bathroom as you did at the turn of the century. All rooms have private baths for the convenience of the modern traveler.

Beautifully restored and furnished with antiques of the late 1800s, this reasonably priced hotel is a delight. In these rather plush Victorian surroundings, the ambience is casual, warm, western, and friendly. The Strater has ninety-four air-conditioned rooms, all of which are decorated and furnished in the mode of the late 1800s. This decorating has obviously been a labor of love. The Strater offers the Opera House and Henry's restaurants as well as the Diamond Belle Saloon. Some parking. Advance reservation deposit required. Mailing address: The Strater Hotel, 699 North Main Avenue, Durango, Colorado 81301. Telephone: 1-303-247-4431 or toll free in the United States 1-800-247-4431 or toll free in Colorado 1-800-227-4431. Low expensive.

The General Palmer Hotel. This hotel sits in an enviable location almost adjacent to the Denver and Rio Grande rail depot and in the midst of numerous restaurants and shops. Originally there was a hotel on this site, which was built in 1890, but it was not until 1964 that the building was converted from other uses back to hotel status and an annex added to give more space. The small lobby gives a strong turn-of-the-century flavor. The hotel's thirty-nine air-conditioned rooms with private baths are restored to late 1800s elegance. Parking lot. No pets. Advance reservation deposit required. Mailing address: The General Palmer

House, 567 Main Avenue, Durango, Colorado 81301. Telephone: 1-303-247-4747 or toll free in the United States 1-800-523-3358 or toll free in Colorado 1-800-824-2173. Moderate and low expensive.

Durango Travel Lodge. In a good position just two blocks from town center. There are thirty-eight air-conditioned rooms with private baths, TV's, and phones. Cafés and restaurants nearby. Heated swimming pool. Mailing address: Durango Travel Lodge, 150 East Fifth Street, Durango, Colorado 81301. Telephone: 1-303-247-0955 or toll free in the United States 1-800-255-3050. Moderate and low expensive.

Rodeway Inn. In an enviable location close to the railway station, this modern structure with 102 air-conditioned rooms is built around a central, enclosed atrium with a heated swimming pool. Amenities include hot tub (as well as over 20 rooms with whirlpool baths), sauna, video-game room, and continental breakfast. Mailing address: Rodeway Inn, 400 East Second Avenue, Durango, Colorado 81301. Telephone: 1-303-385-4980 or toll free in the United States 1-800-228-2000. Low expensive and expensive.

Jarvis Suite Hotel. Conveniently located right in the heart of downtown Durango. The twenty-one air-conditioned units in this historic downtown building offer the comfort and luxury of a small European hotel, and in addition, each has a kitchen. The handsomely appointed accommodations—one-bedroom, two-bedroom, and studio units—all have private baths and offer a quiet, restful place to stay with restaurants and shops a few steps out the door. Parking provided. Mailing address: Jarvis Suite Hotel, 125 West Tenth Street, Durango, Colorado 81301. Telephone: 1-303-259-6190 or toll free in the United States 1-800-824-1024 or toll free in Colorado 1-800-228-9836. Low expensive and expensive.

Red Lion Inn/Durango. Located on the banks of the Animas River, two blocks west of the downtown historic railroad station is this chic, elegant, ultramodern hotel with 159 air-conditioned rooms. The rooms are attractively decorated and most have small balconies. The rooms on the quiet, north side overlook the river. The public rooms are handsome and in the summertime are bustling with activity just like a big city hotel. Heated indoor swimming pool, sauna, exercise room, and dining room with river view. Parking. No pets. Mailing address: Red Lion Inn/Durango, 501 Camino del Rio, Durango, Colorado 81301. Telephone: 1-303-259-6580 or toll free in the United States 1-800-547-8010. Expensive.

Holiday Inn-Durango. Nothing nostalgic nor western here. A fairly typical Holiday Inn, but only a stone's throw from the Animas River and just a few blocks from town center and the railway depot. The larger inner courtyard contains a very nice swimming pool and wading pool, welcome amenities on a warm day. Ideally situated for families with children, it generally offers some kind of family rate. There are 139 air-conditioned units with private baths, TV's, and phones. It has a dining room that offers three meals a day. It is located between Eighth and Ninth streets on Camino Del Rio, which is two blocks west of Main Avenue. Mailing address: Holiday Inn-Durango, 800 Camino Del Rio, Durango, Colorado 81301. Telephone: 1-303-247-5393 or toll free 1-800-238-8000. Low expensive.

Durango Youth Hostel. Conveniently located near downtown, this hostelry provides dormitories, family rooms, and some private rooms at bargain prices. Mailing address: Durango Youth Hostel, 543 East Second Avenue, Durango, Colorado 81301. Telephone: 1-303-247-9905 or 1-303-247-5477. Inexpensive.

Best Western Durango Inn. Pleasantly located just off U.S. Highway 160 (the Mesa Verde-Cortez Highway) about one mile west of the center of town. Spacious rooms. Large spacious grounds with plenty of room to roam and a heated swimming pool. A good place for families. Restaurant. Mailing address: Best Western Durango Inn, Box 3099, Durango, Colorado 81302. Telephone: 1-303-247-3251 or call toll free in the United States 1-800-528-1234. Moderate.

Adobe Inn. Located 1.5 miles north of town center, this motel has twenty-four air-conditioned rooms with private baths, TV's, and phones. It also has a heated indoor swimming pool and sauna. Free guest laundry provided. Mailing address: Adobe Inn, 2178 North Main Avenue, Durango, Colorado 81301. Telephone: 1-303-247-2743 or toll free direct to the motel 1-800-251-8773. High moderate.

Sleepy Hollow Lodge. Also north of downtown, this pleasant motel with a view of the Animas River has thirty air-conditioned rooms with TV's and some with views of the Animas River. Some kitchens. Playground, miniature golf. Advance reservation deposit required. Mailing address: Sleepy Hollow Lodge, 2970 North Main Avenue, Durango, Colorado 81301. Telephone: 1-303-247-1741. Low moderate.

Spanish Trails Motel. Also located along U.S. Highway 550 north of downtown, this motel has forty-one air-conditioned or air-cooled rooms with TV's. Some kitchenettes. Heated pool and playground on spacious grounds. Good family motel. No pets. Mailing address: Spanish Trails Motel, 3141 Main Avenue, Durango, Colorado 81301. Telephone: 1-303-247-4173. Low moderate.

River House Bed and Breakfast. Located less than two miles north of town center off U.S. Highway 550 North on County Road 203 in an excellent and quiet location just across the road and railroad tracks from the Animas River. This is a nicely designed contemporary mountain home. Six guest rooms all with private baths. The public rooms, including a large, enclosed atrium space, are handsomely designed and decorated. There is an outdoor patio just outside on the spacious grounds. Game room. Living room with fireplace. Full breakfast included. Mailing address: River House Bed and Breakfast, 495 County Road 203, Durango, Colorado 81301. Telephone: 1-303-247-4755. Inexpensive.

Edelweiss Motel and Restaurant. This excellent, reasonably priced motel, located two miles north of Durango's center on County Road 203, is nicely situated just below U.S. Highway 550 in the Animas River Valley. Some of its twenty rooms have kitchenettes, all have TV's. Excellent German restaurant. Jacuzzi and sauna are available. Advance reservation deposit required. Mailing address: Edelweiss Motel and Restaurant, 689 County Road 203, Durango, Colorado 81301. Telephone: 1-303-247-5685. Inexpensive.

Iron Horse Resort. Located less than three miles north of the town's center in a picturesque western Colorado setting along the Animas River is this 137-unit, air-conditioned resort-type inn. It boasts an indoor swimming pool, restaurant, saunas, and a hot tub. Many of the nice bilevel rooms have fireplaces. Wood provided in the winter only. Reservations requested. Call for directions. Mailing address: Iron Horse Resort, 25926 U.S. Highway 550 North, Durango, Colorado 81301. Telephone: 1-303-259-1010. Inexpensive.

Quality Inn Summit. Nicely situated along U.S. Highway 550, about four miles out from the center of town, with vistas over the Animas Valley and San Juan Mountains. Ninety-five air-conditioned rooms (some are beginning to look tired) in a multi-story building with a heated, Olympic-size indoor swimming pool and restaurant. Advance reservation deposit required. Mailing address: Quality Inn Summit, 1700 County Road 203, Durango, Colorado 81301. Telephone: 1-303-259-1430 or call toll free in the United States 1-800-228-5151. Low moderate.

Scrubby Oaks Bed and Breakfast. Located about three miles north of Durango's town center in a pleasant site overlooking the Animas River and surrounding mountains. This comfortable and friendly establishment is just like home. Nice public rooms, game room, and sauna. One guest room has a private bath. The other rooms share a bath (two rooms to a bath). The energetic and knowledgeable hostess here prepares a big country breakfast, which can include Belgian waffles. Box lunches can also be prepared. No pets. No smoking. Call for directions. Mailing address: Scrubby Oaks Bed and Breakfast, P.O. Box 1047, Durango, Colorado 81302. Telephone: 1-303-247-

2176. Inexpensive and low moderate.

Tamarron Resort. Located eighteen miles north of Durango on U.S. Highway 550 in a beautiful, forested, high-elevation mountain setting is this full-service ski (close to nearby Purgatory Ski Area) and summer resort. There are 389 luxury units in multistory lodges and townhouses with kitchens. Large heated indoor/outdoor pool, saunas, whirlpools, recreational program, and children's program. And for a fee you can play eighteen holes of golf on the championship golf course, fish, river raft, play tennis and platform tennis, go horseback riding, take jeep tours of the region or work out in the health club. Picnic lunches packed for walks on the spacious property or nearby hiking trails. There are two dining rooms. Reservation deposit required. No pets. Mailing address: Tamarron Resort, P.O. Drawer 3131, Durango, Colorado 81302. Telephone: 1-303-247-8801. Expensive plus.

Bear Ranch. Located seventeen miles north on U.S. Highway 550, this ski lodge in the winter and resort in the summer offers many amenities for those who stay in the small number of condo-style units with cooking facilities. Besides a restaurant, there are clay tennis courts, saunas, and hot tubs as well as nearby horseback riding. Attractive Colorado-modern wood architecture. Mailing address: Bear Ranch, 42570 U.S. Highway 550 North, Durango, Colorado 81301. Telephone: 1-303-247-0111. Expensive.

Wilderness Trails Ranch (Dude Ranch). Twenty-eight miles northeast of Bayfield, Colorado, and thirty-five miles northeast of Durango. Horseback riding, lake fishing, sailboating. No pets. American Plan with weekly rates during the summer season. Mailing address: Wilderness Trails Ranch, 23486 C. R. 501, Bayfield, Colorado 81122. Telephone: 1-303-247-0722.

Lake Mancos Ranch (Dude Ranch). Located at 8,000 feet elevation approximately thirty miles northwest of Durango and approximately five and one-half miles from Mancos. Horseback riding, heated swimming pool, and lake and stream fishing available. Weekly reservations only during summer season. Three-day minimum after August 30. Mailing address: Lake Mancos Ranch, 42688 County Road "N," Mancos, Colorado 81328. Telephone: 1-303-533-7900.

Echo Basin Ranch. This ranch resort and R.V. park is located just east of Mancos, three miles north off U.S. Highway 160. Formerly a 600-acre working ranch, it is now a visitor's haven with two stocked mountain lakes, lush meadows cut by the trout-infested Mancos River, and forest-clad mountainsides. The very reasonable rates include three meals a day in the lodge dining room and accommodations in one of the 18 modern A-frame cabins, some with fireplaces. Fishing, horseback riding, hiking, hay rides, cookouts, and a heated swimming pool and spa are all a part of the scene and some require a fee. Also shaded tent sites and R.V. sites with full hookups. Mailing address: Echo Basin Ranch, 43747 Road M, P.O. Box 788, Mancos, Colorado 81328. Telephone: 1-303-533-7800 or 1-303-533-7000.

Campgrounds

Cottonwood Camper Park. One-third mile west of Durango, U.S. Highway 160. Telephone: 1-303-247-1977.

United Campground. One mile north of Durango, U.S. Highway 550. Telephone: 1-303-247-3853.

Safari Camp. Two and one-half miles west of Durango on U.S. Highway 160 and then about two more miles up Lightner Creek Road. Telephone: 1-303-247-5406.

Alpine Rose. Three miles north of Durango on County Road 203 just off U.S. Highway 550. Telephone: 1-303-247-5540.

Junction Creek Campground. Approximately five miles northwest of Durango on Junction Creek Road or Twenty-fifth Street. Eighteen sites. Telephone: 1-303-247-4874.

K.O.A. Durango East. Seven and one-half miles

east of Durango on Mesa Verde Highway (U.S. Highway 160). Telephone: 1-303-247-0783.

Hermosa Meadows. Nine miles north of Durango, U.S. Highway 550. Telephone: 1-303-247-3055.

Ponderosa K.O.A. Twelve miles north of Durango, U.S. Highway 550. Telephone: 1-303-247-4499.

Food

The Palace Grill. No. 1 Depot Place. Telephone: 1-303-247-2018. Associated with the General Palmer Hotel and located adjacent to the Denver and Rio Grande depot. Its turn-of-the-century decor makes it a very pleasant place to dine. The menu includes a delicious honey duck, numerous continental specialties, steaks, and some additional "down home" western dishes such as chicken and dumplings. Also many continental specialties are available at dinner. Open for breakfast, lunch, and dinner. Moderate and expensive.

Dos Juan's Restaurante y Cantina. 431 East Second Avenue. Telephone: 1-303-259-0550. Just a few blocks from the Durango–Silverton rail depot, this restaurant is adjacent to the Travel Lodge. The nice adobe-style architecture is complemented on the inside with many decorative pieces from south of the border. Good selection of Mexican dishes. An excellent bar. Although you will be able to get better Mexican food than this in the Rio Grande Valley, this is one of the best in southwestern Colorado. Inexpensive and moderate.

Mr. Rosewater's Deli. 552 Main Avenue. Telephone: 1-303-247-8788. A pleasant relaxed kind of a place. Good for lunch or a snack. Excellent homemade soups, salads, and baked goods. Carrot cake is a specialty. Right in the middle of old downtown Durango. Takeout orders available. Breakfast, lunch, and dinner. Inexpensive.

Ore House. 147 East Sixth Street. Telephone: 1-303-247-5707. This old Durango favorite continues to serve a variety of steaks and seafood in an atmosphere evoking the area's mining heyday. Dinner only. High moderate.

Pronto Pizza and Pasta. 150 East Sixth Street. Telephone: 1-303-247-1510. Just a block off Main Avenue is this upscale pizza joint specializing in thin-crust pizza and homemade pastas and gelati. Pleasant sit-down service. Carry-out or delivery service. Inexpensive.

Father Murphy's Pub and Gardens. 636 Main Avenue. Telephone: 1-303-259-0334. There is an Irish theme here with a good selection of beer on tap and "pub grub" consisting of nicely prepared soups and sandwiches. Heartier fare for dinner. Very nice outdoor garden dining room as well as the comfortable and snug indoor eatery and bar. Inexpensive and moderate.

Opera House Restaurant (Strater Hotel). Seventh and Main avenues. Telephone: 1-303-247-4431. A reasonably priced restaurant evoking turn-of-the-century ambience. A casual, fun place to dine offering breakfast, lunch, and dinner. Upon request, they will also pack an excellent picnic lunch. The extensive breakfast menu features full breakfasts, which include a six-ounce breakfast steak with two fried eggs and home-fried potatoes or a simple continental breakfast. Inexpensive and moderate.

New York Bakery. 750 Main Avenue. Telephone: 1-303-259-1007. This bakery restaurant has been at this location since 1883. Serves breakfast, lunch, and dinner with many Italian specialties. Its prices are reasonable. Inexpensive and moderate.

Kachina Kitchen. Located in the Durango Mall, 835 Main Avenue. Telephone: 1-303-247-3536. For lunch or an early dinner, try this informal café, which specializes in food from the American Southwest and Mexico. Navajo tacos, Indian fry bread, and, of course, sopaipillas. Inexpensive.

The Red Snapper. 144 East Ninth Street. Telephone: 1-303-259-3417. Entering this restaurant with its two hundred gallons of fish-filled aquariums is like visiting the waterfront. With a fresh fish menu featuring a "today's catch" section, you'll begin to believe you're seaside instead of mountain bound. Enjoy the wide selection of items from rainbow trout to Boston bluefish. Prime rib and steaks as well. Moderate and expensive.

Hunters Restaurant. 992 Main Avenue. Telephone: 1-303-259-6474. In this elegant but informal dining establishment you can taste some of the wild game of the region (and beyond). Elk, duck, pheasant, and other woodsy types prepared in a variety of delicious ways. But if that is too "regional" for you, you can order any number of standard European-style entrées including veal, seafood, and steaks, all prepared in a caring and knowing fashion. And just for fun, try the hot fudge cream puff, a spoof on that classic French dessert, profiterolles. Children's menu. Soups and sandwiches for lunch. Reservations accepted. Moderate and expensive.

Olde Tymer's Café. 1000 Main Avenue. Telephone: 1-303-259-2990. Located in a restored nineteenth-century building, this café, with its high ceilings and interesting, very pleasant outdoor patio, evokes much of Durango's past. Serving excellent hamburgers, sandwiches, soups, and daily specials, it is open daily for breakfast, lunch, and dinner. Inexpensive and moderate.

Carvers Bakery and Café. 1022 Main Avenue. Telephone: 1-303-259-2545. This tantalizing bakery with table service specializes in German pastries as well as their own fresh creations. Open early enough to grab a bite and catch the first train to Silverton. You will find good coffee here because they roast the beans on the premises. Breakfast and lunch. Inexpensive.

Edelweiss Restaurant. Two miles north of Durango off of U.S. Highway 550 and County Road 203. Telephone: 1-303-247-5685. This excellent restaurant, which makes everything from "scratch," serves a variety of home-style German dishes. Apple strudel is a house specialty. Live Austrian-Bavarian music on the weekends. Breakfast and dinner. Moderate.

Sweeney's Grubsteak. Two miles north on U.S. Highway 550 across the highway from the Iron Horse Resort. Telephone: 1-303-247-5236. The owners call this interesting contemporary wooden building and its pleasant atmosphere "contemporary Durango." The steaks are excellent, and the salad, which not even one hutch of rabbits could finish off, is equally good. Other entrées include seafood, lamb, and (hold your hat) sweet-and-sour frog legs. High moderate.

Bar-D Chuckwagon Suppers. Nine miles north of town on County Road 250 just off U.S. Highway 550. Telephone: 1-303-247-5753. This listing might well be called an "event" rather than a restaurant. The proprietors have done all they can to conjure up the western atmosphere. Although at times you feel you are part of a Hollywood western movie set, it is all good fun and does create some of that Old West feeling. Of course, there is nothing but "ranch" food available. Chuckwagon meals, including barbecued beef, baked beans, and homemade biscuits, are served. There are small shops on the premises that recreate aspects of early Durango life. And to top it off, there is a real western band, complete with fiddles, guitars, and trail songs. Breakfast horseback rides are offered as well. Reservations are required. Moderate.

Tours

The Durango and Silverton Narrow-Gauge Railway Co. From the middle of May through the third week of October, several trains leave Durango daily for Silverton, high in the San Juan Mountains forty-five miles away. There are fewer trains running in the late fall and early spring, and in the winter the train only goes to the halfway point, Cascade Canyon. In the summer, the trains leave at 7:30 A.M., 8:30 A.M., 9:30 A.M., and 10:15 A.M. But remember that boarding times are from 6:30 A.M. to 7:10 A.M. for the 7:30 A.M. train and from 7:30 A.M. to 8:00 A.M. and 8:30 A.M. to 9:00 A.M. and 9:30 A.M. to 9:45 A.M., respectively, for the other three trains. If you have reservations but have not prepaid your ticket, you must confirm your ticket by 6:00 P.M. the evening before your scheduled trip. If you arrive in town without a reservation, a phone call to the depot will get you a place on the train's wait list. Tickets go on sale at 6:00 P.M. the evening prior to departure for wait-listed passengers. Also, a half hour before each train's departure time, tickets from that train's no-shows go on sale. If you have made a reservation ahead of time and have prepaid your ticket (highly recommended), just show up at the station at the scheduled boarding time for your train. The one-way trip takes 3.25 hours. You will have 2 hours to explore Silverton. The early train arrives back in Durango at 3:45 P.M., while the other trains return at 5:00 P.M., 6:10 P.M., and 6:55 P.M. This train is often booked each day throughout the busy summer months. Do reserve your tickets ahead of time if you can. It is possible to purchase one-way seats and request open, gondola-style cars versus closed ones. In addition, another summer season trip for those with less time on their hands (offered some summers but not all) leaves Durango at 4:30 P.M. and makes a round trip to the halfway point, returning to Durango at 8:30 P.M. Snacks, soft drinks, and coffee are available on all trips. If you cannot get on, try driving to Silverton or take the bus there and try to get a return seat to Durango. (See: "Silverton, Tours, Festivals and Events," this section for other interesting train travel options.) Mailing address: Durango and Silverton Narrow-Gauge Railway Co., 479 Main Avenue, Durango, Colorado 81301. Telephone: 1-303-247-2733.

Horse-Drawn Carriages for Hire. Located across the street from the Strater Hotel. Tour historic Durango in a horse-drawn carriage anytime between noon and dusk during the summer tourist season. First come, first serve.

Durango Lift. This intown bus service provides service to most of the Durango area including the airport, every hour. Daily except Sunday. Telephone: 1-303-259-2366.

Durango Transportation Company. Whether you need a taxi, limousine service to or from the airport, or a tour of surrounding old mining towns, Mesa Verde, or Chaco Canyon, this company has it. Telephone: 1-303-259-4818.

Rocky Mountain Stage. This bus company offers daily service to Silverton and service to Alamosa, Pueblo, and Farmington (with connecting service to Albuquerque). Telephone: 1-303-259-2366.

Jamboree Walking Tours. This one and one-quarter-hour tour of Durango's historic district begins with a slide show of early Durango photographs followed by a walk through yesteryear. Telephone: 1-303-259-1290.

O'Farrell Hat Company. 598 Main Avenue. Tour this small factory and retail store, where they use turn-of-the-century tools to manufacture western and traditional felt hats. Telephone: 1-303-259-2517.

Hassle Free Sports. Rent mountain or road bikes, bicycle clothing, and accessories to tour the area. Located at 2615 Main. Telephone: 1-303-259-3874.

Flexible Flyers-Rapid Thrills. Conveniently located across the river from the Holiday Inn is this river raft company which offers one- and two-hour raft trips of the Animas River rapids. Mailing address: 2344 County Road 225, Durango, Colorado 81301. Telephone: 1-303-247-4628 or 1-303-247-8131.

Rocky Mountain Outpost. One-half- or full-day canoeing or kayaking trips on the Animas River. Extended trips to other areas. Mailing address: P.O. Box 2936, Durango, Colorado 81302. Telephone: 1-303-259-4783.

Colorado River Tours. One-half-day raft trips on the Animas River. Mailing address: 1523 Main Avenue, P.O. Box 1386, Durango, Colorado 81301. Telephone: 1-303-259-0708.

Wild Goose Adventures. 707 Main Avenue. River trips similar to the above. Mailing address: P.O. Box 2814, Durango, Colorado 81301. Telephone: 1-303-259-4453.

Mountain Waters Rafting. Economy half-day and full-day river raft trips on the Animas River. Specially arranged longer trips to raft the upper Animas River, the nearby Dolores River, and the Colorado River. Mailing address: 108 West Sixth Street, Durango, Colorado 81320. Telephone: 1-303-259-4191.

High Country Jeep Tours. Four-wheel-drive-vehicle tours into the mountainous backcountry to see old mines and ghost towns. Mailing address: High Country Jeep Tours/Tamarron Resort, 40292 Highway 550 North, Durango, Colorado 81301. Telephone: 1-303-247-8801, ext. 5050 or 5053.

Horseback Riding

Bear Ranch. Breakfast rides as well as one-hour, two-hour, and full-day rides. Located seventeen miles north of Durango on U.S. Highway 550. Mailing address: 42570 U.S. Highway 550, Durango, Colorado 81301. Telephone: 1-303-247-0111.

Bar-D Ranch. Breakfast rides or one-hour and two-hour rides throughout the day. Nine miles north of Durango just off U.S. Highway 550. Mailing address: 8625 County Road 250 North. Telephone: 1-303-247-5755.

South Fork Riding Stables. Breakfast, lunch, and evening chuckwagon supper rides as well as moonlight champagne rides and hourly or daily rides. Overnight regional safaris arranged. Located six miles southeast of Durango. Mailing address: 28481 U.S. Highway 160 East, Durango, Colorado 81301. Telephone: 1-303-259-4871.

Over the Hill Outfitters. Breakfast rides, hourly and daily rides, family pack trips, summer fishing trips, and elk and deer hunts. Located twelve miles north of Durango just off U.S. Highway 550 on County Road 250 (next to the Ponderosa K.O.A.). Mailing address: 3824 County Road 203, Durango, Colorado 81301. Telephone: 1-303-247-9289 or in the summer 1-303-259-2834.

Fishing

If you are an avid trout fisherman, you will want to seek information from one of the many tackle shops or from the United States Forest Service office in Durango. Telephone: 1-303-247-4874. But if you are an amateur with little time on your hands and would like to try catching Rocky Mountain trout, one of the commercial "trout

farms" is a good bet. No license required.

Wildcat Canyon Lodge. One and one-half miles west on U.S. Highway 160. Telephone: 1-303-247-3350.

Twin Buttes Trout Ranch. Three miles west on U.S. Highway 160, then 0.5 mile on Lightner Creek Road (County Road 207). Telephone: 1-303-259-0479.

Hermosa Meadows. Nine miles north on U.S. Highway 550. Telephone: 1-303-247-3055.

Ponderosa K.O.A. Twelve miles north on U.S. Highway 550. Telephone: 1-303-247-4499.

Rainbow Springs Trout Ranch. Ten miles south on U.S. Highway 550, and one mile west on County Road 214. Telephone: 1-303-247-2939.

Silver Streams Lodge. At Vallecito Lake, eighteen miles north of Bayfield, Colorado. Telephone: 1-303-884-2770.

Other Activities

Backpacking and Hiking. If you are interested in hiking the trails of the San Juan National Forest and Weminuche Wilderness Area, contact the United States Forest Service office in Durango for information, trail guides, and maps. It is located in the federal building across from the Holiday Inn. Mailing address: U.S. Forest Service, Federal Building (Room 301), 701 Camino del Rio, Durango, Colorado 81301. Telephone: 1-303-247-4874 or 1-303-247-4879.

Jogging. Opie-Remes Nature and Jogging Trail (see "Durango" for description).

Golf. There is an eighteen-hole golf course at the Hillcrest Golf Club next to Fort Lewis College on College Hill. Follow Eighth Street to Eighth Avenue, turn left, and follow the signs past the college to Hillcrest Municipal Golf Course. Telephone: 1-303-247-1499. Another eighteen-hole course is eighteen miles north of Durango on U.S.

Highway 550 at Tamarron Resort. Telephone: 1-303-247-8801.

Swimming. Municipal Swimming Pool. Twenty-fourth and Main. Telephone: 1-303-247-9876. You may also swim at the Summit Swim Club adjacent to the Summit Quality Inn. Telephone: 1-303-259-1519.

Fairs, Festivals, and Events

Narrow-Gauge Days. Last weekend in May. The Iron Horse Bicycle Classic (including a race to Silverton and mountain bike races), ten-mile run, and parade.

Fourth of July, Durango. Large fireworks display at La Plata County Fairgrounds.

Annual Rock and Mineral Show. Held the third weekend in July at Exhibit Hall in the La Plata County fairgrounds.

Durango Fiesta Days. Held two or three days in late July and early August. La Plata County fairgrounds. Rodeo. Square dancing, parades, and horse racing.

La Plata County Fair. Usually begins around the middle of August. Livestock and agricultural exhibits and judging, plus the popular draft horse pull contest.

Colorfest Festival. A series of special events held in the fall from the middle of September to the middle of October. Events include a three-day bicycle tour from Durango through Ouray, Telluride, and return; historic home tour of Victorian homes; canoe and kayak races; Durango literary conference (featuring writers like Louis L'Amour); playwriting competition at Purgatory; gallery walks; and a Victorian Ball at the Strater Hotel. For each year's update and complete schedule, write Durango Chamber/Resort Association, Box 2587, Durango, Colorado 81302. Telephone: 1-303-247-0312.

Theater

Diamond Circle Theatre. Located in the Strater

Hotel, this theater is open only in the summer. It specializes in the production of melodramas and turn-of-the-century entertainment. Telephone: 1-303-247-4431.

Abbey Theatre. This Abbey Theatre, in Durango not Dublin, is located at 152 East Sixth Street. It offers a broad range of repertory theater year-round. Telephone: 1-303-247-0136.

Gallery Theatre. Fort Lewis College hosts the Repertory Theatre Company del Rio de Las Animas Perdidas, which features a wide selection of historic and contemporary plays in repertory during the fall and winter months. Telephone: 1-303-247-7823.

Summer Theatre at Purgatory. Amid dormant ski lifts, the large theater tent sets the stage for the production of many theatrical classics as well as some newer contemporary plays. During July and August only. Purgatory ski area twenty-five miles north of Durango off U.S. Highway 550. Telephone: 1-303-247-9000, ext. 143.

Parking

A parking garage is available one block west of Main Avenue on Narrow-Gauge Avenue between Eighth and Ninth streets. No charge if you purchase something in the adjacent shopping mall.

A large parking lot is available one-half block east of Main Avenue, just off Fifth Street. Enter by way of the driveway just beyond Swenson's and The Stockman Store.

Shopping

Waldenbooks. 104 East Fifth Street. Telephone: 1-303-259-3728. Not only a good general bookstore, but one with a fine selection of regional books about the West, mining ghost towns, and the historical development of the area. Conveniently located near the rail depot.

Appaloosa Trading Co. 501 Main Avenue. Telephone: 1-303-259-1994. An outstanding selection of leather goods made on the premises (everything from belts and briefcases to flight jackets), plus an outstanding selection of belt buckles and silver and antler jewelry as well as handmade wooden steam locomotive whistles.

Overland Outfitters. 546 Main Avenue. Telephone: 1-303-259-2005. Formerly known as the Overland Sheepskin Co., this shop brings an added dimension to Durango's shopping scene. Warm and nicely designed sheepskin coats, jackets, slippers, and soft sheepskin toys as well as leather and suede outerwear garments.

O'Farrell Hat Company. 598 Main Avenue. Telephone: 1-303-259-2517. If you are looking for a bronc or bull rider felt hat, or for that matter, a "Bogart" fedora or almost any other kind of fur felt hat, this custom hat maker and retailer will probably have it.

Native American Creations Gallery. 145 East Sixth Street. Telephone: 1-303-259-3319. This gallery is a good southwest Indian crafts store with a nice middle range of Navajo rugs, Pueblo pottery, and kachinas. It also has some souvenir-type articles including American Indian incense.

The Greenery. Located at 747 Main Avenue. Telephone: 1-303-259-0663. A bookstore, card, gift, and plant shop all rolled into one. And it works well, as evidenced by the crowds of locals and travelers who congregate there.

Graden's. 777 Main Avenue. Telephone: 1-303-259-1294. Possibly Durango's oldest department store, carrying a wide selection of western gear.

Gallerie Marguerite. 114 East Eighth Street. Telephone: 1-303-259-2377. Just a block off Main Avenue, this fine gallery showcases southwestern art, including bronze and wood sculptures, oil paintings, and watercolors.

Duranglers. Located below street level at 801-B Main Avenue. Telephone: 1-303-385-4081. Claiming to be the most complete fly shop in the Southwest, this store for devoted fly fisherfolk can do everything from custom building a fly rod to making custom flies (the largest collection of hand-tied flies in the Southwest). They also have up-to-date stream reports and specialize in custom-guided

fishing trips. And if you don't know how to fly fish, they will teach you.

Toh-Atin Gallery. 145 West Ninth Street. Telephone: 1-303-247-8277. This gallery puts Durango on the map as a center for southwestern Indian arts and crafts. Here you will find a wide selection of carefully selected Navajo rugs, kachinas, Pueblo Indian pottery, and Indian jewelry as well as an outstanding selection of southwestern Indian paintings and prints, all beautifully displayed. If you are a collector or interested in seeing high-quality Indian arts and crafts, you should not miss this gallery.

Maria's Book Shop. 928 Main Avenue. Telephone: 1-303-247-1438. This shop has an excellent supply of books relating to the cultural and natural history of the High Southwest. Topographic maps for hikers also can be purchased, as well as general books. Also a nice selection of Navajo rugs.

Durango Art Center. 970 Main Avenue. Telephone: 1-303-259-2606. If you are interested in the local and regional art scene, don't miss this excellent gallery featuring juried shows and traveling shows as well as children's educational exhibits.

Piedra's Gallery. 1021 Main Avenue. Telephone: 1-303-247-9395. This gallery carries an excellent selection of contemporary crafts, including an extensive selection of handcrafted jewelry as well as many fine prints and posters (including those of R. C. Gorman and Doug West). Definitely worth a visit.

Honeyville. On U.S. Highway 550, ten miles north of Durango. Telephone: 1-303-247-1474. Shopping is a pleasure at Honeyville, where you can browse the shelves of Colorado high-altitude wildflower honey, combed honey, wild chokecherry jelly, watermelon pickles, and chili sauce. In addition, the kids can watch the bees make the honey. Mail-order catalogue and service. Mailing address: Honeyville, 33633 Highway 550 North, Durango, Colorado 81301.

Telephone Numbers

Chamber of Commerce. Telephone: 1-303-247-0312.

Grand Imperial Hotel, Silverton

United States National Forest Service. Telephone: 1-303-247-4874 or 4879.

Mesa Verde National Park. Telephone: 1-303-529-4461 or 1-303-529-4463 (after hours).

Weather. Telephone: 1-303-247-0007.

Road conditions. Telephone: 1-303-247-3355.

Durango and Silverton Narrow-Gauge Depot. Telephone: 1-303-247-2733.

Taxi. Telephone: 1-303-247-1412.

Bus. Telephone: 1-303-259-LIFT.

Avis Car Rental. Telephone: 1-303-247-9761.

Budget-Rent-A-Car. Telephone: 1-303-259-1841.

National Car Rental. Telephone: 1-303-259-0068.

Thrifty Car Rental. Telephone: 1-303-259-3504.

American West Airline. Telephone: 1-303-247-0033.

Continental Express. Telephone: 1-303-259-3466.

Mesa Airlines. Telephone: 1-303-259-5178.

United Express. Telephone: 1-303-247-9735.

Silverton

Lodging

Grand Imperial Hotel. Built in 1882, this hotel has been restored to some of its past grandeur. Forty rooms with private baths are available, many of which are decorated with period antiques. The lounge and dining room, which serves two meals a day, offer the same turn-of-the-century am-bience. Mailing address: Grand Imperial Hotel, 1219 Greene Street, Silverton, Colorado 81433. Telephone: 1-303-387-5527. Inexpensive and moderate.

Teller House Hotel (Bed and Breakfast). This in-teresting, comfortable hotel offers more modest accommodations in a building built around the turn of the century. The eight rooms and two hos-tel dormitories are on the second floor above the French Bakery Restaurant, and in keeping with the European bed-and-breakfast tradition, the bathroom is down the hall. Breakfast is included in the price of the room. Mailing address: Teller House Hotel, 1250 Greene Street, Silverton, Col-orado 81433. Telephone: 1-303-387-5423. Inex-pensive.

Smedley's Bed and Breakfast. These three very nicely decorated one-bedroom units on the sec-ond floor, each with a living room, kitchen, color TV, and private bath, are located downtown above Smedley's Ice Cream Parlor. Rates include breakfast at the Pickle Barrel Restaurant. No pets. Mailing address: Smedley's Bed and Breakfast, P.O. Box 2, Silverton, Colorado 81433. Tele-phone: 1-303-387-5423 or 1-303-387-5713. Inex-pensive.

The Wyman Hotel. This hotel is also on the second floor of a downtown storefront built in 1902. The eleven spacious rooms with private baths have been brought up to modern standards and are equipped with queen beds and color TV's. No smoking allowed. Mailing address: The Wyman Hotel, 1371 Greene Street, Silverton, Colorado 81433. Telephone: 1-303-387-5372. Inexpensive.

The Alma House. This handsome, historic building (circa 1898) is now a comfortable hotel with turn-of-the-century ambience. The ten rooms, each with a queen bed and color TV, are very comfortable. Shared baths. The tasteful renovation here in this quieter location off Main Street makes you feel like you are a part of historic Silverton. Good mountain views from most rooms. No smoking allowed. No pets or children. Mailing address: The Alma House, 220 East Tenth Street, Box 780, Silverton, Colorado 81433. Telephone: 1-303-387-5336. Inexpensive.

Fool's Gold Bed and Breakfast. This historic home, built in 1883, is up on a hill just a few blocks from downtown, where there is a good panoramic view of the mountains. The three quaintly decorated rooms (two with vanity sinks) on the second floor share a bath, while the guest room on the first floor has a private bath. The friendly, knowledgeable owner-hostess provides a breakfast of brunch proportions featuring her own homebaking. Dinner may be available on weekend evenings. Fresh flowers and homemade soaps also provided. Reservation deposit requested. Mailing address: Fool's Gold Bed and Breakfast, 1069 Snowden, Silverton, Colorado 81433. Telephone: 1-303-387-5879. Inexpensive and moderate.

The Wingate House (Bed and Breakfast). This restored Victorian "gingerbread" house (circa 1886) up on the hillside a few blocks from downtown has four rooms each with a queen bed. The bathroom is down the hall. Breakfast is included in the price of the room and is served at the Pickle Barrel restaurant several blocks away. Guests have use of the kitchen in the house. Nonsmokers preferred. No pets. Mailing address: The Wingate House, P.O. Box 2, Silverton, Colorado 81433. Telephone: 1-303-387-5423. Inexpensive.

Campgrounds

Molas Lake Park. Over sixty sites on ten acres, five miles south of Silverton on U.S. Highway 550. Lake fishing. Mailing address: P.O. Box 776, Silverton, Colorado 81433.

Silverton Lakes Campground. One mile northeast of Silverton on twenty-three acres along Colorado Highway 110. Jeep rentals available. Mailing address: P.O. Box 126, Silverton, Colorado 81433. Telephone: 1-303-387-5721.

Food

The Pickle Barrel Food and Spirits. 1304 Greene Street. Telephone: 1-303-387-5713. This pleasant café is open for breakfast, lunch, and dinner. It features hamburgers and sandwiches, imported beers and cheeses, and a salad bar as well as daily hot meal specials. Closed Wednesday and Thursday for dinner. Inexpensive and moderate.

The French Bakery Restaurant. 1250 Greene Street. Telephone: 1-303-387-5423. Open for breakfast and lunch. Homebaked breads and pastries for breakfast, and deli-style lunches with freshly baked French bread. Inexpensive.

Natalia's 1912 Family Restaurant. 1159 Blair Street. Telephone: 1-303-387-5300. Located near the train station, this lunch and dinner establishment occupies a lovely, historic downtown building. Natalia's serves a traditional American lunch with sandwiches and soups, but it is best known for its excellent dinners. The broad-ranging dinner menu features many delicious entrées including schnitzel, scampi, steak, and prime rib. The chef here knows his business. A good wine list and dessert menu. Closed Monday for dinner. Inexpensive and moderate.

Tours, Festivals, and Events

Silverton is the northern terminus of the Durango and Silverton Narrow-Gauge Railroad. Visitors coming on the train from Durango with round-trip tickets may get off in Silverton and spend a night or two (or longer) and return to Durango at a later time. However, they must arrange for their return to Durango as soon as they arrive in Silverton. Contact the Silverton depot agent at 1-303-387-5416 to arrange this round-trip layover. Round-trip tickets that allow a layover in Durango may also be purchased in Silverton. It is also possible to take a bus to Durango and return the same day to Silverton by train. The bus and train follow separate routes to and from Durango, allowing the traveler to see different scenery both ways. Trains during the busy summer months leave Silverton for Durango at 12:45 P.M., 2:00 P.M., 3:00 P.M., and 3:45 P. M.

And for a trip of a different sort, allowing full expression of your fantasy of the Old West, take a stagecoach ride originating from Old Town Square in Silverton on Blair Street, near the train depot. Telephone: 1-303-387-5707 or 1-303-883-5450.

Throughout the year, Silverton stages a number of interesting events some of which are listed below. The summer starts off with the Kendall Mountain footrace and Fourth of July Celebration in July. Then comes one of the nation's most unique festivals, Hardrocker's Holidays, early in August. This is not a "rock" festival but a mining celebration featuring unique competitive events such as hand and machine mucking, machine drilling, and wheelbarrow racing. That stellar event is followed by the Great Rocky Mountain Brass Band Festival in late August, which in turn, is followed by the Silverton Sky Fest over Labor Day featuring kite flying, hang gliding, and flights of hot-air balloons. And then come a month-long series of Colorfest events, when the leaves begin to turn, including an Antique Car Rally and Quilting Show in late September. For a complete listing of year-round events and their precise dates as well as hiking and fishing information, contact the Silverton Chamber of Commerce, P.O. Box 565, Silverton, Colorado 81433. Telephone: 1-303-387-5654.

Shopping

Silverton has many shops (with numerous rock and mineral and Colorado souvenir shops) greeting the hundreds of rail passengers who land there for a short time each day. Several shops of particular interest are listed below.

Silverton Standard and the Miner. 1257 Greene Street. Telephone: 1-303-387-5477. An interesting bookstore with a good selection of railroad, local, regional, and natural history books as well as hiking books and maps of the area.

The Crewel Elephant. Located on Thirteenth Street between Greene and Blair streets. This very nice gift shop features well-selected, handmade, one-of-a-kind items including jewelry and clothing from the local area and around the world.

Eureka-The Miner and Prospector Store. Near the corner of Greene Street and Eleventh Street. Telephone: 1-303-387-5491. In this local emporium you will find an interesting array of miner's supplies and equipment. Worth a visit even if you aren't heading into the hills looking for gold.

Ouray

Lodging

St. Elmo Hotel (Bed and Breakfast Inn). This handsomely restored, historic, two-story brick hotel has been in continuous service since 1899. Many of the original Victorian and Art Nouveau furnishings remain. Others have been added. Of the eleven rooms, seven have private baths while four guest rooms share two baths. The hotel is conveniently located on Main Street right near the middle of town. The Bon Ton Restaurant, on the premises, serves up excellent meals with an Italian-continental flavor. Room rate includes a very nice continental breakfast. Mailing address: St. Elmo Hotel, 426 Main Street, P.O. Box 667, Ouray, Colorado 81427. Telephone: 1-303-325-4951. Inexpensive and low moderate.

The Main Street House. Located right along Main Street is this renovated turn-of-the-century residence. The three suites (each with a private bath) have decks offering nice views, and two have full kitchens. Landscaped courtyard and play area shared by the three units. Daily and weekly rates. Mailing address: The Main Street House, 334 Main Street, Ouray, Colorado 81427. Telephone: 1-303-325-4317. Inexpensive and moderate.

The Manor Bed and Breakfast. This old house (circa 1881) has been partially converted to accommodate guests. There are six upstairs guest rooms, which share bath and shower. Rates include continental breakfast. Mailing address: The Manor Bed and Breakfast, 317 Second Street, Ouray, Colorado 81427. Telephone: 1-303-325-4574. Inexpensive.

Alpenglow. These condominium units, nicely designed to reflect the "Colorado modern" look, have kitchens and fireplaces furnished with wood. Although close to restaurants and shops, they are in a quiet location one block off Main Street. The units can be rented by the day, week, or month. In addition, a hot tub spa is on the premises. Mailing address: Alpenglow, 440 Second Street, P.O. Box 1855, Ouray, Colorado 81427. Telephone: 1-303-325-4664. High moderate and low expensive.

Circle M Motel. A rather basic motel but with a decidedly western flavor a few blocks off Main Street and close to the river. This motel, with its nineteen ranch-style rooms, is good for families with small children because it has a playground area as well as an expanse of grass for picnics. Mailing address: Circle M Motel, 120 Sixth Avenue, Ouray, Colorado 81427. Telephone: 1-303-325-4394. Inexpensive.

Best Western Twin Peaks. Pleasant, modern motel with western flavor, not far from the river. Offers a natural hot springs whirlpool bath. Good location just four blocks from Box Canyon Falls. There is a total of forty-eight rooms with private baths. No pets. Advance reservation deposit required. Mailing address: Best Western Twin Peaks, 125 Third Avenue, Ouray, Colorado 81427. Telephone: 1-303-325-4427 or call toll free in continental United States 1-800-528-1234. Moderate.

Box Canyon Motel and Hot Springs. Thirty motel units with TV's, near the river and close to the Box Canyon. Mineral springs hot tub. No pets. Advance reservation deposit required. Mailing address: Box Canyon Motel and Hot Springs, 45 Third Avenue, P.O. Box 439, Ouray, Colorado 81427. Telephone: 1-303-325-4981. Moderate.

St. Elmo Hotel, Ouray

Wiesbaden Spa and Lodgings. This interesting motel-lodge is situated up on the hillside. Below its lobby, deep in the ground, is a hot mineral water vapor cave and exercise room. Outdoor hot mineral water pool. Sauna with indoor pool. Sixteen very pleasant rooms with TV's and some with fireplaces. Some kitchens. No pets. Unlimited use of all facilities for guests. Advance reservation deposit required with three-day refund notice. Located on the corner of Sixth Avenue and Fifth Street. Mailing address: Wiesbaden Spa and Lodgings, P.O. Box 349, Ouray, Colorado 81427. Telephone: 1-303-325-4347. Moderate.

House of Yesteryear (Bed-and-Breakfast-style Inn). This large Victorian home is located across the river on the hillside overlooking Ouray town and offers some of the finest views in town . . . not just fine but magnificent! And you can hear the river as it bubbles and gurgles below the house. Yet if you are so inclined, it is just a few minute's walk to downtown. There are three pleasant rooms with private baths (either full or half-bath) downstairs and five nicely furnished guest rooms upstairs, which share two baths. For just one dollar per person you will be served a very nice continental breakfast. Open June through September only. No pets. Call for directions. Mailing address: House of Yesteryear, 516 Oak Street, P.O. Box 440, Ouray, Colorado 81427. Telephone: 1-303-325-4277. Inexpensive.

Campgrounds

4-J + 1 + 1 Trailer Park-RV Park and Campground. In town, three blocks west of U.S. Highway 550 or Main Street, on Seventh Avenue. Some of the eighty sites are on the river. Jeep rentals. Telephone: 1-303-325-4418.

K.O.A. Kampground, Ouray. Drive three miles north on U.S. Highway 550, then turn west on Colorado Highway 23 for one-quarter mile. One hundred and ten sites, some on the river. Jeep rentals. Telephone: 1-303-325-4736.

Amphitheater Campground. Located in the National Forest one mile southeast of town off of U.S. Highway 550.

Main Street, Ouray, Colorado

Food

The Bon Ton Restaurant. Located at 426 Main Street in the old St. Elmo Hotel. Telephone: 1-303-325-4951. This attractive restaurant serves a fine array of tantalizing northern Italian and continental specialties, plus steaks and fresh seafood. Lunches and Sunday brunches are served on the outdoor patio in the summer. Children's menu. Nice Italian wine selection. Moderate.

Le Papillon Bakery and Dog and Burger Bar. 321 Sixth Avenue. Telephone: 1-303-325-4178. This small but good bakery-café with inside tables and a few outdoor benches is a fine spot for breakfast or lunch, just half a block off Main Street. Home-style hamburgers and hotdogs can be followed by homemade donuts, pastries, and cakes. Inexpensive.

Apteka Pharmacy. 611 Main Street. Telephone: 1-303-325-4388. This drugstore, in operation since 1939, comes complete with an old-fashioned soda fountain. Whether it's an ice cream cone, sundae, or milkshake, you'll enjoy it in this truly American setting.

Coachlight Restaurant. 118 West Seventh Avenue. Telephone: 1-303-325-4361. This favorite old Ouray restaurant, located in an old hotel built in 1887, offers a wide selection of food ranging from steaks to French silk pie. Children's menu. Dinner year-round plus breakfast in the summer. Moderate and expensive.

Pricco's. 736 Main Street. Telephone: 1-303-325-4040. A good spot for breakfast or lunch. Features light fare such as omelets, homemade soups, and a wide variety of popular sandwiches. Homemade desserts. Inexpensive.

The Nugget and Top of the Nugget Tavern. 737 Main Street. Telephone: 1-303-325-4476. This restaurant, located in a handsome two-story brick building, serves croissant sandwiches and barbecue for lunch and turns to heartier fare at dinner with jumbo butterfly shrimp and steaks. Inexpensive and moderate.

The Corner Nugget Café. 740 Main Street. Telephone: 1-303-325-4100. Breakfast, lunch, and dinner are served in this family-oriented restaurant, which offers fine views of Cascade Falls in the distance. Soups and sandwiches and other light fare plus homemade pastries. Inexpensive.

Timberline Delicatessen. 803 Main Street. Telephone: 1-303-325-4958. Just what it says it is, this full delicatessen offers a variety of sandwiches, soups, fresh pastries, and drinks. Inside or outside dining, or if you prefer, a box lunch for a picnic. Inexpensive.

Bar C Chuckwagon Supper and Show. Located 4.5 miles north of town on U.S. Highway 550. Telephone: 1-303-325-4423. In a decidedly western setting you can have a chuckwagon outdoor dinner just like in the movies. The dinner is followed by songs of the Old West and a western-style stage show. There are small shops to browse, and the evening ends with a friendship fire.

Tours

Scenic San Juan Jeep Tours. What could be a more southwestern Colorado thing to do than to take a jeep trip into the high mountains to see ghost towns and old mines. There are a variety of one-half to full-day trips. Mailing address: 480 Main Street, P.O. Box 143, Ouray, Colorado 81427. Telephone: 1-303-325-4444 or 1-303-325-4154.

Switzerland of America Jeep Rentals. See the wonders on your own by renting a jeep. Mailing address: 226 Seventh Avenue, Box 367, Ouray, Colorado 81427. Telephone: 1-303-325-4484.

Activities

Backpacking and Hiking. Ouray is a hub for getting into the wilderness. The chamber of commerce and sports stores can give you the details.

Swimming. You should not miss Ouray's famous outdoor Hot Springs Pool in an absolutely breathtaking setting at the north edge of town. Heated to between 85 and 95 degrees by diluting the natural springwater at 156 degrees with cold water, this giant pool (250 feet long by 150 feet wide and varying from 2 to 9 feet in depth) is well worth a stop. The Swim Shop at the Pool rents anything you'll need to have fun, including bathing suits. For a fee, there are large changing rooms, lockers, and showers. Open daily in the summer. For winter hours, telephone 1-303-325-4638.

Bachelor-Syracuse Mine Tour. Located two miles east of Ouray on County Road 14. This tour, which has been mentioned in several national magazines, allows you to ride a mine train 3,350 feet, horizontally, into Gold Hill, the site of an authentic gold and silver mine. There you will actually see silver veins and other mineral deposits as well as have the opportunity to visit some of the miner's work areas. The Treasure Chest, a jewelry store there features gold and silver jewelry. Hourly tours every day from mid-May to mid-September. Mailing address: Bachelor-Syracuse Mine Tour, County Road 14, P.O. Drawer 380, Ouray, Colorado 81427. Telephone: 1-303-325-4500.

San Juan Odyssey. See this production, which features unique panoramic photography of Colorado's San Juan Mountains. Fifteen electronically synchronized projectors are focused on a fifty-foot-wide screen, accompanied by full stereophonic sound tracks featuring the music of Aaron Copland. Nightly at Wrights Opera Hall, Fifth and Main streets. Telephone: 1-303-325-4507 for tickets.

Fairs, Festivals, and Events

Music in Ouray. Chamber music concerts fill the valley with music during the last two weeks in June.

Old Fashioned Fourth of July Celebration. This event is combined with a draft horse pull and show beginning the day before the fourth.

Arts and Crafts Fair. The second weekend in August.

Artist's Alpine Holiday. The second week in August. This is a well-known, juried show of artists' work from all over the Southwest. There are also demonstrations by artists, and films shown relating to art.

Ouray County Fair, RCA Rodeo and Race Meet. First week in September. Sponsored by the Ouray County Sheriff's Posse, this rodeo is held in nearby Ridgway. Steer racing, calf roping, saddle bronc riding by cowboys from all over provide the excitement. Barbecue and parade.

Culinary Arts Show. Third weekend in September. Just as the aspens are turning in the fall, Colorado's finest chefs gather in Ouray for a few days to display their talents and part with some of their

Mineral Hot Springs swimming pool

secrets.

Victorian House Tour. This tour takes place for one day in early September.

Colorfest. The region's month-long celebration of the changing of the seasons during September and October.

Shopping

Ouray has a variety of good shops, all within easy walking distance from each other. A few of special interest are listed below.

Bear Creek Store. 514 Main Street. Telephone: 1-303-325-4700. This book and gift store has a lot to offer. In addition to an excellent selection of southwest regional books, guides (including jeep guides), and maps, the store has a wide selection of southwestern Indian crafts, western prints, bronzes, jewelry, and prospecting supplies.

The Sandman. 330 Sixth Avenue. Telephone: 1-303-325-4071. This unique store features bottles and lamps filled with an unbelievable array of colored sands from the Southwest, which are layered to make designs and pictures. Also unusual gift items such as antler jewelry, aspen wood vases, handcrafted Colorado pottery, and a wide selection of Colorado mineral specimens.

Nava Southwest. 308 Sixth Avenue, one-half block east of Main Street. Telephone: 1-303-325-4850. For high-quality southwestern Indian crafts, this is the shop to visit. The knowledgeable owners have brought together an excellent selection of Navajo sandpaintings and rugs, turquoise and silver jewelry, Pueblo Indian pottery, and American Indian wall art. The shop also features the owner's own museum-quality, beautiful, handcrafted contemporary American Indian jewelry.

Cabin Fever Shop. 612 Main Street. Telephone: 1-303-325-4408. This outdoor equipment store has a good selection of backpacking and fishing supplies and regional topographic maps. And they have a large selection of custom silk-screened T-shirts. This shop is also a good source of informa-

tion about hiking and fishing in the area.

The Viking. 629 Main Street. Telephone: 1-303-325-4412. This is a gift shop with many nice regional crafts and a touch of the old world with some items from abroad. Items like silver-plated Colorado and Ouray souvenir spoons are but a few of the pleasing gift items.

Telephone Numbers

Ouray Chamber of Commerce. Box 145, Ouray, Colorado 81427. Telephone: 1-303-325-4746.

Road and weather report. Telephone: 1-303-249-9363.

Telluride

The lodging price categories listed below are based on the very reasonable "regular" summer rates. But these rates may increase, and in some instances, may even double during some of the more popular summer festivals. And of course, the ski season rates are higher than the off-season summer rates. During the ski season and some of the more popular summer festival weeks, be certain to make reservations far in advance, for there is a lot of competition for the 3,500 pillows here. During those times expect a busy, crowded Telluride. But if you plan a summer visit between festivals, there is usually plenty of room available should you arrive without a reservation. During those times the town is quiet and peaceful, to boot.

Telluride has a regional airport about five miles from town. Shuttle service and rental cars are available there as well as at the airport in Montrose, Colorado, (sixty miles away), where the planes land if the Telluride airport is closed due to bad weather or mud slides.

If you need more information about lodging or summer festival ticket information, contact Telluride Central Reservations, P.O. Box 1009, Telluride, Colorado 81435. Telephone: 1-303-728-4431 or toll free in the United States 1-800-525-3455. For general information about Telluride and

New Sheridan Hotel, Telluride

specific dates of festivals and events, stop by the Telluride Chamber Resort Information Center at 666 West Colorado Avenue as you enter town, or write Telluride Chamber Resort Association, P.O. Box 653, Telluride, Colorado 81435. Telephone: 1-303-728-3041.

Lodging

New Sheridan Hotel. This is a fine place to stay if you want to soak up some of Telluride's past in a comfortable, centrally located hostelry. Sarah Bernhardt and William Jennings Bryan stayed here. So can you. Built in 1895, this historic hotel has been tastefully refurbished. They have even installed an elevator in this three-story building, so you will not have to pant climbing the stairway, 8,745 feet above sea level. All of the thirty rooms have color TV's, and nine have private baths. The excellent dining room and bar are restored to Victorian elegance, and a sauna and Jacuzzi are available to guests. Mailing address: New Sheridan Hotel, 231 West Colorado Avenue, P.O. Box 980, Telluride, Colorado 81435. Telephone: 1-303-728-4351. Inexpensive and moderate.

Black Bear Condominiums. Conveniently located right in the heart of town on Colorado Avenue on the second and third floors of the post office building. These modern, handsomely furnished units all have private baths (the two- bedroom units have two private baths) and color TV's. You can rent a one- or two-bedroom unit with private baths and kitchens (some with fireplaces) or just a room with a private bath. If you stay over two nights the rate drops. Mailing address: Black Bear Condominiums, c/o Resort Rentals, P.O. Box 1278, Telluride, Colorado 81435. Telephone: 1-303-728-4405 or toll free in the United States 1-800-538-7754 or toll free in Colorado 1-800-835-7433. Low moderate and moderate.

Johnstone Inn (Bed and Breakfast). A bed-and-breakfast inn in a centrally located, restored Victorian home. Rooms are tastefully appointed and furnished with turn-of-the-century furniture. One room with private bath, the rest share. Mailing address: Johnstone Inn, 403 West Colorado Avenue, Box 546, Telluride, Colorado 81435. Telephone: 1-303-728-3316. Inexpensive and moderate.

The Victorian Inn. Centrally located, yet off the main street, is this twenty-unit inn. It offers standard motel accommodations with private baths and TV's on the two upper floors, and budget lodging with shared baths on the lowest floor. Sauna, hot tub, and continental breakfast. No pets. Reservation deposit required. Mailing address: The Victorian Inn, 401 West Pacific Avenue, P.O. Box 217, Telluride, Colorado 81435. Telephone: 1-303-728-6601. Low moderate.

Manitou Hotel. This nicely designed three-story frame building with a shed roof is located right on the banks of the San Miguel River, just three blocks from Colorado Avenue. There are ten rooms with private baths and refrigerators, some have nice balconies with superb views. Nice public room with a TV and a large fireplace. Grassy play area alongside riverbank. Continental breakfast. Mailing address: Manitou Hotel, c/o Telluride Accommodations, Box 756, Telluride, Colorado 81435. Telephone: 1-303-728-3803 or toll free in the United States 1-800-237-9292 or toll free in Colorado 1-800-237-0753. Low moderate and moderate.

Riverside Condominiums. These elegant, multi-story condominium units line the south bank of the San Miguel River in an enviable location only two to three blocks from downtown at the foot of South Pine Street. They are nestled into a flat space just below the forested mountainside. These nicely furnished one-, two-, or three-bedroom luxury units have gas fireplaces, washer/dryers, color TV's, and kitchens. Most have outstanding views of the river, town, and the mountains. Outdoor hot tub. Mailing address: Riverside Condominiums, c/o Telluride Lodging, P.O. Box 276, Telluride, Colorado 81435. Telephone: 1-303-728-4311 or toll free in the United States 1-800-852-0015. Expensive.

Viking Hotel. In a beautiful location right on the banks of the San Miguel River at the foot of South Davis Street on Pacific Avenue is this two- and three-story condominium hotel with elevator. The forty-nine spacious one-bedroom units with mini-kitchens, TV's, and private baths offer a Murphy double bed and bunk beds in the bedroom, and a queen sofa bed or queen bed in the living-sitting room, which in the southernmost or riverside building overlooks beautiful views of the river and the mountains. The downstairs units in the riverside building block open onto a grassy lawn leading to the riverbank, where you can soak in the sun or let the river lull you to sleep. Heated outdoor swimming pool and hot tub. Walk across the bridge to mountain trails. Mailing address: Viking Hotel, 651 West Pacific Avenue, P.O. Box 2038, Telluride, Colorado 81435. Telephone: 1-303-728-3291. Low moderate.

Coonskin Inn. Located on the south side of the river at the foot of South Davis Street is this well-maintained, basic two-story inn. The river flows by one side while the forested mountainside, cut by a series of trails, flanks the other side. Seventy-eight of the units are basic motel rooms with private baths, queen beds, and TV's, while eight units have kitchenettes. Hot tub, laundry, and complementary breakfast. Mailing address: Coonskin Inn, P.O. Box 1890, Telluride, Colorado 81435. Telephone: 1-303-728-3181 or toll free in the United States 1-800-852-5822. Low moderate and moderate.

Skyline Guest Ranch. In an absolutely magnificent high-mountain setting at 9,600 feet elevation surrounded by grassy hillsides, wildflower meadows, several small lakes, and groves of aspen and pine is this outstanding guest ranch. Just eight miles south of Telluride. The large, inviting log lodge (part of a former logging camp) with its ten smallish bedrooms (all with private baths) and large, comfortable living room and dining room is only part of the scene. Near the lodge on this multi-acre property are five very comfortable two- and three-bedroom view cabins with full kitchens. The lodge dining room serves three meals a day for the American Plan lodge guests or for the European Plan cabin guests who want to join in. The rates include a variety of activities such as horseback riding and instruction; pack trips; jeep trips to Mesa Verde, old mining towns, and other nearby sights; guided hiking or mountaineering trips; and fishing on the premises. Of course there's picnicking and hiking on the ranch and into the national forest that surrounds it. The knowledgeable, energetic, and hospitable owners seem to know how to make their guests have memorable experiences. Sauna. Wood-fired hot tub. Reservations for summer must be made many months in advance. Mailing address: Skyline Guest Ranch, Box 67, Telluride, Colorado 81435. Telephone: 1-303-728-3757.

Campgrounds

Telluride Town Park and Campground. Just two blocks east of Telluride. Limited camping. Often crowded.

Sunshine Campground. Located eight miles southwest of Telluride on Colorado Highway 145.

Matterhorn Campground. Ten miles southwest of Telluride on Colorado Highway 145.

Food

Coyote Lounge and Rose's Too. 666 West Colorado Avenue. Telephone: 1-303-728-6912. Do not let the name fool you. There's food in this coyote's lair as well as drink. Located above Rose's Victorian deli and next to the Telluride Resort Chamber Visitor Center is this perky establishment, Rose's Too, which offers a cafeteria-style lunch or dinner. Beautiful mountain and sunset views from the modern dining room, lounge, or outdoor patio. Innovative food creations such as Anasazi bean and chicken chili; Quinoa wheat salad; and some familiar favorites like roast chicken and cornbread stuffing with giblet gravy; and chicken, turkey, ham, and beef sandwiches. Homemade deserts. Carry out. Inexpensive and moderate.

Julian's. 231 West Colorado Avenue. Telephone: 1-303-728-3839. Located in the New Sheridan Hotel is this very good restaurant featuring northern Italian cuisine in a pleasant, quiet setting. In addition to the good, carefully prepared food is the authentic Victorian-era bar (circa 1895), which offers a full array of spirits. Reservations accepted. Moderate and low expensive.

The Powder House. 226 West Colorado Avenue. Telephone: 1-303-728-3622. This downstairs restaurant captures some of the flavor of the Victorian period yet definitely has both feet in the modern culinary world. The menu features a good selection of fresh fish and shellfish as well as a variety of steak, veal, and lamb dishes. You can order a full or a light dinner. Children's menu. Moderate and low expensive.

Excelsior Café. 200 West Colorado Avenue. Telephone: 1-303-728-4250. This interesting casual, yet cosmopolitan café offers a light menu of good pastries, fondues, and barbecue beef and chicken. Good breakfasts (outdoors on patio, weather permitting) feature most favorites and homemade coffeecake. Inexpensive.

Baked in Telluride. 127 South Fir Street. Telephone: 1-303-728-4705. A friendly establishment that bakes pastries, donuts, bagels, and a variety of breads for the assorted sandwiches they serve. Continental breakfast is also served, and at lunch there is pizza, potato knish, calzone, spanakopita, and a host of other movable feasts. Carry out. Inexpensive.

La Marmotte. 150 West San Juan. Telephone: 1-303-728-6232. This excellent country French restaurant, located in the old icehouse two blocks south of Colorado Avenue, should not be missed. Specializing in provincial French cooking, the Parisian-born owner has established a highly varied menu that borrows from Switzerland as well as the provinces of France. Fondue and raclette served the way they should be are excellent. Then there are crépes and a variety of beef, veal, and seafood entrées prepared in a number of tantalizing ways. Excellent wine list and outstanding pastries made on the premises. Outdoor patio-garden seating at lunch, weather permitting. Pique-nique baskets on request. Lunch, dinner, and Sunday brunch. Moderate and low expensive.

The Silver Glade. 115 West Colorado Avenue. Telephone: 1-303-728-4943. Located downstairs midway along Colorado Avenue is this new American, fresh seafood restaurant, which brings a taste of the desert to mountainous Telluride with its mesquite charcoal grill. But it is not just some of the fish that get a bite of mesquite, steaks and poultry get some of the same flavorful treatment. Also serves cajun specialties. Extremely nice decor in a very comfortable dining room. Small plate specials. Moderate.

Floradora Saloon. 103 West Colorado Avenue. Telephone: 1-303-728-3888. A Colorado-style lunch and dinner spot, offering a wide variety of omelets, soups, sandwiches, steaks, and homemade desserts. Inexpensive and moderate.

Pandora's Box. 101 East Colorado Avenue. Telephone: 1-303-728-5137. This very pleasant, handsomely decorated lunch and dinner restaurant located downstairs under the post office features a gourmet salad bar and salad menu with such delectables as spinach salad, fresh fruit boat, and grilled raspberry chicken salad plate. The freshly baked breads provide the jackets for a delicious array of sandwiches. Dinner may include entrées of duck, fish, prime rib, Grecian chicken, or salmon en papillote. Sunday brunch. Moderate.

Sofio's. 110 East Colorado Avenue. Telephone: 1-303-728-4882. This interesting restaurant serves good Mexican-style food daily for breakfast and dinner. And the very good breakfast menu includes many standard American favorites. Pleasant atmosphere. Inexpensive and moderate.

The Fly Me to the Moon Saloon. 132 East Colorado Avenue. Telephone: 1-303-728-MOON. Besides light fare and carry out, there is a full list of spirits. But the most spirited scene is the spring-loaded dance floor and the live entertainment featured almost nightly. Inexpensive.

East Side Café. 138 East Colorado Avenue. Telephone: 1-303-728-6424. Return to the ambience of the 1960s with a delicious, nutritious, and fullsome breakfast served on the sunny east-facing patio, weather permitting. Homemade biscuits, fresh fruit and vegetable dishes, and most anything else you would like for breakfast. Sandwiches, special sausages, and grilled specialties for lunch. Inexpensive.

Annabelle's. 123 South Spruce Street. Telephone: 1-303-728-4080. You will dine very comfortably for lunch or dinner in several nicely decorated dining rooms. The kitchen features Louisiana cuisine focusing on cajun cooking, but also has a variety of chicken, veal, and pasta specialties as well as steaks. Reservations recommended. Nice bar. Moderate and low expensive.

Le Gourmet Vite. 217 East Colorado Avenue. Telephone: 1-303-728-6234. This gourmet carry out right downtown offers croissants and fresh coffeecake for breakfast, and homemade French bread, dilled potato salad, tarragon chicken sandwiches, and other delicious fare for lunch. Picnic lunches. Carry out only. Inexpensive.

Tours

San Miguel County Historical Museum. At the head of North Fir Street. Take a self-guided tour of this museum at 317 North Fir Street (telephone: 1-303-728-3344) with its interesting displays relating to the area's western mining past. Helpful museum staff members can give you directions for touring Telluride's historic area.

Telluride Transit. Airport limousine service to and from Grand Junction, Montrose, Cortez, and Durango. Mailing address: Telluride Transit, P.O. Box 307, Telluride, Colorado 81435. Telephone: 1-303-728-4105.

Big Red Jeep Tours. These extensive, guided jeep tours go over rugged terrain to abandoned mines and ghost towns in open-air tour jeeps. Ice chests and water provided. Half-day, morning or afternoon tours. Mailing address: Big Red Jeep Tours, 401 West Pacific Avenue, Telluride, Colorado 81435. Telephone: 1-303-728-6601.

Fantasy Ridge Mountain Guides. This year-round rock-and-snow climbing school and guide service offers instruction by the hour, half-day, or full-day and can arrange multi-day guided trips. Mailing address: Fantasy Ridge Mountain Guides, The Nugget Building, Suite 204, P.O. Box 1679, Telluride, Colorado 81435. Telephone: 1-303-728-3546.

San Juan Balloon Adventures. Half-hour or hour-long flights, balloon-n-brunch flights, and backpacker's drop-off and pick-up service. Mailing address: San Juan Balloon Adventures, 224 East Colorado Avenue, P.O. Box 685, Telluride, Colorado 81435. Telephone: 1-303-728-3895.

Far Flung Adventures. This adventurous group could keep you busy for weeks. Besides gold-panning tours, white-water rafting expeditions on the Dolores, San Miguel or Colorado rivers, fishing guide service, and geology and archaeology field trips in the Four Corners region, they also can arrange horseback trail rides, pack trips, hunting guide service, kayak trips, and jeep trips. And if you don't want them to guide you on a jeep trip, they will rent you one and tell you where to go (where to go jeeping that is). Mailing address: Far Flung Adventures, 224 East Colorado Avenue, Telluride, Colorado 81435. Telephone: 1-303-728-3895.

D & E Outfitters. Summer trail rides, pack trips, Friday evening chuckwagon cookout rides, Sunday morning breakfast rides, and horse-drawn hay wagon rides through Telluride at night. And if that doesn't tire you, they will stop horsing around and take you up the river without a paddle on a guided white-water raft trip on the Gunnison River or provide guide service for a fishing trip. Mailing address: D & E Outfitters, P.O. Box 516, Telluride, Colorado 81435. Telephone: 1-303-728-3200 or 1-303-728-4276.

Activities

Golf. There will soon be an eighteen-hole golf course six miles from town at Telluride Mountain Village.

Bicycles. The Telluride area is an excellent place to ride mountain bicycles. They can be rented at several of the sport shops downtown.

Olympic Sports Rentals. 105 South Davis. Telephone: 1-303-728-4500. Take off down a valley or up a mountain with equipment rented from this eclectic store. Mountain bike, camping, fishing, backpacking, and mountaineering rentals.

The Coonskin Scenic Chairlift Ride. Take the ski lift to a 10,500-foot elevation scenic overlook with views as far west as the La Sal Mountains in Utah and dramatic views of Telluride and environs. Summer hours are Wednesday through Saturday from 10:00 A.M. until 2:00 P.M. Purchase tickets at the Telluride visitor center (666 West Colorado Avenue) or any Telluride sport shop. Telephone: 1-303-728-3041.

Mountain Splendor. This thirty-minute show is run daily in the summer (8:30 P.M.) at the Masonic Hall above Timberline Hardware, 200 East Colorado Avenue. This is a computer-synchronized slide show of the San Juan Mountains. It features the wildlife, birds, and flowers of the region projected on a twenty-eight-foot-long screen and accompanied by stereophonic music. Telephone: 1-303-728-4132.

Fairs, Festivals, and Events

Besides the booming ski industry in the winter, Telluride has become a summer festival town. There are over twenty events scheduled in Telluride each summer. Some of the better-known festivals and events are listed below.

Bluegrass and Country Music Festival. Held the third week in June. Three days of concerts and contests followed by a week of workshops.

Telluride Jazz Festival. Three days of concerts in Town Park, the third weekend in July, followed by a week of jazz workshops.

Telluride Chamber Music Festival. Chamber music over two weekends in late July and early August.

Telluride Film Festival. Held the first week in September, this small, prestigious international festival has helped to put Telluride on the map.

Colorfest. A month-long Four Corners regional celebration from mid-September through mid-October. During this time of the year the Telluride Garden Club sponsors "Behind Closed Doors," a tour through Telluride's finest homes.

Telluride Hang Gliding Festival. This renowned event is held for five days in mid-September and attracts over 250 of the world's most skilled hang-gliding pilots.

Imogene Pass Run. This popular but grueling running event is held the second weekend in September. Runners traverse the steep, rocky mountain terrain between Telluride and Ouray for a distance of eighteen miles.

Other events include a mountain-related film art festival in late May, a wine festival in early June, photography workshops in June, July, and September, a Fourth of July celebration, and a wild mushroom festival and fair in late August. In addition, Town Park is often the site of scheduled popular music and rock concerts (such as the Grateful Dead who rocked the town in 1987). For a complete schedule of these annual events and their precise dates, write Telluride Chamber Resort Association, Box 653, Telluride, Colorado 81435. Telephone: 1-303-728-3041.

Telluride Academy Summer Program. College classes in Telluride focusing on the history of San Juan Mining Camps, the field archaeology of southwestern Colorado, programs in jazz studies, film genre, and women's film. Also children and teen programs including Camp Telluride, jazz camp, wilderness camps, and baseball camp. Mailing address: Telluride Academy Summer Program, Box 2255, Telluride, Colorado 81435. Telephone: 1-303-728-5311.

For additional information on these festivals and more, write the Telluride Chamber of Commerce, Box 653, Telluride, Colorado 81435. Telephone: 1-303-728-3041.

Shopping

Just as in any booming ski town, shops come and go, becoming more upscale with each new rise in rent. There are a number of unique gift and craft shops in Telluride. A few of them are listed below.

Zia Sun. 210 West Colorado Avenue. Telephone: 1-303-728-4031. This outstanding gift shop anchors the shopping on West Colorado Avenue. Here you will find a wide variety of tastefully selected greeting cards, soaps and toiletries, toys, and many handcrafted gifts made in Colorado. The shop's jewelry selection is excellent.

Between the Covers Books and Records. 224 West Colorado Avenue. Telephone: 1-303-728-4504. This full-service bookstore has a fine selection of Southwest, Four Corners, and Colorado-related books. Its stock of general books has been selected as carefully as the regional books. Also records, tapes, and magazines from the United States and around the world, as well as some gift items.

Telluride Gallery of Fine Art. 130 East Colorado Avenue. Telephone: 1-303-728-4242. This gallery is one of the finest in the Four Corners region. Although it has a good selection of Southwest regional and Colorado art, including limited edition prints (by Doug West and other regional artists), paintings, and ceramics, it also displays the works of contemporary national and international artists. Well worth a stop.

The Potters Wheel and Garden of Earthly Delights. 221 East Colorado Avenue. These two neighboring shops specialize in nicely handcrafted Colorado pottery as well as jewelry and other handcrafted gift items from Telluride and Colorado's west slope craftpersons. Also a good selection of Rocky Mountain crystals and rocks.

Telephone Numbers

Snow report. Telephone: 1-303-728-3614.
Telluride Taxi. Telephone: 1-303-728-3275.
Continental Air Lines/Continental Express. Telephone: 1-800-525-0280.
United Air Lines/United Express. Telephone: 1-800-241-6522.
Mesa Airlines. Telephone: 1-800-637-2247.
Budget Rent-A-Car. Telephone: 1-303-728-4862.
Hertz Rent-A-Car. Telephone: 1-303-654-3131.

Mesa Verde National Park

Lodging and Food

Far View Motor Lodge. Located at the summit of Navajo Hill near the visitor center. The lodge is fifteen miles from the park entrance and only five miles from most of the major ruins. The ranger at the park entrance, just off U.S. Highway 160, carries information about room availability at the lodge. There are one hundred rooms with private baths, and many have porches. The accommodations are scattered over the hillside in units containing a variable number of rooms. Most of the rooms have good views out over the mesa top. The restaurant in the lodge has a southwest Indian ambience, which is reflected in such menu items as deep-fried squash blossom appetizers and Indian corn soup. Breakfast, lunch, dinner. Mailing address: Far View Motor Lodge, Box 277, Mancos, Colorado 81328. Telephone 1-303-529-4421. Moderate.

Campgrounds

Morefield Campground. With 490 sites, this large campground is the only one in Mesa Verde National Park (there are several private campgrounds just outside the park). It is located below the mesa just four miles from the entry station and U.S. Highway 160. All sites are designed for both tent and trailer camping and have picnic tables and fireplaces or charcoal burners. Comfort stations. Morefield Campground general store has groceries, camping supplies, and a good Indian arts and crafts store, as well as a good selection of regional interest books. Summer evenings, rangers give talks about the archaeology, history, and natural history of the area. No reservations. Fee. Telephone: 1-303-529-4421 or 1-303-529-4474.

Tours

Guided Bus Tours. These twice-daily bus tours provided by the park's concessionaire depart from Far View Lodge (morning and afternoon) and Morefield Campground (morning). The three-hour tour is comprehensive and includes the major Chapin Mesa sights. Telephone: 1-303-529-4421.

Cortez, Colorado

Lodging

Cortez Inn. Located near the center of town on Main Street is this attractive multistory, one hundred-unit air-conditioned motel, which offers all the amenities. The rooms are nicely furnished and comfortable. There is a nice, large public room with a fireplace. The continental breakfast is served here each morning. Indoor pool with hot tub, spa, and sauna. Mailing address: Cortez Inn, 2121 East Main Street, Cortez, Colorado 81321. Telephone: 1-303-565-6000. Moderate.

Best Western Turquoise Motor Inn. Located near the center of town on U.S. Highway 160. There are forty-six air-conditioned units with private baths. Heated pool. Mailing address: Best Western Turquoise Motor Inn, 535 East Main, Cortez, Colorado 81231. Telephone: 1-303-565-3778 or toll free in continental United States 1-800-528-1234. Moderate.

Arrow Motel. Located three quarters of a mile south on U.S. Highway 666. This motel has thirty air-conditioned units with private baths. Heated swimming pool. Whirlpool bath. Mailing address: Arrow Motel, 440 South Broadway, Cortez, Colorado 81321. Telephone: 1-303-565-3755. Inexpensive.

Kelly Place (Bed and Breakfast). Located just a few miles west of Cortez on a one hundred-acre farm in McElmo Canyon is this unique, remote southwestern-style bed-and-breakfast inn with five large units, each with private bath. The owners call the place "a living history and archaeology preserve." They introduce visitors to a "hands on" approach to archaeology through an exploration of the ruins on this "living history farm," where draft horses are still used. In addition to one-night stands, Kelly Place also offers week-long stays coupled with workshops (for additional fee) in archaeology, Anasazi pottery construction, and native weaving. Covered wagon trips through the remote Ute Tribal Park can be arranged. Mailing address: Kelly Place, 14663 County Road G, Cortez, Colorado 81321. Telephone: 1-303-565-3125. Inexpensive.

Crow Canyon Archaeological Center and Lodge. Under the direction of some of the Southwest's best-known archaeologists is this dynamic center just a few miles northwest of Cortez. Any visitor who is willing to spend a week or more there can try a hands-on course in archaeology at nearby Anasazi sites. Visitors are taught techniques of archaeological excavation and artifact analysis. The center also has group programs for elementary and junior high school students as well as a ten-day teacher workshop. Archaeological tours of surrounding Anasazi sites can be arranged. Visitors stay in very nice, modern dormitories in the attractive, modern southwestern-style lodge or in modern, handsome, hogan-style cabins, with shared baths, that accommodate four people. Dining room. Mailing address: Crow Canyon Archaeological Center and Lodge, 23390 County Road K, Cortez, Colorado, 81321. Telephone: 1-303-565-8975.

Food

Homesteaders. 45 East Main. Telephone: 1-303-565-6253. This excellent western-style restaurant is open for breakfast, lunch, and dinner. Western breakfast favorites include biscuits and gravy and buttermilk hotcakes, while lunch and dinner feature many Mexican-style specialties. Good hamburgers. Children's menu. Inexpensive and moderate.

Stromsted's Restaurant. 1020 South Broadway (U.S. Highway 666). Telephone: 1-303-565-1257. Located in a nicely designed contemporary Colorado-style frame building south of town is this very good dinner restaurant, whose dining rooms offer fine views over the countryside. The menu includes such continental specialties as Chateaubriand for two and scampi. In addition, there are beef kabobs, teriyaki chicken breasts, and a nice selection of appetizers and desserts. Special children's and senior's menus. Moderate.

Tours

Ute Mountain Tribal Tours. If you want to see some remote Anasazi ruins that few people have visited, Ute Mountain and Mancos Canyon Indian Park await you. Here is a good chance to meet the Utes and see their pottery, plants, and beadwork at Tawaoc, Colorado, where the tours begin (fifteen miles south of Cortez on U.S. Highway 666). Reservations must be made in advance. Mailing address: Ute Mountain Tribal Park, Tawaoc, Colorado 81334. Telephone: 1-303-565-3751, ext. 282 or 1-303-565-4684.

Shopping

City Market. 508 East Main. Telephone: 1-303-565-6504. This large, egalitarian grocery store often stocks a good supply of the native pinto beans grown on nearby farms. They come in small gift-size burlap bags and some bags contain a speckled "Anasazi" bean. This store also has a good supply of Colorado's delicious and famous high-altitude honey.

The Quality Bookstore. 34 West Main. Telephone: 1-303-565-9125. This is a good general bookstore, but as you would imagine, it has an extragood selection of hiking, camping, Colorado-focus, and archaeological books. It also stocks topographical maps of Colorado and the three adjacent "Four Corners" states.

There are several regional craft and gift stores worth a stop plus some reliable places to buy Indian arts and crafts, including the Cortez branch of Durango's excellent Toh-Atin Gallery (in the Mesa Verde Pottery building, one-half mile east of Cortez on U.S. Highway 160), Don Woodard's Indian Trading Post and Museum (U.S. Highway 160, one mile east of town), and Notah-Dineh at 309 North Broadway (U.S. Highway 666 at the north edge of town).

Farmington, New Mexico

You will have little trouble finding a fast-food concession for lunch in Farmington. If you want something more, try Della's Spanish Dining Room, a family style restaurant serving Spanish-Mexican food. Open for lunch and dinner Monday through Friday at 202 East Animas. Telephone: 1-505-325-9413. And if you are looking for Indian arts and crafts, do not fail to visit the Foutz Indian Room at 301 West Main, where you will find an excellent selection of Navajo jewelry, kachinas, and Navajo rugs. To see the rugs, you must ask to visit the rug room in the back of the store.

IV

North Central
New Mexico

The Spanish Rio Grande Country

North Central New Mexico

Introduction

If you want to savor the Spanish colonial atmosphere of Old Mexico without leaving the United States, visit northern New Mexico. There, in a broad valley between high mountains whose snowmelt waters feed the Rio Grande that flows through it, you will find the Spanish spirit very much alive. As you drive over highways and walk along streets and roads there, you will be separated by just a few inches of pavement from some of this continent's oldest and most famous western trails. Some were used by the first European settlers to make their homes deep in the interior of the United States, while others were used by Americans who opened up and settled the West. You will pass by graceful, tan adobe buildings, rising easily from the earth they are made of, some built in the name of the king of Spain less than twenty-five years after the Spanish Armada. You will see ruins of seventeenth-century missions, as well as intact missions and churches from the early eighteenth century and later, that were built by Spain's Franciscan Brothers on orders from the pope in Rome. And you will see modest adobe homes with tin roofs whose only ornamentation is a trim of blue around the windows and doors. In Spanish New Mexico, just as in Moorish Spain, blue paint is applied to keep the devil away. And setting off the blue trim will be five-pound strings of bright red chili peppers, called ristras, hanging from the adobe walls as they dry in the bright sun.

If you are an "Anglo," and you are unless you are Spanish American or Pueblo Indian, you will be in for a degree of cultural shock. The Anglo population is the minority population in this high valley north of Albuquerque. The Anglos who reside there have made adjustments in their lives to adopt to the dominant Spanish culture, rather than the other way around. Much of the Spanish tradition lives on. In the cities, towns, and villages of the region, you will hear English spoken with a Spanish accent by Americans of Spanish descent whose heritage in this country goes back over three centuries. In some of the villages, you may also rub shoulders with older people who speak very little English and whose archaic Spanish expressions date from the time of Cervantes. It is no wonder then that most of the Spanish descendants living in northern New Mexico prefer to be called "Hispanic," the Latin term pertaining to the people, speech, or culture of Spain.

You will detect soon enough that this is a land of "poco tiempo," where everything is done "in a little while." In this high country, there is a more relaxed approach to living, similar to that found south of the border in Mexico. Even Anglo residents talk about being more "laid back" than their contemporaries in the East and West. As a visitor, you may find yourself tiring easily and wanting to take a siesta in the afternoons. You should probably give in to this urge. For as you sight-see in Santa Fe, New Mexico's capital, you will be walking in an atmosphere almost as rarified as that of the "alto plano" or high plain where Mexico City rests. Santa Fe's seven-thousand-foot elevation is over a quarter of a mile higher than the much-touted "mile-high city" of Denver, the capital city of

Colorado. Thus it is America's highest capital city as well as the largest city at such a high altitude in the United States. So slow your pace a little and try to absorb some of the centuries-old ambience. Museums and historical monuments abound. Walk and mix with the people. Slow down, look, listen, observe. For more than anything else, it's the people and how they live that make the real difference in northern New Mexico.

The Spanish heritage is so rich and so deep that you will not have to strain to detect it. First there are the names on the land. Spanish names are everywhere. The Rio Grande is Spanish for "Great River." The high mountains to the east were named Sangre de Cristo, a Spanish term meaning "blood of Christ." And Saint John the Baptist was remembered in the mountains and pueblo which carry his Spanish name, San Juan. Many towns, cities, and hamlets have names that can be matched with the names of older towns by the same name in the mother country. Valencia, San Miguel, and Guadalupe counties, as well as Madrid, Santa Cruz, Albuquerque, and Santa Fe were all named for towns and cities either in Spain or Mexico. Where that is not the case, towns often were named for the Spanish or Mexican families who founded them. Even many of the Indian pueblos lost their ancient Indian names long ago and are best known by Spanish place names. San Juan, Santa Clara, and San Ildefonso all carry Spanish names and many of their Indian residents speak Spanish as a second or third language.

Telephone books in this area of New Mexico, like those in Mexico and Spain, list just about every variety of Spanish surname imaginable. In Spanish New Mexico midwives have always been part of the scene, along with curanderas or "good witches" whose healing powers can break the spell of an infermedad puesta or hex placed on someone by a brujo or "bad witch." The topography of the land is sprinkled liberally with Spanish terms such as arroyo and rio, Spanish names for "canyon" and "river." Restaurant menus are studded with Spanish language words—frijoles, guacamole, and tortillas are just a few of the tempting items. The majority of the people are Catholic, so the names of the churches and missions read like a Who's Who of the Spanish and Mexican list of saints and religious figures. San Miguel Mission Church, Santuario de Guadalupe, and Saint Francis Cathedral are just a few of the many you will encounter.

The architecture is one of the distinctive features you will see. Variously called Spanish Pueblo, Pueblo Territorial, and Pueblo Colonial, it will catch your eye and add to the sense of disbelief that you are still in the United States. Adobe houses and buildings rise discretely from the brown earth, their square and rectangular shapes gracefully rounded by time and weather, blending with the high desert, just as their mud-brick counterparts do in Spain and Mexico. The Indians also built great houses out of mud before the Spanish arrived. But it was the Spanish who taught the Indians how to make durable adobes of mud bricks, a skill they in turn had learned from generations of living with the Moors.

So today you will see old Spanish colonial buildings built for the Spanish by their Indian subjects that are still standing almost four hundred years later. The Palace of the Governors is the oldest public building in the United States, dating to 1610. Still standing and still in use by the public as a museum and educational center, its three-foot-thick adobe walls have aged gracefully. But there are not many other seventeenth-century buildings so intact. Most of what the Spanish built was destroyed by their Pueblo Indian conquerors in 1680 when, after nearly one hundred years of servitude and oppression, they rose to destroy every existing memory of their Spanish conquerors. But you will find great delight in rambling through thoroughly intact eighteenth-century and nineteenth-century buildings, churches, and homes that have been well preserved in the high arid environment.

If you are in northern New Mexico at the right time, you may hear the rich, mellow sounds of old bells in adobe churches, calling the faithful to their duty or ringing out in joyous celebration of some special occasion. Although this is a land of great hardship and poverty, lively fiestas with a Latin flair and wonderfully happy celebrations older than the Fourth of July are carried out regularly each year. The preservation of these customs by New Mexico's Spanish population reflects the seriousness of purpose and great sense of duty shown to their long and rich cultural past. This devotion has allowed the Spanish influence to re-

Adobe church,
Saint Francis of Assisi, Ranchos de Taos

main amazingly intact in the mountain fastness of northern New Mexico.

But preceding the Spanish were the Indians. They inhabited this area for hundreds of years before the Spanish arrived. It is thought that most of today's Pueblo Indian ancestors came from the Four Corners area, migrating to the Rio Grande region around 1300. They came from the great Anasazi tradition (see Section II, "A Prehistory of Indian Country") and knew how to build multi-storied houses from hand-shaped, stone building blocks. At first, they came to areas like Frijoles Canyon (Bandelier National Monument) and Puyé, where they built villages resembling the ones they left at Mesa Verde and Chaco Canyon. Then, several hundred years later, for reasons not yet fully understood, they moved down from the canyons onto the high, flat plain next to the Rio Grande.

It was there that Coronado's men found them. By then, the Indians had learned to make houses from mud laid up in courses and from rounded, hand-shaped mud loaves known as turtlebacks. They farmed an estimated twenty-five thousand irrigated acres, made beautiful pots, and wove clothing from cotton. At that time there were thirty to possibly seventy or one hundred villages estimated to have thirty thousand or more inhabitants. Tanoan was their language. Then as now, each village spoke one of the three Tanoan dialects, either Tewa, Tiwa, or Towa, or the Keresan language. Today all up and down the banks of the Rio Grande you will see the ancestors of those very first colonizers. They are called Pueblo Indians, pueblo being a Spanish word for "village." You may wish to visit several of the pueblos, where you will be met with warmth and friendliness. If possible, try to time your visit so you can see one of the many Pueblo ceremonies or dances open to the public.

The Johnny-come-latelies on the scene have been the Americans and other, assorted Anglos. They arrived in the 1800s and have been settling there ever since. It was the Anglo who was responsible for romanticizing and popularizing north central New Mexico. The Spanish did little to spread the reputation of this region. In fact, they did all they could to keep non-Spanish people out. In addition, they did not find anything very special about the area. After all, the mountains were not grander than the Spanish Sierras, and the plains were not browner nor hotter than those of La Mancha and Estremadura. Living with the Indians seemed little different than coexisting with the Moors and the Jews in their native Spain.

It was the Anglo who came to northern New Mexico and was awed by what he saw and felt. For he encountered two unique cultures, the Spanish and the Pueblo Indian, living together but separately in this dramatic, remote land of high mountains and dry plains. It was Kit Carson, D. H. Lawrence, Willa Cather, and many other well-known Anglos who put northern New Mexico on the map. They gave it unprecedented worldwide publicity. Georgia O'Keeffe's paintings of Spanish crosses, old adobes, and bleached cow bones had much the same impact. Partially because of this romanticizing, New Mexico is variously known as the Land of Enchantment and the Land of Contrasts. People talk of the "mystery" of its mountains and the "spell" of its land. For some who rush through it on two- or three-day tours, the buildup seems out of proportion to what they see. To others who stay long enough to savor it, not enough can be said to describe this unique area. For many, the spell of New Mexico takes hold and will not let loose. In spite of changing times and increasing modernization, the area still exerts its magnetic pull. Close to 1.5 million people a year are drawn to Santa Fe alone. You may be next.

If you travel there, keep your ears open as you go from place to place. You may hear something that will be so exciting and mysterious that it will stay with you for a lifetime. On several occasions over the years, while browsing in the Taos Book

Store, I have overheard hushed conversations between the proprietors and some of their customers. The spicy topics have ranged from the secret rites of the Indians to rumors about the Penitentes. Once the conversation centered around alleged threats of a few Taos Indians toward an Anglo writer who had overstepped his bounds and become too intrusive. And, of course, almost everywhere you go you may hear tidbits of information about Greer Garson, Roger Miller, and a host of others who make up northern New Mexico's star-studded cast. So not all the excitement of New Mexico is in the landscape!

Today, north central New Mexico is truly one of the cultural heartlands of the Southwest's high desert country. In wide, open spaces ringed by mountains whose tall peaks reach up to the bluest skies you will ever see, three visions have developed into a human mosaic unlike any other known in the United States. The Pueblo Indian, the Spanish, and the Anglo all live out their lives together, yet separately. They share in community living but retreat, daily, to homes of different values and traditions. Their shared life is called "New Mexican." New Mexicans, regardless of extraction, often prefer pinto beans to green beans, consume tons of chili each year, and dote on the sopaipilla, a cousin to Indian fry bread developed by the Spanish and devoured by thousands of both residents and tourists.

The region's isolation has led to a gentle, mellow entry into the modern world. But all is not as tranquil or content as it would seem. Part of the quaintness and charm you may see in certain areas is as much the product of poverty as it is of isolation and cultural difference. Per capita incomes and educational levels in some of northern New Mexico's counties are the lowest in the country. Unemployment is endemic in certain areas. There is a multitude of tensions, prejudices, and biases as the people of this area struggle with their future development (see "History"). For the most part, differences are worked out cooperatively. In the 1960s and early 1970s, many of America's young people became wrapped up in the romantic idealism of the area without recognizing the realities. In seeking an alternative life-style, they sought a haven in what they thought would be a tolerant, multiethnic, trilingual society. But what

they found was similar to what they discovered elsewhere. No one embraced them with open arms. There was some violence. Northern New Mexico could not easily absorb yet another culture.

The Setting

New Mexico's three cultures have developed in a splendid setting. For it is in north central New Mexico that the Rockies rise in a maze of parallel and conflicting ridges from the Chihuahua Desert to the south, the great Staked Plains to the east, and the Colorado Plateau to the west. It is at this meeting of desert, plain, plateau, and mountains that the Gulf Stream, Pacific Westerlies, and Canadian Northerlies all converge to produce a fascinating scenario of ever-changing weather. These conditions lend to the sense of mystery that prevails in New Mexico. You may experience a part of this when on a warm, sunny, August day, the peaceful morning calm is broken by the sound of thunder as it reverberates through the canyons and bounces off steep mountain faces. Then in a wink, the bright clear air becomes dark and ominous. The dust begins to blow. The mountains become dark, purple, and foreboding. Animals scurry for cover. Then it comes. A few large drops at first, falling "splat" on the dry ground. Then more drops until finally you are pummeled by a torrential downpour so forceful that in moments a thousand gullies are washed out and flooded. In a short while, it's all over. You are left wondering about the magic chemistry of high mountains and rising hot air. Yet in spite of the dramatic summer thunderstorms, howling snowstorms in the winter, and windy, dusty spring days, the sun manages to shine over three hundred days each year making this one of the most sun-drenched regions in America.

Sunny? Yes, and bright, too, for the high elevation tends to make the air less dense. Scientists say that for every nine hundred feet elevation gain, the atmosphere loses one-thirtieth of its density. By the time you reach Santa Fe at seven thousand feet elevation, the air has lost one-fourth of its density. Since the rainfall in some areas is less than ten to twelve inches per year, the air is free of light-distorting moisture particles. In that crystal-clear air that some have described as being "transparent," distant objects seem closer and more sharply outlined, creating a sense of space and openness rarely experienced elsewhere. It is possible on a clear day to see nearly one hundred fifty miles distant. The unfiltered light has a pure quality and a clarity that artists notice immediately when they arrive in the area. So seeing things in a "different light" is not just an abstract expression in New Mexico's high country, it is a reality. You will literally see things differently. That dry, rarified air often carries the pungent aromas of piñon, sage, and juniper, waking yet another of the senses. These sensual changes, plus your body's adjustment to the high elevation, will alter your perceptions considerably. Pretty soon even the "doubting Thomases" begin to believe in the legendary "mystique" of New Mexico's high country.

Most authorities talk about the Rockies petering out in north central New Mexico. But whether the Rockies begin or end in New Mexico depends on which way you are traveling. When I first approached Albuquerque and Santa Fe from the southeast forty years ago, I had the same impression the first Spaniards to the area must have had.

Piñon pine

New Mexico is where the mountains begin. The low eastern plains and southern deserts give way to rolling land, leading to undulating hills. Those hills fade as higher foothills take their place, eventually rising to twelve- and thirteen-thousand-foot peaks. Coming from the west, a similar impression is gained. The Continental Divide is but an imaginary line across a level, high desert. From that desert the high, purple peaks of the Rockies rise to the north.

The Rockies descend from Colorado into New Mexico like a forked stick, with space between the prongs for the Rio Grande and its wide valley. The western range thrusting down is a continuation of Colorado's San Juan Mountains. The Spanish first called this range the Sierra de las Grullas or the Sierra of the Cranes. Today throughout most of northern New Mexico these mountains are referred to as the Jemez Mountains. They are cut and watered by the Chama River, one of the Rio Grande's major tributaries. The Jemez Mountains embrace one of the world's largest extinct volcanic craters, the Valle Grande Caldera, measuring over sixteen miles in diameter. Before it had spent all of its explosive forces, it blasted and forged much of the country you will see west of the Rio Grande. Ash from its eruptions accumulated in depths measured in hundreds of feet and spread as far as today's Oklahoma and Kansas. Over time, the ash hardened to become a honeycombed rock form called "tuff." Nature chiseled caves out of this soft rock which became home to some of the first Anasazi settlers of the region. Today sheep graze and wild flowers grow in peaceful meadows which cover that ancient caldera's scarred surface.

To the east, another great mountain mass comes down into New Mexico from Colorado. These mountains were first named the Sierra Madres since they reminded the Spanish of peaks in their homeland. Later the name was changed to the Sangre de Cristo Mountains. There are many stories about how this name came to be used. The most plausible one relates to a natural phenomenon. At sunset these mountains take on a red glow which reminded the Spanish of the blood of Christ. Thus, "Sangre de Cristo." This range includes New Mexico's highest peaks. Not far from Taos is New Mexico's highest peak, Mount Wheeler, topping out at 13,151 feet. The Sangre de Cristo range fades north of Albuquerque, where the Sandia Mountains drop down to the lower, flatter deserts and plains to the south and east.

But the soaring mountains and their high deserts are not sufficient to make the land livable. In this arid country, there has to be water or man cannot survive. When faced with prolonged drought and depleted soil conditions, the Anasazi abandoned their Mesa Verde, Aztec, Salmon, and Chaco Canyon sites in the Four Corners area (see Section II, "A Prehistory of Indian Country" and Section III, "Indian Past: The Anasazi Circle Tour"). Many of them drifted southeast, looking for a well-watered place to farm. As they migrated east, leaving the lands of the San Juan drainage area behind them, they traveled through northern New Mexico, eventually departing from the Colorado Plateau and entering a wide valley. There they found a welcome river and its tributaries. Cottonwood trees grew along its banks. Its soil was rich in volcanic ash.

So it was that this river and its tributary rivers, like the Euphrates in Mesopotamia, gave birth to the great Pueblo civilization which bloomed in the southern Rockies while Europe was slumbering in the Middle Ages. When the dream of discovering easy riches had eluded the Spanish, it was this river and its valleys that, in the end, attracted them and cradled the first European civilization in the interior of the United States.

The Spanish first discovered this river in 1519 at its terminus. There, in the midst of palm trees and a semitropical setting, it empties into the Atlantic Ocean's Gulf of Mexico. They called it the Rio de las Palmas, "the River of the Palms." Little did the Spanish know at that time, only twenty-seven years after the first voyage of Columbus to America, that the river extended nearly two thousand miles northwest to its source. Later in the sixteenth century, when the river was discovered by the Spanish in New Mexico, they gave it several different names. It was known variously as the Rio del Norte, "the River of the North" and the Rio Bravo del Norte, "the Bold River of the North." Eventually the Spanish in New Mexico would call it the "great river," the Rio Grande.

It is a "great river." It stretches over eighteen hundred miles in length and is either America's second or third longest river, depending on which "fact" you choose to believe. If the Missouri River, a tributary of the Mississippi, is considered as just a segment of the "Father of Rivers," then the Rio Grande earns the distinction of being the second longest river. But local tradition and regional interest frequently overrule the geographers. The Missouri is often considered a river unto itself. In that instance, the Rio Grande slides into third position. The Spanish followed the Rio Grande north from El Paso del Norte, Mexico, where today it serves as the international border between the United States and Mexico. The early Spanish settlers established the El Camino Real ("the Royal Road") alongside it, and farther north they settled along its banks in the Española Valley.

But the Spanish were never inclined to follow the river much farther north. Their maps told them that the Rio Grande orginated near the North Pole. No hot-blooded, gold-seeking, Spanish con-quistador would waste his time going there. They searched for gold and silver to the west and as far east as Kansas, but they never went north. If they had followed their "Great River" just one hundred miles to the north, they might have been richly rewarded. For there, in the San Juan range of the Colorado Rockies, just east of the Continental Divide not far from that 13,838-foot massif known as the Rio Grande Pyramid, winter snows and tor-rential summer rainstorms spawn this river of life. It begins near Stony Pass. That pass, once known as Rio Grande Pass, was the gateway to riches for American prospectors in the 1800s as they strug-gled westward to the fabulous silver and gold mines near today's town of Silverton, Colorado. Whether the Spanish could have fully exploited these riches we will never know. Some say that the Spanish were looking for easy riches and that unless, as in Mexico and Peru, they had had thousands of slaves to do the mining for them, they would not have gone after the plum. Today, much of the crystal-clear Rio Grande water is trapped in several reservoirs just below its source, allowing better control of the river's flow and providing water for Colorado's irrigated farms. From there the river cascades in pristine pureness down to Creede, Colorado, another fabulously rich mining area in the early days. Although silver is still being mined near Creede, Colorado, today the area is best known for a stretch of the Rio Grande nearby. There, Texans, Oklahomans, and Kansans can be heard to boast that the trout are so willing to be caught, they just jump into your pockets.

From Del Norte, Colorado, the Rio Grande winds ever eastward to hit the high plains at Alamosa. There it begins to make close to a ninety-degree turn to the south. Near this location in 1779, the Spaniard de Anza came up from the south to conquer the Comanches. He was the first Spaniard known to have followed the Rio Grande that far north. He discovered to his surprise that the Rio Grande took off to the west at a sharp angle rather than continuing northward to the Pole as the Spanish maps had suggested for two centuries. But de Anza never had a chance to explore the western Rockies. He went on to defeat the Coman-ches and opened the way for more accessible trade routes to Santa Fe.

Before heading south, just east of Alamosa, the river passes within close range of Blanca Peak, that 14,363-foot mass of stone just north of Fort Garland. It is a peak sacred both to the Navajo and to certain Pueblo groups. Reportedly, it can be seen from as far distant as Taos, New Mexico, eighty miles to the south as the crow flies. Now flowing southward, the river passes the place where Lt. Zebulon Pike was captured by the Spanish in 1805 and transported to Santa Fe. The site is now marked as the Pike Historical Monument. From there the river cuts through the wide San Luis Valley. Migration of the Spanish from northern New Mexico to that area in the 1800s established the final northern extension of the Spanish culture. The quiet Spanish farming towns along the valley point to the fact that by the 1800s the settlers from Iberia were not looking for gold, but for better farmland to help them survive in that rough country.

The river then passes over the Colorado border into northern New Mexico. From the border, south, for a distance of forty-eight miles, it flows deep in the shadowy recesses of a gorge where it becomes frenetic in its push southward. The deep canyon walls, the raging white water with drops of 10 to 15 feet, won for this segment of the Rio Grande the designation of the Rio Grande Wild River Area, becoming the first river in America to receive this designation. Many a kayaker and rafter know that the rapids are as challenging there as any place in the country. Near Arroyo Hondo, north of Taos, the crystal-clear waters give up numerous brown trout to the delight of both visiting and local anglers.

Near Taos, the river is deep in a gorge, 650 feet below the surface of the rim of the high sagebrush plain. The tan basalt and sandstone walls are so steep and narrow that sunshine only penetrates to the bottom in the summer at midday. There, on the second highest bridge in the national highway system, you can see the narrow flash of river below. Standing there, you will understand why the Taos and Picuris pueblos, unlike their neighbors to the south, are not situated along the Rio Grande. The river is most inaccessible along this stretch. So Taos and Picuris are situated closer to the mountains where clear streams that eventually feed the Rio Grande are at surface level and are easily reached.

Below the junction of "trouty" Taos Creek, the

Rio Grande Gorge and Bridge

clear water rushes through ever-widening rock walls as the gorge gives way to a broader canyon. Above Pilar, the wild river gasps its last breath over moderate rapids. These rapids are a favorite of local rafting devotees. Then the river faces the first impediment in its long course down from Colorado. A series of small diversion dams takes the water to the surrounding orchards. There apples, peaches, apricots, and cherries flourish in this otherwise dry land. Corn and chilies receive the moisture required to ripen in time for the fall harvest. The Spanish villages of Pilar, Embudo, and Velarde are garden oases. Their green is particularly inviting in this otherwise brown country. At Velarde, thirty miles south of Taos, the canyon ends. Leaving black lava walls behind, the river enters the broad Española Valley. There it is wider, calmer, and very accessible. Continuing south, the river lays claim to a broad fertile valley where it cradled and nurtured three cultures. In prehistoric times, there were thirty to seventy towns along this central and northern segment of the Rio Grande. With irrigation water from the river and its tributaries, it is estimated that twenty-five thousand acres were under cultivation at that time. The Indians grew corn, beans, pumpkins, gourds, and in certain warm, dry areas, cotton.

When the Spanish came, they improved on

the ancient Indian irrigation system. As was their habit, they provided rules to govern the use of the canals. Today, in Valencia, Spain, the Water Tribunal meets every Thursday morning at 10:00 A.M. just as it has done since the Middle Ages. It meets to settle disputes arising from the management of eight great irrigation canals along the Turia River. These were first established by the Romans and later improved by the Arabs. Similarly today, in numerous Spanish villages along the Rio Grande watershed, ancient Spanish rules regulate a hefty bureaucracy that governs the maze of acequias or water ditches on which life in the valley depends. The wooden gates and the ditches are blessed in elaborate ceremonies each spring. Everyone whose land is irrigated by the ditches must provide labor to clear them and ready them for another fruitful season. Just about all the green you see along the Rio Grande is due to the watering of the high dry land by the irrigation ditches. After its annual rainfall of between eight and twelve inches per year, the land is still twenty inches short of sufficient moisture to be productive. Yet in spite of providing enough water for irrigation most years, the Rio Grande has been dubbed "forever undependable." In drought years it fails to supply what is needed, while in other years it may flood uncontrollably.

Just north of Española, the Rio Grande meets its best but dirtiest contributor, the Chama River. The Chama is one of the few perennial streams that does not die in the summertime. It cuts a mighty swath through the San Juan Mountain range. In fact, it divides that range so completely that different names have arisen for the different segments. The mountains north of the river are often called the San Juan Mountains, while the part south of the river is generally known as the Jemez Mountains. The Chama cuts through many red sedimentary layers so that by the time it reaches its confluence with the Rio Grande, the waters are muddy and red, despoiling the crystal-clear waters that come surging out of the gorge below Taos. A large dam has been built on the Chama at Abiquiu to minimize this problem. From the confluence on, the Rio Grande takes on a much more muddy, silty, even sluggish appearance as it proceeds southward. But it was there at the confluence of the two rivers that the Spanish established

the first European town in America's interior and the first capital in what would later be called New Mexico. They called the first permanent capital San Gabriel del Yunque. Today you can see the location of the site just across the river from San Juan Pueblo.

After passing by Santa Clara Pueblo, the river passes through San Ildefonso Pueblo lands, below Black Mesa. Then it enters White Rock Canyon. There it waters the border of the Pajarito Plateau, which is cut by the Rio de los Frijoles and the canyon of the same name. This historic river and canyon gave birth to an early Indian civilization whose history is now preserved in Bandelier National Monument. In White Rock Canyon, the Rio Grande's muddy waters froth over the last rapids it will meet for hundreds of miles. In the canyon the river is fifteen to twenty miles west of Santa Fe and further south receives the waters of the Santa Fe River.

Now, in its southwestern course, the river comes to its first major impediment since the reservoir at its source, Cochiti Dam. It is touted as one of the world's largest earthen dams. Cochiti Lake is too big for the Rio Grande to fill by itself. Water from the San Juan River drainage system is diverted under the Continental Divide to help fill this massive reservoir. Below the dam, the river passes near Cochiti Pueblo not far from Santo Domingo Pueblo on Galisteo Creek. As it enters more open country, it passes near Bernalillo where it is thought Coronado made his first crossing of the river. A little further south at Albuquerque, you will most likely see a dry riverbed. There you may wonder why the river is so "great," especially if that is where you see it for the first time. Much of the Rio Grande water north of Albuquerque is drawn off in a series of canals built for flood and irrigation control. So its greatness is best seen in the benefits it produces. Those are many and include the verdant alfalfa fields and orchards in that rich midsection of the Rio Grande Valley that Albuquerque's citizens call North Valley. Looking at the windswept, arid country around Albuquerque, it is difficult to imagine that finally this river, after serving as the border between the United States and Mexico, will enter the Gulf of Mexico in a semitropical environment of palm trees and citrus orchards where it is known as the Rio Bravo del Norte.

History

Far removed in place and time from today's Santa Fe, New Mexico, yet in a similar environment of arid land and high mountains, Ferdinand and Isabella gathered their considerable forces at Santa Fe de Granada in 1492 to push the Moors, once and for all, out of their Alhambra fortress back into North Africa. The conquest was successful and Spain was purged of the Arabs, who had occupied Spanish lands for over three hundred years. But the influence of those many centuries of Arabic-Moorish culture on the life-style and ways of the Spanish was to remain. In fact, this influence would be spread to the New World. For while still camped at Santa Fe, Isabella and Ferdinand signed papers giving approval to Columbus's first voyage to the Americas. This action set in motion a series of expeditions that would, in just a little over a hundred years, bring settlers to the area known today as northern New Mexico. This in turn would lead to the establishment in 1610 of another town named Santa Fe. It would become the political capital of the northernmost province of New Spain and later the political and cultural capital of New Mexico, U.S.A.

Today in Santa Fe, New Mexico, there is ample evidence that Ferdinand and Isabella purged the Moors from their land but not from their culture. The Spanish explorers who came to the New World brought with them many traditions borrowed from the Moors, who had lived on Spanish soil for so many generations. Perhaps the most important one you will see in your travels is the use of clay or mud bricks for constructing buildings. "Af-fub" is an Arab word meaning brick of clay or mud. The Spanish corruption of that word is "adobe." For centuries Spanish women in New Mexico have adorned themselves with beautiful scarves wrapped around their necks and shoulders. The scarf or rebozo is also Arabic in origin. In addition the Moors also brought to the Spanish their centuries-old tradition of irrigated farming. The Spanish who came to New Mexico carried this knowledge with them and built irrigation canals that are still being used today in modern Santa Fe.

After Columbus discovered the Americas, he made additional voyages, as did other Spanish explorers. Where the Spanish explored, they often set up colonies. Some of the earliest colonies were established in today's Puerto Rico and Cuba. From Puerto Rico, Ponce de Leon sailed to the Florida coast in 1513. In just a little over fifty years, the Spanish would establish America's first city, Saint Augustine, in 1565, near the site where Ponce de Leon landed. In 1518, a Cuban plantation owner, who was eager to seek the kinds of riches found later by Pizarro in Peru, left Cuba to explore the western curvature of the Gulf of Mexico. Cortez landed in Mexico that year and by 1521 had conquered the great Aztec Indian Empire. Within a few years, most of that great civilization had been plundered and destroyed as the Spanish began building a new city on the site of the Aztec ruins. By making slaves of the Aztecs, he was able to accomplish much in a short period of time. New Spain, as the newly conquered land was called, grew by leaps and bounds. Within twenty years, the restless Spanish were looking for more riches.

After all, the Spanish monarchy did have riches in mind when it launched Columbus's first expedition. One of Columbus's missions was to keep an eye out for the legendary Antilla, a mysterious island which rose from the sea, far out in the Atlantic. There, it was said, sea mists hid seven rich cities, the seven cities of Antilla. Legend had it that they were founded by either seven Christian brothers or bishops who had fled with their people from Portugal when it was invaded by the Moors. The seven cities were a refuge provided by the Divine Providence in the west. Columbus did discover the West Indies or the "Antilles," but there were not seven rich cities there. The myth persisted anyway. Ponce de Leon found no such cities in his travels either, but he did find gold on the island of Puerto Rico. Neither did Cortez find the seven fabulously wealthy cities, but he did find the Aztecs, whose rich civilization should have sated even the greediest explorer.

The Aztecs told the Spanish that their ancestors had lived in seven remote cities to the north of their immediate homeland. A seed was planted! Then in 1532 to 1533, the stunning news of Pizarro's conquest of Peru and his rich discoveries there reached New Spain. This seemed to give credence to another legend, the legend of El Dorado. El Dorado is a Spanish term meaning the "Golden Man." Somewhere in the New World, the legend stated, there was a land of great riches where each year the chief of the mythical land was rolled in gold and then placed in a sacred pond where the gold was rinsed from his body. What a find that pond would be, filled with the accumulation of hundreds of years of gold silt! The atmosphere was now ripe in New Spain for an event that would trigger new expeditions to the unexplored lands north of Mexico City.

That event came in 1536 when Cabeza de Vaca, along with a Moorish slave by the name of Estévan and two other Spaniards, reached Culiacán, Mexico, after several years of rugged cross-country travel. They had been part of a Spanish expeditionary and settlement party landing in Florida in 1528. They scrapped their expedition and fled when Indian hostilities intensified. Traveling in crude, handmade boats, they shipwrecked on either Mustang or Galveston Island, just off the coast of today's Texas. Taken captive there by the Indians, de Vaca and his group were able to escape after five or six years. They made their way across today's Texas, New Mexico, and Arizona before turning south to Mexico. It is believed they were the first white men to see the buffalo and were probably the first to see the Rio Grande in New Mexico. But more importantly, they learned from Indians they encountered about other Indians to the north who lived in permanent multistoried houses and who wore cotton garments as well as jewelry of coral and turquoise.

When they reached Mexico and related their fantastic story, the oft-reported tendency of the Spanish to blur illusion with fact took hold. The seven cities must be to the north! An expedition was organized pressing Estévan, de Vaca's black slave, into service as a guide under the leadership of a Franciscan Catholic friar, Marcos de Niza. After a number of months of travel, Estévan did in fact find a cluster of six Zuñi villages spaced over a distance of fifteen miles. Each had multistoried homes, but the streets were of dust not gold. The people were rich in history and culture, but not in gold nor jewels.

Estévan apparently stayed awhile in the villages, but for unknown reasons was murdered by the Indians shortly thereafter. Some of his companions escaped and retraced their route back to Fray Marcos, who had been trailing woefully behind. No one is quite sure what happened at this point, but Marcos returned to Mexico where he told of viewing seven cities from a distance. He described them as a wonder larger than the city of Mexico, and he detailed one city in particular called Cibola. It was the smallest of the cities but very beautiful, having terraced houses made of stone. But Fray Marcos did not stop there. He embellished his story by saying there were "emeralds and other jewels—vessels of gold and silver—whereof there is greater and more abundance than in Peru." No one knows how his imagination led him to stray so far from reality. What he had seen was a Zuñi village of stone and mud. If he had seen it at sunset when the tan sandstone building blocks and the yellow straw in the mud mortar had reflected a golden glow, perhaps he could have concluded that this was a city of gold.

No one questioned Marcos any further. In the minds of the opportunistic Spaniards, the myth was complete—the seven cities had been found. They would be known as the Seven Cities of Cibola since Fray Marcos used the term "Cibola" in his report. Cibola is possibly a Spanish corruption of the Pima Indian word for the Zuñi's sacred mountain range, the "Shiwina." Later the Spanish used the same word to name the buffalo. The Kingdom of Cibola, as it came to be called, had to be explored and, if necessary, conquered. Mounting an expedition of this kind was entirely possible for the powerful Spanish nation. After all, Charles V, the Spanish King, was also the Holy Roman Emperor and he ruled much of Europe from Holland almost down to the boot of Italy.

Thirty-year-old Vasquez de Coronado, the son of a prosperous family from Spain and the Governor of New Galicia in New Spain, was chosen to lead the expedition. By this time, King Charles V, grandson of Isabella and Ferdinand, had received reports about the mistreatment of the Indians by Cortez in New Spain and by other Spaniards elsewhere in the colonies. Influenced by Spanish missionaries such as Bartolomé de las Casas, he implored that the Indians be treated well so their souls could be saved for Christianity. According to his wishes, the "New Law of the Indies," a humanitarian conduct code, was drawn up several years later and was adopted by 1542. Although difficult to enforce and often totally disregarded, it nonetheless may have had a moderating influence on the way the Spanish conquistadores treated the Indians.

In 1540 Coronado amassed a large expeditionary force at Compostela (not far from today's Guadalajara) containing 336 Europeans, of which 275 were cavalrymen. Many were from Charles V's wide-ranging empire. It has been reported that the group included 2 Italians, 5 Portuguese, and 1 German. In addition, he enlisted the aid of 4 friars, including the redoubtable Marcos de Niza. He also recruited 800 Indians to help with the expedition. A total of 10 European and Indian women went along. It is thought that he took over 1,000 horses plus hundreds of other animals including many sheep, goats, and cattle. These would be the first horses and sheep the American Indians had ever seen, and they would be the first horses to roam

Spanish conquistador

the high deserts since the horse became extinct on the North American continent sometime after the last Ice Age (see Section II, "A Prehistory of Indian Country").

In gilded armor and a steel helmet decorated with plumes, Coronado led the expeditionary force, traveling several hundred miles north to Culiacán near the west coast of Mexico. From there it was an arduous one thousand miles to Cibola, in La Tierra Nueva, as the northern frontier was called. His route somewhat paralleled today's Guadalajara–Nogales Highway. Then it ascended the higher country near today's New Mexico–Arizona border. From there, the group went north to the Zuñi villages, de Niza's Cibola, just south of today's Gallup, New Mexico. The Zuñis put up a heavy resistance. Their accurate throwing arms unleashed such a damaging barrage of stones that Coronado was nearly pummeled to death. The Spanish, with their superior weaponry, forced surrender of the pueblo after an hour of fighting. Upon entering the Zuñi farming village of Háwikuh, the Spanish saw no evidence of the wealth of El Dorado. There was nothing to resemble the splendors they had heard about in Peru. In fact, the people seemed to barely be eking out a living in the high, dry desert. Marcos de Niza was discredited and sent back to Mexico in shame.

Coronado made Zuñi his headquarters. From there he sent various expeditions into the surrounding countryside, still looking for the elusive riches that had thus far evaded him. He sent Pedro de Tovar and Fray Juan de Padilla north to the Kingdom of Tusayan (today's Hopi villages) on the hunch that they might be the fabled seven cities (see Section II, "The Hopi: A Long and Continuous Past"). He sent Garcia López Cárdenas to explore reports of a large canyon (the Grand Canyon) with a river running through it. Hernando de Alvarado was sent east to explore the village areas around the Rio Grande and Pecos rivers, in the area of today's New Mexico. These men became famous in time as the first white discoverers of some of the richest scenic and cultural wonders in America. But the wealth of these rich lodes would not be mined for another 350 years when they would be discovered by twentieth-century tourists.

Alvarado explored the Rio Grande Valley north to the Taos Pueblo. But he was most impressed with the area called Tigeux. He sent word that the latter area would be a good place to make winter camp. So Coronado and his party traveled east to a point near today's Isleta Pueblo, then north up the Rio Grande to Tigeux, near today's Bernalillo, close to the site of the Coronado Historical Monument. From there they explored north to Taos and east of Santo Domingo Pueblo to the Cerrillos Hills, where they saw the turquoise deposits that had been mined by the Indians for hundreds of years. During that winter, Coronado and his men came upon a Plains Indian living in the Pueblo at Pecos. He told the Spanish about a land to the east called Quivira where there were villages in which the people made gold jewelry. In fact, he said a gold bracelet had been taken from him by the Pueblo chiefs.

Gold fever rose again! The chiefs were interrogated. They knew nothing about a gold bracelet. The revered chiefs were placed in chains and dogs were set upon them in an attempt to force them to reveal the hiding place of the gold bracelet. Still they insisted they did not know anything about a gold bracelet. Nonetheless, Coronado and his men, smitten with desire, decided that in the spring they would follow the Plains Indian, whom they called the Turk, to the eastern plains to search for those elusive riches. But before spring came, winter had to be conquered. The cold weather and snows were so severe that the Spanish made some of the Pueblo people abandon their villages so they could live there. That act plus the insults heaped upon their chiefs, as well as the confiscation of their winter food supply, made the Indians angry. Soon they began to retaliate.

But the Spanish, tiring of the insolent Indians, decided to put an end to the revolt. They destroyed one village and burned several hundred Pueblo Indians at the stake. Coronado and his men were later put on trial for these and other atrocities committed against the Indians. Coronado was cleared at the trial, but his compatriot, Cárdenas, was found guilty. It seemed that the Spanish government did wish fair treatment of the Indians after all, but La Tierra Nueva was so far from the Spanish seat of government that the law of the frontier took precedence over the humanitarian "New Law of the Indies." This scene was to be repeated over and over again for the next two hundred years. Atrocities would be committed. Later, usually years later, the Spanish official in charge would be recalled to Mexico City or Spain and placed on trial.

Coronado and his men did set out with the Turk to the eastern plains. They passed into what is now part of the Texas Panhandle near Palo Duro Canyon, thence north through Oklahoma until they reached some Indian villages near today's Lyons and Salina, Kansas. The Turk had lied. There was no gold in these poor villages. He was summarily executed. Coronado marched the long way back to Tigeux, where he spent another disconsolate winter. He was injured for the second time when he fell from his horse during some recreational horse racing and was nearly trampled to death. With the coming of spring, the first European expedition to penetrate the continent packed up. With their injured leader, who had to be carried most of the way, they started the long trek, empty-handed, back to Mexico City in 1542. If riches could not be found, perhaps souls could be saved. Three friars were left behind for that purpose. It is believed that all three were later killed by the Indians.

With the myth of easy riches put to rest in the remote northern hinterlands of New Spain, forty years passed before any major expeditions were dispatched to the north. In that period of time, the old Spanish empire in Europe began to fade and its power to diminish. But exciting things were happening in New Spain. The first great silver strike was made at Zacatecas, Mexico, in 1546, leading to the founding of the city of Durango (see Section III, "Durango"). By 1567, another great silver strike had been made in the northernmost province of Chihuahua, centering around the town of Santa Barbara. There were high hopes that more silver might be found further north. Obviously, the disappointing reports of Coronado's expedition had long been forgotten in the intervening forty years.

Fray Augustin Rodríguez and Captain Francisco Chamuscado set forth in 1581 for Tigeux, the region of Coronado's former base camp. They entered New Mexico from Chihuahua, Mexico, and followed the Rio Grande to Tigeux. They established the route that would later be known as El Camino Real or "The Royal Road." They were the first white men to pass through the desolate, extremely parched ninety-mile-long piece of land called the Jornado del Muerto (Spanish for "Journey of the Dead Man") near where, over three hundred years later, the first atomic bomb would be exploded. From Tigeux, they explored in all directions. They finally returned to Mexico, having found neither gold nor silver. But their commercial instincts told them that the cotton goods made by the Pueblo Indians might be useful trade items for the mines in New Spain. Three more friars stayed behind to save the souls of the many Indians encountered along the Rio Grande.

A year later, Antonio de Espejo and Fray Bernaldino Beltrán led another expedition to learn what had happened to the trio of priests since they had not sent any messages south. Of course, Espejo also planned to search for gold and silver. Upon reaching La Tierra Nueva, they discovered that the three friars had been martyred by the Indians. Espejo then traveled west among the Hopi villages in search of gold and silver. He later reported finding some rocks that looked promising. But his report is better known for the new name he gave to this, the most remote of the Spanish colonial outposts. He called it Nuevo Mexico or New Mexico. Before Espejo's visit, it had variously been called La Tierra Nueva and Cibola. Although a provincial governor of Mexico had called it Nuevo Mexico in 1562, Espejo's use of the term began to catch hold. The term Nuevo Mexico implied that this land might be as rich as its namesake to the south, where silver mines had made many a Spaniard wealthy.

But Espejo's "PR" was not enough. Once again, except for an abortive, unauthorized expedition by Don Gaspar Castaño de Sosa in 1590, Nuevo Mexico slid into obscurity, receiving little attention from Mexico City or Madrid. After a number of years, when the church in Spain finally began to hear about the thousands of Indians along the Rio Grande whose souls needed saving and the shocking stories of the martyred priests, Spanish interest was once again renewed. But another event also placed the Spanish spotlight on New Mexico. In 1579, Sir Francis Drake raided some Spanish ships off the Pacific coast of South America. He made such a quick retreat that the Spanish thought he had found a new, secret passage from the Pacific to the Atlantic. Although Drake had taken the conventional route back to England, the Spanish believed he took a quick sea route back to the Atlantic. They imagined this sea passage to be just north of New Spain. They called it the Strait of Anian and placed it on their maps where it appeared just north of New Mexico. Eager to find evidence of this new sea route and always eager to save new souls and to explore for riches, the Spanish decided to establish a permanent settlement in northern New Mexico in 1598.

By then Spain, under Philip II, had been badly defeated by England when the Spanish Armada was destroyed in 1588. Philip himself was dying the summer of 1598. But New Spain was vigorous and, by now, producing its own sons born in the New World. So it is no surprise that Juan de Oñate, the son of a wealthy miner from Zacatecas and a native of New Spain, was chosen to lead the settlement expedition. Although many of these New World Spaniards were of Spanish stock, some historians have pointed out that others were apparently of Spanish–Indian descent. Oñate's wife was one of these, being a descendent of both Cortez and Montezuma, the Aztec chief.

Oñate's expedition stretched the length of four miles as it traveled the route of the Camino

Oxcart

Real. There were four hundred men. About one hundred thirty of the men were accompanied by their wives and families. They carried all of their earthly belongings in eighty-three carretas or ox-carts, which were followed by seven thousand head of livestock. The expedition marched under two flags, the royal flag of the Spanish crown and the banner of the Catholic church. The latter was held high by eleven members of the order of Friars Minor, followers of Saint Francis of Assisi, who preached the brotherhood of man and the joys of poverty.

One of the first stops the group made was at a mountain pass named El Paso del Norte, near the site of today's El Paso, Texas. There, on Holy Thursday of 1598, the expedition stopped for religious observances. Part of the ritual of the Third Order of Saint Francis included the custom of scourging or beating oneself. Don Juan and his soldiers beat their backs until they drew blood. Arriving in northern New Mexico, Oñate established the religious center for the new Spanish kingdom at Santo Domingo Pueblo. Moving north, he established the first political capital and European settlement deep in America's interior on July 11, 1598.

There, near the confluence of the Rio Grande and the Chama River in a wide, fertile valley surrounded by the Sangre de Cristo Mountains to the east and with rugged lava cliffs and the Jemez Mountains to the west, he took over an Indian village, O'ke or Ohke. He called the new town San Juan de los Caballeros. In naming it, he honored Saint John the Baptist and his own Saint's Day and noted the virtues of the "caballeros" or gentlemen like himself and his followers. Soon, Oñate moved the settlement to the west side of the Rio Grande to the Indian pueblo of Yuqueyunque, leaving the name of San Juan behind. Oñate named the new permanent settlement San Gabriel del Yunque.

Almost immediately he ordered a chapel constructed. The colonists set to work to make a new life for themselves. By September, they were sufficiently settled that they could stage the popular play, Los Moros y Los Christianos, commemorating the expulsion of the Moors from Granada, Spain. This celebration was revived a number of years ago and is celebrated at Chimayó, New Mexico, on the feast day of Santiago, near the end of July. Only partially excavated ruins attest to the presence of this first Spanish capital in North America and the town that would later gain for New Mexico the title of the oldest of the fifty states in terms of having the first organized government. Life was very difficult for the first settlers. Although they were allowed to exact a certain amount of free labor from the Indians, there were not enough Indians available to do all the work. So the early Spanish settlers did much of their own farming.

Oñate and his group made several expeditions from the new settlement. On one, he sent his nephew Juan de Zaldivar to take food from the Ácoma Pueblo for the Spanish settlers. The Ácoma Pueblo Indians, not warming to the idea, attacked Zaldivar. They killed him and twelve others. Oñate, seeking revenge led an expedition of seventy men and assaulted the pueblo. With considerable violence, he conquered it, leaving in his wake from six to eight hundred dead Ácoma Indians. He then rounded up all of the other villagers and took them to the mission capital of Santo Domingo. There all males over the age of twenty-five had one foot cut off and sixty girls were carted away to convents in New Spain. By 1601, more Pueblo unrest was met by the Spanish with the burning of three pueblos, killing nine hundred people and taking four hundred more captive.

These actions and others like them would eventually come back to haunt the Spanish. One day the Pueblo Indians would avenge themselves.

By 1607, the year Jamestown was established by the British on America's East Coast and the year before Champlain established the French city of Quebec, Oñate was having difficulty with the leadership of the new Spanish settlement. He was not well respected and he was frequently absent, spending much of his time on exploratory missions. Twice he went to the Sea of Cortez or the Gulf of California. Once upon returning from there, he carved a message on a sandstone rock not far from the Ácoma Pueblo. Roughly translated, it reads: "There passed by here Don Juan de Oñate, from the discovery of the South Sea in 1605." That ancient message carved in sandstone is preserved today as a tourist attraction known as Inscription Rock at El Morro National Monument. While Oñate was exploring and writing on rocks, Cervantes in Spain was writing the last pages of his first volume of *Don Quixote*.

In Oñate's absence, there was much unrest. The settlers were unable to produce much from the land. The difficult living conditions prompted such a high desertion rate at one point that there were only forty Spanish adult males and their families remaining. By 1608, the year Cervantes's first volume of *Don Quixote* was published, Oñate was recalled to Mexico City where he was eventually placed under investigation, tried, and found guilty of a number of charges, including misconduct in office.

The viceroy of Mexico appointed Pedro de Peralta to replace Oñate. He was given the mandate to move the provincial capital of the kingdom of New Mexico to a militarily defensible location where there would be good grazing for the settlers' livestock and where there would be no conflict with the Indians over water. Since there was little apparent wealth there, the area was to be continued mostly as a missionary province.

Peralta did move the capital to a well-watered higher location along the Santa Fe River, near the site of an old abandoned pueblo village. The town was laid out in 1609–1610, and occupied in 1610. It was called Villa de Santa Fe, but later became known as La Villa Real de Santa Fe. Still later, it was known as La Villa Real de Santa Fe de San Francisco. Since that time, regardless of which nation controlled it, Santa Fe has continuously been the capital city of the area. This makes it the oldest capital city in the United States. The capitol buildings, or casas reales, were built in 1610. One of those buildings, El Palacio Real, better known as the Palace of the Governors, is the oldest continuously occupied public building in the United States.

Mission churches were built at an astounding pace all over the Rio Grande Valley. By 1625, the busy Franciscans had fifty churches in place and were claiming to have saved thousands of souls among the Pueblo Indian population. By 1680, the number of mission churches had increased to eighty. Today two of these early seventeenth-

Palace of the Governors, Santa Fe

century mission churches are still intact and in use. They are without doubt the two oldest churches in the United States. The mission church at Isleta Pueblo was built between 1613 and 1630 while the mission church at Ácoma, to the west, was built in 1629.

Although the Indians already knew how to construct multistoried houses out of mud, the Franciscan missionaries taught the Indians how to build, using techniques their culture had borrowed from the Moors. They taught the Indians to make sun-dried rectangular building bricks called adobes and showed them how to construct a building from those bricks. The Franciscans saw to it that their churches would last a long time. Using Indian labor, they had forty-foot beams hand carried to the building sites from many miles away. They made sure that the adobe walls, often rising thirty-five feet in height, were five to eight feet thick. Twin towers were often twenty-five feet taller than the buildings.

The law allowed a certain amount of Indian labor to be donated each year. But the governors of Nuevo Mexico, in their eagerness for profit, often made the Indians perform more gratis work than they were supposed to. From tilling fields, to building adobe missions, to weaving garments in sweatshops for trade in Mexico, the Indians came to be overworked and abused. By the middle of the seventeenth century, the Indians, for all practical purposes, were slaves. Apparently, both the priests and the government officials were guilty of this offense, each bitterly accusing the other of mistreating the Indians. As the mission churches went up around the countryside and the Indians were subjected to more and more bondage, the ninety or so Pueblo villages that Oñate observed in 1598 had shrunk to half that number by 1650. By 1630–40, the Indians had had enough. Rebels at Jemez and Taos pueblos killed their Spanish priests. After that, the Pueblos were so savagely subdued that no further resistance was offered for awhile.

But things were not going well for the Spanish colonists and their charges either. The rugged land was exacting its toll. Persistent drought, epidemics of one sort or another, and marauding Apaches made living conditions there barely tolerable. Being eight hundred miles from civilization in Mexico, they were isolated. Supplies from the south only came every three years. By 1675, the Franciscans were upset that many of the Pueblo Indians were still practicing their old rituals. In concert with the governor of Nuevo Mexico, the decision was made to suppress these practices. Systematically, all estufas or kivas were burned and destroyed. Later all the religious leaders or shamans of the Pueblos, whom the Spanish termed "wizards," were rounded up and tried for sorcery and witchcraft. Three were hanged and more would have met the same fate, but for the seventy Pueblo warriors who stormed the Palace of the Governors demanding release of their brothers. They threatened that if the shamans were not released, they would not help the Spanish fight the Apaches, a group who had acquired Spanish horses and was increasingly a menace.

One of the Indians released, called Popé, fled to Taos Pueblo, further away from watchful Spanish eyes than his own San Juan Pueblo. There with a half-Spanish, half-Indian Taos resident named Naranjo, an Indian revolt was planned. At the time of the revolt there were from sixteen to thirty thousand Pueblo Indian people and about twenty-four hundred Spanish, including many Spanish sympathizers who were of mixed descent. Popé and Naranjo, in concert with other Pueblo leaders, set a date for the rebellion. Runners were to carry knotted cords to each pueblo. Each day a knot was to be untied. When all the knots had been removed, it was time to strike. On August 11, 1680, all the Pueblos were to rise up and kill every Spanish sympathizer, including men, women, and children.

The Spanish governor got wind of the plot. Knowing of this, the Indian leaders again dispatched runners to tell the pueblos to rise up on the tenth rather than the eleventh. In the first few days, four hundred Spanish in the outlying areas were killed, as were twenty-one of the thirty-two priests who were in New Mexico at the time. Those who survived took refuge in the Palace of the Governors in Santa Fe. That great, fortified building, with its impenetrable walls, allowed the Spanish to hold out for ten days, during which they killed three hundred Indians and captured and shot forty-seven more. The Indians, tiring of the battle, cut the water ditch to the palace. With this act, Governor Otermín realized he was beaten. He led the one thousand Spanish refugees in a retreat and headed south to friendly Isleta Pueblo. In their hasty retreat, it is said that the Spanish people took time to gather up a three-foot-tall crowned, wooden statue of the Virgin Mary which had stood in the parish church since it had been brought to Santa Fe from Mexico in 1625. The defeated Spanish left with their beloved Madonna on August 21, 1680. At Isleta, they met up with other refugees and eventually evacuated all the way to the state of Chihuahua in Mexico. There they began plotting a reconquest.

Meanwhile, the Indians took over the Palace of the Governors and redesigned its interior to their liking. They then set about to destroy all material evidence of the Spanish occupation. Santa Fe became the capital for a loose federation of Pueblo tribes. The Isleta Mission Church and the Ácoma Mission Church were the only two churches of the eighty or so built before 1680 that were not completely destroyed in that revengeful spree. These two ancient churches are still in use today. Governor Otermín attempted a reconquest in November of 1680, but upon arriving at Isleta, he found that the Indians were ready to entrap him to the north. He abandoned the plan and returned to Mexico with close to four hundred Isleta Indians for whom he feared reprisals. They eventually settled at a site near today's El Paso, Texas, known as Ysleta.

Perhaps being conquered by the Pueblo Indians and losing New Mexico was just another example of what was happpening to declining Spain. Between 1621 and 1665 under Philip III and Philip IV, the Spanish had lost the Thirty Years War and had lost Portugal as well. By 1680, Spain was truly a lesser nation headed for the doldrums, led by Charles II who was apparently mentally incompetent.

It would be twelve years before another reconquest of New Mexico would be attempted. The indomitable Spanish would not give up, especially since La Salle and the French landed on the Texas coast of the Gulf of Mexico in 1684. It was thought they might threaten Spanish holdings in New Mexico or their silver mines in New Spain. La Salle had arrived on the gulf largely due to infor-

mation given to France by a Spanish traitor, Don Diego de Peñalosa, who, ironically, had been governor of New Mexico from 1650 to 1655. Like most Spanish governors of New Mexico, he was accused of misconduct in office, tried, and stripped of his wealth. But instead of retiring to lick his wounds, he became a turncoat and aided France in its New World interests.

In 1692, Captain General Diego de Vargas Zapata Lujan Ponce de León y Contreras marched resolutely back into New Mexico. He found little resistance to his expeditionary force. He went peaceably up and down the Rio Grande and even traveled to the Hopi mesas without event. In his report, he used the word "moqui," derived from a Zuñi word to describe the Hopi. He also stopped by Inscription Rock. There, not to be outdone by Juan Oñate, he inscribed the following: "Here was General Don Diego de Vargas who conquered for our Holy Faith and the Royal Crown all New Mexico at his own expense in 1692." After four months traveling around as the "reconquistador," he returned victorious to Mexico.

In 1693, he led a resettlement expedition back up the Camino Real to Santa Fe with one hundred soldiers, seventy-three families, eighteen Franciscan priests, some Pueblo Indians, and four thousand animals. This resettlement party returned to Santa Fe with the little wooden statue of the Virgin they had taken with them in 1680. They took solace from the Virgin as they camped outside Villa de Santa Fe that winter. As the weather became colder and the Spanish food supplies dwindled, the Spaniards suggested that the Indians give them the Palace of the Governors and also find food for them. In this request, the Indians saw in these "new Spaniards" the same traits present in the Spanish twelve years before. They resisted and a battle ensued. The Spanish immediately cut the water ditches to the palace, forcing the Indians to surrender. The Spanish executed seventy of the resisters and took four hundred others as captives to be used as servants.

It was not a peaceful reconquest. Over the next few years, some of the bloodiest battles in the history of the region were fought at San Ildefonso, Jemez, and Ácoma pueblos. Many Rio Grande Pueblo people, fearing reprisals, fled west to live with the Navajo and the Hopi (see Section II, "The

La Conquistadora

Hopi: A Long and Continuous Past"). By 1696, most of the villages had been subdued by de Vargas's heavy hand. But the Hopi remained adamant, slaughtering some of their own people who were about to invite a Franciscan priest to live in their village rather than submit to Spanish control. The resolute Hopi offered a home to Rio Grande Indian refugees who feared Spanish reprisals. Spain finally regained some lost territory in this far distant colonial empire. The little wooden statue of the Virgin became known as La Conquistadora, since it was to her that the Spanish colonists attributed their victory. La Conquistadora became the focus of a procession and festival of thanksgiving that began in 1716 and has continued to this day. The statue of the Virgin was carried from the church to the place where the Spanish colonists waited while the battle for the Palace of the Governors ensued. This venerated figure can still be seen today in Saint Francis Cathedral in Santa Fe. Divine intervention aside, de Vargas was tried for misconduct, imprisoned, and dishonored. But as was usually the case, his name was eventually cleared and he even returned to New Mexico to serve a second term as governor.

By 1695, fifteen hundred more colonists had arrived from Mexico. Often on the last night before entering Santa Fe, the weary travelers would spend the night near today's La Cienaga at El Rancho de las Golondrinas. This ancient ranch with its torreons or towers dating back to the 1650s has been restored and is open to the public on a limited basis. Now firmly in control, the Spanish set about seriously to colonize this area. A second villa, Santa Cruz de Cañada, was established as de Vargas issued the first recorded settler grant in

New Mexico. The third villa to be established was Villa de Albuquerque in 1706.

The greatest threat to the newly resettled colony in the early part of the 1700s came from the Apaches. They threatened the lives and livelihood of both the Pueblo Indians and the Spanish. Consequently, the Spanish and Pueblo people found some common ground as they both fought a hated enemy. The other common denominator uniting the two was survival in this rugged country. Each learned from the other a variety of lifeways that made living not just possible but a little easier. Learning from the land's native inhabitants was critical for the Spanish New Mexicans since Spain gave them very little attention during this time and they had to rely more and more on themselves. It has been said that while the rest of the world flourished and technology grew by leaps and bounds in the 1700s, the Spanish in New Mexico were defeated by distance and time, finally having to live much like their former enemies the Pueblo Indians, in a static state where survival was the name of the game.

The Apache threats lessened after 1720, when the Comanches became more of a problem. Within time, the Utes were also threatening the Rio Grande settlements. To cope with the problem, the Spanish established settlement grants at Abiquiui, Belen, Tomé, and San Miguel, which were to be settled predominantly with Indians of obscure identity, known as genizaros. They were usually captured Ute, Apache, and Comanche slaves. With these people serving as the first line of defense against Indian raids, it was thought the Spanish settlers would not be bothered quite so much. The vanguard of most Spanish expeditions in pursuing the marauding Apaches and Comanches were the Pueblo Indians.

The year of 1739–40 saw the beginning of French explorers making their way across the plains to the Rockies. Within a few years, they were trading at the Taos summer fair, a wild event in which Indians, both friendly and hostile, traded with the Spanish. Upon leaving the fair, the Utes or Comanches would often raid the countryside. Fearful of further French encroachment from the east, the Taos trade fair was closed to the French in 1752. In 1763, the French were driven from the North American continent when England took

Canada. Shortly after that, to keep England from grabbing up Louisiana, France ceded that territory to Spain. Spain could breathe a sigh of relief, at least for a while. The French were no longer a threat. Later Spain, supporting the American Revolution, declared war on England. Years later Spain would come to distrust the new American government.

In the last quarter of the 1700s, an amazing man entered the scene. It was said that by the time he died, he had ridden over twenty thousand miles on horseback. In 1774, Juan Bautista de Anza helped settle California to help ward off the threat of the Russians along the Pacific Coast. In 1776, the year the American colonists declared independence from Great Britain, he founded the city of San Francisco. That same year, the Spanish crown took the northern Spanish provinces out from under the control of the viceroy of Mexico and created "provincias internas" or internal provinces to be directed by a military officer known as the commandante general who was to be stationed in Chihuahua, the Mexican state which borders New Mexico today.

The tireless de Anza was appointed the first governor of New Mexico under the new system. In 1779, he launched an entirely innovative and very clever attack on the great Comanche leader Cuerno Verde. On this punitive expedition, he became the first Spaniard to follow the Rio Grande north to today's Colorado. There, doing battle with the Comanches, he discovered that the river took a sharp turn to the west, rather than going on to the North Pole as the Spanish maps had shown for years. With his defeat of the main Comanche elements, he was able to temporarily enlist their support in fighting the Apache, who had once again become a menace. More amazingly he was able to pacify the Moqui or Hopi in 1780, the last defiant pueblo to make peace.

By that time, the Hopi had been through a series of severe droughts and numerous, devastating epidemics of smallpox, a disease unknown in the New World until the Spanish came. By 1786, one year before the United States Constitution was completed, de Anza was able to strike a lasting peace with the Comanches, opening up trade to the East. Soon Pedro Vial, a French explorer hired by Spain, blazed a trail from Santa Fe to the Span-

ish Presidio at San Antonio. He also explored a route to St. Louis that eventually would lead to the development of the Santa Fe Trail. In 1776, the Domínguez–Escalante expedition left Santa Fe to explore trade routes to California (see Section I and Section III). In spite of the discovery of these new routes, northern New Mexico was still isolated except for the regular trading up and down the Camino Real, a distance of over five hundred miles from Taos to the trade centers in Chihuahua, taking six months for a packtrain to leave and return.

In 1800, the victorious Napoleon forced Spain to give Louisiana back to France. To Spain's dismay and Thomas Jefferson's delight, Napoleon sold the whole Louisiana Territory to the United States three years later, in 1803. Now New Spain would have to be wary of its former ally, the United States. In fact it was just two years later that those fears would be heightened. For in 1805, twenty-seven-year-old Lt. Zebulon Pike set out on an exploratory expedition to determine the extent of the lands the United States had acquired in the Louisiana Purchase. His travels led him to the Rockies. There, thinking he was near the Red River, he built a stockade just a few miles from the Rio Grande as it courses through the San Luis Valley. For reasons not entirely clear, one member of his group headed for Santa Fe. There, in the New Mexico capital, he was questioned. He told the Spanish about Pike's stockade in the San Luis Valley. Spanish forces headed north, picking up Pike and his men. They were taken to Santa Fe, questioned, and then sent back to the United States via a circuitous route to the south. No doubt Pike was able to observe the Spanish lands and their defenses.

But Pike and his men were not the first Americans to be seen by Santa Feans. A few months earlier, several American-based trappers had made their way to Santa Fe. From this point on, more and more American traders and trappers would find their way to New Mexico, especially to Taos which became a prime trading and commercial center. Soon the unrest which was spreading through New Spain like wildfire and which was manifested in the revolutionary acts of the inspired Mexican priest, Hidalgo, crept northward into New Mexico. The Mexico revolution of 1810–15 finally led to establishing Mexico's independence from

Salt Lake City ●

UTAH

COLORADO

Moab ●

**Old
Spanish Trail**

*To Independence,
Missouri*

● Durango

**Santa Fe
Trail**

*To Los Angeles,
California*

Taos ●

Flagstaff ●

● Gallup

Santa Fe ●

Phoenix ●

Albuquerque ●

*To Salina,
Kansas*

ARIZONA

NEW MEXICO

**Chihuahua
Trail
(El Camino
Real)**

**Coronado's
Route**

*To Veracruz,
Mexico*

El Paso ●

TEXAS

CHIHUAHUA

Historical Trails

Spain in 1821. Under the new Mexican law, the Pueblo Indians were granted full citizenship. Restrictive trade laws that had been adopted by the paranoid Spanish were abandoned and Taos, a local trade center for the Spanish and Indians for many years, now became a major trade center.

In 1812, St. Louis merchants were sending good-sized trade expeditions to Taos. By 1821, William Becknell brought the first major trade caravan over part of the same route Pedro Vial had traveled earlier. This route, called the Santa Fe Trail, originated at Independence, Missouri, near America's westernmost river port along the Missouri River. It ended eight hundred jarring miles later in Santa Fe. But it became a beehive of activity when both New Mexican and American traders began to realize that it was one thousand miles shorter than the Camino Real or Chihuahua

Trail route to Veracruz, the closest Mexican water port. Soon, more goods were rolling into Santa Fe at cheaper prices. Over the years, the Santa Fe Trail carried so much traffic that even today you will be able to see traces of wagon ruts near Fort Union National Monument, northeast of Santa Fe. Huge, red-wheeled freight wagons, pulled by spans of mules or yokes of oxen, brought hardware and calico to Santa Fe and hauled furs, hides, and Mexican mules and burros to Missouri. Yes,

Freight wagon

Burros

the legendary Missouri mules originally came from Mexico!

Within a short time, Santa Fe and Taos became major way stations as American traders pushed south along the Camino Real into northern Mexico, returning all the way home with pesos jingling in their pockets. All this activity in northern New Mexico attracted the likes of Kit Carson, Peg-leg Smith, Antoine Robidoux, and other well-known American mountain men. Kit Carson was so enthusiastic about Taos that he was reported to have said, "No man who has seen the women, heard the bells or smelled the piñon smoke of Taos will ever be able to leave." Needless to say, Carson married a Spanish woman and settled in Taos. His home there is still standing and has become an excellent museum accurately portraying early nineteenth-century life in northern New Mexico. Possibly because of new information brought back to New Mexico by the American mountain men, who had explored to the west, the Old Spanish Trail was developed within a few years (see Section I, "History"). Packtrains traveled its route from Santa Fe to Los Angeles, making Santa Fe an important commercial hub.

In the late 1820s, gold was discovered south of Santa Fe near Mount Chalchihuitl, not far from the ancient site of the Indian turquoise mines. By 1830, another strike was made at Tuerto. These were the first gold strikes west of the Mississippi and preceded the discovery of gold in California by twenty years. Now for the first time, northern New Mexico, the distant cousin of Spain and the ignored half brother of Mexico, began to flourish on its own.

But all was not well with the New Mexican people. In the late 1700s and early 1800s, the Spanish decided that if the Indians weren't converted to Christianity after 162 years, they never would be. The expense of maintaining missions in that remote country was more than Spain could afford. Consequently, the Franciscan priests were gradually withdrawn from the Indian pueblos. The removal of the Franciscans became even more widespread after the takeover by Mexico. The Mexicans, having just freed themselves from oppressive Mother Spain, were eager to rid their country of all Spanish influence, including religious influence. They ordered all Spanish-born Franciscans out of New Mexico in 1828.

Needless to say, the Spanish villagers of New Mexico were unhappy about the loss of contact with the mother church. From that point on, religious duties came more and more into the hands of secular clergymen and laymen. Over the years, they developed a unique form of Catholicism which continues to influence the area to this day. Carrying the belief of salvation through penance to its limits, the "Penitente" movement became more radical in its practices. Some of the rites of self-flagellation and punishment became so abhorrent to the mother church that the Penitentes were not allowed in traditional churches and were forced to build their own chapels. These they called "Moradas." Of course, the chapels had to be decorated without help from the organized church, so villagers began decorating the chapels themselves.

From this beginning sprang the fine tradition of New Mexican Spanish carvers and craftsmen who continue to turn out some of the most

Bulto

beautiful and unique pieces of religious and secular art in the United States today. The "santeros," as the craftsmen were called, became revered figures who often went from house to house carving and painting three-dimensional statues called bultos and painting religious figures on wood or tin, called retablos. In the early 1800s, almost all non-Indian Catholics belonged to the Penitente sect. It has been said that the Indians viewed the severe practices of this sect as a form of Spanish dementia.

In addition to resenting the loss of their beloved Franciscan priests, the New Mexicans bitterly resented the high taxes imposed on them from a distant, impersonal capital. This resentment came to a head in 1836, when Mexico reorganized the country, changing New Mexico's political status and installing a Mexican, rather than a native-born New Mexican, as governor. The atmosphere was once again ripe for revolt.

For the first time in New Mexico's long history, Spanish-Mexican villagers united with Pueblo Indians in an alliance that would spearhead two revolts in the following ten years. In 1837, some Taos residents, led by a General Chopón, established revolutionary headquarters at Santa Cruz. There, in a clash with government troops, the Mexican governor was forced to retreat. However, in anticipation of this, his escape route was cut off and he was captured at Santo Domingo Pueblo, where he was summarily killed and decapitated.

The insurgents took over the capital. The General Assembly of New Mexico joined the revolt by electing Jose González, an Indian living at Taos Pueblo, as governor. For the second time in history, the Palace of the Governors was occupied by a revolutionary leader from Taos Pueblo. But his rule was short lived. A little over a month later, General Manuel Armijo, representing the Mexican government, was appointed chief of a liberating army by that government. Reinforced with troops from Mexico, he marched from Albuquerque to Santa Fe. González and his followers, seeing the handwriting on the wall, retreated to Santa Cruz where they finally were overwhelmed. Armijo had González shot on the spot.

But the atmosphere was ripe for rebellion in other parts of Mexico as well. In 1835, settlers in Texas revolted and ran the Mexican citizens out of that part of Mexico, declaring their independence from Mexico in 1836. After being defeated by the Mexicans at the Alamo, the Texans came back to win the day at the Battle of San Jacinto. Texas became an independent nation. But the Republic of Texas was not to be annexed into the United States for another ten years. In 1841, the president of the newly independent Republic of Texas sent expeditionary forces to take the New Mexican capital at Santa Fe. Armijo, fresh from quelling rebellion there, got wind of the expedition and captured the Texas troops. Some were killed. Others were sent to Mexico in chains.

In 1845, the Republic of Texas was annexed into the United States. This brought an immediate break in diplomatic relations between Mexico and the United States. In spite of this break in relations, the United States government continued to seek control of California and New Mexico. The United States placed special emphasis on the notion that all the land claimed by the Republic of Texas east of the Rio Grande should be transferred to the United States because of the annexation of Texas. Mexico was unwilling to negotiate such a transfer. Consequently, in 1846, President James Polk declared war on Mexico. Gen. Stephen Watts Kearny, leader of the "Army of the West," first led his troops into New Mexico and then on to California. His arrival in New Mexico was a fateful day for General Armijo. First he took his troops over Apache Pass near Pecos to fend off the American Army. But then, for reasons not quite clear, he withdrew his resistance and retreated to Mexico. Kearny entered Santa Fe without a bullet being fired. The Americans called this takeover an occupation rather than a conquest. A third national flag now flew over Santa Fe, marking the end of 248 years of Spanish and Mexican rule.

Within a few weeks, Kearny ordered the building of Fort Marcy. This massive, star-shaped adobe fort, located north of the plaza, was the first American military post in the Southwest. It is no longer standing today. Having completed only part of his mission, Kearny appointed Charles Bent of Taos as first governor of the New Mexico area. Leaving Santa Fe in the hands of a subordinate, Kearny headed west to California. A few months later in January of 1847, intrigue was brewing once again at Taos. The Spanish were fearful the United States would interfere with their land rights. A plot originating among the Spanish, which enlisted the aid of the Taos Pueblo Indians, was devised.

In January 1847, the Spanish and Pueblo Indians struck at Taos, killing the Catholic prefect, the prosecuting attorney, and the sheriff. But the final prize was finding Governor Bent in Taos. He had come there to celebrate Christmas with members of his family. The marauders stormed his home, scalped Bent alive, and then riddled him with bullets. United States troops from Santa Fe immediately came to the rescue. With the help of several veteran American mountain men like Dick Woottan and Jim Beckworth and able American soldiers like Col. Sterling Price and Capt. John Burgwin, the insurgents were defeated at Santa Cruz and Embudo. In the final battle, the Americans stormed the mission church at Taos Pueblo where the last renegades had taken cover.

With cannons blazing, they blew holes in the thick adobe walls. They routed the Indians from the demolished church. Two hundred Indians were killed. Those who lived were tried and executed on the spot.

But it wasn't until the signing of the Treaty of Guadalupe Hidalgo in 1848 that New Mexico was officially transferred to the United States. In 1850, Congress paid the state of Texas for its claims to the land east of the Rio Grande and established the territory of New Mexico. By 1853, the western borders of New Mexico were established after purchasing land from Mexico in the Gadsden Purchase. Northern New Mexico, now a territory of the United States, continued to suffer from Apache, Navajo, and Comanche raids. The United States government built several protective forts. Fort Union, the first one to be constructed in 1851, stood ninety miles east of Santa Fe.

Wagon trains or stagecoaches found the fort a welcome oasis in a desert filled with marauding Comanche and Kiowa Indians. Today, you can visit the ruins of the fort. They are highlighted by an interpretive trail through them. Most of the American forts remained active until about 1886, when the Apache Indians were finally subdued. Another fort to be established was Cantonment Burgwin, which was built in 1852 to help ward off Comanche attacks from the east. With Comanche raids drying up, the fort was closed and its detachment of troops of the First Dragoons left in 1860. You will be able to see parts of this reconstructed log fort today on the outskirts of Taos (see "A Day Traveling through Spanish New Mexico: A Narrative Account").

Aside from the political and military intrigue

Cantonment Burgwin

of the mid-1800s, life in the villages went on much as before. Nonetheless, the takeover by the United States brought two major changes directly to the people, which established the tone for many of the cultural nuances you will see today. The 1848 Treaty of Guadalupe Hidalgo stated that property rights legally held under Mexican law would be respected by the United States. But the concept of land ownership held by the newly arrived Americans was entirely different from the concepts practiced by the Spanish and Mexicans. Conflict arose on several points which, over the years, would create an atmosphere of rancor and bitterness.

Many of the native New Mexicans lost land in the attempt to translate their holdings into the rigid system of surveys and measurements taken by the Americans. The Spanish had used natural objects like trees and rocks to define the boundaries of their property. Strict surveys employed by the Americans often diminished the size of certain parcels of land. Under Spanish and Mexican law, land grants had not only been made to Spanish families for plots of land around their homes and adjacent to the acequias or irrigation ditches, but to each village as well. This large community-owned parcel of land outside the village was called the "ejido" or the commons. All families in the village shared in its use. Over time, the Spanish lost much of this ejido land because the concept of community-held land was foreign to the American system of land ownership and was therefore subject to question and could easily be challenged. The Spanish and Mexicans did not impose taxes on land. The United States government did. Not only taxes but also assessments of one sort or another were placed on property.

Probably, the bulk of the land was lost through foreclosure when the Spanish landowners could not afford to pay the taxes or just did not understand what taxes were all about. After all, the Americans in power did not issue tax statements in the Spanish language. Those foreclosed lands were eventually sold to speculating Anglos. Of the original thirty-five million acres of land held by native New Mexicans before the United States took over, those early Spanish families now own very little. That which was not wrested away from them by United States law the Spanish people have held

onto faithfully.

This devotion to the land has given rise to the phrase still heard today that he who sells his land sells his mother. This strict retention of small family plots has led to so much subdivision of the land that some pieces of property have taken on strange proportions. Some have cited parcels of property that are 26 inches wide by 1.5 miles long and that are owned by seven or eight heirs. You will notice, as you travel around the Spanish villages, the land takes on the appearance of a postage stamp album, with each little square or oblong rancho fenced and farmed separately from the adjacent properties.

The United States occupation also had an effect on the vital religious life of the original Spanish and Mexican residents. Over the years, they had known many changes in their religious leadership. First there were the Franciscans, provided by the Spanish, and then came the secular leadership of the very devout laity. Finally, the people came under the leadership of a few native priests, like José Martinez of Taos, who were born in New Mexico but who were trained in the churches of Mother Mexico.

The United States ecclesiastical authorities made yet another change. They appointed a dynamic Frenchman, Jean Baptiste Lamy, as bishop of the new diocese. Although he had been working in Cincinnati, his heart was still in France. He began a crash program of bringing European Catholicism back to New Mexico. He filled vacant missions and parishes with priests imported from France and other locations in Europe. In 1852, he brought the Sisters of Loretto (from Kentucky) to establish a girls' academy at Santa Fe. Shortly thereafter, he brought an order of the Christian Brothers from France to found Saint Michael's College. He imported French architects and Italian stonemasons to begin construction of the Romanesque Cathedral of Saint Francis in Santa Fe in 1869. He also ordered the construction of the Gothic chapel of Our Lady of Light, the Loretto Chapel. But it was not long after the American takeover that the first Protestants would also make the scene. The first Protestant church, built by the Baptists, was constructed in 1854. That building is no longer standing, but today you can see a lovely old adobe built in the early 1900s by the

Presbyterians, who have occupied that site since 1866 (see "Half-Day Tour of Santa Fe, North of the River").

Lamy immediately came into conflict with the Penitentes, the sect that had grown out of the Third Order of Saint Francis and that had flourished in its own peculiar way in the absence of the Franciscan priests. Los Hermanos de Luz or the Brothers of the Light, as these Penitentes were known, had continued the development and perpetuation of severe religious practices in the fifty-year hiatus when there were so few priests. Flagellations had become so severe that often people were thrashed until the flesh was torn away to the bone. Others were allegedly crucified on the cross at Eastertime.

In spite of these excesses, the Penitentes engaged in many good works. They ministered to village people at times of sickness and death. In difficult times, their unfailing belief in their religious practices helped to keep their faith alive. One of the lasting legacies of the Penitente movement was the development of the great santero tradition, where artisans traveled from village to village carving bultos, three-dimensional religious figures carved from wood, and retablos, religious figures painted on tin or wood. But in 1856, Lamy took a strong stand to limit some of the Penitente practices. Since that time there has been gradual moderation of the Penitente rituals. It is estimated that twenty-five hundred Penitentes exist in northern New Mexico today, contributing to the rich cultural mix you will see in your travels.

By the 1860s, another lode of gold had been discovered in New Mexico, leading to a minor boom that brought more American settlers. The American influence on the area was growing and even becoming visible in the architecture. The previous architecture, variously called Spanish Colonial, Franciscan, or Pueblo, gave way to Territorial Pueblo, showing traces of the neo-Grecian and Victorian influences which were sweeping the middle part of the United States at that time. You will see many examples of this style of architecture. One of the best is the Pinckney R. Tully House in Santa Fe. American technological advances replaced dirt floors with wood, introduced kiln-fired bricks to cap adobe side walls, and brought in glass for windows. The Americans also brought with them the design for pitched roofs which slowly began to show up among the flat-roofed adobe homes.

During this period of increased settlement, the gold strikes in Colorado were underway and the Civil War broke out. Shortly after the war started, there was another invasion of New Mexico from Texas. This time it was under the Confederate flag. The invasion force streamed north out of El Paso, hoping to conquer New Mexico and thereby gain control of the rich Colorado gold mines and interrupt the flow of gold and trade goods from California to the north. In 1862, the upstart Confederate troops marched through Albuquerque and on to Santa Fe without contest. They raised the fourth flag over the Palace of the Governors. Their rule was short-lived, for a few weeks later the Confederates were defeated at the "Gettysburg of the West" en route to attempt the takeover of the Union stronghold, Fort Union. Confederate troops, misjudging the strength and position of the Union forces, retreated back to Texas, and once again the United States flag was raised over Santa Fe and New Mexico. A third invasion by Texas would not occur until later in the twentieth century, when Texas tourists "discovered" northern New Mexico and began to flock there in unprecedented numbers.

In 1866, gold was discovered near Elizabethtown north of Taos. But by 1879, more significant strikes were made near the location of the earlier gold strikes in New Mexico, south of Santa Fe. Cerrillos, Madrid, and Golden became boomtowns. By the 1880s, Albuquerque had become a railroad town, even boasting a large number of Irish railroad workers, and soon, Santa Fe, previously neglected by the major lines, would have its own railroad. The Denver and Rio Grande pushed down from Chama to Española, finally reaching Santa Fe. The line was dubbed the "Chili Line" as it transported carload after carload of famous New Mexican Rio Grande Valley peppers out of the state. By 1890, most of the mineral boom days in northern New Mexico were over and the territory concentrated on moving toward statehood, finally reaching that goal in 1912, as the forty-seventh state.

With the excitement of the gold rush gone, northern New Mexico settled down to become the agriculturally based, sheep-raising culture it had been under Spanish rule, when the first churro and merino sheep were brought to New Mexico in the livestock herds of Coronado, Oñate, and others. It was from these animals that the sheep industry got its start. Both the Indians and the Spanish grazed sheep in the pastoral mountain valleys of northern New Mexico and on the community lands, mentioned earlier, that were granted by the Spanish and Mexican governments. Eventually though, overgrazing of the grass and excessive cutting of the timber led to such severe erosion that, by the end of the nineteenth century, the grazing lands were not productive.

In 1906, the United States government, in its zealousness to put natural country into the public domain, grabbed up much of this "ejido" or community land. In Taos County, the United States Forest Service came to own 44 percent of the county. Although the people were able to obtain grazing permits from the government, it was easier for some than for others because of the politics involved. Too often favoritism was the name of the game. Within time, the United States government felt the land was being overgrazed and the number of grazing permits was reduced, hitting at the lifeblood of many of the people. Land around Indian reservations was also taken by the government about the same time. In one of these land grabs, twelve miles from Taos Pueblo, the government gobbled up, without compensation, Taos Pueblo's sacred Blue Lake, site of religious rites and ceremonies since A.D. 1200. After years and years of politicking, debate, and bitterness, the Taos Indians, in 1971, won their long-fought battle and the United States government returned this hallowed ground to them.

The Spanish people were not so fortunate. Less organized and unable to wield the clout at the federal level that the Pueblo Indians did, some sat in smoldering anger until 1967, when all hell broke loose. Led by a Texas-born Hispanic, who had formed an alliance called Alianza Federal de Mercedes (Federal Alliance of Land Grants), which sought to regain the ejido land for New Mexico's Spanish descendants, a violent revolt once more hit New Mexico in the summer of 1967. Occasionally you will still hear mention of the courthouse raid in Tierra Amarilla, where three law officers were wounded and a deputy sheriff and news-

paper reporter were abducted. That was the highwater mark for the Alianza. After that, several factions developed among its members and the movement lost much of its impetus. Although the "raid" focused national attention on the issue, the ownership of the lands in question remains unchanged.

But these days you are apt to read and hear more about the explosion of the arts in Santa Fe than anything else. Perhaps the first intimation that northern New Mexico was to become an inspirational haven for writers and artists came during the term of Gov. Lew Wallace (1878–81) who, while occupying the Palace of the Governors in Santa Fe, wrote the famous epic *Ben Hur,* the first Biblical novel in United States history. He was certainly a cut above the rowdy frontier types who had prevailed until then. His predecessors were known to have thrown valuable state documents helter-skelter into back rooms under leaky roofs. At other times, when no one knew what to do with the increasing mounds of public records, the problem of storing these was allegedly solved by stuffing them down the outhouse "two holer." Gov. William A. Pile is most often accused of these acts.

Into this colorful, stranger-than-fiction atmosphere came two well-known American artists in 1898. Bert Phillips was one of the first. He had heard about northern New Mexico from one of his teachers in Paris, Joseph Henry Sharp, who had come through the area earlier. With his fellow artist, Ernest L. Blumenschein, he set out from Colorado on a sketching trip to Mexico. Their wagon broke down north of Taos. Phillips left Blumenschein and went into Taos to have the wheel repaired. While riding along, he was inspired and overwhelmed by the scenery and the people. These two men settled in Taos and were later joined by Sharp who, with his earlier visit in the 1880s, is credited as the first artist to come to New Mexico. Then came Berninghaus, Higgins, Ufer, and Dunton.

But it was not until Mabel Dodge arrived from New York with her painter husband Maurice Sterne, in 1916, that the town began to buzz. Mabel had previously been married to architect Edwin Dodge. She had established herself as a wealthy socialite and arts patron when she and her husband renovated the Villa Curoni in Florence, Italy

There, for ten years, they held court, hosting the likes of Gertrude Stein and Alice B. Toklas. Wherever Mabel went, she made a big splash and her career was carefully watched by writers and artists alike early in the twentieth century. She began extending invitations to her friends to come to Taos.

Mabel called and the famous and famous-to-be came. Before she died, her guest list read like a Who's Who in American arts and literature. John Marin, Georgia O'Keeffe, Robert Henri, Marsden Hartley, E. A. Robinson, Edward Weston, Willa Cather, and D. H. Lawrence were but a few who visited Taos at her invitation. Some of these people returned to New Mexico and took up residence there. So it is not by happenstance that Taos, a town of a little more than three thousand inhabitants, has over eighty arts and crafts galleries and more than one hundred resident painters. Stemming from a small nucleus of five painters in the 1920s who became known as the Los Cincos Pintores, Santa Fe has become equally blessed with an even larger component of painters and writers, as well as an unprecedented number of arts and crafts galleries for a city of its size.

The tourist industry began in earnest in the 1920s and 1930s. The relative isolation of the area, especially after abandonment of the "Chili Line," meant that Santa Fe, Taos, and all that was between would not be hit as hard by the variety of technological changes sweeping the country. The growth of the area remained fairly steady until World War II. In 1943, the Los Alamos Ranch School on the Pajarito Plateau was taken over by the United States government as a secret hideaway for Robert J. Oppenheimer and his compatriots to work on developing the atomic bomb. The population and economy of the state have been greatly influenced by a variety of federal projects since that time.

Today, the three linked, but never-to-be-united cultures go about their separate ways. Things are peaceful in northern New Mexico, but all is not well. Poverty is on a level with that of Appalachia. The mean level of education is well below high school for the Hispanics. Although better now, in the 1970s the average level of education for a Hispanic over age twenty-five was five years of schooling. Unemployment is high. None-theless, the richness of the three cultures that you will see as a tourist still sustains the people. Modern technology is finally making life easier, but the old ways often persist.

In your visit to New Mexico, you may see Hispanic ladies from distant villages give each other a warm kiss and embrace, European style, at one of the colorful religious feast days. Or you may see people from a Spanish village follow their Spanish-born priest to the acequias or water ditches in May in a centuries-old procession which honors San Ysidro de Labrador, the patron saint of the fields, to pray for the fertility and productivity of the land. And you may also see in the pueblos the village chief, the cacique or religious priest, announce on a fine spring day that it is time to plant the fields because the sun has reached the right spot along the mountain's ridgeline. Then that hooded, mysterious figure, the pregonero, will climb to the top of the pueblo and, like the town criers of old, announce to all that it is time to plant. Nowhere else but in northern New Mexico will you discover such a unique center of foreign culture slapdab in the heart of "Apple Pie America."

Seeing the Spanish Rio Grand Country

Albuquerque

Vibrant, expanding Albuquerque, rapidly approaching a half million citizens, is finally overcoming its past reputation as a place to "get through" as more and more it becomes a place "to go to." Situated out of the mountains above the northern edge of the high, but flat, sunbaked Chihuahuan Desert, at 5,300 feet elevation, Albuquerque has always been either too hot, too windy, too dusty, too cold, or too barren for most travelers' tastes. A decade or two ago, cars on old U.S. Highway 66 used to roar through the town, their occupants looking neither right nor left as they sped towards far-flung destinations to the east and west or sought the cooler elevations of the mountains to the north and south. The Santa Fe train stopped there, back then, just as Amtrak does now. There was always a brief stop to see the Indians selling their wares on the station platform before speeding on to Chicago or Los Angeles. And still today, travelers disembarking at the Albuquerque airport often rush pell-mell to the mountain heartland towns of Spanish New Mexico, Santa Fe, and Taos, hardly taking notice of New Mexico's largest city.

But things are changing. More and more travelers are finding that although disjointed, sprawling Albuquerque may be hard to love, it is easy to like and is an interesting, pleasant place to spend some time. Modern Albuquerque, the hot-air balloon capital of the world, is also the educational, industrial, medical, and commercial jet air capital of New Mexico. Growing University of New Mexico with its twenty-four thousand students and able faculty has brought considerable life to this desert city. Once a cultural dustbin, Albuquerque is out to change its image as new stores, shops, galleries, and museums reflect a level of sophistication previously unknown there. The city seems filled with new, vibrant, young residents from Maine to California who have joined this city's progressive New Mexicans in the effort to create a better place to live.

More and more, Albuquerque has realized its potential as host city to thousands of jet travelers who rely on the only commercial jet airport for miles around. There in the comfortable surroundings of the modern airport, whose architecture reflects the ambience of the region, you will catch a glimpse of New Mexico's three cultures. Pueblo Indians in traditional dress prepare to board a plane to Seattle, Washington, where they will give seminars about the way they dig their clay and make their pottery. From New Mexico's eastern plains, Anglo cowboys dressed like they were born that way discuss an upcoming helicopter trip to look after their oil and gas holdings. Meanwhile, a group of Spanish New Mexicans who hold government jobs in Santa Fe buzz excitedly in Spanish about their upcoming trip to Washington, D.C.

Some Albuquerque Tour Sites

A more in-depth introduction to north central New Mexico's diverse cultures has been arranged by Albuquerque's city fathers. "Old Town" Albu-

San Felipe de Neri Church, Albuquerque

querque has been beautifully preserved to capture the essence of the Spanish tradition of this city which proudly boasts a Hispanic population of over 36 percent. Old Town is one of the most interesting and charming sections of this 276-year-old settlement. In fact, the city got its start there when about a dozen families from the Bernalillo area created a new community in 1706, the third major "villa" to be developed in New Mexico. In the center of this approximately five-square-block area located between Rio Grande Boulevard on the west, Mountain Road on the north, and Central Avenue on the south, is a grassy, tree-shaded plaza from which all activity stems. There Texans and New Yorkers mingle near two old Confederate cannons, reminders that the Confederate government ruled Albuquerque for a short time in 1862. Anchoring the north side of the plaza is San Felipe de Neri Church. Although that lovely old adobe building is not the original structure, having been enlarged and remodeled many times, church services have been held at this location every Sunday without fail since 1706 when the original church was first constructed on this site.

Across the street from the west side of the plaza and fronting the church is the visitor center on Romero Street. You can pick up useful information about Albuquerque there. From the plaza, spreading in all directions for several blocks, the adobe and territorial-style buildings, many former homes of Spanish families, line the streets offering the traveler a variety of shops and restaurants. There are several fine Indian arts and crafts shops,

as well as one of the finest contemporary craft shops in the region. Within walking distance, on the northwest corner of Old Town, is the Albuquerque Museum on Mountain Road. The rotating art exhibits and the museum shop are worth a visit. The shop carries some regional crafts as well as an excellent supply of books about the area. Walking tours of Old Town depart from the museum several days a week. For inquiries, telephone 1-505-766-7878.

But don't stop there. Walk from the museum across the street (Mountain Road) to the large, sand-colored modernistic building that houses the New Mexico Museum of Natural History. Touted as the only state-sponsored museum of its kind to be built in the United States in this century, it is well worth a visit. Its attractions are many. The most modern technological advances in digital sound systems, edge-lit fibre optics, and polarizing filters are used to recreate a variety of ancient prehistoric phenomena, making this museum an experience not to be missed. The museum's well-conceived, almost magical exhibits transform you into a time traveler by taking you on a journey spanning 4.5 billion years of this region's natural history. As you go sleuthing through the museum following the well-laid out Timetracks, you will learn about the forces that helped create the earth as it is today, including the development of the phenomenon known as the Continental Divide, which splits our continent into two distinct watersheds. Along the way, you will have a chance to walk into the heated inferno of a simulated volcano (complete with a realistic illusion of flowing magma), view unique three-dimensional kinetic light collages that depict prehistoric scenes, and stroll through the cool, damp interior of an Ice Age cave complete with incredibly realistic stalagmites and stalactites. And if you are fascinated by the Rio Grande, you will be glad to see it laid out in a detailed miniature form of it coursing through New Mexico. The museum is designed, wherever possible, with hands-on exhibits, most notable of which are in the section called the Age of Giants where replicas as well as actual reconstructed skeletons of dinosaurs, mammoths, and flying reptiles can be experienced firsthand.

The museum's gift shop is an experience in itself with a wide selection of books, replicas, models, and toys that echo the biological, geological, and paleontological exhibits of the museum. This museum is the sort of place that will have a lasting educational effect on young and old learners alike. In addition, the museum offers a series of expedition tours to many of the natural history sites in the Southwest. Open daily. For more information, write New Mexico Museum of Natural History, P.O. Box 7010, Albuquerque, New Mexico 87194. Telephone: 1-505-841-8836.

There is one natural history site you can find on your own without having to take a tour. In just a few minutes you can drive from the eighty-five-foot-long, true-to-life model of the Rio Grande in the New Mexico Museum of Natural History to the actual banks of that fabled river. There near the east bank is the Rio Grande Nature Center State Park. Although located in the city limits, the center seems far removed from the urban environment. The bunkerlike, glass-enclosed, low-slung concrete building that serves as a visitor center rests in the middle of a bosque. Bosque is the Spanish word for forest or grove of trees. And how well it applies to the 270 acres of century-old cottonwood groves, salt cedar and tamarisk thickets, and mature Russian olive trees, which comprise this narrow verdant strip along the river's edge. Bosques occur many places along the course of the Rio Grande, and where they do, they serve as a refuge for all sorts of wildlife giving them sanctuary from the harshness of the adjoining desertlands. Coyote, fox, muskrat, and beaver share these verdant living spaces with turtles, roadrunners, and owls, while all seem to tolerate the temporary visitation of migrating Canada geese and sandhill cranes.

Visitor center exhibits range from such river-related topics as ecology and geology. The glass enclosed library and observation room focuses on the brimming bird life around a three-acre pond and marsh area where you may see some of the over 260 species of resident and migrating birds that inhabit the Rio Grande bosques throughout the year. There you are just as apt to see a pied-billed grebe as a black phoebe. Over two miles of trails through the Rio Grande bosque and along the riverbank reveal even more of the natural flora and fauna as they wind through forests, grasslands, and sandflats. At certain times of the year you can catch glimpses of many species, including ash-throated flycatchers, blue grosbeaks, and black-capped chickadees. There are naturalist-led walks on Sunday afternoon. The small bookstore and gift shop have a nice selection of titles on Southwest ecology, birds, wildflowers, and other natural history subjects. Open daily except for major holidays. To find the Rio Grande Nature Center, drive from the New Mexico Natural History Museum to Rio Grande Boulevard and turn right or north. Travel about one and one-half miles to Candelaria Road. Turn left or west on Candelaria and follow it a little over one-half mile to the visitor center. Telephone: 1-505-344-7240.

Although Albuquerque has a very small Indian population, it has recently become the home of the Museums of the Indian Pueblo Cultural Center, two blocks north of U.S. Interstate Highway 40 West on Twelfth Street Northwest. Telephone 1-505-843-7270. Opened to the public in 1976, it is jointly owned by the nineteen Indian pueblos of New Mexico, some of which are but a few miles out of Albuquerque. It provides a fine introduction to the Pueblo Indian life you will see later as you drive north along the Rio Grande. Try to see it if you can. The museum is in a beautiful contemporary structure, which echoes the graceful architectural lines of prehistoric Pueblo Bonito at Chaco Canyon. Its excellent permanent exhibits detail Pueblo Indian life from prehistoric to modern times. The favorite of many visitors is the exhibit of contemporary Pueblo life. There each pueblo is individually showcased with photo-

Indian Petroglyph State Park

graphs of the villages to demonstrate how the people live. In addition, a complete selection of handcrafts made in each village is displayed to familiarize the visitor with this important and increasingly well-known aspect of Pueblo life. So if you are seriously interested in Indian crafts, be certain to drop by there to see this informative exhibit. An hour there will familiarize you with the best of the Pueblo Indian arts and crafts. On Sunday afternoon, Indian dances are held at the center. The cultural center also has a large shop selling high-quality Indian crafts. The Pueblo Kitchen Restaurant offers typical Pueblo and Indian foods at modest prices in a well-designed, comfortable, modern setting. There you can sample Indian fry bread, posole, and Indian tacos, as well as some of New Mexico's favorites such as tamales, chili, and burritos (see "Albuquerque–Food").

If the exhibits at the Pueblo Cultural Center inspire you, take another hour or two to walk the trails at Indian Petroglyph State Park on the west side of Albuquerque. On Albuquerque's West Mesa within sight of over a half-dozen volcanic cinder cones, you will find some of the Southwest's finest examples of prehistoric rock art. They were carved by the resourceful ancestors of the Pueblo Indians sometime between A.D. 1100 and 1600. And they must have kept busy. For packed into the boulders and other lava formations along a serpentine seventeen-mile-long, three-block-wide volcanic escarpment are an estimated fifteen thousand petroglyphs. The incised lines appear gray or white against the dark surfaces of the porous lava rock.

The state park, managed by the city of Albuquerque, presently preserves only a small portion of this prehistoric art gallery. Much of it backs up to several of Albuquerque's rapidly expanding west side subdivisions bounded by the Volcanic Cliffs development to the south and the Paradise Hills addition to the north. An ongoing conflict between developers and preservationists may soon be solved by the National Park Service, which is interested in giving national monument status to an expanded preservation area. Meanwhile there is plenty to see along the state park's three major walking trails. The main paved trail slowly takes you to the top of the lava heap. Along the way you will encounter rock art images reflecting the prehistoric artist's view of himself, the sun, stars and, of course, southwestern clouds. And there are ceremonial designs and kachinalike figures, not to mention a whole menagerie of plant, insect, bird, and animal likenesses. And if that isn't enough, atop the ridge of these volcanic cliffs, you can see forever as your gaze stretches from the Rio Grande and its valley eastward toward the Sandia Mountains. Picnic shelters and water are available in the park, which is open daily except Tuesdays, Wednesday, and major holidays. Extended hours and days in the summer. Telephone: 1-505-823-4016. The park is approximately eight miles from both the Indian Pueblo Cultural Center or Old Town. To get there, take Interstate 40 west across the Rio Grande bridge to the first exit, the Coors Boulevard-Rio Rancho Exit 155. Follow Coors Road north to the fourth stoplight, which is at the junction with Montano Road. Turn left on Montano Road and travel west about two miles until reaching Unser Boulevard. Turn right on Unser Boulevard and follow it about one-half mile to the park. The park entrance is at 6900 Unser Boulevard at the base of the lava cliffs.

The University of New Mexico contributes greatly to the culture of the city. It is unique in the world, as all of its architecture is in the Spanish Pueblo style. It is a pleasant campus with tree-shaded walkways and refreshing fountains. The Maxwell Museum of Anthropology is located on the west end of the campus. Its permanent exhibit, "People in the Southwest," traces the history of earliest man in the area to modern times. Its superbly mounted rotating exhibits feature both regional and world cultures in depth. The museum gift shop offers a wide array of Pueblo, Navajo, Mexican, and South American crafts. The museum is located on Redondo Drive just off University Boulevard one block north of Grand Avenue. No fee is required. Telephone: 1-505-277-4404. Also free and on the campus is the outstanding Geology Museum, the Jonson Gallery, featuring contemporary art (1-505-277-4967), and the Institute of Meteorites Museum (1-505-277-2747). For further inquiries, call the University of New Mexico's Information Office at 1-505-277-0111. Just two blocks south of the university is the informative but small Spanish History Museum, which tells the story of the Spanish people in this country from early times to present. The exhibits include information on the founding families of New Mexico, Spanish heraldic coats-of-arms, and the influences of the Spanish on the history and culture of New Mexico. A small gift shop sells books relating to Spanish-American history as well as framed, illustrated Spanish coats-of-arms. Located at 221 Lead Southeast between Harvard and Yale. Open only on Saturday and Sunday except by appointment on weekdays. For hours and other information, telephone 1-505-268-7805.

And if you have more time while in this area, travel east from the University of New Mexico on Central Avenue or U.S. Highway 66 about four and one-half miles to Wyoming Boulevard. Turn right on Wyoming Boulevard and drive approximately one and one-half miles to the air force security station. Just beyond the Kirtland Air Force Base security gate in Building 20358 is the National Atomic Museum. Exhibits reveal all aspects of atomic power from wartime to domestic energy production. Energy production is a second major focus of the museum since it emphasizes other energy sources such as geothermal and solar. Solar power gets more than its share of attention in the sunny Southwest, especially in New Mexico where all kinds of solar technologies are incorporated into the fabric of everyday living. In fact one of the most eye-catching and intriguing exhibits you will see is the Power Tower just south of the museum. There you will witness one of the most sophisticated solar collectors in the world. Acres of solar mirrors nearby focus the power of their reflected light on the solar collector at the top of the

tower. There a chamber of molten salt receives the collected, concentrated light and converts it to heat. You must stop at the Wyoming Boulevard gate for a free pass before entering the museum. Open daily. Tours of the Tower Power Monday through Friday afternoons. Telephone: 1-505-844-8443.

Tours Around Albuquerque

Coronado State Monument and Park by way of Corrales, New Mexico

The monument is located just outside of Bernalillo, a small community just north of Albuquerque. To reach Coronado State Monument by way of a scenic route from Albuquerque, take the Rio Grande Boulevard Exit from Interstate 40 and follow Rio Grande Boulevard (New Mexico Highway 194) through the very nice Los Ranchos de Albuquerque residential district approximately six and one-half miles to Alameda Road (New Mexico Highway 46). Turn left or west onto Alameda Road, cross the bridge over the Rio Grande and in slightly less than one mile, at the corner of the Las Tiendas de Corrales Shopping Center, turn right onto Corrales Road. Follow it north as it leads you into the historic, rural Spanish settlement of Corrales. Watch your speed for as the sign posted on the outskirts of town a few years ago admonished, "Drive slow and see the town, drive fast and see the Judge." Corrales is a picturesque rural community with its many lovely old adobes and ranchitos scattered along the lush Rio Grande bosque where the fertile soil yields up an abundance of corn, chiles, and apples. For such a small community it has an abundance of good luncheon and dinner restaurants as well as a small and charming bed-and-breakfast inn. (See "Staying There—Albuquerque—Lodging.") Continue on north through Corrales about six and one-half miles to the junction with New Mexico Highway 528. Turn right (in the direction of Cuba and Farmington) and drive four and one-half miles to the junction with

Kiva mural, Coronado National Monument

New Mexico Highway 44. Take a right and watch for the signed spur road to the monument taking off to the left in less than a mile.

Although dedicated to Coronado, this excellent museum and the ruins around it focus mostly on the Indian culture that Coronado found at this location, rather than on the early Spanish culture, which archaeologists had hoped to find at this site. Little evidence has been found to support the notion that Coronado stayed at this village called Kuaua, one of the Tigeux Pueblos. But scientists did find an astonishing number of kiva murals painted one on top of another, that span the years between A.D. 1350 and 1600. The original murals were removed from the kiva walls and are displayed in the museum. Please note that this is one of the most outstanding exhibits of its kind in the Southwest. These murals resemble the intricacy and beauty of the Hopi art found in the ruins of ancient Awat'ovi (see Section II, "The Hopi: A Long and Continuous Past").

In addition to the display inside, you can tour the ruins outside on well-marked trails around the museum. There you can descend a ladder into a reconstructed kiva where the original murals were found. You will see replicas of some of the murals

that have been reproduced on the walls. Most of the partial mud walls of the ruins are twentieth-century reconstructions. They were rebuilt using Spanish-style adobe bricks rather than the original Pueblo Indian construction of mud turtlebacks or mud laid up in courses. A small gift shop sells some crafts from the pueblos and a few books related to the Pueblo culture. A picnic area and campground are nearby. Almost all of the monument lands offer good views of the Rio Grande. Open daily except major holidays. Telephone: 1-505-867-5351.

After leaving the monument travel New Mexico Highway 44 east back across the Rio Grande. You can then return to Albuquerque by turning right or south on New Mexico Highway 313 through Bernalillo. This is a slower, scenic route roughly paralleling the old Camino Real. Or you can travel a little farther east to Interstate 25 where you can either turn north to Santa Fe or return to Albuquerque. The round-trip driving distance from Albuquerque is a little less than forty miles.

Sandia Peak and Sandia Tramway

For panoramas out over the desert, either drive to Sandia Peak or take the tramway up to the top, elevation 10,678 feet. The views up there will knock your socks off daytime or nighttime as eleven thousand square miles of desert, mountains, and plateaus unfold before you. Some have called the Sandia Mountains an "afterthought" of the Rockies. Sandia means watermelon in Spanish. That place name was given to the mountain, as well as the pueblo of the same name, by the Spanish. No one is certain why. Some say it was because of the watermelons that grew in the valley near the pueblo. A more popular notion has it that the Spanish thought the Sandia Mountains resembled a watermelon, either because of the striped appearance of the rocks along the west face or because of the pink reflection of the mountain's rocks at sunset.

To reach Sandia Crest by car, drive east 16 miles on U.S. Interstate Highway 40. Take exit 175 north on New Mexico Highway 14 through Cedar Crest. Turn left on New Mexico Highway 44 and follow the signs to the top. One-way driving time is about forty-five minutes. Alternatively, you can take the Sandia Aerial Tramway up the west side of the mountain. That 2.7-mile, fifteen-minute-long ride is the longest tramway ride in the United States. The tram terminal can be reached by driving 5 miles north of Albuquerque on U.S. Interstate Highway 25 to Tramway Road Exit, then 4.5 miles east to the station. There is a fee for parking as well as a tram fee. Telephone: 1-505-298-8518. A restaurant and complete facilities are available on top.

Continue north on New Mexico Highway 14 for an interesting alternative route to Santa Fe. This excellent two-lane paved road, dubbed the Turquoise Trail, winds through the scenic high desert to the old mining towns of Golden, Madrid, and Cerrillos. Mining relics of a bygone era dot the countryside. The old mining towns are not ghost towns any longer. Some of New Mexico's finest artists and craftspeople now inhabit these isolated towns, finding them a haven for their creative work. All along the route, you will see old buildings that have been converted into shops and galleries that market the visual arts produced there.

A Three-Quarters-of-a-Day Auto Tour West of Albuquerque to Ácoma Pueblo

Sixty-five miles west of Albuquerque at a cloud-scraping elevation of 7,000 feet is the oldest and most dramatically situated Indian pueblo in New Mexico. Sometimes called the Sky City, Ácoma Pueblo spreads out across 70 acres of a flat mesa top, which caps a huge, malformed hunk of sandstone jutting like an island in the sky 367 feet above the surrounding desert. Blending with the tan rock from which it rises, this exposed yet almost completely camouflaged sentinel village of rocks and mud overlooks 344,000 acres of arid Ácoma farming and grazing land where corn fields are patiently nurtured, and cattle and sheep graze. It is a scene of splendid isolation and solitude that has been on hand since the village was first inhabited in the twelfth century. The Ácoma people, who speak the ancient western Keresan language, proudly assert that theirs is the oldest continually inhabited city in the United States. And who is to quibble, except of course their western pueblo neighbors at Old Oraibi village on the Hopi Reservation who assert a similar claim. Atop the mesa you know you have stepped far back into time as you walk the dusty streets, for you will see weathered kiva ladders stretching skyward, reminding you that an ancient religion is still being practiced

there. And you will see one of the oldest, largest, and noblest Spanish mission churches ever to be built in the Southwest, with its two bell towers reaching to the heavens—a symbol of the first white contact in 1540, and a reminder of the bitter struggles with the Spanish that subsequently ensued. (See this section, "History.") There are only a few people who continue to live on the mesa nowadays. Ácoma's three thousand citizens began drifting away several decades ago when it became evident that parents and their children living in this remote village would have to be separated in order for the children to receive an education. In addition, the lack of an adequate water supply and modern energy sources there made the subzero winter temperatures and the one-hundred-degree and above summer temperatures intolerable for most of Ácoma's citizens. Over the past few decades almost all have moved closer to the schools in the well-watered modern villages of Ácomita, McCarty's, and Anzac along the Rio San José. Nonetheless they return regularly to their ancestral homes and kivas, staying on the mesa several days and even weeks at a time during certain important ceremonial occasions.

When you arrive at the base of the mesa follow all signs and instructions with respect. You will be asked to enter the visitor center to purchase an entry and tour permit. You will also need a camera permit if you want to take pictures. The visitor center has several good permanent exhibits detailing Ácoma's history and culture. There is also a snack bar with sandwiches and cold drinks. The gift shop stocks a good supply of Ácoma pot-

Pottery Vessel, Ácoma Indian Pueblo

Ceramic Owl, Ácoma Indian Pueblo

tery, the art form that has brought fame and fortune to some of the better Pueblo artists. Many of the artists also sell from their homes both on the mesa and below it. Look for signs in windows, yards, or on fences that say "Pottery." The strong, thin-walled vessels produced at Ácoma are an attribute of the special, fine, light gray clay that is dug on the reservation. Once the vessel is formed, it is typically covered with a white Kaolin clay slip, which is then polished with a smooth rock before being painted and fired. Vessels with an all-white corrugated surface (a surface with numerous indentations made with a tool or fingernail), black on white, white on black, and polychromes of orange, black, and brown on white are the most common surface colors. These color combinations are used to paint arabesque swirls, hatched sections, geometric designs, and figures of birds, deer, and flowers. In addition, you will see figurines of owls and turtles and beautifully decorated canteens. You will join about fifteen others in a small bus that travels the short but steep road to the top of the mesa. The required one-hour- to one-and-a-half-hour-long guided tour by a tribal member is informative and interesting. You will see the natural cisterns on the mesa top, which catch rain water and provide the only water source there. You will see the entrances to the square kivas which are typical of the western pueblos of Zuñi, Hopi, and Ácoma. You will walk the timeless, treeless streets between the three long rows of historic two-story and terraced, three-story adobe apartment dwellings. And you will soak in views, views, views!

Everywhere views. East to Mesa Encantada or the Enchanted Mesa where Ácoma legend has it that the pueblo first began, north to 11,301-foot-high Mount Taylor, a mountain sacred to many southwestern Indians, and south and west as far as your eye will take you. Some of the permanent residents will invite you to look over their pottery wares, which are displayed for sale on small tables outside their apartments. And finally, after passing by the picturesque cemetery at the mesa's edge, you will tour the interior of the large San Esteban Rey Mission Church where the insulating effects of its ten-foot-thick adobe walls, constructed between 1629 and 1640, provide instant relief from the heat. You will hear about the tragic conflict with the early Spanish. You will learn how the original forty-foot-long heavy wooden beams were carried on the shoulders of Ácoma men from the Cebelleto forest near Mount Taylor, a distance of over thirty miles. And you may begin to wonder why the Spanish decided to build such a large church in this remote inaccessible location when you discover that each adobe brick as well as the dirt for the church floor and cemetery had to be laboriously carried up the sides of the steep escarpment from the desert below. In this church without pews, you will walk over the smooth, hard-packed clay floor to view or-

Ladder, Ácoma Indian Pueblo

nate Spanish altarpieces, reredos, and the venerated bulto or carved statue of Ácoma's patron, Saint Stephen, which date back as far as the seventeenth century. You will hear the remarkable story about the miracle-giving painting of Saint Joseph, which was presented to the Ácoma Pueblo by the King of Spain in the seventeenth century. Stolen by Laguna Pueblo, it was later regained by Ácoma only through legal action. Indeed before the walking tour ends you will enjoy these and other interesting facts and anecdotes told by your Ácoma guide atop this rocky mesa far removed from the Blarney Stone. Allow two hours for the visitor center and tour. At the conclusion of the tour you can ride the bus back to the visitor center or return by walking down the mesa via the narrow path called the Padre's trail. If you choose to walk down the steep hillside of eroded, malformed rocks, you will know why the Spanish thought that Ácoma Pueblo was an impregnable fortress.

To reach the pueblo drive west from Albuquerque on Interstate 40 for approximately fifty miles until you reach the junction with New Mexico Highway 23 at the Ácoma Exit 108. Then travel approximately thirteen miles south on Highway 23 to the visitor center. Along the way you will pass by the legendary home of the Ácoma people, Katzimo, better known today at the Enchanted Mesa as it rises four hundred feet from the desert floor. If you wish to shop further for crafts, return to Albuquerque by way of the modern Ácoma villages. Take the good, paved Indian Reservation Highway 32 to Ácomita and 38 to Anzac and McCarty. Then follow Reservation Highway 30 or 33 to Interstate 40. In the summer it may be best to tour Ácoma Pueblo in the cool of the early morning or in the early evening. Hours are variable but summer hours are usually from 8:00 A.M. until 7:00 P.M. Visitors are welcome on certain special festival and dance days but are not allowed on the mesa for others. It is best to check ahead of time. One of the several festivals that is open to the public is San Esteban Feast Day held in early September and celebrated with a Corn Dance and an arts and crafts fair. For information about other events open to the public at other times of the year, contact Pueblo of Ácoma Tourism, P.O. Box 309, Pueblo of Ácoma, New Mexico 87034. Telephone: 1-505-552-6604 or 1-505-252-1139.

For side trips north of Albuquerque to Santo Domingo and Cochiti pueblos, and Las Golondrinas Spanish Museum at La Cienega, see the Santa Fe section. For further information about Albuquerque and environs, contact the Albuquerque Convention and Visitors Bureau, P.O. Box 26866, Albuquerque, New Mexico 87125 or telephone 1-505-243-3696.

Santa Fe

Santa Fe makes an excellent base for touring northern New Mexico. It offers the traveler a harmonious blend of the old and the new. Its seven-thousand-foot altitude, its small size (less than fifty thousand people), its ethnic mix (55 percent Hispanic, 43 percent Anglo, and 2 percent Indian), and its tendency to attract visitors and residents who are interested in art and music make Santa Fe a unique city. Its 1.0 to 1.5 million visitors per year attest to the fact that Santa Fe is a major attraction. But it is also a real city, a working, capital city. It has evolved into its present unique form over a period of 370 years. Santa Fe was never shut down and later rebuilt as a tourist attraction. So do not expect the fantasy-perfect world of a Williamsburg or a Sturbridge Village. Yet Santa Fe does have a large number of homes and buildings on the National Historic Register and many others that are plaqued by state and local historical societies. It preserves the past gracefully, yet it is definitely a part of the modern world.

The only major attempt to control Santa Fe's outward appearance came in 1957, when an ordinance was passed requiring all new construction in the older area, comprising about one-third of the city, to be in character with Old Santa Fe architecture. Most of the newer buildings in these areas are in good taste, but some look like a developer's attempt to push the ordinance to its limits. Nonetheless, the city has a warm, friendly atmosphere that I think comes in part from the rounded earth-tone adobes that meet your eye everywhere.

While the ancient El Palacio Real or Palace of the Governors sits regally on the north side of the plaza, teenagers in souped-up low riders drag the plaza, burning rubber a few hundred feet away from that seventeenth-century structure as they speed devilishly down the Old Santa Fe Trail Road. Meanwhile, on any warm evening, young and old alike jam into the ice cream parlor on the south side of the plaza, not far from the terminus of the old Camino Real, to slake their thirst and feed their appetites like modern Americans everywhere.

Lying deep in the heart of America's high desert, Santa Fe evolved from a different set of circumstances than the rest of America (see Section IV, "History"). It has retained much of its differentness because of the strong character of its people and because it still remains isolated. Although it was the hub of commerce for wagon trains and pack mules going every which way in the 1800s, the twentieth century has left it relatively isolated. There is no commercial jet airport in New Mexico's capital city. There is not even a passenger railroad. Its namesake, the Santa Fe line (now Amtrak), stops at Lamy, twenty long, dusty miles from Santa Fe. Even the interstate highways just about missed Santa Fe until the U.S. Interstate Highway 25 spur was pushed down from Denver to Albuquerque in 1972. That road tends to relieve some of Santa Fe's isolation.

If you drive up to Santa Fe from Albuquerque, you will drive on U.S. Interstate Highway 25. Upon approaching Santa Fe, do not be tempted to take the first exit that says Santa Fe. Go on to exit number 284 that says Santa Fe via the Old Pecos Trail. Turn left onto the Old Pecos Trail, New Mexico Highway 85, U.S. Highway 285. This way you will be entering Santa Fe from the east via the Old Pecos Trail, which then merges with Old Santa Fe Trail Road. Follow the signs to the capitol as you head down the Old Santa Fe Trail into town. This route provides a dramatic entry, winding through narrow streets between old adobe buildings until reaching the Santa Fe River and the old part of the city centered around the plaza. There you will find most of the accommodations.

Resting on a high plain, twenty miles east of the Rio Grande, Santa Fe is surrounded by pine-clad foothills and the towering peaks of the Sangre de Cristo Mountains. Far to the west are the Jemez Mountains. To the south are the Ortiz and Sandia mountains. Nestled next to the Santa Fe River, which cuts through the center of town, the city commands beautiful views in all directions. Approaching Santa Fe from any direction is like finding an oasis in the desert. Its treelined, shady, sometimes narrow, winding streets offer relief from the frequently relentless New Mexico sun. The Santa Fe Opera, the Santa Fe Chamber Music Group, and the over one hundred art and craft galleries there provide a cultural mecca for this sparsely populated region of the country, which the media has recently dubbed as an American Salzburg. So allow enough time to see the "city different," as the chamber of commerce likes to call it. Take off your boots, put your feet up, and rest for a few days in Santa Fe. You will not be bored. In fact, you will discover so much to see and do that you may find yourself soaking your feet, swollen from long days of walking and sight-seeing.

It is often said that Santa Fe is a walking city. And it is. There are several different, excellent walking areas, but they are sufficiently far apart to require your car or one of the privately operated tour buses or trolleys that operate during the busy summer season. Santa Fe still has no year-round public transit system. In fact, until just a few years ago, there were hardly any taxicabs. Then it might have been easier to rent a horse than find a cab. But now there is a larger fleet of cabs that meets most everyone's needs year-round. You may want to arrange transportation between the plaza and the Canyon Road shops. Sure, it is only a mile or so from downtown, but with the heat and high altitude depleting your energy, you will probably be more comfortable using "wheels" for the trip there and to the museums out in the hills southeast of town.

Driving in Santa Fe is a bit tricky. The street names read like an extended history of northern New Mexico. Streets which have evolved in chronological order over 320 years are no substitute for lettered or numbered streets in some kind of logical sequence. The original layout of the city in 1609, ordered by the King of Spain, must have made sense to its creator, Governor Pedro de Peralta. But as the city grew new streets were apparently added in a wandering, random fashion without much concern for what went on before. Imposed on this hodgepodge of streets are a few obstacles such as one-way streets in unlikely locations and unexpected diagonal access routes to major arterials. Will Rogers reportedly once said after visiting Santa Fe, "Whoever designed this town did so while riding on a jackass backwards and drunk." The traffic is never particularly bad; it is the pathfinding that can get you down. You may even want to augment the accompanying map with a more detailed version from the chamber of commerce and mark your route before setting out. Doing this will save you a lot of headaches.

It is possible you will want to spend the first day in Santa Fe, taking it easy and adjusting to the altitude. If you are an early riser, you will find you may have the city to yourself as Santa Fe seems to take its waking slow. In the early morning and late evening, the streets are practically abandoned. Those are good times to see and appreciate the beautiful lines of the old adobe buildings, without scads of cars and people to block your view. The very historic plaza is a particularly nice place to sit before the hustle-bustle of the day's activities begins (see "Revisiting the Plaza and a Day with the Pueblo Indians North of Santa Fe: A Narrative Account"). But even with its throngs of visitors and all of its sophistication, Santa Fe's pace never reaches the frenetic state of most American cities. A small-town pace definitely prevails and that is one of its charms.

The main old portion of the city is divided by the Santa Fe River. This is not a river like the Seine. It is small, even inconspicuous during the dry summer as it trickles through the city. But you know it is there because of its very visible moisture-laden banks, which are verdant with shade trees and other vegetation. Sidewalks, walking paths, and picnic tables abound in the plentiful shade. It is no wonder the Spanish dubbed this greenbelt, the Alameda, the Spanish word for a park with a grove of trees, and carried the name over to the street that parallels the river. One half-day walking tour can include the sights north of the river, while in another half day you can cover the sights south of the river.

Half-Day Tour of Santa Fe, North of the River

One of the best places to start a walking tour of Santa Fe is the plaza, north of the river. The amount of history the plaza has seen is enough to fill at least one good-sized history text. Some of the most famous events that occurred there are marked by monuments. Walk over to the obelisk. It commemorates some of the turbulent history of the 1800s. The plaque tells about the difficult times faced by white settlers in northern New Mexico because of marauding Apache and Comanche Indians. And it tells about the Confederate occupation of Santa Fe. Later in the nineteenth century, Billy the Kid was allegedly kept in chains in the plaza until he could be removed to a sturdy jail. Previous to these events and under Mexican rule, the plaza contained a bullring.

At the southeast corner of the plaza, diagonally across from the La Fonda Hotel, is a plaque on a rock commemorating an even older historical landmark. It is a reminder that the eight-hundred-mile-long Santa Fe Trail, starting first in Franklin and then later in Independence, Missouri, ended right there after six arduous weeks of travel across the plains. All goods coming in from the United States had to be taxed and cleared at the customs building, formerly on the east side of the plaza.

Although the plaza has shrunk over the years, it is still the pulsating heart of the city, where fiestas and fairs are held annually. But to visualize the plaza as it was in Spanish times requires some imagination. Then it was longer and extended without obstacles to the parroquia or parish church on the site of today's Saint Francis Cathedral. The church, the Palace of the Governors, and the houses around the plaza were enclosed by a thick adobe wall. For all intents and purposes, Santa Fe was a seventeenth-century European walled city. West, just across from the plaza, is a small tourist information office, which is open only in the summer.

But probably the main reason to visit the plaza is to lay your eyes on the oldest public building in the United States, the Palace of the Governors. It covers the entire north side of the plaza. Up and down its long portico or porch, Pueblo Indian artisans, some in traditional garb and some in contemporary dress, display and sell their goods. After browsing along the portico, go inside the Palace of the Governors, for it contains an excellent regional, historical museum. Telephone: 1-505-827-6483. There you will see some of the most interesting historical artifacts in America and gain an appreciation for much that you will see later as you explore more of New Mexico. A considerable amount of New Mexico's eventful history took place within these walls, which were constructed about 1610. In addition, the museum maintains a superb shop, where some of the finest Indian and Spanish crafts can be

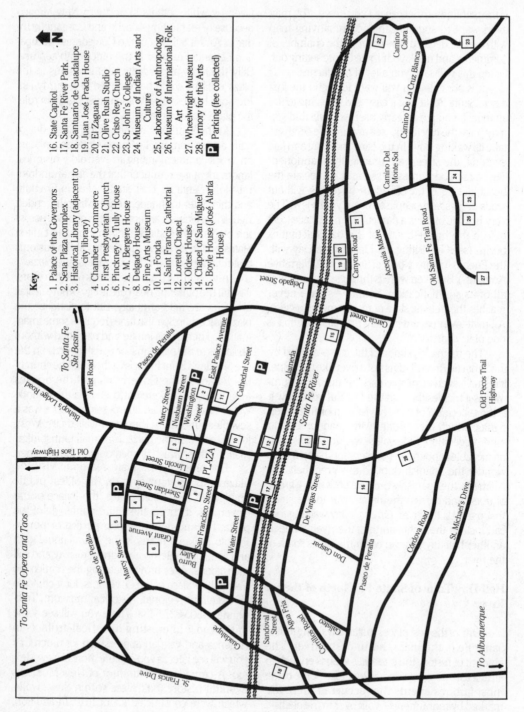

Key

1. Palace of the Governors
2. Sena Plaza complex
3. Historical Library (adjacent to city library)
4. Chamber of Commerce
5. First Presbyterian Church
6. Pinckney R. Tully House
7. A. M. Bergere House
8. Delgado House
9. Fine Arts Museum
10. La Fonda
11. Saint Francis Cathedral
12. Loretto Chapel
13. Oldest House
14. Chapel of San Miguel
15. Boyle House (José Alaria House)
16. State Capitol
17. Santa Fe River Park
18. Santuario de Guadalupe
19. Juan José Prada House
20. El Zaguan
21. Olive Rush Studio
22. Cristo Rey Church
23. St. John's College
24. Museum of Indian Arts and Culture
25. Laboratory of Anthropology
26. Museum of International Folk Art
27. Wheelwright Museum
28. Armory for the Arts
P Parking (fee collected)

Santa Fe

Sena Plaza Building, Santa Fe

purchased. This shop offers an excellent supply of regional books and magazines, ranging from cookbooks to monographs by local artists and writers. Note the sturdy construction of this building, which was originally known as the Casa Real. Inside, walk around the grassy courtyard or plaza and note how the thick adobe walls create a quiet haven from the noise outside.

After touring the Palace of the Governors, return to the street that fronts it, Palace Avenue, and turn left. Cross Washington Avenue and in a short distance you will enter a portal or long porch, fronting numerous small stores trimmed in white. This is the Arias de Quiros site. De Quiros, from Asturias, Spain, was given this site by General de Vargas, the reconquistador, for his services in helping to regain New Mexico from the Indians in 1693. The original structure probably deteriorated. Many of the early adobes have simply "melted" through the years. Adobe brick walls will succumb to moisture over time, eroding much the way sandstone erodes. This is especially true of the early adobes. Those sun-dried adobe brick walls were not capped by the harder, more resilient surfaces commonly used today, so the water from torrential thunderstorms easily could get a foothold in the soft brick. In addition, many of the earlier adobes were not plastered on the outside, thus opening the full length of the walls to weathering from rain and freezing conditions.

The structures you see on this site probably were built in the nineteenth century, although it is thought part of one of the structures may date back to the eighteenth century. Of recent note, the most famous unit, the location of a travel agency now, is 109 East Palace, which served as the first office for the Manhattan Atomic Bomb Project in 1943. The citizens of Santa Fe were kept in the dark about this project until several years after the clandestine office was set up. The small plaza just west of the 109 address is Trujillo Plaza. The 113½ East Palace location is well known for another reason. Its zaguan or covered entryway leads into a small courtyard, Prince Plaza, and one of Santa Fe's most popular lunchtime restaurants.

At 125–127 East Palace Avenue the doors are trimmed in blue. This is the Sena Building. Turn into the courtyard where the sign above the door says Sena Plaza. You will now find yourself in the secluded, flower-filled patio that once belonged to José Desiderio Sena. He lived at this location with his family, which included eleven children. His grand Spanish colonial home with its interior placita or plaza was built in the mid-1800s. It is a classic example of the "Mexican Surprise." For even today in Spanish colonial Old Mexico, doorways along dusty busy streets like Palace Avenue, flanked by cracked and peeling plaster walls, open into the most exquisite and lush interior plazas imaginable. Many homes in Santa Fe are arranged in a similar way to give relief from the commotion outside the walls. The Sena Plaza garden is in constant bloom most of the summer, but it is especially beautiful in May when the redbud trees and lilacs are in bloom. It is one of Santa Fe's best sights. Shops and small businesses line the courtyard, and located on the backside of the garden is one of Santa Fe's most atmospheric restaurants.

Return toward the plaza. Cross Washington Avenue and turn right or north. You will immediately notice the entrace to the Palace of the Governors' Museum Shop, and at 110 Washington is the Museum of New Mexico's History Library. There are many local historical artifacts on display in this research library, which is open to the public. Continue walking along Washington Avenue for one long block until it intersects treelined Marcy Street. Notice the building on the corner. It is one of Santa Fe's recently constructed bank and office buildings. Its more contemporary lines, underground parking garage, and the trendy shops and restaurant inside seem to reflect many of the changes Santa Fe is experiencing now. Across the street in the recently refurbished old City Hall Building is the public library. A block farther east on Marcy, located in a renovated Santa Fe home on the north side of the street, is one of Santa Fe's all-time favorite family-operated luncheon spots. Turn left or west onto Marcy. In this block are several luncheon cafés as well as apparel and gift shops. As you continue west along Marcy, you will notice a small shop handling museum-quality Spanish and Mexican folk art pieces, set back a short distance from the southeast corner of Lincoln and Marcy. The owner's fine sense of the Santa Fe style provides unique and interesting window displays. Continue on Marcy to Sheridan where you will notice across the street the Sweeney Convention Center. Located inside is the Santa Fe Convention and Visitors Bureau, which along with the chamber of commerce across town at 333 Montezuma, offers up-to-date useful information to travelers. Continue walking west on Marcy to Grant. Cross Grant to the attractive, large adobe structure on the corner, the First Presbyterian Church, designed by well-known Santa Fe restoration architect, John Gaw Meem (see "History," first protestant church site).

Now walk south, cross Griffin Street, and turn left. Almost immediately to your right you will see a red brick structure with white trim. This is the Pinckney R. Tully House at 136 Grant Avenue. Built in 1851 by one of Santa Fe's prosperous traders, it is a fine example of territorial-style architecture. Note that the brickwork is fake. The outline of rectangles, simulating the shape of brick,

has been applied with white paint over red plaster, giving the appearance of a brick surface. Over the years, there have been no major structural changes affecting the appearance of this building, a rarity in Santa Fe. Since the house is used for business purposes, it is open to the public only on a limited basis from 10:00 A.M. to 4:00 P.M. on the third Thursday of each month or by appointment. For more information on this or other historic homes, call the Historic Santa Fe Foundation. Telephone: 1-505-983-2567.

Across the street at 135 Grant Avenue is the A. M. Bergere House. This house was built in the 1870s as officers' quarters for the Fort Marcy Reservation located on that site. The apricot and other fruit trees planted by the home's Italian immigrant owner in the early 1900s still blossom and fruit each year. (Not open to the public.) And notice at 122 Grant Avenue the Grant Corner Inn on your right. Housed in an historic older home built in the early 1900s, this inn is typical of the several warm and charming bed-and-breakfast inns that have cropped up around Santa Fe.

Continue on down Grant Avenue past the courthouse to Palace Avenue. Across the street on the northeast corner of Grant and Palace avenues is the Palace Court Building with its specialty retail stores and restaurants. Cross Palace. Immediately facing you is Burro Alley on the west side of the Palace Restaurant property. Walk a short distance up the alley and see the large mural on the wall to the right depicting the alley's historical use. This narrow street connecting Palace Avenue and San Francisco Street was for many years a donkey parking lot. Firewood was brought from the mountains, piled high on the backs of burros who plodded down Canyon Road and who finally came to rest at this point while their owners hawked firewood in town.

Walk east on Palace past the Palace Restaurant building until you come to a doorway with a sign indicating entry to Downtown Subscription, a newsstand, coffee bar, and quick breakfast stop in the Palacio Francisco courtyard. Enter and take the corridor past interesting shops and studios to the delightful flower filled outdoor courtyard with its potted shade trees. From here you can follow a corridor south from the courtyard to San Francisco Street or retrace your steps to Palace Avenue. Continuing east up Palace toward the plaza is the

Pinckney R. Tully House, Santa Fe

*Detail of painting
false bricks at Tully House*

Pueblo Mission or Spanish-Pueblo style, sparked a rebirth of that type of native architecture, which led to the construction of many more buildings in that mode. The Museum of Fine Arts houses a permanent collection of paintings, photographs, and statues. In addition, it has a rotating display of contemporary artwork which has from time to time included works from the private collection of Georgia O'Keeffe and photography by Ansel Adams. The museum's Saint Francis auditorium, built to resemble the interior of a Spanish church, is often host to such prestigious music groups as the Santa Fe Chamber Group. Attending a Santa Fe Chamber concert or rehearsal there is always a

lovely old Delgado House, built of adobe in the 1890s and later modified to fit the trends of the time, including the interesting Victorian additions on the second level. Its original owner was also a prosperous trader since Santa Fe was a hub of commerce during much of the nineteenth century. Before the house was built, the site was used by traders to store their wagons as it was near the end of the Santa Fe Trail. This home has been converted to business use and to that extent can only be visited the first Monday of each month from 9:00 A.M. until 4:00 P.M.

Now cross Palace Avenue to the large adobe building in the direction of the plaza. It is The Museum of New Mexico's Museum of Fine Arts Telephone: 1-505-827-4468. This lovely adobe was built in 1917 on ground that was previously occupied by part of the first United States fort in the area, Fort Marcy. This museum, constructed in

Delgado house, Santa Fe

special experience. There is an excellent fine arts bookstore on the first floor. And, of course, the museum's permanent art collections as well as the special exhibits and traveling shows often displayed there are well worth a visit. Leaving The Museum of Fine Arts, continue east on Palace to the west side of the Palace of the Governors. There note the blue, carved wooden doors with the plaque to the side that tells their history.

Now cross Palace Avenue to the plaza. Walk across the plaza at a diagonal to its southeast side. There fight your way through the crowds (this is probably the most crowded corner in Santa Fe) to the large multistoried adobe building, across the street, the La Fonda Inn. Built in 1920 on the site of several previous "fondas" or inns, it is an imposing sight. Its public rooms are well worth a visit, even if you are not staying there. Its spacious, cool, shop-lined lobby and covered court offer welcome relief on a warm day. Paintings by some of Santa Fe's more traditional artists hang from the lobby's walls.

From the La Fonda, cross San Francisco Street and walk to the right up to the Saint Francis Cathedral. Both the cathedral and the street honor Santa Fe's venerable Saint Francis. You cannot

miss the cathedral, with its stubby European, Romanesque, double towers which, because of lack of funds and other complexities, were never finished off with their proposed 160-foot-tall steeples. On Sunday and on special occasions, the bells from the cathedral ring out for all Santa Fe to hear. The construction of today's church was started in 1869, over twenty years after the American occupation. The site had been the location of several previous churches or parroquias. In fact, during the almost twenty years it took to construct the building, services in the old church continued without interruption as the new building was built around it.

The old building was finally taken down section by section as the new building was being completed. Many of its adobe bricks were used in constructing the north walls of the new church. One small chapel of the early church, dating to 1714, remains intact. There you may see America's oldest Christian religious statue, the famous figure carved from willow wood, La Conquistadora (see "History"). Every year the statue is carefully lifted from its age-old resting place in Saint Francis Cathedral and taken to the Rosario Cemetery, northwest of the city, to com-

Saint Francis Cathedral, Santa Fe

memorate the difficult winter of 1692, resulting in the final reconquest of New Mexico. The paintings surrounding the statue are part of a "reredos," or a Spanish mural. Two of the early priests are buried in the wall of the chapel. This beautiful church is definitely worth seeing, especially its nineteenth-century stained-glass windows from Clermont-Ferrand, France. Of interest, too, is the Hebrew religious symbol on the keystone over the main entrance to the cathedral. The symbol was allegedly placed there in appreciation of Santa Fe's Jewish citizens who contributed funds to help build this edifice. Archbishop Lamy, made famous in Willa Cather's novel, *Death Comes for the Archbishop*, is buried in the crypt behind the altar (see "History").

Now you may be fully saturated after seeing the sights. If so, it is time for either lunch at one of the many good restaurants north of the river or for a siesta. Another pleasant alternative is to have a picnic lunch at the shady Santa Fe River Park just two blocks south of the plaza. (See the Santa Fe restaurant section for restaurant-deli's that have fixings for picnics.)

Half-Day Tour of Santa Fe, South of the River

For another half day of walking in the plaza area, go to the southeast corner of the plaza, cross the street, and walk down the Old Santa Fe Trail Road alongside the La Fonda Hotel. Cross East

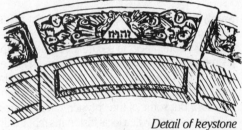

*Detail of keystone
in Saint Francis Cathedral*

Water Street and you will be facing the Loretto Chapel or "The Chapel of Our Lady of Light" at 219 Old Santa Fe Trail. This lovely little chapel was just about squeezed out of existence when the Sisters of Loretto sold most of the grounds to the Best Western Motel chain for construction of the new Inn at Loretto. It was another of Bishop Lamy's enterprises, modeled after the Sainte Chapelle Church in Paris, France.

One story has it that the French architect for the chapel became enamored with the wife of Bishop Lamy's nephew. The nephew discovered the tryst and did the architect in, so plans for the chapel were never completed. One of the essential features that did not make it onto the design boards was a stairway from the chapel floor to the choir loft. By all indications, there was not enough room for a conventional stairway. So the Sisters of Loretto prayed for a solution. In answer to their prayers, so the legend goes, a carpenter appeared one day. In no time he constructed from wood a

Loretto Chapel, Santa Fe

twenty-three-foot-high spiral staircase that made two complete turns and had thirty-three steps, using only wooden pegs to secure it. He then disappeared as mysteriously as he had come. Hence, the stairway was dubbed the "mysterious staircase." Indeed, it is a marvel in its design and construction. But some of the "mystery" was cleared up in recent years when local historians reportedly identified the builder as a man by the name of Hadwiger, who was a master carpenter from Austria visiting in Colorado at the time. A small entry fee is charged.

Now continue your walk south past the handsome Inn at Loretto and cross East Alameda and the Santa Fe River Bridge. The river is often dry in the summer, pointing up the fact that water is a scarce commodity in this part of the high desert. If current growth continues, the present marginal supply from wells and diversion projects will not be sufficient and the city will have to go twenty miles away to the Rio Grande for additional supplies. Water rates here are already some of the highest in the United States and would become astronomical if the Rio Grande had to be tapped. As you cross the river, note the sidewalk paralleling it. The "river walk" is a pleasant excursion you may want to take advantage of some evening. It is also a good jogging trail.

Continue south on the Old Santa Fe Trail Road. Underneath the pavement lies the dusty Santa Fe Trail as it came winding down the hill towards the plaza and the inn at the end of the trail, eight hundred miles from the starting point in Missouri. Next you will come to De Vargas Street. Turn left to view what is purported to be the oldest house in the United States. It most certainly could win honors as being the oldest house in Santa Fe, but it has not been officially recognized as the oldest house in the United States. A Spanish house was built around an earlier Indian dwelling on this site that dates back more than eight hundred years.

But this is not the oldest Indian house in the United States either. Pueblo houses at Ácoma Pueblo and at Old Oraibi in Hopiland are older. The Spanish portion is thought by some to have been added before 1628. Yet tree ring specimens taken from the oldest Spanish section only date back to 1740–67. So it is not the oldest European-built house still standing in America since one house in Saint Augustine has been reliably dated to 1727. It is too bad that the entryway to the oldest house contains a glut of curios that makes this venerable shrine look like a sequel to Coney Island. Nonetheless, when I visited this house at age ten, I was greatly impressed and it somehow altered my sense of historical perspective.

Regardless of all the hokiness and unsubstantiated claims, this is truly one of the oldest buildings in the United States and should not be missed. Its value is to reveal how circumstances and environment reduced the Spanish to living much like the Indians. Any notion that the very early Spanish lived in great haciendas will be quickly and realistically dispelled by your visit to this house. Survival took precedence over aesthetics in those days and the Spaniards lived no more regally than did the American pioneers on the prairie in their dark sod houses. Some of the walls of the oldest house were made by the Indians of puddled adobe

"Oldest House," Santa Fe

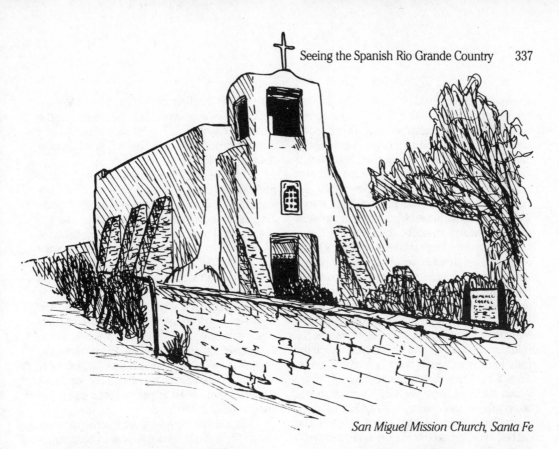

San Miguel Mission Church, Santa Fe

and taper toward the ceiling. Other walls were made during the Spanish period of adobe brick. The Spaniards also added entryways to this Indian house from the side rather than from the roof and contributed a fireplace with a chimney, rather than fire pits whose only outlet for the smoke was the entry hole in the roof. Of course, the Spanish added furniture made out of wood and utensils out of metal, but these improvements did not alter the fact that the early Spanish, like the Indians, lived in dark spaces behind mud walls.

Leave the oldest house and cross De Vargas Street to the south. There on the corner is the old San Miguel Mission. The Christian Brothers who own it claim that it is the oldest church in the United States. Again, this has not been made official by any certifying historical society. The original chapel was built before 1626, perhaps as early as 1610 to 1615, as a house of worship for the Tlaxcalan Indians whom the Spanish brought with them from Mexico. That first church was destroyed in the Pueblo Rebellion of 1680 and was not reconstructed until 1710. It was completely rebuilt then, using a different foundation. But the new chapel was built over the remains of the old

seventeenth-century chapel. Those remains can be viewed through peepholes in front of the altar.

It is on the basis of these remains, which have been dated back to the early 1600s, that the claims of being the oldest church have been made. But many would claim that the oldest of the Spanish churches still standing in the United States are the mission churches located at Ácoma and Isleta pueblos. These churches were also built in the early 1600s and, although parts of them have been rebuilt from time to time, they are essentially still standing as they were then. So here again the controversy of what is the "oldest" in the United States rages on. The issue may never be settled. But just for the record, the oldest Christian church (one of the three above), one of the oldest most continually inhabited villages, Ácoma, and the oldest public building still in use in America reside in New Mexico, whereas the oldest wooden school building and the oldest masonry fort still standing in the United States are in our oldest city, Saint Augustine, Florida.

Whether San Miguel's is the oldest church or not is a moot point. Be sure to visit it, for inside are some precious religious art objects. Upon entering the chapel, your eye will be drawn immediately to the painted, wooden altarpiece or altar screen which the Spanish call a reredos. This one was constructed in 1798 and is the oldest dated wooden altarpiece remaining in New Mexico. Note particularly the salomónicas or spiraled columns, a design used frequently in both Spain and New Spain. Also note how a beautifully designed, elegant screen like this enhances the stark plainness of the white plastered walls of an adobe church.

Also note the largest of the several paintings of Saint Michael. It was executed by Captain Bernardo Miera y Pacheco, who served the Spanish as mapmaker for the region in the eighteenth century. Some of his maps of New Spain, which became famous over time, are in the British Museum today. Of interest, too, are the religious paintings on deerskin and buffalo hide, which the early Franciscan priests used in teaching the Indians about Christianity. Another highlight is the gilded statue of Saint Michael. This statue was taken around the countryside in 1709 to aid in solicitation of funds for rebuilding the church. The old bell in the gift shop is alleged to be from Spain and is alleged to date back to 1356. But recent, more objective data would suggest that the bell was cast in 1856 in New Mexico. Both the oldest house and the San Miguel Mission Church were a part of Santa Fe known as Barrio de Analco. Analco is a term derived from an Indian word meaning "the other side of the water." This was where the Tlaxcalan Indian slaves lived who had been brought up from Mexico by the Spanish.

Altar screen, San Miguel Chapel

Note the old building south of San Miguel Mission built in 1878 by the Christian Brothers. It is the former home of Santa Fe College and served as a dormitory for Saint Michael's School. It now houses state offices.

Continue one more block south on Old Santa Fe Trail to the unusual territorial-style New Mexican State Capitol whose shape was inspired by the Zia Pueblo Indian sun symbol. You may want to visit several of the public rooms and galleries there. Or from San Miguel Mission, you can walk east on De Vargas Street past several interesting old adobe homes, including the historic Boyle House, a late eighteenth-century home with adobe walls four feet thick. Boyle, one of its later owners, was a New Mexican agent for an English land speculator in the late 1800s. Continue walking east to the intersection of De Vargas and Paseo de Peralta, where you will find a museum-quality gallery of early Indian and Spanish crafts on the southeast corner. Canyon Road intersects Paseo de Peralta just one block to the north.

Still another interesting alternative from San Miguel Mission is to retrace your steps back across the Santa Fe River and turn to the left or west on East Alameda, taking the treelined river walk on the sidewalk paralleling the river. Follow the river west, past numerous picnic sites. Soon you will see approximately four blocks to the west, directly in front of you, the Santuario de Nuestra Señora de Guadalupe, on the corner of Guadalupe and Agua Fria streets on the west side of Guadalupe. The santuario, with its simple lines and beautiful grounds, is one of the most attractive churches in New Mexico. Its light, uncluttered interior allows you to focus on some of the building's more interesting features.

Note the choir loft, where you will see some handsome carved vigas or ceiling beams and their supporting vertical corbels or posts. Perhaps it is the removal of the pews from the chapel that has given the interior a sense of spaciousness that enhances its simple elegance. The chapel, built around 1765, alongside New Mexico's historic lifeline, El Camino Real, was dedicated to the Virgin of Guadalupe, a venerated figure in the section of New Spain that would become Mexico. The chapel is now used as a museum and performance hall. Arts and crafts exhibits relating to New Mexico's

Santuario de Guadalupe, Santa Fe

Spanish tradition are the primary focus. Telephone: 1-505-988-2027. In addition, the chapel contains some very old religious objects taken from the military chapel on the plaza, La Castrense, after it was dismantled in the 1800s. Notice the deep red altar wall. The color comes from mixing oxblood with plaster.

Now after several hours of walking and sightseeing, you may want to stroll on your tired dogs a block or two south on South Guadalupe Street where you can take refreshment at one of the small cafés or deli's located there. Along the way you will pass the numerous small shops and specialty stores that have made South Guadalupe Street a major attraction for visitors. After you get your second wind, you might want to continue on down South Guadalupe Street to Montezuma Avenue. There on the northeast corner is the Santa Fe Chamber of Commerce at 333 Montezuma Avenue, where you can receive personalized help in planning your Santa Fe visit. You can wander on down South Guadalupe another block or two and see some of the older buildings, which served as the terminus of Santa Fe's historic Chili Line Railway. Several have been renovated, and one is the home of a popular Santa Fe restaurant. Or you can walk west on Montezuma Avenue passing near several restaurants and shops in newly renovated railway station buildings and a movie house to the handsomely renovated old warehouse buildings at 500 Montezuma, known as the Sanbusco Market Center. This nicely designed, mostly commercial center has a large wine and imported beer shop, luncheon deli, and a restaurant or two. The

Chile Line trolley makes a stop here. Alternatively, you can walk east along Montezuma from South Guadalupe to Las Tres Gentes, a marketplace where a large high-ceilinged building is divided into small shops and stalls. There you will find a coffee and tea shop as well as several small cafés, delis, and a bakery. And now, if your feet are aching, you might as well return to the downtown historic district in style by trying to catch one of the trolleys that sporadically visit the Sanbusco Market Center.

A Three-Quarters-of-a-Day Auto Tour of Southeastern Santa Fe

If you are hardy and young, without children, and are looking for a challenging sight-seeing hike at high altitudes, you might want to leave your car downtown and walk this one. But if you are the average traveler, swallow your pride and hop into the American version of the Spanish horse and drive to the Paseo de Peralta. On the south side of the Santa Fe River, turn off Peralta to the left or east at the sign designating Canyon Road. Canyon Road is a paved-over version of an ancient Indian trail that went from the Pueblo villages near today's Santa Fe to Pecos Pueblo to the east. In the early days of Santa Fe, this route to and from the Sangre de Cristo Mountains was the entry point for wood vendors, who brought their products heaped high on the backs of sturdy burros. There is still a dusty, rural feeling to this street, but it has mostly become a shopping street. Although many kinds of goods are sold there, most of its shops specialize in the arts and crafts of the region and elsewhere. Many artists have their studios on or around Canyon Road. Canyon Road is a one-way street for approximately four or five blocks up to Camino del Monte Sol. Try to find a parking place in the shade, if possible, as close to Peralta or Garcia as you can, then walk up Canyon Road. This venture can take several hours. Hardened, veteran shoppers might even spend half a day there.

You will find Canyon Road to be an interesting, if not exhausting, experience. There are many shops to see and numerous little back alleys and placitas to explore. You will have to sort the wheat from the chaff as numerous, curio-type stores are also part of the scene. For galleries and shops of particular note in this area, see the shopping section under Santa Fe in "Staying There." While shopping on Canyon Road, you may wish to note several of Santa Fe's historic homes. On the left at 519 is the Juan José Prada House, a private residence, built perhaps as early as 1768. At 545 is El Zaguan. These private apartments are in the original residence, which was built before 1849. One of the units, number five, just to the right as you enter the porch, is the home of the Historic Santa Fe Foundation. Telephone: 1-505-983-2567. This helpful organization has a wealth of important information about historic Santa Fe and can answer many of the questions you might have. The garden to the west side, originally laid out by Adolf Bandelier, contains several large, old horse chestnut trees and is open to the public for viewing. Farther down the road on the right is the Olive Rush Studio Home at 630 Canyon Road. Olive Rush, a Quaker artist, purchased this nineteenth-century adobe home in the early 1900s. It is now a meeting house for the Santa Fe Religious Society of Friends. At 724 Canyon Road is the Borrego House. Parts of the house date to 1753, while the more modern sections were built in the late 1800s. The Carriage Trade Restaurant is there now.

After you are shopped out, your pocketbook is flat, and your eyes are bulging from fatigue, return to your car and drive east on Canyon Road, retracing the route you have just walked. At the T intersection, make a right turn on Camino Cabra leading to upper Canyon Road. To your right, note the Church of Cristo Rey. This is the largest adobe church in America, containing nearly two hun-

Stone reredos, Cristo Rey Church, Santa Fe

dred thousand adobe bricks. Even though this church was not constructed until 1939–41, the old Spanish custom of making adobe bricks by hand from the dirt at the building site was followed. The church was built to commemorate the four hundredth anniversary of Coronado's expedition to the Southwest. The walls vary from two to seven feet in thickness to guarantee that this building will be intact on the eight hundredth anniversary! Inside the church is one of the most famous pieces of church art in New Mexico, a carved, stone altar screen or reredos which was executed by craftsmen from Mexico in 1760. Cut from local stone, this rendering is thought to have been the model for many of the altar screens produced later by native New Mexican santeros.

From the Cristo Rey Church, travel to the end of Upper Canyon Road to the Randall Davey Audubon Center. Telephone: 1-505-983-4609. The distance is less than two miles and all but the last half-mile is paved. Be certain to bear right when you come to the Y in the road. The good dirt road will take you to the parking lot adjacent to the visitor center. A few steps away amid grassy lawns, large cottonwoods, aspen and pine forests, and beautiful vistas, you will find the Randall Davey home. The home rests on 6 developed acres of grassy lawns, orchards, and gardens, amid 135 acres of undeveloped meadow and forest land, now a wildlife sanctuary owned by the National Audubon Society. Trails branch out in several directions taking you into the heart of this peaceful place. Once there it seems incredible that you are only a few miles from the busy, congested downtown area. One hundred species of birds call this oasis their home during various times of the year and they don't seem to mind sharing it with the 120 plant and wildflower species that grow so abundantly there. Migrating osprey, blue heron, and egrets may be seen along with brown creepers, yellow-bellied sapsuckers, and lazuli buntings. Bears periodically pay visits to the old orchards on the property, and raccoons and coyotes are sometimes spotted at night along with an occasional mountain lion or bobcat, who has found his way into this pocket of civilization on the border of the Santa Fe National Forest. The old adobe home, formerly a sawmill built in 1847, was refurbished and occupied by its internationally known artist and bon vivant owner, Randall Davey, from the early 1920s until his death in 1964. The National Audubon Society received the historic property in 1983 and now uses it as a wildlife refuge and educational center. Open daily for exploring the nature trail, El Temporal (a comprehensive self-guiding trail booklet is available at the visitor center), which meanders uphill into forest and down dale into meadows and across the Acequia del Llano. The tastefully decorated home, with its New Mexican and European accents and its flamboyant wall murals painted by Davey, can be toured on Sunday afternoons from Memorial Day to Labor Day. Lecture programs and workshops for adults are often held on Saturdays. Do take time to see orientation exhibits in the visitor center. Telephone: 1-505-983-4609.

Return to the Cristo Rey Church and retrace your route back down the two-way stretch of Canyon road to Camino del Monte Sol. Turn left on Camino del Monte Sol and drive south for several miles. Many of Santa Fe's picturesque adobe residential sections are in this area on little dirt roads along the Acequia Madre or in the foothills. At the junction with Mount Carmel Road, note the building to the left on the north side of the road. This is the Santa Fe Preparatory Academy. Further up the same road on the south side is the stringently academic Saint John's College, a twin to the college of the same name in Baltimore, Maryland. Soon, Monte del Sol intersects with Old Santa Fe Trail Road. Turn right on that road and travel for a short distance to Camino Lejo Street and the sign directing you to the Camino Lejo Museum Complex, which includes the Museum of Indian Arts and Culture (telephone: 1-505-827-8000), the Laboratory of Anthropology (telephone: 1-505-827-8941), the Museum of International Folk Art (telephone: 1-505-827-8350), and the Wheelwright Museum (telephone: 1-505-982-4636). Driving up Camino Lejo to the Laboratory of Anthropology, the vistas increase as the road climbs, offering nice views of Santa Fe, the foothills, and environs.

The newest pearl in the string of the Museum of New Mexico's superlative showcases is the Museum of Indian Arts and Culture. It is an offshoot of the Laboratory of Anthropology, whose spectacular collection of thousands of Southwest Indian artifacts has never had a proper showroom. Now, through rotating displays, it is possible for many of those artifacts to be displayed properly for the first time in the spacious and handsome 31,000-square-foot passive solar building, which is located to the left of the Laboratory of Anthropology as you drive up Camino Lejo. The basement alone will eventually contain the ten thousand-piece Indian pottery collection in an open storage format, which visitors can view. In addition to these rarely seen artifacts, the museum focuses on the Indian people of the Southwest, with interesting photographic displays that poignantly tell the story of individuals, pueblos, and tribes as they were in the past and as they are today. These exhibits also focus on the beautiful art and many crafts that are such an important part of Indian cultural life. The museum devotes space to craft exhibits and demonstrations. The museum's shop features some Indian crafts, books, and gift items. Next door the renowned Laboratory of Anthropology will continue to offer the services of its outstanding research library to scholars and others wanting to know more about the history and culture of the Southwest Indian people. The laboratory is part of the Museum of New Mexico and was given to the state by John D. Rockefeller, Jr., in 1949. Next door to the laboratory is another branch of the New Mexico Museum system, the International Folk Art Museum, which now contains the Alexander Girard collection of folk art. This is without doubt the largest museum in the world dedicated exclusively to the folk art of the world. It is appropriate that northern New Mexico, with its intense concentration of folk artists, should host such a fine museum. Of course, the museum's collection of local Spanish colonial craftwork is superb. If folk art and folk costumes interest you, do not miss this museum. A small shop in the lobby is the source of some very good folk art crafted by local Spanish carvers and other artisans.

Adjacent to the Folk Museum is the Wheelwright Museum of the American Indian. It was formerly known as the Museum of Navajo Ceremonial Art, even though there are no Navajo towns in the Rio Grande Valley. For a long time, this was the only museum in the Southwest dedicated to preserving the best of that Four Corners culture (see Section II). The Navajo tribe is preserving its heritage on its own reservation now (see Section II, "Back to Navajoland: Keams Canyon to Ganado via Hubbell Trading Post and on to Window Rock . . ."), so the Wheelwright Museum has expanded its interest to all southwestern Indians. The exhibits at the Wheelwright are of the highest quality and are nicely displayed in a large building shaped like a Navajo hogan. A few years ago, shortly after the death of Maria Martinez, the famed San Ildefonso potter, the museum staged an outstanding retrospective exhibit of her works. In the basement of this very unique building is the Case Trading Post, done up in Navajo trading post style. Specializing in quality Indian crafts, it serves as the shop for the gallery upstairs.

Now drive back down the hill to the Old Santa Fe Trail Road. Turn left onto that road and follow it approximately two miles back to the plaza in downtown Santa Fe. If you just want to take a trip to the museums and not visit Canyon Road, get on the Old Santa Fe Trail Road downtown and follow it all the way to the museums, being certain to take the left fork at the intersection with the Old Pecos Trail.

Tours Around Santa Fe

Revisiting the Plaza and a Day with the Pueblo Indians North of Santa Fe: A Narrative Account

The sun is already bright this morning. It is comfortable in the sun, but in the shade it is still cool. I am up early, the rest of the family still sleeping. (We were up late last evening, not returning to our room until after midnight.) I walk out of the inn and stroll south to the plaza. I have walked this treelined street many times in the last twenty-five years. Particularly, I remember the profusion of lilacs in bloom along this street in May. The sun's warmth will not penetrate the leaves of these trees for another few hours, but looking up I can see the sunlight beginning to come through as it reflects off of the shiny green leaves.

All the shops along the front of Sena Plaza are quiet this morning. They will not open for another hour or so. As I round the east corner of the Palace of the Governors and look down the long, empty portal, I realize I have arrived before the Indian vendors who will take their places along the portico later in the day to sell their crafts. Anglo vendors are not allowed here, just Pueblo Indians. I think to myself that is the way it should be. After all, these stalwart people had the first villages along the Santa Fe River long before the Spanish came. And later, in historical times, when they were subjected to the "civilizing influences" of the Spanish, Mexicans, and Americans, they revolted several times, capturing and occupying the very same building they will sit in front of today.

I find a bench in the plaza and sit down across from the Palace of the Governors. My gaze fixes on that old adobe which the Spanish called El Palacio Real. Built in 1610, it is the oldest public building in the United States and has always symbolized to me the enduring strength of this region. It was built to last, with adobe walls up to five feet thick in places. Someone has said that two or three men can turn out five to six hundred adobe bricks each day. The bricks for this building were probably obtained from the mud taken from the building site. The mud, mixed with straw to give it strength, was then poured into wooden molds to make bricks approximately fifty-six by thirty centimeters or twenty-two inches by twelve inches. After drying in the sun, these molded rectangular bricks were most often laid end to end, forming a wall approximately four feet thick. Mud mortar was used between the bricks, and after the walls were laid up, they were then plastered to a warm smoothness. Yesterday, in spite of the intense midday heat, the Palace of the Governors was a cool haven due to the fine insulating qualities of those old adobe walls.

A few more people are out now. The town is

Blue doors, west side of Palace of the Governors, Santa Fe

waking up. I reflect that I first sat in this plaza forty years ago. The plaza has not changed much. But I do recall my astonishment a few years ago when I realized how much Santa Fe had changed when I returned here after a four-year hiatus. Houses were being built on the hills north of town, fast-food places had cropped up all over the place, and the world's most splendid hole-in-the-wall steak house, Tony's U and I Café, had disappeared. The Inn at Loretto was under construction. The La Fonda was undergoing a variety of changes and the traffic was heavier and seemed uglier. A "jillion" little shops had cropped up.

For awhile I thought all my pleasant memories of Santa Fe had been destroyed. Then I came and sat here in the plaza on a morning like this. I sat and looked around. It was quiet and peaceful. The old landmarks were still here—the La Fonda anchoring the southeast corner, the Saint Francis Cathedral looming up to the east, and the Palace of the Governors buttressing the north side. The center had held! Today as I look at the storefronts across from the plaza, I see new names and fancier, more expensive stores. Although it is possible the plaza will someday be just a shopping mall for affluent visitors, that is not true just yet. Yesterday there was, as there always has been, a wide mix of Santa Fe's citizens using and enjoying this pleasant area in the heart of the city. The center still holds. The center in Santa Fe, hopefully, will always hold. No one would dare screw up this centuries-old plaza!

The warm sun is breaking through the trees. I shed my sweater and start walking back to the inn from this plaza that has seen so much. I decide to walk around the west side of the Palace of the Governors to see my favorite Santa Fe antique. It is a set of ancient doors, painted blue, framed by lovely old beams which blend naturally into the old adobe wall that supports them. The wooden plaque on the adobe wall states that "from 1610 to 1910" this building, originally known as El Palacio Real, was "the residence of over a hundred Governors and Captains General."

Perhaps through these very doors rode messengers from the king of Spain in Madrid and the viceroy of New Spain in Mexico City. Near these walls, both Spanish and Indians were killed as battles took shape around this building. Perhaps Popé, the San Juan Pueblo Indian leader, entered these doors after conquering the Spanish in 1610. Or perhaps it was through these portals that the venerable Spanish Madonna, *La Conquistadora,* was lovingly carried in 1692 when the Spanish regained control of this, the Casa Real, their Royal House. And possibly, secret messages were slipped under the doors telling of the impending revolution in New Spain that would eventually place this royal seat of government under Mexican rule rather than Spanish domination. It may have been through these doors that captured trespassers onto Spanish lands, like America's Lt. Zebulon Pike, were brought to face their Spanish inquisitors. And Pike, whether he knew it or not, presaged the entrance through these portals forty-one years later of United States General Kearny and his victorious American Army of the West.

But before that, no doubt some mules left this passageway heading for St. Louis along the Santa Fe Trail and to Los Angeles along the Old Spanish Trail. In addition, my active imagination has pictured Gov. Lew Wallace slipping quietly out these side doors, away from the clamor and din of the seat of New Mexican territorial government, to walk the quiet side streets while he pulled his thoughts together to write another series of lines for his best seller, *Ben Hur.* And I am sure that some of Santa Fe's Los Cincos Pintores (The Five Painters) must have looked at this historic wall and doors as I am doing now and seen the beauty of it all as the morning sunlight illuminates the vibrant blue of the old doors framed by smooth, rounded, sand-colored walls.

When I see these blue doors, I am reminded that the Spanish brought with them from the Old Country a superstition borrowed from their Moorish-Arabic enemies. It is said the color blue helps to keep the devil away. Blue doors, blue window frames, even blue roofs help protect homes as well as public buildings. Ironically the Indians, long before the Spanish came, believed that turquoise would keep the evil spirits away. So another shade of blue, used for the same reason, adorns many a Pueblo Indian home.

Now I rapidly return to the inn, realizing that I have spent more time here wrapped in reverie than I should have. Sure enough, my family is up, fed, and raring to go. We find the Paseo de Peralta and follow it until we see signs to U.S. Highway 84–285 to Taos. We quickly leave the city behind as we pass the Rosario Cemetery, the home of the Rosario Chapel, and head into the sagebrush hills. In seven miles, we see the modern structure of the Santa Fe Opera Building on the left in the Tesuque hills and many modern adobe homes in the hills to the right. As we continue north, we notice on the left the several weirdly eroded sandstone formations, including Camel's Rock, that have delighted us for years. From Santa Fe, we drive approximately fifteen miles to the junction marked Los Alamos. This is New Mexico Highway 502 and is also the road to San Ildefonso Pueblo. We turn left or west on Highway 502. Now the road goes up and down but mostly down, as we drive the approximately five and one-half miles to the pueblo access road near the Rio Grande.

We spot the pueblo in the distance to the right. At the marker sign, we turn to drive the approximately one mile into the pueblo. We enter the plaza and turn left until reaching the Popovi Da Studio. We park in front and get out. The physical aspects of the village are little changed since my first visit here over forty years ago, especially the extra-large, bare, dusty plaza, with its fine sense of openness. I show my children, as my parents showed me, the solitary, lonely old cottonwood tree in the plaza which provides cool relief from the midday sun.

Forty years ago, the plaza was full of people, especially children. Today the plaza is quiet, attesting to the fact that many Pueblo men and women work at jobs away from the village in towns like Los Alamos and that others have moved away, leaving a stable population of only five hundred. Farming the land here no longer provides enough income for all the people. Often in coming here we have seen smoke curling up to the sky from the pottery fires. Today no one is firing pottery, although we notice that a few of the homes still have signs up, indicating that their occupants will sell craftwork from their doors.

Of course, this was the pueblo home of the famous potter, Maria Martinez. Maria possibly made the finest pots ever constructed, using the coil method. Only a few have even come close to duplicating the thin walls and lifelike forms of her pots. Her talented hands had a delicate touch, the sure touch of a master. Her sister hand-rubbed the pots patiently with a smooth stone, burnishing them to a high, rich gloss. Then her husband Julian, and later her son Popovi Da and later other relatives, put designs on her pots. I recall the first black on black San Ildefonso pot I ever saw. I was fascinated by its utter smoothness, as I traced the beautifully executed serpent design all the way around the pot.

My father had purchased the pot for a few dollars and some jelly beans. Both the seller and the buyer felt they had completed a good deal. That was in the late twenties when the Pueblos were just reviving their pottery craft after having been exposed to some of the fine pottery produced by their ancestors, which was just then being turned up in the archaeological digs of the time. I tell my children about my first visit here in the 1940s, when the plaza was filled with activity and

San Ildefonso clay vessel

Ceremonial chamber, San Ildefonso

the smoke trailed up from the beehive ovens, those remnants of Moorish Spain, as they slowly baked some of the best bread I have ever tasted in my life.

We walk around the empty plaza. One of the large kivas here is built into the adobe house block on the north. It is from this ceremonial kiva that many of the dancers will emerge on festival days. To our right is the large, beautiful circular ceremonial chamber that we passed as we drove in. It is harmoniously designed to fit in beautifully with the Pajarito Plateau that rises behind it in the distance. My daughter asks why the stair rails are notched. That one stumps me. But as we look at those notches and see rising behind them a billowy thunderhead cloud with terraced edges forming over the mountain, we wonder if we have not found the answer.

We have read that this plaza is lined up with "toonyopeeng/ya" or Black Mesa, a sentinel fortresslike rock structure exactly to the north. Black Mesa is a sacred structure and its flat top holds several ancient ruins. It also was used as a fortress. When the Spanish returned to New Mexico in the 1690s, San Ildefonso was one of the last Pueblo strongholds to be reconquered. To strengthen their position, the village residents moved to the top of Black Mesa. From its craggy heights which they used as a fortress, they fended off the Spanish for several years before being subdued.

Looking toward the west end of the plaza, we see the Catholic church, newly reconstructed, outside the plaza. We have learned that most of the residents here are Catholic and that many have Spanish surnames. But the Indian religion and the Indian way supercede both of these influences. In spite of the great pressure the Spanish imposed on the Puebloans to give up their old religion, the Indians were able to keep their religion and culture intact. Spanish law stated that the Indians should be left on their own lands. So the Spanish, who had some experience in coexisting with a second, alien culture on their native soil, the Moors, learned to live side by side with the Indians here. Unfortunately, as much cannot be said for their European counterparts in the eastern part of the United States who displaced the Indians from their lands. Today in the East, there are no Indian villages that have been continuously inhabited as long as those in the Southwest. The large, wooden structure just east of the church catches our attention. It is called the "Hollywood Gate," for it is a relic from the Hollywood movie set for a movie made at the pueblo. Before leaving, we visit the new Pueblo Museum next to the church and browse awhile in the Popovi Da Shop.

Returning to the car, we drive back to New Mexico Highway 502, turn right, and head for Bandelier National Monument. It is thought that the ancestors of today's San Ildefonso's residents lived to the west of the present pueblo on the Pajarito Plateau. Specifically, it is thought that their ancestral home on the plateau was in a canyon called Frijoles. Bandelier National Monument is dedicated to the preservation of the Frijoles Canyon ruins. After leaving the pueblo, we cross the Rio Grande. It is very dry, with only a few puddles of water standing. It looks so different here than it does in Colorado where its clear, fast-flowing waters sparkle in the sunlight. Perhaps in Spanish times and even later it flowed more freely. Today, much of the water is diverted to the farms and ranches of southern Colorado before it ever reaches New Mexico. Nevertheless, the river and its tributaries still provide much of the water required for farming in this region.

The road begins to climb fairly quickly now as

Bandelier National Monument

we head west to Bandelier and ascend the Pajarito Plateau. We wind and weave through interesting rock formations. The rock with all the holes in it that looks like honeycomb is called "tuff." Tuff is petrified volcanic ash. Ash covered this region in great depth after the eruption of the volcano just west of here, thousands of years ago. When that volcano blew its stack, it left an immense bowl, the Valle Grande Caldera, one of the world's largest extinct volcano craters (see "The Setting").

We disregard the cutoff to Los Alamos and follow New Mexico Highway 4 as it turns south or left, winding all the way to Bandelier, forty-six miles northwest of Santa Fe. Bandelier National Monument (telephone: 1-505-672-3861) was established in 1916 and covers almost thirty thousand acres. It is named for Adolf Bandelier, a Swiss archaeologist who began studying this area in 1882. We pay the small admission fee and enter the tree-shaded parking area and visitor center near the El Rito de los Frijoles or "The Little River of the Beans." The shade is very welcome now as the sun hits high noon. We find a nice picnic area near the stream and enjoy the cool breeze at sixty-one hundred feet above sea level. The cold drinks from the lunchroom at the visitor center help

soothe our parched throats.

We take a quick tour of the museum, which houses many of the artifacts from the ruins here. We purchase the inexpensive guide entitled "The Trail to Frijoles Ruins," and take off on a self-guided tour of the area. We walk the dusty trail in the canyon bottom that was probably used by the inhabitants during the three hundred years the canyon was occupied. Some of the first occupants probably trickled down from the great Anasazi civilizations in the Four Corners area around 1250, when for unknown reasons they left their home there. This well-watered canyon must have looked good to them. We pass by the ruins of a circular kiva or ceremonial chamber (see Section II, "A Prehistory of Indian Country" and Section III, "Seeing Mesa Verde") and are reminded of the kivas we have seen at Mesa Verde and Aztec National Monument, as well as the one we saw this morning at San Ildefonso.

Now we come across a small hill or mound next to the trail. This is the way an unexcavated site often appears. When archaeologists see mounds like this, they begin to look in the dust around them for pottery shards or other evidence of habitation. Such evidence frequently leads to the decision to excavate the area. We now reach the famous ruin of Tyuinyi, a word in the Keres language meaning "meeting place." Although practically leveled now, this complex once stood three stories high and contained four hundred rooms. Perhaps one hundred people lived here. This large site was excavated in 1909–10. From artifacts found at sites like this and others on the Pajarito Plateau, the Pueblo Indians were able to discover much about their past early in the twentieth century. This rediscovery of early pottery and design motifs was thought to be instrumental in sparking the renaissance of fine Pueblo crafts near the beginning of this century.

We now continue on the trail to the cliff ruins. Here we explore in some detail the caves carved out of the soft volcanic tuff. Some of the caves we see, though, are natural. Many of them look too small to be occupied. Our children climb several of the ladders to peek into the caves. I do the same and find several cave roofs darkened with black soot from ancient cooking fires. Now we come to Talus House, resting on a talus or rock slope beneath the cliff. Here the walls are intact and the ancient viga timbers supporting the roof still protrude dramatically from the walls. The walls are of stone and to our eye look very similar to the buildings we have seen in the Four Corners area.

In the "cave kiva," we see long poles fastened to the ceiling, which served as supports for the upper portion of an ancient loom. The lower horizontal bar of the long, vertical loom was anchored to supports imbedded in the small holes we see in the floor. Like the Egyptians, the Pueblo people wove cotton which they grew in selected areas along the Rio Grande. When the Spanish came and discovered that the Pueblo people manufactured cotton clothing, they began to see dollar signs. Profit could be made by shipping cotton garments to the increasingly populated mining regions of northern Mexico.

We come to a fork in the trail. We have been walking and looking for about forty-five minutes. Instead of turning back to the center, we take the trail to the right, to Long House Ruin. We have heard that it abounds in petroglyphs and pictographs. Now the trail ascends through some interesting, narrow passageways between the rock cliffs. Long House was probably the largest settlement in the canyon. Only a few intact stone walls remain, but they are dramatically situated under the sheer cliff face that rises hundreds of feet above them. Here we see a pictograph outlining the same terraced stair-step design we saw this morning on the stairway of the round kiva at San Ildefonso. In subtle tones of terra cotta and cream, this beautiful design tells us that the Anasazi Pueblo people have been superb artists for years.

At this point, we can either turn right to the ceremonial cave or cross the River of Beans and return to the visitor center. We choose to do the latter. As we walk back along the river, we encounter an excellent self-guided nature trail which graphically tells about the high desert vegetation. This extremely well-designed exhibit helps us to identify vegetation such as rabbitbrush, sage, box elder, and of course New Mexico's state flower, the yucca plant. We all agree that this unexpected natural history find is a nice bonus to our very pleasant two hours here at Bandelier. We return to the visitor center and refresh ourselves with a cool drink. As we walk back to the car, we discuss the fact that the

Yucca (New Mexico State flower)

Indians left here sometime in the 1500s. By the time the first Europeans arrived in 1540, the Frijoles Canyon area was practically abandoned.

Returning to New Mexico Highway 4, we can either choose to continue west to the Valle Grande volcanic crater and Jemez State Monument or retrace our steps. We choose to do the latter. In less than twenty miles we come to the junction leading to Los Alamos. We resist the temptation to stop there. On previous visits we have seen the excellent Bradbury Science Hall with its atomic bomb and nuclear science exhibit, as well as the instructive Los Alamos Historical Museum. Los Alamos continues to be an interesting, scientific town with more Ph.D.'s in residence than you can shake a stick at. Many are employed at the National Scientific Laboratory or its support facilities. From previous experience, we have learned not to drive New Mexico Highway 4 after 3:00 P.M., for the traffic leaving Los Alamos and heading east toward the valley is nightmarish and slow, as many commuting government workers return to their homes along the Rio Grande.

It is now 2:00 P.M. and we seem to be just ahead of the traffic. Instead of crossing the Rio Grande, we turn off Highway 502 to New Mexico Highway 30 at the junction just west of the river. We pass the entrance to the Puyé cliff dwellings and bypass Santa Clara Pueblo. Santa Clara, like San Ildefonso, is one of the great Pueblo pottery villages. We reflect that our many visits there have been very enjoyable and that we have often seen some of the fine Santa Clara potters firing their distinctive burnished black pottery. Now, we enter Española. We find our way through a confusing array of streets to U.S. Highway 285 and New Mexico Highway 68 North, where in approximately four and one-half miles a sign marks the turnoff to the left or the west, one mile, to San Juan Pueblo.

We are all excited to return here as it is a very

enjoyable pueblo to visit. It is not architecturally stunning like Taos, but it is laid out in a pleasant way along the Rio Grande, amid great old cottonwood and Chinese elm trees. We all agree as we drive along the shaded road that the Spanish chose well when they sited this spot for the first European settlement in the interior of America (see Section IV, "History"). But the San Juan Indians knew this was a special place long before the Spanish came. They established their village O'ke here sometime in the 1300s and, as far as we know, it has been continuously occupied since then. This is the largest of the Tewa-speaking villages, having a population in excess of seventeen hundred. It is also the most northerly of the Tewa communities. It is surrounded on two sides by the Spanish-speaking community of Chamita.

Parking in front of the O'ke Oweenge Crafts Cooperative, we notice that it is very quiet this afternoon in the outer plaza of the pueblo. We note the Catholic church to the west and the Pueblo chapel to the east, as we walk over to the Pueblo's craft cooperative, O'ke Oweenge. It is interesting that the San Juan residents have chosen their Tewa name O'ke for their traditional crafts shop. We are greeted warmly by several of the San Juan women behind the counter. Our daughter strikes up a conversation with one of the women about a painted gourd she likes. She is told that this nicely decorated piece was made by one of the young girls in the pueblo, not too much older than she is. We inquire about several carved, wooden, craft objects and once again receive the full story about the people who made them, including some interesting facts about their roles in the life of the village.

After admiring a white, cotton, woven "rain" sash, a type of sash made here and on the Hopi reservation, we note excellent displays of finely crafted brown and red, plain black, and plain red pottery. Once again, the Pueblo women eagerly tell us who made them and how they are used. We leave the front display room and enter another, larger room in the back. Here there are ribbon shirts and other craft items made in the pueblo. And today, in one of the small craft rooms, several Pueblo women are doing handwork, and in yet another room, several San Juan wood-carvers are at work. We purchase a few items, return them to the car and then walk across the plaza. The smaller church to the east is the church the Pueblo uses. The one across the plaza, larger and more formal, is the one built for residents of Chamita. We walk around the church and enter the main plaza of the pueblo.

It is very quiet and almost empty this afternoon. This is very different from what it was like on a June day two years ago. Then we visited the pueblo to attend the San Juan Feast Day festivities, which included a Buffalo Dance. The plaza was crowded that June day with many Pueblo Indians who had come home for this important event and some Anglos as well. Circulating in the crowd were a number of San Juan men whose job it was to make certain that all cameras, sketching equipment, etc., were duly registered and fee permits issued to their owners. We had our 110 camera along with us. After it was inspected and we were queried about the purpose of the pictures we were going to take, we paid a three-dollar fee and were given a permit which we were asked to display. We jockeyed for position in the plaza for the best viewing spot. The drums began to beat as five men carrying large, handsomely handcrafted Pueblo drums entered the plaza. Over the course of the afternoon, we saw some beautiful costumes, watched some fine dancing, and enjoyed being a part of a happy, spirited crowd for whom the dances had more meaning than we would ever know.

But today in the plaza it is so quiet that we can hear the cottonwood leaves rustle as we walk back to the car. The traffic is heavy in the opposite lane as we drive out. Many San Juan residents are returning from jobs elsewhere. We drive the short distance back to Española, which some have dubbed a Spanish island in a sea of pueblos, realizing that in many ways this Hispanic community is the cultural hub of northern New Mexico. There are six Pueblo villages within twenty miles of here and there are over a dozen Hispanic villages equally close. With much anticipation, we find our way through busy, sprawling Española to the family-run Rio Grande Café (see "Food—Santa Fe"). We are starved. We know from past experience that the Archeleta family will fill our stomachs with delicious New Mexican food without depleting our pocketbook. Full and content, we should be back to Santa Fe by 9:00 P.M., just in time to join

Buffalo Dance, San Juan Pueblo

the evening crowd for ice cream on the plaza.

There are two interesting sights south of Santa Fe—El Rancho de las Golondrinas and Santo Domingo Pueblo. They can be seen either as part of a day trip out of the capital city or, because of their proximity to the freeway, can be visited as you drive to or from Albuquerque. Seeing both sites takes over half a day.

El Rancho de las Golondrinas (Ranch of the Swallows) near La Cienega

If you would like to learn more about the early Spanish settlers in New Mexico and capture the flavor of their life-style, this village museum is the place to go. It has one of the best historical displays in New Mexico, but tours are available only on certain days. It is open from the first weekend in April through the last weekend in October. On the first weekend in May and October, this live Spanish museum becomes the Sturbridge Village of New Mexico as Spanish wood-carvers, musicians, embroiderers, weavers, and tinsmiths show their stuff, while Spanish cooks stoke the fires of ancient adobe fireplaces and ovens, turning the rancho's kitchens or cocinas into a frenzy of culinary activ-

ity. The rest of the summer, Las Golondrinas returns to being the sleepy but superb museum it is.

Unfortunately, the rancho is closed more than it is open. It is only open to the public on a drop-in basis on the first Sunday of June, July, August, and September from 10:00 A.M. to 4:00 P.M. It is open for guided tours every Wednesday and Saturday during June, July, and August, but you should call ahead to make reservations for these tours. Groups of ten or more who have made reservations several weeks in advance are allowed in at other times. If you are in the area on a day when the rancho is not regularly open, call the rancho office anyway, for often they will allow individuals or families to accompany some of the groups that may be touring the rancho. But if there are no groups going through on the day you want to go and it is not a regularly scheduled day, you can walk through the village but the exhibits will not be open for viewing.

What is all the fuss about anyway? It is about a four hundred-acre authentic Spanish village developed in this century on the site of an old rancho, which in turn was built early in the eighteenth century on ground which contained a defensive torreon or tower constructed around 1650 by orders of the king of Spain. This small valley was a well-watered place kept so moist by flowing springs that the Spanish named it "Cienega" or "marshy place." Because of its location along the Camino Real and its close proximity to Santa Fe, it became a paraje or stopping place for travelers going to or coming from the capital city. Fifteen miles was a long distance in those days. But as time went on and the Camino Real was replaced with other trails and roads, La Cienega ceased to function as a paraje and became a typical Spanish rancho. The Spanish family who had owned the land for over two hundred years eventually sold four hundred acres of it to an Anglo family from out of state in 1932. Most of the buildings had weathered away or were otherwise in disrepair by then.

Shortly after that, in the 1940s, a Finnish diplomat met and married one of the owners. This couple took up residence on the old rancho and decided to reconstruct it. With great dedication and care, they bought up old Spanish buildings from all over New Mexico and carted them piece by piece to the site, where they were reconstructed. In addition, they collected a wealth of artifacts and furniture relating to the early culture of the Spanish. The property is now operated by the Colonial New Mexico Historical Society. Besides the main house, there are over twenty other buildings which contain three fully equipped cocinas and their adobe fireplaces, several capillas or chapels with many religious artifacts, a wide variety of handcrafted Spanish New Mexican furniture, and a rich selection of kitchen, craft, and farm tools.

You will see the typical New Mexican well houses called norias as well as the outdoor beehive ovens called hornos, both of which are still being used in the Spanish villages to the north. While walking up hill and down dale of the village, look for barn swallows or las golondrinas for which the ranch was named. Also keep an eye out for New Mexico's state bird, the spritely roadrunner which the Spanish call el paisano. If you tour the whole rancho, you will have walked 1.75 miles round-trip. Allow at least 2.5 hours for a guided tour visit. There is also a museum shop with books and information about the rancho and the Spanish in New Mexico. For information, write the rancho at Route 14, Box 214, Santa Fe, New Mexico 87505. Telephone: 1-505-471-2261.

To reach Las Golondrinas, leave Santa Fe via

El paisano or roadrunner
(New Mexico State bird)

U.S. Interstate Highway 25 South. Just past Santa Fe Downs Racetrack, at approximately twelve miles, take exit 271 to La Cienega. In about a mile as you head west, you will pass an excellent contemporary craft shop and ceramics studio just before reaching a T junction. Take a right at the junction, following the signs until you come to the rancho. A small entry fee is charged. Along this same road is a sign marking the way up another road to prehistoric camel tracks a few miles away in the direction of the Santa Fe River (see Section II, "A Prehistory of Indian Country").

Santo Domingo Pueblo

The major jewelry making village along the Rio Grande is Santo Domingo. On any warm summer day, you will see expert craftsmen there working in the shade of hastily constructed ramadas adjacent to their homes, their electric grinders and polishers going at a clip. The workmanship from this pueblo's best craftsmen is very good, with much of the work still being done by hand. The Santo Domingo jewelers come by their trade honestly. Pueblo residents from this area have been making shell and turquoise jewelry for centuries. In fact, the Santo Domingo Pueblo claims ownership of the ancient Indian turquoise mines at Mount Chalchihuitl in the Cerrillos hills just east of the pueblo. One of the specialties at Santo Domingo is the crafting of heishi necklaces. Shells are cut into round shapes, hand drilled, polished to

Church at Santo Domingo Pueblo

an exquisite fineness, and then strung on a cord. Silver jewelry, especially the style called liquid silver, is also made at the pueblo.

The Keres-speaking Santo Domingoans are known as excellent traders and, like the Taos Indians, are extremely conservative. Intent on keeping their ancient ceremonies and rituals intact, they maintain a healthy suspicion of Anglo intentions. Although Oñate made his first stop at Santo Domingo and established ecclesiastical headquarters there for all the Indians of the region, the village is more of a mecca for traditional ways than it is a Christian Vatican for the Pueblo world. Even the beautiful Catholic mission church dedicated to the thirteenth-century Spanish preacher and founder of the Dominican order, Saint Dominic, is outside the village proper, being separated from it by an irrigation ditch.

The mission church is as unique a building as you will see along the Rio Grande. Its single, terraced adobe bell tower caps a rectangular adobe structure with a bright, sky blue balcony. The front facade is painted with the figure of two horses facing one another, signaling almost immediately that the pueblo is a farming community first and foremost. Its lands bordering the Rio Grande on both sides of the river are easily irrigated and productive. So the people chose well centuries ago when they moved off the Pajarito Plateau to the valley. But they did not foresee the ravishing Rio Grande floods that would finally destroy the old village in 1886. The pueblo and church you see have all been rebuilt since then.

See the beautiful altar screen in the church and walk for awhile in this village of over twenty-five hundred inhabitants. Jewelry and pottery, as well as some willow and yucca baskets, can be bought there. A few of the many fine jewelers living there are Clara Reano, Lorenzo Tortellita, Percy Reano, Joe B. and Terry Reano, Old Joe Reano, and Angie Reano Owen. If you are in the area the first weekend in August, do not miss Santo

Domingo Feast Day and Corn Dance, a spectacle of over five hundred dancers that rivals the Santa Fe Opera in costuming and comes close to matching the drama of the dances on the Hopi mesas to the west. If you have more time upon leaving Santo Domingo Pueblo, you may want to continue on New Mexico Highway 22 approximately nine miles to Cochiti Pueblo where fine drums, clay storyteller figures and nacimientos or nativity scenes are made.

To reach Santo Domingo Pueblo, leave Santa Fe via U.S. Interstate Highway 25 South in the direction of Albuquerque. At approximately twenty-five miles, take the New Mexico Highway 22 exit and head west on Highway 22, about six miles to the pueblo.

A Day Traveling Through Spanish New Mexico: A Narrative Account

Today is one of those incredibly beautiful summer mornings in Santa Fe. The light is bright, the air cool, dry, and invigorating. A few minutes ago, the waitress seated us at this table in the sun here on the patio at La Posada. My daughter is

Storyteller clay figure, Cochiti Pueblo

reading Willa Cather's *Death Comes for the Archbishop.* I reach over and borrow the book for a moment and thumb through it to this passage: "In New Mexico, he always awoke a young man; not until he rose and began to shave did he realize he was growing older. His first consciousness was a sense of the light dry wind blowing in through the windows, with the fragrance of hot sun and sagebrush and sweet clover; a wind that made one's body feel light and one's heart cry 'To-day, to-day,' like a child's." My family chides me for my romanticism, but all agree that Cather caught the essence of mornings like this one in that passage. We have ordered huevos rancheros, a favorite dish in New Mexico. A fried egg is placed atop a corn tortilla and over that is poured a fresh sauce of tomatoes, onions, chili peppers, and oregano. While we devour this mildly piquant or hot dish we make our plans for the day.

We are going to Taos. Instead of taking the major highway north from Española, New Mexico Highway 68, the "low road" that follows the Rio Grande, we will take the scenic eighty-mile route by way of New Mexico Highway 76 through the mountains, the so-called "high road to Taos." Besides being an excellent, paved, two-lane road, it winds through some of the more remote and interesting Spanish villages. We leave Santa Fe the "back way" to head northwest on Bishop's Lodge Road, an extension of Washington Avenue. At the confusing intersection of Washington Avenue and Paseo de Peralta, we continue straight across the intersection, staying on Washington as we follow the sign that says Ski Basin Road. We are now on Bishop's Lodge Road (New Mexico Highway 590) and we continue straight ahead, disregarding the spur road that comes in a short distance leading to Artist Road and the Santa Fe Ski Basin. At approximately 3.5 miles, we pass the intersecting road leading to Bishop's Lodge which we see to our right. This famous Santa Fe resort was constructed on the grounds of Archbishop Lamy's home where his chapel is still intact.

In a little less than 2.5 miles further on, we make a stop at Ben Ortega's home, studio, and sales gallery on the right side of the road. Ben lives here with his wife and family. His ten children have been raised here. Now several sons and daughters-in-law are part of this "cottage industry."

Wooden statue of Saint Francis

Ben is a Spanish wood-carver and has developed a unique art form. He collects pieces of wood and stumps from the surrounding area. With wonderful imagination, he converts these lifeless forms into small statues that resonate with personality. Most of the statues are of some of the more popular saints. Two of his statues, one of San Pascual, the patron saint of the kitchen, and one of Saint Francis of Assisi, complete with two beautifully carved birds on his arms, grace our home. On a visit a few years ago, we were met by one of the older daughters since Ben and his wife were away. Her greeting was so warm and friendly that we were reminded of the Spanish phrase that has prevailed here for years: Mi casa es su casa—my house is your house. Our son and daughter took her literally and found their way through the house to the work area in the back courtyard. There one of Ben's sons greeted us and invited us to watch him work. He was shaping a large piece of cottonwood that would eventually become a Saint Francis. This piece of wood was chosen, he told us, because there was a large burl at the top that resembled a Franciscan friar's hood. From that spot, a head would be attached and with the natural bend in the log giving it a human shape, arms and feet would be attached to aid in the final conversion of an inanimate object to a statue that truly resembled a person. After talking with Ben and viewing his new work, we return to the car.

Continuing north on Bishop's Lodge Road or New Mexico Highway 590, we pass the Tesuque post office and finally the spur road to Rancho Encantado before entering U.S. Highway 84, U.S. Highway 285. For a few miles, we retrace the route we took two days ago to San Ildefonso. Today we pass by that exit and continue north to Española where New Mexico Highway 76 intersects U.S. Highway 285, twenty-five miles north of Santa Fe. We see the sign to New Mexico 76, and Chimayó and Penasco to the right just before the intersection and then we see our identifying landmark, McDonald's, across the highway from the U.S. Highway 285 and New Mexico Highway 76 junction. We turn right or east onto New Mexico Highway 76.

Even though we will stay down in the valley for the next twelve miles or so, we are now, for all practical purposes, on the high road to Taos, the heartland of Spanish New Mexico. In less than one-half mile we pass a lovely small adobe chapel dedicated to the local saint, San Niño de Atocha. In another half mile we see the large old Santa Cruz

Church at Santa Cruz

Chile ristra

Mission Church off the road to the left, with its thick adobe walls and its tin roof shining in the morning sun. Built in 1733, it was one of New Mexico's leading churches in the eighteenth century, serving the village of Santa Cruz founded in 1695, the second villa or city to be established by the Spanish government in New Mexico. Already we feel transported to another age, another time, and we are only one mile away from urban sprawl.

In a few more miles, we reach the outer barrios or sections of Chimayó. Originally a compact village, Chimayó is now spread out along the Santa Cruz River. We come to an intersection with paved Santa Fe County Road 88 leading back through interesting and beautiful countryside to U.S. Highways 84 and 285 via the Hispanic villages of La Puebla and Arroyo Seco. We continue on to the left past adobe houses with ristras or strings of chili peppers hanging from their walls, with flowering plants climbing their fenced courtyards, and with dusty yards scattered with stands of multicolored hollyhocks, their long flowering stems belligerently blooming out of the dry soil. We see the lilac hedges that were in bloom last May when we were here, and in front of several of these homes we see the quaint water well houses or norias. Signs advertising peppers and fruit for sale dot the road. A small café advertises homemade tamales and enchiladas.

It is said that not too many years ago, every

other house here contained a handloom. For this is the home of the brightly colored, handsome, woven, wool Chimayó blankets. Weaving has a long history in this region and some believe the link between the famous Saltillo serapes in Mexico and the later development of Navajo weaving is right here in Chimayó (see Section II, "The Navajo: Nomads and Survivalists"). In a few minutes we come to Trujillo's Weaving Shop on the left-hand side of the road. We have often stopped here to see the weavers at work on the several different sizes of handcrafted looms (see "Shopping"). A short distance further, just past the sign to Santuario de Chimayó, is the junction of New Mexico Highway 76 and New Mexico Highway 520, approximately eight and one-half miles from Española. We turn right onto New Mexico Highway 520 and pass by Ortega's large weaving and Spanish craft shop to the right. In half a mile we pass the Rancho de Chimayó Restaurant on the left, as we drive several miles further to the barrio of Potrero.

We park near the entrance to the Santuario de Chimayó. We are now facing one of the most venerated and charming adobe structures in New Mexico. We have visited this church three or four times and have taken many pictures of it. Yet today we are once again awed by its setting beneath the Sangre de Cristo Mountains and by its simple charm. We have been told that the spot where the

Chimayó weaving

church was built was also a sacred place to the early Indians of the area. And we have read that the lovely pyramid-shaped mountain rising behind the santuario is the sacred mountain of the east for San Juan Pueblo. So here is the sacred church lying under the ancient sacred mountain of the Tewa Indians. No wonder, then, that this plaza is filled with both Hispanics and Indians several times each year.

Once again we find ourselves intrigued with the notion of the intermixing of Spanish Catholicism and Indian religion. Even the name Chimayó is a Spanish corruption for the name of the Tewa Indian village that once occupied this area, Tsimayo. That Tewa word means "good flaking stone," referring to the obsidian found in the area. On Good Friday, it is said that ten thousand Hispanic and Indian pilgrims swarm to this tiny church, some hiking or hitchhiking distances of over three hundred miles while some bear rough, hand-hewn crosses on their shoulders. The devout have called the santuario here at Chimayó the Lourdes of America. Perhaps it is the Fatima as well. We re-

flect that the plaza, so quiet this morning, must once again be jammed late in July on the feast day of Santiago or Saint James, the patron saint of Spain. At that time, there is a ceremonial enactment commemorating the Spanish victory in driving the Moors out of Spain. The festival is called Los Moros y Los Cristianos, the Moors and the Christians. In costumes reminiscent of each faction, men on horseback stage a dramatic mock battle, resulting in a Christian victory.

We enter this small church that was built between 1814 and 1816. It was constructed as a public church, but financed by one man and his family. Its purpose was to serve as an auxiliary to the larger church at Santa Cruz so that people in the new village of Chimayó would not have to travel so far to worship. It is said that this building was constructed entirely without nails. Our eyes seem to make a slow adjustment from the very bright light outside to the very dim interior in here. Even though the whitewashed walls help accentuate the light, it is still fairly dark. This is an exquisitely beautiful interior, splashed with color from

Santuario de Chimayó

Bulto, Señor Santiago de Chimayó (San Juan)

the altar screen in front and from the various reredos and painted bultos on both sides of the nave. Our son immediately points out his favorite figure, the bulto or statue known locally as Señor Santiago de Chimayó on the right side of the altar. It is a local representation of Saint James. So revered was Saint James of Compostela that Spanish soldiers often shouted "Santiago" before they charged their enemies. The glass case around the statue is to keep it safe from devout, loving hands, which at one time just about destroyed it. We note that this New Mexican version of Saint James depicts him in caballero dress with boots, long spurs, and a straw hat.

Our eyes now focus on the colorful altar screen made by New Mexico's greatest santero, Molleno, who is sometimes called the "Chili Painter." At the bottom of the large niche which holds the crucifix are painted representations of wheat and grapes. In the center is the six-foot-tall crucifix of Our Lord of Esquipulas, a Guatemalan Christ figure. We wonder how it got here. Local legend has it that on a Good Friday early in the 1800s, the head of the family who finally built the church saw a burst of light centering somewhere in the area of today's santuario. He thought the light was coming from a particular spot in the ground, so to sate his curiosity he felt compelled to dig at that spot. When he did so he unearthed a crucifix with a dark green cross and a darkened

Christ figure. Some said it resembled crucifixes carved in Esquipulas, Guatemala, where the "Black Christ" is worshipped. At any rate, the discovery caused quite a stir. In addition to helping its discoverer overcome an illness, it speeded along his earlier request for a church to be built near this site.

When the church was built, it was constructed near the site of some springs which the Indians thought had healing properties. We walk in to the small room to the left of the altar and then into a smaller room off of that called El Pozito or the little well room. We see a hole in the floor exposing the dirt underneath. For over one hundred fifty years, thousands upon thousands of the faithful have come to take small bits of this healing clay soil, either to ingest or to apply to various afflicted body parts. There is no mystery why the hole is not deeper. The priest and his assistants keep filling it up with more clay and dirt. Still they come.

In this same room, we see a smaller crucifix of the Esquipulas Christ. We ask someone, who tells us that this is the crucifix discovered in the ground and that the one in the main sanctuary is an enlarged replica. We step back into the little prayer room where we see an astonishing array of crutches, braces, and other testaments to the healing power of this shrine hanging from every wall surface. We also see a bulto of Santo Niño de Atocha, the venerated local saint. He also is credited with healing powers. The belief is that he does his good work by walking through the surrounding communities each night, keeping them safe and protecting them from harm. In accomplishing this task, Santo Niño, the Holy Child, wears out his shoes nightly so that every day he must have a new pair.

We walk back to the entrance and step outside. We are all squinting in the bright sun as we get in the car and drive the short distance on Highway 520 back to Rancho de Chimayó, seeking the restorative powers of an early lunch. We turn off the road into the long driveway leading to the old hacienda. The rancho not only is a picturesque place of historical interest, but it also has some of the best Mexican-style food in America today—bar none! After making that statement, I ask for a vote. Three eager hands of three hungry pilgrims to this gourmet shrine shout "right on." As we pull into

Rancho de Chimayó

the parking lot, we again notice the old apricot trees bending under the weight of their ripening fruit. We are greeted warmly by the hospitable owners, who have had family ties with the ranch since it was constructed late in the nineteenth century.

Because of the authentic decor and varied architectural features of the several rooms, we have a hard time deciding where we want to sit. One cold day in February, while eating here, we sat in the room that has the corner adobe fireplace. That fireplace is so well designed that the piñon fire burning in it penetrated us with its warmth at a table ten feet away. But today we consider the more open and lighter room near the bar with its authentic shepherd's bed or hooded fireplace. In the old days, its adobe ledge right above the fire provided a warm place for some tired shepherd to sleep. But we decide instead to sit on the patio outdoors rather than inside. This delightful patio in the shade of the building and some young cottonwood trees is always pleasant on a warm day. Today is no exception. The kids scurry off to the play area on the terrace above us and to the "shop," where some very nice Spanish crafts are sold.

Meanwhile, we sit and sip a Chimayó cocktail, made from local apples and tequila, while waiting for lunch.

Finished with lunch and a tour of the kitchen to see just how the best sopaipillas in New Mexico are made, we return to New Mexico Highway 520 and retrace our route to New Mexico Highway 76, where we turn right or east. Now the road begins to live up to its name as we climb steadily in an easterly direction to Cordova. The brown, dry earth meets a bright blue sky this afternoon, but there are a few thunderheads building over Truchas Peak to the east. Now a little more than three miles from the New Mexico Highways 76 and 520 junction, we look for a small sign that will direct us, rather suddenly, off New Mexico Highway 76, down a moderately steep dirt road to the village of Cordova.

At the bottom of the hill, we see a few small ranchos with signs out in front advertising wood carvings. We see the sign in front of the home of George Lopez whose carvings, along with those of his famous father, José Dolores, we have seen in several regional museums. Today we stop briefly to see what the Lopez family have on the sales "table" inside their house. George and his daughter greet us warmly and invite us inside. George tells us that he is no longer carving, but his children and grandchildren are. Their fine work graces his sales table. We purchase several carvings and thank the Lopez family for their gracious hospitality.

Now we descend further into the village, keeping to the left as we negotiate the dusty streets. In a few minutes we pass the post office and the center of this small village. We park and walk over to a small store that sells cold drinks. We talk briefly with the proprietor, who responds in English with a very strong Spanish accent. Refreshed, we walk up the narrow road to the Catholic chapel, Saint Anthony of Padua. It is not open today, but in the past we have seen the lovely altar screen in the back and the many carved bultos of various religious figures. Most of the carving done in this village is from white pine, red juniper, and aspen. These carvings are extremely handsome and the lines are generally clean and simple. As we walk back over the dusty road through the narrow street, we have a mounting feeling that we are walking a village street somewhere in the high dry plains of Spain.

Returning to Highway 76, we continue to wind and ascend through the Sangre de Cristo foothills. We can see great distances from up here as the car rolls along this high ridge road. We feel like we are sitting on top of the world. Now, eighteen miles from Española and at an elevation of 8,600 feet, we reach the picturesque village of Truchas perched on a high bench of the Sangre de Cristo Mountains. The village is situated across a deep valley from Truchas Peak, New Mexico's second highest mountain at 13,102 feet. Truchas is the Spanish word for trout, an abundant fish in these mountain streams.

Exiting from the highway to enter the village, we drive several blocks down the narrow street which follows the edge of the escarpment and then pull off the road to park. We get out and walk a few blocks, seeing some very old, weathered houses and noticing how the architecture differs up here close to the pine forests. Instead of flat roofs, we predominantly see steeply pitched, corrugated tin roofs designed to help shed the large amount of winter snow this area receives. Although many homes have adobe walls, we also see quite a number of homes with walls made of logs and other materials. In the middle of the block is the Truchas Senior Citizens Community Center and Craft outlet. We laugh when someone comments that we never pass up the opportunity to visit this kind of center. That is true. Stops like this allow us to meet some of the local people, which broadens our experience and helps us to understand a variety of lifeways we otherwise would not be exposed to. Today is no exception.

As we wind our way back down the narrow street to New Mexico Highway 76, we pull over at times to allow cars to pass. Now we continue in a northeasterly direction to Las Trampas. There are few tourists up here today so, when we stop in the Spanish villages, we seem to be the only Anglos around. Over and over today we have noticed that the older people speak Spanish among themselves, not English. The young people speak English, but with a strong Spanish accent. Our daughter points out that some of the Spanish terms used by the older women are different from the Spanish she is learning in school.

Indeed, it is, for I have read that in this part of New Mexico, partially because of isolation and partially because of resistance to change, some archaic Spanish terms dating back to the time of Cervantes in the early 1600s are still in use. Some of the priests in residence here from Spain are often astounded by this language phenomenon that is a direct result of the isolation of these small villages. The twelve- to thirteen-thousand-foot peaks of the Sangre de Cristos loom large to our right, but they do not seem that overwhelming since the roadbed we are on is well over eight thousand feet elevation. Large quantities of piñon wood are stacked near most of the farmhouses and smoke curls up from some of the chimneys, as it is no longer hot. The weather is changing rapidly up here, becoming very cloudy and cool in the last fifteen to twenty minutes. We see the sheets of rain dancing over the Sangre de Cristos and know it will be here before long.

We pass through the small sleepy village of Ojo Sarco. The farmhouses come closer together now as we approach Las Trampas. Our kids spot a few hornos or ovens in front of several homes. Our

Church at Las Trampas

son asks if there will be tramps in Las Trampas. I explain that "trampas" is a Spanish word for traps or snares and that the town is named for the river that flows through it, which was well known in Kit Carson's day as a fine place to trap beavers. Almost immediately upon entering Las Trampas, our eyes are drawn to the church, San José de Gracia. The historical marker in front of the church tells us in Spanish that the town was founded in 1751 by families who came here from Santa Fe. Many have likened Las Trampas to an eigheenth-century walled, Spanish colonial village. Because of many of the old adobes remaining and because of the beauty and intactness of the Spanish colonial mission church, San Jose de Gracia, the area was declared a National Historic Landmark. It is also thought to be one of the centers of the Penitente movement of this region (see "History").

We stand in the plaza admiring the church. Completed in 1776, it was dedicated to the Twelve Apostles. Legend has it that only twelve men were allowed to build it. Perhaps that is why it took twenty years to complete it. Money for building materials came from the villagers, who gave one-sixteenth of their crops each year until it was finished. This is one of the few adobe structures remaining that has genuine mud-plastered walls rather than the artificial commercial materials more commonly used these days to achieve the same effect. Rising gracefully above the heavy,

four-foot-thick adobe walls are two bell towers made of wood. We now notice that the portal to the plaza has the same terraced, cloud pattern we saw on the stairway of the kiva at San Ildefonso. This is not an Indian village, yet the same imagery is used. The exterior choir loft is an unusual feature of the church and we admire the fine carving of its vertical members. Here in the ceiling of the choir loft we see an excellent example of latillas or the peeled juniper or aspen poles which are laid over the roof beams. And we see the vigas or logs of pine and spruce used as roofing beams, extending under the balcony. The door and lintel are beautifully carved.

In spite of efforts to raise the caretaker to unlock the door, we can find no one. We try with some success to peek through the keyhole. The unattached structure on the east side of the church, bordering on the cemetery, catches our attention. This is a morada, a special place for Penitente services. We have read that it contains many interesting religious objects, including a Penitente death cart. The cart holds a carved, wooden statue of the death angel Dona Sebastina, better known as La Muerta. This unique piece of folk religious art was first developed by Nasario Lopez, the father of Jose Dolores Lopez of Cordova, who is the father of the man we just visited, George Lopez. We return to the car and then drive up a few of the village streets. Small gardens growing squash, corn,

La muerta, "death cart"

chilies, and apple trees abound. We now exit this Spanish village, reflecting that it was founded in 1751 as a distant outpost to protect the people of Santa Cruz from Comanche raids.

Once again we enter New Mexico Highway 76, the road to Taos. We continue to lose altitude as we approach the village of Chamisal, named for the chamiza or rabbitbrush that abounds in this area. We note the special visual treat of small, well-tended fields and recall the much-used phrase of "postage stamp ranchitos." Much to our amazement we see an old horse-drawn wagon with large wooden wheels approaching us from the other direction. For a moment we doubt our senses, for we thought that carts like these disappeared from the highway many years ago. But as it comes closer there is no doubt that it is a carro de vestias. One of our favorite New Mexican authors, Rudolfo Anaya, has written about just this type of wagon which his grandfather used many years ago to drive into town to sell produce. We stop and wave as I point to my camera. The driver smiles and nods his head so I take a picture. We say adios and are on our way again in this "Land of Enchantment." Midway between Chamisal and Peñasco, New Mexico Highway 76 intersects New Mexico Highway 75. The latter highway connects, via Dixon, New Mexico, with the other main route to Taos. Dixon is fast becoming a popular place for many of New Mexico's artists and craftspeople to live, and a few small galleries have opened there and in the nearby village of Embudo. Once we took an excursion to the Indian pueblo of Picuris from this junction by turning left and traveling a short distance on New Mexico Highway 75, following the signs to the pueblo. We enjoyed the fine museum there and purchased one of the very durable micaceous clay bean pots in the museum shop. We also shopped door to door and met several potters, enjoying the hospitality of their homes. But today we turn right onto New Mexico Highway 75 and continue toward Taos. We pass other Spanish villages in their quiet settings along the road with names such as Peñasco, Vadita, and Placitas. Since leaving Chimayó, we have seen no motels, inns, hotels, nor restaurants with a tourist orientation. Once again we comment on the remoteness of these villages. Now that we have descended to an elevation of about seven thousand feet, some of the mystery we felt in that higher country is gone.

Just beyond Placitas, New Mexico Highway 75 intersects New Mexico Highway 518. We turn north onto Highway 518. At the top of a long incline called U.S. Hill, we catch glimpses of New Mexico's highest peak, snowcapped Mount Wheeler at

Chamiza (rabbitbrush)

Church at Talpa

13,161 feet. We are now in a pine–aspen forest. As we descend to Fort Burgwin Research Center, we find ourselves back to scrub country, loaded with juniper, piñon, scrub oak, cottonwood, and sagebrush. A large historical marker on the left side of the road interests us so we turn off the road to stop and read it. It tells us that a cantonment or fort was built here in 1852 and was occupied by a troop of the First Dragoons who had several skirmishes with hostile Indians. This fort was built after the Taos Revolt in 1847 and its name commemorates the death of Captain John Burgwin who was killed in that clash (see "History"). We drive down the long entryway to park in the signed lot.

The authentically restored log fort is an imposing site and the only restored fort of its kind in northern New Mexico. The fort and surrounding buildings serve as headquarters for a research unit from Southern Methodist University who study the military and Indian history of the area. Inside the fort we see a few military relics. The parade grounds, now planted with grass and trees, offer quiet seclusion and some amount of cooling shade this afternoon. We find a door that opens to a small museum and display area which gives some of the details about the fort and the prehistoric Indian culture which preceded it. Archaeological work is

being done in the hills nearby where several hundred Indian ruins are being studied. We walk outside the fort's walls and notice a small stream. It will eventually flow into an excellent trout fishing river, the "Little Rio Grande." We spot several bluebirds and are delighted to see several magpies swoop by.

Refreshed after the stop at Burgwin, we continue on toward Taos, still ten miles north. To our left, we see the skeletal remains of an old adobe house, beautifully framed under billowing white clouds in the blue, blue sky. Now a little further at six miles from Taos, we see the sparse, quaint village of Talpa, formerly called Rio Chiquita, after the river of the same name that flows nearby. This little village was founded around 1823 during the restless years of Mexican rule of New Mexico. A small lane leads to the church of San Juan de los Lagos, Saint John of the Lakes. We get out of the car and walk over to the church. Our children comment that there are not any lakes nearby so how did it get its name? I explain that I had read that some of the early settlers were devotees of a small statue of Our Lady of the Immaculate Conception that had graced a church in Jalisco, Mexico, in a town called Saint John of the Lakes. These New Mexican devotees named their church in honor of that shrine. We are disappointed that we are unable to arouse an attendant to enter the church, for inside is another fine altar screen by the old master, Molleno, one of New Mexico's best nineteenth-century santeros. But the beauty of the little church with its simple, centrally located bell tower is sufficient reward. Framed by the blue sky and the surrounding adobes, it is a perfect camera subject. Driving on, there is an especially picturesque, Hispanic cemetery on the right, framed by Taos Mountain in the background. Colorfully festooned with flowers, white crosses of all shapes, sizes, and materials, there is a certain aura of optimism and acceptance evoked by this scene.

We now pass Ranchos de Taos to our left, four miles south of Taos. It is a small village on the outskirts of Taos proper that has retained much of its old charm. It is fully anchored by what is unquestionably the most picturesque Spanish church in New Mexico, Saint Francis of Assisi Mission Church. We turn left on to New Mexico Highway 68 to catch a glimpse of the church. Admiring its fine exterior features, we pass it by this afternooon since we are tired and the heat is beginning to take its toll. We will come back here for a longer visit later this evening or tomorrow. Now we return to New Mexico Highway 68 and drive on to Taos, about four miles north. Taos has sprawled considerably in this direction in the last few years. This approach, which used to offer beautiful vistas to the north as we looked across the sagebrush plain to Taos, is now cluttered with many unattractive, view-blocking commercial establishments spread out alongside the road. But our enthusiasm returns as we enter town and find the plaza and several other familiar landmarks much the way we remember them. We pull into the narrow driveway that leads to the parking lot of the Taos Inn, our favorite resting spot here. We get out of the car, walk into the historic old lobby, order some drinks and sit down to rest. We can check in later!

Taos

"Taos" is a place name used in the title of three separate and very different communities. Trav-

elers are often confused by this. The principal community by that name is, simply, Taos, formerly known as Fernando or Fernandez de Taos. Taos is predominantly a Hispanic community with 86 percent of its full-time population of a little over three thousand belonging to that group. It is the touring base for the area around it. Three miles to the northeast is Taos Pueblo. This very conservative, traditional Indian village with a population of two thousand has carried the name Taos longer than either of the other two communities bearing that name. In fact, the name "Taos" is probably a Spanish corruption of the Tewa Indian name for this Tiwa-speaking village which means down at the village. Ironically, this name, of Indian origin, was used to later name the nearby Spanish community of Taos. This is unusual since the Spanish usually hispanicized the names of the Indian pueblos to suit them and generally did not name their settlements after Indian villages. The other community that uses the word Taos in its name is Ranchos de Taos, a small Hispanic community four miles south of Taos, centered around the beautiful and historic Saint Francis of Assisi Church.

You will certainly enjoy your visit to Taos. Resting on a high plain like Santa Fe, it is in many ways more dramatically situated. The flat, undulating sagebrush plains roll right up to it from the west, while Taos Mountain and the Sangre de Cristo range snug close up and dominate it to the east. The immediacy of the mountains to the east with the wide, open spaces to the west lend an aura of mystery to Taos that I have found in only a few other places in northern New Mexico. Storms build up almost over your head in Taos, then let loose their barrage of rain pellets as they spread west over the dry sage plain, somehow releasing the pungent aroma of sagebrush into the air. Otherworldly? It often seems so in Taos.

But Taos is very much a part of this world, too, and changes every year. In the late 1940s and early 1950s when I first visited there, I remember quiet, tree-shaded streets, little traffic, and many dusty unpaved roads. There were some shops, but not many, and the town seemed relaxed and laid back. Today, in midsummer, traffic snarls the main entrance to town. Pay parking lots are increasing as on-street parking becomes even more dear. Shops by the hundreds, so it seems, line the formerly sleepy old streets and, heaven forbid, even shopping malls have made their way close to the heart of Taos. The plaza has been updated and refurbished and a chamber of commerce booth has been placed there in the summer to help travelers.

But much of the Taos that captured my heart as a boy remains. The plaza and buildings that surround it are pretty much the same as they were, except for the modern development to the east. The low adobe buildings with their wide porches still attract and evoke nostalgic sighs of relief from me. The shady, grassy parks, the narrow passageways and alleyways between old adobes, and even some unpaved, dusty streets, remain. The same slow, nonchalant, poco tiempo pace continues in most areas. The Taos Book Store anchors the east end of town where it is still possible to linger in its cool interior on a hot day and overhear conversation by Anglo locals who talk in hushed tones about mysterious things going on out at the pueblo or about the curanderas, midwives, and brujos who are part of life in Taos County's large Hispanic population.

So in spite of modern change, the center holds. This town, founded in 1615 but not incorporated until 1934, offers the tourist much by way of its rich past (see"History"). Its cultural mix means that you will experience different foods and see different styles of living than you are used to. Taos is not a rich town. From starving artists and struggling Hispanic subsistence farmers to aging hippies, the standard of living is low. In the 1970s per capita income in Taos County was less than four thousand dollars annually. At times, almost half of the county's twenty thousand inhabitants has received financial assistance of one sort or another. The literacy rate is much lower than the national average. And some have reported that within the Taos city limits, almost half the dwellings lack inside plumbing. Taos County is an undeveloped country in the heart of the United States. As charming and beautiful as it is, these charms, as local author John Nichols has so poignantly written, are bittersweet in terms of the misfortunes that strike many of the families who live year-round in this beautiful, but terribly harsh land.

A Three-Quarters-of-a Day Walking Tour of Taos

Because the town is small and reasonably compact, many interesting sites can be seen in a short time. Taos is more conducive to walking than driving. A good starting point for a tour is the plaza. If you are staying in one of the motels or inns right in town, walk to the plaza. If you are staying outside of town you may want to drive in, park your car, and then walk to the plaza. Unless you drive into town early in the morning, before 9:00 A.M. in the summer, on-street parking will be hard to find. In that event, park in one of two municipal lots. These are close in, yet well camouflaged from view. If traffic is backed up along North Pueblo Road and you are approaching from the south, turn left onto Placitas Street which intersects South Santa Fe Road about one block below the plaza intersection. Follow Placitas, always keeping to the right as it doglegs around the town. It will take you to the marked municipal parking lot north of the plaza or all the way around town to New Mexico Highway 522, U.S. Highway 64, heading north.

In the plaza, note the flagpole with the American flag flying. By tradition and special approval of the United States Congress, the flag flies day and night. This does not especially mean that the people there are super-patriotic. The tradition stems back to the Civil War when Confederate citizens kept taking down the American flag from the plaza. A few Union sympathizers like Kit Carson did not like their antics so they went into the mountains and brought back to Taos one of the tallest and sturdiest timbers they could find. Then they nailed the flag to it and planted the pole deeply, thereby raising a permanently installed flag high above the plaza. Just to make sure no one tried to remove the flag, they stationed sentries on the rooftops of the plaza. Then they patrolled the plaza day and night, armed with rifles, with orders to shoot anyone wanting to remove the flag. Rumors had it that Kit Carson and his cohorts were pretty good shots, so the flag flew without incident twenty-four hours a day until it finally wore out.

Since that time, the flag has continued to fly day and night and in a special ceremony each year in May, near Memorial Day, a new flag replaces the worn, tattered one. The plaza goes back to

1710 when the town was rebuilt after the Pueblo Revolt of 1680. The buildings faced the plaza. They completely encircled the plaza space, their rear walls offering fortresslike protection to the Spanish settlers from the marauding Plains Indians. Walk to the south side of the plaza, cross the street, and enter the La Fonda Hotel, not to be mistaken for the large hotel by the same name in Santa Fe. Toward the back of the beautiful old lobby, with its fine collection of Navajo rugs, you can pay a small fee to view some of D. H. Lawrence's paintings. His paintings apparently caused as much of a stir in the early days as his books did, even though neither Lady Chatterley nor her lover are the subjects of his paintings!

Return to the front of the hotel. Turn left and left again onto the small side street which leads south to Placitas Street. Cross Placitas and enter Ledoux Street. Now with the hustle and bustle of the plaza behind you, walk this dusty, narrow, quiet street bordered by some of the loveliest adobe homes and courtyards you will see in New Mexico. One of the restored adobes is the former home of R. C. Gorman. It is now a gallery open to the public (see "Taos–Shopping"). The modern treatment of its interior has only enhanced the beauty of this fine old adobe, where Mr. Gorman, a renowned Navajo painter, sculptor, and print-maker, exhibits his work.

Continue down Ledoux Street to the Ernest L. Blumenschein Memorial Home (telephone: 1-505-758-4741), a registered National Historic Landmark. Blumenschein, one of the cofounders of the first art colony in Taos, purchased this old Spanish home, built in 1797, on returning from Paris to make Taos his permanent residence in 1919. The intact furnishings are representative of the years Blumenschein and his talented wife made their home and studio there. It is well worth a visit. Re-enter Ledoux Street with its many walled, flower-filled patios on each side and proceed to the Harwood Foundation Building at 25 Le Doux Street (telephone: 1-505 758-3063), another fine adobe owned and administered by the University of New Mexico. The large building and the adobes around it are some of the oldest in Taos. They house a fine historical and cultural library, a children's library, and an art gallery displaying representative pieces of most of the artists who have lived for awhile or settled in Taos since the 1890s. You will also see some antique Spanish furniture, a few local Spanish handcrafts, and a collection of New Mexican retablos displayed there. With the availability of this research center, it is easy to understand why writers and artists go to Taos, taking up residency there to do serious work on the history and culture of the Southwest.

Retrace your steps approximately two long blocks east, back to the plaza. Walk by the store fronts on the west end of the plaza where most of the stores and shops still retain a local, small town flavor. Then enter Teresina lane, a pedestrian side street extending from the northwest corner of the plaza. Follow it passing along the way several small shops and galleries. Then turn right to enter the municipal parking lot. Cross the parking lot and enter historic Bent Street. This street of shops and small restaurants (some with shaded outdoor dining areas) is very touristy, yet it retains some of the flavor of old Taos and is especially noted for the Governor Bent House, Museum, and Gallery. Bent was massacred there by a Spanish and Indian coalition who was not pleased with the American takeover of the areas in 1846 (see "History").

Walk east along Bent Street to the very busy North Pueblo Drive. Cross the street, if you can, and enter the quiet lobby of the Taos Inn, secluded behind thick adobe walls. The lobby was formerly the open courtyard or placita of a Spanish home. The courtyards in those days were special places of beauty and peace. The home which the hotel now occupies was built in the early 1800s. Find your way from the hotel lobby through the restaurant to discover another Mexican surprise, a pool and a grassy outdoor patio surrounded by small casitas. Although one placita has been lost to enclosure and modernization, another one has been made from the open space at the back of the hotel. Return to the Taos Inn lobby and exit on North Pueblo Road. Turn right and walk to the Stables Art Center next door. This dynamic center, operated by the Taos Art Association, offers a good overview of the arts and crafts scene in Taos today.

In the courtyard behind the center is one of the region's best contemporary craft galleries (see "Taos–Shopping"). Return to North Pueblo Road, turn right, and walk north. In less than the distance of a half block you will come to the sign marking one of the pedestrian entrances into the twenty-acre Kit Carson Memorial State Park with its tree-shaded picnic tables, cooking grills, and playgrounds. You may want to stroll to the back of the park to the historic cemetery to see the graves of Kit Carson and his family, as well as those of Padre Martinez, Mabel Dodge Luhan, and other historic Taos figures.

Now continue north two more blocks until you come to a sign indicating the Fechin House. For many years this beautiful adobe, set back some distance from the road yet visible from it, brought excited exclamations from vacationing flatlanders as they traveled up North Pueblo Road. Most travelers knew that someone special had to have built a home like that, but most never took time to find out who. Then in 1979, the home was listed on the National Register of Historic Places. Shortly after that, in 1981, the home became more visible to the public with the formation of the Fechin Institute, named after the longtime occupant of this historic Taos adobe. The institute was formed to commemorate the one hundredth anniversary of Nicolai Fechin's birth. Nicolai Fechin was born in 1881 in Kazan, Russia, a trading center along the Volga River. His artistic talents, which were recognized at an early age, led to a career as an artist and art teacher. In 1923 at the age of 42, Fechin, along with his wife and daughter, emigrated to the United States. In 1926, Fechin left New York to visit a friend in Taos. As with many other artists who visited Taos in the twenties, Fechin was immediately taken with the region and within a year established residence there. He soon purchased an adobe house at this site and set about to renovating it. The result, both inside and out, is nothing short of spectacular, for Fechin was an artist's artist. He was at home with wood carving, ceramics, sculpture, and architecture as well as the impressionistic oil paintings, which brought him fame.

If you have time to see the interior of only one of Taos's many famous adobes that are open to the public, this is the one to see. It offers the rarest and most beautiful blend of two worlds that you are apt to find anywhere. For inside this twentieth-century New Mexican adobe rests the spirit of historic Russia. Pursuing his oil painting career during the best daylight hours, this complete artist put aside his brushes in the evening to wield adze, chisel, and mallet as he shaped wood and adobe to resurrect the spirit of his homeland in this remote American hinterland. There is a feeling of richness and warmth in these rooms, which makes you want to linger. You wonder what artistic magic has created such nurturing comfortable spaces. Is it the artist's profound use of light and proportion or is it his remarkable knowledge of the centuries-old techniques of wood carving and surface finishing that creates the wonder here? Beautifully carved wood panels, doors, mantels, and furniture will no doubt please your aesthetic senses, but it is the sculptured adobe fireplace that makes you feel like you have just entered the portals of aesthetic heaven. The institute hosts musical events and rotating art exhibits. Of course, Fechin's works are showcased several times during the year. The home, adjacent studio, and the Fechin Institute are operated by the artist's daughter and granddaughter. During the summer it is open to visitors in the afternoons, Wednesday through Sunday. Open by appointment other days in the summer and throughout the year. For more information, write The Fechin Institute, Box 832, Taos, New Mexico 87571. Telephone: 1-505-758-1710.

Now return to North Pueblo Road, turn left, and walk three long blocks back to Kit Carson Road. (You might choose to visit the Kit Carson Memorial Park now. If so, you can walk through the park to the cemetery and then to the south border of the cemetery, where you can enter Dragoon Lane. From there it is only two blocks to Kit Carson Road.) Turn left or east onto Kit Carson Road and walk up this street with its many shops and galleries.

Now about a block from the Kit Carson Road junction at the plaza, enter the narrow walkway to the Kit Carson Home and Historical Museum. This is one of the most thoroughly delightful small museums in the area. Not only are the lives of the famous Indian scout and explorer, Kit Carson, and his Spanish wife detailed completely, but there are excellent regional historical and archaeological displays there in addition. In the museum you will learn about the Taos trappers, the American and French mountain men of the early 1800s who lived and worked using Taos as a base for their expedi-

Las Palomas, Taos

tions into the unknown mountain country to the west (see Section I, "History," Old Spanish Trail).

Further up Kit Carson Road and across the street is the venerable Taos Book Store, a veritable mecca for books about D. H. Lawrence, New Mexico, and the Southwest. At this point if you have more time and you are not too tired, you can continue to walk further east on Kit Carson Road, past Dragoon Road turning left at the second intersection. This is Morada Road. Now heading in a northerly direction, you will reach in about one-half mile Las Palomas, the former seventeen-room palatial adobe home of Mabel Dodge Luhan on the edge of the Taos Pueblo property. By the time this house was built, Mabel Dodge had married for the fourth time to a traditional Taos Indian, Tony Luhan, a marriage that was to last forty years until her death in 1962. It was through the efforts of this spirited woman that Taos become nationally and internationally known as a haven for artists and writers.

Las Palomas, the "big house" as the locals call it, saw it all. Las Palomas is now operated by a private nonprofit educational organization, Las Palomas de Taos, offering courses for school teachers, senior citizens, and others in the history, art, and culture of the Southwest. A bed-and-breakfast inn and an elderhostel are also on the premises. Tours of the home are given at certain times of the year

Write P.O. Box 3400, Taos, New Mexico 87571, or telephone 1-505-758-9456. On the edge of the property is an old morada or Penitente chapel presently used by the Kit Carson Museum Foundation. From the Dodge house, you can retrace your steps back to Kit Carson Road.

A One-Day Auto Tour around Taos: A Narrative Account

Last evening while it was still light, we drove south of town a short distance, turning off the highway onto a secondary road heading west. We got out of the car and walked along the road and through the sage for awhile. The view from any of these open areas was splendid. As far as we could see there was open space. In the distance, the San Juan Mountains were visible to the west. Close at hand, the pungent scent of sage permeated the air. We intensified the aroma by breaking off small pieces of sage and pinching them with our fingernails to release a double-distilled dose of that lovely incense. After about a mile, we turned back to the car. Facing east, Taos Mountain loomed above us. The sunlight hitting this peak bathed it in a reddish glow. This reddish blush on the mountains so impressed the Spaniards that they named these mountains east of the Rio Grande, the Sangre de Cristos or the "Blood of Christ" Mountains. As the reddish glow faded, we saw the moon rising behind Taos Mountain, and we immediately felt a cool breeze. The warmth of the car felt good as we drove back to the inn. As we approached the inn in the purple of twilight, the aroma of sagebrush gave way to the delicious fragrance of piñon smoke drifting down from the chimneys of the adobe fireplaces in the casitas. After lighting our own piñon fire, we fell asleep in just minutes, exhausted from the day's activities.

But this morning we feel refreshed and ready to face another day of sight-seeing as we walk into the inn's restaurant. We eat breakfast with gusto and prepare to leave for the day. It is chilly this morning, but we know that by midafternoon we will be sweating instead of shivering. We get in the car and drive south or left on North Pueblo Road. We pass the junction at the plaza and head south on New Mexico Highway 68. Our first visit today will be to the small Spanish village of Ranchos de Taos, approximately four miles south of Taos. We turn left or east at the scenic marker across the highway from the post office and park in the designated space near the Mission Church of Saint Francis of Assisi. Out of the car now, we stop and look at this old adobe church built sometime around 1776, the year of our Declaration of Independence. That event probably passed unnoticed here, for it would have meant very little to the colonists of Spanish descent who were struggling to survive in one of Spain's most remote colonies.

This lovely church commands our attention. We walk around to the back of it, for architecturally and aesthetically the back side is the most famous section of the church. The massive adobe buttresses seem to flow from the earth, supporting the walls like great hands. Although we have visited

Ranchos de Taos Church

this church many times, our reaction today is just as intense as it was before. We stand for a few moments just taking it all in. A beautiful, old church rising out of the ground on the flat plain, as if to echo the heights of the Sangre de Cristo Mountains behind it. We slowly walk around it until we find a view of the buttresses, reminding us of the painting of this church by Georgia O'Keeffe in 1929.

O'Keeffe used to point out that most artists must paint this church, just as sometime in their careers they feel compelled to paint a self-portrait. We are also reminded of the excellent contemporary photographs of this church done a few years ago by Ruffin Cooper. Except for a few puffy, white clouds, the sky is brilliantly blue this morning, just as it was in both of those well-known artistic efforts. The light brown-colored church rises into that vastness of blue and white, providing a combination of shapes and colors that fixes our attention.

Now at the front of the church, we enter the sanctuary, finding it cool and dim. Our eyes have trouble adjusting. In a few minutes we can see better. What we see is a fine collection of Spanish art. In the east transept is one of the largest altar screens in New Mexico. Its 425 square feet of surface is beautifully painted and decorated, lending light and brilliance to the dim room. The salomónicas that we saw in the San Miguel Mission Church in Santa Fe are also part of the altar screen here. The image on the altar screen is that of Esquipulas, the Christ of Guatemala. We remember the wonderful legend behind that image from our visit to the Santuario de Chimayó the day before yesterday. This altarpiece is also the work of Molleno, one of New Mexico's great native santeros. Again, we note the balance struck between the plain whitewashed walls of the church and the colorful religious artwork. We see also the painting of Christ done by Henry Ault in 1896. Between June and September at 9:00 P.M. each evening, a showing of the painting and a lecture about it is given. In complete darkness, the painting changes form as a cross appears on the left shoulder of Jesus and a halo emerges above his head. More of the mystery of New Mexico!

We leave the church, return to New Mexico Highway 68, and head back to Taos. On the way, we pass the junction of New Mexico Highway 240 (Lower Ranchitos Road) to the left. A few years ago we took that very scenic, rural route four miles west and north to tour the newly restored Hacienda de Don Antonio Severino Martinez (telephone: 1-505-758-4741), an early fortified Spanish colonial house that belonged to an important figure in the history of Taos. But today we pass it by and drive through town, thankful that the congestion near the plaza is minimal as we head north on North Pueblo Road (New Mexico Highway 522, U.S. Highway 64). We travel approximately four miles from the plaza until we spot a blinking caution light and in front of it a sign to the Millicent Rogers Museum. We turn left immediately at the Texaco station onto a good dirt road before reaching the blinking light. We follow the road less than a mile south to the parking lot of the Millicent Rogers Museum (telephone: 1-505-758-2462). We walk into the reception area of this handsome building and pay a fee to enter what I call the Alhambra of New Mexico, a monument to the architecture, arts, and crafts of the region.

Millicent Rogers was an heiress to the Standard Oil fortune. She visited Taos in 1947 and decided, like Blumenschein, Dodge, and others before her, to stay. She became enamored with the local Spanish and Indian art. With the realization that this indigenous art might vanish someday, she wisely began collecting crafts of these cultures. Between then and her death about six years later, at age fifty, she collected an incredibly rich cache of folk art. After her death, her son established a museum to keep his mother's valuable collection intact. The museum opened in 1956. In 1968 it was moved to this site, formerly an elegant private home. There have been several tasteful additions to this former adobe residence, which over the years has come to look more and more like a museum. For a long time this adobe hacienda-turned-museum retained many of the characteristics of the original home and gave rise to the fantasy that we were visiting someone's beautiful home. And when I would look out the windows and see broad, unbroken vistas of sage plain and purple mountains through the adobe-encircled windows, I was always tempted to move to Taos— immediately if not sooner! Although we have not been here for a number of years, we have fond memories of the displays we saw then, which included many items from the museum's perma-

nent collection of Native American jewelry, pottery, textiles, and Hispanic arts and crafts. We begin our tour of the museum's ten gallery spaces by spending some time in the textile gallery. We particularly like this gallery where there are beautiful examples of both Indian and Hispanic weavings with an interesting commentary on the history of each and how to distinguish one type from the other. From there we go to the Maria Poveka (Martinez) Family Collection. We never seem to tire of looking at the museum's stunning collection of burnished, black San Ildefonso pottery created by Maria and her family. We then see an exhibit on Native American Clown Paintings, which revive memories of the wonderful Koshare clowns we have seen over the years at dances on the Hopi mesas. We quickly move on to the Hispanic Collection, one of our favorites, which details the Hispanic settlement of the area by exhibiting their agricultural tools as well as their superb art. There is a fine collection of santos, retablos, and bultos here along with a beautiful example of the death cart with its defiant looking skeletal occupant, La Muerta. We then spend a few moments looking at the permanent jewelry collection, which has several extraordinary pieces of jewelry on display by the outstanding Hopi artist, Charles Loloma. Finally we finish up by seeing the newly curated, but temporary exhibit, "Coyote: A Myth in the Making," a selection of the works of the famous American Indian artist, Harry Fonseca. This exhibit, rich in humor and symbol, has us all laughing as we see the various antic poses of the irascible trickster coyote. I anxiously glance at my watch and realize that our quick run through the museum has taken well over an hour and comment that we must move on. The reply is that when the going gets tough the tough go shopping, so we spend a few minutes in the excellent museum shop with its wide assortment of Southwest Indian and Hispanic arts and crafts for sale. (see "Taos–Shopping").

We return to the car and drive back to the highway. At the intersection with the blinking light, we make a left onto U.S. Highway 64 to Tres Piedras, which will take us to the Rio Grande Gorge Bridge seven miles away or approximately fifteen miles from Taos. The wind is blowing some this morning, perhaps presaging an early afternoon thundershower. Since we plan to picnic near the gorge, we hope it holds off. Now, several miles in the distance, as we look west across what seems to be the flattest stretch of land in the United States, we see many cars and people—specks in the distance—gathered at the edge of the gorge. We pull into the parking lot and join the other gorge watchers. This narrow, steep gorge, truly a deep slot into the bowels of the earth, is so long that it extends from north to south as far as we can see, giving us the impression that it is a huge fault that splits the continent. Of course, it is not a fault and it does not go on forever. It is a slot carved by the constantly flowing water of the Rio Grande as it cuts deeper and deeper into the hard basalt rock. If the rock here had been soft sandstone, the river would have carved a wide canyon rather than the narrow gorge we see.

We walk to the edge and look down. We are bathed in sunlight, but the Rio Grande is still in shade 650 feet below us. We begin to wonder how deep 650 feet really is. The gorge would easily contain the 555-foot-high Washington Monument. Then someone says that if you could place the Eiffel Tower in the gorge, 350 feet of the narrow top portion would protrude above the surface. Getting into this imaginary frame of mind, we look up to see just how high it would protrude. As we look up, we see a few thunderheads building above us, so we quickly cross the second highest bridge in the national highway system to the west side of the gorge. There we enjoy the protection of one of the picnic shelters, while the dark clouds are rapidly forming. The wind is blowing many miles away across the sage plain, where we see numerous dirt devils or whirlwinds, those small funnels of dirt that are set into motion by the action of the wind.

Lightning zigzags across the sky, its thunder reverberating across the plain. We see sheets of rain moving toward us. It starts—a few giant drops at a time—s-p-l-la-a-t! Suddenly more drops. And now we are grateful for the shelter as the rain pounds the ground around us. In about five minutes the storm is over. There is an incredibly sweet, fresh smell in the air. The aroma of sage is very intense now. Where else could air be so fresh, so clear, so fragrant? Refreshed by the cool breeze and a good lunch, we get back into our newly "washed" car.

We retrace our route back across the bridge and along U.S Highway 64 until we reach the junction with New Mexico Highway 522. Instead of going on into town, we make a left turn from the intersection at the blinking light and follow New Mexico Highway 522 to the northwest, as though we were going to Questa. We follow this road about six miles to Arroyo Hondo and another three and one-half miles beyond that town until we see a sign to the Lawrence Ranch directing us six miles up a road to the right. We follow the dirt road through rolling sage lands toward the mountains. This road can sometimes be difficult during very wet periods. Although a little water is still standing in the potholes, the road has been graded recently and is in good shape. D. H. Lawrence's modest house, really a small cabin in the pines, and his ranch now belong to the University of New Mexico where every summer a writers-in-residence program is convened. Frieda, Lawrence's wife, allegedly traded Mabel Dodge Luhan Lawrence's manuscript of *Sons and Lovers* for this property, which Lawrence eventually named Kiowa.

As we drive up the road through the pines, our daughter recalls her favorite painting by Georgia O'Keeffe, *The Lawrence Tree.* It was done in 1929 and was based on the artist's experience at the Lawrence Ranch about a year before Lawrence died in France in 1930. It is a fanciful, imaginative painting of an old tree near the Lawrence cabin that reflects what I have so often experienced here. The ordinary takes on a different character in this remote mountain fastness of New Mexico. In her rendition of the tree, O'Keeffe painted the brown tree bark at night a deep shade of plum. There is in that evocative painting a wonderful sense of the mysterious and intense beauty to be found in this heartland of the Southwest.

We pull into the parking lot below the shrine. In spite of all the talk about D. H. Lawrence's Taos, Lawrence did not spend much time here. He visited Taos three times between 1922 and 1925, spending about six months each time. On the last visit in 1925, he was ill with the tuberculosis that would end his life five years later. In Europe, ill and yearning nostalgically to return to New Mexico, he wrote a piece, at Mabel's request, for the publication, *Survey Graphic* (1 May 1931), that summed up his feelings about New Mexico. Of his arrival there in 1922 with Frieda and in 1924 with Frieda and Lady Dorothy Brett, he wrote, "I think New Mexico was the greatest experience from the outside world that I have ever had. It certainly changed me for ever. Curious as it may sound, it was New Mexico that liberated me from the present era of civilization, the great era of material and mechanical development.... But the moment I saw the brilliant, proud morning shine high up over the deserts of Santa Fe, something stood still in my soul, and I started to attend. There was a certain magnificence in the high-up day, a certain eagle-like royalty,... In the magnificent fierce morning of New Mexico one sprang awake, a new part of the soul woke up suddenly, and the old world gave way to the new."

In the short time he was in New Mexico, Lawrence did a lot of work, completing, revising, or composing some of his best works. Lawrence was intrigued with the Indians, especially the Taos Pueblo Indians and the Hopi Indians to the west. He was fascinated by the closeness with which they lived to nature. Loving the rare beauty found in this cultural vortex of America, he wrote that from his viewpoint one of the first commandments of the Indian's religion was "Thou shalt acknowledge the wonder." For it seemed to him that the Indians were truly in touch with their magnificent surroundings in a way that white men rarely are. Even steeped in the traditions of Europe, he felt he had no permanent sense of religion until he came to New Mexico and attended many of the Indian ceremonies and religious dances. He wrote, "For the Red Indian seems to me much older than Greeks, or Hindus or any Europeans or even Egyptians. The Red Indian, as a civilized and truly religious man... is a remnant of the most deeply religious race still living... [with] a tribal integrity and a living tradition going back far beyond the birth of Christ, beyond the pyramids, beyond Moses. A vast old religion which once swayed the earth lingers in unbroken practice there in New Mexico...."

As we walk the steep trail up to the shrine, the incense of pine lingering in the air, we begin to understand why Lawrence loved this ranch. He and Frieda had not been happy down at Las Palomas in Taos, but it was here at this mountain retreat that he would find peace and would be moved to write that he had never experienced

D.H. Lawrence shrine, northeast of Arroyo Hondo

anything like New Mexico. As he walked, hoe in hand, along a ditch to the canyon at the ranch, he witnessed a beauty that inspired him to rhapsodize about mountains "blue as chalcedony, with the sage-brush desert sweeping grey-blue in between, dotted with tiny-cube crystals of houses, the vast amphitheatre of lofty, indomitable desert..." So it was here at the ranch that Lawrence broke through the "shiny sterilized wrapping," as he called civilization, and "touched" the country. When you do this in New Mexico, he wrote, "...you will never be the same again."

We see Frieda's grave in front of the handsome stone shrine and Lawrence's remains encased in concrete inside the shrine. Frieda brought his ashes from Europe to the ranch. Some say she was fearful that Mabel Dodge Luhan might try to get hold of the ashes, so she had them buried in concrete. Although she remarried, she spent the rest of her life loyally promoting Lawrence's image and his works. On the way down, we are even more taken with the views from the ranch which range out over the Rio Grande Valley. Piñon jays flit from one pine to another. The small picnic table in the pines makes us wish we had brought our lunch up here today. It is quiet and the light is as pure as Lawrence described it. It is as Lawrence wrote, "...so beautiful. God! so beautiful!"

The three talented women in Lawrence's life lived out the rest of their lives in the Taos area. It is said that they developed a sense of loyalty to one another over the years. Frieda occupied the ranch until her death in 1956. Mabel Dodge Luhan, who authored numerous books on the region, died in 1963, and Lady Dorothy Brett, who had become well known for her paintings of the Taos Indians, died in Taos in 1977.

Returning to the car, we drive back to the highway, turning left to drive to Taos. On the way back to town, we decide to visit Taos Pueblo. We turn left or east off U.S. Highway 64, New Mexico Highway 522, at the Mobil station this side of the Kachina Lodge, just before entering Taos. We drive the little over two miles through the lush, irrigated meadows watered by the Taos River. I recount for my family that although I first came here in the 1940s, I have been here many times since. In my mind, there is hardly a more beautiful valley in the world. Over five hundred years ago, the Taos Indians were directed by their legends to settle here. In Lawrence's terms, the Taos Indians have indeed "acknowledged the wonder" in choosing this location for their home. For here the sage plain gives way to lush green meadows watered by the Taos Pueblo River whose source is high in the mountains above us at Blue Lake, the sacred lake of the Taos people. We can see the pueblo in the distance as it rests peacefully below Taos Mountain, a wonderfully rounded, symmetrical pine-clad hunk of massive rock which cradles beautiful, jewellike Blue Lake. If there ever was a central place where heaven and earth meet, it is here. No wonder Blumenschein was enthralled. No wonder world-traveler Lawrence was stopped in his tracks, becoming a born-again New Mexican almost overnight.

Beyond the backdrop of the mountains in front of us is one of the few ancient passes to the eastern plains. Over the years the Taos Indians were greatly influenced by the Apaches, Kiowas, and Comanches to the east. Being near the portal to the east, the Taos Indians traded with these eastern Plains Indians and in doing so acquired some of their cultural traits, not found in the other Pueblo groups. We drive on past meadows with beautiful horses, sleek cattle, and even buffalo and the work yard of a Taos drum maker at the edge of the pueblo. Now we catch glimpses of the everyday life surrounding the pueblo that is thought to have been occupied continuously from sometime between 1370 and 1450 until the present. Some say the Taos Indians, like the other Pueblo people,

Piñon jay

migrated west from the Four Corners area, while others point out that their language is related to the Kiowa language, a language used by a group of eastern Plains Indians who now reside in Oklahoma.

But whatever their origins, the Taos people settled here. And today we catch glimpses of their everyday life as we pass near the ruin of the old mission church destroyed by Captain Burgwin and the other soldiers of the First Dragoons in 1847 (see "History"). We join the line of cars bottlenecked at the admission booth just outside the plaza. I get out and walk over to the booth. While I wait in line, I muse about this whole process. The Taos Indians have cleverly figured out a way to let tourists see a little of their pueblo and their lifestyle, without revealing all. Over the years, the Taos Indians have survived drought conditions, cold winters, and marauding Indian enemies. They have protected themselves from the onslaught of the Spanish, the Mexicans, the Americans, and since the early 1900s, the tourists. They are aware of the powerful impact of their village on tourists.

The large plaza, cut in the middle by the sparkling clear Taos River and surrounded by multistoried adobe buildings supporting long ladders jutting into the sky, is quite a sight and a photographer's dream. They also know that tourists tend to be snoopy, intrusive and in some instances, overly aggressive. By charging a parking fee and a photographer's/artist's fee and by keeping the tourists in a specified area, the Taos Indians are in control of their own village, as they should be. While we wander through the historic plaza, we hear distant drumbeats, signifying that more meaningful village functions are being performed in other areas of the reservation not open to the public. Thus Taos Pueblo maintains a public front and a private side simultaneously. The money we pay here at the admission booth will be used for financing segments of the Pueblo government and helping to carry out some of its programs for the people. The Taos Indians are known as good traders. In their transaction with the tourist, I think a fair bargain has been struck. The person in front of me pays his fee. It is for his camera only. He has parked his car several blocks away outside the plaza to avoid paying a parking fee. I decided to park in the plaza, so I pay both the parking fee and the camera fee for the use of my still camera.

I return to the car and drive into the large, open plaza and park. The pueblo is bustling with activity this afternoon. We understand that all of these ancient "apartment houses" are occupied. The villagers go about their everyday activities without much notice of us. One of the first things we see are the beehive ovens or hornos, which are believed to have been introduced to the Pueblo by the Spanish. They are in full operation. As we walk close to one, the aroma of freshly baked bread is more than we can resist. From a very friendly Pueblo lady we buy two loaves. In a few seconds we have torn one loaf into pieces and devoured it. Now we take a walk along the river that courses

through the middle of the plaza. It irrigates Pueblo lands before dumping into the Rio Grande. The water is clear and cool. Signs urge us not to despoil the water in any way as it is used for drinking by the villagers. Sitting along the grassy edge of the river, we finish the second loaf of bread.

We cross the small bridge to the other side of the village and walk among the adobe structures. Today one family and their friends are applying a mudlike plaster to a newly constructed adobe building. They are having a good time. They laugh and joke in a language we do not understand. They are talking in Tiwa, a dialect of the Tanoan language. The building they are plastering looks like a new building, but all the buildings around it look very old. It is thought that some of the sun-dried mud houses here are exactly as they were in 1540 when Hernando de Alvarado, one of Coronado's men, first saw them. He, like us today, was impressed with these multistoried buildings and irrigated fields. Now we look at the building blocks to the north and the south of the river. In places on the north side, the buildings rise to five stories. Their stepped-back or terraced appearance relieves the harshness of the line, giving these buildings a warm and inviting feeling. Ladders reach from one level to another. In the olden days, the units had no doors as we know them. Entry was through a hole in the roof. We walk back over

Hornos or beehive ovens at Taos Pueblo

Taos drum maker

the log bridge towards the north building block. We see numerous open wooden structures in front of the adobe buildings, which we learn are ramadas or drying racks for corn, peppers, etc. In the winter, some of them are covered with bundles of hay, providing shelter for many of the domestic animals.

We see a sign on one of the apartment doors. The sign just says "crafts." When we knock on the side of the open door, an elderly Taos Indian greets us with a warm, toothless smile and asks us to come in. The apartment is immaculately clean. The dirt floor is packed so tight that it almost shines. The furniture is simple but comfortable. Our host shows us the bows and arrows he makes. He is very proud of them. We purchase one and say good-bye. On the way out, we notice that the apartment contains no plumbing and that water is still carried in. But we do learn that modern conveniences have been installed in the new homes springing up around the pueblo. The old part is being kept "traditional."

We walk across the plaza near the admission booth and stand in front of the chapel of San Geronimo de Taos. Geronimo is the Spanish name for Saint Jerome. The terraced portal to its courtyard and the nonobtrusive bell towers seem very much in harmony with the surroundings. We enter the courtyard of the small church. Its brightly colored interior seems to lend light to the room.

Church at Taos Pueblo

Pregonero, Taos Pueblo

We learn that this chapel was built after the 1847 revolt when the older chapel, which we passed on the way in, was destroyed. As we admire the building, we discuss the fact that this Christian chapel is visible and easy to find, while six or more kivas are much less obtrusive. But often this afternoon we have heard drums beating in the distance. We are told that their source was one of the kivas outside the area where tourists are allowed. So the people here continue to practice their ancient rituals as well as being active participants in their adopted religion, Catholicism.

The Taos Indians fought the Spanish tooth and nail and, aside from the Hopi people to the west, were the most intransigent of the Pueblo people, being one of the last groups to submit to Anglo domination. Today their enemy is creeping urbanism, a formidable foe. Yet at Christmas Eve each year, this church is the site of one of the most interesting rituals performed anywhere in the world. It occurs during the period the Taos Indians call "The Time for Staying Still," a forty-day period of quiet and rest beginning on December 10 and ending January 20, during the interval between the death and rebirth of Mother Earth. But the quiet is broken for a Christian ceremony on Christmas Eve, when after vespers in the mission church of San Geronimo, the pueblo's inhabitants burst into the moonlit plaza carrying the figure of the Madonna Mary, firing rifles, and chanting to the pulsating rhythms of drums which reverberate through the night air. Cracking piñon pitch bonfires called luminarias light the way.

Returning to the plaza, we notice that most of the tourists are gone. Tourists are required to leave the pueblo at 6:00 P.M. We see several men with blankets over their heads and upper torso, reminiscent of Arab burnooses. They round the corner, walking with a resoluteness in their moccasin boots. Now we look up and see several more men with striped, pastel, cotton blankets wrapped around their heads and upper bodies ascend to the top of the pueblo. They are silhouetted against the darkening blue sky as they stand next to the smooth, rounded corner of the mud walls. Watching this ritual, we feel the mystery of Taos Pueblo as a foreign sound emits from one man's lips. He is the pregonero or the Pueblo crier and he is performing an ancient ceremony whose true meaning will always remain obscure to us Anglos. But we know the sun is about to set and it is time for us to leave. As we drive back to Taos, I continue to think about the friendly Taos Indians we have met today. There are over two thousand residents living in the pueblo. The community is intact, independent, and knows where it is going. We feel certain that Taos Pueblo will continue to be here to greet us in the future just as it always has in the past.

Staying There

Lodging

In north central New Mexico you will often have a choice between two different kinds of accommodations. There are motels that resemble modern motels in any part of the United States. But there are also inns, posadas, fondas, lodges, bed-and-breakfast establishments, ranchos, and even motels that evoke the spirit of the region, either through their architecture, interior design, or their location. In most instances, their prices will be higher than those of the standard motels down the road from them. Wherever possible, accommodations with a southwestern ambience will be listed. Some of the accommodations do not have air conditioning since the nights are generally cool in this very high country.

Food

In most of the restaurants of north central New Mexico, you will see menus that refer to native foods, regional cuisine, local foods, Spanish American, and Mexican foods. All these notations generally mean a type of food similar to what is called "Mexican food" in most parts of the United States. Chili, enchiladas, tamales, burritos, tacos, and many other similar dishes are all part of the scene. But there is a distinct New Mexican influence on most menus. You will likely be served a basket of sopaipillas, little pillows of bread made from flour, lard, sugar, and milk, which is rolled very thin, cut into small triangles or squares, and deep fried. Usually honey or a fruit syrup is served with the sopaipillas. The idea is to poke a hole in the fried puff bread and put the sweetener inside. Sopaipillas filled with honey are a fine antidote to some of the "picante" or hot chili dishes. Sopaipillas resemble Indian fry bread, which you will see in the pueblos and at Indian dances and fairs. The fry bread is equally delicious, but thicker and flatter.

Sometimes the tortillas you are served will be made from blue cornmeal. This is a product made from the bluish black, sometimes dark slate gray kernels of Indian corn that have been grown by the Pueblo Indians for centuries. Other colors of corn are also cultivated by the Indians, but it is the cob that contains all blue kernels that is prized by the Hopi for making delicate, flat piki bread and by other Pueblo Indians for making a hot cereal known as atole. Further hybridization of blue corn has led to a blue corn popcorn. Instead of mashed refried beans, you will often be served delicious whole brown beans that have simmered many hours with seasoning. Generally, that is the way the Indians have cooked beans since they threw away the basket and replaced it with a clay cooking vessel over one thousand years ago. Bean pots of micaceous clay are still fashioned and sold at Nambe, Taos, and Picuris pueblos. But instead of beans, you may be served posole. Posole is like hominy and it, too, has been a staple in the region for many years. And then there is carne adovada.

Pork or beef is marinated for about twenty-four hours in a tangy paste of ground chiles, herbs, and vinegar. The meat is then baked just prior to serving. In ordering New Mexican food in the regional restaurants, you can often choose between a mild red chili sauce and a hotter green one. If you are unsure about how picante or hot the sauce is, ask for the sauce to be served on the side. Then you can titrate your own gastronomic distress. Some Santa Feans say that the proper titration is reached when you begin to sweat. But there is no requirement that you turn your dinner into a sauna bath.

Tours, Fairs, Festivals, Fiestas, and Events

If you are planning to be in northern New Mexico for one of the area's major unique summer weekend fairs, festivals, or fiestas, reserve your lodging months ahead of time and prepare yourself for a crowded city. If you are not interested in the special events in the area, schedule your visit there so it does not correspond with those busy dates. For a complete schedule of where to go, what to do, and exact times for important events, write New Mexico Tourism and Travel Division, Joseph M. Montoya Building, 1100 Saint Francis Drive, Santa Fe, New Mexico 87503. Telephone: 1-505-827-0291 or toll free in the continental United States, except in New Mexico 1-800-545-2040.

The Indian pueblos around Santa Fe open their doors to the public during a number of their celebrations and dance days. These are well worth seeing if you are in the area. A partial list of some of the more popular events appears in the "Fairs, Festivals, and Fiestas" section. There are many other celebrations that you can find out about by calling the chamber of commerce in Santa Fe (1-505-983-7317) or the Santa Fe Convention and Visitors' Bureau (1-505-984-6760 or toll free 1-800-528-5369) or by calling the Taos Chamber of Commerce (1-505-758-3873 or toll free 1-800-732-8267) or by calling the pueblos directly (see individual listings under "Indian Pueblo Telephone Numbers" at the end of the Santa Fe section).

Shopping

At best, it is very difficult for the average traveler who has come to north central New Mexico for a few days or a week or two to make any sense out of the several hundred galleries and shops selling traditional regional and contemporary arts and crafts. Although the galleries and shops listed are but a few of many, it is hoped this preselection will help you gain a better perspective about the art market and aid you in finding what you want as quickly as possible. There are many other establishments on the scene not listed here that are worthy of your attention if you have the time to locate them. You may also want to check the bibliography for material related to the region's art scene.

Many northern New Mexican cities and towns, such as Santa Fe and Taos, are predominantly Hispanic in their population, yet they have gained much of their popularity and notoriety from the various groups of Pueblo Indians who live in small pueblos up and down the Rio Grande Valley. Only a very small percentage of Indians live in the major cities of the region, yet the cities are the major marketplace for Pueblo Indian arts and crafts. Without a doubt, Albuquerque, Santa Fe, and Taos are excellent places to buy pottery, jewelry, woven goods, and drums from the Acoma, Cochiti, Jemez, Picuris, San Ildefonso, San Juan, Santa Clara, Santo Domingo, Taos, Tesuque, and Zia pueblos. You will also find that these towns are the best places to buy Hispanic or Spanish crafts, including woven rugs, wood carvings, and tin and iron work. In addition, there are many shops that import handcrafted items from Mexico. Although Navajo rugs and Hopi kachinas are featured in many stores, they are brought in from the Navajo and Hopi reservations in the Four Corners area. Similarly, Zuñi handcrafted work is brought in from western New Mexico. So if you plan to include "Indian Country" (Section II) or western New Mexico in your travels, you might want to wait and see what is available there. Sometimes better values as well as a wider selection of crafts can be found closer to the craft source. But no matter where you choose to purchase traditional southwestern Indian arts and crafts (Navajo rugs, Pueblo pottery, silver and turquoise jewelry) please read this book's buying guide found in Section II, Indian Country, "Staying There," "Shopping (Consumer Tips for Buying Indian Arts and Crafts)". The brief guide you will find there is designed to help you sort out and deal with some of the complexities in today's marketplace. Do read it if you are planning to purchase traditional southwestern Indian crafts.

Because Santa Fe is the home of the prestigious Institute of American Indian Art and has been associated for so many years with the Indian arts and crafts revival movement, it has become the contemporary Indian art capital of the United States. You will see excellent paintings, prints, sculpted pieces, and ceramics representing this movement. Many of these pieces are outstanding in their design and execution. Northern New Mexico has also attracted many fine Anglo and Hispanic contemporary artists working in similar media. Artistically, this is a rich area.

Albuquerque

As each year goes by Albuquerque seems to increase the number and quality of facilities and services for the traveler. The result is that more people are not only discovering Albuquerque but are returning to soak up more of what it has to offer. No doubt this trend will continue, given Albuquerque's stunning natural setting, its multi-ethnic ambience, its delightful fairs and festivals, and its unique regional museums. And when visitors discover the increasing number of new and diverse accommodations and good restaurants available there, a return visit may just be inevitable.

The majority of the accommodations listed here center around some of the locations of the major sight-seeing areas this book emphasizes, particularly Old Town, the Indian Pueblo Cultural Center, and the sights west of the Rio Grande. One of the downtown listings, La Posada de Albuquerque, is worth seeing whether you stay there or

not (see details pertaining to that hotel in this section). Where possible, small inns and bed-and-breakfast accommodations, which convey the ambience of the region, are included. Sometimes this type of accommodation is away from the core of the city but not so far that you cannot easily slide into town to see the sights.

As with most growing sunbelt cities, Albuquerque has experienced a restaurant boom in this decade, which is unparalleled in its history. Although this book lists good restaurants, which serve American, continental, and ethnic foods of all sorts, the "Food" section primarily emphasizes the food of the region. You can eat native New Mexican fare in large, upscale, trendy restaurants or in small, modest family-operated, "hole-in-the-wall" cafés. You will find the full range listed here.

The airport is located in the southeastern part of the city not far from the University of New Mexico campus. Most of the sights mentioned in this book are located in the west end of town near Old Town, not far from the Rio Grande. The accommodations, restaurants, and shops listed are also centered around that area. You will not have trouble getting from one end of town to another as Albuquerque has an excellent, still uncrowded freeway system feeding all four quadrants of the city. It is well marked and easy to negotiate. Should you need assistance in any way, contact the Albuquerque Convention and Visitors' Bureau, 625 Sixth Street Southwest, Suite 210, P.O. Box 26866, Albuquerque, New Mexico 87125. Telephone: 1-505-243-3696 or toll free 1-800-284-2282 or in New Mexico 1-800-843-3659. An information center is also in Old Town at 305 Romero Northwest just across from the plaza. Telephone: 1-505-243-3215. After hours, call for a taped message on current local events. Telephone: 1-505-243-3696. International visitors seeking bilingual assistance should call the Albuquerque Council for International Visitors. Telephone: 1-505-888-1867.

Lodging

Sheraton Old Town Inn. Located within easy walking distance of "Old Town," Albuquerque, this relatively new, locally owned and managed, modern and tastefully designed hotel offers one of the most pleasant places to stay in Albuquerque.

From its upper stories there are excellent territorial views of the city and environs. A large outdoor swimming pool and patio area, two tennis courts, and a shopping mall complete the scene of this air-conditioned oasis. In addition, Tigeux Park, several blocks from the hotel's north entrance, is a nice place to jog. The interior of the hotel is tastefully decorated with both regional antiques and contemporary arts and crafts, which create a modern New Mexican, southwestern atmosphere. The inn has an excellent, moderately priced coffee shop that has a good breakfast menu. The 190 air-conditioned rooms are spacious and comfortable. Some have private patios outside. This is a revitalizing place to spend one night after a long, fatiguing air or automobile journey. TV's and telephones. Airport transportation provided. Mailing address: Sheraton Old Town Inn, 800 Rio Grande Boulevard Northwest, Albuquerque, New Mexico 87104. Telephone: 1-505-843-6300. Expensive.

Best Western Rio Grande Old Town Hotel. Also located on the west side of Albuquerque, this modern hotel is only four blocks from Old Town and within easy reach of the Indian Pueblo Cultural Center. This no-nonsense hotel offers 170 comfortable air-conditioned rooms for less money. Heated swimming pool. Airport transportation provided. Pets allowed. Dining room. Mailing address: Rio Grande Old Town Hotel, 1015 Rio Grande Boulevard Northwest, Albuquerque, New Mexico 87104. Telephone: Call Best Western Reservations Center in continental United States 1-800-528-1234 or phone 1-505-843-9500. Moderate.

Old Town Bed and Breakfast. This conveniently located adobe-style bed-and-breakfast home is located just two blocks from historic Old Town Plaza and museums in a very nice, quiet, tree-shaded residential area. Its second-story guest room is air cooled and has a private bath and shower, a color TV, and a separate entrance. Leave your car at the house and take the pleasant ten-minute walk through Tigeux Park to Old Town and the museums. Continental breakfast served on the patio or in the dining room. Hot tub available. Reservation deposit required. Call for directions. Mailing address: Old Town Bed and Breakfast, 707 Seventeenth Street Northwest, Albuquerque, New Mexico 87104. Telephone: 1-505-842-6410. Inexpensive.

William E. Mauger Estate Bed and Breakfast. This historic Victorian home, only ten blocks from Old Town, has been thoroughly renovated to its previous splendor and is now a wonderfully comfortable inn. Built in 1897, it is one of the oldest homes of this style in Albuquerque. There are eight air-conditioned rooms each with private bath and shower. A full continental breakfast is served in the handsome and spacious public rooms. Mailing address: William E. Mauger Estate Bed and Breakfast, 701 Roma Northwest, Albuquerque, New Mexico 87107. Telephone: 1-505-242-8755. Inexpensive and moderate.

Monterey Motel. This small (fifteen units) air-conditioned motel is just two blocks from Old Town on Central Avenue (from Interstate 40 take the Rio Grande Boulevard Exit). The price is right for families or budget travelers. Color TV's are available in all rooms and a coin-operated laundry is on the premises. Heated swimming pool. Many Old Town restaurants are nearby. Mailing address: Monterey Motel, 2402 Central Southwest, Albuquerque, New Mexico 87104. Telephone: 1-505-243-3554. Inexpensive.

Motel 6. This larger, attractive, 130-room two-story motel is located just west across the Rio Grande, which means that it is within easy reach of Old Town Plaza and the museums. Take the South Coors Road Exit from Interstate 40 and travel one block south to Iliff Road Northwest. In addition to air-conditioned rooms with color TV's, there is a heated swimming pool with whirlpool bath. Furr's Cafeteria adjacent. Mailing address: Motel 6, 6015 Iliff Road Northwest, Albuquerque, New Mexico 87105. Telephone: 1-505-831-3400 or 1-505-891-6161. Inexpensive.

La Posada de Albuquerque. If the rebuilt, modern glass and steel high-rise core of downtown Albuquerque has a heart and soul, it resides in the ten-story low-rise at 125 Second Street Southwest.

There, Conrad Hilton built his pride and joy in 1939. You get there from Interstate 25 by taking the Central Exit and traveling Central to Second Street. The Albuquerque Hilton, as La Posada de Albuquerque was known in those days, saw the famous and the soon-to-be famous enter its stunning New Mexican-style lobby. Conrad Hilton honeymooned with Zsa Zsa Gabor in room 821. Jimmy Stewart checked in on weekends when he was stationed at the nearby air base during World War II. And Lucille Ball, along with a host of other movers and shakers, made pilgrimages to this most elegant hotel, which soon became the center of Albuquerque's social life. In the 1970s the deteriorating stucco and brick territorial-style building was placed on the National Register of Historic Places and in the mid 1980s, this landmark hotel was restored to its original splendor, and its rooms updated to contemporary standards. Today its spacious territorial-style lobby with pueblo deco motifs is popular with locals and visitors alike. The combined effect of its earthy tile floors, massive carved vigas, carved wooden door lintels, large tin chandeliers, New Mexican-style fireplace, ornate tile-fringed fountain, restored wall murals, and lobby bar is to produce a sense of comfort and southwestern ambience not found elsewhere in the city. Evenings often find the lobby filled with live piano music or the soft refrains of a jazz quartet. But the liveliest nighttime scene to be found in downtown Albuquerque's otherwise quiet business core is in the upstairs ballroom on the mezzanine level. There, feet fly over the smooth parquet wood floors to the music of some of the best local bands. Eulalia's Restaurant, just off the lobby, is one of the city's finest (see "Food," this section), and the hotel is just across the street from the chic underground Galeria with its contemporary shops, galleries, and boutiques. The 114 spacious air-conditioned rooms and suites with color TV's are also decorated in southwestern style with Spanish-style bedsteads and wall art of the region. Located only about ten minutes from Old Town Plaza. Airport transportation provided. Some parking. Reservation deposit required. Mailing address: La Posada de Albuquerque, 125 Second Street Northwest, Albuquerque, New Mexico 87102. Telephone: 1-505-242-9090 or toll free from out of state 1-800-621-7231. Moderate and expensive.

El Centro Plaza Hotel. This multi-storied hotel is pleasantly situated near a tree-shaded park and, like the other accommodations along busy Central Avenue, is within easy reach of Old Town. There are 145 air-conditioned rooms. Heated pool. Airport transportation. Attractive dining room. Several good restaurants nearby. Mailing address: El Centro Plaza Hotel, 717 Central Avenue Northwest, Albuquerque, New Mexico 87102. Telephone: 1-505-247-1501. Inexpensive and moderate.

Lorlodge Motel West. Similar to the above motel except more basic. Closer to the cultural sights of Albuquerque's west side with sixty air-conditioned rooms. TVs and small pool. One-half mile west on U.S. Highway 66. Mailing address: Lorlodge Motel West, 1020 Central Avenue Southwest, Albuquerque, New Mexico 87101. Telephone: 1-505-247-4023. Inexpensive.

Quality Inn Northeast. A large, conveniently located motel near the junction of U.S. Interstate Highways 40 and 25 at 2120 Menaul Northeast. There are 218 air-conditioned units, pool, and coin-operated laundry. Restaurants nearby. Take the Carlisle Boulevard Exit from Interstate Highway 40. Mailing address: Quality Inn Northeast, 2120 Menaul Boulevard Northeast, Albuquerque, New Mexico 87107. Telephone: 1-505-884-0250 or 1-800-328-5151. Moderate.

Amberley Suite Hotel/Quality Inn. This large three-story motor hotel is located north of Albuquerque just off the main route to Santa Fe, Interstate 25. Take Exit 231 from Interstate 25 and follow the frontage road to Pan American Freeway Northeast. All of the 170 units are suites, which have two rooms plus bath. The living area includes a kitchen with full-sized refrigerator, microwave oven, and built-in coffee maker. The bedroom is furnished with either a king bed or two double beds. Of course, the rooms are air conditioned, and each suite has a color television. Heated pool, whirlpool bath, sauna bath, health club, coffee shop, deli, bar, and convenience store on premises. And don't miss the landscaped courtyard with fountains. Children free in room with parent. Pets with deposit. Mailing address: Amberley Suite Hotel, 7620 Pan American Freeway Northeast, Albuquerque, New Mexico 87109. Telephone: 1-505-823-1300 or 1-800-228-5151. Expensive.

Corrales Inn. This bed-and-breakfast inn, with its French country restaurant nearby is a little bit of Europe in old Corrales. Located about twelve miles from Old Town, Albuquerque and the museums. Corrales is a small, historic, rural New Mexican community that exudes charm at every turn. The handsome adobe-style inn has six air-conditioned and very nicely furnished spacious rooms with private baths. Some of the rooms have fireplaces. Twin, queen, and king beds are available. The large, comfortable living room has as many books lining the wall as you might see in a small library. There you might curl up in a chair with one of the many excellent books on the region and relax thoroughly. The owner knows the region like the back of her hand, so when the books do not have the answer, she probably will or know where to find it. And just a few steps away is an excellent walking and jogging trail along the banks of the acequia. Hot tub. A gourmet breakfast is taken in the French Country Inn, a short walk away. Breakfast is included in the tariff and is different each day. From Interstate 40 take the Rio Grande Exit and travel six and one-half miles to Alameda Road. Turn left on Alameda, cross the Rio Grande, and in just less than a mile turn right onto Corrales Road at the first major intersection (where Alameda Road meets Coors Road). Travel about two and one-half miles from there to the inn, which is on the left and set back from the road behind the restaurant. A less scenic but faster route is to travel Interstate 40 west across the Rio Grande and take the first exit to the north (155) to Coors Boulevard and road. Follow Coors Road north into Corrales. Reservation deposit taken. Discount for longer stays. Mailing address: Corrales Inn Bed and Breakfast, Plaza San Ysidro, P.O. Box 1361, Corrales, New Mexico 87048. Telephone: 1-505-897-4422. Moderate and expensive.

Casita Chamisa Bed and Breakfast. Located in Albuquerque's cottonwood-shaded North Valley not far from the Rio Grande is this bed-and-breakfast establishment. The separate guest house, Casita Chamisa, with its southwestern decor, has two bedrooms, a living area with a kitchenette and fireplace, and a private bath. It sleeps up to six people. But it is rented to only one party at a time whether it be one or six. The rate increases slightly for each additional person. The second room, also with a fireplace and private bath, is in the owner's home. Enclosed pool and hot tub are available to guests. The knowledgeable owners also share with their guests what is known about the seven hundred-year-old Pueblo Indian village that has been excavated on their property under the auspices of the Maxwell Museum of Anthropology. Breakfast, included in the rate, features homemade breads and coffeecake served with jams and honey that are prepared on the premises. Fifteen minutes from Old Town and museums. Nearby walking and jogging trails. Reservation deposit required. Call for directions. Mailing address: Casita Chamisa Bed and Breakfast, 850 Chamisal Road Northwest, Albuquerque, New Mexico. Telephone: 1-505-897-4644. Moderate.

Food

Pueblo Kitchen Restaurant. Located two blocks north of U.S. Interstate Highway 40 West at 2401 Twelfth Street Northwest. From Interstate 40 West, take the Sixth and Twelfth streets exit, turn right at second stoplight onto Twelfth Street Northwest. From Old Town, take Rio Grande Boulevard north, pass under Interstate 40 West and turn right on Indian School Road, which becomes Menaul Boulevard. Turn right from Menaul Boulevard to Twelfth Street Northwest. Located in the Indian Pueblo Cultural Center. Telephone: 1-505-242-4943 or 1-505-843-7270. This restaurant, open for breakfast and lunch, is a must if you are new to this area. It is the place to "break in" on the foods of the region. The menu includes many native Indian dishes, as well as a large variety of New Mexican specialties. Lunch daily. Breakfast except on Sundays. Inexpensive.

Golden Crown Bakery (Panadería). This regional bakery is conveniently located, one-half mile east of Old Town Plaza at 1103 Mountain Road. Telephone: 1-505-243-2424. It specializes in bakery goods often found in the bakeries of Mexico. Try the little hard rolls or bolillos, the sweet breads such a span dulce, or the chili bread, either mild or hot. An interesting stop for a fast take-out breakfast or for picking up bread or desert for a picnic. Inexpensive.

La Placita Dining Room. In Old Town on San Felipe Street across from the plaza. Telephone: 1-505-247-2204. This establishment has been delighting both travelers and locals for several decades. Built in 1706, its thick adobe walls, once enclosing one of the first Spanish homes in Albuquerque, wrap around an inner courtyard, which is now covered for year-round use. The other rooms of this old hacienda make up the rest of the restaurant. The food is good simple regional fare such as tamales, enchiladas, and chiles rellenos. The sopaipillas are excellent. Standard American fare is also served. Historically and architecturally, this 275-year-old building is worth a visit by itself. Guitarists sing and play a medley of Latin tunes several nights a week. Open for lunch and dinner. Moderate.

La Hacienda Restaurant. Located just down the street from La Placita at 302 San Felipe Northwest are the dining rooms of this longtime visitors' favorite in a large turn-of-the-century hacienda that also houses several rooms with curios and crafts. In the attractive, no nonsense, Mexican-style dining rooms you can have a fine enchilada, chiles rellenos, or other regional specialties along with sopaipillas for a modest price. Open daily for lunch and dinner except for major holidays. Inexpensive and moderate.

High Noon Restaurant and Saloon. Located just across from the Sheraton Old Town Inn at the corner of 425 San Felipe Northwest and Mountain Road is this attractive restaurant, part of which is in one of Albuquerque's oldest buildings dating back to 1750. Telephone: 1-505-765-1455. There are several small, intimate dining rooms, one of which has a beehive fireplace. The whitewashed plastered adobe walls and other New Mexican architectural elements give this restaurant a lot of charm. The informal luncheon menu, which includes hamburgers and barbecued beef as well as more elaborate dishes, gives way in the evening to a more formal list of continental selections such as steak Diana, a variety of veal and fish dishes, Caesar salad, and flambéed deserts. But you can get a good steak here, too. Reservations advised. High moderate and expensive.

Stephens. 1311 Tijeras. Telephone: 1-505-842-1773. Located just off Central Avenue not far from Old Town Plaza is this casual but elegant very good restaurant with a territorial-style dining room, a pueblo-style bar with dining area and a Victorian-style dining room. Outdoor dining on the patio in the summer. Fresh seafood, steaks, and grilled chops abound on the menu as well as specialities such as Heart of Palm Salad, Chicken Breast Piccata, and other of Chef Stephens' favorites. Southwest specialties with a unique gourmet flair also find their way onto the menu. Excellent wine list. Lunch and dinner served Monday thru Saturday.

Christopher's. This Old Town restaurant is just one-half block from the plaza at 323 Romero Northwest. Telephone: 1-505-242-0202. Christopher's is a family-run, informal establishment with a lot of charm, and a good place to grab a quick bite to eat at lunchtime. A wide selection of excellent sandwiches as well as many New Mexican favorites—enchiladas, burritos, and compuestas. Plans are in the works to expand the menu and the hours—Thursday through Sunday—to include dinner and to serve wine and beer. Inexpensive and moderate.

Napoleon's. Located at 308 San Felipe Northwest in the heart of Old Town. Telephone: 1-505-842-9866. This deli-café with an Italian touch features lunch and more with an upscale menu that includes such tasty dishes as cucumber soup, green chili chicken, potato salad with dill, fettucini, and a host of traditional deli sandwiches on homemade breads. This is also a good place to pick up pastry and cappuccino. Carry out available. Excellent for lunch and early dinner. Inexpensive.

M and J Restaurant and Sanitary Tortilla Factory.

Located at 403 Second Street Southwest in an older section of downtown that the wrecking ball missed. Telephone: 1-505-242-4890. This mecca of native Mexican food has received rave national reviews, not for its location or beautiful surroundings, but for its food. Sometimes the best is the simplest, and that is what you have at the very plain but equally authentic family-owned and operated M and J. The food is prepared for the natives not travelers, so watch out! Go easy on the hot sauce unless you know your limits. And if you have no limits, you will be in picante heaven. Fresh tortillas are made on the premises, and freshly prepared chips with homemade salsa are but a few of the joys here. The five hongo burrito, a burrito filled with carne adovada, is a specialty, and the chiles rellenos are outstanding as are most of the other regional entrées, which are served with either a homemade red or green chili sauce. And since you will need plenty of sopaipillas and honey for an antidote, they, too, are available. Children's menu. Breakfast (especially huevos rancheros) and lunch until 4:00 P.M. Closed Sunday and major holidays. Inexpensive and low moderate.

Eulalia's. You will find this restaurant, which specializes in continental and Southwest cuisine, just off the lobby of La Posada de Albuquerque at 125 Second Street Northwest. Telephone: 1-505-242-9090. For the weary traveler who is checking into the hotel in the evening, this excellent, comfortable, bordering on elegant restaurant is a godsend. The entrées include veal, served in a variety of ways, pheasant, and a good selection of fresh fish creatively prepared. Simpler fare is also on the menu ranging from prime rib to regional southwestern specialties. The wine list is excellent, and the service is friendly and prompt. Desserts are outstanding. The restaurant's furnishings and accessories are derivative of the Southwest and of Mexico. The many large banquettes provide both privacy and comfort. Open daily for breakfast, lunch, and dinner. Sunday brunch. Reservations recommended. High moderate and expensive.

Artichoke Café. Located at 424 Central Avenue Southeast. Telephone: 1-505-842-8740. If you are looking for good French cooking in Albuquerque, this is the place to come. Fresh food is the byword in this very nice corner café next door to Albuquerque's finest fresh seafood market. This handsome, comfortable, intimate restaurant has just the right touch of elegance. It serves a tantalizing array of European gourmet specialties including fresh fish entrées such as halibut champagne, and salmon moutard along with numerous outstanding veal and beef dishes. Excellent desserts. Lunch and dinner. Open for lunch only on Sunday and Monday. High moderate and expensive.

Barelas Coffee House. Just south of the downtown Civic Plaza area at 1502 Fourth Southwest near the Barelas Bridge. Telephone: 1-505-843-7577. This down-home, native food café has legendary green chili sauce. In addition to enchiladas (maybe slathered in some of that green sauce), burritos, and carne adovada, you can also order that Pueblo Indian favorite, posole. Hamburgers. Fresh tortillas are made on the premises as are the dessert empanadas. Or you can soothe your membranes with a deliciously smooth and cooling tapioca pudding. Breakfast, lunch, and dinner before 4:30 P.M. Closed Sunday. Inexpensive.

Mary's and Tito's. Located at 2711 Fourth Northwest. Telephone: 1-505-344-6266. In the northwest sector of Albuquerque you will find this modest neighborhood restaurant which serves up some of the best and least expensive regional Mexican food in Albuquerque. Here, the carne adovada is the specialty of the house, but it almost takes a back seat to the superb red chili and green chili enchiladas. You'll want to go easy on the sauce unless you know how flameproof you are. But if your teeth can walk on fire, then go after the hottest with gusto. No sopaipillas here, just good, fresh tortillas. No American food except a hamburger served on a tortilla. Children's plates available without the hot stuff. There is no beer or wine but there is a plentiful supply of soft drinks. Open for breakfast, lunch, and dinner. Closed Sunday. No personal checks or credit cards. Inexpensive.

Sadie's Cocinita. Located at 6132 Fourth Street Northwest. Telephone: 1-505-345-5339. Located on the mezzanine of the B. G. Valley Bowl building overlooking the bowling lanes. This very popular and comfortable dining room featuring well-prepared, consistently good New Mexican food. On certain days it seems that all of Albuquerque has piled into this bustling, busy, somewhat noisy egalitarian place, where students, businessmen, families, and the older set are all having a great time. Most who come here order their favorites all the time. Almost every dish comes with papitas—tasty, diced Spanish-style potatoes—which help offset the spicy and delicious carne adovada, chiles rellenos, and enchiladas slathered with red or green chili sauce. But some are quite content to just order Sadie's Spanish-influenced taco, a unique blend of potatoes, sausage, beef, and spices cradled in a fresh-fried corn tortilla shell. Open for lunch and dinner. Inexpensive.

Garduno's Tortilla 'N' Tequila Junction. Located northeast of town at 5400 Academy Road Northeast. Telephone: 1-505-821-3030. This large, lively, upbeat Mexican restaurant packs them in. Here you will find both local citizens and travelers often waiting together for a table, especially in the evenings on the weekend. Wall-to-wall Mexican decor with a large menu of authentic as well as Garduno-style food from south of the border. Specializes in chicken, beef, and shrimp fajitas as well as fruit margaritas. Lunch and dinner. Inexpensive and moderate.

El Pinto Restaurant. Located at 10500 Fourth Street Northwest. Telephone: 1-505-898-1771. Located nine miles north of Old Town in Albuquerque's North Valley. The short but scenic drive to this country Spanish restaurant through some of Albuquerque's lovely residential areas is well worth the trip. The handsome territorial-style restaurant sets on spacious landscaped grounds. Meals are served either in the nicely appointed dining rooms or outdoors on the garden patio. Of course, New Mexican food is the specialty of the house. Included are carne adovada, tamales, chiles rellenos, burritos, and very good enchiladas along with tasty sopaipillas. To get to El Pinto from Interstate 40, take the Rio Grande Avenue Exit and drive north six and one-half miles to Alameda Road. Turn right onto Alameda and drive about one mile to the junction with Fourth Street Northwest New Mexico Highway 313. Turn left on Fourth Street and drive about one mile to the restaurant on the right side of the road. Lunch and dinner. Closed Monday. Inexpensive and low moderate.

The Desert Rose. Corrales, New Mexico. Telephone: 1-505-898-2269. Located in Corrales, approximately eleven miles from Old Town, Albuquerque. This café-restaurant in an atmospheric adobe offers family style New Mexican cooking. Meals are served indoors or outside on the patio. The beef and chicken fajitas are legendary as is the paparitos, a burrito filled with potatoes, scrambled eggs, and chorizo (sausage) and then slathered with red or green chili sauce and cheddar cheese. There are, of course, the usual regional specialties, but the diverse kitchen does more. There are gourmet specials on the menu each evening, which give an international gourmet flare to this flowering Desert Rose. Good regional desserts. Lunch and dinner. Breakfast, lunch, and dinner Saturday. Brunch Sunday. Closed Monday. For directions to Corrales, see Corrales Inn under "Lodging" this section. Inexpensive and low moderate.

Corrales Inn—French Country Cuisine. Plaza San Ysidro, Corrales, New Mexico. Telephone: 1-505-897-4411. Located about eleven scenic miles from Old Town, Albuquerque. The talented and eclectic chef here knows not only French cuisine but international cookery as well, and he uses nothing but the freshest ingredients. In the country inn atmosphere evoked by the nicely appointed, informal, comfortable dining room you can begin your meal with a delicious homemade soup, appetizer, or savory salad. The list of entrées might include English beef salad, coq au vin, medallions of pork, a curry dish, or a fresh seafood preparation. Whatever you choose, you won't be disappointed. Excellent desserts prepared on the premises. Outdoor dining, weather permitting. Dinner only. Closed Monday and Tuesday. For directions to the Corrales Inn, see Corrales Inn under "Lodging" this section. Reservations required. Moderate.

Rancho de Corrales. Located in Corrales. Telephone: 1-505-897-3131. This restaurant benefits from the sure hand of one of the Southwest's leading restauranteurs who turned a remote restaurant in Chimayo into a legendary mecca of Northern New Mexico cuisine. And he's done it again in this renovated, charming, historic old adobe providing Albuquerque and environs with the finest in regional, native cuisine. For directions to Corrales see Corrales Inn under "Lodging" this section. Lunch and dinner daily. Moderate.

Tours

Albuquerque Trolley Co. For special sight-seeing tours of the Albuquerque area or for just getting from place to place, these special motorized buses, which look like old-fashioned trolleys, are a convenient and fun way to get around the city. They routinely stop at Old Town, downtown hotels, the University of New Mexico campus, and other attractions. You can always catch one just off Interstate 40 and Commercial Street at the Antique Mall. The drivers are knowledgeable and fill you in on the history and culture of the area. Daily. Telephone: 1-505-242-1407.

American West Tours. This group gives personalized tours of the Albuquerque area. They have also produced a cassette auto-tour tape of the Albuquerque–Santa Fe region and the Turquoise Trail, which is available for sale at the American Automobile Association Office, 10501 Montgomery Boulevard Northeast, Albuquerque 87111. Telephone: 1-505-291-6611. American West Tours is located at 500 Kinley Avenue Northeast, Albuquerque, New Mexico 87125. Telephone: 1-505-242-1407.

Tours of Enchantment. This tour operator offers regional sight-seeing services and hot-air balloon rides for groups or individuals. Mailing address: 5801 Jones Northwest, Albuquerque, New Mexico 87120. Telephone: 1-505-831-4285.

Horseback Riding

Los Amigos Stables. Rides along the Rio Grande bosques and along other trails as well as Chuckwagon cookouts in the barn and hayrides along the Rio Grande. Located on the Sandia Indian Reservation at 10600 Fourth Northwest, P.O. Box 10359, Alameda, New Mexico 87184. Telephone: 1-505-898-8173.

Tramway Riding Stables. Offers short or long rides at the base of the Sandia Mountains. You may want to time your ride to view the magnificent sunsets at this location. Located at 25 Tramway Boulevard, adjacent to the Sandia Tramway. Telephone: 1-505-293-1270.

Fairs, Festivals, and Fiestas

Annual New Mexico Arts and Crafts Fair. This colossal event, involving several hundred craftspersons from New Mexico, is held the last weekend in June at the state fairgrounds, 2745 San Mateo Northeast. The participants, who include some of New Mexico's best Spanish, Indian, and Anglo artists, bring their finest ceramics, fiber arts, glass, sculptures, and more for the largest event of this kind in New Mexico. Telephone: 1-602-884-9043.

Fiesta Artistica. Not to let Santa Fe and Taos steal all the thunder about New Mexico's Spanish heritage, Albuquerque stages this fair to commemorte its Hispanic roots. The event takes place at the Albuquerque Convention Center and Civic Plaza. In addition to entertainment that fits the occasion, Spanish craftspersons from all over New Mexico bring their best carvings, weavings, and other crafts to sell. A folk mass is held during this celebration, which occurs the last weekend in August or first weekend in September. Telephone: 1-505-768-355 or 1-505-848-1334.

New Mexico State Fair. This stellar event is held over a two-week period in September starting the weekend after Labor Day. In addition to the usual displays at most state fairs, this one includes exhibits of Navajo rugs, Spanish weaving, Indian pottery and jewelry, as well as many other crafts. And there is entertainment in the Indian Village and Villa Hispanic replicas, with native music, dances, songs, and costumes. There is also horse racing and a rodeo. Held in the fairgrounds at Central Avenue and San Pedro. Telephone: 1-505-265-1791.

International Balloon Festival. This event, held seven or eight days spanning the first two weekends in October, has been important in putting Albuquerque on the map. Most Americans and many Europeans have by now seen magazine or newspaper pictures of hundreds of hot-air balloons as they ascend above the desert over Albuquerque. Although balloons go up all week, the mass rising only occurs at sunrise on the first and last weekends. Mailing address: Albuquerque International Balloon Fiesta, 4804 Hawkins Northeast, Albuquerque, New Mexico 87109. Telephone: 1-505-344-3501 or toll free 1-800-321-6979.

Southwest Arts and *Crafts Festival.* This large exhibition of arts and crafts from the Southwest as well as across the nation is an invitational, juried show in early November. The participants display their work for sale at the New Mexico State Fairgrounds. Telephone: 1-505-262-2448.

Shopping

There are many excellent shops in Albuquerque that sell both traditional Indian and contemporary crafts from this region. Many of the better shops are in the Old Town area in west Albuquerque. The shops listed here have been favorites over the years and have a reputation of dependability and reliability. Generally speaking, you will get what you pay for in these shops.

Gift Shop/Market of Indian Pueblo Cultural Center. Located at 2401 Twelfth Street Northwest. Telephone: 1-505-843-7270. In this shop you will find a wide variety of carefully chosen Indian pottery, basketry, weaving, and jewelry from the nineteen participating pueblos. This is a good shop that is associated with a museum of Pueblo crafts to help acquaint you with the subject.

The Adobe Gallery. Located at 413 Romero Street. Telephone: 1-505-243-8485. The owner of this spacious Old Town museum-quality gallery and his staff know their stuff and have good contacts with Pueblo Indian craftspeople. A wide price range is represented, which should please the casual buyer or the collector. Pueblo Indian pottery is a specialty here, but there are also kachinas,

Navajo rugs, and ceremonial sashes, as well as contemporary Southwest Indian paintings. In addition to the tastefully displayed craft and art pieces (which include an excellent selection of miniatures), the gallery has a full selection of books about Southwest Indian arts and crafts. And do not forget to see their outstanding selection of Pueblo Indian figurine pottery pieces (storyteller figures and nacimientos)—one of the best to be found anywhere.

Mariposa Gallery. Located at 113 Romero Street Northwest. Telephone: 1-505-842-9097. If you are interested in fine contemporary crafts, you should not miss this gallery housed in an old adobe near the plaza in Old Town. It is one of the best in the Southwest, possibly in the nation. The gallery is tastefully divided into several rooms. Each room or cluster of rooms showcases different types of crafts. The contemporary ceramics that have been selected for sale there are unique and are of the highest quality. The fabric art is equally stunning. There is a large collection of handcrafted wearables and a fine collection of contemporary jewelry. The knowledgeable and artistic owners have done their job well.

The Navajo Gallery. Located at 323 Romero Street Northwest in Old Town. Telephone: 1-505-843-7666. This gallery is owned by Navajo artist R. C. Gorman. It is a showcase for many of his paintings, prints, and sculpted pieces. Other contemporary artists are also shown. Gorman has another gallery in Taos where he lives.

The Christmas Shop. Located at 400 Romero Street Northwest. Telephone: 1-505-843-6744. There are Christmas shops and then there is this truly unique store that sells high-quality Christmas decorations that reflect the Indian and Spanish heritage of the Southwest, as well as Mexico and the Americas. Ingenious is the word for their wax candle luminarias and chile pepper Christmas light covers.

The Card Shop. Located at 1919 Old Town Road Northwest in a small shopping complex about one-half block east of the Old Town plaza. Telephone: 1-505-247-9634. Some of the most unusual and beautiful greeting cards from all over the world are gathered together here. In addition to a wide selection of southwest regional cards, the shop prints its own very fine silk-screened cards, depicting southwestern Christmas scenes, Rio Grande Pueblo pottery, and Navajo rug patterns.

Andrews Pueblo Pottery and Art Gallery. Located at 400 San Felipe Northwest, Old Town. Telephone: 1-505-243-0414. This well established Southwest Indian art gallery is worth a stop. But the stop may be a long one as this gallery's selection of kachinas, paintings, graphics, and baskets is extensive and outstanding. Also you will see many old, pre-Columbian Pueblo pots. Open daily.

Covered Wagon. Located at 2034 South Plaza Northwest, on a prominent corner across from the old church in Old Town. Telephone: 1-505-242-4481. This large emporium is known best by natives and visitors alike, for its excellent selection of Navajo and Zuñi turquoise and silver jewelry. Much of the time there are Indian silversmiths on the premises making high-quality natural turquoise and sterling silver jewelry. Also if you are in the market for a bolo tie this is the place to come. They have inexpensive, souvenir bolos as well as more expensive, fine, handcrafted traditional and contemporary bolos. But that's not all. In their American Indian Gallery they stock a fine selection of Pueblo pottery, kachinas, and Navajo rugs. In short, you can find the whole gamut of Southwest Indian crafts. But there's more yet. It's worth mentioning that there are many curios and souvenirs here, more than just about anybody else in town. In fact it can be overwhelming.

Casa Talavera. Located at 621 Rio Grande Boulevard Northwest. Telephone: 1-505-243-2413. If you have an interest in handmade tiles from Talavera, Mexico, and other areas across the border, do not miss this shop. It carries every size, shape, and configuration of handmade, glazed, and unglazed tiles. In addition, it has a fine selection of Mexican handcrafts.

Museum Shop Maxwell Museum of Anthropology. University of New Mexico campus. Located on Redondo Drive just off University Boulevard, one block north of Grand Avenue. Telephone: 1-505-277-4404. This small, but well-stocked shop carries crafts from the Rio Grande region as well as from the Navajo reservation, Mexico, Central America, and South America. Ceramics, wood carvings, baskets, jewelry, and fabrics are but a few of the media you will find there. The book section is wide ranging and encompasses local as well as worldwide ethnic and cultural subjects. The museum also sells its own books, such as *Southwestern Weaving* and *Seven Families in Pueblo Pottery,* classics in the craft field.

Salt of the Earth Books. Located at 2128 Central Avenue Southeast near the University of New Mexico. Telephone: 1-505-842-1220. You won't find a better bookstore to meet your Southwest travel needs or pique your curiosity about Southwest archaeology or, for that matter, the cultures of some of the Mayan and Mesoamerican civilizations to the south. Outstanding selection of titles pertaining to American Indian arts and crafts of the Southwest as well as general art and photography books and natural history books.

Telephone Numbers

Road and Weather Conditions. Telephone: 1-505-841-8066.
National Forest Service, Southwestern Region. Telephone: 1-505-842-3292
Avis Rent-A-Car. Telephone: 1-505-842-4080.
Budget Rent-A-Car. Telephone: 1-505-884-2666.
Hertz Rent-A-Car. Telephone: 1-505-842-4235.
Thrifty Car Rental. Telephone: 1-505-842-8733.
Taxi Service. Telephone: 1-505-247-8888.
Shuttlejack to Santa Fe. Telephone: 1-505-243-3244.
Albuquerque Trolley Co. Telephone: 1-505-242-1407.
Airport bus service to Española and Taos. Telephone: 1-505-758-1144.

Santa Fe

If you are flying into the area, you will quickly find that Santa Fe does not have a commercial jet airport. Most visitors fly into Albuquerque International Airport and then either rent a car or take one of the convenient, modern buses that carry travelers daily from Albuquerque to Santa Fe on a regular schedule. Shuttlejack offers this service, as well as return service to the airport, but requires a reservation six hours in advance. Telephone: 1-505-243-3244 during the week or 1-505-982-4311 on weekends. Or, during the week, toll free in the United States 1-800-452-2665. Amtrak offers passenger rail service to Lamy, New Mexico, which is eighteen miles south of Santa Fe. Transportation to Santa Fe daily via the Lamy Shuttle Service. Telephone: 1-505-982-8829.

In Santa Fe, it is possible to eat and sleep in settings that feed your fantasies about the area without totally breaking your pocketbook, although prices in Santa Fe are some of the highest in this book. And if you wish to go first-class, you will find your wish can be fulfilled in several of America's most distinctive hotels and resorts and in some of the High Southwest's finest restaurants. Over the years Santa Fe has become more and more crowded in the summer as its reputation has spread through the many magazine and newspaper articles, both here and abroad, which have sung its praises. In recent years, just about every music, art, and craft magazine has featured the artistic boom that is going on there from opera and chamber music to painting and ceramics. Background photographs of Santa Fe often appear in glossy fashion magazines. And home decorating magazines and books have repeatedly featured the "Santa Fe Style" of living, many elements of which are being duplicated in homes throughout the United States. With more affluent, sophisticated travelers coming to Santa Fe, the character of the downtown area is changing rapidly. Many of the locally owned utilitarian shops and stores along the plaza have been faced with increasingly high rents and congested traffic and have moved off the plaza to other downtown locations or to outlying shopping centers. They have been replaced by upscale boutiques, galleries, and trendy restaurants, some of which have national affiliations. Still Woolworth's and a scattering of older, practical stores remain, reminding all of us visitors that when we leave at the end of the summer, life in Santa Fe goes on just as it has for several hundred years. Then, many locals who have assiduously avoided the plaza during the busy summer months, return to enjoy the heart of their city.

But the plaza and its surrounding streets do not represent the only shopping areas for travelers. For many years Canyon Road, southeast of the plaza, has been (and still is) a visitors' favorite with its many interesting galleries and restaurants. But now travelers are also discovering the South Guadalupe Street-Montezuma Avenue area, southwest of the plaza centered near the junction of those two streets and including many newly renovated older buildings near the former terminus of the historic Chili Line Railway. This developing area is now the home of the Santa Fe Chamber of Commerce, and there is talk of a future convention center nearby. The area includes the many shops and restaurants stretching along South Guadalupe Street from the Santuario de Guadalupe to Montezuma Avenue, and there is budding activity along Montezuma Avenue west of South Guadalupe Street to the Guadalupe Station area and the Sanbusco Market Center. There are also new shops and galleries west of South Guadalupe Street along Aztec, Garfield, Montezuma and Read streets to Las Tres Gentes, a large indoor marketplace-pavilion with a number of small market stalls and a few shops and cafés.

The Santa Fe season begins in May. It is a season that lasts until mid- to late October. Reservations for lodging in the place of your choice are necessary during most of those months, particularly between Memorial Day and Labor Day. In fact, to get any decent reservations at all during the major summer holidays such as Memorial Day or during special weekends such as Indian Market in late August, reserve far in advance of your arrival. In the winter things slow down a bit, but then there is Christmas in Santa Fe, a unique time of the year there that has been popularized by national television specials. And, of course, there is both downhill and cross-country skiing in the nearby mountains, which keeps some activity going all winter. All of this does not mean that you cannot find a place to stay if you arrive impromptu. But if you want anything special—a room with a view, an adobe fireplace, or a patio—then you had better try to tie your wishes down a few months ahead of time. Many of the restaurants do not take reservations. Some do. For them, it is wise to call the day before or the morning of your projected visit to make a reservation.

Almost all of the accommodations in Santa Fe that evoke the spirit of the region are in the downtown, historic area within a five- or six-block radius of the plaza. With the exception of a few rooms in some of the bed-and-breakfast inns and a few of the larger establishments, most of the accommodations downtown are in the high moderate to high expensive range. Some are very expensive. But the convenience of the downtown inns and hotels to the major sights and the Santa Fe scene is truly a plus. However, if you require less expensive accommodations, you must, unfortunately, leave the city's historic center and drive out to the busy "strip," Cerrillos Road. Most of the motels there are quite adequate, but with one or two exceptions, they do not offer the charm or the convenience that visitors seek when they come to Santa Fe. For the increasing number of return visitors to the area and for those who for one reason or another do not choose to stay in the city, a number of options are available. There are two superb resorts a short distance north of Santa Fe, which are in the luxury category, while the resort south of Santa Fe is less expensive and has some rooms in the moderate range. Meanwhile more modest, somewhat less expensive accommodations are cropping up outside of Santa Fe in the form of small bed-and-breakfast inns. Some are located within a few miles of the city but many are about thirty minutes out. They offer a different, more pastoral scene since almost all of the accommodations are in beautiful rural locations and are frequently housed in charmingly renovated historic old adobes.

Santa Fe is truly a city of wonderful museums. The five museums of New Mexico (The Palace of the Governors, Museum of Fine Arts, Museum of International Folk Art, Museum of Indian Arts and Culture, and the Laboratory of Anthropology) operated by the state of New Mexico's office of Cultural Affairs are all superb. Try to allow time to see them for they, along with the Wheelwright Museum, should not be missed. There is a description of each of these museums along with their telephone numbers in the "See the Spanish Rio Grande Country: Santa Fe" section of this book. In this section of the book there are several other museums listed under "tours" including the Institute of American Indian Arts Museum, the Center for Contemporary Arts of Santa Fe, and the Santa Fe Children's Museum.

For visitors from other countries, the Santa Fe Council on International Relations, located on the mezzanine of the La Fonda Hotel, 100 East San Francisco Street, has a "meeting Americans program." This program helps international visitors locate inexpensive accommodations in Santa Fe homes and will provide support services, including information brochures in German, French, Italian, Spanish, and Japanese. Mailing address: Santa Fe Council on International Relations, P.O. Box 1223, Santa Fe, New Mexico 87504. Telephone: 1-505-982-4931. In addition budget accommodations are available for both international travelers and Americans in a dormitory setting at the International Visitors Hostel, 1412 Cerrillos Road. Telephone: 1-505-988-1153 or 1-505-983-9896.

And all visitors can receive last-minute, up-to-date information on activities and events from the Santa Fe Chamber of Commerce, 333 Montezuma Avenue, P.O. Box 1928, Santa Fe, New Mexico, 87504. Telephone: 1-505-983-7317. During the summer the chamber of commerce maintains a booth on the west side of the plaza. Also, visitors may contact the Santa Fe Convention and Visitors Bureau, Sweeney Center, 201 West Marcy Street, P.O. Box 909, Santa Fe, New Mexico 87504. Telephone: 1-505-984-6760 or toll free in the United States, except New Mexico 1-800-528-5369.

Please note below the listing labeled "Parking." Read that section carefully and notice some of the parking locations on the small Santa Fe map that accompanies this section. If these lots are full, you might try the underground parking garage at the corner of Washington Avenue and Marcy Street, the large pay lot at the Inn of Loretto, or the new parking garage at the La Fonda Hotel. Alternatively you can park out from the city center and take the Chile Line trolley into town. These gas-operated bus-trolleys travel throughout the city during the summertime, connecting the historic downtown area with peripheral shopping malls, scenic sights, museums, major hotels, and other well-traveled destinations.

Lodging

La Posada de Santa Fe. If you are looking for Santa Fe's "in" place where the veteran Santa Fe visitor is apt to stay and where artists, performers, and directors of Santa Fe's famous music, opera, and drama programs frequently hang their hats, this is it. And there is good reason for their choice. Located out of the congestion on six acres of quiet, tree-shaded, landscaped grounds within two long blocks of the plaza, this adobelike "posada" with its wide variety of interesting rooms decorated in the New Mexican mode, is a restful place to stay. You can choose between about a dozen less expensive, small hotellike rooms, more expensive rooms with kitchens or kitchenettes, suites, or casitas with adobe fireplaces. Many of the 103 units have adobe fireplaces or wood stoves. Some of the rooms in the less expensive category seem a little tired but still have charm. And no matter how many times a day the maids try to sweep away Santa Fe's historic and ever-present dust, it and the leaves from the beautiful old trees tend to accumulate on the outdoor porches. Some of us wouldn't have it any other way.

A few rooms are on a peninsula surrounded by entry and exit roads and are a little noisy at certain times. Since the rooms are not air-conditioned (Thank goodness! Who needs it at this elevation anyway?), you may lie awake with your window open on certain busy weekend nights, listening to cars bounce over speed bumps. But, if you are under forty or over sixty and sleep like a bear, this will not bother you. For quietness and more privacy, try to request one of the many rooms in other sections of the property. Especially good are the rooms on the south end of the grounds behind and to the east of the swimming pool. But beware. Rooms at La Posada are so popular that they are sometimes completely filled a year in advance. It is essential that you call or write ahead for reservations. The amenities are many. The lobby, wonderfully atmospheric restaurant, and three watering holes including the Garden Room, are located in the oldest section of La Posada, the Staab Mansion, built in the late 1800s. In the summer, the lovely outdoor patio is open for breakfast most mornings and for lunch. The heated outdoor

La Posada, Santa Fe

swimming pool is in a nice location overlooking the grounds. So if you like a relaxed informality, where the ambience is so thick it haunts you at every turn, you will enjoy the wonderful "real Santa Fe" atmosphere at La Posada. Children under twelve free if in parents' room and do not require a rollaway bed. No pets. Parking is free and generally quite close to your room if not in front of it. Mailing address: La Posada, 330 East Palace Avenue, Santa Fe, New Mexico 87501. Telephone: 1-505-983-6351 or toll free in the United States 1-800-531-6424. Moderate and expensive.

La Fonda Hotel. One of the questions you may be asked by friends when you return home from your trip to Santa Fe is whether or not you stayed at La Fonda. Over the years that venerable, old, adobe inn has been as much a part of the scene as the plaza and many of the area's historical sights. Grand and impressive as it is, it is not really that old. The present hotel was constructed during the period of Pueblo architectural revival in the 1920s. Previous to that, other hotels had profited from the same location at the end of the Santa Fe Trail. Today's rambling but commanding old adobe has a wide range of accommodations from "standard" rooms to fifth-story suites with adobe fireplaces, furnished with fine examples of Spanish colonial furniture, crafts, and accessories. The average "deluxe" room is also apt to have ornate Spanish colonial bedsteads with high headboards painted in a fanciful array of colors and designs evoking the area's Spanish heritage. With all the traffic outside, some of the outside rooms can be noisy.

The hotel and its welcome parking garage cover a full city block and are the best situated of all Santa Fe's lodgings for seeing the city. But be warned. In midsummer the hotel and the streets around it are the most congested in this capital city. The beautiful old lobby with its white plastered walls and heavy, ornate beams and tile floors always buzzes with activity. The lobby contains an excellent display of old paintings by some of Santa Fe's prominent artists of the last fifty years. The small newsstand in the lobby carries a wide variety of newspapers from all over the United States and an excellent supply of local and regional magazines. In addition, there are several shelves jammed full of books about the region. On the ground floor of the hotel is a variety of shops. The inner courtyard of the hotel has been enclosed to create the dining area, La Plazuela, which serves three meals a day in a very pleasant, informal atmosphere. The beautiful hand-painted glass windows there are well worth seeing. And high up on the fifth floor (high up for Santa Fe, anyway) in the bell tower is a bar where you can catch great views of the city and wonderful mountain panoramas, especially at sunset. In addition there is outdoor terrace dining on the third floor during the summer season. The 160 rooms are air-conditioned and have TV's and phones. There is a heated swimming pool. No pets. Advance reservation deposit required. No charge for children under twelve years of age. Special off-season rates. Mailing address: La Fonda Hotel, 100 East San Fran-cisco Street, Box 1209, Santa Fe, New Mexico 87501. Telephone: 1-505-982-5511. High expensive.

Best Western Inn at Loretto. If you want the adobe ambience but also want a modern, updated, clean-as-a-whistle, no-loose-strings-attached kind of hotel, head straight for the Inn at Loretto. This beautifully designed hotel is so efficiently run that it is hard to believe it is in Santa Fe. Located on grounds that formerly belonged to the Sisters of Loretto, one block south of the plaza, this modern, multistory Pueblo-style adobe harmoniously and tastefully echoes the architecture of La Fonda Hotel to the north. Built in the shape of an L, the building's walls enclose a large sun-drenched area on the east side, where you will find a pleasant patio and heated swimming pool. The dining room, with the traditional viga and latia ceiling members and corner adobe fireplace, is a handsome room and a pleasant place for breakfast or lunch. The multilevel bar with its large fireplace is also attractive. The shops lining its first floor corridor offer some of the best selections of traditional and contemporary art in the city. The 139 air-conditioned rooms are nicely furnished with modern fixtures. A few rooms have fireplaces, king beds, and patios. Children twelve and under are free if in the same room with parents. No pets. Advance reservation deposit required if arriving after 4:00 P.M. Three-day refund notice. Mailing address: Best Western Inn at Loretto, 211 Old Santa Fe Trail, P.O. Box 1417, Santa Fe, New Mexico 87501. Telephone: 1-505-988-5531 or toll free in the United

La Fonda, Santa Fe

States 1-800-528-1234. High expensive.

Hotel St. Francis. Commanding one of the best downtown locations just one block from the plaza and yet one step removed from the crowds and congestion is this wonderfully atmospheric hotel. A thorough and imaginative renovation has turned the historic De Vargas Hotel into an upbeat, cheerful place to stay. It has all the modern conveniences today's travelers demand without sacrificing the charm and warmth of the handsome architectural features of the old hotel, which dated back to 1924. The tan stucco building creates a distinctly Spanish, old-world atmosphere with its rounded moorish arches, tiled floors, and wrought iron work. Although the eighty-five rooms and suites vary in size, most have high ceilings and are equipped with small refrigerators as well as lock boxes for valuables. The brass and iron beds with colorful and fluffy comforters are complemented nicely by the cherrywood and marble period furniture. In short, these rooms are delightfully comfortable. From the attractive plant-filled lobby to the delightful outdoor garden court, this intimate hotel satisfies again and again. Breakfast, lunch, and dinner can be taken at Francisco's, the hotel's attractive restaurant, which also offers seasonal outdoor dining on the tree-shaded garden patio. Afternoon tea is served daily in the lobby and on the veranda, which also serves as a favorite watering hole for hotel guests and others especially in the late afternoon before dinner. Complementary parking. Children under twelve are free provided they occupy the same room as their parents and don't need a rollaway bed. No pets. Handicap access. Reservation deposit required. Mailing address: Hotel St. Francis, 210 Don Gaspar Avenue, Santa Fe, New Mexico 87501. Telephone: 1-505-983-5700 or toll free in the United States, except New Mexico 1-800-552-0070 ext. 102. Moderate and expensive.

Eldorado-A Clarion Hotel. If you enjoy the ambience, comfort, and prestige of the best big city hotels, the Eldorado will make you feel right at home. In an enviable location a little over two blocks from the plaza, this sleek, almost imposing, more-modern-than-most, pueblo- and territorial-style, tan, stucco five-story building blends amaz-

ingly well into its historic site. Not only is it Santa Fe's largest hotel, it is also its most elegant and priciest hostelry. In excavating the spacious underground parking garage, workers no doubt unearthed a whole history book full of artifacts. The site was once occupied by Louis Robidoux, trapper and explorer, whose brother founded Saint Joseph, Missouri.

In the mid 1800s a hotel called the Eldorado was erected on this site. It was the namesake for the present hotel. The old hotel and the site underwent several changes of use until the 1920s when the property was taken over by the Big Jo Lumber Company, the namesake for the new Eldorado's oysterbar. So it would seem that all the elegance comes with a pedigree of sorts. But you don't need to know this hotel's past in order to give it your stamp of approval. It pleases in every way. From the spacious, atriumlike lobby with its lounge and café, where you can eat breakfast, lunch, or dinner, or drink your favorite libation, to the rooftop outdoor heated swimming pool, which offers unparalleled views of Santa Fe and vistas of the surrounding mountains, you will appreciate this landmark hotel. And in between those two wonders are four floors with 218 rooms and suites, most with stocked bar refrigerators, some with fireplaces, wet bars, Jacuzzi tubs, and balconies. The air-conditioned rooms are spacious, quiet, and very comfortable, and the attractive decor is southwestern. Besides the lobby-atrium restaurant and bar, the Eldorado Court, there is an elegant, more formal restaurant and bar, The Old House, Big Jo's Oyster Bar, and a shopping arcade. Children seventeen and under free if in same room with parents. Mailing address: Eldorado-A Clarion Hotel, 309 West San Francisco Street, Santa Fe, New Mexico 87501. Telephone: 1-505-988-4455 or toll free in the United States 1-800-CLARION. High expensive plus.

Hilton Inn in Santa Fe. Conveniently located at the west end of San Francisco Street about three long blocks from the plaza, this large territorial-style hotel with 150 air-conditioned units offers all the amenities in pleasant surroundings. Heated swimming pool in very pleasant courtyard area. Dining room and coffee shop. Children accompanied by their parents and in the same room are free. Advance reservation deposit required. Mailing address: Hilton Inn in Santa Fe, 100 Sandoval Street, Box 2387, Santa Fe, New Mexico 87501. Telephone: 1-505-988-2811 or toll free in the United States 1-800-445-8667. High expensive.

The Inn of the Governors. Approximately three blocks from the plaza, the Inn of the Governors rests across from the Santa Fe River at Alameda and Don Gaspar streets. The Spanish-style building with its enclosed flower-lined courtyard provides a pleasant ambience. For the most part, the one hundred air-conditioned rooms are decorated in a modern fashion, but almost half have adobe fireplaces and most have stocked refrigerators. The restaurant offers inside as well as patio dining. Advance reservation deposit required. The inn offers two classes of rooms: "red carpet" and the less expensive "standard" rooms. Pets allowed. Mailing address: The Inn of the Governors, Alameda and Don Gaspar streets, Santa Fe, New Mexico 87501. Telephone: 1-505-982-4333 or toll free in the United States, except New Mexico 1-800-552-0070. Moderate and expensive.

Garretts' Friendship Desert Inn. Looking like a motel almost anywhere, it seems strange that this inn is right in the center of the historic district alongside the Santa Fe River, two blocks south of the plaza. Nevertheless, it is and that fact, besides its being extremely well run, is why it is almost always full. The eighty-three air-conditioned rooms are decorated in motel modern. Heated swimming pool. Restaurant with outside dining. No pets. Advance reservation deposit required during the summer season. Mailing address: Friendship Garrett's Desert Inn, 311 Old Santa Fe Trail, Santa Fe, New Mexico 87501. Telephone: 1-505-982-1851 or toll free in the United States 1-800-453-4511. Expensive.

Inn on the Alameda. Well situated near Canyon Road's shops and yet just three blocks from the plaza is this charming adobe, which functions with all the amenities, friendliness, and personal service of a small elegant, European bed-and-breakfast hotel. And it is just across from the shady Alameda, which borders the Santa Fe River. The thirty-six air-conditioned rooms with private baths and cable TV's are beautifully furnished with south-western decorative touches, and some rooms have private balconies. You may take your generous continental breakfast (included in the room rate) in your room or in the handsomely decorated country kitchen downstairs adjacent to the comfortable living room-library area with its kiva fireplace. Whirlpool tub. Free parking. Mailing address: Inn on the Alameda, 303 East Alameda, Santa Fe, New Mexico 87501. Telephone: 1-505-984-2121 or toll free in the United States, except New Mexico 1-800-552-0070 ext. 289. High expensive.

El Paradero en Santa Fe (Bed and Breakfast). This delightful adobe is just a short walk from the state capitol and just a few more blocks to the historic district. It offers much Santa Fe ambience. There are twelve well-designed, nicely furnished adobe-style rooms, several with adobe fireplaces. Some rooms have private baths, while in others, tastefully designed baths are shared. This place, with its delightful homey atmosphere, is run by an owner-manager family who live on the premises. The breakfast, included in the price, varies from eggs Benedict to homebaked goods, sausages, and pancakes. Advance reservation deposit required. Mailing address: El Paradero en Santa Fe, 220 West Manhattan Street, Santa Fe, New Mexico 87501. Telephone: 1-505-988-1177. Inexpensive, moderate, and expensive.

Preston House (Bed and Breakfast). One of Santa Fe's old, late-1800 Victorian-style homes that is conveniently situated three blocks from the plaza on a quiet street one block north of La Posada de Santa Fe. Some of the eight bedrooms have private baths, while the others have shared baths. The rooms are nicely furnished and beautifully renovated. Some have fireplaces. Two of the bedrooms are in a small cottage on the property. Continental breakfast included. No pets. Children under fifteen not encouraged. Two-day minimum stay for weekends. Advance reservation deposit required. Mailing address: Preston House, 106 Faithway Street, Santa Fe, New Mexico 87501. Telephone: 1-505-982-3465. Low moderate and expensive.

Grant Corner Inn (Bed and Breakfast). Advantageously located one block from the New Mexico

Museum of Fine Arts and less than two blocks from the plaza, this beautifully restored, three-story, historical colonial manor home with warm stucco exterior and red-tiled roof is truly a haven. Its thirteen guest rooms are tastefully decorated and comfortable as is the detached casita with its two guest rooms, private bath, and fireplace. Southwest artifacts grace the hallways, and the downstairs living areas, which are shared by all the guests, are just like home. And then there's breakfast, a not-to-be-missed gourmet's delight, served to all the guests and open to the public by reservation. Afternoon tea, also open to the public, is equally delicious. The owners are gracious hosts, who are careful to attend to your needs. Both private and shared bath facilities available. Advance reservation deposit required. Mailing address: Grant Corner Inn, 122 Grant Avenue, Santa Fe, New Mexico 87501. Telephone: 1-505-983-6678. Low moderate and expensive.

Travelodge of Santa Fe. This motel, part of a large chain, is at the intersection of Guadalupe Street and Cerrillos Road, six blocks from the plaza and only three blocks from the many shops and restaurants along Guadalupe Street. It is the most conveniently situated to downtown of all the motels on Cerrillos Road. In this complex, there are forty-eight air-conditioned units with a heated pool. Mailing address: Travelodge of Santa Fe, 646 Cerrillos Road, Santa Fe, New Mexico 87501. Telephone: toll free in the continental United States 1-800-255-3050 or 1-505-982-3551. Inexpensive and moderate.

Budget Inn of Santa Fe. This large, plain motel with 160 air-conditioned units is located along Cerrillos Road close to the Travelodge and the intersection of Guadalupe Street and Cerrillos Road. As the shops and restaurants along Guadalupe move farther and farther south, this inn and the Travelodge become closer to the action. TV in each room. Heated swimming pool. No pets. Mailing address: Budget Inn of Santa Fe, 725 Cerrillos Road, Santa Fe, New Mexico 87501. Telephone: 1-505-982-5952. Moderate.

Preston House, bed-and-breakfast inn, Santa Fe

El Rey Inn. Although located along busy Cerrillos Road, this very attractive air-conditioned adobe-style inn is situated on over three acres of beautifully landscaped grounds, which isolates it from all the hubbub and makes it a peaceful haven. Some of its fifty-six nicely furnished southwestern-style rooms with kiva fireplaces as well as refrigerators and TV's are situated around a lovely courtyard with adobe walls. Five kitchenettes. Some of the rooms employ passive solar architecture, and others have private patios. Some of the units are on the terrace by the pool. Coin-operated laundry. Large outdoor heated pool. Ample parking and children's play areas. Just two miles from the plaza, this is your best bet if everything downtown is full or if you want southwestern ambience at a lower price. Complimentary coffee in the attractive lobby. No pets. Mailing address: El Rey Motel, 1862 Cerrillos Road, Box 130, Santa Fe, New Mexico 87504. Telephone: 1-505-982-1931. Inexpensive and moderate.

Alamo Lodge. Two and one-half miles southwest on U.S. Highway 85 at 1842 Cerrillos Road is this modern, comfortable, eighteen-unit air-conditioned motel with TV's. Telephone: 1-505-982-1841. Inexpensive.

Sunrise Springs Inn. This resort and spa, as well as conference center, is located ten miles south of Santa Fe. Travel south on Cerrillos Road, take the frontage road toward the Santa Fe Downs Racetrack. Turn only two miles from the racetrack at Decker's Supply and go for two and one-half miles to the resort on thirty-three acres with a large freshwater pond. Sunrise Springs Inn has been developed from modernized, old adobe farmhouse buildings and several new, well-designed modern outbuildings. There are many health-oriented facilities, including classes in yoga and meditation. There is swimming in a junior Olympic-size pool as well as tennis, nature trails, a quarter-mile jogging and roller skating track. When you are through with all the activity, you can relax in one of the saunas or hot tubs. There are thirty-two garden rooms with full baths. Some have fireplaces and refrigerators. Botanical gardens. Breakfast, lunch, and dinner are available at the inn, which also operates the handsome Blue Heron Restaurant.

The setting and the well-wrought artistic touches throughout make this inn a relaxing, pleasant place to stay. Mailing address: Sunrise Springs Inn, Route 14, Box 203, (La Cienega) Santa Fe, New Mexico 87505. Telephone: 1-505-471-3600 or toll free in the United States 1-800-772-0500. Expensive.

Bishop's Lodge. Located three and one-half miles north of Santa Fe on Bishop's Lodge Road (New Mexico Highway 590) is this impeccably fine resort, which provides enough southwestern atmosphere, comfort, and services to empty most pocketbooks in a few days. But unquestionably, you get what you pay for. The "Bishop" in the lodge's name was Santa Fe's Bishop Lamy. He loved this place then as you will now and as Joseph Pulitzer and his family did when they purchased this property after Lamy's death. Lamy's chapel is still on the grounds. Today, just as in 1918, the property belongs to the Thorpe family, who established a guest ranch there in the 1900s. The sixty-five air-conditioned rooms are spread among five Pueblo-style adobe buildings. The interiors of some rooms contain interesting southwestern artifacts and adobe-style fireplaces. Others have more modern furnishings that do not quite seem to fit in. Amenities—the lodge has them. In the first place, the ranch covers over one thousand acres, allowing for a full horseback riding program (fee), and a series of trails where you can walk through gardens and orchards or into the surrounding pine-clad foothills. Good fishing is available in a stocked pond, as well as in nearby streams. There are five tennis courts (fee), a large heated swimming pool, and a skeet and trap shooting range. There are also saunas, whirlpool baths, a children's playground, and a social program for kids. Anything else? The dining room prides itself on its continental and New Mexican specialties and is open to the public by reservation only. No pets. Modified American Plan only from June through the first week in September. The European Plan is available with reduced rates from March until June and from early September through October. Advance reservation deposit required. Fifteen percent gratuity or service charge. Mailing address: Bishop's Lodge, P.O. Box 2367, Santa Fe, New Mexico 87501. Telephone 1-505-983-6377. Expensive plus.

Rancho Encantado, north of Santa Fe

Rancho Encantado. From Santa Fe head north on U.S. Highways 285 and 84, the road to Los Alamos, Española, and Taos. Take the Tesuque Exit (not the Tesuque Pueblo Exit) on the right-hand side of the highway and follow the road for three miles. On the right will be New Mexico Highway 590 with a sign indicating Rancho Encantado. Turn on Highway 590 and follow the signs to the rancho. About eight miles from Santa Fe, the Rancho Encantado is a place the bishop might have liked just as well as well or better if he could have found it before Betty Egan did in 1967. She and her family have developed one of the finest resorts anywhere out of a slumbering old ranch lodge built in chaparral country in the late 1920s. The ranch's setting is on 168 acres in spectacular country that looks like what New Mexico is supposed to. No watering down for the dudes there. This is the real stuff. As you climb from the Tesuque Valley on the dusty road to the ranch, vistas begin to open up. By the time you are at the ranch, you have the whole Rio Grande Valley to look out on as well as the Pajarito Plateau to the east. At night the lights from Los Alamos, many miles away across the valley, twinkle at you as you sit in resplendent comfort in a dining room full of good cheer and southwestern charm. But the rancho has more than views; it has gusto. It pleases and then some more. The white Spanish territorial-style adobe buildings enclose twenty-two tastefully decorated rooms (most with fireplaces and some with refrigerators), while across the road at Pueblo Encantado Condomin-iums are thirty-six one- and two-bedroom apartment units with kitchens. Many of the guest rooms are filled with southwestern Spanish and Indian crafts. From your room you can walk out over the rolling hills, home to innumerable desert cottontail rabbits, or repair to one of the most delightful courtyards in New Mexico. This place exudes "Southwest" and "New Mexico" at every turn. The environment has been carefully preserved, and the atmosphere is so casual and relaxed that within a few hours you begin to feel like a born-again New Mexican. But there is more to do than just bask in the rancho's warm hospitality. There are two professional tennis courts (no fee), horseback riding (fee), as well as swimming, horseshoes, shuffleboard, and a complete recreation center. The dining room serves three meals daily and offers spectacular views out over the countryside. It is open to the public by reservation only. European Plan only. Mailing address: Rancho Encantado, Route 4, Box 57C, Santa Fe, New Mexico 87501. Telephone: 1-505-982-3537. Expensive plus.

Hacienda Rancho de Chimayó. Out in the New Mexico countryside in a lovely and peaceful high-desert setting, this bed-and-breakfast-style country inn in the Chimayó area (just across the road from the owner's renowned restaurant, Rancho de Chimayó) is sure to please. Seven handsomely renovated rooms filled with regional antiques face the central courtyard of this historic and charming one-hundred-year-old adobe home. Continental breakfast in your room, outdoors, or in one of the public rooms. Advance reservations advised. The inn is closed in January. For directions to the hacienda, see directions to Rancho de Chimayó Restaurant. Mailing address: Hacienda Rancho de Chimayó, P.O. Box 11, Chimayó, New Mexico 87522. Telephone: 1-505-351-2222. Inexpensive, moderate, and expensive.

Chinguague Compound. Far from the madding crowd is this tranquil and comfortable bed-and-breakfast establishment, which snuggles right up to the banks of the Rio Grande and its bird-filled bosques in the valley just north of San Juan Pueblo. Although only minutes from New Mexico Highway 68, you will experience a sense of adventure as you travel over short stretches of unpaved gravel and dirt roads winding your way through giant cottonwoods to the front gate of the compound. Once you enter the compound you feel an immediate sense of serenity. The giant trees and fruit orchards offer midday shade, the coyote fences and old adobes remind you of where you are, the beautiful rose bushes provide familiarity, and the owners' truly gracious and warm hospitality melt all your cares away. Three very old and authentic adobes have been renovated to just the right level of comfort. One with its large screened-in porch has a kitchen, fireplace, and two bedrooms, each with private bath. Then there is a smaller cottage with one bedroom, private bath, fireplace, and kitchen. The third unit has one bedroom, private bath, living room with kiva fireplace and sofa bed, as well as a kitchen and an enclosed porch. And for breakfast, the owner's cornmeal pancakes and homemade breads served with honey from the compound's hives, can't be beat. Near the Rio Grande just north of San Juan Pueblo, midway between Santa Fe and Taos. Call for directions. Mailing address: Chinguague Compound, Box 1118, San Juan Pueblo, New Mexico 87566. Telephone: 1-505-852-2194. Moderate.

Camping

Hyde Memorial State Park. Located just off the road to the ski area (New Mexico Highway 475 or Hyde Park Road), approximately eleven miles northeast of the plaza. From the northeast corner of the plaza travel one-half mile north on Washington Avenue, then east on Artist Road to New Mexico Highway 475 or Hyde Park Road. Seventy sites on 350 acres. Telephone: 1-505-827-7465.

Black Canyon. This National Forest Service campground is located approximately ten miles northeast of the plaza off New Mexico Highway 475. Follow the directions to Hyde Memorial State Park, above. Forty-one sites on sixteen acres at an elevation of 8,400 feet. Telephone: 1-505-753-7331.

Ranchero de Santa Fe Camping. Located approximately ten and one-half miles east of the plaza off frontage road, which parallels Interstate 25 as it heads toward Las Vegas, New Mexico. One hundred and twenty sites on 122 acres. Reservation deposit required. Telephone: 1-505-983-3482.

Food

La Posada's Staab House Restaurant. 330 East Palace Avenue. Telephone: 1-505-983-5800. Inside or outside, where the patio catches the morning sun, this is a very enjoyable and cheery spot for breakfast. Traditional or continental breakfast as well as huevos rancheros. Lunch and dinner in the dining room with its attractive southwestern decor. Inexpensive, moderate, and expensive.

The Shed. 113 ½ East Palace Avenue, Prince Plaza at Sena Plaza Complex. Telephone: 1-505-982-9030. Both locals and knowledgeable travelers alike start lining up at 11:00 A.M. at this popular luncheon spot. And there is good reason. You'll dine inside one of Santa Fe's old adobes or outdoors on the patio, and you will be treated to some good food. Besides well-prepared soups and sandwiches, delicious charbroiled hamburgers, and the savory Pueblo Indian dish, posole, the specialty of the house is blue corn tortillas, which are used to make some out-of-this-world blue corn enchiladas. Good homemade desserts, too. Open only from 11:00 A.M. to 2:30 P.M. No reservations accepted. You will have to stand in line, but it's worth

Desert cottontail rabbit

it. Closed Sundays. Inexpensive.

La Casa Sena. 125 East Palace Avenue. Located one block east of the plaza in Sena Plaza courtyard at 20 Sena Place. Telephone: 1-505-988-9232. Nicely situated adjacent to the Sena Plaza gardens, this busy restaurant serves up New Mexican and continental specialties for breakfast, lunch, and dinner in the handsomely refurbished interior of the historic old Sena home and in season on the lovely outdoor garden patio. From the fresh trout baked in clay to the chiles rellenos con queso and green chiles enchiladas accompanied by whole wheat sopaipillas, you can't go wrong. And then there is La Cantina, the lively Spanish bar, which serves tapas, those delicious Iberian appetizers, several times weekly and provides entertainment by strolling troubadour waiters singing many popular and favorite songs. Moderate and expensive.

The Burrito Company and Poster Gallery. Just half a block north of the plaza at 111 Washington Avenue (telephone: 1-505-98-CHILE) is this always busy, informal, fun, egalitarian eatery with its numerous outdoor tables spread out in front. A good stop for a quick lunch, a snack, or just a good cold drink on a hot day. Many New Mexican specialties prepared with red chiles from Chimayó and green chiles from Hatch, New Mexico. Breakfast, lunch, and dinner, but mostly a short-order haven. Take out food available. Inexpensive.

Santa Fe Gourmet. 72 West Marcy Street. Telephone: 1-505-982-8738. Located on the street just behind the Palace of the Governors is this small "gourmet" lunch café, which has excellent soups and sandwiches. Regional food is also served with many creative variations. Picnic lunches prepared. Also open for continental breakfast. Closed Sundays. Inexpensive.

Josie's Casa de Comida. 225 East Marcy Street. Telephone: 1-505-983-5311. This old home turned into a family-operated lunch café is a local favorite at noon. Very good New Mexican food in an informal atmosphere. You can't go wrong with the carne adovada burrito, the blue corn enchiladas and soft tacos, or the outstanding selection of wonderful homemade desserts, which include a wide selection of mouth-watering pies. The line outside the door moves fast, but even if it doesn't, it's well worth waiting. Closed Saturdays and Sundays. Inexpensive.

Santacafé. 231 Washington Avenue. Telephone: 1-505-984-1788. Located just beyond Marcy Street in the historic Padre Gallegos House several blocks from the hustle and bustle of downtown. If you are a seeker of the best-prepared food an area has to offer, then you should make a reservation here, fast. The setting is remarkable for the blend of old territorial-style architecture on the outside and the elegant contemporary treatment of the superb restaurant inside. Carefully prepared from the freshest of ingredients are innovative continental, haute American, and new international gourmet dishes that are just outstanding, if not ambrosial. The eclectic, free-wheeling menu offers a variety of dishes including small, gourmet pizzas, Chinese dumplings stuffed with spinach and shrimp and served in an excellent ginger sauce, homemade ravioli filled with a variety of tasty fillings, and Chinese cinnamon bark chicken along with other well-prepared pasta, beef, and fresh fish specialties. The dessert menu is equally tantalizing. If the weather permits, eat outdoors in the lovely courtyard for lunch or dinner. Inside guests may see the old water well, covered and lighted for viewing, or between courses, doodle on the paper tablecloths with the crayons provided by the owner, who just wants you to know that you are dining at the Santacafé, the restaurant that's different! Reservations highly recommended. Closed Sundays. High moderate and expensive.

Grant Corner Inn. 122 Grant Avenue. Telephone: 1-505-983-6678. This centrally located bed-and-breakfast inn, located about two blocks west of the plaza, has decided to share its outstanding breakfasts with the public. You can eat inside in the dining room of the lovely renovated historic home or on the patio in the summer. Featuring blue corn waffles, dutch babies, eggs Benedict and huevos rancheros, along with mouth-watering, flaky homemade pastries and fresh fruit frappes, the Grant Corner Inn knows how to do breakfast! Reservations required. Inexpensive and moderate.

Chez Edouard. 239 Johnson Street. Telephone: 1-505-982-9800. Located three blocks west of the plaza is this handsomely appointed chef-owned and -operated restaurant, which offers classic French country-style cuisine in an ambient southwestern setting. Some outdoor patio dining in season. The menu includes cassoulet, pepper steak, seafood brochette, and several chicken and veal dishes laced with calvados and raspberry vinegar sauces. Brunch is served on Sunday. Reservations advised. Closed Monday. Moderate and expensive.

The Palace. 140 West Palace Avenue. Telephone: 1-505-982-9891. This Santa Fe restaurant has been at it for decades. The motif is Victorian, the atmosphere more formal and reserved. The food is continental and northern Italian with a Swiss touch, but there are also New Mexican specialties on both the lunch and dinner menus. The outdoor patio is a very pleasant place for lunch in the summertime, and the bar is a favorite watering hole for many influential Santa Feans. Reservations advised. Closed Sundays. Moderate and expensive.

Downtown Subscription (Newsstand). 130 West Palace Avenue. Telephone: 1-505-983-3085. If you are feeling isolated from the rest of the world, try this convenient outlet for newspapers and magazines, which serves excellent coffee, tea, and pastries as well. It is located in the pleasant, tree-filled courtyard of the Palacio San Francisco. An ideal place for a quick breakfast. You can enter either from San Francisco Street, just west of Origins or from Palace Avenue, east of the Palace Restaurant, where a signed entranceway opens to the shops of Palacio San Francisco and the corridor leading to the courtyard. Inexpensive.

Santa Francisco Street Bar and Grill. 114 West San Francisco Street. Telephone: 1-505-982-2044. A chic gourmet short-order house might be a good description of this popular and very good modern-style restaurant downstairs at the Plaza Mercado (across the street from El Paseo Theater). Open for lunch and dinner with many specials but regularly featuring superb hamburgers, sandwiches, homemade soups, and salads. Homemade sausages served with herbs and green chiles. Inexpensive.

Comme Chez Vous. Located on the third floor of the Plaza Mercado at 116 West San Francisco Street. Telephone: 1-505-984-0004. If you would like to back away from New Mexican specialties and try some very good French and continental cuisine in a lovely setting, this may be the place to try. You can choose, among other entrées, fresh seafood with delicate innovative sauces, veal medallions, duck, or rack of lamb. Outdoor patio dining, weather permitting, with very nice views out over the city. Lunch and dinner daily. Brunch and dinner on Sunday. Reservations advised. Moderate and expensive.

La Plazuela. In the La Fonda Hotel, San Francisco Street and Old Santa Fe Trail Road. Telephone: 1-505-982-5511. This enclosed, roofed courtyard or patio is an excellent place for breakfast or lunch. You can have traditional or continental breakfast or a regional specialty, huevos rancheros. Very pleasant atmosphere. And then upstairs, on the third floor you can dine outdoors on the Carriage House Terrace where you will be treated to a splendid view of the city and mountains at sunset. An even more superb view is available on the fifth floor in the Bell Tower bar where you can sip your drink as the sun slips behind the mountains. Also open for dinner. Moderate and expensive.

The French Pastry Shop Crêperie, and Restaurant. La Fonda Hotel. Telephone: 1-505-983-6697. San Francisco Street side. This busy place serves excellent croissants and other French delights for breakfast. Good soups and sandwiches for lunch. A favorite breakfast spot if you do not mind the crowds. Revel in these authentic and delicious French pastries as you remember the history of the cathedral just down the street, which was so heavily influenced by French priests in the 1800s (see "History"). Inexpensive.

Café Pasqual's. 121 Don Gaspar at Water Street. Telephone: 1-505-983-9340. Just a little over a block south of the plaza. This centrally located restaurant makes an ideal stop for lunch or a snack. You can get breakfast all day and lunch when it should be or until midafternoon. Excellent soups, salads, omelets, and innovative New Mexican fare, including a special blue corn burrito that will fill you right up. The homemade desserts are worth a trip by themselves. Breakfast and lunch only. Closed Wednesday. Inexpensive.

Coyote Café. 132 West Water Street. Telephone: 1-505-983-1615. A little over two blocks southwest of the plaza and up one long nicely designed flight of stairs is one of the most upbeat, fun, and innovative restaurants in Santa Fe. Architecturally, the dining room is a work of art that should not be missed. Its high ceiling and sparsely but elegantly decorated stucco walls give a sense of openness to the room not unlike the wide-open spaces around Santa Fe itself. The large bar and grill curve gracefully around one corner of the spacious room where the stucco wall has been sculpted to the shape of a giant kiva fireplace. From coyotes etched on glass, to oversized folk art jackalopes, coyotes, and rabbits to colorful dancing buffalo mobile sculptures and Navajo eye dazzlers, the creative interior decor is a delight. But this is no coyote's trick. The decor is no more pleasing or inventive than the food, which is outstanding. For starters try the tequila, black bean quesadilla, or the chorizo quesadilla with mango salsa. Then when you really get going try one of the delicious soups or salads concocted from the freshest ingredients and served with a basket of homemade herb and red chile breads. For an entrée try something like red chile quail with baby greens or the chiles rellenos with corn and mushroom filling in crème fraiche. Or try any one of the fresh fish or meat dishes, which are grilled over pecan wood. For dessert the jalapeño sorbet will make you howl at the Coyote. But its your fault, you should have

chosen the blueberry-ginger crème brûlée or the raspberry mousse. Lighter fare, such as hamburgers can be found in the seasonal outdoor cantina (up a half-flight of stairs) on the rooftop with very nice views of the city. Lunch Monday through Friday. Dinner daily with brunch and dinner on Sunday. Moderate and expensive.

Galisteo News and Ticket Center. Located two blocks southwest of the plaza at 201 Galisteo at Water Street (telephone: 1-505-984-1316) is this innovative establishment where you can pick up your opera tickets, read an out-of-town newspaper, browse through their excellent regional book selection, or quaff delicious espresso drinks and pastries. Good spot for breakfast on the run or a snack. Inexpensive.

The Periscope. 221 Shelby Street. Telephone: 1-505-988-2355. This small, but outstanding restaurant offers a variety of carefully prepared international and continental dishes with an Italian touch. Dinner on Saturdays only further establishes this small restaurant's reputation as one of the best gourmet kitchens in town. The outstanding, fixed-price seven-course dinner allows you to choose among three entrées. Lunch, Tuesdays through Saturdays. Reservations required. High moderate to expensive.

The Pink Adobe. 406 Old Santa Fe Trail Road. Telephone: 1-505-983-7712. A trip to Santa Fe is not complete without a visit to this venerable old restaurant located in one of the oldest districts in Santa Fe. You will dine in an atmosphere that evokes northern New Mexico and the Spanish Southwest. In addition, the food has been consistently good for the last twenty years, at least. New Mexican, creole, and gourmet specialties are served. Excellent homemade desserts are also part of the scene. The bar across the driveway is a beauty and a good place to catch a before- or after-dinner drink. The character of the place is more formal than it used to be. Lunch, Mondays through Fridays. Dinner, daily. Reservations should be made in advance most of the year, especially in the summer, when you may have to call a day ahead of time. Moderate and expensive.

Patis Corbae Bakery and Café. 422 Old Santa Fe Trail next to the Capitol. Telephone: 1-505-983-2422. If you are up touring around the oldest church, stop at this European-style sidewalk café. Specializes in butter croissants, plain or stuffed with a variety of fillings. Soups, salads, fruit plates, and of course, desserts. Good for breakfast or lunch. Also, carry out available. Inexpensive.

Rincon Del Oso. 639 Old Santa Fe Trail. Telephone: 1-505-983-5337. From the whole wheat sopaipillas to the excellent chiles rellenos and blue corn enchiladas, you know you are dining at an establishment that puts a lot of care into its food preparation. No wonder it's a Santa Fe favorite. Homemade desserts are part of the reason for going, and they include mocha pie and flan. Inexpensive and low moderate.

The Compound. 653 Canyon Road. Telephone: 1-505-982-4353. This is Santa Fe's most elegant dinner house and continental restaurant. If you need a change from regional specialties to continental fare and you want to splurge a bit, this is where you may want to go. A beautifully appointed restaurant, designed by Alexander Girard (architect and folk art collector), is enclosed within tree-shaded adobe walls with an ambience evoking the Southwest. Also open for lunch. Reservations advised. Closed Mondays. Expensive.

Aunt Babe's Restaurant Bar and Gallery. 731 Canyon Road. Telephone: 1-505-983-3512. Located on Canyon Road near the Camino Del Monte Sol intersection, this upbeat, large, pleasant, flower-filled, garden atrium dining room is a good place to have lunch after shopping hard all morning. You can get a pizza or a sandwich or delve into either Italian or New Mexican cuisine before resuming the afternoon's activities. Moderate.

El Farol. 808 Canyon Road. Telephone: 1-505-983-9912. Superb Spanish tapas and gourmet entrées in this popular very atmospheric restaurant and bar. This is a favorite watering hole for local artists. Informal live music in the evening may vary from folk and country to flamenco. Outdoor dining in the summer. Dinner only, Tuesday–Saturday. Bar open nightly. Reservations for dinner advised. Moderate.

Andrea's Mexican Restaurant. 802 Canyon Road. Located on Canyon Road at the intersection of Camino Del Monte Sol. The informal outdoor patio here is a convenient stopping point to order a cold drink and a short order of something good. Lunch and dinner daily. Breakfast on weekends only. Inexpensive.

La Tertulia. 416 Agua Fria Street. Telephone: 1-505-988-2769. No wonder both visitors and native Santa Feans like this restaurant. Numerous picturesque dining rooms in a restored historic adobe convent across the road from Santuario de Guadalupe. From the black bean soup and sopaipillas through the well-prepared entrées (which include flavorful Spanish dishes like paella, New Mexican specialties, and steaks) to the dessert natilla, this restaurant pleases again and again. Friendly, enthusiastic staff. Spanish colonial art in several rooms. Outdoor dining in the summer. Open for lunch and dinner. Reservations advised. Closed Mondays. Moderate.

The Guadalupe Café. 313 South Guadalupe Street. Telephone: 1-505-982-9762. This little gem of a café serves breakfast, lunch, and dinner. Creative New Mexican specialties prevail at all three meals, but are augmented by American, Italian, and French specialties including pasta and crêpes. A warm, friendly environment. Open Tuesday through Friday for lunch with brunch on Saturday and Sunday. Open for dinner Tuesday through Friday. Closed Monday. Inexpensive and moderate.

The Swiss Bakery and Restaurant. 320 Guadalupe Street. Telephone: 1-505-988-3737. This excellent bakery, restaurant, and espresso bar is a fine place to go for either breakfast or lunch. The quiches, crêpes, and pastries are excellent, and the sandwiches on a variety of homemade breads are also good. Outdoor patio dining available. Picnic lunches. Closed Sundays. Inexpensive and moderate.

Zia Diner. 326 South Guadalupe Street. Telephone: 1-505-988-7008. American cooking at its best in this one-hundred-year-old adobe warehouse. Art-deco 1950s interior with patio dining in the summer is the scene for lunch and dinner snacks or full-course meals. And for your sweet tooth there are homemade pies as well as soda fountain delights. Full dinners can include fresh fish, pork chops with red chile sauce, and mashed potatoes done the hard way. Inexpensive and moderate.

The Winery. 510 Montezuma in Sanbusco Center. Telephone: 1-505-982-9463. This wine shop with its extraordinary selection of fine wines and beers also serves light lunches featuring a range of tasty deli sandwiches and salads. Inexpensive.

Tomasita's. 500 South Guadalupe Street. Telephone: 1-505-983-5721. This New Mexican restaurant located in the old Chili Line Railway freight depot is a bustling place with a lot of charm. Local Santa Feans out for a night of margaritas and good New Mexican food mingle and rub shoulders with the travelers who find this spot. But no matter where you are from, you will have to wait for a table in the evenings. The price is right and the food is good. Also open for lunch. Closed Sundays. Inexpensive and low moderate.

Las Tres Gentes Market Center. 418 Cerrillos Road. Located close to the intersection of Montezuma and Cerrillos, one long block east of South Guadalupe Street. Here you will find the excellent, gourmet Carry-Out Café (order ahead by calling 1-505-984-3003) where everything is made from scratch and from the freshest ingredients. Ideal for picnic lunches. Limited seating. Although you can pick up your food by just driving by the Carry-Out's pickup window, you may want to walk through the market to see the small shops and take in the other specialty foods available there. While you're there, you may want to visit the Chocolate Maven, a bakery specializing in chocolate brownies, tortes, and other chocoholic favorites.

La Choza. 905 Alarid Street. Telephone: 1-505-982-0909. Located southwest of downtown. Take Paseo de Peralta to South Guadalupe Street. Cross Guadalupe Street and travel west on Paseo de Peralta to Alarid Street. Or from Cerrillos Road turn north on Alarid (one block east of the Cerrillos Road, St. Francis intersection), cross the railroad tracks and look for the restaurant on your right. This informal café in a restored old adobe ranch house is owned by the wizards who hold forth at the Shed, downtown. So if for any reason you can't get into the Shed at lunchtime, you can try La Choza, which is open for both lunch and dinner. The regional New Mexican menu is similar and well worth the trip, especially for those blue corn enchiladas. Carry-out meals also available. Closed Sunday. Inexpensive.

Tecolote Café. 1203 Cerrillos Road. Telephone: 1-505-988-1362. If you are staying out on Cerrillos Road this is a convenient place to stop in for breakfast or lunch. The breakfasts are famous at this family-run restaurant, where you will feel right at home. From the New Mexican specialties such as the breakfast burrito to western favorites like flapjacks, you will start the morning right here. Inexpensive and moderate.

Old Mexico Grill. 2434 Cerrillos Road. Telephone: 1-505-473-0338. Located out on Cerrillos Road on the south side of the College Plaza Shopping Center. This very nicely appointed restaurant is popular with many New Mexicans who want a taste of Old Mexico. The open grill, fueled by mesquite, and the rotisserie cook the meats for the excellent beef and chicken fajitas and the tacos al carbón, a soft taco with a beef, chicken, or sausage filling. There are also enchiladas, flautas, and chalupas done the way they do them south of the border. Unique and different salads and soups, derived from Mexican-based recipes, are featured. The eclectic dessert menu includes items like apricot torte and key lime pie. And for you Mexican beverage fans, a treat. The Grill stocks thirteen varieties of Mexican beer, ten different varieties of tequila, and a complete selection of Peñafiel soda pop, a delightfully different fruit-based soda pop made in Mexico. Lunch and dinner. Inexpensive and moderate.

Bobcat Bite. Five miles south of town on Old Las Vegas Highway. From the plaza take Old Santa Fe Trail south and continue south on Old Pecos Trail toward Interstate 25. About one hundred yards before reaching the interstate, at the location of several roadside vendors, take a left on Old Las Vegas Highway, which parallels the interstate highway. Travel 4.1 miles to the Bobcat Bite. Telephone: 1-505-983-5319. If you are visiting the museums southeast of Santa Fe and are hungry for a hamburger, drive down Camino Lejo to Old Pecos Trail and turn left, following the directions above. In a few miles you will come to this café which serves up the best hamburger in the region, bar none. Also excellent steaks. Open for lunch and early dinner. Closed Sunday and Monday. Traveler's checks, local checks, or cash only. No credit cards. Inexpensive and moderate.

Tesuque Village Market. Located in Tesuque, north of Santa Fe (for directions to Tesuque see "A Day Traveling through Spanish New Mexico: A Narrative Account"). Telephone: 1-505-988-8848. This is an art gallery, restaurant, delicatessen, wine shop, and grocery store all rolled into one. Breakfast and lunch are served, and of course, there are lots of goodies to carry out for picnics. Homemade breads and muffins as well as delectable desserts are specialties. Homemade soups, sandwiches, and enchiladas for lunch. Picnic lunches made to order. Closed Sunday. Inexpensive and moderate.

El Nido. Located seven miles north of Santa Fe in Tesuque. Take New Mexico Highway 590 from downtwon Santa Fe. Telephone: 1-505-988-4340. For many years this local favorite has been known as a steak house worth patronizing. Not only is the drive pleasant but the southwestern ambience is thick. It is a large restaurant and almost always seems busy and full of life. In addition to quality cuts of aged beef, seafood and a variety of New Mexican specialties are served. Dinner only. Closed Monday. Reservations advised. Moderate and expensive.

Rancho Encantado. Eight miles north of Santa Fe. (See driving instructions under "Lodging.") Telephone: 1-505-982-3537. The dining room of this famous resort is open to the public by reservation only. Breakfast, lunch, and dinner are served. American, continental, and New Mexican specialties comprise the menu. The food is good, but the views are magnificent, especially at sunset. Ask for a view table. Before or after lunch or dinner, spend some time walking through the rolling hills around the ranch. Well worth the trip. Closed January through March. Reservations required. Moderate and expensive.

Rancho de Chimayó. Approximately a thirty-minute drive from Santa Fe to the north. (See "A Day Traveling through Spanish New Mexico: A Narrative Account" for directions.) A more direct alternate route is to take U.S. Highway 285 north approximately sixteen miles. Then, just beyond the Los Alamos Exit, take New Mexico Highway 503 east at Nambe and drive eleven miles, partly via New Mexico Highway 520, to the ranch on the right. Telephone: 1-505-351-4444. Lunch and dinner served daily during the summer. Dinner daily after Labor Day except Monday. Lunch on seasonal schedule after summer, but almost always served on Sundays. Closed Christmas Day and approximately the last three weeks of January. If you like New Mexican regional food, you should visit the rancho. This is probably one of the finest restaurants of its kind in the United States and certainly outshines all competition in the region. The setting is perfect. Whether in the historic ranch house or the tree-shaded patio you won't find a more pleasant place to dine. (See detailed description of interior in "A Day Traveling through Spanish New Mexico: A Narrative Account.") The regional foods are magnificently prepared. No apologies for the hyperbole. Try their Chimayó cocktail for starters, then follow that with one of the superb entées, which include pork adovada and the best enchiladas, tamales, and chiles rellenos you will ever taste. You will not be disappointed with anything on the menu. The steaks, trout, and fried chicken are well pepared. Outstanding sopaipillas. Reservations advised. Moderate.

Rio Grande Café. In Española at the Los Alamos turnoff, one block south of U.S. Highway 84 intersection. Telephone: 1-505-753-2125. If you are in or around Española at lunch or dinnertime, do not miss this family-owned and-run regional café that has been serving up excellent New Mexican specialties since 1948. At this restaurant the food is called "native" food. Informal cafélike, very clean, and very authentic. Closed

Saturdays and Sundays. Inexpensive.

Jo Ann's Ranch O Casados Restaurant. In Española along U.S. Highway 84/285 at the Big Rock Shopping Center. Telephone: 1-505-753-2837. This small restaurant owned by the well-established New Mexican family that has for many years produced much of the posole and other staples that are sold to stores and restaurants in the region and beyond, is as authentic as you can get. With a wide-ranging regional menu that includes chiles rellenos, stuffed sopaipillas, carne adovada, huevos rancheros, posole, chicos, and homemade tamales as well as homemade corn and blue corn tortillas, you can sample some of the Rio Grande Valley favorites. American dinners and sandwiches also available. And for dessert you can fill up on panoche pudding or biscochitos. Breakfast, lunch, and dinner. Closed Sunday. Inexpensive.

Anthony's at the Delta. It seems a little difficult to believe that one of the most aesthetic and elegant restaurants in the Santa Fe area is along the river in Española. Yet it's true. Anthony's, family-owned and fastidiously operated, is worth seeing whether you're hungry or not. You will find it by driving north from Santa Fe to Española. There look for the Chama Highway, U.S. Highway 84, and the Delta Bar sign. The restaurant is located just off the highway at 228 Onate Northwest. Telephone: 1-505-753-4511. In numerous, beautifully appointed dining rooms decorated with Hispanic and Native American art and fronting on exquisite adobe-walled courtyards filled with fragrant fresh flowers (over three hundred rose bushes and enough geraniums to fill every window box in a large Swiss village) and exotic plants, you will dine on well-prepared entrées of fresh fish, prime rib, and steaks. Outdoor dining in the rose garden including Sunday brunch, weather permitting. Reservations advised. Moderate and expensive.

Tours

Santa Fe Detours. This consortium of tour operators, offering their services under the umbrella of one tour operation, makes it easy to find a tour to fit your specific needs. You can choose a walking tour of the city's historic areas with the tour organization known as Santa Fe Walks, or see some of the same sights as well as some more distant ones by touring in an open-sided bus, the Roadrunner. In the summer you can catch the Roadrunner at the corner of Palace and Lincoln for its hour-and-a-half city tour. By air-conditioned Grey Line bus you can explore out-of-town sights such as Santa Clara Pueblo, Bandelier National Monument, and Taos. Or you can join Southwest Safaris for flight-seeing trips in the region, which include time on the ground in areas like Monument Valley and the Grand Canyon. At Detours you can also go another direction by taking exciting river raft trips through stretches of white water offered by Southwest Wilderness Center, steam rail trips on the Cumbres and Toltec line, or arrange for horseback riding at Blue Sky Ranch, by the day or overnight. You can make arrangements at the office in the lobby of the La Fonda Hotel, 100 East San Francisco, Santa Fe, New Mexico 87501. Telephone: 1-505-983-6565 or toll free in the United States, except New Mexico, 1-800-DETOURS.

Historical Walking Tours of Santa Fe. Learn how native Santa Feans feel about their city and get their perspective on the cultures of the area during these three-hour tours of historic Santa Fe. Las Tres Gentes Market Center, 418 Cerrillos Road, Santa Fe, New Mexico 87504. Telephone: 1-505-984-8235.

New Wave Rafting. Raft the Rio Grande, Chama, or other regional rivers with expert guides. Pickup and return to Santa Fe. Half-, full-day and overnight trips. Located at 107 Washington Avenue. Mailing address: New Wave Rafting, Route 5, Box 302 A, Santa Fe, New Mexico 87501. Telephone: 1-505-984-1444.

Rojo Tours. This tour and service group also offers a wide range of personalized tours for individuals or groups, from walking tours of the city, river rafting, or biking (these interesting bike tours are handled by Desert Wind Excursions) to steam railroad and bus tours of the region including tours to the Indian Pueblos, Indian festivals and dances, and Chaco Canyon. Located across from the Inn at Loretto. Mailing address: Rojo Tours, 228 Old Santa

Fe Trail Road, Santa Fe, New Mexico 87501. Telephone: 1-505-983-8333.

Rocky Mountain Tours. This multi-tour operator can arrange for everything from a car and driver and white-water rafting to sight-seeing tours of the Indian pueblos. Located at 102 West San Francisco. Telephone: 1-505-984-1684.

Discover Santa Fe. This organization specializes in group tours of the area and has the capability of making all arrangements for any group or convention in Santa Fe. Mailing address: Discover Santa Fe, P.O. Box 2847, Santa Fe, New Mexico 87501. Telephone: 1-505-982-4979.

Escortguide. This consortium of Santa Fe and New Mexico specialists focus on custom-designed travel planning and specialized services for individuals or groups. Their book *Escortguide, The People Connection to New Mexico* is a fine resource directory to services, consultants, professional guides, and unusual resources for anyone planning an extended visit to the area.

Footsteps Across New Mexico. This is a good tour to take if you want to sit still awhile and see and learn a lot. In a semicircular theatre with comfortable seats, you can sit back and take in the history and culture of New Mexico thanks to the latest in visual and sound production equipment. This nine projector, computer-controlled show starts every half hour and is a real winner. And when it is over, you can browse the complete bookstore with many special Southwest titles. Conveniently located in the Inn at Loretto, just a block and a half from the plaza. Daily. Fee. Telephone: 1-505-982-9297.

Behind Adobe Walls Tours. House and garden tours of Santa Fe, sponsored by the Santa Fe Garden Club, are given the last two Tuesdays in July and the first two Tuesdays in August. Here is your chance to see the Santa Fe style at the source, as you tour some of Santa Fe's most interesting and beautiful adobe homes and gardens. Fee. For more information, telephone 1-505-982-2500.

The Center for Contemporary Arts of Santa Fe. 291

East Barcelona. Located next door to the Armory for the Arts (1050 Old Pecos Road). Telephone: 1-505-982-1338. This handsome and nicely renovated art center concentrates on contemporary art in its mixed media exhibits. Its compact auditorium allows for both live film and live art performances.

School of American Research Indian Arts Research Center. 660 East Garcia Street. Telephone: 1-505-982-3584. This prestigious group of scholars has gathered together one of the finest collections of traditional Indian work, particularly ceramics, baskets, and fabrics, that you will find anywhere. Collection may be viewed by appointment only under the direction of a tour guide. Call for tour dates and times. In addition, the grounds of the school are particularly attractive.

Institute of American Indian Arts Museum. You may make a self tour to this prestigious museum, which focuses on contemporary art of Native Americans from the Southwest and throughout the nation. In addition to seeing the works of well-known artists, you will also view the work of many of the talented students at the IAIA. Perhaps they will follow in the path of many successful former students like Fritz Scholder and T. C. Cannon. Closed Saturday and Sunday. Telephone: 1-505-988-6281.

Santa Fe Children's Museum. 1050 Old Pecos Trail. Adjacent to the Armory for the Arts. Telephone: 1-505-989-8359. The development of special museums for children around the country has not escaped Santa Fe. This excellent, hands-on, tuned-into-the senses museum will delight most children.

Horseback Riding

Bishop's Lodge Stables. See "Lodging" for directions to the lodge. You can take two-hour trail rides into the Sangre de Cristo Mountains, except in the busy part of the summer when lodge guests have first priority. Telephone: 1-505-983-6377.

Double Arrow Stable. Five miles southwest of the plaza on Old Santa Fe Trail Road. Hourly rides for a minimum of two and longer tours through the Sangre de Cristo Mountains, by reservation. Telephone: 1-505-983-1561.

Events

Santa Fe Opera. One of the best-known opera companies in the United States performs from early July through late August in an impressive outdoor theater, seven miles north of Santa Fe just off U.S. Highways 84 and 285. Take warm clothing and rain gear. Performances begin at 9:00 P.M. Seating starts at 8:30 P.M. Arrive a little early to avoid all the congestion. Cameras, recording equipment, food, and beverages are not allowed inside. One hundred and fifty inexpensive standing room spaces go on sale at 8:00 P.M. at the opera box office on the night of the performance. For further information and schedule of performances, write Santa Fe Opera, P.O. Box 2408, Santa Fe, New Mexico 87504-2408. Business office telephone: 1-505-982-3851. In the summer, tickets can be purchased at the opera theater box office or at the Galisteo News and Ticket Center at 201 Galisteo Street. For telephone orders, call 1-505-982-3855.

Santa Fe Chamber Music Festival. The prestigious Santa Fe Chamber Music Group is in residence in Santa Fe during most of July and through the middle to the end of August. During that time, they perform at the New Mexico Museum of Fine Arts in the acoustically superb Saint Francis Auditorium. Visitors may attend rehearsals at the Fine Arts Museum. Dates and times of the rehearsals are usually posted in the museum lobby. Tickets can be purchased on the mezzanine of the La Fonda Hotel. For further information, write Santa Fe Chamber Music Festival, P.O. Box 853, Santa Fe, New Mexico 87504-0853. Telephone the festival office: 1-505-983-2075 or the box office 1-505-982-1890 for tickets or toll free in the United States 1-800-962-7286.

Santa Fe Desert Chorale. This professional vocal ensemble performs from June through early August in the Santuario de Guadalupe on the corner of Agua Fria and Guadalupe. This fine group presents a wide range of choral music. For further information, write Santa Fe Desert Chorale, P.O. Box 2813, Santa Fe, New Mexico 87504-2813. Telephone: 1-505-988-7505.

Summerscene Concerts. For two months, from the last weekend in June through the last weekend in August, the chamber of commerce and the city of Santa Fe present a series of noon and evening concerts (usually on Tuesday and Thursday, but may change from year to year) and other free events on the plaza, at Fort Marcy Amphitheater or at the Sweeney Convention Center. Mailing address: Santa Fe Chamber of Commerce, 333 Montezuma Avenue, P.O. Box 1928, Santa Fe, New Mexico 87504. Telephone: 1-505-983-7317.

Santa Fe Community Theatre. This well-established drama group (now over sixty years old) gives performances throughout the summer in the theatre at the Armory for the Arts. From hilarious melodramas to sophisticated contemporary dramas, this experienced group of local players do an outstanding job. Mailing address: Santa Fe Community Theatre, 142 East DeVargas Street, Santa Fe, New Mexico 87501. Telephone: 1-505-988-4262.

The Armory for the Arts. Located at 1050 Old Pecos Trail, this outstanding theatre facility hosts a variety of musical, drama, dance, and other fine art and pop productions during the summertime, some local, some imported. For more information, write Armory for the Arts, 1050 Old Pecos Trail, Santa Fe, New Mexico 87501. Telephone: 1-505-988-1886.

British American Theatre Institute. This group puts on a summer training program in Santa Fe during the middle part of the summer. In addition to performances, there are lectures, demonstrations, and public rehearsals. The events are held in the Greer Garson Theatre. For further information, write Greer Garson Theatre Center, College of Santa Fe, Saint Michael's Drive, Santa Fe, New Mexico 87501. Telephone: 1-505-473-6511.

Greer Garson Theatre Center. Located on the campus of Santa Fe College, this theatre, named for the illustrious actress who now calls Santa Fe her home, stages a number of excellent drama productions throughout the year. The season starts after school begins and continues throughout the winter and spring. For further information, write Greer Garson Theatre Center, College of Santa Fe, Saint Michael's Drive, Santa Fe, New Mexico 87501. Telephone: 1-505-473-6511.

The María Benítez Dance Company. Throughout the summer this outstanding Flamenco dancer and her talented Estampa Flamenca Spanish dance company perform to enthusiastic audiences at the Sheraton de Santa Fe Hotel, 750 North Saint Francis Drive. Touted as the most outstanding performer of this style of dance in the United States, the evening shows are usually jammed. Reservations advised. Telephone: 1-505-982-5591.

Horse Racing, Santa Fe Downs. The Santa Fe Downs racetrack is five miles south of town, just off U.S. Interstate Highway 25. The season is from May until Labor Day. Telephone: 1-505-471-3311.

Fairs, Festivals, and Fiestas

Spring Arts, New Mexico/Spring Arts Festival. This festival, held the last week of May and the first week of June, ushers in the fine arts season for Santa Fe. Memorial Day crowds are treated to a variety of music, drama, and dance programs as well as special visual art exhibitions during this special time. Telephone: 1-505-988-3924.

La Conquistadora Procession. June, the Sunday after Corpus Christi Feast Day or the ninth Sunday after Easter. During this annual event, the La Conquistadora Madonna is taken from the old North Chapel of Saint Francis Cathedral and carried in procession to the Rosario Chapel northwest of the city in the cemetery by the same name, which was built for the purpose of receiving the Madonna (see "History"). This was the approximate location of the De Vargas encampment prior to retaking Santa Fe. After a novena of masses, the statue is returned to the cathedral the following Sunday.

Rodeo de Santa Fe. Three days centering around the second weekend in July. This large, colorful event is augmented by a parade and entertainment at the rodeo grounds. Telephone: 1-505-983-3658.

Zozobra, Fiesta de Santa Fe

Spanish Market. Usually held the last weekend in July, this is the place to see and buy the best of the crafts by New Mexico's Hispanic citizens. Wood carving (bultos), retablos, furniture, and colcha embroidery are but a few of the crafts represented. The market is held in front of the Palace of the Governors. Mailing address: Spanish Market, P.O. Box 1611, Santa Fe, New Mexico 87501. Telephone: 1-505-988-8888 or toll free in the United States, except New Mexico 1-800-528-5369.

Indian Market. This annual event held the third weekend in August is a nationally famous fair and market. Indians from around the Southwest and beyond bring their crafts to the plaza and fill it with display and sales booths. You will see many fine crafts there, and moreover, you will have the opportunity to see and meet some of the best-known Indian potters, sculptors, weavers, painters, and basketmakers in the country. For more information, write Indian Market, P.O. Box 1964, Santa Fe, New Mexico 87501, or call the Southwest Indian Affairs office at 1-505-983-5220.

Fiesta de Santa Fe. First weekend after Labor Day. Labeled as the oldest community celebration of its kind in the United States, this four-day celebration commemorates the Spanish reconquest of New Mexico by De Vargas (see "History"). During this event, a giant forty-foot-tall effigy of Zozobra or Old Man Gloom is burned. In addition, parades and a candlelight procession, mariachi music, Spanish colonial dancers, and musicians perform daily in the plaza. For a complete guide to fiesta activities, write the Santa Fe Chamber of Commerce, 333 Montezuma Avenue, Santa Fe, New Mexico 87504.

Festival of the Arts. This important festival, staged for seven days in mid-October, has been instrumental in boosting Santa Fe's image as a city of the arts. The main event is the juried show of New Mexican fine arts, photographs, and contemporary crafts in the gallery space on the second floor of the downtown public library. Many of the city's art galleries mount special shows of national importance at this time. For further information, write Festival of the Arts, 628 Paseo de Peralta, Santa Fe, New Mexico 87501. Telephone: 1-505-988-3924.

Christmas in Santa Fe. For the very special and unique events held during the Christmas season in Santa Fe and the pueblos and villages in the area, contact the Santa Fe Chamber of Commerce, P.O. Box 1928, Santa Fe, New Mexico 87501 or call 1-505-983-7317.

Santa Cruz Day. Cochiti and Taos pueblos. Green Corn Dance. First weekend in May.

San Antonio Feast Day. Taos, San Ildefonso, and Santa Clara pueblos. Corn Dance. Second Sunday in June.

San Juan Feast Day. San Juan and Taos pueblos. Held the third weekend in June. Buffalo and Comanche dances at San Juan (see "Revisiting the Plaza and a Day with the Pueblo Indians North of Santa Fe: A Narrative Account") and Corn Dance in Taos.

San Pedro Feast Days. The last weekend in June. Santo Domingo, San Felipe, Santa Ana pueblos. Corn Dance at Santa Ana.

Viva La Oñate Festival. Three days over the second weekend of July. In Española. Commemorating the Spaniard Oñate's expedition to northern New Mexico. The celebration includes raft races on the Rio Grande, a torch run from Santuario de Chimayó, fireworks, and mariachi music in this Hispanic town. For further information, write Valley Chamber of Commerce, 417 Big Rock Center, Española, New Mexico 87532. Telephone: 1-505-753-2831 or 1-505-465-2244.

San Buenaventura Feast Day. Cochiti Pueblo. Corn Dance. The second weekend in July.

Eight Northern Pueblos Arts and Crafts Fair. Held on a rotational basis in one of the participating pueblos the third weekend in July. This is an outstanding event with the best in Pueblo Indian pottery, weaving, jewelry, and other crafts on display and for sale. For more information, call 1-505-852-4265.

Santo Domingo Feast Day. Santo Domingo Pueblo. Held the first weekend in August. Features the Corn Dance. This is probably the granddaddy of them all, with over five hundred dancers participating. Full of pageantry, beauty, and mystery. In spite of the heat and crowds, it is worth every minute of the hassle.

Santa Clara Feast Days. Santa Clara Pueblo. The second weekend in August. A variety of important and beautiful dances at this ancient Rio Grande pueblo.

For more complete and up-to-date information about the Pueblo Indian ceremonies, dances, and other inquiries you may have, contact the Rio Grande pueblos listed under "Indian Pueblo Telephone Numbers." A central telephone number for most of the pueblos north of Santa Fe is 1-505-852-4265.

Parking

In the summer months parking is very tight in Santa Fe's Historic District, around the plaza. These municipal lots are available within a few blocks of the plaza and are in the locations listed below. The rates may vary from lot to lot, but generally they are quite inexpensive.

Lot bounded by East Water Street and Don Gaspar Street across from the De Vargas Hotel and west of El Centro Mall.

Lot bounded by West Marcy Street and Sheridan Street across from the chamber of commerce, adjacent to Sweeney Convention Center.

Lot bounded by Sandoval Street and East Water Street across from the Hilton Hotel.

Lot behind Sena Plaza accessed via Nusbaum Street from Washington Street.

Lot east of the Loretto Chapel and the Inn at Loretto between Cathedral Place and Paseo de Peralta north of Alameda.

Shopping

Museum of New Mexico Shop. Palace of the Governors. Museum of New Mexico Foundation. Telephone: 1-505-982-3016. The museum shop can be entered from the museum itself if you have paid the entry fee and are touring the museum, or from Washington Avenue (east and around the corner from the main museum entrance on Palace Avenue), where there is a direct entrance to the shop only, no fee required. This excellent store has knowledgeable buyers who are well respected by both Pueblo Indians and Spanish craftsmen. Their fine selection of Indian pottery, basketry, jewelry, Navajo rugs, kachina dolls, and Hispanic folk art is one of the best in the city. You get what you pay for. The prices at this shop can serve as a guide to determine what similar crafts should sell for elsewhere. In addition, the book and magazine section is one of the best in the city, covering a wide range of local and regional topics of consequence. From the museum shop, enter the outdoor patio. Follow it around to the right until you come to the museum's Palace Print Shop (telephone: 1-505-827-6477). There you can purchase interesting posters as well as reprints of old documents and Indian sayings.

The Mudd-Carr Gallery. 227 Otero Street. Telephone: 1-505-982-8206. On the corner of Paseo de Peralta and De Vargas Street. This gallery, located in a handsome territorial-style building, carries older, rare Navajo rugs, Pueblo textiles, Pueblo pottery, pawn jewelry, kachinas, Mexican masks, and fine antique regional Spanish crafts including New Mexican and Mexican furniture. Other folk arts from around the world make up the rest of the scene here.

W. S. Dutton—Rare Things. Number 10A Sena Plaza (enter from the east side of the courtyard area). Telephone: 1-505-982-5904. If you are looking for old, rare, hard-to-find southwestern Indian pots, baskets, weavings, ceremonial garb, or brass or silver jewelry, this respected shop is apt to have it.

Señor Murphy-Candymaker. 131 East Palace Avenue (Sena Plaza complex) and La Fonda Hotel (on Old Santa Fe Trail entrance). No trip to New Mexico is complete without a visit to this confectioner who makes candy from the wonderful piñon nuts of the region and from other piñon growing areas like Spain and Portugal. Roasted and salted piñon nuts and piñon nuts for cooking are also available, as well as red and green chili jellies. Mailing address: Señor Murphy-Candymaker, P.O. Box 2505, Santa Fe, New Mexico 87501. Telephone: 1-505-988-4311.

Ross Lew Allen Jewelry. "Earcuff." 105 East Palace Avenue. Telephone: 1-505-983-2657. Ross Lew Allen is one the Southwest's best-known contemporary jewelers. His "earcuffs" are legendary. Working in sterling silver and gold he has produced many unique earrings and bracelets evoking Southwest themes. New Mexico safari bracelets and a series of pieces that use folk images of trout and snakes are also in his repertoire.

Davis Mather. 141 Lincoln Avenue. Telephone: 1-505-983-1660. This museum-quality shop stocks a nice selection of Hispanic crafts that evoke the Santa Fe style. Particularly prominent here, from time to time, are wood carvings of porcupines, pigs, coyotes, and other regional animals hand carved by prominent Hispanic wood-carvers. Unusual handcrafts from some of Mexico's finest craftspeople are also displayed.

Burnt Horses-A Bookstore. 225 E. DeVargas. Telephone: 1-505-982-4799. A book lovers delight. There are three charming rooms around a courtyard filled with well-selected books on a variety of topics including the Southwest. Also unusual and out-of-print books.

La Mesa of Santa Fe. 225 Canyon Road. Telephone: 1-505-984-1688. Located in a compound of shops and galleries near the entrance to Canyon Road. There's more than just something for the tabletop at La Mesa. Some of New Mexico's best-known artists and craftspeople are represented there. The emphasis is on functional pieces, but in this gallery/shop, art and function are one and inseparable. And the displays are extraordinary, a credit to the knowledgeable and helpful owners.

The Elaine Horwitch Galleries. 129 West Palace Avenue. Telephone: 1-505-988-8997. In the past, this well-known gallery, with branches in Scottsdale and Sedona and Palm Springs, has displayed the works of Georgia O'Keeffe, Jean Miro, Harry Fonseca, R. Lee White, R. C. Gorman, Ruffin Cooper, and Fritz Scholder, and has become a focal point for the best contemporary art in the Southwest. But regional folk art is not forgotten, as the gallery often has a nice selection of museum-quality Spanish carvings and frequently focuses on Native American Art. This gallery bills itself as the major contemporary art gallery in the Southwest. That is probably not an overstatement.

The Gallery Wall. 50 East San Francisco. Telephone: 1-505-988-4168. Fine contemporary art with an emphasis on stone and bronze sculpture. This large gallery often features the work of renowned Indian sculptor, Allan Houser, and other contemporary Native American Artists.

Los Llanos Bookstore. 500 Montezuma in Sanbusco Center. Telephone: 1-505-982-9542. One of Santa Fe's largest and oldest bookstores, with a good selection of general and southwestern titles including regional guidebooks and arts and crafts books. Also children's books and cookbooks. Outstanding selection in most all categories.

Dewey Galleries. 74 East San Francisco Street. Telephone: 1-505-982-8632. A large gallery located on the north side of the plaza. It has a wide assortment of extrafine Navajo rugs, Indian and Spanish collector's items, plus Indian jewelry. Also, Western art is now part of the gallery's offerings.

The Contemporary Craftsman. 100 West San Francisco Street. Telephone: 1-505-988-1001. This excellent gallery represents many of New Mexico's best potters, weavers, fabric artists, contemporary basketmakers, glass blowers, and furniture makers. The gallery is just down the street from the plaza's west side.

Santa Fe Center for Photography. 104 West San Francisco Street. Telephone: 1-505-984-7299. This gallery's commitment to exhibiting the best photographic work available anywhere is deserving of your attention. Shows have included Eliot Porter's 35-mm color photographs of New York, and the works of several photographers from Spain have been showcased.

Cristof's. 106 West San Francisco Street. Telephone: 1-505-988-9881. Another showcase gallery with an excellent selection of Navajo rugs, Hopi kachinas, and many fine contemporary Indian paintings. Also an outstanding selection of both contemporary and traditional fine Indian jewelry.

Nambe Showrooms. 112 West San Francisco Street in the Plaza Mercado and 924 Paseo de Peralta. These retail outlets and the Nambe shop on U.S. Highways 84 and 285 between Santa Fe and Española at Nambe, New Mexico, offer a truly useful and beautiful handcrafted product. Nambeware, as it is called, is freeze-proof, oven-proof ware, sandcast from a special alloy that has the appearance of fine silver. A truly unique, easy-care product made in Santa Fe. Seconds and firsts available in the outlets. For catalog, write Nambe Mills, 1127 Siler Road, Santa Fe, New Mexico 87501.

Origins. 135 West San Francisco Street. Telephone: 1-505-988-2323. A large shop carrying an unbelievably wide selection of traditional ethnic clothing from around the world, as well as some locally made clothes.

The White Hyacinth-Posters of the West. Located at 137 West San Francisco Street. Telephone: 1-505-983-2831. Specializing in fine art, photographic and southwest posters signed and unsigned by artists such as West, Gorman, Pena, and O'Keeffe. At last, a gallery having all those wonderful Santa Fe fiesta, fair, and general southwestern posters under the same roof. And if you get home without one, don't worry, a mail-order catalog is available.

Mailing address: Posters of the West, 137-D West San Francisco Street, Santa Fe, New Mexico 87501.

Santa Fe Bookseller. 203 West San Francisco Street. Telephone: 1-505-983-5278. This bookstore specializes in art books covering the world as well as the regional scene. A large and good selection of southwestern titles pertaining to the contemporary and traditional arts and crafts of the region. Both new and out-of-print art books and exhibition catalogs.

The Shop. 208 West San Francisco. Telephone: 1-505-983-4823. Featuring an incredible range of handcrafted items from New Mexico, this shopper's delight presents Christmas all year long with an extraordinary and diverse selection of southwestern tree ornaments and special regional Christmas decorations.

Collected Works Bookshop. 208-B West San Francisco Street. Telephone: 1-505-988-4226. Anchoring the west end of San Francisco Street is this bookstore, with a good selection of general books as well as mystery and southwestern regional titles including guidebooks and books about the Indian and Spanish cultures of the area.

Packard's Indian Trading Company. 61 Old Santa Fe Trail Road. Telephone: 1-505-983-9241. This very visible shop and gallery of Southwest Indian arts and crafts is on the corner across from the La Fonda Hotel. From Rio Grande pottery to Hopi kachinas, they have a large selection of authentic and high-quality pieces, which are well displayed. Friendly, knowledgeable staff.

La Fonda Newsstand. La Fonda Hotel lobby. Telephone: 1-505-988-1404. Good selection of newspapers and magazines, as well as many southwestern books including history, archaeology, and regional arts and crafts titles. Nice selection of regional greeting and postcards.

Santa Fe East. 200 Old Santa Fe Trail Road. Telephone: 1-505-988-3103. Located across from the Inn at Loretto, this gallery is divided into two sections. Traditional, one-of-a-kind, designer Indian jewelry and crafts occupy one space, while southwestern prints, paintings, and sculpture can be found in the other section.

The Santa Fe Store. 211 Old Santa Fe Trail Road and the Inn at Loretto. Telephone: 1-505-982-2425. This interesting store, whose knowledgeable proprietress has a good eye for the best in locally crafted items, carries an unusually fine selection of women's clothing with both a Southwest and south of the border flair. In addition to apparel, this shop also carries an excellent selection of beautiful handcrafted jewelry and regional folk art, including Spanish wood carvings and retablos. The shop's regional diversity makes it well worth visiting.

Handwoven Originals. 211 Old Santa Fe Trail. In the Inn at Loretto. Telephone: 1-505-982-4118. Original jewelry by one of the area's finest contemporary jewelry artists, Richard Lindsay. Unique silver and gold pieces featuring a menagerie of animals including folk rabbits, trout, cats, and his now famous road-killed animals series. Necklaces, pins, drops, earrings are all made by this talented artist. Also features beautiful handwoven clothing including ponchos and other southwestern favorites and creative accessories.

The Chile Shop. 109 East Water Street. Telephone: 1-505-983-6080. This well-thought-out shop has truly captured the essence of Santa Fe and the Southwest. There are enough unique items of the region gathered together under one roof here to fill several home-bound suitcases with gifts as well as mementos for yourself. From unique chile lights for the Christmas tree to all the blue corn, chile products, and native herbs and condiments you'll ever need to duplicate those delicious New Mexican dishes at home, this creative store seems to have it all. In addition chile greeting cards, folk art gourds, handmade tabletop accessories (salsa jars, chip and dip platters), table and door decorations made with dried native plant materials, and chile ristras and wreaths are all available, plus replicas of the old Santa Fe Railway dining car china with its interesting mimbres decorations.

Foreign Traders (Old Mexico Shop). 202 Galisteo Street. On the corner of Galisteo and Water streets. Telephone: 1-505-983-6441. This large shop carries handcrafted items from Mexico and Central

America. Merchandise ranges from Guatemalan fabrics to large pieces of furniture from Mexico. This shop also has a mail-order service for such items as ristras or dried chile peppers on strings. Mailing address: Foreign Traders, P.O. Box 1967, Santa Fe, New Mexico 87501.

Overland Sheepskin Co. 215 Galisteo Street. Telephone: 1-505-983-4727. This store serves as an outlet for beautiful sheepskin garments from long coats to vests and sheepskin pillows, all made in Taos. It also carries a large selection of leather hats and belts.

Lujan's Place. 218 Galisteo Street. Telephone: 1-505-983-9610. A priceless Santa Fe relic, this store, in one form or another, has been selling New Mexican cooking supplies for more years than the congenial owner will admit to. It is small, but crammed full of interesting kitchenware items and one of the largest selections of bulk herbs and spices you will ever encounter. Lujan packages posole, chicos (another form of preserved corn), and most especially, blue cornmeal, blue corn harina (for making blue corn tortillas), and a variety of dried chile peppers in small quantities, making it easy for travelers to cart these delicacies home.

Artesanos Imports of Mexico. 222 Galisteo Street. Telephone: 1-505-983-5563. All in all, this is one of the most interesting large shops to browse through in Santa Fe. The owner, originally from Mexico, has an excellent selection of Mexican crafts, from furniture and textiles to baskets and tiles. The outdoor courtyard carries some outstanding, large sculpted stone garden pieces from Michoacan, Mexico. If you are interested in Mexican pottery, tiles, and glassware, do not miss this shop.

Marilyn Butler Fine Art. 225 Galisteo. Telephone: 1-505-988-5387. This excellent gallery focuses on new and important contemporary art in the Southwest. It features many Native American and Hispanic artists in this gallery and its gallery in Scottsdale.

Handcrafters Gallery. 227 Galisteo Street. Telephone: 1-505-982-4880. Contemporary crafts (pottery especially, and jewelry and fiber) from all over the United States, including the Southwest, can be seen under one roof here. Much of the high-quality work shown is on the leading edge of the contemporary American craft movement.

The Artists' Gallery. 228 Galisteo Street. Telephone: 1-505-988-2582. This gallery is a cooperative effort of some of the region's better artists. The range of works varies from paintings, graphics, batiks, and jewelry to stoneware, raku, and porcelain pottery. This is a very nice small gallery, offering some of the best local contemporary work in the area.

Scheinbaum and Russek Gallery of Photography. 328 South Guadalupe Street. Telephone: 1-505-988-5116. Located just off Agua Fria Street behind the Santuario de Guadalupe west of Guadalupe Street. This small but distinguished gallery has rotating exhibits of twenty photographers, including world-famous Santa Fe color photographer, Eliot Porter. Besides the excellent contemporary exhibits, there are alos rare and limited-edition portfolios on hand. The helpful owners are knowledgeable about regional photography workshops.

Cookworks. 316 South Guadalupe Street. Telephone: 1-505-988-7676. There are a lot of kitchen stores around these days, but few with the scope and quality of this one. There are plenty of useful items for the kitchen all right, but in addition, there is a good supply of both regional and general cookbooks, numerous gourmet spices and condiments, and many gift items.

Tresspassers William Children's Bookstore. 330 Garfield. Telephone: 1-505-982-4100. This excellent children's bookstore is located just east of south Guadalupe Street, one block north of Montezuma Avenue. Regional children's books as well as general children's books are featured.

The Santa Fe Pottery-Gallery and Studio. 323 South Guadalupe Street. Telephone: 1-505-983-9011. Santa Fe Pottery is both a studio and retail gallery, which sells the very nice functional pottery produced by six local potters. From utilitarian pottery lamps and tableware to many other accessories for home and kitchen. This pottery shop produces consistently high-quality ware.

Rettig y Martinez Gallery. 500 Montezuma Avenue.

Sanbusco Center. Telephone: 1-505-983-4640. This small but artistically rich gallery represents some of the finest contemporary artists of the region, whose work covers just about all the bases from sculpture and prints to painting and photography.

Fenn Galleries. 1075 Paseo de Peralta. Telephone: 1-505-982-4631. When native Santa Feans take guests to see a showplace gallery in town that captures the essence of the arts and crafts of the Southwest, they often take them here. Antiques and rare items such as pre-Columbian and historic Southwest crafts are beautifully displayed. There are many fine historic western paintings for sale from such prestigious artists as Nicolai Fechin and Leon Gaspard, as well as sculpture and contemporary American paintings.

Munson Gallery. 225 Canyon Road. Telephone: 1-505-983-1657. This well-established, well-run, handsome art gallery is worth a visit as you begin your cruise up Canyon Road. It exhibits a fine selection of southwest contemporary painting, sculpture, and graphics, including the works of Doug West, Forrest Moses, and Walter Cooper.

Linda Durham Gallery. 400 Canyon Road. Telephone: 1-505-988-1313. This fine art gallery, one of Santa Fe's best known, is located in a historic old school building just to the right as you enter Canyon Road. The artists represented in this gallery are some of the finest contemporary painters and ceramic sculptors in the country. This well-known gallery has produced exhibitions in San Francisco, Toronto, and Edinburgh, Scotland.

Bellas Artes. 301 Garcia at Canyon Road. Telephone: 1-505-983-2745. Next door to the Linda Durham Gallery on the Garcia Street side, just off Canyon Road. Here you will find some of the nicest contemporary ceramic, glass, and textile art in the city. And that's not all. This gallery also exhibits and sells some outstanding pieces of pre-Columbian art.

The Sombraje Collection. 403 Canyon Road. Telephone: 1-505-988-5567. You need not go all the way out to the Dixon, New Mexico, art colony to see the beautiful work being produced there. The Sombraje Collection shop and gallery brings it right here to Santa Fe. This wonderful collection of elegant branch-covered screens and New Mexico contemporary designed furniture painted in magnificent colors and fitted with branch-covered doors is exhibited along with the ceramic tiles, ollas, bowls, and fabric accessories handcrafted by Dixon's well-known artists.

Morning Star Gallery. 515 Canyon Road. Telephone: 1-505-982-8187. If you have time to see just one Canyon Road gallery featuring American Indian arts, see this one. It is devoted to securing the very finest historical and contemporary Native American art from across America. From southwestern textiles and pottery to jewelry, sculpture, and paintings you probably will not find such a large and complete collection anywhere else but a museum. Here you will also see Northwest Coast Indian masks and Plains Indian artifacts. The handsome gallery-showrooms are well designed, and the staff is knowledgeable and helpful.

Running Ridge Gallery. 640 Canyon Road. Telephone: 1-505-988-2515. This is another gallery on the leading edge of the American craft movement. If you are walking out on Canyon Road, take a look at their contemporary ceramics from around the United States, as well as their excellent selection of graphics, jewelry, and other art forms.

The Museum of New Mexico Shop Branches. Located at the Museum of International Folk Art (telephone: 1-505-982-5186) and the Museum of Indian Arts and Culture (telephone: 1-505-982-5057). (For driving directions, see "A Three-Quarters-of-a-Day Auto Tour of Southeastern Santa Fe.") Each of the small branch shops has a different focus. At the Folk Art Museum, there is often a good selection of native Spanish wood carvings as well as an excellent jewelry selection, often with some fine pieces from Mexico and other areas. Crafts and toys from the region and around the world are also for sale. At the Indian Arts and Culture Museum shop, there are books on Native American crafts and archaeology as well as a small but good selection of Southwest Indian arts and crafts.

Case Trading Post. 704 Camino Lejo. Telephone: 1-505-982-4636. Wheelwright Museum (see driving instructions in "A Three-Quarters-of-a-Day

Auto Tour of Southeastern Santa Fe"). This excellent shop is downstairs from the gallery of the Wheelwright Museum. In addition to a large selection of Navajo rugs and Ácoma pottery, you will find a good selection of regional Indian jewelry, pottery, basketry, and weaving. Some contemporary crafts by Indian artists in the area are also showcased. As at the other museum shops, the dependability and reliability is high.

Farmer's Market. Adjacent to Sanbusco Center. Farmers from the villages around Santa Fe bring in their produce to sell. In the summer only, on Tuesdays and Saturdays.

Jackalope Pottery. 2820 Cerrillos Road (telephone: 1-505-471-8539) and 213 Galisteo (telephone: 1-505-989-7494). The largest of these two stores and probably the most fun to visit is out on Cerrillos Road. This large emporium, which is a cross between a curio, souvenir store and a folk arts store, has many items from Mexico, Central America, and South America as well as from throughout New Mexico. It makes for interesting browsing.

Ben Ortega's El Dulce Hogar-Art Gallery and Studio. This gallery-studio is located approximately six miles north of Santa Fe on New Mexico Highway 590 (Bishop's Lodge Road) just south of the Tesuque junction. Telephone: 1-505-982-3020. Here one of the finest representational wood-carvers in the Southwest sells his work and that of his talented family. The sales "garden" outside his home is usually filled with lovely images of Saint Francis, San Pasquale, nativity scenes, and other favorite regional subjects. For a more detailed description, see the Santa Fe "Seeing the Spanish Rio Grande Country" section for the narrative account "A Day Traveling through Spanish New Mexico."

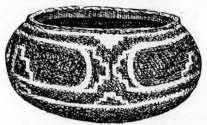

Santa Clara bowl

Shidoni Sculpture Gallery and Foundry. Located on eight acres between Santa Fe and Tesuque just off New Mexico Highway 590 or Bishop's Lodge Road. Telephone: 1-505-988-8001. This indoor and outdoor sculpture gallery is in a beautiful location which serves as a fine natural background for the contemporary, unique sculpture work produced here. Most of the pieces are bronze or steel fabrications. The work of other nationally known sculptors and artists are also exhibited. Tours of the foundry are sometimes given on Saturdays.

Popovi Da Studio of Indian Arts. San Ildefonso Pueblo. Telephone: 1-505-455-2456. Located on the pueblo's plaza, this small but excellent gallery sells the fine pottery for which the pueblo and adjacent pueblos are so well known. Jewelry and other fine crafts are sold here also. Many pieces by the owner's famous mother, the late Maria Martinez, and other museum-quality pieces can be viewed.

O'ke Oweenge Crafts Cooperative. San Juan Pueblo. Telephone: 1-505-852-2372. (See "Revisiting the Plaza and a Day with the Pueblo Indians North of Santa Fe: A Narrative Account.") Beautiful handwoven San Juan rain sashes, ribbon shirts, pottery, painted gourds, and jewelry made from corn, squash, and watermelon seeds, as well as other materials are but a few of the excellent high-quality crafts found in this large, most reliable and friendly shop where prices are reasonable.

Herman Valdez Fruit Stand. P.O. Box 218, Velarde, New Mexico 87582. Telephone: 1-505-852-2129. Do not miss this bastion of Spanish crafts located on the west side of New Mexico Highway 68, fourteen miles north of Española on the "low road" to Taos. The art of weaving peppers, corn, gourds, pomegranates, and pine cones into decorative wreaths and table centerpieces is at its peak in this shop. In addition, if you have been hankering for a ristra (long strings of chile peppers or corn cobs) to hang from your door, this is a good place to buy one. Excellent mailing service. Catalog on request. Exhibition of wreaths and ristras the last weekend in October. This stand also carries local fruit in season.

Sopyn's Fruit Stand. Located in Rinconada, just

north of the Dixon junction on New Mexico Highway 68, the road to Taos. Telephone: 1-505-579-4233. This unpretentious fruit stand on the west side of New Mexico Highway 68 is where you will find many of those unusual dried chile and corn decorations for door and table that you see decorating restaurants and shops. The talented artisan has an excellent eye and a good touch when it comes to making a unified decoration from the regional dried flowers, vegetables, grasses, and weeds. And what's more, the prices for these expertly done pieces are very reasonable.

Trujillo's Weaving Shop. Chimayó, New Mexico. Located on the west side of New Mexico Highway 76, the high road to Taos, just before that road intersects with New Mexico Highway 520 to Rancho de Chimayó and Santuario de Chimayó. See members of this talented Spanish family, artisans all, at work weaving beautiful blankets and rugs in the classic contemporary and historic styles of the region. The quality of the weaving is excellent. All sizes of tapestries are made, and special orders are taken. In addition there is a very good selection of local Spanish wood carving for sale as well as a few other crafts indigenous to the area.

Ortega's Weaving Shop and Galeria Plaza del Cerro. Chimayó, New Mexico. Telephone: 1-505-351-4215. Located just off the high road to Taos on New Mexico Highway 520, the highway to Santuario de Chimayó and Rancho de Chimayó. This large shop, also family run, has many Chimayó area blankets and rugs for sale, as well as a large selection of Spanish wood carvings. Good regional book selection. This shop will enhance your understanding of the Spanish influence in northern New Mexico. Weavers at work. Adjacent to the weaving shop is Galeria Plaza del Cerro, a gallery of fine contemporary northern New Mexican arts and crafts in a historic old adobe building.

Hand Artes Gallery. Truchas, New Mexico. Follow the main street through Truchas till you see sign. Telephone: 1-505-689-2243. This excellent shop/gallery in a striking rural setting, features southwest paintings of Donna Clair and others, textiles, wood, clay and glass. Also local Hispanic woodcarvings and quality crafts from Mexico.

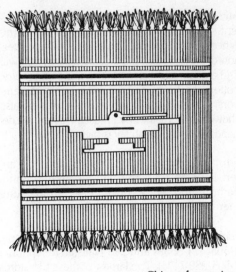

Chimayó weaving

Indian Pueblo Telephone Numbers

Cochiti. Telephone: 1-505-465-2244.
Nambe. Telephone: 1-505-455-7692.
Picuris. Telephone: 1-505-587-2519.
Santa Clara. Telephone: 1-505-753-2424 or 1-505-753-7326.
Santo Domingo. Telephone: 1-505-465-2214.
San Ildefonso. Telephone: 1-505-455-2273.
San Juan. Telephone: 1-505-852-4400.
Taos. Telephone: 1-505-758-8626 or 1-505-758-9593.

Telephone Numbers

Shuttlejack. Shuttle to and from Albuquerque International Airport to Santa Fe. Telephone: 1-505-982-4311.
Chile Line (trolley transportation in Santa Fe). Telephone: 1-505-989-8595.
Taxicab service. Telephone: 1-505-982-6172 or 1-505-988-1211 or 1-505-983-2090.
Avis Rent-A-Car. Telephone: 1-505-982-4361.
Budget Rent-A-Car. Telephone: 1-505-984-8028.
Hertz Rent-A-Car. Telephone: 1-505-982-1844.
Santa Fe Opera. Telephone: 1-505-982-3855.
Lamy (Amtrak) Shuttle Service. Telephone: 1-505-982-8829.
Weather. Telephone: 1-505-988-3437.

Santa Fe Chamber of Commerce. Telephone: 1-505-983-7317.

Santa Fe Convention and Visitors' Bureau. Telephone: 1-505-984-6760 or toll free in the United States, except New Mexico 1-800-528-5369.

Santa Fe Central Reservations: Telephone: toll free in the United States 1-800-982-7669.

Historic Santa Fe Foundation. Telephone: 1-505-983-2567.

American Automobile Association. Located at 1509-1511 Fifth Street in Santa Fe. Telephone: 1-505-982-4633.

Albuquerque International Airport. Telephone: 1-505-842-4366.

Golf reservations at Santa Fe Country Club. Telephone: 1-505-471-0601.

Fishing information and licenses. Telephone: 1-505-827-7882.

Hiking and Camping information. Telephone: toll free in the United States, except New Mexico 1-800-545-2040.

Packaging and shipping of parcels. Telephone: 1-505-982-8527.

Taos

Taos used to come alive a few months during the summer and then slip back into a quiet restful period the remainder of the year. To some extent this is still true, but winter and spring are becoming busier months there as skiing and white-water rafting in the area become increasingly popular. But it is still the summer season with four months jam-packed with events and festivals (listed in this section) in town and out at Taos Pueblo that creates all the excitement. And then, of course, there are Taos's museums and art galleries, which attract visitors like a magnet most of the year, but especially during the busy summer. Many of them are described in the several walking and automobile tours detailed in the section of the book, "Seeing the Spanish Rio Grande Country," "Taos."

Taos is long on good accommodations, many having the kind of ambience that brought you to New Mexico in the first place. The restaurant scene is neither as good nor as varied as in Santa Fe, but then Taos is a town of just over three thousand, rather than fifty thousand, and receives fewer visitors than Santa Fe. Nonetheless, you will not starve in Taos. In fact, in several restaurants you will eat some fine continental, regional, and alternative-style dishes that are equal to any in the region. With one or two notable exceptions, many of the accommodations and restaurants are within a few blocks of the plaza, making Taos an excellent walking town.

Like Santa Fe, but on a smaller scale, Taos has had its problems with traffic and congestion during certain times of the year. The prime bottleneck is just east of the plaza along the major north–south arterial. This has become a particular problem because of the development of numerous large motels along that arterial south of the plaza. They are just far enough out from the plaza that most visitors feel compelled to drive into the city center. A partial solution, at least, has been found with the development of a shuttle-bus service from the motels into the plaza area.

The helpful Taos County Chamber of Commerce, located one block south of the plaza on the east side of South Santa Fe Road adjacent to the Indian Hills Inn, can be reached by writing P.O. Drawer I, Taos, New Mexico 87571 or phoning 1-505-758-3873 or toll free in the United States, except New Mexico 1-800-732-8267.

Lodging

The Taos Inn. This attractive, adobe hostelry right in the center of town is overflowing with the region's Spanish charm. Its location, just a block and a half north of the plaza, and its unbeatable ambience make it the best place to stay in Taos. Part of the inn, once a Spanish home, is over one hundred and fifty years old. The lobby is where the courtyard used to be and in the middle of it, preserved for all to see, is the site of the old Taos water well. Today, the lobby, like the well in days gone by seems to serve as a gathering place for both visitors and Taos natives. The spirit of Taos is alive and well at the Taos Inn! Some of the rooms are in the three-story adobe structure that fronts on Pueblo Road, while many others, which could best be described as casitas, are out back around a delightful courtyard. Many of these rooms have adobe fireplaces. The rooms are tastefully furnished with carefully selected items from the region and from Mexico that evoke the southwestern spirit. Just off the lobby is the hotel restaurant, Doc Martin's, and bar. The ever-busy Adobe Bar is on the other side of the lobby and is a friendly place popular with visitors as well as locals. Just off the dining room is an outdoor dining patio, a quiet welcome haven for breakfast, lunch, or dinner. Beyond that are a heated swimming pool and an indoor Jacuzzi, which front a grassy, open courtyard circled by numerous secluded rooms. None of the rooms is air-conditioned. Only on a rare, warm evening is that a problem; then, fans can be obtained from the desk. Generally reservations are needed in advance for the forty rooms in this delightful gem of an inn, which fills quickly. No pets. Advance reservation deposit required. Mailing address: The Taos Inn, P.O. Drawer N, North Pueblo Road, Taos, New Mexico 87571. Telephone: 1-505-758-2233 or toll free in the United States 1-800-826-7466. Moderate and expensive.

La Posada de Taos. This bed-and-breakfast inn has a location just two and a half blocks west of the plaza. Four charming rooms with private bath in a handsomely renovated old adobe house and an adobe casita, dubbed the honeymoon house, also with private bath, await the traveler. From adobe fireplaces and woodburning stoves to a room with a Jacuzzi bathtub, the amenities are many. The main public room is a warm, pleasant living space decorated southwestern-style with comfortable reading chairs and good lighting. Breakfast is served in a sunny location at the far end of this room. Truly a full breakfast with many New Mexican touches. Advance reservation deposit required. Call for directions. Mailing address: La Posada de Taos, P.O. Box 1118, Taos, New Mexico 87571. Telephone: 1-505-758-8164. Inexpensive, moderate, and expensive.

El Rincon Bed and Breakfast. Centrally located, just one-half block from the plaza behind the oldest trading post in Taos by the same name and under the same family ownership is this very charming bed-and-breakfast establishment, which exudes southwestern ambience. The five nicely decorated rooms, all with private baths, and several with fireplaces, are on three different levels of a lovely adobe. Some have views, some have a terrace or a patio, and one has a hot tub. All of the rooms, some of which are small, are handsomely decorated and most have TV's with VCR's. The continental breakfast is taken downstairs in the dining room or out on the patio, weather permitting. And it is only a short walk to galleries and restaurants. Mailing address: El Rincon Bed and Breakfast, P.O. Drawer Q, 110 East Kit Carson Street, Taos, New Mexico 87571. Telephone: 1-505-758-4874. Inexpensive, moderate, and expensive.

El Monte Motel. Located in the pine woods just one-half mile (four longish blocks) east of Taos on U.S. Highway 64, this adobe-style motel is a real charmer. Some of the units have fireplaces and the piñon wood is free for the asking. The thirteen units are spread around the small, but well-kept grounds in several separate buildings. At the El

Taos Inn

Monte, you can have your own casitalike room without paying an arm and a leg for it. Four of the units have kitchens. Pets allowed. Advance reservation deposit required. Ten-day refund notice must be given. Mailing address: El Monte Motel, Box 22, Taos, New Mexico 87571. Telephone: 1-505-758-3171. Moderate.

The Mabel Dodge Lujan House. This bed-and-breakfast establishment is located at the end of Morada Road (see "Half-Day Walking Tour of Taos") about one-half mile northeast of the plaza. Eleven rooms in this historic home are available to travelers, including Mabel's bedroom, which is the most expensive. Beautiful setting overlooking Taos Indian Reservation lands and the Sangre de Cristo Mountains. Shared or private bath. The home is used for other functions, which makes rooms scarce during certain times of the year. So make inquiries at least three weeks ahead of time. Mailing address: Mabel Dodge Lujan House, P.O. Box 3400, Taos, New Mexico 87571. Telephone: 1-505-758-9456. Moderate and expensive.

American Artists Gallery House. This adobe-style bed-and-breakfast home, situated behind a low–lying adobe wall in a quiet spot about a mile and a half from the plaza, provides beautiful unobstructed views of Taos Mountain from its patio and some of the rooms. The view of the mountain from this vantage point is truly remarkable. There is art on the walls throughout the four nicely appointed guest rooms and the attractive public rooms, and there are sculptural pieces sharing the garden with the hollyhocks and roses. Most of the art, collected by the knowledgeable and congenial owners from local Native American and Anglo artists, is for sale in this gallery-house. Three of the four rooms have kiva fireplaces as well as private baths. The fourth guest room is a cottage located in the garden. Its bathroom is in the main house. There is a hot tub for those who can stop watching the ever-changing light and shadows on the mountain long enough to use it. The gourmet, full breakfast is a real treat. Call for directions. Reservation deposit requested. Moderate and expensive. Mailing address: American Artists Gallery House, P.O. Box 584, Taos, New Mexico 87571. Telephone: 1-505-758-4446. Inexpensive and moderate.

Ramada Inn. Located a little over a mile south of the plaza, just off New Mexico Highway 68 (Santa Fe Road South), is this 124-unit, modern, two-story, harmoniously designed, large structure, which blends features of the historic adobes of the region with more contemporary elements. The comfortable, spacious rooms are nicely decorated with Southwest touches, and guests have available to them a heated indoor pool with Jacuzzi. Most rooms have excellent views of the sagebrush plain and the mountains. Cafe Fennel located on premises. Air conditioned. Mailing address: Ramada Inn, Box 6257, Taos, New Mexico 87571. Telephone: 1-505-758-2900. Low expensive.

Hacienda Inn. Located about two and a half miles south of the plaza is this two-story New Mexico-style motel, which blends nicely with the architecture of the region. The fifty-one spacious rooms, all with two queen beds and cable TV's are very comfortable. Many of the rooms have views of the sagebrush plains and mountains. Children under twelve years free in room with their parents. Enclosed heated swimming pool and restaurant on premises. Reservation deposit required. Mailing address: Hacienda Inn, South Santa Fe Road, P.O. Box 5751, Taos, New Mexico 87571. Telephone: 1-505-758-8610. Moderate.

Sagebrush Inn. The Sagebrush Inn is located three miles south of the plaza on the west side of New Mexico Highway 68. This adobe inn was built in 1929. Over the years it has hosted many of Taos's famous and near-famous guests, including Georgia O'Keeffe. Out on the sagebrush plain where the inn is situated, there are fine views of Taos Mountain and the rest of the Sangre de Cristo Mountains. North of the Sagebrush Inn, formerly isolated sage desert has given way to urban sprawl. But the views to the west, overlooking the most scenic sage plain in America, are as fine as they ever were. Those who have known the Sagebrush Inn in the past will be surprised at the many changes and additions there, which, architecturally, do not detract too much from this fine adobe structure. Even though the place is feeling more and more like a ski lodge than a desert retreat, it is still one of the more enjoyable places to stay in or near Taos. Pleasant, tree-shaded patios, atmospheric rama-

Sagebrush Inn, Taos

das, swimming pool, Jacuzzi, and tennis courts as well as new condominium units are all part of the scene. You can eat in the Sagebrush Dining Room or the Los Vaqueros steak house. Lobby bar with live music at times. No air conditioning. Many of the rooms have adobe fireplaces, and the giant piñon woodpile is close by. There is a slightly worn, comfortable-as-an-old-shoe quality in some of the eighty-two rooms. Mailing address: Sagebrush Inn, P.O. Box 557, Taos, New Mexico 87571. Telephone: 1-505-758-2254. Moderate and expensive.

El Pueblo Motor Lodge. Located just off busy New Mexico Highway 522 and U.S. Highway 64, one-half mile (about four long blocks) north of the plaza is this pueblo-style motel with forty-six rooms. Some of the rooms have kitchens or efficiencies, and some have fireplaces. You can choose between either modern or southwestern-style rooms. Three condominium units also available. Heated swimming pool. Advance reservation deposit required. Thirty-day refund notice. Mailing address: El Pueblo Motor Lodge, Box 92, Taos, New Mexico 87571. Telephone: 1-505-758-8641. Moderate.

Hacienda de Sol. This bed-and-breakfast home is located about one mile north of the plaza just off New Mexico Highway 522 and U.S. Highway 64 (Pueblo Road North). Although just a short distance off the busy highway, the hacienda rests peacefully under the largest cottonwood trees you may ever see on an acre of ground offering views out over Taos Indian Reservation lands to the mountains. There are three rooms, each with private bath, and two with kiva fireplaces in this historic adobe. Or choose a two-bedroom adobe home with fireplace and kitchen (stocked for breakfast), which will accommodate six people. Creative homemade breakfast in the main house in the handsomely decorated southwestern-style dining room. Call for directions. Mailing address: Hacienda del Sol, Box 177, Taos, New Mexico 87571. Telephone: 1-505-758-0287. Moderate.

moderate, and expensive.

Quail Ridge Inn. Out on the sage plain, five miles northeast of the plaza on Ski Valley Road (New Mexico Highway 150), is this tastefully designed two-story contemporary southwestern-style resort-lodge, which has all the amenities, including tennis (six outdoor, two indoor courts), swimming (covered pool), racquetball (four courts), and volleyball. The 116 spacious rooms, with some elements of southwestern decor, have fireplaces, balconies or patios, and over half have fully equipped kitchens. Outstanding views of the high sage plain and Sangre de Cristo Mountains. Mailing address: Quail Ridge Inn, P.O. Box 707, Taos, New Mexico 87571. Telephone: 1-505-776-2211 or toll free in the United States 1-800-624-4448. Moderate and expensive.

Mountain Light Bed and Breakfast. Located twelve miles north of Taos on New Mexico Highway 522, on a hill overlooking the village of Arroyo Hondo, New Mexico. This attractive adobe home with rustic vigas and traditional fireplaces offers views over the countryside that won't stop. The three rooms have shared bathroom facilities, and the common kitchen may be used by the guests. Mailing adress: Mountain Light Bed and Breakfast, Box 241, Taos, New Mexico 87571. Telephone: 1-505-776-8474. Inexpensive and low moderate.

Camping

Taos Valley R. V. Park. Located just off New Mexico Highway 68 three miles south of the plaza. Seventy-five sites on twelve acres. Telephone: 1-505-758-4469.

Capulin. This National Forest Service campground is located 5.6 miles east of Taos on U.S. Highway 64. Ten sites on six acres. Reservation deposit required. Telephone: 1-505-758-2911.

La Sombra. This National Forest Service campground is located six miles east of Taos on U.S. Highway 64. Thirteen sites on three acres. River fishing. Telephone: 1-505-758-2911.

Rio Grande Gorge State Park. Located approximately sixteen miles southwest on New Mex-

ico Highway 68 near Pilar, New Mexico. Sixteen sites on 1,300 acres. River fishing. No telephone.

Food

The Apple Tree Restaurant. This restaurant, located in an old adobe at 26 Bent Street, one block from the plaza, is a good bet for lunch or dinner. Telephone: 1-505-758-1900. On nice days, lunch and dinner are served in the comfortable outdoor patio shaded by several old apple trees. The inside dining room in the old adobe is also very pleasant. Regional specialties like blue corn soft tacos and enchiladas sprinkle the somewhat international menu. The excellently prepared food includes many unique variations of seafood, chicken, and gourmet vegetarian dishes. Try their licuados, a nonalcoholic, popular fruit drink from south of the border. Beer and wine available. Sunday brunch. Reservations for dinner advised. Moderate.

Hopi coiled basket

Taos Trading Co. 212 North Plaza. Telephone: 1-505-758-3012. Sometimes on a hot day it is nice to know of a place to get an ice cream cone or a cold drink. The old-fashioned soda fountain at the Taos Trading Co. provides the answer with its malts, milkshakes, and soda fountain drinks. Also cards and T-shirts.

Ogelvie's Bar and Grille. Enviably located on the east side of and overlooking Taos Plaza. Telephone 1-505-758-8866. In this lively restaurant you can sate your lunch or dinner appetite with excellent sandwiches, southwestern regional dishes, and fresh seafood selections. The bar is as popular as the restaurant, and live jazz is provided on some weekends. Dinner reservations accepted. Moderate and expensive.

Doc Martin's. This restaurant is located in the Taos Inn just one-half block up North Pueblo Road (New Mexico Highway 522, U.S. Highway 64) from the plaza. Telephone: 1-505-758-2233. Thick, old adobe walls provide a quiet but informal setting, which includes an outdoor patio. Regional specialities on the menu are numerous and good. A nice variety of steak and seafood dishes completes the bill of fare. A highly varied and good breakfast menu. Also open for lunch. Moderate.

Roberto's. Located in an adobe compound reached from East Kit Carson Road about two blocks from the plaza, across from the Kit Carson Museum. Telephone: 1-505-758-2434. Taos has seen many restaurants come and go but for over twenty years this one has remained. In a handsome, old adobe building with lots of ambience, you will be able to choose from northern New Mexican and Mexican entrées. The chiles rellenos and tacos are especially good. But then you can't argue about the sopaipillas or the refried beans or the cooked dried, sweet corn kernels called chicos. Lunch and dinner. Inexpensive and moderate.

Michael's Kitchen. Located one-quarter mile north of the plaza on North Pueblo Road (New Mexico Highway 522 and U.S. Highway 64). Telephone: 1-505-758-4178. This establishment, which has grown from a bakery and breakfast place, now serves three meals a day. Both regional and American food are served in an informal, lively atmosphere. Good place for families. The food is good and reasonably priced. Best for breakfast and lunch. Inexpensive.

Brett House. Located about four miles north of the plaza. Telephone: 1-505-776-8545. Take New Mexico Highway 522 and U.S. Highway 64 (Pueblo Road North) to the junction with the blinking light. Take a right onto the Ski Valley Road, New Mexico Highway 150, where you will find the restaurant immediately to your right. This fine dinner restaurant is located in the historic Dorothy Brett House. If it is well-prepared new Southwest and international (including continental) food you are seeking, this is the place to come. You might try the roasted quail on corncakes with sweet pepper relish, or the shrimp-crab relleno or the veal scallopini. If those don't suit, try the New York steak, roast duck, or blue corn crêpe. And somehow there's room for fresh fish on the menu as well. Outdoor patio dining, weather permitting. Extensive and well selected wine list. Tasty desserts. Reservations recommended. Closed Mondays. High moderate and expensive.

The Chile Connection. Located about five miles north of the plaza just off New Mexico Highway 150 (Taos Ski Valley Road) near the Quail Ridge Inn. Telephone: 1-505-776-8787. This restaurant specializes in foods of the region (try the green chiles rellenos and blue corn enchiladas) as well as chicken, steaks, and shrimp. Dinner is served between 6:00 P.M. and 10:00 P.M. Pleasant atmosphere in a fine setting out on the high desert. Well-prepared food. Bar. Moderate.

Casa Cordova. This truly epicurean restaurant in a wonderful adobe that offers fine vistas of the mountains rests eight miles north of Taos on the Taos Ski Valley Road. (From New Mexico Highway 522, turn right on New Mexico Highway 150 and travel four and a half miles to the restaurant, at Arroyo Seco.) Telephone: 1-505-776-2200. Features Italian cuisine (particularly northern Italian) and continental dishes with a light touch. On many nights it is one of the best dinner houses in the area. Caring, personal touches are always in evidence, such as the handpicked, fresh mushrooms from the local countryside. Although neither stuffy nor pretentious in any way, this is a more formal restaurant than some in the area and caters to customers who appreciate fine food. Closed Sunday. Reservations. High moderate and expensive.

Casa De Valdez. Located in an A-frame building on the southeast corner of South Santa Fe Road and Estes Road, about three miles south of the plaza. Telephone: 1-505-758-8777. Here you will find on the menu a southwest regional favorite, hickory pit barbecue, as well as many excellently prepared northern New Mexican dishes and char-broiled steaks. And the owners, natives to Taos County, know how to make super sopaipillas. Lunch and dinner. Dinner only on Wednesday and Sunday. Inexpensive and moderate.

Sagebrush Inn. Located three and a half miles south of the plaza just off New Mexico Highway 68 or South Santa Fe Road. Telephone: 1-505-758-2254. There are two restaurants at this country inn. The Dining Room serves breakfast and din-ner, featuring native New Mexican and gourmet American food. Los Vaqueros, a steak house, is open for dinner only, serving such items as prime rib, rack of lamb, London broil, and of course, steaks. Lunch daily except Wednesday and Sun-day. Dinner daily. Moderate and expensive.

Andy's La Fiesta Restaurant. Located four miles south of Taos across from the Ranchos de Taos Church in a two-century-old building in historic Saint Francis Plaza. Telephone: 1-505-758-9733. You will dine informally on excellent native New Mexican food, especially the carne adovada. Steaks and seafood are available, and this casual establishment serves up one of the best margaritas in the area. Dinner only. Carry out available. Closed Sunday and Monday. Moderate.

The Stakeout. Located eight miles south of Taos on New Mexico Highway 68. Telephone: 1-505-758-2042. If you are a sunset aficionado and you want to see a "ten" sunset, this is the place to come. Viewing a sunset from this location may make you feel like you have died and gone to heaven barefoot, for the sunset view which stretches for over one hundred miles will knock your socks off. And while you are there, you might have a drink in the bar or dinner in this antique-filled adobe house. Grilled Long Island duck, chicken Gio-vanna, scallops provençal, and of course, a long list

of steaks, which gave this place its name (if you like to play on words, that is). Closed Tuesday. Moderate and expensive.

Tours

The Taos Shuttle. If you are without wheels or do not want to drive into the plaza, ride the shuttle. This convenient bus stops at most major motels north and south of the plaza as well as some of the parking lots, and you can take the shuttle as far north as the Millicent Rogers Museum. Watch for "Ride the Shuttle" buses.

Taos Historic Walks. The walks, which depart from the Kit Carson House Museum on Kit Carson Road, include a historical and cultural commen-tary by the guide and cover most of the historic dis-trict of Taos. For more information, telephone 1-505-758-3861.

Rio Grande Raft Trips. For one-day raft trips through the exciting Taos Box or the Lower Gorge and for two- and three-day trips through the Rio Grande Wild and Scenic River area, contact Sierra Outfitters and Guides, P.O. Box 2756, Taos, New Mexico 87571. Telephone: 1-505-758-1247. Or contact Rio Grande Rapid Transit. Telephone: 1-505-758-9700 or toll free in the United States, ex-cept New Mexico 1-800-545-4020 or toll free in New Mexico 1-800-222-7238. Or try Far Flung Ad-ventures, telephone 1-505-758-2628.

Cumbres and Toltec Scenic Railroad. From Taos, you can drive to either Chama, New Mexico, or Antonito, Colorado, for a seven-hour-long, round-trip, steam narrow-gauge railway trip into the Sangre de Cristos. The tracks are part of the Den-ver and Rio Grande system built for the mining booms of the 1880s. For more details, write P.O. Box 789, Chama, New Mexico 87520. Telephone: 1-505-756-2151. Or write P.O. Box 668, Antonito, Colorado 81120. Telephone: 1-303-376-5483.

Horseback Riding

Taos Indian Horse Ranch. Located at Taos Pueblo. This well-established stable offers hour-long rides for novices at the pueblo, as well as two-hour rides for intermediate and advanced riders. Also available are overnight trips into the Rio Grande Gorge and the Sangre de Cristo Mountains. Mailing address: Taos Indian Horse Ranch, P.O. Box 3019, Taos, New Mexico, 87571. Telephone: 1-505-758-3212.

Lobo Ranch and Taos Equestrian Center. Located twenty minutes north of Taos, just outside of Arroyo Hondo. The center offers daily trail rides into the Carson National Forest in the summer. English and western riding are offered, as well as pony riding for children. Trips into the Sangre de Cristo Mountains. Mailing address: Lobo Ranch, Box 1101, Taos, New Mexico 87571. Telephone: 1-505-776-8526.

Fairs, Festivals, and Fiestas

To confirm dates of festivals and dances at Taos Pueblo, it is best to check with the pueblo visitors center. Telephone: 1-505-758-8626

Santa Cruz Day. Close to the first weekend in May. Green Corn Dance at Taos Pueblo.

Taos Meet the Artist Series. This series, where the public has a chance to participate in informal sessions with Taos-based artists and beyond, is held at the Taos Inn. It includes studio tours, lectures, and demonstrations and is held twice a year. The first session is from the middle of May through the third week of June. The second session is from mid-October through the second week of December. Telephone: 1-505-758-2233 or toll free in the United States, except New Mexico 1-800-732-8267.

Spring Arts Celebration. From the third week in May to the second weekend in June. Taos comes out of its slow season fast now with this celebration, which includes studio tours, seminars, concerts, and art workshops. For more information, write Spring Arts Celebration, Box 3163, Taos, New Mexico 87571. Telephone: 1-505-758-0516 or toll free in the United States, except New Mexico 1-800-732-81267.

San Antonio Feast Day. Second weekend in June. Corn Dance at Taos Pueblo.

San Juan Feast Day. Midweek, around the fourth week in June. Corn Dance at Taos Pueblo.

Annual Chamber Music Festival. Midweek beginning around the second week in June. In addition to the concerts staged by professional musicians, there are numerous student chamber music concerts held throughout June, July, and the first week of August. Sponsored by the Taos School of Music and held in the Taos Community Auditorium. Mailing address: Annual Chamber Music Festival, Box 1897, Taos, New Mexico 87571. Telephone: 1-505-758-2388.

Annual Taos Pueblo Powwow. Around the second weekend in July costumed Indian dancers from around the United States gather for this major powwow and dance competition held on reservation land behind the Overland Sheepskin Co. north of town. Arts and crafts booths and many, many traditional dances. A festive event well worth seeing. Special Native American foods. Telephone: 1-505-758-1538.

Fiesta de Santiago y Santa Ana. This Taos fiesta occurs the fourth weekend in July. Taos's largest celebration commemorates the feast days of Saint Anne and Saint James. Street dances, arts and crafts fair, and entertainment with a Spanish flavor. There is also a Fiesta Mass, Candlelight Procession from Our Lady of Guadalupe Church to the plaza. During the same weekend Taos Pueblo stages the Fiestas de Taos with Santiago Day Corn Dance. Telephone: 1-505-758-0239.

Taos Arts Festival. The last week in September and the first week in October. Large, juried show of arts and crafts. Retrospective exhibition of famous Taos artists over the years. Studio tours, theater, and music performances. The Wool Festival, which also takes place during this time, features educational demonstrations and weaving exhibits and sales areas. For more information, write Drawer I, Taos, New Mexico 87571. Telephone: 1-505-758-3873 or 1-800-732-8267.

Old Taos Trade Fair. Also held during the last week in September, and a major part of the Taos Art Festival, this gala affair is a re-creation of the early nineteenth-century trade fairs held in this remote outpost. Sponsored by the people who should know more about this kind of thing than anybody else, the Kit Carson Foundation really captures the spirit of former times as they stage traditional-style caravans complete with Indian, Spanish settler, and mountain men look-alikes. Craft demonstrations, native foods, and authentic Spanish music and dances. Telephone: 1-505-758-0505.

San Geronimo Feast Day. The last week in September at Taos Pueblo. This two-day occasion begins with a ceremonial dance at sunset on the first day, followed by more dances, war games, foot races, and an arts and crafts fair the next day.

Taos Mountain Balloon Rally. Held the third weekend in October, this hot-air balloon festival includes parades, dances, and an arts and crafts fair. Telephone: 1-505-758-8100.

Parking

You will find municipal parking lots in the following locations. These lots are not visible from the major pedestrian and auto byways.

Lot bounded by Bent Street (just south of Bent Street) and Placitas Road. Behind the shops that border the north side of the plaza.

Lot entered from North Pueblo Road through a narrow lane leading east, just south of Martha's of Taos Dress Shop. It also can be entered from Kit Carson Road via the first narrow lane east of the Kit Carson Road and North Pueblo Road junction (the plaza stoplight).

Lot entered from North Pueblo Road. Turn east on the first road just north of the Stables Art Center. This is the Taos Community Auditorium parking lot.

Shopping

Magic Mountain Gallery. Located on the north side of the plaza toward the east end. Telephone: 1-505-758-9604. This excellent, well-respected gallery bridges the gap between traditional Indian crafts and contemporary crafts of the region. A good selection of both types of crafts can be found there

as well as fine art paintings and sculpture evocative of the region.

Bryans Gallery. North Plaza Art Center. Telephone: 1-505-758-9407. This exceptional gallery (accessed from the plaza's north side or from the municipal parking lot behind) is a treasure trove of unique, unusual, and fine contemporary art ranging from fine paintings to exquisite ceramics and sculpture, many evoking the Southwest but certainly not limited to that idiom.

Fernandez de Taos Bookstore. Located on the north side of the plaza. Telephone: 1-505-758-4391. A conveniently located general bookstore featuring magazines, posters, and film, as well as a good selection of general and southwest regional books.

Open Space/A Cooperative Gallery. Located in the Plaza Real on Taos Plaza. Telephone: 1-505-758-1217. The works of fourteen Taos and northern New Mexico mixed-media artists and craftspeople are shown in this attractive gallery space. This is an excellent gallery to visit since it gives a superb overview of the current northern New Mexico arts and crafts scene. Pottery, weaving, glass, jewelry, and most other media.

Galeria Nativa. West side of the plaza. Mailing address: P.O. Box 1185, Taos, New Mexico 87571. Telephone: 1-505-758-2416. This shop, featuring Spanish handcrafts of the area, specializes in Spanish wood carvings, weavings, and some furniture.

Tally Richards Gallery. 2 Ledoux Street. One and one-half blocks southwest of the plaza. Telephone: 1-505-758-2731. This well-known contemporary art gallery features the work of some of the country's best artists. Probably the best gallery in Taos to see the leading edge of contemporary art.

Navajo Gallery. 5 Ledoux Street. Telephone: 1-505-758-3250 or 1-505-776-8313. This beautiful gallery is located in an old adobe, formerly the home of talented and famous Navajo artist R. C. Gorman. It is an interesting gallery containing many of Gorman's paintings, prints, sculptures, and painted ceramic pieces. The artist has given many personal decorative touches to the gallery. If you are a Gorman fan, you will find a wide selection of his work for sale there.

Moby Dickens—A Taos Bookshop. Bent Street. Telephone: 1-505-758-3050. General books with a nice selection of regional and children's titles.

Dwellings Revisited. 8 Bent Street. Located near the corner of Bent Street and North Pueblo Road. Telephone: 1-505-758-3377. If you are planning to build or renovate your home in the Santa Fe style or Mexican style, this is the place to come. Architectural antiques and accessories as well as Spanish, Mexican, and primitive furniture. And for the entrance of your home, antique Mexican doors. Stained-glass windows and more. Mailing address: Dwellings Revisited, P.O. Box 470, Taos, New Mexico 87571.

Taos Artisans: Cooperative Gallery of Fine Arts. Located at 8 Bent Street near the intersection of Bent and North Pueblo Road. Telephone: 1-505-758-1558. Some of northern New Mexico's best artists and craftspeople, working in a variety of media, are represented here. Ceramics, wood carvings, jewelry, glass, and woven tapestries and wearables.

Salobra. 6 Bent Street. Telephone: 1-505-758-1128. This gallery features the works of several well-known Taos area artists, whose painting, raku pottery, and glass are quite unique. Also brightly patterned, handsome bolo ties and other jewelry, designed by one of the artists, depicting Indian and cowboy western themes.

Morgan Gallery. 4 Bent Street. Telephone: 1-505-758-2599. Ed Morgan is a master engraver and that is quite evident from the exquisitely beautiful work that is the central focus of this gallery. His highly unusual, very complex, colorful embossed prints are stunning. Many Southwest themes are explored in his work. The gallery also features one of a kind limited edition jewelry and other art forms.

Brodsky's Bookshop. On North Pueblo Road next door to the Taos Inn. Telephone: 1-505-758-9468.

Stables Art Center. On North Pueblo Road between the Taos Inn and Kit Carson Park. Mailing address: P.O. Box 198, Taos, New Mexico 87571. Telephone: 1-505-758-2036. This gallery is an arm of the Taos Art Association and is located in the historic Manby House, where its eight exhibition rooms and outdoor sculpture garden focus on the arts and crafts of Taos County and New Mexico. Sales gallery, excellent gift shop, rotating exhibitions, and special shows. Instruction in the visual arts is offered during certain times of the year.

Clay and Fiber (Gallery, Shop, and Studio). In the courtyard behind the Stables Art Center and adjacent to the Taos Community Auditorium parking lot. Telephone: 1-505-758-8093. This mother lode of contemporary crafts is hidden from view as you walk along North Pueblo Road. But if you are interested in contemporary crafts and contemporary design, search it out, as it is one of the finest galleries in the region. The owners' considerable knowledge and excellent eye for the best work available are reflected in their selection of ceramics, fiber art, unusual fabrics and wearables, blown glass, and contemporary jewelry. Another room has been added with a wide selection of baskets, contemporary furniture, and some folk crafts. The gallery changes shows monthly to focus on the finest in regional and national crafts.

Martha of Taos. Located next to the Taos Inn and about one block from the plaza. This custom dress store designs and makes southwestern dresses and skirts, broomstick skirts, Navajo skirts, and velvet Navajo skirts and dresses. A unique shop well worth a visit. Telephone: 1-505-758-3102.

Weaving Southwest. 116A Paseo Del Pueblo Sur. Telephone: 1-505-758-0433. Located about one block south of the plaza is this contemporary weaving gallery, which features weavings by artists of the three cultures of New Mexico. Also equipment and supplies for weavers.

El Rincon. On Old Kit Carson Road. Mailing address: Box Q, Taos, New Mexico 87571. Telephone: 1-505-758-9188. Located just one-half block east of the plaza on Kit Carson Road. Probably the oldest trading post in Taos, this excellent shop is a fine place to buy Indian jewelry (some jewelry made on the premises), Spanish wood carvings, and many fine Indian crafts, both old and new. This shop has a museum section in the back that is well worth seeing.

Carson House Shop. On Old Kit Carson Road next to the Kit Carson House Museum. Telephone: 1-505-758-0113. In this location for many years, this shop carries a nice selection of local and regional Indian crafts. The popular high-top Indian moccasins as well as Taos drums, Hopi kachinas, Navajo rugs, and Pueblo pottery can be purchased there.

Taos Book Shop. 216 East Kit Carson Road. One block east of the plaza. Telephone: 1-505-758-3733. A fine, old, established Taos landmark with a large general book section, as well as special sections on D. H. Lawrence, Taos, New Mexico, and the Southwest. Old and rare books relating to the Southwest. Magazines of regional interest. In addition, this shop has a good selection of children's books and a mail-order catalog for its customers interested in southwestern history and culture.

El Taller. Located on Kit Carson Road just north of the plaza. Telephone: 1-505-758-4887. This major southwestern art gallery beautifully displays a wide variety of art media, from southwestern paintings, graphics, and posters to sculpture, weavings, and jewelry. The works of Amado Pena and other Southwest artists are carried in depth.

Veloy Vigil Gallery. 110 Morada Road. Telephone: 1-505-758-8384. Do not miss seeing the works of this well-known contemporary artist, who has his roots in Colorado and the Southwest. His abstractions and use of color, which evoke the southwestern spirit, are truly remarkable.

The Taos Gallery. North Pueblo Road. Telephone: 1-505-758-2475. This spacious gallery about four blocks north of the plaza, has an outstanding selection of traditional western art and southwest impressionism, in watercolor, oils, bronze, and sculpture.

Overland Sheepskin Co. Three miles north of town on New Mexico Highway 3. Telephone: 1-505-758-8822. This is the home of the company that fashions interesting clothes and decorative items from sheepskins.

Red Shirt Drum Shop. On the left-hand side of the road leading to Taos Pueblo. Stop at this workshop to see Taos drums made. Drums may also be purchased there.

Taos Pueblo Visitor Center. Located at the entrance to Taos Pueblo. Telephone: 1-505-758-8626. This helpful visitor center managed by the pueblo often has a good selection of Pueblo crafts for sale, including Taos bean pots, drums, and many other interesting items.

Millicent Rogers Museum Shop. North of Taos. For directions, see "A One-Day Auto Tour around Taos: A Narrative Account." Telephone: 1-505-758-2462. This excellent shop, with reasonable prices and buyers who know what they are doing, has a wide variety of Pueblo, Four Corners, and Navajo Indian crafts, as well as a fine selection of Spanish wood carvings. The bookstore there is also well worth a visit for its good selection of books on regional subjects.

Treats and Sweets and Something More. Located south of Taos in Ranchos de Taos in historic Saint Francis Plaza just across from the church. Telephone: 1-505-758-1990. Señor Murphy's Piñon nut candy specialties as well as light lunches, special coffees, and excellent baked goods are featured in this gallery setting.

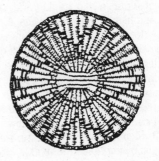

Hopi wicker plaque

Going There

There are two variables you may wish to consider before planning a trip to the High Southwest, the weather and the crowds.

Weather

Winter in the High Southwest can be severe, with below-freezing temperatures and sudden snowstorms, often of blizzard proportions, that can turn the landscape and roads into a slippery dangerous mess in minutes. If you plan to ski, then of course winter is the time to visit the High Southwest. But if you are visiting to see the sights, it is best to wait until the weather settles, usually in early May. By then the snow is gone, even from the higher elevations listed in this book, and late spring is breaking in all of its glory with sunshine, warmth, and high desert wild flowers. Although it is possible to be caught in a freak snowstorm at higher elevations in early May, that risk diminishes considerably by the middle of the month. During that time of year, if it is cold and raining at one location and you are planning to drive to a higher location, be certain to check with the highway patrol to be sure the road is free of snow. It can be raining in Moab, elevation four thousand feet, while it is snowing down the road at Monticello, elevation seven thousand feet.

June is often a dry month, sometimes hot and windy. In July and August the daily heat, which may reach one hundred degrees in some of the lower areas but which seldom exceeds ninety degrees in the higher elevations, is dramatically broken by afternoon thunderstorms which clear the air and cool it. Although the days are often hot in the summer, the air is so dry and the elevation is so high that if you get out of the sun into the shade you will experience immediate relief. Although it is hot in the High Southwest in the summer, it is comfortable compared to the lower deserts to the south and west and the plains states to the east and the south. For many who live in other parts of the United States, the High Southwest is the best place to escape the unrelenting summer heat and humidity.

The heat in the High Southwest varies considerably with the elevation. Most of the towns and cities covered in this book range from four thousand feet elevation to over nine thousand feet elevation. It is generally accepted that the temperature goes down three degrees Fahrenheit for every one thousand feet of increase in elevation. Consequently if it is ninety-five degrees in Moab, Utah, elevation four thousand feet, it is probably going to be eighty-three degrees at the rim of Bryce Canyon or eighty-six degrees in Santa Fe, New Mexico. But almost everywhere in the High Southwest there is a cooling effect when the sun goes down so that nights are considerably cooler. In many of the higher locales like Santa Fe, New Mexico, air conditioning is not essential to a good night's sleep. But in towns at a lower elevation, most of the facilities are air-conditioned.

The fall through mid-October is also an excellent time to travel the High Southwest. But beyond the middle of September there is an increased likelihood of an occasional early snowstorm at the higher elevations. The weather is usually sunny and warm in the daytime, but the nights become very cool as the aspen leaves begin to turn and reveal their golden fall foliage. After mid-October, the chance of capricious unfavorable winter weather increases.

Crowds

Some people flock to the High Southwest in the summer to seek relief from the heat in their home states, while others choose that time of year to travel because it is the only time they can bring their children to see this beautiful and educational part of the United States. July and August are the peak travel months. May, June, September, and October are considerably less crowded. You will particularly notice the summer crowds in the Santa Fe area, especially when there is a special event going on. Durango, Mesa Verde, and Bryce Canyon are also crowded in the summer. In most of the other areas covered by this book the crowds are not a problem, even in the peak summer months, so you can generally find some of the solitude for which this area is famous.

Preparing to Go There

During the best travel months, from May through September, plan on sunny, warm to hot days. If you are accustomed to covering up in the sun, then bring a hat with a brim, plenty of suntan lotion or screen, and lightweight long-sleeved shirts and pants. For comfort's sake, these garments should be made of lightweight cotton or a cotton-polyester blend which is nearly half cotton. (Most polyester fabrics do not breathe, so they tend to trap the heat next to your body.) If you feel comfortable in the sun with fewer clothes rather than more, bring cutoffs, shorts, sleeveless blouses, cool skirts, etc., and a good supply of your favorite tan-

ning lotion. Unless you want to bring more formal clothes, casual, informal dress is usually the order of the day and night in most of the towns and cities covered by this book. The exceptions to this general rule, depending on what you want to do there, may be Santa Fe and Albuquerque, where some travelers choose to dress more formally in the evening.

The air is dry in the Southwest, a fact that contributes to many of its more favorable climatic factors. But it is so dry that it can chap and crack your lips in less than a day, especially if it is windy. So bring along a chapstick or lip balm to prevent this uncomfortable condition. Other useful items to bring along are insect repellent (for mosquitoes and flies), binoculars, sunglasses, and a pair of good sturdy, walking or tennis shoes or boots with soles that offer good traction. These will get you by walking the short trails listed here; but if you plan to do more extensive hiking either on or off the trails, you should unquestionably wear high-top boots with good Vibram or traction soles. Also, be certain to bring a lightweight rain jacket in case you get caught in a sudden cloudburst out in the open. A small day pack is an excellent item to bring along to tote water, snacks, cameras, and other necessities as you hike some of the scenic trails this book describes. To carry water you may want to bring along several plastic or poly bottles or one-quart canteens. Water not only tastes good on the trails, but it is also a refreshing aid as you drive through arid, isolated stretches of high desert without facilities offering cold drinks. It is very easy to get dehydrated in the High Southwest. So if you plan to do a full day of hiking, carry along one gallon of water per person for each full day of hiking, just as the park rangers suggest.

And of course, do not forget your camera. When you buy your film, take into account that the light is very intense in the High Southwest and extremely bright.

Getting There

It is possible to reach the High Southwest by driving your family auto or by taking a plane, train, or bus from most parts of the United States. But once you get there, you should have a car. The major sights are miles apart and the accommodations are equally isolated from one another. Rental cars are available at most entry points. However, if you are just touring a small area covered by this book, you may be able to do without a car. Many interest points in northern New Mexico are interconnected by good public bus service or by special tour buses from one town to another. Similarly, the Durango and Mesa Verde area can be toured without a car since tour buses regularly leave Durango for both Mesa Verde and the towns of the Silver Circle. But easy access to the remaining areas of this book are best seen by car.

Being There

Driving

Be certain your car is in good operating condition before you leave home or depart from the rental car agency. Because towns are far apart and a few of the areas are fairly remote, you want to be sure you have a good spare tire and equipment to change tires if you need to. Also, it helps to have tires with good treads, since you will be traveling in hot weather and occasionally over dirt or graveled roads.

In the summer, air conditioning is definitely a plus, especially if you are not used to hot climates or if you have children who do not tolerate the heat. Driving without air conditioning in the summer, especially at the lower elevations of four thousand to six thousand feet, can be very fatiguing, for the hot dry air coming in through open windows seems to sap every bit of energy you have. But if you do drive without air conditioning, you should consider sun shades or screens for at least some of the windows. These are often available at auto supply or trailer supply stores. They reflect the sun's rays, but let you see out. They are also helpful in cars with air conditioning. If you have a choice of automobiles to drive, try to get a light-colored one. White is best. Light colors reflect the sun's rays, while dark ones absorb

them. Now you know why the Bedouins wear white robes! You may also want to try to schedule the longest drives in your unair-conditioned car during the early morning hours or early evening hours when it is cooler.

Whether you have an air-conditioned car or not, you should carry plenty of cold water, pop, and juice to drink. Small, inexpensive ice chests are available at most discount and hardware stores and they are ideal for cooling your drinks or keeping picnic lunches from spoiling in the heat. These little ice chests will literally save the day for you when temperatures are soaring in the high desert to one hundred degrees and your spirits are flagging in the dehydrating heat. You may also want to bring an old blanket or tablecloth to spread under the shade of a piñon tree for an inexpensive lunch in one of the many excellent picnic areas along the way.

All of the roads mentioned in this book can be driven by the average driver in the average family car, except for those few which are listed for four-wheel-drive vehicles only. Of course, if you have a four-wheel-drive vehicle and are comfortable operating it under subadverse conditions, there are many jeep trails open to you that are not available to the average motorist.

The only truly mountainous driving you will find routed in this book is the stretch of road between Durango and the old mining towns to the north. On those high mountain roads, be certain to stay in the center of the road and drive slowly, taking care not to pass over the yellow center stripe as you make the curves. At higher altitudes, your car will lose much of its power, especially if you are going uphill. On the way down, use your brakes, of course, but also shift into lower gear, which helps to slow you down without placing too much wear on your brakes. Do not slip into neutral gear on the way down. Coasting is very dangerous. Before you start out on a mountainous stretch, be certain that you have plenty of water in your radiator and that your water hoses are in good shape. The altitude and grade can heat an engine up rapidly. If your car stalls at higher altitudes, it may be suffering from vapor lock, a condition that may be remedied by placing a damp cloth over the fuel pump to cool it down. If that does not work, keep the hood up to signify distress and get back in your car to await help from either the highway patrol or helpful fellow travelers. I have driven for nearly thirty years in the High Southwest and have not experienced vapor lock, while others seem to be plagued by it.

Most of the roads you will travel are good, paved, two-lane highways. But a few of the highways are not elevated and follow the lay of the land. Certain stretches of these roads are marked with signs "Flash Floods Next 5 Miles" or "Road Subject to Flooding Next 5 Miles" or "Do Not Enter if Raining." Do heed these signs. In the High Southwest, an afternoon thunderstorm can let loose an unbelievable amount of water in just a few minutes, flooding absolutely dry gullies and washes so that they become raging rivers before you realize it. These gully washers have been known to wash both people and cars away.

If you are driving and you enter a rain or dust storm that diminishes your visibility so you cannot see, look for a safe place to turn off the road. Stop there until the storm abates. But do not stop in soft sand or at the mouth of a wash or gully. It is generally advised to wait the storm out with your lights off. Those dramatic blinding storms are usually over in five to fifteen minutes, usually rewarding you with cool air, rainbows, and sun-

shine. If there is lightning associated with the storm, do not touch anything metal in your car and turn your radio off. Do not seek protection under a tree during a lightning storm as trees attract lightning. If you are worried about a storm or the road conditions ahead, look for roadside signs giving information about where to turn your radio dial to receive updated storm alerts.

If you have need to pull off some of the roads without shoulders, be certain you are not pulling into a sandy area. But if you happen to find yourself getting stuck in sand or deep mud, do not allow the car to stop until you are out of it. However, do not accelerate rapidly or you will just dig yourself in more. Apply steady, slow pressure while in low gear, just as you would in snow. If that does not get you out, rock back and forth by switching from drive to reverse and back again, pressing gently on the accelerator. If this fails, you can try deflating your tires somewhat and then attempting to drive out. If you have a shovel, you can dig the sand or mud away from the tires and then place tree limbs or other materials in front of all four tires to give you sufficient traction to pull out. If all else fails, wait for a park ranger or the highway patrol.

Some perfectly good dirt and clay roads become slippery when wet. So slow down under

Colorado River Bridge, Moab, Utah

Travel Access

Arrival Point	Interstate Highways	*Air Service	Train
Denver, Colorado	76, 70, 25	Commercial and Commuter	Amtrak
Albuquerque, New Mexico	40, 25	Commercial and Commuter	Amtrak
Santa Fe, New Mexico	25	Shuttle flights to and from Albuquerque (nine passenger, single engine)	Amtrak to Lamy, New Mexico
Salt Lake City, Utah	80, 15	Commercial and Commuter	Amtrak
Phoenix, Arizona	17, 10	Commercial and Commuter	Amtrak
Thompson, Utah	70	No	Amtrak
Grand Junction, Colorado	70	Commuter or shuttle flights from Denver, Albuquerque, and Phoenix	Amtrak
Telluride, Montrose, Colorado	None	Commuter or shuttle flights from Denver, Albuquerque, and Phoenix	No
Durango, Colorado	None	Commuter or shuttle flights from Denver, Albuquerque, Phoenix, and Southern California	No
Flagstaff, Arizona	40, 17	Commuter or shuttle flights from Phoenix and Las Vegas	Amtrak
Las Vegas, Nevada	15	Commercial and Commuter	Amtrak

*Commercial jet service utilizes larger jets usually carrying more than one hundred passengers. Commuter or shuttle services utilize much smaller planes carrying sixty passengers or fewer.

Bus	National Car Rentals	**Destination	***Approximate Miles to Destination
Yes	Yes	IV–Santa Fe	310
		III–Durango	350
		I–Moab	390
Yes	Yes	IV–Santa Fe	60
		II–Hopi Reservation	255
Yes	Yes	III–Durango	225
Yes	Yes	I–Moab	240
		II–Monument Valley	386
		III–Durango	398
Yes	Yes	II–Hopi Reservation	281
Yes	No	I–Moab	40
		II–Monument Valley	186
		III–Durango	200
Yes	Yes	I–Moab	115
		III–Durango	168
		II–Monument Valley	261
Yes	Yes	III–Durango	108
		I–Moab	175
Yes	Yes	III–Durango	0
		I–Moab	158
		II–Canyon de Chelly	170
		IV–Santa Fe	230
Yes	Yes	II–Navajo Reservation	55
		II–Hopi Reservation	130
		IV–Santa Fe	384
		I–Moab	330
		III–Durango	325
Yes	Yes	I–Bryce Canyon	240
		II–Flagstaff	250

**Roman numerals correspond to Sections I–IV of the book.
***Mileages over 400 miles not listed.

wet conditions. If you begin to slide, treat your car as if you were on snow and turn your steering wheel in the direction the rear end of your car is skidding.

Occasionally you will see signs warning you of high winds. If the winds are high as you drive through these areas, just slow down until your car feels firm and steady in its forward progress and then proceed.

When you drive at night, look for critters on the road in the unfenced areas or where you see a warning sign with the picture of a deer on it. In the High Southwest, deer share the road with you in the evenings, but hitting a deer can be fatal to both you and the deer. But deer are not all you will see on the highways. On the Indian reservations, where there are few fences, cattle, sheep, and goats often roam the highway at night, so be careful.

Be certain to obey the speed limits in the small towns you will travel through. In one small town in New Mexico which some would consider a wide place in the road of little consequence, a sign on the road going into town says: "Drive slowly and see the town, Drive fast and see the Judge." And be especially careful about observing speed limits on the Indian reservations in towns like Kayenta and Tuba City, for they are strictly enforced. If driving ten or fifteen miles per hour seems ridiculous to you, just wait to see what your reaction is to a seventy-five-dollar speeding ticket.

When you leave your car in a parking area to walk a trail, be sure to lock it. And if you are going to be out of sight of your car for awhile, be certain to put cameras, radios, and other valuables out of sight. Yes, even the remote High Southwest suffers from vandalism.

Distances between towns and gas stations can sometimes be great, so be sure you have plenty of gas in the tank and know where you can fill up again. Except for Mesa Verde National Park, none of the other national parks in this book offers automobile services.

Hiking

For hiking the trails listed in this book, very little special equipment is needed. But there are some practices you should try to observe. First, stay on the designated trail and in areas of switch-backs do not make your own trail by cutting through from one level to another. This causes erosion of the trail. Also, do not throw rocks upon the trail nor from canyon nor mesa rims. Someone like yourself may be hiking far below you. If you have young children, do not let them run ahead to a rim or a viewing point. Some rims are fenced and protected, but many others are open. It is often a long way to the bottom. Also, be careful about standing on mesa edges or rims when you take photographs. More than one would-be photographer has walked over the rim while his eye was glued to his range finder. Sandstone ledges at cliff rims are often undermined by erosion of softer rocks underneath. Your weight may be enough to aid nature's erosional forces by splitting the rim rock and widening the canyon. And, of course, do not walk up dry stream beds, washes, or arroyos if it is raining or about to rain.

People often wonder about snakes in the High Southwest. Most travelers will visit there and may hike many trails without ever seeing a sign of a live snake. But there are plenty of dead ones along the highways to let you know they are there. However many, like the garter and bullsnake, are harmless. The poisonous ones are generally of the rattlesnake variety and can vary from twelve to fourteen inches to twenty to twenty-four inches. Believe it or not, they are more afraid of you than you are of them. Given the least opportunity to run from your approaching footsteps, they will, for they sense the vibrations your feet make on the ground and their immediate instinct is to flee. If you hike the trails in this book, you probably will never see a snake, much less hear one slithering away from you in the grass. But hiking cross country you may well encounter the sounds of snakes as they attempt to avoid you. In either circumstance, do not stick your hands in rock crevasses or on rock ledges without first seeing what is on top, and if you walk through thick grass go slowly, making as much noise as you can with your feet. Snakes, sluggish from their sunbaths on rock ledges, may not hear your approach, and if your hand interrupts their nap they may get irritated. In a like fashion, if you do any walking at night along the highway still warm from the afternoon's sun, carry a flashlight and do not accidentally interrupt a snake taking a snooze on his warm pad. In addition to snakes, you will see many lizards, all harmless in the High Southwest. You will hear a lot of talk about scorpions, insects which can sting something fierce when they attack you with their stinger tail. Generally they will not be a problem unless you are camping. Shake out your boots before putting them on and place mosquito netting over your tent entrance, securing it at the bottom of the opening, and you should never have to suffer the pain of a scorpion bite.

Throughout the book, you will see the term "slickrock." Most of the sandstone you will be walking over is a form of slickrock. The rock really is not slick unless it is wet. Nonetheless, it does not offer the traction of cement or asphalt since the grains of sand act as roller bearings and could send you tumbling if you are wearing slick leather soles. Tennis shoes, walking shoes, and boots with good treads all offer safety on dry slickrock. If it is wet, though, you should exert caution even with good footgear. If you plan to do a lot of cross-country hiking, you should definitely wear high-top hiking boots with thick Vibram soles or equivalent. Not only will the high tops help to keep dirt and sand away from your feet, but they will offer additional support and traction on the rougher steeper ground away from the trails.

The average summer travelers who want to hike some of the trails may want to consider doing their hiking in the morning before the afternoon thunderstorms, which can start as early as late June and last through July and August. This way you avoid the danger of flash floods, slippery rock, and the discomfort of becoming thoroughly soaked. Another alternative is to plan some hiking after the daily showers in the late afternoon. In both instances, the temperatures are cooler and you will enjoy your hike more. Plan to take a siesta during the afternoon thundershowers or sit it out in a protected place where you can enjoy these beautiful and dramatic storms.

Try to allow time to see the various sights at their best. Do not plan such a busy schedule that you are constantly rushing from one place to another. Slow down a bit to nature's pace and you will enjoy your trip more. If you find yourself getting overheated while you are hiking, seek a shaded area and rest for a few minutes. It is cool in the dry air at these higher altitudes when you are out of the sun.

Health

The High Southwest is a healthy environment for most, but for those with certain types of heart disease or disabling lung conditions, the altitude can be a detriment. If you have one of these debilitating conditions, you may wish to travel the lower parts of the High Southwest. Table B lists some of the elevations you may want to take into consideration or use to consult with your physician.

Most everyone has some temporary reaction to the higher elevations over six thousand feet, which is often more noticeable if they have flown into the High Southwest rather than traveled there by surface. But do not worry. Your body's initial reactions of sluggishness and shortness of breath will diminish as you adjust to the altitude in a matter of hours or within a day or two of your arrival. Some visitors find that cutting down their alcohol intake the first day helps to make the adjustment easier.

People often ask, "Is it safe to drink the water?" Absolutely. The same high standards which apply to public water supplies in the rest of the United States prevail in the High Southwest and on the Indian reservations. But generally it is not safe to drink water from streams, ponds, creeks, and other natural sources, except at the very highest elevations where man does not live. Even then you should seek the advice of the United States Forest Service or National Park Information Services about the specific area you are going to.

Rabies is a problem in certain areas of the High Southwest, especially in northern New Mexico. If you should be bitten by any animals, dogs, squirrels, chipmunks, or bats, be sure to contact a local physician in that area or seek help at one of the nearby ranger stations immediately.

Meeting the Indians

In most instances your contact with the Indian people will be pleasant and rewarding. As with many people who live in small towns and rural areas, there is generally an attitude of openness and a desire to be helpful. But there are a few sen-

Sample Altitudes in the High Southwest

Place	Altitude Above Sea Level
Bryce Canyon National Park	8,000 feet
Capitol Reef National Park, visitor center	5,400 feet
Moab, Utah	4,000 feet
Arches National Park	5,000 feet
Monument Valley	5,000 feet
Hopi mesas–Second Mesa	6,300 feet
Canyon de Chelly	5,500 feet
Mesa Verde	7,000 feet
Durango, Colorado	6,500 feet
Silverton, Colorado	9,032 feet
Santa Fe, New Mexico	7,000 feet
Albuquerque, New Mexico	5,300 feet

sitivities you should be aware of before entering Indian Country.

After reading this book, you will be aware of some of the historical roots that have affected the relationship between the whites and the Indians in the High Southwest. Many of the negative aspects of these roots have extended into modern times when twentieth-century white tourists and visitors have, on occasion, roused the ire of the Indians. Not too many years ago, well-meaning but insensitive fortune seekers plundered ancient ruins that seemed to belong to no one, carting off the relics and selling them for profit. Not too many years later, intrusive visitors with cameras would snap photos of the Indians and sell them for profit to be used on postal cards or for other commercial enterprises. Later, when the Indians discovered what had been done, they were infuriated. Once again it seemed the white man had profited from the Indian.

The Hopi banned cameras from their ceremonies in 1907 and the Taos Indians have carefully regulated white visitors for decades. The ban or regulation on cameras is still present today and in fact has been extended to include sketching, drawing, tape recording, and all other mechanical means of reproducing a real-life situation. The Hopi are probably the most adamant today about the use of cameras and the like. Most Hopi will not give permission to have their pictures taken and most of the village chiefs will not give permission for you to bring your camera into the villages. For all practical purposes, the camera and all devices like it are banned on the Hopi reservation. So the best place for your camera when you visit the Hopi villages is in the glove compartment of your car, not around your neck or in your hands. And of course, these devices are strictly banned at the ceremonial dances.

The Rio Grande Pueblo people are a little more tolerant. In most instances they regulate rather than ban image-making equipment. The procedure there is to ask the village chief for permission to take pictures of the village. You may have to pay a fee to do so. The Taos Indians have different fees for the different kinds of equipment you want to bring in. It costs more to obtain a permit for a movie camera than a 110 still camera. Nonetheless, with a permit and the inevitable restrictions that go along with it, you can still take pictures of some of the Rio Grande Pueblos and their ceremonial dances. If you involve individuals other than those in a crowd scene, you should ask for their permission. They may turn you down, charge you a fee, or just say "okay."

The Navajo seem to be more tolerant than the Hopi. Since they live in widely spread family clusters, you must negotiate with each family or individual whose picture you may want to take. Again, you will probably be asked to pay a fee to take a picture.

In general, I would suggest that you just put your camera away and work on formulating visual images in your memory. For much of what you see is so dramatic and strikingly different that it will leave an indelible imprint far more true than any photo or slide that you may take.

Not infrequently you will see travelers drive into a village park and embark on an aggressive sight-seeing tour, including cupping their hands and looking in the windows of houses. It is doubtful that these people would do the same thing in their own town or city or in a neighboring town. So treat and respect the privacy of the Indians as you would your own. Be courteous and remember you are a guest visiting them. Do not stand and point at people or things. As intriguing as they are, stay away from the sacred kivas and do not let children climb on kiva ladders. Respect these religious objects. If you need information or help, do ask someone in the village. I have never found the Indians to be anything but responsive and helpful in this situation. If you plan more than just a brief visit to a village, be sure to obtain the approval of the village chief.

In conversations with the Indians, do not ask questions relating to their religious or ceremonial life. If you do, you will be rebuffed quickly, for in the Indian's mind his religion is none of your business no matter how good your intentions are. For many whites who often talk openly and easily about their religion, this difference is particularly hard to understand. But it makes perfectly good sense to the Indian people, whose religion is very private and does not condone proselytism.

You should also be warned that the Indians of the High Southwest come from an ancient and timeless culture where the concern about timeliness and punctuality is not the same as it is in the white culture. In order for you not to be disturbed by this, you will find yourself having to slow your reaction time to the pace of their culture, rather than expect the opposite to happen. Perhaps in being patient rather than angry the lesson learned is that their culture has been in existence for over nine hundred years. The white American culture has only been at it for a little over two hundred years.

Many of the High Southwest Indians will sell their crafts directly to visitors from their homes. You may get a better price or you may not, but the selection may be different than in a shop or trading post and you also have the opportunity to custom order something you might want. So visit the craftsperson who has made an object you have seen in a shop that has caught your eye. Or if you are visiting a village, ask someone who makes kachinas or pottery or who does weaving. You will be directed to someone's door. You may very well be invited to watch the craftsperson work. If you do not find what you want to buy, do not feel badly. Treat your Indian fellow citizen as a peer and you will get along fine.

You will seldom see traditional southwest Indian adults wearing shorts in their villages. In fact, shorts are banned at many of the Hopi ceremonial dances. One hot, summer afternoon, our daughter was wearing shorts as we left the car and headed for the plaza where the Snake Dance was to be performed. After parking outside the village, we got out of the car. Immediately we were face to face with a Hopi policeman who gently and sensitively informed us that our daughter would not be permitted at the ceremony wearing shorts. She quickly changed in the car and we were then given a warm smile and nod from the Hopi policeman and proceeded to the ceremony.

When visiting Indian or public lands in the Southwest, it is wise to remember that the Federal Antiquities Law passed in 1906 is still in effect and has recently been reinforced by the Archaeological Protection Act of 1979. It is against the law to remove any Indian relics or artifacts from these lands. To do so could result in stiff fines as well as imprisonment in some cases.

Camping

Although this book does not pretend to be a camping guide, numerous campsites are listed in areas where camping seems particularly enjoyable. Some of the campsites at lower elevations are plagued with heat, dust, and bugs, whereas higher elevation campsites are more pleasant. Details on these campsites and others are outlined in several books on the market, including Woodall's *Campground Directory,* Western Edition, and the American Automobile Association's *Southwestern Camping Book* which is available to members only.

Bibliography

I. Southeastern Utah: Canyon Country

General Descriptive/Historical/Cultural

Abbey, Edward. *Desert Solitaire: A Season in the Wilderness.* New York: Ballantine Books, 1968.

Abbey, Edward, and Hyde, Philip. *Slickrock: The Canyon Country of Southeast Utah.* San Francisco: Sierra Club, 1971. (pictorial book in color)

Bakker, Elna, and Lillard, Richard G. *The Great Southwest: The Story of a Land and Its People.* The Great West Series. Palo Alto: American West Publishing Co., 1972.

Barnes, F. A. *Canyon Country Scenic Roads.* Salt Lake City: Wasatch Publishers, Inc. 1977.

Crampton, C. Gregory. *Standing Up Country: The Canyon Lands of Utah and Arizona.* New York: Alfred A. Knopf/University of Utah Press, 1965.

Findley, Rowe. "Canyonlands: Realm of Rock and the Far Horizon." *National Geographic* 140 (July 1971): 71–91.

Folsom, Franklin. *America's Ancient Treasures.* New York: Rand McNally and Co., 1974.

Grant, Campbell. *Rock Art of the American Indian.* New York: Promontory Press, 1967.

Hafen, Leroy R., and Hafen, Ann W. *Old Spanish Trail.* Glendale, Cal.: Arthur H. Clark Co., 1954.

Lavender, David. *Colorado River Country.* New York: E. P. Dutton, Inc., 1982.

Leigh, Rufus Wood. *Five Hundred Utah Place Names.* Salt Lake City: Desert News Press, 1961.

Plateau. "Canyonlands National Park." *Plateau, Magazine of the Museum of Northern Arizona* 52 (1980): 1–32. (entire issue)

Roylance, Ward J. *Seeing Capitol Reef National Park: A Guide to the Roads and Trails.* Salt Lake City: Wasatch Publishers, Inc., 1979.

———. *Utah Part 2. A Guide to the State.* Salt Lake City: A Guide to the State Foundation, 1982.

Stegner, Wallace. "The High Plateaus." *Sierra* 66 (1981): 9–17.

Stegner, Wallace, and Stegner, Page. *American Places.* New York: Elsevier-Dutton Publishing Co., 1981.

Sunset Books and Sunset Magazine Editors. *National Parks of the West.* Menlo Park, Cal.: Lane Publishing Co., 1980.

Trimble, Stephen. *The Bright Edge.* Flagstaff, Ariz.: Museum of Northern Arizona Press, 1979.

Natural History

Baars, Donald L. *Red Rock Country: The Geologic History of the Colorado Plateau.* Garden City, N.Y.: Doubleday/Natural History Press, 1972.

Barnes, F. A. *Canyon Country Geology for the Layman and Rockhound.* Salt Lake City:

Wasatch Publishers, Inc., 1978.

Bezy, John. *Bryce Canyon: The Story Behind the Scenery.* Las Vegas: K. C. Publications, 1981.

Dodge, Natt N. *Roadside Wildflowers of Southwest Uplands.* Globe, Ariz.: Southwest Parks and Monuments Association, 1963.

Doolittle, Jerome, and the editors of Time-Life Books. *Canyons and Mesas.* New York: Time-Life Books, 1974.

Hintze, Lehi F. *Geologic History of Utah.* Brigham Young University Geology Studies, vol. 20, pt. 3. Provo, Utah: Brigham Young University Press, n.d.

Hoffman, John F. *Arches National Park: An Illustrated Guide and History.* San Diego: Western Recreational Publications, 1981.

Lamb, Samuel H. *Woody Plants of the Southwest.* Santa Fe: The Sunstone Press, 1977.

Olson, Virgil J. *Capitol Reef: The Story Behind the Scenery.* Las Vegas: K. C. Publications, 1975.

Redfern, Ron. *Corridors of Time.* New York: Times Books, 1980.

Rigby, Keith J. *Northern Colorado Plateau.* K/H Geology Field Guide Series. Dubuque, Iowa: Kendall/Hunt Publishing Co., 1976.

Stokes, Wm. Lee. *Scenes of the Plateau Lands and How They Came to Be.* Salt Lake City: Publishers Press, 1969.

Trimble, Stephen. *The Hickman Natural Bridge Trail.* Torrey, Utah: Capitol Reef Natural History Association, n.d.

Fremont Indian petroglyph

Welsh, Stanley L., and Ratcliffe, Bill. *Flowers of the Canyon Country.* Provo, Utah: Brigham Young University Press, 1977.

Yundell, Michael D., ed. *Photographic and Comprehensive Guide to Zion and Bryce Canyon.* Casper, Wyo.: National Parks Division of Worldwide Research and Publishing Co., 1972.

Some of the above books may be purchased from the following sources:

Capitol Reef Natural History Association, Capitol Reef National Park, Torrey, Utah 84775. Telephone: 1-801-425-3791.

Southwest Parks and Monuments Association, 221 North Court Avenue, Tucson, Arizona 85701. Telephone: 1-602-792-0239.

Maps

Southeastern Utah, Utah Multipurpose Map, Utah Travel Council.

Southeastern–Central Utah, Utah Multipurpose Map, Utah Travel Council.

American Automobile Association Maps: Western States, Utah–Nevada, and A Guide to Indian Country.

The Utah multipurpose regional maps, helpful brochures, and other useful, generally free information can be obtained by writing the Utah Travel Council, Department HL 73, Council Hall/State Capitol, Salt Lake City, Utah 84114. Telephone: 1-801-538-1030. Maps are available without charge to members of the American Automobile Association at 560 East Fifth South Street, Salt Lake City, Utah 84102. Telephone: 1-801-364-5615.

Additional site and trail maps as well as general information brochures, updated entrance fee rates and visitor center opening and closing hours can be obtained without charge from the following:

The Utah Division of Parks and Recreation, Information Services, 1636 West North

Temple, Salt Lake City, Utah 84116. Telephone: 1-801-533-6011 or 6012.

The Bureau of Land Management, 2370 South 2300 West, Salt Lake City, Utah 84119.

You may obtain detailed maps of the national parks throughout the High Southwest by writing for a copy of the U.S. Geological Survey index map, which lists availability of topographic maps for each park. Index and maps can be ordered from: USGS Western Distribution Branch, Box 25268, Federal Center, Denver, Colorado 80225.

II. Northeastern Arizona: Indian Country

Background Information: The Indians on the Colorado Plateau

Arizona Highways. "A Special 46-page Salute in Color to Canyon de Chelly." *Arizona Highways* 53(March 1977):1–48. (entire issue)

———. "Special Edition: Touring the Navajo Nation." *Arizona Highways* 55(1979):1–48. (entire issue)

———. "The Hopi Tricentennial." *Arizona Highways* 56(September 1980):1–48. (entire issue)

Arnold, David A. "Pueblo Artistry in Clay." *National Geographic* 162(November 1982): 593–605.

Bahti, Tom. *Southwestern Indian Ceremonials.* Las Vegas: K. C. Publications, 1970.

Bates, Caroline. "Pueblo Indian Breads." *Gourmet Magazine* 37(November 1977): 48–53, 120–24, 130–34.

Belknap, William, Jr. "20th-Century Indians Preserve Cliff Dwellers' Customs." *National Geographic* 125(February 1964): 196–211.

Bowman, Eldon. "Beale's Historic Road: By Camel, From the Zuñi Villages to the Rio Colorado." *Arizona Highways* 60(July 1984): 2–10 and 15.

Canby, Thomas Y. "Search for the First Americans." *National Geographic* 156(September 1979): 330–63.

———. "The Anasazi: Riddles in the Ruins." *National Geographic* 162(November 1982): 554–92.

De Lauer, Marjel. "A Century of Indian Traders and Trading Posts." *Arizona Highways* 51(March 1975): 6–14.

———. "The Bi-Millennium of the Southwest." *Arizona Highways* 52(January 1976): 3–9.

Dutton, Bertha P. *The Rancheria Ute and Southern Paiute Peoples: Indians of the American Southwest.* Englewood Cliffs, N.J.: Prentice-Hall, Inc., 1975–76.

Eggan, Fred. *Social Organization of the Western Pueblos.* Chicago: University of Chicago Press, 1950.

Hillerman, Tony. *The Blessing Way.* New York: Harper and Row, 1970.

———. *Dance Hall of the Dead.* New York: Harper and Row, 1973.

———. *Listening Woman.* New York: Harper and Row, 1978.

Hodge, Carl. "Arizona's First Farmers." *Arizona Highways* 52(November 1976): 2–6.

———. "Museum of Northern Arizona." *Arizona Highways* 58(June 1982): 12–17.

Jacka, Jerry. "The Miracle of Hopi Corn." *Arizona Highways* 54(March 1978): 3–15.

Klinck, Richard E. *Land of Room Enough and Time Enough.* Salt Lake City: Peregrine Smith Books, 1984.

Laughter, Albert. "Our People, Our Past." *National Geographic* 156(July 1979): 81–85.

Lipe, William D. "The Southwest." Chap. 8 in *Ancient Native Americans,* edited by Jesse D. Jennings, 327–401. San Francisco: W. H. Freeman and Company, 1978.

Lister, Robert H., and Lister, Florence C. *Those Who Came Before.* Tucson, Arizona: The University of Arizona Press, 1983.

Looney, Ralph. "The Navajos." *National Geographic* 142(December 1972): 740–81.

Lowenkopf, Anne N., and Katz, Michael W. *Camping with the Indians.* Los Angeles: Sherbourne Press, Inc., 1974.

Marquis, Arnold. *A Guide to America's Indians: Ceremonials, Reservations, Museums.* Norman, Okla.: University of Oklahoma Press, 1960.

May, Karl. *Winnetou: A Novel.* Translated by Michael Shaw. New York: Seabury Press, 1977.

McAllester, David P., and McAllester, Susan W. *Hogans, Navajo Houses, and House Songs.* Irvington, N.Y.: Columbia University Press, 1980.

Muench, David, and Pike, Donald. *Anasazi: Ancient People of the Rock.* Palo Alto, Cal.: American West Publishing Co., 1974.

Nelson, Lisa. "Electricity Lights Up Lives of Navajo Families." *Winds of Change: A Magazine for American Indians.* 1(December 1986): 15–16.

Nequatewa, Edmund. *Truth of a Hopi.* Flagstaff, Ariz.: Northland Press, 1967.

Noble, David Grant. *Ancient Ruins of the Southwest.* Flagstaff, Ariz.: Northland Press, 1981.

Olin, George. *Mammals of the Southwest Mountains and Mesas.* Globe, Ariz.: Southwest Parks and Monuments Assoc., 1961.

Page, Jake, and Page, Suzanne. "Inside the Hopi Homeland." *National Geographic* 162(November 1982): 607–29.

Page, Suzanne, and Page, Jake. *Hopi.* New York: Harry N. Abrams, 1982.

Plateau: Magazine of the Museum of Northern Arizona. "Wupatki-Sunset Crater." *Plateau* 49(2):1–33. (entire issue)

Rigby, J. Keith. *Southern Colorado Plateau.* K/H Geology Field Guide Series. Dubuque, Iowa: Kendall/Hunt Publishing Co., 1977.

Rock Point Community School. *Between Sacred Mountains Navajo Stories and Lessons from the Land.* Chinle, Ariz.: Rock Point Community School, 1983.

Romero, Manny. "Flagstaff: One Century Old." *Arizona Highways* 52(July 1976): 16–20.

Schaafsma, Polly. *Indian Rock Art of the Southwest.* School of American Research: Santa Fe, 1980.

Scully, Vincent. *Pueblo/Mountain, Village, Dance.* New York: The Viking Press, 1975.

Sunset Magazine: "The Land of the Hopi and the Navajo." *Sunset Magazine.* (May 1987): 96–109.

Supplee, Douglas, and Anderson, Barbara. *Can-*

yon de Chelly: The Story Behind the Scenery. rev. ed. Las Vegas: K. C. Publications, 1981. Reprint. New York: Penguin Books, 1982.

Weaver, Thomas, ed. *Indians of Arizona: A Contemporary Perspective.* Tucson, Ariz.: The University of Arizona Press, 1979.

Webb, William, and Weinstein, Robert A. *Dwellers at the Source: Southwestern Indian Photographs of A.C. Vroman, 1895–1904.* New York: Grossman Publishers, 1973.

Wilson, Maggie. "Men, Myths, and Rituals." *Arizona Highways* 55(September 1979): 2–9.

———. "The Sacred Mountains." *Arizona Highways* 56(May 1980): 12–33.

Witherspoon, Gary. *Navajo Kinship and Marriage.* Chicago: University of Chicago Press, 1975.

Wormington, H. M. *Prehistoric Indians of the Southwest.* Denver, Colo.: The Denver Museum of Natural History, 1973.

Navajo and Hopi Crafts

Allen, Laura Graves. *Contemporary Hopi Pottery.* Flagstaff: Museum of Northern Arizona, 1984.

Arizona Highways. "Turquoise Attitude." *Arizona Highways* XLX(January 1974): 1–48. (entire issue)

———. "Prehistoric Pottery of Arizona." *Arizona Highways* 50(February 1974):1–48. (entire issue)

———. "Southwestern Pottery Today." (Special edition) *Arizona Highways* 50(May 1974): 1–48. (entire issue)

———. "Indian Weaving." (Special Edition) *Arizona Highways* 50(July 1974): 1–48. (entire issue)

———. "Indian Jewelry." *Arizona Highways* 50 (August 1974): 1–48. (entire issue)

———. "American Indian Basketry." (Special Edition) *Arizona Highways* 51(July 1975): 1–47. (entire issue)

———. American Indian Artists Series. *Arizona Highways* 52(August 1976): 1–48. (entire issue)

———. "Collector's Edition: The New Look in Indian Jewelry." *Arizona Highways* 55(April 1979): 1–48. (entire issue)

———. "The New Individualists: A Spectacular Visual Journey through the Realm of Native American Fine Art." *Arizona Highways* 62:(May 1986): 1–47. (entire issue)

Bahti, Mark. *A Consumer's Guide to Southwestern Indian Arts and Crafts*. Tucson, Ariz.: Bahti Indian Arts, 1975.

Bahti, Tom. *Southwestern Indian Arts and Crafts*. Flagstaff, Ariz.: K.C. Publications, 1966.

Collins, John E. *Hopi Traditions in Pottery and Painting*. Alhambra, Cal.: NuMasters Gallery, 1977.

Deedra, Don. *Navajo Rugs: How to Find, Evaluate, Buy and Care for Them*. Flagstaff: Northland Press, 1975.

Gertzwiller, Steve. *The Fine Art of Navajo Weaving*. Tucson, Arizona: Ray Manley, 1984.

James, H. L. *Posts and Rugs: The Story of Navajo Rugs and Their Homes*. Globe, Ariz.: Southwest Parks and Monuments Association, 1977.

Lister, Robert H., and Lister, Florence C. *Anasazi Pottery*. Albuquerque: University of New Mexico Press, 1978.

Maxwell, Gilbert S. *Navajo Rugs—Past, Present and Future*. Santa Fe: Heritage Art, 1984.

McCoy, Ron. "Naalye he Bahooghan: Where the Past is Present" (Indian Country Trading Posts) *Arizona Highways* 63(June 1987): 6–15.

Mora, Joseph. *The Year of the Hopi: Paintings and Photographs 1904–06*. With essays by Tyrone Stewart, Frederick Dock Stader, and Barton Wright. New York: Rizzoli International Publications, Inc., 1979.

Plateau. "Hopi and Hopi-Tewa Pottery." *Plateau, Magazine of the Museum of Northern Arizona* (Winter 1977):1–32. (entire issue)

Rosnek, Carl, and Stacey, Joseph. *Skystone and Silver: The Collector's Book of Southwest Indian Jewelry*. New York: Prentice-Hall, 1976.

Tanner, Clara Lee. *Prehistoric Southwestern Craft Arts*. Tucson, Ariz.: University of Arizona Press, 1976.

Trimble, Stephen. *Talking with the Clay: The Art of Pueblo Pottery*. Santa Fe: School of American Research, 1987.

Washburn, Dorothy K., ed. *Hopi Kachina Spirit of Life*. San Francisico: California Academy of Sciences, 1980.

Wright, Barton. *Hopi Kachinas: The Complete Guide to Collecting Kachina Dolls*. Flagstaff, Ariz.: Northland Press, 1977.

Wright, Barton, and Roat, Evelyn. *This Is a Hopi Kachina*. Flagstaff, Ariz.: Museum of Northern Arizona, 1973.

Wright, Margaret. *Hopi Silver: The History and Hallmarks of Hopi Silversmithing*. Flagstaff, Ariz.: Northland Press, 1972–74.

Maps

Guide to Indian Country, Automobile Club of Southern California and California State Automobile Association, 2601 South Figueroa Street, Los Angeles, California 90007. An indispensable map.

Arizona Road Map. *Arizona Highways* Magazine, 2039 West Lewis Avenue, Phoenix, Arizona 85009. Issued for free distribution.

An Arizona State map and detailed county map sheets are available for a fee from the Arizona Department of Transportation, Mail Drop 134A, 206 South Seventeenth Avenue, Phoenix, Arizona 85007. Telephone: 1-602-255-7011. Additionally, free maps plus general tourist information are available from the Arizona Office of Tourism, 1480 E. Bethany Home Road, Phoenix, Arizona 85014. Telephone: 1-602-255-3618. Maps and travel information can also be obtained from the American Automobile Association (free of charge to members) at 748 East McDowell Road, Phoenix, Arizona 85006. Telephone: 1-602-252-7751.

III. Southwestern Colorado and Northwestern New Mexico: Rocky Mountain Frontier Country

General Descriptive/Historical

Beckner, Raymond M. *Guns Along the Silvery San*

Juan. Cannon City, Colo.: Masber Printers, distributed by Raymond M. Beckner, 1975.

Brown, Robert. *An Empire of Silver: History of San Juan Silver Rush.* Caldwell, Idaho: Caxton Printers Ltd., 1965.

Chronic, Halka. *Roadside Geology of Colorado.* Missoula, Mont.: Mountain Press Publishing Co., 1980.

Dawson, Frank J. *Place Names in Colorado.* Denver: Golden Bell Press, 1954.

Eichler, George R. *Colorado Place Names.* Boulder: Johnson Publishing Co., 1977.

Elmore, Francis H. *Shrubs and Trees of the Southwest Uplands.* Globe, Ariz.: Southwest Parks and Monuments Association, 1976.

Fisher, Vardis, and Holmes, Opal Laurel. *Gold Rushes and Mining Camps of the Early American West.* Caldwell, Idaho: Caxton Printers Ltd., 1968.

Goetzmann, William H. *Exploration and Empire.* New York: W. W. Norton & Co., Inc., 1966.

Johnson, Robert Neil. *Southwestern Ghost Town Atlas.* Susanville, Cal.: C. Y. Johnson and Son, 1977.

Landi, Val. *The Great American Countryside.* New York: Macmillan, Inc., 1982.

Lavender, David. *The Rockies.* Lincoln, Nebr.: University of Nebraska Press, 1968.

———. *The Telluride Story.* Boulder: Wayfinder Press, 1987.

Miller, Millie. *Kinnikinnick: The Mountain Flower Book.* Boulder: Johnson Publishing Co., 1980.

Newberry, Friederica. *Specialty of the House.* Durango, Colo.: Sojourner Press, 1979.

Nord, Myrtle. *Durango Early Times,* vol. 1. Durango, Colo.: TriState Printing Co., n.d.

Osborne, Douglas. "Solving the Riddles of Wetherill Mesa." *National Geographic* 125(February 1964): 155–95.

Osterwald, Doris B. *Cinders and Smoke.* 1st ed. Lakewood, Colo.: Western Guideways, 1965. (13th printing, 1980)

Silverton Standard and the Miner. *Silverton–San Juan Vacation Guide, 1980–1981 and 1982.* Silverton, Colorado: Silverton Standard and the Miner, 1980.

Smith, Duane Allen. *Rocky Mountain Mining Camps: The Urban Frontier.* Bloomington,

Ind.: Indiana University Press, 1967.

———. *Colorado Mining: A Photographic History.* Albuquerque: University of New Mexico Press, 1977.

Sprague, Marshall. *The Great Gates.* Lincoln, Nebr.: University of Nebraska Press, 1964.

Sumner, David. *Colorado/Southwest: The Land, the People, the History.* Denver: Sanborn Souvenir Co., Inc., 1973. (text)

Weber, David J. *Taos Trappers.* Norman, Okla.: University of Oklahoma Press, 1971.

Wenger, Gilbert R. *The Story of Mesa Verde.* Denver: Mesa Verde Museum Associates, Inc., 1980.

Wolle, Muriel Sibell. *From Stampede to Timberline.* Chicago: Sage Books, 1949.

———. *Timberline Tailings.* Chicago: The Swallow Press, Inc., 1977.

Yount, Michael D., ed. *National Parkway Photographic and Comprehensive Guide to Mesa Verde and Rocky Mountain National Parks.* Casper, Wyo.: Worldwide Research and Publishing Co., 1975.

Zwinger, Ann. *Beyond the Aspen Grove.* 1970. Reprint. New York: Harper and Row, Publishers, Inc., 1981.

——— *Land Above the Trees. A Guide to American Alpine Tundra.* New York: Harper and Row, Publishers, Inc., 1972.

Maps

A free Colorado State map can be obtained from the Colorado Board of Tourism, 1625 Broadway, Suite 170, Denver, Colorado 80202. Telephone: 1-800-433-2656. If you are a member, you

Panning for gold

can receive free maps of the region from the American Automobile Association at either of the following locations: 4100 East Arkansas Avenue, Denver, Colorado 80222 (telephone: 1-303-750-4985) or 1840 North Twelfth Street, Unit C, Grand Junction, Colorado 81501 (telephone: 1-303-245-2336).

IV. North Central New Mexico: The Spanish Rio Grande Country

General Descriptive

Armstrong, Ruth, and *New Mexico Magazine* Staff. *New Mexico Magazine's Enchanted Trails.* Santa Fe: New Mexico Magazine Press, 1980.

Bowman, Jon. "Los Alamos and Española." *New Mexico Magazine* 65(1987) 10:63–71.

Ellis, William S. "A Goal at the End of the Trail: Santa Fe." *National Geographic* 161(March 1982): 323–45.

Hagan, Bob. "West Mesa Petroglyphs." *New Mexico Magazine* 65(1987)2:16–21, 59–60.

Hazen-Hammond. "Farmington." *New Mexico Magazine* 64(1986)5:54–55, 58–60.

Hillerman, Tony, ed. *The Spell of New Mexico.* Albuquerque: University of New Mexico Press, 1976.

Kuhn, I. C. "Christmas in Santa Fe." *Gourmet Magazine* 38(December 1978):20–24, 82–88.

Lawrence, D. H. *Mornings in Mexico and Etruscan Places.* Middlesex: Penguin Books, 1967.

Lawrence, D. H. "New Mexico." *Survey Graphics* 1 May 1931. Also collected in *Phoenix: The Posthumous Papers of D. H. Lawrence.* Edited by Edward McDonald. New York: Viking, 1936.

Laxalt, Robert. "New Mexico: The Golden Land." *National Geographic* 138(September 1970): 299–345.

———"New Mexico's Mountains of Mystery." *National Geographic* 154(September 1978): 416–36.

Muench, David, and Hillerman, Tony. *New Mexico.* Portland: Charles H. Belding, 1974.

O'Keeffe, Georgia. *Georgia O'Keeffe.* 1976. Reprint. New York: Penguin Books, 1977.

Pearce, M. T., ed. *New Mexico Place Names: A Geographical Dictionary.* Albuquerque: University of New Mexico Press, 1965.

Roach, Archibald W. *Outdoor Plants of the Southwest.* Dallas: Taylor Publishing Co., 1982.

Sagar, Keith, ed. *D. H. Lawrence and New Mexico.* Salt Lake City: Gibbs M. Smith, Inc., 1982.

Sutton, George Miksch. *Oklahoma Birds.* Norman, Okla.: University of Oklahoma Press, 1967.

Thompson, Waite, and Gottlieb, H. Richard. *The Santa Fe Guide.* Santa Fe: The Sunstone Press, 1980.

Young, John V. *The State Parks of New Mexico.* Albuquerque: University of New Mexico Press, 1984.

Historical/Cultural

Anaya, A. Rudolfo. *Bless Me, Ultima.* Berkeley: Tonatiuh International, Inc., 1972.

Cather, Willa. *Death Comes for the Archbishop.* New York: Random House, Inc., 1971.

Dutton, P. Bertha. *Let's Explore Indian Villages Past and Present.* Santa Fe: Museum of New Mexico Press, 1962.

Fergusson, Erna. *New Mexico: A Pageant of Three Peoples.* Albuquerque: University of New Mexico Press, 1964.

Historic Santa Fe Foundation. *Old Santa Fe Today.* Albuquerque: University of New Mexico Press, 1982.

Hogan, Paul. *The Heroic Triad.* New York: World Publishing, 1970.

Jenkins, Myra Ellen, and Schroeder, Albert H. *A Brief History of New Mexico.* Albuquerque: University of New Mexico Press, 1974.

La Farge, Oliver. *Santa Fe.* Norman, Okla.: University of Oklahoma Press, 1959.

Langseth-Christensen, Lillian. "The Kitchens of El Rancho de las Golondrinas." *Gourmet Magazine* 34(August 1979): 44–48, 94.

Lavender, David. *The Southwest.* New York: Harper and Row, Publishers, Inc., 1980.

Morrill, Claire. *A Taos Mosaic: Portrait of a New Mexico Village*. Albuquerque: University of New Mexico Press, 1973.

Nichols, John, and Davis, William. *If Mountains Die: A New Mexico Memoir*. New York: Alfred A. Knopf, 1979.

Querry, Ronald B. *Growing Old at Willie Nelson's Picnic and Other Sketches of Life in the Southwest*. College Station, Tex.: Texas A & M University Press, 1983.

Shishkin, K. H. *The Palace of the Governors*. Santa Fe: Museum of New Mexico Press, 1972.

Smith, Griffin, Jr. "The Mexican Americans: A People on the Move." *National Geographic* 157(June 1980):780–809.

Stein, Rita. *A Literary Tour Guide to the United States: South and Southwest*. New York: William Morrow & Co., Inc., 1979.

Weber, J. David. *The Taos Trappers*. Norman, Okla.: University of Oklahoma Press, 1968.

Fine Arts and Traditional Arts and Crafts

Babcock, Barbara A., and Monthan, Guy and Doris. *The Pueblo Storyteller: Development of a Figurative Ceramic Tradition*. Tucson: University of Arizona Press, 1986.

Barry, John W. *American Indian Pottery*. 2d ed. Florence, Ala.: Books Americana, 1984.

Boyd, E. *Popular Arts of Spanish New Mexico*. Santa Fe: Museum of New Mexico Press, 1974.

Broggs, L. Charles. *The Wood Carvers of Córdova, New Mexico*. Knoxville: University of Tennessee Press, 1980.

Dickey, F. Roland. *New Mexico Village Arts*. Albuquerque: University of New Mexico Press, 1949.

Dittert, Alfred E., Jr., and Plog, Fred. *Generations in Clay*. Flagstaff, Ariz.: Northland Press, 1980.

Jacka, Jerry. *Pottery Treasures*. Portland: Graphic Arts Center Publishing Co., 1976.

Jeter, James, and Juelke, Paula Marie. *The Saltillo Serape*. Santa Barbara: New World Arts, 1978.

Kent, Kate Peck. *Pueblo Indian Textiles: A Living Tradition*. Seattle: University of Washington Press, 1983.

Lambert, Marjorie F. *Pueblo Indian Pottery: Materials, Tools and Techniques*. Santa Fe: Museum of New Mexico Press, 1966.

LeFree, Betty. *Santa Clara Pottery Today*. Albuquerque: University of New Mexico Press, 1975.

Lister, H. Robert, and Lister, C. Florence. *Anasazi*

Truchas, New Mexico

Pottery. Albuquerque: University of New Mexico Press, 1978.

Marriott, Alice. *Maria: The Potter of San Ildefonso*. Norman, Okla.: University of Oklahoma Press, 1948.

Martinez, Levi. *What is a New Mexico Santo?* Santa Fe: The Sunstone Press, 1978.

Mather, Christine, and Woods, Sharon. *Santa Fe Style*. New York: Rizzoli International Publications, 1986.

Maxwell Museum of Anthropology. *Seven Families in Pueblo Pottery*. Albuquerque: University of New Mexico Press, 1974.

Monthan, Guy, and Monthan, Doris. *Nacimientos*. Flagstaff, Ariz.: Northland Press, 1979.

Wroth, William, ed. *Hispanic Crafts of the Southwest*. Colorado Springs: Colorado Springs Fine Arts Center (Taylor Museum), 1977.

Zeigler, George M. *Art in Santa Fe*. Chicago: Lake Shore Press, 1987.

Maps

Free maps and tourist information are available from the New Mexico Tourism and Travel Division, 1100 St. Francis Drive, Santa Fe, New Mexico 87503. Telephone: 1-505-827-0291 or toll free in the United States, except New Mexico 1-800-545-2040. Additionally, maps are available without charge to members of the American Automobile Association at both of the following addresses: 10501 Montgomery Boulevard Northeast, Albuquerque, New Mexico 87111. Telephone: 1-505-291-6611 or 1509 and 1511 Fifth Street, Santa Fe, New Mexico 87501 (telephone: 1-505-982-4663). The American Automobile Association map, "A Guide to Indian Country" is excellent for much of north central New Mexico. See Section I of the Bibliography for mailing address.

Glossary

acequia	irrigation ditch
adovado	the name of a sour seasoning paste for meat made of ground chilies, herbs, and vinegar
arrastra	a rudimentary mill for pulverizing ores containing valuable minerals like gold
arroyo	the wide, water-carved, flat-floored channel of an intermittent stream in dry country
barrio	a district or section of a town
bolillo	a small, elongated, oval bread roll, often with a slightly sweet taste
brujo	a witch or sorceror who performs black magic and is capable of influencing others adversely
bulto	a three-dimensional carved figure or statue, often of a saint
cacique	a word brought to the Southwest by the Spanish from Cuba which means chief. It was applied to the religious leaders of the Pueblos.
curandera	a healer who is skilled in the use of herbs, but who also is endowed with certain powers to counteract the evil influence of the brujo
Dineh	a word used by the Navajo to refer to themselves, which means "The People"
fetish	a natural or a man-made object resembling a natural object, which is believed to hold a spirit that will protect or aid its owner
fonda	inn or restaurant
frijoles	beans
hogan	a Navajo house
horno	a beehive or inverted cone-shaped outdoor oven of Moorish-Arabic origin, brought to the Southwest by the Spanish
kachina	a supernatural Hopi deity.

(katsina) There are over three hundred kachinas, representing the various forms of life who reside in the San Francisco Peaks. Dolls are often made in their image.

kikmongwi a village leader in a Hopi village

kiska covered passageway in a Hopi village between the buildings, which connects part of the village to the plaza

kiva Pueblo Indian ceremonial chamber which is sometimes underground or partially underground

latia (latillas) small peeled poles of juniper or aspen used in the construction of ceilings in adobe buildings

mariachi a group of folk musicians (including a guitarist, violinist, and singers) which had its origin in Mexico

nacimiento a representation of the Nativity scene through one of several media, including clay or carved wood figures

pahaana the Hopi word for a white person

pan dulce sweet roll

paraje a stopping place for travelers

parroquia a parish church, as opposed to a mission church

Penitente short for Los Hermanos Penitentes, the Penitente Brothers, a religious order of laymen known for their severe religious practices

petroglyph an image that has either been pecked, carved, scratched, or abraded on the face of a stone

pictograph an image that has been painted on the surface of a stone

placer a gravel or sand deposit, usually along a stream bed, which contains small particles of gold or other valuable minerals washed down from larger deposits upstream

placita a small courtyard, square, or plaza located either in the center of a private home or in the center of a complex of buildings

portal a long covered porch supported by vertical posts

posada an inn or place of lodging; also a Christmas festivity lasting nine days

posole the name given to a soup or stew of meat and corn, as well as the name of the special corn used in the stew which is prepared by boiling it in lime water until it is free of hulls

pregonero a crier in Pueblo villages who announces the time to open the irrigation ditches and other important events

rancho small ranch

rebozo a shawl made of cotton or silk

reredos altar screen

retablo   a religious picture, usually
            painted on wood or tin or
            other flat surfaces

ristra   a string of either chilies, corn,
            or garlic, hung up to dry
            or strung for ornamental
            purposes

santero   a local craftsman who makes
            religious statues or paintings

santuario   a sanctuary

shard   a fragment of a broken
            pottery vessel; also called
            a potsherd

sing   a Navajo ceremonial occasion
            where, in addition to social
            dancing, there are healing
            ceremonies presided over by
            a Navajo medicine man or
            "singer" whose singing and
            chanting is an important part
            of the healing ceremony

sipaapuni   small hole in the floor of
            kivas which, in the Hopi
            religion, symbolizes the place
            of man's emergence from
            the earth

tailings   the mounds of accumulated
            waste debris from ore-
            processing mills

talus   piles of fallen, broken rock
            that accumulate at the base of
            a ridge or a cliff

viga   log used as a ceiling beam in
            adobe houses

villa   an early-day Spanish town or
            city that served as an ad-
            ministration center

zaguan   a covered passageway joining
            separate buildings, often serv-
            ing as an entryway to a
            placita

Zozobra   a Spanish word meaning
            foundering, sinking, or worry,
            which has been used to
            name a forty-foot-tall puppet
            figure representing Old Man
            Gloom that is burned every
            September at fiesta time in
            Santa Fe

Index

Also of Interest from
The Globe Pequot Press

"The Recommended Country Inns" *series: Arizona, New Mexico, and Texas; West Coast; Rocky Mountain Region; Midwest; South; Mid-Atlantic States and Chesapeake Region; New England*

The Seattle GuideBook

Alaska's Southeast: Touring the Inside Passage

Guide to Western Canada

Guide to Eastern Canada

Bed and Breakfast in California

Guide to the National Park Areas: Western States

Guide to the National Park Areas: Eastern States

Colorado: Off the Beaten Path

Northern California: Off the Beaten Path

Southern California: Off the Beaten Path

Day Trips from Phoenix/Tucson/Flagstaff

Day trips from Houston

Rocky Mountain National Park Hiking Trails

Whitewater Rafting in Western North America

Available at your bookstore or direct from the publisher. For a free catalogue or to place an order, call 1-800-243-0495 (in Connecticut, call 1-800-962-0973) or write to the Globe Pequot Press, Box Q, Chester, Connecticut 06412.